MARIANNE M. JENNINGS
...

BUSINESS
ETHICS

CASE STUDIES AND SELECTED READINGS

Marianne Moody Jennings

Arizona State University

FIFTH EDITION

THOMSON

SOUTH-WESTERN

Australia · Brazil · Canada · Mexico · Singapore · Spain · United Kingdom · United States

Business Ethics: Case Studies and Selected Readings, Fifth Edition
Marianne M. Jennings

VP/Editorial Director:
Jack W. Calhoun

Publisher:
Rob Dewey

Acquisitions Editor:
Steven Silverstein, Esq.

Developmental Editor:
Bob Sandman, Brian Coovert

Executive Marketing Manager:
Lisa L. Lysne

Production Editor:
Heather Mann

Manager of Technology, Editorial:
Vicky True

Technology Project Editor:
Christine A. Wittmer

Web Coordinator:
Scott Cook

Manufacturing Coordinator:
Charlene Taylor

Production House:
Cadmus Communications

Printer:
Thomson West
Eagan, MN

Art Director:
Michelle Kunkler

Internal Designer:
Kenn Tompos/Straight Face Studio

Cover Designer:
Kenn Tompos/Straight Face Studio

Cover Image:
© Amy DeVoogd/Artville

Library of Congress Control Number: 2004115439

For more information about our products, contact us at:

Thomson Learning Academic Resource Center 1-800-423-0563

Thomson Higher Education
5191 Natorp Boulevard
Mason, Ohio 45040
USA

Contents

UNIT 3

Foundations of Business Ethics: What Is the Role of Business in Society? Shareholders vs. Stakeholders 61

Section A: The Role of Business in Society 62

Section B: Applying Social Responsibility and Stakeholder Theory 82

UNIT 4

Individuals, Individual Values, and the Business Organization 121

Section A: Trust and Employment 123

Section B: Taking Advantage 142

UNIT 5

Individual Rights and the Business Organization   153

UNIT 6

Business Operations: Financial Issues 257

UNIT 7

Business Operations: Workplace Safety Risks, Systems, and International Operations 349

Preface

"What is right is right even if no one is doing it. What is wrong is wrong even if everyone is doing it."

— SOURCE UNKNOWN

"Never trust the people you cheat with."

— MARIANNE M. JENNINGS

"Goodness is the only investment that never fails."

— HENRY D. THOREAU, *WALDEN*; HIGHER LAWS

"Three people can keep a secret if two are dead."

— HELL'S ANGELS (QUOTING BEN FRANKLIN)

"We're the good guys. We are on the side of angels."

— JEFFREY SKILLING, former CEO of Enron, awaiting trial on fraud and other federal charges

A 2003 joint survey by Deloitte Touche and Junior Achievement found that 45 percent of high school students believed that business leaders were unethical. Another 38 percent weren't sure whether business leaders were ethical. Only 18 percent of that group of young people were willing to say that they felt business leaders were ethical. In its 2004 data on cheating in high school, the Josephson Institute reported that 62 percent of those students surveyed said that they had cheated on an exam in the past year, and 83 percent said that they had copied someone else's homework to turn in for credit. The Center for Academic Integrity at Duke University and Professor Donald McCabe of Rutgers report that college cheating has grown from 11 percent in 1963 to 49 percent in 1993 to 75 percent in 2003.[1] By longitudinal measures, we are in a decline. And the decline does not result, as many like to argue, from our being more honest about ethical breaches. The Josephson Institute also found that the high school students who reported that they cheated felt very comfortable about their behavior, with 92 percent saying they were satisfied with their character and ethics and 83 percent believing that they would be listed by their friends as one of the most ethical people they knew.

---

[1] *Professor Donald McCabe conducts the Rutgers study on a regular basis. See http://www.rutgers.edu for more information on Professor McCabe and his work on academic integrity.*

The following events from the past few years offer some insight into the current issues in business ethics:

- The Securities and Exchange Commission (SEC) filed fraud charges against Sunbeam, its former CEO Albert J. Dunlap (often called "Chainsaw Al" for his career pattern of downsizing companies and making deep and swift cuts in the size of their workforces in order to quickly restore profitability), and its auditors for allegedly overstating earnings by, among other things, recording sales that did not really occur.[2] Mr. Dunlap has settled his case by agreeing to pay shareholders $15 million. Arthur Andersen settled with the shareholders for $110 million.[3]
- Jonathan G. Lebed began trading stock when he was twelve and, through the Internet, was able to pump and dump his way from an initial investment of $8,000 all the way to $800,000 until the SEC moved in and filed its first fraud charges against a minor, collecting almost $600,000 in gains and leaving his parents with only the funds to pay the income taxes on young Jonathan's three-year run.[4]
- FINOVA, Inc., a financial corporation, and Enron, an energy trading firm, both consistently named among the top ten companies to work for in the United States, had to issue corrected financial statements. The final fallout from information about debts and write-downs not revealed to shareholders was that both companies now sit in Chapter 11 bankruptcy with their shares valued at under $1 each, down from highs of $70–$80 per share. These were the largest and seventh-largest bankruptcies in the history of the United States, until WorldCom knocked them down a notch with its own failure, and the root causes of their failure rest in ethical lapses.
- Congress has passed the most extensive ethical and corporate governance standards and regulations in the history of the securities markets to prevent conflicts of interest, require disclosures, and ensure that all employees of publicly traded companies understand ethics and ethical issues.
- General Motors lost a case on a Chevrolet Malibu that exploded on impact, and the jury awarded the family injured in the fiery crash over $4.9 billion (later reduced to $1.2 billion on appeal), because the evidence included internal memos documenting GM's knowledge of a design defect involving the gas tank and its placement that GM would not correct.[5]
- Martha Stewart sold her shares in ImClone the day before the company, which was run by a good friend of hers, announced that its premier drug, Erbitux, would not be approved by the FDA. Ms. Stewart saved about $40,000 by selling before the public announcement, but then was convicted of obstruction of justice after she and her brokers tried to concoct a story and alter records to prove the sale was preplanned. Ms. Stewart spent five months in prison and was, at this writing, under house arrest for an additional five months, even as her own company, Martha Stewart Omnimedia, struggled to regain the revenue that declined upon her indictment and had remained flat.
- WorldCom capitalized $9 billion in ordinary expenses, a clear violation of accounting rules that made its revenues seem fabulous. Its former CFO, Scott Sullivan, entered a guilty

[2] Floyd Norris, "They Noticed the Fraud but Figured It Was Not Important," The New York Times, May 18, 2001, p. C1.

[3] Kelly Greene, "Dunlap Agrees To Settle Suit Over Sunbeam," The Wall Street Journal, January 15, 2002, p. A3.

[4] Michael Lewis, "Jonathan Lebed: Stock Manipulator, S.E.C. Nemesis—and 15," The New York Times, February 25, 2001, at http://www.nytimes.com and also p. 24 of The New York Times Sunday Magazine.

[5] Milo Geyelin, "How an Internal Memo Written 26 Years Ago Is Costing GM Dearly," The Wall Street Journal, September 29, 1999, pp. A1, A6.

plea to fraud and other charges, then agreed to testify against his boss, CEO Bernie Ebbers, who was convicted on all counts of the federal charges brought against him.

Pressures for profits and high returns on investments still exist. Those pressures translate into earnings management that then crosses over into accounting fraud. Weak product designs produce defective products and often chains of internal company memos about employee concerns over the products' safety. College sports, baseball, and politics all have their ethical issues. Each day brings news of another ethical lapse. Businesses do exist to make a profit, but business ethics exist to set parameters for earning that profit. This book of readings and cases explores those parameters and their importance. This book teaches us, through detailed study of the people and companies previously mentioned, that business conducted without ethics means a short-term existence, a company that will fall to the earth like the flash of a meteor. Long-term personal and business success demand ethics. This book connects the moral sentiments of markets with the wealth of nations. Business without ethics is self-destructive.

In 1986, before Ivan Boesky was a household name and Michael Douglas was Gordon Gekko in *Wall Street*, I began teaching a business ethics course in the MBA program in the College of Business at Arizona State University. The course was an elective. I had trouble making the minimum enrollments. However, two things changed my enrollments and my fate. First, the American Association of Collegiate Schools of Business (AACSB) changed the curriculum for graduate and undergraduate business degree programs and required the coverage of ethics. The other event was actually a series of happenings. Indictments, convictions, and guilty pleas by major companies and their officers—from E.F. Hutton to Union Carbide to Beech-Nut to Exxon—brought national attention to the need to incorporate values in American businesses and business leaders.

Whether out of fear, curiosity, or the need for reaccreditation, business schools and students embraced the concept of studying business ethics. My course went from a little-known elective to the final required course in the MBA program. In the years since, the interest in business ethics has only increased. Today nearly 100 percent of the Fortune 500 companies have a code of ethics. Under the provisions of the Sarbanes-Oxley Act and in order to minimize sentencing under the U.S. sentencing guidelines, companies must also provide their employees with regular training in ethics.

Application of ethical principles in a business setting is a critical skill. Real-life examples are necessary. Over the past eighteen years, since my ethics course first began, I have collected examples of ethical dilemmas, poor ethical choices, and wise ethical decisions from newspapers, business journals, and my experiences as a consultant and board member. Knowing that other instructors and students were in need of examples, I have turned my experiences into cases and coupled them with the most memorable readings in the field to provide a training and thought-provoking experience on business ethics.

The cases come not only from nearly 30 years of teaching and business experience, but also from my conviction that a strong sense of values is an essential management skill that can be taught. The cases apply theory to reality; hopefully, they will nurture or reinforce a needed sense of values in future business leaders.

A new realization came to me while using the fourth edition over the past few years: My students did not have sufficient grounding in ethics in life, not to mention business. Further, the magnitude of the mistakes the business people in the cases were making showed that they were not grappling with or puzzled by close calls. Something must have gone awry in their ethics training in business school for them to have drifted so far from virtue. I realized that it was important to relate the materials we were discussing to students' personal lives and to help them see that personal ethics and business ethics are one and the same: Virtue is the goal in all aspects of our lives, and businesses are not asking us to behave differently. The result is the addition to this fifth edition of a new introductory unit on personal ethics to help motivate students and teach both theory and application. The addition of ethical theory is also a tip of the hat to my good colleagues who felt the students needed more grounding there before they could tackle the more difficult business issues in the remainder of the book. Combined into one exciting introduction section then are theory and practice, with all new cases and discussion questions to get students really thinking about life, business, and ethics.

The fifth edition continues the features students and instructors embraced in the first, second, third, and fourth editions, including both short and long cases, discussion questions, hypothetical situations, and up-to-the-moment current, ongoing, and real ethical dilemmas. Some of the longstanding favorites are back by popular demand—such as the Nestlé infant formula experience with its longstanding lessons in doing the right thing.

The fifth edition still continues the classic readings in business ethics that provide insight into the importance of ethics in business and how to resolve ethical dilemmas. The readings remain integrated throughout the book to provide substantive thoughts on the particular areas covered in each section. The organizational structure and indexes, modified from the fourth edition, make material easy to locate. A case can be located using the table of contents, the topical index, or the product index, which lists both products and companies by name. An index for business disciplines groups the cases by accounting, management, and the other disciplines in colleges of business.

Supplements

Business Ethics: Case Studies and Selected Readings offers a comprehensive and well-crafted supplements package for both students and instructors. Contact your Thomson Learning/West Legal Studies in Business Sales Representative for more details, or visit the Jennings Web site at http://jennings.westbuslaw.com.

Instructor's Manual (ISBN: 0-324-30371-8). This edition's instructor's manual is updated with more sample test objective- and essay-answer questions of varying lengths and structures. The questions have been coded for topic and even some for case-specific questions so that exams can be created by subject area. The transparency master package, which includes illustrative charts to assist instructors in walking classes through the more complex cases, has been updated and expanded. Qualified instructors can also download the instructor's manual at http://jennings.westbuslaw.com.

West's Digital Video Library. Featuring more than 60 segments on the most important topics in business law, West's Digital Video Library helps students make the connection between their textbook and the business world. Access to West's Digital Video Library is free when bundled with a new text, and students with used books can purchase access to the video clips online. New to this edition are LawFlix, twelve scenes from Hollywood movies with instructor materials for each film clip. The clips were chosen by the author, and the instructor's materials were written by the author; they include elements such as goals for the clips, questions for students (with answers for the instructor), background on the film and the scene, and fascinating trivia about the film, its actors, and its history. For more information about West's Digital Video Library, visit http://digitalvideolibrary.westbuslaw.com.

West Legal Studies in Business Resource Center.   This Web site offers a unique, rich, and robust online resource for instructors and students. Visit http://www.westbuslaw.com for customer service and product information, links to all text-supporting Web sites, and other cutting-edge resources such as *NewsEdge* and **Court Case Updates.**

LegalTrac™.   An excellent resource for research and writing assignments, *LegalTrac* provides indexing for approximately 875 titles, including major law reviews, legal newspapers, bar association journals, and international legal journals, and also contains law-related articles from more than 1,000 additional business and general interest titles. *LegalTrac* is available as an optional package with a new text.

The Business and Company Resource Center.   *The Business & Company Resource Center (BCRC)* is a premier online business research tool that allows you to seamlessly search thousands of periodicals, journals, references, financial information, industry reports, company histories, and much more. Visit http://bcrc.swlearning.com to learn more about this powerful tool. BCRC is available as an optional package with a new text.

The Wall Street Journal.   For a nominal additional cost, any new West Legal Studies in Business text can be packaged with a card entitling students to a fifteen-week subscription to both the print and online versions of *The Wall Street Journal.* Instructors with at least seven students who activate subscriptions will automatically receive their own free subscription.

Student Guide to the Sarbanes-Oxley Act.   This brief overview for undergraduate business students explains the Sarbanes-Oxley Act, what is required of whom, and how it might affect students in their business life. Available as an optional package with the text.

West Legal Studies in Business VHS Video Library.   VHS videotapes on many business law issues are available (with some restrictions) to qualified adopters of West Legal Studies in Business texts. For more detailed information about the videos, please visit http://video.westbuslaw.com.

Acknowledgments

This book is not mine. It is the result of the efforts and sacrifices of many. I am grateful to the reviewers for their comments and insights. Their patience, expertise, and service are remarkable.

Dr. Kenneth Bigel
Lander College for Men

Dr. Gary McMahan
University of Texas at Arlington

Nicholas J. Chabra
University of North Carolina at Greensboro

Jane Hass Philbrick
Savannah State University

Dr. Diane Dolezal
St. Thomas Aquinas College

Kathleen Suchon
University of Massachusetts Dartmouth

Dr. Sandra Gill
Benedictine University

I am fortunate to have Brian Coovert as the editor for this edition. His calm and steady guidance make him an author's choice for editor-of-the-year. I am grateful to Rob Dewey for his continuing support of all my work. I continue to love editors. Where I see only deadlines, they see both the big picture of the book and its details: They have vision. And many blessings upon the marketers, especially those like Steve Silverstein and Lisa Lysne, who understand why ethics is important in business, live it, and want to see it in the next generations of students who will enter the business world and take charge with a vision of virtue.

I am grateful to my parents for the values they inculcated in me. Their ethical perspective has been an inspiration, a comfort, and, in many cases, the final say in my decision-making processes. I am especially grateful to my father for his continual quest for examples of ethical and not-so-ethical behavior in action in the world of business. I am grateful for my family's understanding and support. I am most grateful for the reminder their very presence gives me of what is truly important.

Marianne M. Jennings

Professor of Legal and Ethical Studies in Business

W.P. Carey School of Business

Arizona State University

Marianne.jennings@asu.edu

About the Author

Marianne M. Jennings earned her undergraduate degree in finance and her J.D. from Brigham Young University. She is a member of the Department of Supply Chain Management in the W.P. Carey School of Business at Arizona State University. She has been named professor of the year in the College of Business three times and was the recipient of a Burlington Northern teaching excellence award. She joined the faculty at ASU in 1977 as an assistant professor. Professor Jennings was promoted to associate professor in 1980 and to full professor in 1983. She has worked with the federal public defender and U.S. attorney in Nevada and has served as a consultant to many law firms, businesses, and professional groups. She is the author of more than 130 articles in academic, professional, and trade journals and 6 textbooks. Her weekly columns are published throughout the country, and her work has appeared in the *New York Times, Chicago Tribune, Washington Post,* and *Wall Street Journal.* Her book on companies that paid dividends for 100 years was published in 2002. In addition, Professor Jennings is a legal commentator for National Public Radio. She has conducted more than 200 workshops and seminars in the areas of business, personal and professional ethics, legal ethics, real estate, credit management, legal issues for academic administrators, law for CPAs, and legal and political strategic planning. Professor Jennings is a member of the Arizona bar. Her most recent book, *A Business Tale: A Story of Ethics, Choices, Success (and a Very Large Rabbit)* has received several awards, including recognition by *Library Journal* and Business Editors of America.

Introduction

"The reputation of a thousand years is determined by the conduct of one hour."

— JAPANESE PROVERB

"A quiet conscience makes one so serene."

— BYRON

"There is no pillow as soft as a clear conscience."

— KENNETH BLANCHARD AND NORMAN VINCENT PEALE
THE POWER OF ETHICAL MANAGEMENT

"What once seemed black and white

Turns to so many shades of gray

We lose ourselves in work to do and bills to pay"

— BRUCE SPRINGSTEEN, *BLOOD BROTHERS*[1]

Why Business Ethics?

A cover story in *Fortune* magazine, entitled "The Payoff from a Good Reputation" (*Fortune*, February 10, 1992), quotes a vice chairman of an advertising agency as saying, "The only sustainable competitive advantage any business has is its reputation." The same could be said about individual business persons. Reputation cannot be found in the annual 10K filing the Securities and Exchange Commission requires of a firm and won't be reflected in the net worth recorded on the firm's balance sheet. But its loss can be so devastating that if it were quantifiable, the failure of a firm to disclose that its ethical values were waning would constitute fraud under the federal securities laws. A business lacking an ethical commitment will, eventually, bring about its own demise.

A May 14, 2001, cover for *Fortune* magazine asks this question: "Can we ever trust again?" As we discover some of the creative accounting of the dot-com companies and the all-too-close relationships and conflicts among analysts, underwriters, and their clients, those who have invested are wondering how there could have been so many breaches of trust with so few people willing to express concerns. The burst of the dot-com bubble offers its share of ethical missteps that may have contributed to or exacerbated the scope of the economic downturn.

---

[1] *Copyright © 1995 Bruce Springsteen (ASCAP). Reprinted by permission.*

But the dot-coms with creative accounting and conflicts of interest are not unique. Examining the fates of companies such as Union Carbide, Beech-Nut, E.F. Hutton, Salomon Brothers, Johns-Manville, Exxon, Phar-Mor, Kidder Peabody, Bausch & Lomb, Sunbeam, FINOVA, Nike, Ford, Firestone, and others whose very public ethical mishaps resulted in tremendous losses supports the notion that a lack of commitment to ethical behavior is a lack of commitment to a firm's success.

Many people consider the term "business ethics" an oxymoron. Nonetheless, in keeping with the observations in *Fortune*, compelling reasons support choosing ethical behavior in a business setting. Courses in finance and accounting teach us that the primary purpose and obligation of a business is to earn a profit. The immediate pursuit of the bottom line occasionally can distort even the most conscientious perspective. The fear of losing business and consequently losing profits can lead individuals and companies to make decisions that, while not illegal, raise concerns about fairness, equity, justice, and honesty.

In their 1994 book *Built to Last*, James C. Collins and Jerry I. Porras noted that the common thread among companies with long-term growth and profits was a strong commitment to values. These successful companies had high standards for product quality, concern for employees and employee safety, and reputations for fairness and good service. In short, the ethical components of business were a common thread in their success.

A firm must pursue the positive figure for its bottom line with a long-term perspective in mind. Running a successful and ethical business is like running a marathon, not a sprint. Studies show that firms that perform better financially over time are those with a commitment to ethical behavior. A study by the Lincoln Center for Ethics and Professors Louis Grossman and Marianne Jennings at Arizona State University demonstrated that the fifteen U.S. corporations that have paid dividends for at least one hundred years without interruption also had a strong commitment to values. These companies knew what they had to do to be successful, but they also knew what they would *not* do to achieve that success.[2] What they would not do is compromise their values.

A 1997 study in the *Academy of Management Journal* concludes that firms involved in ethical difficulties (including criminal violations, regulatory citations, and product liability suits) experience earnings declines for at least five years following the public announcement of their problems.[3]

There is something to the correlation between business ethics and business success. While not every ethical person is guaranteed business success, every business that engages in unethical behavior is guaranteed a setback and the costs of trying to restore that invaluable reputation.

---

[2] *The results of this study appear in* Building and Growing a Business: The Remarkable Stories of Fifteen Companies Each with 100 Years of Consistent Dividends, *Greenwood Press, 2002.*
[3] *Melissa S. Baucus and David A. Baucus, 40* Academy of Management Journal, *1997, p. 129.*

Foundations of Ethics: Virtue and Values

BEFORE WE BEGIN THE STUDY OF BUSINESS ETHICS, we should do some introspection: what does ethics mean to me personally? The purpose of this unit is to provide you with a personal look at ethics and you before we bring in the business component and cover you, ethics, and business.

Virtues, Values, and Why We Care About Ethics

This unit explains three things: what ethics are, why we should care about ethics, and how to resolve ethical dilemmas. The materials in this unit serve as the foundation for the study of particular issues in business ethics. We begin with a personal look at ethics, discuss why it matters, and then decide how to resolve ethical dilemmas.

1A

Defining Ethics

READING 1.1
What Are Ethics?

When we read a story about former Senator Bob Torricelli, an elected official who accepted a Rolex watch from a constituent who was looking to court the senator's vote on some important trade issues, we think, "He's unethical." When we read about Jayson Blair, a young reporter with the *New York Times* discovered to have fabricated his stories and lifted large segments of his work from other reporters' work in other papers, we say, "That's unethical!" When we read about Dennis Kozlowski, the former CEO of Tyco, purchasing a $6,000 shower curtain with lavish bonuses and through officer loan programs not always approved by Tyco's board of directors, we think, "Where are his ethics?" (See Unit 6 to study the Tyco case.)

Situations such as these happen every day. Some conduct is more harmful, such as those situations in which there is a violation of a criminal statute. For example, Mr. Kozlowski was tried for fraud for his use of company programs and funds. In some ethical breaches, there may be a right to bring a civil lawsuit for the harm caused. For example, the journalist whose work was used by Mr. Blair, along with her newspaper, has the right to sue for copyright infringement. But in Mr. Torricelli's case the FBI found no violation of criminal laws, and there is no civil right of action that voters can bring against elected officials who accept gifts. But, the Senate Ethics Committee censured Mr. Torricelli for his conduct and he did resign from the Senate. His conduct was not a criminal or a civil breach, but a committee found clear ethics violations.

In Mr. Kozlowski's case, he was tried for violations of state law including fraud and embezzlement, but the jury was a hung jury; it could not reach a verdict in the case. One of the jurors in the case wrote in an opinion piece that explained the jury's deliberations: criminal intent is difficult to prove. Mr. Kozlowski's conduct may have been outrageous with his lavish spending and decadent parties at corporate expense. His use of company funds was unethical, but if the money was spent with others knowing and authorizing it, he did not commit a crime. Those who authorized it were perhaps not paying enough attention and Mr. Kozlowski took advantage of others, a form of an ethical breach, but the jury had difficulty finding that crimes were committed.

Still, regardless of the application of law or the right to sue, we look at the conduct of Mr. Torricelli, Mr. Blair, and Mr. Kozlowski and conclude, "It's just not right!" We are probably unanimous in our conclusion that they all behaved unethically. We may not be able to zero in on what bothers us about their conduct, but we know an ethics violation, or an ethical breach, when we see one.

But what is ethics? What do we mean when we say that someone has acted unethically? Ethical standards are not the standards of the law. In fact, they are a higher standard. Sometimes referred to as normative standards in philosophy, ethical standards are the generally accepted rules of conduct that govern society. Ethical rules are both standards and expectations for behavior, and we have developed them for nearly all aspects of life. For example, there is no statute in any state that makes it a crime for someone to cut in line in order to save the waiting time involved by going to the end of the line. But we all view those who "take cuts in line" with disdain. We sneer at those cars that sneak along the side of the road to get around a line of traffic as we sit and wait our turn. We resent those who tromp up to the cash register in front of us, ignoring the fact that we were there first and that our time is valuable too.

If you have ever resented a line-cutter, then you understand ethics and have applied ethical standards in life. Waiting your turn in line is an expectation society has. "Waiting your turn" is not an ordinance, a statute, or even a federal regulation. "Waiting your turn" is an age-old principle developed because it was fair to proceed with first-in-time, first to be served. "Waiting your turn" exists because when there are large groups waiting for the same road, theater tickets, or fast food at noon in a busy downtown area, we found that lines ensured order and that waiting your turn was a just way of allocating the limited space and time allotted for the movie tickets, the traffic, or the food. "Waiting your turn" is an expected but unwritten behavior that plays a critical role in an orderly society.

So it is with ethics. Ethics consists of those unwritten rules we have developed for our interactions with each other. These unwritten rules govern us when we are sharing resources or honoring contracts. "Waiting your turn" is a higher standard than the laws that are passed to maintain order. Those laws apply when physical force or threats are used to push to the front of the line. Assault, battery, and threats are forms of criminal conduct for which the offender can be prosecuted. But the law does not apply to the stealth line-cutter who simply sneaks to the front, perhaps using a friend and a conversation as a decoy for edging into the front. No laws are broken, but the notions of fairness and justice are offended by one individual putting himself above others and taking advantage of others' time and position.

Because line-cutters violate the basic procedures and unwritten rules for line formation and order, they have committed an ethical breach. Ethics consists of standards and norms for behavior that are beyond laws and legal rights. We don't put line-cutters in jail, but we do refer to them as unethical. There are other examples of unethical behavior that carry no legal penalty. If a married person commits adultery, there is no crime, but there is a breach of trust with his or her spouse. We do not put adulterers in jail, but we do label their conduct with adjectives such as "unfaithful" and even use a lay term to describe adultery: "cheating."

Speaking of cheating, looking at someone else's paper during an exam is not a criminal violation. You may be sanctioned by your professor and there may be penalties imposed by your college, but you will not be prosecuted by the county attorney for cheating. But your conduct was unethical because you did not earn your standing and grade under the same set of rules applied to the other students. Just like the line-cutter, your conduct is not fair to those who spent their time studying. Your cheating is unjust because you are getting ahead using someone else's work.

In these examples of line-cutters, adulterers, and exam cheaters, there are certain common adjectives that come to our minds: "That's *unfair!*" "That was *dishonest!*" "That was *unjust!*" You have just defined ethics for yourself. Ethics is more than just common, or normative, standards of behavior. Ethics is honesty, fairness, and justice. The principles of ethics, when honored, ensure that the playing field is level, that we win using our own work and ideas, and that we are honest and fair in our interactions with each other, whether personally or in business.

A great many philosophers have gone round and round trying to define ethics and debate the great ethical dilemmas of their time and ours. They have debated everything from the sources of authority on what is right and what is wrong to finding the answers to ethical dilemmas. An understanding of their language and views might help you explain what exactly you are studying and can also provide you with insights as you study the cases about personal and business ethics. Ethical theories have been described and evolved as a means for applying logic and analysis to ethical dilemmas. The theories provide us with ways of looking at issues so that we are not limited to concluding, "I think . . ." The theories provide the means for you to approach a dilemma to determine why you think as you do, whether you have missed some issues and facts in reaching your conclusion, and if there are others with different views who have points that require further analysis.

Divine Command Theory

The Divine Command Theory is one in which resolution of dilemmas is based upon religious beliefs. Ethical dilemmas are resolved according to tenets of a faith, such as the Ten Commandments for the Jewish and Christian faiths. Central to this theory is that decisions in ethical dilemmas are made on the basis of guidance from a divine being. In some countries the Divine Command Theory has influenced the law, as in some Muslim nations in which adultery is not only unethical but also illegal and sometimes punishable by death. In other countries, the concept of natural law runs in parallel with the Divine Command Theory. Natural law proposes that there are certain rights and conduct controlled by God, and that no matter what a society does, it should not drift from those tenets. For example, in the United States, the Declaration of Independence relied on the notion of natural law, stating that we had rights because they were given to us by our Creator.

Ethical Egoism Theory

Ethical egoism holds that we all act in our own self-interest and that all of us should limit our judgment to our own ethical egos and not interfere with the exercise of ethical egoism by others. This view holds that everything is determined by self-interest. We act as we do and decide to behave as we do because we have determined that it is in our own self-interest.

One philosopher who believed in ethical egoism was novelist Ayn Rand, who wrote books about business and business leaders' decisions in ethical dilemmas, such as *The*

Fountainhead and *Atlas Shrugged*. These two famous books made Ms. Rand's point about ethical dilemmas: the world would be better if we did not feel so guilty about the choices we make in ethical dilemmas and just acknowledged that it is all self-interest. Ms. Rand, as an ethical egoist, would maintain order by putting in place the necessary legal protections so that we did not harm each other.

Ms. Rand subscribed to the school of thought of philosopher Thomas Hobbes, who also believed that ethical egoism was the central factor in human decisions. Hobbes also warned that there would be chaos because of ethical egoism if we did not have laws in place to control that terrible drive of self-interest. Hobbes felt we needed great power in government to control ethical egoism.

Although he too believed that humans act in their own self-interest, and so was a bit of an ethical egoist, Adam Smith, a philosopher and an economist, also maintained that humans define self-interest differently from the selfishness theory that Hobbes and Rand feared would consume the world if not checked by legal safeguards. Adam Smith wrote, in *The Moral Sentiments of Markets,* that humans are rational and understand that, for example, fraud is in no one's self-interest. That is, many believe that they can lie in business transactions and get ahead. Adam Smith argues that while many can and do lie to close a deal or get ahead, they cannot continue that pattern of selfish behavior because just one or two times of treating others this way results in a business community spreading the word: don't do business with him because he cannot be trusted. The result is that they are shunned from doing business at least for a time, if not forever. In other words, Smith believed that there was some force of long-term self-interest that keeps businesses running ethically and that chaos only results in limited markets for limited periods as one or two rotten apples use their ethical egoism in a selfish, rather than self-interest sense, to their own temporary advantage.

The Utilitarian Theory

Philosophers Jeremy Bentham and John Stuart Mill moved to the opposite end of ethical egoism and argued that resolution of ethical dilemmas requires a balancing effort in which we minimize the harms that result from a decision even as we maximize the benefits. Mill is known for his "greatest happiness principle," which provides that we should resolve ethical dilemmas by bringing the greatest good to the greatest number of people. There will always be a few disgruntled souls in every ethical dilemma solution, so we just do the most good that we can.

Some of the issues to which we have applied utilitarianism include providing health care even as costs escalate; protecting the environment even as we generate electricity, drive cars, and operate factories; and outsourcing manufacturing of clothing to developing countries. Utilitarianism is a theory of balancing that requires us to look at the impact of our proposed solutions to ethical dilemmas from the viewpoints of all those who are affected.

The Categorical Imperative and Immanuel Kant

Kant's theories are complex, but he is a respecter of persons. That is, Kant does not allow any resolution of an ethical dilemma in which human beings are used as a means by which others obtain benefits. That might sound confusing, so Kant reduced to simplest terms is that you cannot use others in a way that gives you a one-sided benefit.

Everyone must operate under the same usage rules. In Kant's words, "One ought only to act such that the principle of one's act could become a universal law of human action in a world in which one would hope to live."

Philosophers are not the easiest fellows to follow, so an illustration will help us grasp this deep thought. For example, there are those who find it unethical to have workers in developing nations labor in garment sweatshops for pennies per hour. The pennies-per-hour wage seems unjust to them. However, suppose the company was operating under one of its universal principles: Always pay a fair wage to those who work for it. A "fair wage" in that country might be pennies, and, the company owner could argue, "I would work for that wage if I lived in that country." The company owner could also argue, "But, if I lived in the United States, I would not work for that wage, would require a much higher wage and would want benefits, and, we do provide that to all of our U.S. workers." The employer applies the same standard, but the wages are different.

The company has developed its own ethical standard that is universally applicable, and those who own the company could live with it if it were applied to them, but context is everything under the categorical imperative. The basic question is: are you comfortable living in a world operating under the standards you have established or would you deem them unfair or unjust?

There is one more part to Kant's theory: you not only have to be fair; you have to want to do it for all the right reasons. Self-interest was not a big seller with Kant, and he wants universal principles adopted with all good will and pureness of heart. So, to not engage in fraud in business because you don't want to get caught is not sufficient basis for a rule against fraud. Kant wants you to adopt and accept these ethical standards because you don't want to use other people as a means to your enrichment at their expense.

The Contractarians and Justice

Blame John Locke and John Rawls for this theory, sometimes called the theory of justice and sometimes referred to as the social contract. Kant's flaw, according to this one modern and one not-so-modern philosopher, is that he assumed we could all have a meeting of the minds on what were the good rules for society. Locke and Rawls preferred just putting the rules into place via a social contract that is created under circumstances in which we reflect and imagine what it would be like if we had no rules or law at all. If we started with a blank slate, or tabula rasa as these philosophers would say, rational people would agree, perhaps in their own self-interest, or perhaps to be fair, that certain universal rules must apply. Rational people, thinking through the results and consequences if there were not rules, would develop rules such as, "Don't take my property without my permission," and "I would like the same type of court proceeding that rich people have even if I am not so rich."

Locke and Rawls have their grounding in other schools, such as natural law and utilitarianism, but their solution is provided by having those in the midst of a dilemma work to imagine that there are not only no existing rules, but that they don't know how they will be affected by the outcome of the decision, i.e., which side they are on in the dilemma. With those constraints, Locke and Rawls argue, we would always choose the most equitable and fairest resolution of the dilemma. The idea of Locke and Rawls is to have us step back from the emotion of the moment and make universal principles that will survive the test of time.

Rights Theory

The rights theory is also known as an entitlement theory and is one of the more modern theories of ethics, as philosophers go. Robert Nozick is the key modern-day philosopher on this theory and it has two big elements: (1) Everyone has a set of rights; and (2) It's up to the governments to protect those rights. So under this big umbrella of ethical theory we have the protection of human rights that includes issues such as sweatshops, abortion, slavery, property ownership and use, justice (as in court processes), animal rights, privacy, and euthanasia. Nozick's school of thought faces head-on all the controversial and emotional issues of ethics including everything from human dignity in suffering to third-trimester abortions. Nozick hits the issues head-on, but not always with resolutions because governments protecting those rights are put into place by egoists, Kantians, and divine commandment followers.

Moral Relativists

Moral relativists believe in time-and-place ethics. Arson is not always wrong in their book. If you live in a neighborhood in which drug dealers are operating a crystal meth lab or crack house, arson is ethically justified. If you are a parent and your child is starving, stealing a loaf of bread is ethically correct. The proper resolution to ethical dilemmas is based upon weighing the competing factors at the moment and then making a determination to take the lesser of the evils as the resolution. Moral relativists do not believe in absolute rules, virtue ethics, or even the social contract. Their beliefs center on the pressure of the moment and whether the pressure justifies the action taken.

Back to Plato and Aristotle: Virtue Ethics

While it seems odd that Aristotle and Plato are last in the list of theories, there is reason to this ethical madness. Aristotle and Plato taught that solving ethical dilemmas requires training, that individuals solve ethical dilemmas when they develop and nurture a set of virtues. Aristotle taught the importance of cultivating virtue in his students and then having them solve ethical dilemmas using those virtues once they had become an integral part of their being through their virtue training. One of the purposes of this book is to help you develop a set of virtues that can serve as a guide in making both personal and business decisions. You will learn those virtues by studying the history of business through individual case studies. You will learn what constitutes a good ethical choice in business and what brought disastrous results for a business. From contrasting those differing results, you can develop your list of virtues.

Some modern philosophers have embraced this notion of virtue and have developed lists of what constitutes a virtuous business person. The following list of virtue ethics was developed by Professor Robert Solomon:

Virtue standard	Definition
Ability	Being dependable and competent
Acceptance	Making the best of a bad situation
Amiability	Fostering agreeable social contexts

Virtue standard	Definition
Articulateness	Ability to make and defend one's case
Attentiveness	Listening and understanding
Autonomy	Having a personal identity
Caring	Worrying about the well-being of others despite power
Charisma	Inspiring others
Compassion	Sympathetic
Coolheadedness	Retaining control and reasonableness in heated situations
Courage	Doing the right thing despite the cost
Determination	Seeing a task through to completion
Fairness	Giving others their due; creating harmony
Generosity	Sharing, enhancing others' well-being
Graciousness	Establishing a congenial environment
Gratitude	Giving proper credit
Heroism	Doing the right thing despite the consequences
Honesty	Telling the truth; not lying
Humility	Giving proper credit
Humor	Bringing relief; making the world better
Independence	Getting things done despite bureaucracy
Integrity	Being a model of trustworthiness
Justice	Treating others fairly
Loyalty	Working for the well-being of an organization
Pride	Being admired by others
Prudence	Minimizing company and personal losses
Responsibility	Doing what it takes to do the right thing
Saintliness	Approaching the ideal in behavior
Shame (capable of)	Regaining acceptance after wrong behavior
Spirit	Appreciating a larger picture in situations
Toughness	Maintaining one's position
Trust	Dependable
Trustworthiness	Fulfilling one's responsibilities
Wittiness	Lightening the conversation when warranted
Zeal	Getting the job done right; enthusiasm[1]

[1] *Robert C. Solomon, A Better Way to Think about Business (New York: Oxford University Press, 1999), p. 18. See also, Kevin J. Shanahan and Michael R. Hyman, "The Development of a Virtue Ethics Scale," 42 Journal of Business Ethics, 2002, pp. 197, 200.*

The list offers a tall order for virtue in business because these are difficult traits to develop and keep. But, as you study the companies, issues and cases, you will begin to understand the mighty role that these various schools of thought on ethics play in seeing the ethical issues, discussing them from all view points, and finding a resolution that ensures that the business survives over the long term.

Discussion Questions

1. Your friend, spouse, child, or parent needs a specialized medical treatment. Without the specialized treatment, they cannot survive. You are able to get that treatment for them, but the cost is $6,800. You don't have $6,800, but you hold a job in the Department of Motor Vehicles. As part of your duties there, you process the checks, money orders, and other forms of payment sent in for vehicle registration. You could endorse these items, cash them, and have those funds. You feel that because you open the mail with the checks and money orders no one will be able to discover the true amounts of funds coming in, and you can credit the vehicle owners' accounts so that their registrations are renewed. Under the various schools of thought on ethics, evaluate whether the embezzlement would be justified.

2. What is the difference between virtue ethics and utilitarianism?

3. Give an example of a situation in which moral relativists would feel that theft is justified.

4. Could businesses use moral relativism to justify false financial reports? For example, suppose that the CFO says, "I did fudge on some of the numbers in our financial reports, but that kept 6,000 employees from losing their jobs." What problems do you see with moral relativism in this situation?

READING 1.2
The Types of Ethical Dilemmas

The following twelve categories were developed and listed in *Exchange*, the magazine of the Brigham Young University School of Business:

Taking Things That Don't Belong to You

Everything from the unauthorized use of the Pitney Bowes postage meter at your office for mailing personal letters to exaggerations on travel expenses belongs in this category of ethical violations. Using the copy machine at work for your personal copies is another simple example of the type of conduct that fits into this category. Regardless of size or motivation, unauthorized use of someone else's property or taking property under false pretenses still means taking something that does not belong to you. A chief financial officer of a large electric utility reported that after taking a cab from LaGuardia International Airport to his midtown Manhattan hotel, he asked for a receipt. The cab driver handed him a full book of blank receipts and drove away. Apparently the problem of accurately reporting travel expenses involves more than just employees.

Saying Things You Know Are Not True

This category deals with the virtue of honesty. Assume you are trying to sell your wrecked and repaired car. If the potential buyer asks if the car has been in an accident and you reply, "No," then you have given false information. If you take credit for someone else's idea or work, then you have, by your conduct, said something that is not true. If you do not disclose an accident that you had in the last year on an insurance application, you have not told the truth. If you put down that you have a college degree on your résumé, but have not yet graduated, you have committed an ethical breach.

Giving or Allowing False Impressions

This category of ethical breach is the legal technicality category. What you have said is technically the truth, but it does mislead the other side. For example, if your professor asks you, "Did you have a chance to read the assigned ethics cases?" Even if you had not read the cases, you could answer a "Yes!" and be technically correct. You had "a chance" to read the cases; but, you did not read them. The answer is not a falsehood, because you may have had plenty of chances to read the cases, but you didn't read the cases.

If you were to stand by silently while a co-worker was blamed for something you did, you would leave a false impression. You haven't lied, but you allowed an impression as to blame to continue.

A landscaping company that places decorative rocks in a drawing and bid for a customer has created the impression that the rocks are included in the bid. If, after the customer signs the contract the landscaper reveals that the rocks require additional payment, the customer has been misled with a false impression that came from the drawing including the rocks.

Buying Influence or Engaging in Conflict of Interest

This category finds someone in the position of conflicting loyalties. An officer of a corporation should not be entering into contracts between his company and a company that he has created as part of a sideline of work. The officer is conflicted between his duty to negotiate the best contract and price for his corporation and his interest as a business owner in maximizing his profits. In his role as an officer, he wants the most he can get at the lowest price. In his role as a business owner, he wants the highest price he can get with the fewest demands. The interests are in conflict, and this category of ethical breach dictates that those conflicts be resolved or avoided.

Conflicts of interest need not be as direct as an officer of the company self-dealing. For example, there would be a conflict of interest if a company awarded a construction contract to a firm owned by the father of the state attorney general while the state attorney general's office is investigating that company. A county administrator responsible for awarding the construction contract for a baseball stadium who accepts from contractors interested in bidding on the project paid travel around the country to other stadiums that the contractors have built would be conflicted. His job as a county employee is to hire the most qualified contractor at the best price. However, his acceptance of benefits, and how much those benefits impress him, conflict with that interest of his employer, the county.

These examples illustrate conflicts of interest. Those involved in situations such as these often protest, "But I would never allow that to influence me." The ethical violation is the conflict. Whether the conflict can or will influence those it touches is not the issue, for neither party can prove conclusively that a *quid pro quo* was not intended. The possibility exists, and it creates suspicion. Hence, conflicts of interest are to be avoided or, at a minimum, disclosed.

Hiding or Divulging Information

Taking your firm's product development or trade secrets to a new place of employment constitutes an ethical violation: divulging proprietary information. Failing to disclose the results of medical studies that indicate your firm's new drug has significant side effects is the ethical violation of hiding information that the product could be harmful to purchasers. A bank that sells financial and marketing information about its customers without their knowledge or permission has divulged information that should be kept confidential.

Taking Unfair Advantage

Many current consumer protection laws were passed because so many businesses took unfair advantage of those who were not educated or were unable to discern the nuances of complex contracts. Credit disclosure requirements, truth-in-lending provisions, and new regulations on auto leasing all resulted because businesses misled consumers who could not easily follow the jargon of long and complex agreements. One of the newer issues on credit cards is that the late fees have increased, as well as the fees for charging more than the card balance. In addition, companies have been shortening the billing cycle so that customers have less time to pay and establishing the cut-off times for payment earlier in the day. If payment must be received by 9 AM on a particular day, this cut-off means that the customer must pay one day earlier because mail does not arrive by 9 AM. These fees and practices are legal right now, but many have questioned their fairness to consumers.

Committing Acts of Personal Decadence

While many argue about the ethical notion of an employee's right to privacy, it has become increasingly clear that personal conduct outside the job can influence performance and company reputation. Sometimes our conduct in our personal lives does have an impact on how well we perform our jobs, and perhaps, even whether we can perform our jobs safely. For example, a company driver must abstain from substance abuse because with alcohol or drugs in his blood, he creates both safety and liability issues for his employer. Even the traditional company Christmas party and picnic have come under scrutiny as the behavior of employees at, and following, these events has brought harm to others in the form of alcohol-related accidents.

Perpetrating Interpersonal Abuse

A manager who keeps asking an employee for a date not only violates the laws against sexual harassment, but also has committed the ethical breach of interpersonal abuse. Interpersonal abuse consists of conduct that is demeaning, unfair, hostile, or involves others so that privacy issues arise. A manager who is verbally abusive to an employee falls into this category. The former CEO of HealthSouth, Richard Scrushy, held what his employees called the "Monday morning beatings." These were meetings during which managers who had not met their numbers goals were upbraided in front of others and subjected to humiliating criticism. A manager correcting an employee's conduct in front of a customer has not violated any laws, but has humiliated the employee and involved outsiders who have no reason to know of any employee issues. In some cases in this category, there are laws to protect employees from this type of conduct. However, many situations are simply ethical violations, or, again, the forms of conduct that we are able to look at and instantly conclude, "It's not fair," or "It's not right."

Permitting Organizational Abuse

This category covers the way companies treat employees. Many U.S. firms with operations overseas, such as Nike, Levi Strauss, The Gap, and Esprit, have faced questions related to organizational abuse. The questions focus on the treatment of workers in these companies' international operations and plants. The critical issues raised are child labor, low wages, and too-long hours. While a business cannot change the culture of another country, it can perpetuate—or alleviate—organizational abuse through standards of fairness and respect in its operations there.

Violating Rules

Many rules, particularly those in large organizations that tend toward bureaucracy from a need to maintain internal controls or follow lines of authority, seem burdensome to employees trying to serve customers and other employees. Stanford University experienced difficulties in this area of ethics when it used funds from federal grants for miscellaneous university purposes. Questions arose about the propriety of the expenditures, which quite possibly could have been approved through proper channels, but weren't. The rules for the administration of federal grant monies used for overhead were not followed. The results were not only an ethical violation but damage to Stanford's reputation and a new president for the university. While rules can be revised and studied because of problems they create, they should be honored by employees until those changes are made.

Condoning Unethical Actions

In this category, the wrong is actually a failure to report an ethical breach in any of the other categories. What if you witnessed a fellow employee embezzling company funds by forging her signature on a check that was to be voided? Would you report that violation? What if you knew that an officer of your company was giving false testimony in a deposition? Would you speak up and let the court or lawyers know that the testimony is false? A winking tolerance of others' unethical behavior is in itself unethical. Suppose that as a product designer you were aware of a fundamental flaw in your company's new product—a product predicted to catapult your firm to record earnings. Would you pursue the problem to the point of halting the distribution of the product? Would you disclose what you know to the public if you could not get your company to act?

Balancing Ethical Dilemmas

In these types of situations, there are no right or wrong answers; rather, there are dilemmas to be resolved. For example, Levi Strauss struggled with its decision about whether to do business in the People's Republic of China because of known human rights violations by the government there. Other companies debated doing business in South Africa when that country's government followed a policy of apartheid. In some respects, the presence of these companies would help by advancing human rights and, certainly, by improving the standard of living for at least some international operations workers. On the other hand, their ability to recruit businesses could help such governments sustain themselves by enabling them to point to economic successes despite human rights violations.

These 12 categories are resources for you to use as you analyze the cases in this book. As you read, think through the 12 categories and determine what ethical breaches have occurred. These categories help you in spotting the ethical issues in each of the cases.

Discussion Questions

1. Why do we have these categories of ethical dilemmas? How is it helpful to have this list?

2. Consider the following situations and determine which category of the 12 each issue fits into.

   a. A parent has to travel out of town for work, and the night she will be gone is the night of her son's junior high honors assembly. The school has called to let her know that her son will be receiving several awards. She is proud of her son and very supportive, but she promised she would make this trip almost 4 months ago, long before the honors assembly was scheduled.

   b. A manager at a bank branch requires those employees who arrive late for work to clean the restrooms at the bank. The branch does have a janitorial service, but the manager's motto is, "If you're late, the bathrooms must look great." An employee finds the work of cleaning the bathrooms in her professional clothes demeaning.

   c. Jack Walls is the purchasing manager for a small manufacturer. He has decided to award a contract for office supplies to Office Mart. No one knows of Jack's decision yet, but Office Mart is anxious for the business and offers Jack a 3-day ski vacation in Telluride. Jack would love to take the trip but can't decide if there is an ethics question. Help Jack decide if there is.

READING 1.3
How We Avoid Ethical Dilemmas

We often are able to see ethical issues and we understand what ethics is about and why it is important. But, we are often reluctant to raise ethical issues, or, in many cases, we use certain strategies to avoid facing ethical issues. This section covers the rationalizations and avoidance techniques we use so that we never really have to face the ethical issue.

Call It by a Different Name

If we can attach a lovely label to what we are doing, we won't have to face the ethical issue. For example, some people, including U.S. Justice Department lawyers, refer to the downloading of music from the Internet as "copyright infringement." However, many who download music assure us that it is really just the lovely practice of "peer-to-peer file sharing." How can something that sounds so generous be an ethical issue? Yet there is an ethical issue because copying copyrighted music without permission is taking something that does not belong to you or taking unfair advantage.

Yet another example is the financial practice of juggling numbers in financial statements, sometimes referred to as "smoothing earnings," but less eloquently known as "cooking the books." That description helps us to see that we have an ethical issue in the category of telling the truth or not leaving a false impression. But if we call what we are doing "smoothing out earnings" or "earnings management," then we never have to face the ethical issue because we are doing something that is finance strategy, not an ethics issue. One investor, when asked what he thought about earnings management said, "I don't call it earnings management. I call it lying." The categories are the tool to use to be sure we are facing the issue and not skirting it with a different name.

Rationalizing Dilemmas Away: "Everybody Else Does It"

We can feel very comfortable and not have to face an ethical issue if we simply assure ourselves that "Everybody else does it." We use faulty ethical reasoning to conclude that it must be right because so many people are doing it. A good day-to-day example is, "Everybody speeds, and so I speed." There remains the problem that speeding is still a breach of one of the ethical categories: following the rules. While you may feel the speed limit is too low or unnecessary, your ethical obligation is to follow those speed limits unless and until you successfully persuade others to change the laws because of your valid points about speed limits.

Rationalizing Dilemmas Away: "If We Don't Do It, Someone Else Will"

This rationalization is one used frequently by business people as they face tough competition. They seize this rationalization because they can ignore the ethical issue in the name of business survival. They are saying that someone will do it anyway and make money, so why shouldn't it be us? For Halloween 1994, there were O. J. Simpson masks and plastic knives and Nicole Brown Simpson masks and costumes complete with slashes and blood stains. When Nicole Simpson's family objected to this violation of the basic standard of decency, a costume-shop owner commented that if he didn't sell the items, someone down the street would. While nothing about the marketing of the costumes was illegal, the ethical issues that surround earning a profit from an event as heinous as the brutal murder of a young mother abound.

Rationalizing Dilemmas Away: "That's the Way It Has Always Been Done"

When we hear, "That's the way it's always been done," our innovation feelers as well as our ethical radar should be up. We should be asking, "Is there a better way to do this?" Just as "everybody does it" is not ethical analysis, neither is relying on the past and its standards a process of ethical reasoning. Business practices are not always sound. For example, the field of business ethics has taught for years that a good board for a company has independent directors; that is, directors who are not employed by the company or under consulting contracts with the company or related to officers of the company. Independent boards were good ethical practice, but many companies resisted because their boards had always been structured a certain way and they would stick to that saying, "This is the way our board has always looked." With the collapses of Enron, Adelphia, and WorldCom and the substantial officer loans at Tyco, both Congress through the Sarbanes-Oxley legislation and the Securities and Exchange Commission in follow-up regulations now mandate an independent corporate board. A conflict of interest existed when board members were employees or under contract with the corporation for consulting or legal services; but everybody was doing it, and it was the way corporations had always been governed. But the typical and prevailing practice resulted in lax corporate boards and company collapses. Unquestioning adherence to a pattern of practice or behavior often indicates an underlying ethical dilemma.

Rationalizing Dilemmas Away: "We'll Wait until the Lawyers Tell Us It's Wrong"

Many people rely only on the law as their ethical standard, but that reliance means that they have resolved only the legal issue, not the ethical one. Lawyers are trained to provide only the parameters of the law. In many situations, they offer an opinion that is correct in that a company's conduct does not violate the law. Whether the conduct they have passed judgment on as legal is ethical is a different question. For example, a team of White House lawyers concluded in a memo in March 2003 that international law did not ban torture of prisoners in Iraq because they were technically not prisoners of war. However, when pictures of prisoner abuse at the Abu Ghraib prison in Iraq emerged, the reaction of the public and the world was very different. The nonlegal and ethical analysis was that the torture and abuse were wrong, regardless of the legality under treaty law. Following the abuse scandal, new standards for interrogation of prisoners, well above legal standards, were imposed on the U.S. military. While the lawyers were perfectly correct in their legal analysis, that legal analysis did not cover the ethical breaches of interpersonal and organizational abuse.

Rationalizing Dilemmas Away: "It Doesn't Really Hurt Anyone"

We often think that our ethical missteps are just small ones that don't really affect anyone else. We are not thinking through the consequences of our actions when we rationalize rather than analyze ethical issues in this manner. For example, it is probably true that one fraudulent insurance claim is not going to bankrupt an insurance company. However, if everyone who believes his or her fraud is singular and isolated submitted a false insurance claim, we could create what happened in California when fraud overtook its workers' compensation system. Employers' insurance rates for workers' compensation climbed as much as 700% in a 2-year period. In analyzing ethical issues, we turn to Kant and other schools of thought and ask, "What if everyone behaved this way? What would the world be like?"

When we are the sole rubberneckers on the freeway, traffic remains unaffected. But if everyone rubbernecks, we have a traffic jam. All of us making poor ethical choices would cause significant harm. A man interviewed after he was arrested for defrauding insurance companies through staged auto accidents remarked, "It didn't really hurt anyone. Insurance companies can afford it." The second part of his statement is accurate. The insurance companies can afford it—but not without cost to someone else. Such fraud harms all of us because we must pay higher premiums to allow insurers to absorb the costs of investigating and paying for fraudulent claims.

Rationalizing Dilemmas Away: "The System Is Unfair"

Somehow an ethical breach doesn't seem as bad if we feel we are doing it because we have been given an unfair hand. The professor is unreasonable and demanding, so why not buy a term paper from the Internet? Often touted by students as a justification for cheating on exams, this rationalization eases our consciences by telling us we are cheating only to make up for deficiencies in the system. Yet just one person cheating can send ripples through an entire system. The credibility of grades and the institution come into question as students obtain grades through means beyond the system's standards. As we see events unfold in China, Italy, and Brazil, with government employees awarding contracts and rights to do business on the basis of payments rather than on the merits of a given company or its proposal, we understand how such bribery only results in greater unfairness within and greater costs to those countries. As noted in Reading 2.3 in the following unit, many economists have noted that a country's businesses and economy will not progress without some fundamental assurance of trust.

Rationalizing Dilemmas Away: "I Was Just Following Orders"

In many criminal trials and disputes over responsibility and liability, many managers will disclaim their responsibility by stating, "I was just following orders." In fact, when WorldCom collapsed because it had capitalized $9 billion in ordinary expenses and, as a result, overreported its earnings, one of the accountants involved in making the entries indicated that she was just following orders from the controller and chief financial officer. However, she did not deny that she knew such capitalization of ordinary expenses was wrong. She has responsibility, both legally and ethically, for the financial misstatements.

There are times when individuals cannot follow the directions of supervisors, for they have been asked to do something illegal or immoral. Judges who preside over the criminal trials of war criminals often remind defendants that an order is not necessarily legal or moral. Good ethical analysis requires us to question or depart from orders when others will be harmed or wronged. Again, the example of the prisoner abuse scandal in Iraq illustrates that even if the soldiers were following orders, they could not call their abusive conduct ethical.

Discussion Questions

1. Give some examples, other than the speeding example in the reading, of the types of things we do that we are able to feel comfortable with because "everybody does it."

2. Give some examples from history of how following orders resulted in horrific harm to many.

3. A man has developed a license plate that cannot be photographed by the red light and speeding cameras. When asked how he felt about facilitating drivers being able to break the law he replied, "I am not the one with my foot to the gas pedal. They are. I make a product they can use." What rationalization(s) is he using?

4. A parent has instructed his young son to not mention his Uncle Ted's odd shoes and clothing. "If Uncle Ted asks you how you like his clothes or shoes, just tell him they are very nice." His son said, "But that's not the truth, Dad." The father's response was, "It's a white lie and it doesn't really hurt anyone." Evaluate the father's ethical posture.

1 B

Resolving Ethical Dilemmas

READING 1.4

Some Simple Tests for Resolving Ethical Dilemmas

Nearly every business professor and philosopher has weighed in with models and tests that can be used for resolving ethical issues. The following sections offer summaries of the thoughts and models of others in the field of ethics.

Management Guru—Dr. Peter Drucker

An internationally known management expert, Dr. Peter Drucker offers the following as an overview for all ethical dilemmas: *primum non nocere*, which, translated means "above all do no harm." The motto of the medical profession, Dr. Drucker's simple ethical test in a short phrase encourages us to make decisions that do not harm others. This test would keep us from releasing a product that had a defect that could cause injury. This test would have us be fair and decent in the working conditions we provide for workers in other countries. This test would also prevent us from not disclosing relevant information during contract negotiations.

Laura Nash: Harvard Divinity School Meets Business

Ethicist Laura Nash, of the Harvard Divinity School, has one of the more detailed decision-making models, with 12 questions to be asked in evaluating an ethical dilemma. Those 12 questions are:

1. **Have you defined the problem accurately?** For example, often philosophical questions are phrased as follows: would you steal a loaf of bread if you were starving? The problem might be better defined by asking, "Is there a way other than stealing to take care of my hunger?" The rephrasing of the question helps us think in terms of honoring our values rather than rationalizing to justify taking property from another.

2. **How would you define the problem if you stood on the other side of the fence?** This question asks us to live by the same rules that we apply to others. For example, if someone hits your car in the parking lot and does not leave a note, you are angry and may exclaim, "I can't believe someone would do such a thing!" But, when asked if you would leave a note on a car that you hit, you might hesitate and say, "They could stick

me with a big insurance bill!!!!" This question forces us to look at our standards in a more universal way.

3. **How did this situation occur in the first place?** This question helps us in the future. We use it to avoid being placed in the same predicament again. For example, suppose that an employee has asked his supervisor for a letter of recommendation for a new job the employee may get, if the references are good. The supervisor has always had difficulty with the employee, but found him to be tolerable and kept him on at the company, but never really discussed any of his performance issues with him or even put those concerns in his annual evaluation. Does he make things up for the letter? Does he refuse to write the letter? Does he say innocuous things in the letter such as, "He was always on time for work." This reluctant supervisor is in this situation because he or she has never been honest and candid with the employee. The employee is not aware that the supervisor had any problems or issues with him because the fact that he has asked for the reference shows that there has not been forthright communication.

4. **To whom and what do you give your loyalties as a person and as a member of the corporation?** Suppose that you know that your manager has submitted false travel invoices to the company. The expenses are false, padded and unnecessary. No one in the accounting or audit department has caught his scheme. Saying something means you are loyal to your company (the corporation), but you have sacrificed your loyalty to your manager.

5. **What is your intention in making this decision?** Often we offer a different public reason for what we are doing as a means of avoiding examination of the real issue. An officer of a company may say that liberal accounting interpretations help the company, smooth out earnings, and keep the share price stable. But, his real intention may be to reach the financials and numbers goals that allow him to earn his bonus.

6. **How does this intention compare with the likely results?** Continuing with the previous example, the stated intention of increasing or maintaining shareholder value may work for a time, but, eventually, the officer and the company will need to face the truth about its real financial picture. And the officer's real intention will be foiled as well because under the new federal statutes that regulate financial reporting (known as Sarbanes-Oxley), officers who earn bonuses based on false financial statements must repay those bonuses and face criminal penalties as well.

7. **Whom could your decision or action injure?** Under this question, think of not only the direct harm that can result from a poor ethical choice, but all the ripple effects as well. For example, the direct effects of a false financial statement are that shareholders and those who sell or buy stock based on that financial picture are misled and possibly harmed financially. Employees who have invested in their companies are also affected when the financial picture is misrepresented because they base their decisions to buy stock in the company or other retirement and pension investments based on how well their company is doing. For example, at Enron, Ken Lay, the former CEO, is charged with fraudulent statements for telling a group of employees that his "personal belief is that Enron stock is an incredible bargain at current prices." Mr. Lay was selling off blocks of the stock even as he told the employees of his belief. Another direct effect is that the banks that loan money based on those financial statements are also harmed when those statements are false. Even suppliers who have extended credit are harmed because they too have relied on that financial picture in making their decision to extend credit. There will also be indirect or ripple effects from these misstatements. For

example, nonprofit organizations that have benefited from a corporation's donations will lose that source of funding if the company falls into financial ruin. If the company is a critical part of a state or local economy, there will be an indirect effect on all businesses in the state or community. Ethical missteps cut a wide swath of harm, and this question asks us to consider all that harm before we make a final decision.

8. **Can you engage the affected parties in a discussion of the problem before you make your decision?** If you are considering "cheating" on a spouse or significant other, you face an ethical dilemma. The fact that you could not discuss what you are about to do with a person who has been very close to you and who you would betray indicates that your secret decision and action crosses an ethical line.

9. **Are you confident that your position will be as valid over a long period of time as it seems now?** Sometimes cheating on an exam or purchasing a paper on the internet seems to be an expedient way of solving time pressures, financial worries about going to school, and even just the concerns about finishing a semester or a degree. However, this question asks you to think about this small decision over the time frame of your life. When you look back, how will you feel about this decision? Or, what if your friend, roommate, or even someone who happens to see you cheat carries that knowledge of your ethical indiscretion with them? You always have the worry that they will know of your misstep and perhaps would be involved in your future in such a way that this knowledge could affect your potential. For example, what if someone who knows you cheated works for a company you very much want to work for. Suppose further that the person interviewing you sees that you went to the same school as their employee. One question to that employee might be, "Say, I see you went to school at Western U. I interviewed a Josh Blake from Western U. He wants to work with us. Do you know him? And what do you think of him?" Think ahead to their response, "Yes, I knew him at school. He cheated." Interestingly, this feedback is what happened to Joseph Jett, a Wall Street investment banker who was at the heart of a trading scandal at Kidder Peabody. When his credentials of a Harvard MBA emerged, someone from the school emerged to let the world know that while he had finished his course work at Harvard he did not have his degree because he had not paid some fees. The fees might have been unpaid parking tickets. The fees may have been library fines. What seemed expedient budget decisions at the time he was a graduate student turned out to be something that harmed Mr. Jett's credibility when he was most in need of a good reputation. Over the long term your decision might not seem as good as it did during the pressure crunch of college.

10. **Could you disclose without qualm your decision or action to your boss, your CEO, the board of directors, your family, or society as a whole?** This question asks you to evaluate your conduct as if it were being reviewed by those who run your company. If you are thinking of padding your expense account, realize that you could not talk about your actions with these people because you are betraying their trust. This question also has a second part to it: could you tell your family? Sometimes we rationalize our way through business conduct or personal conduct, but know that if we had to face our families, we would realize we landed on the wrong side of the ethical decision. In the movie "While You Were Sleeping," Peter is a wealthy lawyer who has fallen away from his parents' simple values. When his mother learns that Peter is engaged to marry an already married woman she exclaims, "You proposed to a married woman?" Peter looks very sheepish. What seemed to be a fine decision in the confines of his social life suddenly looked different when his family was told.

11. **What is the symbolic potential of your action if understood? If misunderstood?**
A good illustration for application of this question is in conflict of interest questions. For example, Barbara Walters is a network correspondent for ABC News as well as a co-host of the ABC prime-time news show *20/20*. In December 1996, Ms. Walters interviewed British composer Andrew Lloyd Webber, now Sir Andrew Lloyd Webber, and the interview aired the same month as a segment on *20/20*.

    Two months after the interview aired, a report in the *New York Post* revealed that Ms. Walters had invested $100,000 in Webber's Broadway production of his musical, *Sunset Boulevard*. ABC News responded that had it known of the investment, it would have disclosed it before the interview aired. ABC does have a policy on conflicts that permits correspondents to cover "businesses in which they have a minority interest."

    Webber's *Sunset* cost $10 million to produce and investors received back 85% of their initial investment. Ms. Walters' interest in Sunset was one percent.

    Applying this question, even if everyone understands Ms. Walters' good intentions, the appearance is that of a conflict: she has an investment in Webber's production, and regardless of its size the public is likely to perceive that the favorable journalism piece was done to pump up the production and, hence, assure a return on her investment.

12. **Under what conditions would you allow exceptions to your stand?** You may have a strong value of always being on time for class, events, meetings, and appointments. You have adopted an absolute value on not being tardy. However, sometimes other values conflict. For example, suppose that your friend became ill and needed someone to drive her to the hospital, making you late for a meeting. You would be comfortable with that variance because your exceptions relate to the well-being of others. Likewise, you would drive more slowly and carefully in a storm to get to your meeting, something that will make you late. But, again, your exception is the safety and well-being of others. You won't be late because you stopped to talk or you didn't leave your apartment on time, but you are comfortable being late, an exception to your rule on punctuality, when safety and well-being are at stake.

These Nash questions help us gain perspective and various views on the issue before us, and, at least two of the questions focus on the past—what brought us to the dilemma.

A Minister and a One-Minute Manager Do Ethics: Blanchard and Peale

The late Dr. Norman Vincent Peale, an internationally known minister, and management expert Kenneth Blanchard, author of *The One Minute Manager,* offer three questions that managers should ponder in resolving ethical dilemmas: Is it legal? Is it balanced? How does it make me feel?

If the answer to the first question, "Is it legal?" is no, a manager should not proceed any further. Officers of companies cannot trade in their company's stock when they have information that has not yet been released to the public. So, when Dr. Sam Waksal, the CEO of ImClone, Inc. learned that the FDA was not going to approve ImClone's anticancer drug, Erbitux, for release to the market, he had information that (a) was not available to the public; and (b) is the type of information that would affect someone's decision to buy the stock and at what price. Certainly that information when released would influence the market price for ImClone's shares. Nonetheless, Dr. Waksal sold large blocks of his shares before ImClone announced to the public that FDA approval would not be forthcoming. The sales were just plain illegal, and Dr. Waksal is serving a prison term as a result of those stock sales.

Answering the second Blanchard and Peale question, "Is it balanced?" requires a manager to step back and view a problem from other perspectives—those of other parties, owners, shareholders, or the community. For example, an M&M/Mars cacao buyer was able to secure a very low price on cacao for his company because of pending government takeovers and political disruption. M&M/Mars officers decided to pay more for the cacao than the negotiated figure. Their reason was that some day their company would not have the upper hand, and then they would want to be treated fairly when the price became the seller's choice.

Answering "How does it make me feel?" requires a manager to do a self-examination of his or her comfort level with a decision. Some decisions, though they may be legal and may appear balanced, can still make a manager uncomfortable. For example, many managers feel uncomfortable about the "management" of earnings when inventory and shipments are controlled to maximize bonuses or to produce a particularly good result for a quarter. Although they've done nothing illegal, managers who engage in such practices often suffer such physical effects as insomnia and appetite problems.

The Oracle of Omaha: Warren Buffett's Front-Page-of-the-Newspaper Test

This very simple ethical model requires only that a decision maker envision how a reporter would describe a decision or action on the front page of a local or national newspaper. For example, with regard to the NBC News report on the sidesaddle gas tanks in GM pickup trucks, the *USA Today* headline read: "GM Suit Attacks NBC Report: Says Show Faked Fiery Truck Crash." Would NBC have made the same decisions about its staging of the truck crash if that headline had been foreseen?

When Salomon Brothers' illegal cornering of the U.S. government's bond market was revealed, the *Business Week* headline read: "How Bad Will It Get?"; nearly two years later, a follow-up story on Salomon's crisis strategy was headlined "The Bomb Shelter That Salomon Built." During the aftermath of the bond market scandal, the interim chairman of Salomon, Warren Buffett, told employees, "Contemplating any business act, an employee should ask himself whether he would be willing to see it immediately described by an informed and critical reporter on the front page of his local paper, there to be read by his spouse, children, and friends. At Salomon we simply want no part of any activities that pass legal tests but that we, as citizens, would find offensive."

Dow Corning might have made different decisions about disclosures on its silicone breast implants if it had envisioned such headlines as "Breast Implants: What Did the Industry Know, and When?" from *Business Week* shortly after a woman won a $4 million verdict for permanent injury resulting from her implants.

The purpose of this test is to have you step back from the business setting in which decisions are made and view the issue and choices from the perspective of an objective outsider. Their views and perceptions can be quite different because they are not subject to the same pressures and biases. The purpose of this test is to help managers envision how their actions and decisions look to the outside world.

The Wall Street Journal Model

The *Wall Street Journal* model for resolution of ethical dilemmas consists of three components: (1) Am I in compliance with the law? (2) What contribution does this choice of action make to the company, the shareholders, the community, and others? and (3) What are the short- and long-term consequences of this decision? Like the Blanchard-Peale model, any proposed conduct must first be in compliance with the law. The next step requires an evaluation of a decision's contributions to the shareholders, the employees, the community, and the customers. For example, furniture manufacturer Herman Miller decided both to invest in equipment that would exceed the requirements for compliance with the 1990 Clean Air Act and to refrain from using rain forest woods in producing its signature Eames chair. The decision was costly to the shareholders at first, but ultimately they, the community, and customers enjoyed the benefits.

Finally, managers are asked to envision the consequences of a decision, such as whether headlines that are unfavorable to the firm may result. The initial consequences for Miller's decisions were a reduction in profits because of the costs of the changes. However, the long-term consequences were the respect of environmental regulators, a responsive public committed to rain forest preservation, and Miller's recognition by *Business Week* as an outstanding firm for 1992.

Other Models

Of course, there are much simpler models for making ethical business decisions. One stems from Immanuel Kant's categorical imperative (see p. 5), loosely similar to the Golden Rule of: "Do unto others as you would have them do unto you." Treating others or others' money as we would want to be treated is a powerful evaluation technique in ethical dilemmas. Another way of looking at issues is to apply your standards in all situations and think about whether you would be comfortable. In other words, if the world lived by your personal ethical standards, would you be comfortable or would you be nervous? As noted earlier, many of us are terribly shocked when someone dents our car in a parking lot and fails to leave a note, but would we leave a note when we are the ones who have done the damage?

Discussion Questions

1. Take the various models and offer a chart or diagram to show the common elements in each.

2. After viewing the chart, make a list of the kinds of things all those who have developed the models want us to think about as we resolve ethical dilemmas.

READING 1.5

Pressure and Temptation: The Parable of the Sadhu[2]

Now that you have background on ethics and a set of skills for evaluating ethical issues, the application to real-life dilemmas seems fairly straightforward. However, there is one additional aspect of ethical decision-making that causes complexities in the simple

[2] *Reprinted by permission of Harvard Business Review. From "The Parable of the Sadhu" by Bowen H. McCoy, September/October 1983. Copyright © 1983 by the Harvard Business School Publishing Corporation; all rights reserved.*

tests and application of questions presented in the models. That aspect is pressure. We may know that human life is a paramount value and we do honor it, but what if human life got in the way of one of our personal, critical and lifetime goals? The following reading provides a Wall Street investment banker's view of pressure, the value of human life, and ethical dilemmas.

Bowen H. McCoy

[In 1982], as the first participant in the new six-month sabbatical program that Morgan Stanley has adopted, I enjoyed a rare opportunity to collect my thoughts as well as do some traveling. I spent the first three months in Nepal, walking 600 miles through 200 villages in the Himalayas and climbing some 120,000 vertical feet. On the trip my sole Western companion was an anthropologist who shed light on the cultural patterns of the villages we passed through.

During the Nepal hike, something occurred that has had a powerful impact on my thinking about corporate ethics. Although some might argue that the experience has no relevance to business, it was a situation in which a basic ethical dilemma suddenly intruded into the lives of a group of individuals. How the group responded I think holds a lesson for all organizations no matter how defined.

The Sadhu

The Nepal experience was more rugged and adventuresome than I had anticipated. Most commercial treks last two or three weeks and cover a quarter of the distance we traveled.

My friend Stephen, the anthropologist, and I were halfway through the 60-day Himalayan part of the trip when we reached the high point, an 18,000-foot pass over a crest that we'd have to traverse to reach the village of Muklinath, an ancient holy place for pilgrims.

Six years earlier I had suffered pulmonary edema, an acute form of altitude sickness, at 16,500 feet in the vicinity of Everest base camp, so we were understandably concerned about what would happen at 18,000 feet. Moreover, the Himalayas were having their wettest spring in 20 years; hip-deep powder and ice had already driven us off one ridge. If we failed to cross the pass, I feared that the last half of our "once in a lifetime" trip would be ruined.

The night before we would try the pass, we camped at a hut at 14,500 feet. In the photos taken at that camp, my face appears wan. The last village we'd passed through was a sturdy two-day walk below us, and I was tired.

During the late afternoon, four backpackers from New Zealand joined us, and we spent most of the night awake, anticipating the climb. Below we could see the fires of two other parties, which turned out to be two Swiss couples and a Japanese hiking club.

To get over the steep part of the climb before the sun melted the steps cut in the ice, we departed at 3:30 A.M. The New Zealanders left first, followed by Stephen and myself, our porters and Sherpas, and then the Swiss. The Japanese lingered in their camp. The sky was clear, and we were confident that no spring storm would erupt that day to close the pass.

At 15,500 feet, it looked to me as if Stephen were shuffling and staggering a bit, which are symptoms of altitude sickness. (The initial stage of altitude sickness brings a headache and nausea. As the condition worsens, a climber may encounter difficult breathing, disorientation, aphasia, and paralysis.) I felt strong, my adrenaline was flowing, but I was very concerned about my ultimate ability to get across. A couple of our porters were also suffering from the height, and Pasang, our Sherpa sirdar (leader), was worried.

Just after daybreak, while we rested at 15,500 feet, one of the New Zealanders, who had gone ahead, came staggering down toward us with a body slung across his shoulders. He dumped the almost naked, barefoot body of an Indian holy man—a sadhu—at my feet. He had found the pilgrim lying on the ice, shivering and suffering from hypothermia. I cradled the sadhu's head and laid him out on the rocks. The New Zealander was angry. He wanted to get across the pass before the bright sun melted the snow. He said, "Look, I've done what I can. You have porters and Sherpa guides. You care for him. We're going on!" He turned and went back up the mountain to join his friends.

I took a carotid pulse and found that the sadhu was still alive. We figured he had probably visited the holy shrines at Muklinath and was on his way home. It was fruitless to question why he had chosen this desperately high route instead of the safe, heavily traveled caravan route through the Kali Gandaki Gorge. Or why he was almost naked and with no shoes, or how long he had been lying in the pass. The answers weren't going to solve our problem.

Stephen and the four Swiss began stripping off outer clothing and opening their packs. The sadhu was soon clothed from head to foot. He was not able to walk, but he was very much alive. I looked down the mountain and spotted below the Japanese climbers marching up with a horse.

Without a great deal of thought, I told Stephen and Pasang that I was concerned about withstanding the heights to come and wanted to get over the pass. I took off after several of our porters who had gone ahead.

On the steep part of the ascent where, if the ice steps had given way, I would have slid down about 3,000 feet, I felt vertigo. I stopped for a breather, allowing the Swiss to catch up with me. I inquired about the sadhu and Stephen. They said that the sadhu was fine and that Stephen was just behind. I set off again for the summit.

Stephen arrived at the summit an hour after I did. Still exhilarated by victory, I ran down the snow slope to congratulate him. He was suffering from altitude sickness, walking fifteen steps, then stopping, walking fifteen steps, then stopping, walking fifteen steps, then stopping. When I reached them, Stephen glared at me and said: "How do you feel about contributing to the death of a fellow man?"

I did not fully comprehend what he meant.

"Is the sadhu dead?" I inquired.

"No," replied Stephen, "but he surely will be!"

After I had gone, and the Swiss had departed not long after, Stephen had remained with the sadhu. When the Japanese had arrived, Stephen had asked to use their horse to transport the sadhu down to the hut. They had refused. He had then asked Pasang to have a group of our porters carry the sadhu. Pasang had resisted the idea, saying that the porters would have to exert all their energy to get themselves over the pass. He had thought they could not carry a man down 1,000 feet to the hut, reclimb the slope, and get across safely before the snow melted. Pasang had pressed Stephen not to delay any longer.

The Sherpas had carried the sadhu down to a rock in the sun at about 15,000 feet and had pointed out the hut another 500 feet below. The Japanese had given him food and drink. When they had last seen him he was listlessly throwing rocks at the Japanese party's dog, which had frightened him.

We do not know if the sadhu lived or died.

For many of the following days and evenings Stephen and I discussed and debated our behavior toward the sadhu. Stephen is a committed Quaker with deep moral vision. He said, "I feel that what happened with the sadhu is a good example of the breakdown between the individual ethic and the corporate ethic. No one person was willing to assume ultimate responsibility for the sadhu. Each was willing to do his bit just so long as it was not too inconvenient. When it got to be a bother, everyone just passed the buck to someone else and took off. Jesus was relevant to a more individualist stage of society, and how do we interpret his teaching today in a world filled with large, impersonal organizations and groups?"

I defended the larger group, saying, "Look, we all cared. We all stopped and gave aid and comfort. Everyone did his bit. The New Zealander carried him down below the snow line. I took his pulse and suggested we treat him for hypothermia. You and the Swiss gave him clothing and got him warmed up. The Japanese gave him food and water. The Sherpas carried him down to the sun and pointed out the easy trail toward the hut. He was well enough to throw rocks at a dog. What more could we do?"

"You have just described the typical affluent Westerner's response to a problem. Throwing money—in this case food and sweaters—at it, but not solving the fundamentals!" Stephen retorted.

"What would satisfy you?" I said. "Here we are, a group of New Zealanders, Swiss, Americans, and Japanese who have never met before and who are at the apex of one of the most powerful experiences of our lives. Some years the pass is so bad no one gets over it. What right does an almost naked pilgrim who chooses the wrong trail have to disrupt our lives? Even the Sherpas had no interest in risking the trip to help him beyond a certain point."

Stephen calmly rebutted, "I wonder what the Sherpas would have done if the sadhu had been a well-dressed Nepali, or what the Japanese would have done if the sadhu had been a well-dressed Asian, or what you would have done, Buzz, if the sadhu had been a well-dressed Western woman?"

"Where, in your opinion," I asked instead, "is the limit of our responsibility in a situation like this? We had our own well-being to worry about. Our Sherpa guides were unwilling to jeopardize us or the porters for the sadhu. No one else on the mountain was willing to commit himself beyond certain self-imposed limits."

Stephen said, "As individual Christians or people with a Western ethical tradition, we can fulfill our obligations in such a situation only if (1) the sadhu dies in our care, (2) the sadhu demonstrates to us that he could undertake the two-day walk down to the village, or (3) we carry the sadhu for two days down to the village and convince someone there to take care of him."

"Leaving the sadhu in the sun with food and clothing, while he demonstrated hand-eye coordination by throwing a rock at a dog, comes close to fulfilling items one and two," I answered. "And it wouldn't have made sense to take him to the village where the people appeared to be far less caring than the Sherpas, so the third condition is impractical. Are you really saying that, no matter what the implications, we should, at the drop of a hat, have changed our entire plan?"

The Individual vs. the Group Ethic

Despite my arguments, I felt and continue to feel guilt about the sadhu. I had literally walked through a classic moral dilemma without fully thinking through the consequences. My excuses for my actions include a high adrenaline flow, a superordinate goal, and a once-in-a-lifetime opportunity—factors in the usual corporate situation, especially when one is under stress.

Real moral dilemmas are ambiguous, and many of us hike right through them, unaware that they exist. When, usually after the fact, someone makes an issue of them, we tend to resent his or her bringing it up. Often, when the full import of what we have done (or not done) falls on us, we dig into a defensive position from which it is very difficult to emerge. In rare circumstances we may contemplate what we have done from inside a prison.

Had we mountaineers been free of physical and mental stress caused by the effort and the high altitude, we might have treated the sadhu differently. Yet isn't stress the real test of personal and corporate values? The instant decisions executives make under pressure reveal the most about personal and corporate character.

Among the many questions that occur to me when pondering my experience are: What are the practical limits of moral imagination and vision? Is there a collective or institutional ethic beyond the ethics of the individual? At what level of effort or commitment can one discharge one's ethical responsibilities?

Not every ethical dilemma has a right solution. Reasonable people often disagree; otherwise there would be no dilemma. In a business context, however, it is essential that managers agree on a process for dealing with dilemmas.

The sadhu experience offers an interesting parallel to business situations. An immediate response was mandatory. Failure to act was a decision in itself. Up on the mountain we could not resign and submit our résumé to a headhunter. In contrast to philosophy, business involves action and implementation—getting things done. Managers must come up with answers to problems based on what they see and what they allow to influence their decision-making processes. On the mountain, none of us but Stephen realized the true dimensions of the situation we were facing.

One of our problems was that as a group we had no process for developing a consensus. We had no sense of purpose or plan. The difficulties of dealing with the sadhu were so complex that no one person could handle it. Because it did not have a set of preconditions that could guide its action to an acceptable resolution, the group reacted instinctively as individuals. The cross-cultural nature of the group added a further layer of complexity. We had no leader with whom we could all identify and in whose purpose we believed. Only Stephen was willing to take charge, but he could not gain adequate support to care for the sadhu.

Some organizations do have a value system that transcends the personal values of the managers. Such values, which go beyond profitability, are usually revealed when the organization is under stress. People throughout the organization generally accept its values, which, because they are not presented as a rigid list of commandments, may be somewhat ambiguous. The stories people tell, rather than printed materials, transmit these conceptions of what is proper behavior.

For twenty years I have been exposed at senior levels to a variety of corporations and organizations. It is amazing how quickly an outsider can sense the tone and style of an organization and the degree of tolerated openness and freedom to challenge management.

Organizations that do not have a heritage of mutually accepted, shared values tend to become unhinged during stress, with each individual bailing out for himself. In the great takeover battles we have witnessed during past years, companies that had strong cultures drew the wagons around them and fought it out, while other companies saw executives, supported by their golden parachutes, bail out of the struggles.

Because corporations and their members are interdependent, for the corporation to be strong the members need to share a preconceived notion of what is correct behavior, a "business ethic," and think of it as a positive force, not a constraint.

As an investment banker I am continually warned by well-meaning lawyers, clients, and associates to be wary of conflicts of interest. Yet if I were to run away from every difficult situation, I wouldn't be an effective investment banker. I have to feel my way through conflicts. An effective manager can't run from risk either; he or she has to confront and deal with risk. To feel "safe" in doing this, managers need the guidelines of an agreed-on process and set of values within the organization.

After my three months in Nepal, I spent three months as an executive-in-residence at both Stanford Business School and the Center for Ethics and Social Policy at the Graduate Theological Union at Berkeley. These six months away from my job gave me time to assimilate twenty years of business experience. My thoughts turned often to the meaning of the leadership role in any large organization. Students at the seminary thought of themselves as antibusiness. But when I questioned them they agreed that they distrusted all large organizations, including the church. They perceived all large organizations as impersonal and opposed to individual values and needs. Yet we all know of organizations where people's values and beliefs are respected and their expressions encouraged. What makes the difference? Can we identify the difference and, as a result, manage more effectively?

The word "ethics" turns off many and confuses more. Yet the notions of shared values and an agreed-on process for dealing with adversity and change—what many people mean when they talk about corporate culture—seem to be at the heart of the ethical issue. People who are in touch with their own core beliefs and the beliefs of others and are sustained by them can be more comfortable living on the cutting edge. At times, taking a tough line or a decisive stand in a muddle of ambiguity is the only ethical thing to do. If a manager is indecisive and spends time trying to figure out the "good" thing to do, the enterprise may be lost.

Business ethics, then, has to do with the authenticity and integrity of the enterprise. To be ethical is to follow the business as well as the cultural goals of the corporation, its owners, its employees, and its customers. Those who cannot serve the corporate vision are not authentic business people and, therefore, are not ethical in the business sense.

At this stage of my own business experience I have a strong interest in organizational behavior. Sociologists are keenly studying what they call corporate stories, legends, and heroes as a way organizations have of transmitting the value system. Corporations such as Arco have even hired consultants to perform an audit of their corporate culture. In a company, the leader is the person who understands, interprets, and manages the corporate value system. Effective managers are then action-oriented people who resolve conflict, are tolerant of ambiguity, stress, and change, and have a strong sense of purpose for themselves and their organizations.

If all this is true, I wonder about the role of the professional manager who moves from company to company. How can he or she quickly absorb the values and culture of different organizations? Or is there, indeed, an art of management that is totally transportable? Assuming such fungible managers do exist, is it proper for them to manipulate the values of others?

What would have happened had Stephen and I carried the sadhu for two days back to the village and become involved with the villagers in his care? In four trips to Nepal my most interesting experiences occurred in 1975 when I lived in a Sherpa home in the Khumbu for five days recovering from altitude sickness. The high point of Stephen's trip was an invitation to participate in a family funeral ceremony in Manang. Neither experience had to do with climbing the high passes of the Himalayas. Why were we so reluctant to try the lower path, the ambiguous trail? Perhaps because we did not have a leader who could reveal the greater purpose of the trip to us.

Why didn't Stephen with his moral vision opt to take the sadhu under his personal care? The answer is because, in part, Stephen was hard-stressed physically himself, and because, in part, without some support system that involved our involuntary and episodic community on the mountain, it was beyond his individual capacity to do so.

I see the current interest in corporate culture and corporate value systems as a positive response to Stephen's pessimism about the decline of the role of the individual in large organizations. Individuals who operate from a thoughtful set of personal values provide the foundation of a corporate culture. A corporate tradition that encourages freedom of inquiry, supports personal values, and reinforces a focused sense of direction can fulfill the need for individuality along with the prosperity and success of the group. Without such corporate support, the individual is lost.

That is the lesson of the sadhu. In a complex corporate situation, the individual requires or deserves the support of the group. If people cannot find such support from their organization, they don't know how to act. If such support is forthcoming, a person has a stake in the success of the group, and can add much to the process of establishing and maintaining a corporate culture. It is management's challenge to be sensitive to individual needs, to shape them, and to direct and focus them for the benefit of the group as a whole.

For each of us the sadhu lives. Should we stop what we are doing and comfort him; or should we keep trudging up toward the high pass? Should I pause to help the derelict I pass on the street each night as I walk by the Yale Club en route to Grand Central Station? Am I his brother? What is the nature of our responsibility if we consider ourselves to be ethical persons? Perhaps it is to change the values of the group so that it can, with all its resources, take the other road.

Discussion Questions

1. Consider the closing questions Mr. McCoy poses. How do they apply to you personally and to businesses?

2. Why do you think no one made sure the sadhu was going to be fine? What would they have had to do to be sure that the sadhu would live?

3. Are the rules of the mountain different from the rules of our day-to-day lives? Is it survival of the fittest on the mountain?

4. Why do you think Mr. McCoy wrote about his experience?

READING 1.6
Trying Out Your Ethics Skills

While you now have a list of the categories of ethical breaches and many different models for resolution, you may still be wondering about the process for analyzing cases. What follows is a suggested approach for these cases so that you can provide an in-depth analysis from all perspectives.

Steps for Analyzing Ethical Dilemmas and Case Studies in Business

1. Make sure you have a grasp of all of the facts available. Be sure you are familiar with all the facts.
2. List any information you would like to have but don't and what assumptions you would have to make, if any, in resolving the dilemma.
3. Take each person involved in the dilemma and list the concerns they face or might have. Be sure to consider the impact on those not specifically mentioned in the case. For example, product safety issues don't involve just engineers' careers and company profits; shareholders, customers, customers' families, and even communities supported by the business are affected by a business decision on what to do about a product and its safety issue.
4. Develop a list of resolutions for the problem. Apply the various models for reaching this resolution. You may also find that as you apply the various models to the dilemma you find additional insights for questions 1, 2, and 3. If the breach has already occurred,

consider the possible remedies and develop systemic changes so that such breaches do not occur in the future.

5. Evaluate the resolutions for costs, legalities, and impact. Try to determine how each of the parties will react to and will be affected by each of the resolutions you have proposed.

6. Make a recommendation on the actions that should be taken.

In some of the cases you will be evaluating the ethics of conduct after the fact. In those situations, your recommendations and resolutions will center on reforms and perhaps recompense for the parties affected.

Each case in this book requires you to examine different perspectives and analyze the impact that the resolution of a dilemma has on the parties involved. Return to these models to question the propriety of the actions taken in each case. Examine the origins of the ethical dilemmas and explore possible solutions. As you work through the cases, you will find yourself developing a new awareness of values and their importance in making business decisions. Try your hand at a few before proceeding to the following sections. The following, rather short, cases offer an opportunity for application of the materials from this section and give you the chance to hone your skills for ethical resolutions.

CASE 1.7
The Movie Ticket

You and your friend have purchased a movie ticket to see *The Bourne Supremacy*. After seeing the movie you realize as you are walking down the multiplex hallway that no theater employees are there and that you could slip into *Spiderman 2* and see that at absolutely no cost. Your friend says, "Why not? Who's to know? Besides, it doesn't hurt anyone. Look at the price of a movie these days. These people are making money!"

You find you hesitate just a bit. Should you take in the extra movie for free?

Discussion Questions

1. Be sure to apply the questions from the model.

2. Offer your final decision on the second free movie and your explanation for your decision.

CASE 1.8
The All-You-Can-Eat Buffet

You are taking your mom out to eat at Joe's Shrimp Shack. Joe has an all-you-can-eat buffet for $9.99. Joe has a sign over the buffet, "Remember, we can handle the world's biggest appetites, but only while they are here. Please don't take food from the premises."

After you and your mom enjoy a good meal, you realize that your mom has come fully prepared. Her purse is lined with foil and she is loading it up with shrimp, biscuits, and Sweet'n Low.

Discussion Questions

1. Apply the various models to your dilemma.

2. Do you say anything to Mom? Do you ask her not to take the food?

CASE 1.9
Puffing Your Résumé

The résumé is a door opener for a job seeker. What's on it can get you in the door or cause the door to be slammed in your face. With that type of pressure, it is not surprising to learn that one 1997 study by a group of executive search firms showed that 25 percent of all résumés contain misstatements. A 1988 Equifax study (Equifax is a credit-reporting agency often used by employers for background checks) also found the following:

Eleven percent of all applicants lied about their reasons for leaving a previous job;

Four percent fudged job titles on their résumés;

Three percent listed fake employers;

Three percent fabricated jobs; and

Three percent pretended to have a college degree[3]

Ed Andler, an expert in credential verification, says that one-third of all résumés contain some level of "creative writing." Mr. Andler notes that assembly-line workers don't mention misdemeanor convictions and middle-managers embellish their educational background. One reference-checking firm looked into the background of a security guard applicant and found he was wanted for manslaughter in another state.

Vericon Resources, Inc., a background check firm, has found that 2 percent of the applicants they investigate are hiding a criminal past. Vericon also notes, however, that potential employers can easily discover whether job candidates are lying about previous employment by requesting W-2s from previous employers.

In one résumé "puffing" case, according to Michael Oliver, a former executive recruiter who is presently director of staffing for Dial Corporation, a strong candidate for a senior marketing management position said he had an MBA from Harvard and four years' experience at a previous company, where he had been a vice president of marketing. Actually, Harvard had never heard of him, he had worked for the firm for only two years, and he had been a senior product manager, not a vice president.

[3] Dan Barry, "Cheating Hearts and Lying Resumes," The New York Times, December 14, 1997, pp. WK1, WK4.

In a wrongful firing case brought against Honeywell by a former employee, a federal court permitted Honeywell to use the defense that the employee had lied on her résumé (over eight years before the litigation) by stating that she had a college degree when she had taken only six courses (two as audits) and that she had managed property during a time when she owned no property and was unemployed. Her discharge had nothing to do with the puffing on her résumé, but the court ruled that "an employer may defend a wrongful discharge claim on the basis of facts unknown at the time of discharge." A subsequent court decision has held that a previously unknown fact is not a defense to discrimination, but it can always be used as grounds for termination.[4]

In 1997, Dianna Green, a senior vice president at Duquesne Light, left her position at that utility. The memo from the CEO described her departure as one that would allow Ms. Green to pursue "other career interests she has had for many years." While the memo expressed sadness at her departure, Ms. Green had been fired for lying on her résumé by stating that she had a master's degree in business administration when, in fact, she had no master's degree.[5]

Ms. Green had worked her way up through the company and had been responsible for handling the human resources issues in Duquesne's nine years of downsizing. At the time of her termination, she was a director at Pennsylvania's largest bank and known widely for her community service.

On the day following her termination, Ms. Green was found dead of a self-inflicted gunshot wound.[6]

....

Discussion Questions

1. Would it be wrong to engage in résumé puffing and then disclose the actual facts in an interview? Be sure to apply the models.

2. Suppose that you had earned but, due to a hold on your academic record because of unpaid debts, had never been formally awarded a college degree. Would you state on your résumé that you had a college degree?

3. Suppose that, in an otherwise good career track, you were laid off because of an economic downturn and remained unemployed for thirteen months. Would you attempt to conceal the thirteen-month lapse in your résumé?

4. Won't complete candor prevent you from ever getting a job?

5. Is puffing a short-term solution in a tight job market?

---

[4] Id.

[5] The information was revealed after Ms. Green was deposed in a suit by a former subordinate for termination. Because Ms. Green hesitated in giving a year for her degree, the plaintiff's lawyer checked and found no degree and notified Duquesne officials. Duquesne officials then negotiated a severance package.

[6] It should be noted that Ms. Green was suffering from diabetes to such an extent that she could no longer see well enough to drive. Also, during the year before her termination, her mother had died of a stroke and her youngest brother also had died. Carol Hymowitz and Raju Narisetti, "A Promising Career Comes to a Tragic End, And a City Asks Why," The Wall Street Journal, May 9, 1997, pp. A1, A8.

6. Was the tragedy of Ms. Green avoidable? Was Duquesne Light justified in terminating her?

7. What dangers arise if applicants are not honest?

8. James Joseph Minder was appointed to the board of gun manufacturer Smith & Wesson, headquartered in Scottsdale, Arizona, in 2001. In early 2004, he assumed the position of chairman of the board. One month later, he resigned as chair of the board because the local newspaper, the *Arizona Republic*, reported that Mr. Minder had completed a 3.5- to 10-year prison sentence for a series of armed robberies and an escape from prison. He had carried a sawed-off shotgun during the string of robberies, committed while he was a student at the University of Michigan. Mr. Minder indicated that he had never tried to hide his past. In 1969, when he was released from prison, he finished his degree and earned a master's from the University of Michigan. He spent 20 years running a successful nonprofit center for inner-city youth until his retirement in 1997, when he moved to Arizona. Mr. Minder's position is that the subject of his troubled youth and criminal past never came up, so he never disclosed it.[7] Evaluate Mr. Minder's position and silence. What do you think of Smith & Wesson's press release indicating that Mr. Minder "had led an exemplary life for 35 years"? Mr. Minder remains on the board. Why did the public react so negatively to his past and position?

CASE 1.10

Radar Detectors

Just recently the state of Connecticut legalized the use of radar detectors, reversing a previous statute that permitted state police to fine motorists for using the devices.[8] Representative Alex Knopp, one of the legislators who objected to the legalization of the devices, stated, "The bottom line is that speeding kills and that radar detectors will cause more speeding in the state of Connecticut." In 1993, Congress passed a law banning the use of radar detectors by tractor-trailer drivers. Senator Frank R. Lautenberg of New Jersey stated, "It's unacceptable to have devices designed to thwart the law. I want to get rid of these things."[9]

Discussion Questions

1. Are radar detectors a means of breaking the law and avoiding getting caught?

2. Is it morally wrong to speed?

3. Is it morally wrong to use a radar detector?

4. Is it possible that speeding laws constitute positive law but do not reflect any ethical or moral standard?

---

[7] http://money.cnn.com/2004/02/27/news/smith_wesson/?cnn = yes
[8] Kirk Johnson, "Connecticut Lawmakers Legalize Radar Detectors," The New York Times, *June 23, 1992, p. A6.*
[9] "U.S. Acts to Ban Radar Detectors in Big Trucks," The New York Times, *November 12, 1993, pp. A1, A16.*

CASE 1.11

The Ethics of Looking Busy

"Some bosses just like you to be there, whether you need to be there or not. So I've come up with ways to look like a workaholic," Jane Nugent said. "I can be off shopping or on a two-hour lunch, and everyone back at the office thinks I'm still there," she noted, smiling. Jane then listed her strategies:

- Before leaving, place a fresh, steaming cup of coffee on your desk; people will assume you'll be right back;
- Always leave the lights on and the computer running;[10]
- Hang around at the office until the last supervisor leaves—then go;
- Arrive early and let them see you, your car, and your office up and running, and then leave for the morning;
- Go in on Saturday and stay for a few hours—you don't need to work, just make sure someone sees you;
- If you leave early, call back in and ask someone to look something up in your office— they'll assume you're at an out-of-office meeting;
- If you must make personal calls, always have a pad in front of you, write on it frequently and speak firmly (the rest of the office will think you're negotiating); and
- Leave personal belongings (coat, jacket) in your office to give the impression that you're returning.[11]

Discussion Questions

1. Evaluate Jane's strategies from an ethical perspective.

2. Should Jane consider flexible hours?

3. Does Jane have enough to keep her busy at her job? Is it dishonest for her to continue her facade?

4. How should Jane's secretary respond to being asked to go in and jump around in Jane's office so that Jane can be gone?

5. Are Jane's actions just a response to management's basis of evaluation that time spent in the office equals performance?

CASE 1.12

Cell Phone Alibis

The *New York Times* recently ran an article entitled, "For Liars and Loafers, Cell Phones Offer an Alibi."[12] The article explains, among other things, that 20-year-old Kenny Hall

[10] Note: Some offices have motion-detector energy savers. When activity in the office ceases, the lights go off. Therefore, Jane notes, instruct your secretary to go into your office periodically and jump around while you're gone.

[11] Sue Shellenbarger, "How to Look Like a Workaholic While Still Having a Life," The Wall Street Journal, December 28, 1994, p. B1.

[12] Matt Richtel, "For Liars and Loafers, Cell Phones Offer an Alibi," The New York Times, June 26, 2004, pp. B1, B14.

wished to spend a weekend in Boulder, Colorado with a woman other than his girlfriend. Mr. Hall sent out text messages seeking help from a network of individuals who help each other miss dates, get out of obligations, cancel blind dates, ditch work and school, and generally provide alibis to each other. Mr. Hall's text message yielded a response from someone at the University of Colorado, Boulder who offered to call Mr. Hall's girlfriend, posing as the soccer coach from that university and indicate that Mr. Hall needed to be there for a try-out. The area code from the young volunteer's cell phone matched that of the university.

The article points out that there are even freelance deceivers who will make these types of calls for $2.99 each. One of the owners of such a freelance company indicates, "It lets you control your environment." An owner of a European alibi club shut his business down after he got a new girlfriend, "She thought it was immoral. Imagine that!"

Discussion Questions

1. Do you agree with the new European girlfriend?

2. Are these alibi clubs immoral?

3. Would you participate in an alibi cell phone club? Explain your decision using the models you have applied.

CASE 1.13
Travel Expenses: A Chance for Extra Income

The New York Times Magazine profiled the problems with employees' submissions for travel and entertainment expenses reimbursement. American Express reported that employees spend $156 billion annually on travel and entertainment related to business. Internal auditors at companies listed types of expenses for which employees have sought reimbursement: hairdresser, traffic tickets, and kennel fees.

While the IRS raised the amount allowable for undocumented expenses to $75, most companies keep their limit for employees at $25. One company auditor commented that all taxi cab rides now cost $24.97 and if the company went with the IRS limit, the cab fares would climb to $74.65.

Some of the horror stories submitted by auditors on travel and entertainment expenses submitted by employees:

One employee submitted a bill for $12 for a tin of cookies. When questioned, he could not explain how it had been used but asked for reimbursement anyway because all he would have to do is "make up" a couple of taxi rides to get it back anyway;

$225 for three hockey tickets, except that the names on the tickets were the employee's family members;

$625 for wallpapering. The employee had included it with her other travel expenses and even had the wallpaper receipt written in a different language in order to throw off any questions; and

$275 sports jacket submitted as a restaurant bill. The travel office called the number listed on the receipt and asked if food was sold there. The response was, "No, we're a men's clothing store."[13]

Discussion Questions

1. The auditors noted that employees who are confronted often respond with similar justifications:

   "The company owes it to me."

   "It doesn't really hurt anyone."

   "Everybody does this."

   Are these justifications or rationalizations?

2. Why do employees risk questionable expenses?

3. Who is harmed by dishonest expense submissions?

CASE 1.14

Do Cheaters Prosper?

In a book entitled *Cheaters Always Prosper: 50 Ways to Beat the System Without Being Caught*,[14] James Brazil (a pen name), a college student from the University of California at Santa Barbara, has provided 50 ways to obtain a "free lunch." One suggestion is to place shards of glass in your dessert at a fancy restaurant and then "raise hell." The manager or owner will then come running with certificates for free meals and probably waive your bill.

Another suggestion is, rather than spend $400 on new tires for your car, rent a car for a day for $35 and switch the rental car tires with your tires. So long as your car tires are not bald, the rental car company employees will not notice, and you will have your new tires for a mere $35.

Discussion Questions

1. Are these suggestions ethical?

2. Was publishing the book with the suggestions ethical?

3. Do any of these suggestions cost anyone any money?

[13] Paul Burnham Finney, "Hey, It's on the Company!" The New York Times Magazine, March 8, 1998, pp. 99–100.
[14] Citadel Press, October 1996.

Foundations of Business Ethics: Virtue, Values, and Business

2A

Defining Business Ethics

READING 2.1

What Is Business Ethics?

Based on your readings in Unit 1, you understand that society recognizes the value of ethics. But the reality, especially over the period from 2001 through 2004, is that companies and their employees have not always perceived or properly resolved the ethical dilemmas that confront them. Many firms simply adopt a standard of complying with positive law, or any law enacted at any level of government that carries some sanction or punishment for noncompliance. While such compliance promotes many ethical values and moral principles, many actions that comply with positive law raise ethical issues. For example, many of the executives who have been brought to trial because of the financial collapses of their companies have said, "I didn't break the law. I used a loophole in the law," or "I had the approval of the board of directors for all my bonuses and loans, and that's all that the law requires." Their defenses center around strict compliance with the law that ignores the underlying ethical issues of fairness and the other standards and categories you studied in Unit 1.

In 2000, many Arizona businesses used a hastily passed state statute providing tax credit for vehicles with alternative fuel tanks. The statute and the tax credits were intended to create incentives for autos using non-polluting fuels, and the tax credits were so extensive that large and expensive sport utility vehicles (SUVs) could be purchased for the cost of a Geo. Further, dealers and others were just adding a 2-gallon propane tank to the vehicles, including Chevrolet Suburbans and Ford Expeditions, to meet the alternative fuel requirements. The statute produced a land office business for car dealers and businesses specializing in the installation of alternative fuel tanks. The results were that the environmental incentives of the statute were ignored and the total cost to the state for the tax credits was over $600 million before the program could be contained with meaningful requirements. No buyer or business did anything illegal, but the ethics of skirting the intent of law present a different question.

This unit examines the role of basic virtues such as honesty, loyalty, and even compliance with the law in business. This section begins with a brief reading that groups together the various areas of business operations and the topical ethical issues in each. Following are excerpts and readings that present various views on what business ethics is. Philosopher, business ethicist, and corporate governance expert Dr. Michael Novak provides his thoughts on business ethics. Albert Carr's piece, *Is Business Bluffing Ethical?* provides a different perspective on virtue ethics. Finally, management expert Dr. Peter Drucker offers his thoughts on our ethics in our role as business managers. With these pieces you have differing perspectives on what business ethics is. Coupled with the tools from Unit 1, you have a business perspective for the analysis of the ethical issues that follow in the remaining units.

READING 2.2
The Areas of Ethical Challenges[1]

The remaining pages of this book present more readings and cases that illustrate ethical dilemmas faced by businesses and business people. The cases require critical examination of one's moral standards and the impact poor ethical decisions can have on individuals and companies. The cases are divided into categories based on The Conference Board's groupings of ethical dilemmas in business. (The Conference Board is a private research and information group that focuses on corporate and business issues.) Each category represents a grouping of the types of ethical dilemmas that were ranked most important by CEOs in a 1991 survey conducted by the Ethics Resource Center. The topics in each category are listed here.

Individual Values and the Business Organization
    Employee Conflicts of Interest
    Inappropriate Gifts
    Security of Company Records
    Personal Honesty

Individual Rights and the Business Organization
    Corporate Due Process
    Employee Screening
    Employee Privacy
    Sexual Harassment
    Affirmative Action/Equal Employment Opportunity
    Employment at Will
    Whistle-Blowing
    Employee Rights
    Comparable Worth

[1] *Used by permission of The Conference Board.*

Business Operations
    Financial and Cash Management Procedures
    Conflicts between the Corporation's Ethical Code and Accepted Business
    Practices in Foreign Countries
    Unauthorized Payments to Foreign Officials
    Workplace Safety
    Plant Closures and Downsizing
    Environmental Issues
    Purchasing: Conflicts and Bribery

Business and Its Competition
    Advertising Content
    Appropriation of Others' Ideas
    Product Pricing

Business and Its Product
    Contract Relations
    Product Safety
    Product Quality
    Customer Privacy

Business and Its Stakeholders
    Shareholders' Interests
    Executive Salaries
    Corporate Contributions
    Social Issues

Business and Government
    Government Employees
    Government Contracts
    Government Responsibilities

....

Discussion Questions

Place the following issues and topics in the appropriate categories.

1. A credit card company selling purchasing information about its customers to various marketing firms

2. A former employee taking proprietary customer lists to his new employer

3. A company offering employment to a government official who is in a position to award contracts to that company

4. Paying a bribe to a government official in another country

5. An employee purchasing her retail employer's gift cards using her employee discount and then selling those cards on the Internet

6. Stock options for executives as a method of giving bonuses

Business Ethics and the Role of the Corporation[2]

Michael Novak

Business ethics means a great deal more than obeying the civil law and not violating the moral law. It means imagining and creating a new sort of world based on the principles of individual creativity, community, realism, and other virtues of enterprise. It means respecting the right of the poor to their own personal economic initiative and their own creativity. It means fashioning a culture worthy of free women and free men—to the benefit of the poor and to the greater glory of God.

In this light, business ethics means meeting the responsibilities of corporations and small businesses. Some of these responsibilities may not seem like "ethics" at all. They are simply the behaviors necessary to make a business succeed. But that's the point. Quite *internal* to business are significant moral hurdles that need to be jumped—before you even come to the ethical requirements imposed on business from the outside in, by the standards of religious convictions, moral principles, an adequate humanism, and human rights.

Other business ethicists do not notice these internal moral imperatives. But if they would inspect cultures in which these internal responsibilities are not respected (such as Russia in the 1990s)—in which the murderous law of the jungle prevails—they might see that internalized virtues and practices, even if silent and kept tacit, are crucially important.

. . . [w]e turn now to "seven plus seven" business responsibilities. Such weighty responsibilities demand participants who have mastered the habits needed to fulfill them.

. . . Parents sometimes try to impose on one of their children an ideal of behavior appropriate to another of their children. This often ends up hurting the second child. It might have been better to listen for what is distinctive in that child. Perhaps the lifetime ideal of that child is different from that of their other children—even different from their own—yet altogether proper to that child. It may be wrong to impose on one child ideals that worked very well for another. Similarly, it is wrong to impose aristocratic or socialist ideals on business. It is destructive to impose a social democratic framework on a system that has a different (I think, better) aim, . . .

A business corporation is not a church; not a state; not a welfare agency; not (except rarely) a religious association; not a political association. It is not a "total institution." Thus, it is of considerable importance to discern, first of all, the moral ideals inherent in business as business.

---

[2] From Business as a Calling: Work and the Examined Life, by Michael Novak. New York: Free Press, 1996. Reprinted with permission.

Business is an economic association which, simply by being what it is, serves the common good of the community in several ways. Accordingly, among the corporate responsibilities of business that spring from its own nature are at least these seven:

1. To satisfy customer with goods and services of real value.
2. Make a reasonable return on the funds entrusted to the business corporation by its investors.
3. To create new wealth.
4. To create new jobs.
5. To defeat envy through generating upward mobility and putting empirical ground under the conviction that hard work and talent are fairly rewarded. The best way to do this (defeat envy) is to generate economic growth through as many diverse industries and economic initiatives as possible, so that every family has the realistic possibility of seeing its economic condition improve within the next three or four years.

   Businesses should avoid fomenting envy; they can do so by supplying employees with opportunities and incentives. In addition, people in business should avoid some things that are otherwise innocent in themselves. Conspicuous privilege, ostentation, and other forms of behavior, even when not necessarily wrong, typically provoke envy. Unusually large salaries or bonuses, even if justified by competition in a free and open market (since high talent of certain kinds is extremely rare), may offer demagogues fertile ground on which to scatter the seeds of envy. It is wise to take precautions against these eventualities.
6. To promote invention, ingenuity, and, in general "progress in the arts and useful sciences" (Article I, Section 8 U.S. Constitution). The heart of capitalism is *caput:* the human mind, human invention, human enterprise.
7. To diversify the interests of the republic. One of the least observed functions of the business corporation is to concretize the economic loyalties of citizens and to sort out their practical knowledge into diverse sectors of life. The interests of road builders are not those of canal builders, or builders of railroads, or of airline companies. The sheer dynamism of economic invention makes far less probable the coalescing of a simple majority, which could act as a tyrant to minorities. The economic interests of some citizens are, in an important sense, at cross-purposes with the economic interests of others, and this is crucial to preventing the tyranny of a majority.

Seven Responsibilities from Outside Business

1. To establish within the firm a sense of community and respect for the dignity of persons, thus shaping within the firm a culture that fosters virtue.
2. To protect the political soil of liberty. Businesses are plants that do not grow in just any soil; they depend on specific sorts of political environments. People in business therefore have a responsibility to be watchful over their political society, even as a matter of survival. . . . Businesses should encourage their employees, retirees, and shareholders to take political ideas and policy issues seriously, to participate in electoral campaigns, and to vote.
3. To exemplify respect for the law. Businesses cannot survive without the rule of law. Long-term contracts depend for their fulfillment on respect for law.
4. Social justice. Business is a crucial (perhaps *the* crucial) institution of civil society. Civil society (and business, too) depends on the rule of law, on the one side, and on a potent set of moral and cultural institutions, on the other. For its own well-being and

survival, business therefore depends on its personnel being active in civil society: in politics, the law, churches, the arts, charitable works and other civic activities.

5. To communicate often and fully with their investors, shareholders, pensioners, customers, and employees.

6. To contribute to making its own habitat, the surrounding society, a better place. The business firm . . . has a responsibility to become a leader in civil society. To this end, it should contribute to the good fortune of other mediating structures in the private sector, whether in areas such as education and the arts, healthful activities for youth, the environment, care for the elderly, new initiatives to meet the needs of the homeless and the poor, and other such activities.

7. To protect the moral ecology of freedom. In fully free societies, commercial sponsors pay for television time. Although I am reluctant to propose that they should have control (have a censor's power over) program content, such sponsors do control their own advertising—and they also have responsibility for the content their advertising budgets pay for. Most executives, it appears, have not accepted responsibility for the ecology of the television environment.

> *Happy is it for me to be in a situation in which, while their passions inspire in them the thought of being wicked, it is nevertheless, to their interest not to be.*
> — MONTESQUIEU

Discussion Questions

1. Why does Dr. Novak have two sets of responsibilities for his definition of business ethics?

2. What does Dr. Novak say about the rule of law and its relationship to businesses?

3. What does he mean by moral ecology?

4. At the Super Bowl halftime show for 2004, Justin Timberlake tore part of Janet Jackson's costume off during their joint musical number. The result was that Ms. Jackson's breast was exposed on national television. What responsibilities would Dr. Novak say the sponsors of the Super Bowl had regarding this incident?

READING 2.4

The Ethics of Responsibility[3]

Peter Drucker

Countless sermons have been preached and printed on the ethics of business or the ethics of the businessman. Most have nothing to do with business and little to do with ethics.

One main topic is plain, everyday honesty. Businessmen, we are told solemnly, should not cheat, steal, lie, bribe, or take bribes. But nor should anyone else. Men and women do not acquire exemption from ordinary rules of personal behavior because of

[3] From *Management: Tasks, Responsibilities, Practices,* by Peter F. Drucker. New York: Harper & Row, 1974. Reprinted with permission.

their work or job. Nor, however, do they cease to be human beings when appointed vice-president, city manager, or college dean. And there has always been a number of people who cheat, steal, lie, bribe, or take bribes. The problem is one of moral values and moral education, of the individual, of the family, of the school. But there neither is a separate ethics of business, nor is one needed.

All that is needed is to mete out stiff punishments to those—whether business executives or others—who yield to temptation. In England a magistrate still tends to hand down a harsher punishment in a drunken-driving case if the accused has gone to one of the well-known public schools or to Oxford or Cambridge. And the conviction still rates a headline in the evening paper: "Eton graduate convicted of drunken driving." No one expects an Eton education to produce temperance leaders. But it is still a badge of distinction, if not privilege. And not to treat a wearer of such a badge more harshly than an ordinary workingman who has had one too many would offend the community's sense of justice. But no one considers this a problem of the "ethics of the Eton graduate."

The other common theme in the discussion of ethics in business has nothing to do with ethics.

Such things as the employment of call girls to entertain customers are not matters of ethics but matters of esthetics. "Do I want to see a pimp when I look at myself in the mirror while shaving?" is the real question.

The first responsibility of a professional was spelled out clearly 2,500 years ago, in the Hippocratic oath of the Greek physician: *Primum non nocere:* "Above all, not knowingly to do harm."

No professional, be he doctor, lawyer, or manager, can promise that he will indeed do good for his client. All he can do is try. But he can promise that he will not knowingly do harm.

Discussion Questions

1. Does Dr. Drucker believe personal ethics and business ethics can be separated?

2. What is the Drucker test for ethics for business managers?

READING 2.5

Is Business Bluffing Ethical?[4]

Albert Z. Carr

In the following classic reading, Albert Carr compares business to poker and offers a justification for business bluffing. Mr. Carr provides a different perspective from the previous discussion with its various models and categories geared more toward absolutes.

[4] Reprinted by permission of Harvard Business Review. From "Is Business Bluffing Ethical?" by Albert Z. Carr, Vol. 46, January/February 1968. Copyright © 1968 by the Harvard Business School Publishing Corporation; all rights reserved.

A respected businessman with whom I discussed the theme of this article remarked with some heat, "You mean to say you're going to encourage men to bluff? Why, bluffing is nothing more than a form of lying! You're advising them to lie!"

I agreed that the basis of private morality is a respect for truth and that the closer a businessman comes to the truth, the more he deserves respect. At the same time, I suggested that most bluffing in business might be regarded simply as game strategy—much like bluffing in poker, which does not reflect on the morality of the bluffer.

I quoted Henry Taylor, the British statesman who pointed out that "falsehood ceases to be falsehood when it is understood on all sides that the truth is not expected to be spoken"—an exact description of bluffing in poker, diplomacy, and business. I cited the analogy of the criminal court, where the criminal is not expected to tell the truth when he pleads "not guilty." Everyone from the judge down takes it for granted that the job of the defendant's attorney is to get his client off, not to reveal the truth; and this is considered ethical practice. I mentioned Representative Omar Burleson, the Democrat from Texas, who was quoted as saying, in regard to the ethics of Congress, "Ethics is a barrel of worms"[5]—a pungent summing up of the problem of deciding who is ethical in politics.

I reminded my friend that millions of businessmen feel constrained every day to say *yes* to their bosses when they secretly believe *no* and that this is generally accepted as permissible strategy when the alternative might be the loss of a job. The essential point, I said, is that the ethics of business are games ethics, different from the ethics of religion.

He remained unconvinced. Referring to the company of which he is president, he declared: "Maybe that's good enough for some businessmen, but I can tell you that we pride ourselves on our ethics. In thirty years not one customer has ever questioned my word or asked to check our figures. We're loyal to our customers and fair to our suppliers. I regard my handshake on a deal as a contract. I've never entered into price-fixing schemes with my competitors. I've never allowed my salesmen to spread injurious rumors about other companies. Our union contract is the best in our industry. And, if I do say so myself, our ethical standards are of the highest!"

He really was saying, without realizing it, that he was living up to the ethical standards of the business game—which are a far cry from those of private life. Like a gentlemanly poker player, he did not play in cahoots with others at the table, try to smear their reputations, or hold back chips he owed them.

But this same fine man, at that very time, was allowing one of his products to be advertised in a way that made it sound a great deal better than it actually was. Another item in his product line was notorious among dealers for its "built-in-obsolescence." He was holding back from the market a much-improved product because he did not want it to interfere with sales of the inferior item it would have replaced. He had joined with certain of his competitors in hiring a lobbyist to push a state legislature, by methods that he preferred not to know too much about, into amending a bill then being enacted.

In his view these things had nothing to do with ethics; they were merely normal business practice. He himself undoubtedly avoided outright falsehoods—never lied in so many words. But the entire organization that he ruled was deeply involved in numerous strategies of deception.

[5] The New York Times, *March 9, 1967.*

Pressure to Deceive

Most executives from time to time are almost compelled, in the interest of their companies or themselves, to practice some form of deception when negotiating with customers, dealers, labor unions, government officials or even other department[s] of their companies. By conscious misstatements, concealment of pertinent facts, or exaggeration—in short, by bluffing—they seek to persuade others to agree with them. I think it is fair to say that if the individual executive refuses to bluff from time to time—if he feels obligated to tell the truth, the whole truth, and nothing but the truth—he is ignoring opportunities permitted under the rules and is at a heavy disadvantage in his business dealings.

But here and there a businessman is unable to reconcile himself to the bluff in which he plays a part. His conscience, perhaps spurred by religious idealism, troubles him. He feels guilty; he may develop an ulcer or a nervous tic. Before any executive can make profitable use of the strategy of the bluff, he needs to make sure that in bluffing he will not lose self-respect or become emotionally disturbed. If he is to reconcile personal integrity and high standards of honesty with the practical requirements of business, he must feel that his bluffs are ethically justified. The justification rests on the fact that business, as practiced by individuals as well as by corporations, has the impersonal character of a game—a game that demands both special strategy and an understanding of its special ethics.

The game is played at all levels of corporate life, from the highest to the lowest. At the very instant that a man decides to enter business, he may be forced into a game situation, as is shown by the recent experience of a Cornell honor graduate who applied for a job with a large company.

This applicant was given a psychological test which included the statement, "Of the following magazines, check any that you have read either regularly or from time to time, and double-check those which interest you most. *Reader's Digest, Time, Fortune, Saturday Evening Post, The New Republic, Life, Look, Ramparts, Newsweek, Business Week, U.S. News & World Report, The Nation, Playboy, Esquire, Harper's, Sports Illustrated.*"

His tastes in reading were broad, and at one time or another he had read almost all of these magazines. He was a subscriber to *The New Republic*, an enthusiast for *Ramparts*, and an avid student of the pictures in *Playboy*. He was not sure whether his interest in *Playboy* would be held against him, but he had a shrewd suspicion that if he confessed to an interest in *Ramparts* and *The New Republic*, he would be thought a liberal, a radical, or at least an intellectual, and his chances of getting the job, which he needed, would greatly diminish. He therefore checked five of the more conservative magazines. Apparently it was a sound decision, for he got the job.

He had made a game player's decision, consistent with business ethics.

A similar case is that of a magazine space salesman who, owing to a merger, suddenly found himself out of a job:

This man was 58, and, in spite of a good record, his chance of getting a job elsewhere in a business where youth is favored in hiring practice was not good. He was a vigorous, healthy man, and only a considerable amount of gray in his hair suggested his age. Before beginning his job search he touched up his hair with a black dye to confine the gray to his temples. He knew that the truth about his age might well come out in time, but he calculated that he could deal with that situation when it arose. He and his wife decided that he could easily pass for 45, and he so stated his age on his résumé.

This was a lie, yet within the accepted rules of the business game, no moral culpability attaches to it.

The Poker Analogy

We can learn a good deal about the nature of business by comparing it with poker. While both have a large element of chance, in the long run the winner is the man who plays with steady skill. In both games ultimate victory requires intimate knowledge of the rules, insight into the psychology of the other players, a bold front, a considerable amount of self-discipline, and the ability to respond swiftly and effectively to opportunities provided by chance.

No one expects poker to be played on the ethical principles preached in churches. In poker it is right and proper to bluff a friend out of the rewards of being dealt a good hand. A player feels no more than a slight twinge of sympathy, if that, when—with nothing better than a single ace in his hand—he strips a heavy loser, who holds a pair, of the rest of his chips. It was up to the other fellow to protect himself. In the words of an excellent poker player, former President Harry Truman, "If you can't stand the heat, stay out of the kitchen." If one shows mercy to a loser in poker, it is a personal gesture, divorced from the rules of the game.

Poker has its special ethics, and here I am not referring to rules against cheating. The man who keeps an ace up his sleeve or who marks the cards is more than unethical; he is a crook, and can be punished as such—kicked out of the game or, in the Old West, shot.

In contrast to the cheat, the unethical poker player is one who, while abiding by the letter of the rules, finds ways to put the other players at an unfair disadvantage. Perhaps he unnerves them with loud talk. Or he tries to get them drunk. Or he plays in cahoots with someone else at the table. Ethical poker players frown on such tactics.

Poker's own brand of ethics is different from the ethical ideals of civilized human relationships. The game calls for distrust of the other fellow. It ignores the claim of friendship. Cunning deception and concealment of one's strength and intentions, not kindness and openheartedness, are vital in poker. No one thinks any the worse of poker on that account. And no one should think any the worse of the game of business because its standards of right and wrong differ from the prevailing traditions of morality in our society.

Discard the Golden Rule

This view of business is especially worrisome to people without much business experience. A minister of my acquaintance once protested that business cannot possibly function in our society unless it is based on the Judeo-Christian system of ethics. He told me:

"I know some businessmen have supplied call girls to customers, but there are always a few rotten apples in every barrel. That doesn't mean the rest of the fruit isn't sound. Surely the vast majority of businessmen are ethical. I myself am acquainted with many who adhere to strict codes of ethics based fundamentally on religious teachings. They contribute to good causes. They participate in community activities. They cooperate with other companies to improve working conditions in their industries. Certainly they are not indifferent to ethics."

That most businessmen are not indifferent to ethics in their private lives, everyone will agree. My point is that in their office lives they cease to be private citizens; they become game players who must be guided by a somewhat different set of ethical standards.

The point was forcefully made to me by a Midwestern executive who has given a good deal of thought to the question:

"So long as a businessman complies with the laws of the land and avoids telling malicious lies, he's ethical. If the law as written gives a man a wide-open chance to make a killing, he'd be a fool not to take advantage of it. If he doesn't, somebody else will. There's no obligation on him to stop and consider who is going to get hurt. If the law says he can do it, that's all the justification he needs. There's nothing unethical about that. It's just plain business sense."

This executive (call him Robbins) took the stand that even industrial espionage, which is frowned on by some businessmen, ought not to be considered unethical. He recalled a recent meeting of the National Industrial Conference Board where an authority on marketing made a speech in which he deplored the employment of spies by business organizations. More and more companies, he pointed out, find it cheaper to penetrate the secrets of competitors with concealed cameras and microphones or by bribing employees than to set up costly research and design departments of their own. A whole branch of the electronics industry has grown up with this trend, he continued, providing equipment to make industrial espionage easier.

Disturbing? The marketing expert found it so. But when it came to a remedy, he could only appeal to "respect for the golden rule." Robbins thought this a confession of defeat, believing that the golden rule, for all its value as an ideal for society, is simply not feasible as a guide for business. A good part of the time the businessman is trying to do unto others as he hopes others will *not* do unto him.[6] Robbins continued:

"Espionage of one kind or another has become so common in business that it's like taking a drink during Prohibition—it's not considered sinful. And we don't even have Prohibition where espionage is concerned; the law is very tolerant in this area. There's no more shame for a business that uses a secret agent than there is for a nation. Bear in mind that there already is at least one large corporation—you can buy its stock over the counter—that makes millions by providing counterespionage service to industrial firms. Espionage in business is not an ethical problem; it's an established technique of business competition."

"We Don't Make the Laws."

Wherever we turn in business, we can perceive the sharp distinction between its ethical standards and those of the churches. Newspapers abound with sensational stories growing out of this distinction:

- We read one day that Senator Philip A. Hart of Michigan has attacked food processors for deceptive packaging of numerous products.[7]

[6] See Bruce D. Henderson, "Brinkmanship in Business," *Harvard Business Review, March–April 1967, p. 49.*
[7] The New York Times, *November 21, 1966.*

- The next day there is a Congressional to-do over Ralph Nader's book, *Unsafe At Any Speed,* which demonstrates that automobile companies for years have neglected the safety of car-owning families.[8]
- Then another Senator, Lee Metcalf of Montana, and journalist Vic Reinemer show in their book, *Overcharge,* the methods by which utility companies elude regulating government bodies to extract unduly large payments from users of electricity.[9]

These are merely dramatic instances of a prevailing condition; there is hardly a major industry at which a similar attack could not be aimed. Critics of business regard such behavior as unethical, but the companies concerned know that they are merely playing the business game.

Among the most respected of our business institutions are the insurance companies. A group of insurance executives meeting recently in New England was startled when their guest speaker, social critic Daniel Patrick Moynihan, roundly berated them for "unethical" practices. They had been guilty, Moynihan alleged, of using outdated actuarial tables to obtain unfairly high premiums. They habitually delayed the hearings of lawsuits against them in order to tire out the plaintiffs and win cheap settlements. In their employment policies they used ingenious devices to discriminate against certain minority groups.[10]

It was difficult for the audience to deny the validity of these charges. But these men were business game players. Their reaction to Moynihan's attack was much the same as that of the automobile manufacturers to Nader, of the utilities to Senator Metcalf, and of the food processors to Senator Hart. If the laws governing their businesses change, or if public opinion becomes clamorous, they will make the necessary adjustments. But morally they have, in their view, done nothing wrong. As long as they comply with the letter of the law, they are within their rights to operate their businesses as they see fit.

The small business is in the same position as the great corporation in this respect. For example:

In 1967 a key manufacturer was accused of providing master keys for automobiles to mail-order customers, although it was obvious that some of the purchasers might be automobile thieves. His defense was plain and straightforward. If there was nothing in the law to prevent him from selling his keys to anyone who ordered them, it was not up to him to inquire as to his customers' motives. Why was it any worse, he insisted, for him to sell car keys by mail, than for mail-order houses to sell guns that might be used for murder? Until the law was changed, the key manufacturer could regard himself as being just as ethical as any other businessman by the rules of the business game.[11]

Violations of the ethical ideals of society are common in business, but they are not necessarily violations of business principles. Each year the Federal Trade Commission orders hundreds of companies, many of them of the first magnitude, to "cease and desist" from practices which, judged by ordinary standards, are of questionable morality but which are stoutly defended by the companies concerned.

---

[8] *Nader R.* Unsafe At Any Speed: The Designed-In Dangers of the American Automobile. *New York: Grossman Publishers, Inc., 1965.*

[9] *U.S. Senator Lee Metcalf, Vic Reinemer.* Overcharge: How Electric Utilities Exploit and Mislead the Public, and What You Can Do About It. *New York: David McKay Company, Inc., 1967.*

[10] The New York Times, *January 17, 1967.*

[11] *Cited by Ralph Nader in* "Business Crime," The New Republic, *July 1, 1967, p. 7.*

In one case, a firm manufacturing a well-known mouth-wash was accused of using a cheap form of alcohol possibly deleterious to health. The company's chief executive, after testifying in Washington, made this comment privately:

> "We broke no law. We're in a highly competitive industry. If we're going to stay in business, we have to look for profit wherever the law permits. We don't make the laws. We obey them. Then why do we have to put up with this 'holier than thou' talk about ethics? It's sheer hypocrisy. We're not in business to promote ethics. Look at the cigarette companies, for God's sake! If the ethics aren't embodied in the laws by the men who made them, you can't expect businessmen to fill the lack. Why, a sudden submission to Christian ethics by businessmen would bring about the greatest economic upheaval in history!"

It may be noted that the government failed to prove its case against him.

Cast Illusions Aside

Talk about ethics by businessmen is often a thin decorative coating over the hard realities of the game:

> Once I listened to a speech by a young executive who pointed to a new industry code as proof that his company and its competitors were deeply aware of their responsibilities to society. It was a code of ethics, he said. The industry was going to police itself, to dissuade constituent companies from wrongdoing. His eyes shone with conviction and enthusiasm.
>
> The same day there was a meeting in a hotel room where the industry's top executives met with the "czar" who was to administer the new code, a man of high repute. No one who was present could doubt their common attitude. In their eyes the code was designed primarily to forestall a move by the federal government to impose stern restrictions on the industry. They felt that the code would hamper them a good deal less than new federal laws would. It was, in other words, conceived as a protection for the industry, not for the public.
>
> The young executive accepted the surface explanation of the code; these leaders, all experienced game players, did not deceive themselves for a moment about its purpose.

The illusion that business can afford to be guided by ethics as conceived in private life is often fostered by speeches and articles containing such phrases as, "It pays to be ethical," or, "Sound ethics is good business." Actually this is not an ethical position at all; it is a self-serving calculation in disguise. The speaker is really saying that in the long run a company can make more money if it does not antagonize competitors, suppliers, employees, and customers by squeezing them too hard. He is saying that oversharp policies reduce ultimate gains. That is true, but it has nothing to do with ethics. The underlying attitude is much like that in the familiar story of the shopkeeper who finds an extra twenty-dollar bill in the cash register, debates with himself the ethical problem—should he tell his partner?—and finally decides to share the money because the gesture will give him an edge over the s.o.b. the next time they quarrel.

I think it is fair to sum up the prevailing attitude of businessmen on ethics as follows:

> We live in what is probably the most competitive of the world's civilized societies. Our customs encourage a high degree of aggression in the individuals striving for success. Business is our main area of competition, and it has been ritualized into a game of strategy.

The basic rules of the game have been set by the government, which attempts to detect and punish business frauds. But as long as a company does not transgress the rules of the game set by law, it has the legal right to shape its strategy without reference to anything but its profits. If it takes a long-term view of its profits, it will preserve amicable relations, so far as possible, with those with whom it deals. A wise businessman will not seek advantage to the point where he generates dangerous hostility among employees, competitors, customers, government, or the public at large. But decisions in this area are, in the final test, decisions of strategy, not of ethics.

The Individual and the Game

An individual within a company often finds it difficult to adjust to the requirements of the business game. He tries to preserve his private ethical standards in situations that call for game strategy. When he is obliged to carry out company policies that challenge his conception of himself as an ethical man, he suffers.

It disturbs him when he is ordered, for instance, to deny a raise to a man who deserves it, to fire an employee of long standing, to prepare advertising that he believes to be misleading, to conceal facts that he feels customers are entitled to know, to cheapen the quality of materials used in the manufacture of an established product, to sell as new a product that he knows to be rebuilt, to exaggerate the curative powers of a medicinal preparation, or to coerce dealers.

There are some fortunate executives who, by the nature of their work and circumstances, never have to face problems of this kind. But in one form or another the ethical dilemma is felt sooner or later by most businessmen. Possibly the dilemma is most painful not when the company forces the action on the executive but when he originates it himself—that is, when he has taken or is contemplating a step which is in his own interest but which runs counter to his early moral conditioning. To illustrate:

- The manager of an export department, eager to show rising sales, is pressed by a big customer to provide invoices which, while containing no overt falsehood that would violate a U.S. law, are so worded that the customer may be able to evade certain taxes in his homeland.
- A company president finds that an aging executive, within a few years of retirement and his pension, is not as productive as formerly. Should he be kept on?
- The produce manager of a supermarket debates with himself whether to get rid of a lot of half-rotten tomatoes by including one, with its good side exposed, in every tomato six-pack.
- An accountant discovers that he has taken an improper deduction on his company's tax return and fears the consequences if he calls the matter to the president's attention, though he himself has done nothing illegal. Perhaps if he says nothing, no one will notice the error.
- A chief executive officer is asked by his directors to comment on a rumor that he owns stock in another company with which he has placed large orders. He could deny it, for the stock is in the name of his son-in-law and he has earlier formally instructed his son-in-law to sell the holding.

Temptations of this kind constantly arise in business. If an executive allows himself to be torn between a decision based on business considerations and one based on his private ethical code, he exposes himself to a grave psychological strain.

This is not to say that sound business strategy necessarily runs counter to ethical ideals. They may frequently coincide; and when they do, everyone is gratified. But the major tests of every move in business, as in all games of strategy, are legality and profit. A man who intends to be a winner in the business game must have a game player's attitude.

The business strategist's decisions must be as impersonal as those of a surgeon performing an operation—concentrating on objective and technique, and subordinating personal feelings. If the chief executive admits that his son-in-law owns the stock, it is because he stands to lose more if the fact comes out later than if he states it boldly and at once. If the supermarket manager orders the rotten tomatoes to be discarded, he does so to avoid an increase in consumer complaints and a loss of goodwill. The company president decides not to fire the elderly executive in the belief that the negative reaction of other employees would in the long run cost the company more than it would lose in keeping him and paying his pension.

All sensible businessmen prefer to be truthful, but they seldom feel inclined to tell the *whole* truth. In the business game truth-telling usually has to be kept within narrow limits if trouble is to be avoided. The point was neatly made a long time ago (in 1888) by one of John D. Rockefeller's associates, Paul Babcock, to Standard Oil Company executives who were about to testify before a government investigating committee: "Parry every question with answers which, while perfectly truthful, are evasive of *bottom* facts."[12] This was, is, and probably always will be regarded as wise and permissible business strategy.

For Office Use Only

An executive's family life can easily be dislocated if he fails to make a sharp distinction between the ethical systems of the home and the office—or if his wife does not grasp that distinction. Many a businessman who has remarked to his wife, "I had to let Jones go today" or "I had to admit to the boss that Jim has been goofing off lately," has been met with an indignant protest. "How could you do a thing like that? You know Jones is over 50 and will have a lot of trouble getting another job." Or, "You did that to Jim? With his wife ill and the all the worry she's been having with the kids?"

If the executive insists that he had no choice because the profits of the company and his own security were involved, he may see a certain cool and ominous reappraisal in his wife's eyes. Many wives are not prepared to accept the fact that business operates with a special code of ethics. An illuminating illustration of this comes from a Southern sales executive who related a conversation he had had with his wife at a time when a hotly contested political campaign was being waged in their state:

> "I made the mistake of telling her that I had had lunch with Colby, who gives me about half my business. Colby mentioned that his company had a stake in the election. Then he said, 'By the way, I'm treasurer of the citizens' committee for Lang. I'm collecting contributions. Can I count on you for a hundred dollars?'

---

[12] Babock in a memorandum to Rockefeller (Rockefeller Archives).

"Well, there I was. I was opposed to Lang, but I knew Colby. If he withdrew his business, I could be in a bad spot. So I just smiled and wrote out a check then and there. He thanked me, and we started to talk about his next order. Maybe he thought I shared his political views. If so, I wasn't going to lose any sleep over it.

"I should have had sense enough not to tell Mary about it. She hit the ceiling. She said she was disappointed in me. She said I hadn't acted like a man, that I should have stood up to Colby.

"I said, 'Look, it was an either-or situation. I had to do it or risk losing the business.'

"She came back at me with, 'I don't believe it. You could have been honest with him. You could have said that you didn't feel you ought to contribute to a campaign for a man you weren't going to vote for. I'm sure he would have understood.'

"I said, 'Mary, you're a wonderful woman, but you're way off the track. Do you know what would have happened if I had said that? Colby would have smiled and said, "Oh, I didn't realize. Forget it." But in his eyes from that moment I would be an oddball, maybe a bit of a radical. He would have listened to me talk about his order and would have promised to give it consideration. After that I wouldn't hear from him for a week. Then I would telephone and learn from his secretary that he wasn't yet ready to place the order. And in about a month I would hear through the grapevine that he was giving his business to another company. A month after that I'd be out of a job.'

"She was silent for a while. Then she said, 'Tom, something is wrong with business when a man is forced to choose between his family's security and his moral obligation to himself. It's easy for me to say you should have stood up to him—but if you had, you might have felt you were betraying me and the kids. I'm sorry that you did it, Tom, but I can't blame you. Something is wrong with business!'"

This wife saw the problem in terms of moral obligation as conceived in private life; her husband saw it as a matter of game strategy. As a player in a weak position, he felt that he could not afford to indulge an ethical sentiment that might have cost him his seat at the table.

Playing to Win

Some men might challenge the Colbys of business—might accept serious setbacks to their business careers rather than risk a feeling of moral cowardice. They merit our respect—but as private individuals, not businessmen. When the skillful player of the business game is compelled to submit to unfair pressure, he does not castigate himself for moral weakness. Instead, he strives to put himself into a strong position where he can defend himself against such pressures in the future without loss.

If a man plans to take a seat in the business game, he owes it to himself to master the principles by which the game is played, including its special ethical outlook. He can then hardly fail to recognize that an occasional bluff may well be justified in terms of the game's ethics and warranted in terms of economic necessity. Once he clears his mind on this point, he is in a good position to match his strategy against that of the other players. He can then determine objectively whether a bluff in a given situation has a good chance of succeeding and can decide when and how to bluff, without a feeling of ethical transgression.

To be a winner, a man must play to win. This does not mean that he must be ruthless, cruel, harsh, or treacherous. On the contrary, the better his reputation for integrity, honesty, and decency, the better his chances of victory will be in the long run. But from time to time every businessman, like every poker player, is offered a choice between certain loss and bluffing within the legal rules of the game. If he is not resigned to losing, if he wants to rise in his company and industry, then in such a crisis he will bluff—and bluff hard.

Every now and then one meets a successful businessman who has conveniently forgotten the small or large deceptions that he practiced on his way to fortune. "God gave me my money," old John D. Rockefeller once piously told a Sunday school class. It would be a rare tycoon in our time who would risk the horse laugh with which such a remark would be greeted.

In the last third of the twentieth century even children are aware that if a man has become prosperous in business, he has sometimes departed from the strict truth in order to overcome obstacles or has practiced the more subtle deceptions of the half-truth or the misleading omission. Whatever the form of the bluff, it is an integral part of the game, and the executive who does not master its techniques is not likely to accumulate much money or power.

Discussion Questions

1. Do you agree or disagree with Carr's premise?

2. Does everyone operate at the same level of bluffing?

3. How is the phrase "sound ethics is good business" characterized?

2 B

Resolution of Business Ethics Dilemmas

The resolution of ethical dilemmas in business is often difficult, even in firms with a code of ethics and a culture committed to compliance with ethical models for decision making. Managers need guidelines for making ethical choices.

READING 2.6

Trying Out the Models and a Resolution Approach

While you now have a list of the categories of ethical breaches and many different models for resolution, you may still be wondering about the process for analyzing cases. What follows is a suggested approach for these cases so that you can provide an in-depth analysis from all perspectives.

Steps for Analyzing Ethical Dilemmas and Case Studies in Business

1. Make sure you have a grasp of all of the facts available.
2. List any information you would like to have but don't and what assumptions you would have to make, if any, in resolving the dilemma.
3. Take each person involved in the dilemma and list the concerns they face or might have. Be sure to consider the impact on those not specifically mentioned in the case. For example, product safety issues don't involve just engineers' careers and company profits; shareholders, customers, customers' families, and even communities supported by the business are affected by a business decision on what to do about a product and its safety issue.
4. Develop a list of resolutions for the problem. Apply the various models for reaching this resolution. You may also find that as you apply the various models to the dilemma you find additional insights for questions 1, 2, and 3. If the breach has already occurred, consider the possible remedies and develop systemic changes so that such breaches do not occur in the future.

5. Evaluate the resolutions for costs, legalities, and impact. Try to determine how each of the parties will react to and will be affected by each of the resolutions you have proposed.
6. Make a recommendation on the actions that should be taken.

In some of the cases you will be evaluating the ethics of conduct after the fact. In those situations, your recommendations and resolutions will center on reforms and perhaps recompense for the parties affected.

Each case in this book requires you to examine different perspectives and analyze the impact that the resolution of a dilemma has on the parties involved. Return to these models to question the propriety of the actions taken in each case. Examine the origins of the ethical dilemmas and explore possible solutions. As you work through the cases, you will find yourself developing a new awareness of values and their importance in making business decisions. Try your hand at a few before proceeding to the following sections. The three following, rather short, cases offer an opportunity for application of the materials from this section and give you the chance to hone your skills for ethical resolutions.

The first case here is one in which you have the conduct and the outcome. In these types of cases you are studying why they made the decision they made, what questions or models they might have used to help them see what are the consequences you can see in hindsight, and what pressures made them make these choices. These types of historical cases offer experiences for learning as well as definitive patterns of consequences from short-sighted ethical decisions that do not employ the analysis you have learned.

CASE 2.7
....
Boeing and the Recruiting of the Government Purchasing Agent[13]

Darlene Druyun was a lifetime government employee, working her way up through the system to a position of Air Force acquisition officer. In the last quarter of 2002, Ms. Druyun was nearing her retirement and interested in job opportunities after leaving government service.

Ms. Druyun's daughter, Heather McKee, was an employee at the St. Louis facilities for Boeing, Inc., a company that does a significant amount of business with the federal government. In court documents, Ms. Druyun indicated that Mr. Sears helped place her daughter in her job at Boeing. In September 2002, Ms. McKee sent an e-mail to Michael Sears, Boeing's CFO and the man considered to be in line to be the next CEO, to let him know that her mother was planning to retire.

---

[13] The author has done consulting work on ethics with Boeing to help with employee training on ethical issues. The facts in this case are drawn strictly from public accounts.

As a result of this contact, Mr. Sears met with Ms. Druyun in October 2002, which was one month before Ms. Druyun recused herself from working on any contract decisions involving Boeing as a bidder. At the end of the meeting, Ms. Druyun has testified, Mr. Sears said, "This meeting never took place." When he returned to the offices, however, Mr. Sears sent e-mails out indicating that Ms. Druyun was receptive to employment.

At some point late in 2002, the two reached an employment arrangement because Ms. Druyun went to work for Boeing in its Chicago offices as a vice president. Pending before the Air Force at the time was a bid by Boeing to supply the Air Force with 100 Boeing 767 refueling tankers.

Also during this time, John Judy, a Boeing lawyer who was moving from Boeing offices in St. Louis to the Washington, DC area, purchased Ms. Druyun's home from her. Ms. Druyun began work in January 2003 at Boeing's Chicago Facilities.[14]

During the summer of 2003, Boeing began an internal investigation of the circumstances surrounding Ms. Druyun's hiring. Ms. Druyun and Mr. Sears exchanged memos and e-mails with a timeline that was reconstructed and that did not reflect accurately what had really happened and what was easily traceable through meeting places and witnesses. Based on its internal investigation that revealed "compelling evidence" that the two had conspired to employ Ms. Druyun while she still had contracting authority and their subsequent attempts to cover up their conduct, Boeing dismissed both Ms. Druyun and Mr. Sears. Their dismissal for cause cost them any severance benefits.[15]

Ms. Druyun was charged by the federal government with violations of procurement statutes and conspiracy. She entered a guilty plea to conspiracy in April 2004 and told the court, "I deeply regret my actions and I want to apologize."[16] Ms. Druyun was originally scheduled to be sentenced to six months in prison, because she had agreed to cooperate with federal investigators. However, she was ultimately sentenced to nine months because federal investigators established that she had lied when asked whether she had ever showed favoritism to Boeing in awarding defense contracts. She initially stated that she had not, but, after failing a lie detector test, she disclosed that she had given Boeing several contracts and pricing breaks in exchange for hiring her daughter and son-in-law. She also indicated that she had approved a settlement with Boeing that was too high. Boeing and the defense department are renegotiating that settlement. Boeing CEO Harry Stonecipher pledged that the company would address "any inadequacies that need to be corrected." Ms. Druyun's daughter no longer works for Boeing.[17]

[14] Leslie Wayne, "Boeing Dismisses 2 In Hiring of Official Who Left Pentagon," The New York Times, November 25, 2003, pp. A1, C2.

[15] J. Lynn Lunsford and Andy Pasztor, "Boeing Dismisses Two Executives For Violating Ethical Standards," The Wall Street Journal, November 25, 2003, pp. A1, A8.

[16] J. Lynn Lunsford and Andy Pasztor, "Former Boeing Official Pleads Guilty to Conspiracy," The Wall Street Journal, April 21, 2004, pp. A1, A9.

[17] Leslie Wayne, "Ex-Pentagon Official Gets 9 Months For Conspiring to Favor Boeing," The New York Times, October 2, 2004, pp. B1, B13.

Discussion Questions

1. What category of ethical dilemma is involved here?

2. What questions or models did Mr. Sears miss in choosing to recruit Ms. Druyun when he did? What was he hoping would happen?

3. What were Ms. Druyun's motivations? What questions or models did she miss in making her decision to meet with Mr. Sears?

4. Evaluate the conduct of Ms. Druyun's daughter, Heather.

Some Help with the Boeing Case

Some additional information that would help would be the content of the e-mails. Having those available could provide a better timeline as well as the intent of the parties.

Ms. Druyun: She was facing retirement and was looking for a job and income. She forgot to consider issues such as the long-term impact of this behavior on her prospects for employment as well as on her future. The conduct was not just unethical, as a conflict of interest, it violated federal law. It carries a penalty of up to 5 years and $250,000. She may have thought she was simply using her contacts, but to be able to use those contacts she had to eliminate her conflict of interest. She focused on the short-term, not the long-term.

Mr. Sears: His company was in tight competition for a major contract and Ms. Druyun had influence and power over that decision. Having her know that a job awaited her was, he felt, a way of ensuring Boeing getting the contract. However, he failed to apply the simple question of whether the conduct was legal. He did not analyze the conflict of interest and did not consider the impact to his reputation and Boeing's. The conduct proved personally destructive for him, Ms. Druyun, and others. That notion of distrust and corruption creeps into perceptions about corporations and government when this kind of ethical indiscretion emerges.

Heather: Ms. Druyun's daughter was in her position because Mr. Sears and Ms. Druyun had already exercised their influence on each other to obtain her employment. She became used to the pattern and set up the contact for the two. She facilitated a conflict after gaining her job through the use of a conflict of interest.

Now apply your knowledge and skills to the following historical-type case.

CASE 2.8
The Rigged Election

The Finance Club at Harvard University is a prestigious organization for Harvard MBA students. The student members have the opportunity to interact with public officials like Senator William Proxmire and business executives such as Bruce Wasserstein. The Finance Club also serves as a network for job hunting.

Each spring, the club holds elections for its officers, including two co-presidents. In the spring of 1992, after initial balloting, there was a tie between two teams of two co-presidents. Murry Gunty was one member of one of the teams and busily recruited students to vote in a run-off election. Two of the students he recruited voted under names of absentee members of the Finance Club. The new votes gave Mr. Gunty his victory. However, two of the votes were from students who were not members of the club, but used someone else's name to vote.[18]

After an anonymous tip, the elections were set aside and the runners-up installed as co-presidents. Mr. Gunty was required to write a paper on ethics.[19]

Discussion Questions

1. In the words of the school newspaper publisher, "Why would anyone do this? It's just a club."

2. Was anyone really hurt by the conduct?

3. Would you have reported the conduct anonymously or disclosed it publicly?

4. What are the long-term implications for Mr. Gunty?

In the following case, you are playing a different role in that you are analyzing from the perspective of offering a solution in a situation where the conduct has not already been undertaken. In this type of case, you are asked to conduct the ethical analysis without the benefit of hindsight. You have to be certain that you apply all the questions and use the models to help give you insight.

CASE 2.9
The Loan Officer and the Debtors

Ben Garrison is a senior loan officer with First National Federal Bank, the second-largest financial institution in Wyoming. Ben, who has been with First National Federal for ten years, handles loan applications from all over the state.

Following the savings and loan debacle of the late 1980s, First National Federal implemented many institutional changes. Some of the changes were operational; others involved the bank's lending policy. A change that Ben found frustrating was an increasing emphasis on ethics. Ben complained to one of his loan officers, "I don't get this ethics stuff. If it's legal, I'm ethical." One of the loan officers, Shelby Grant, a recent graduate of the University of Wyoming School of Business, replied, "Well, sometimes doing what's ethical helps you avoid legal problems." Ben replied, "Sometimes doing what's ethical just costs you more money!"

Later that morning, following their discussion, Ben appeared in Shelby's office with a loan application from Doug Whitton, a rancher in the northwestern part of the state. He told Shelby that they needed to take a trip to evaluate the proposed collateral for the

[18] Gilbert Fuchsberg, "Harvard Has Some Crimson Faces Over a Lesson in Practical Politics," The Wall Street Journal, April 9, 1992, p. B1.

[19] "Harvard Student Rigging Election Must Write Paper," The Wall Street Journal, April 24, 1992, p. A3.

loan. An on-site evaluation of collateral is a required procedure for loan processing at First National Federal. Ben added, "Whitton's paying our way up there for the evaluation." Shelby asked, "Shouldn't the bank pay our way, since we may not make the loan and we wouldn't want to be obligated to Whitton?" Ben responded, "Now why in the hell would I want to pay our way up there and increase my costs when he's offering to pay?" Shelby was uncertain about the propriety of the proposal.

Ben added that First National Federal's annual fundraiser picnic was coming up and that they were planning to have the usual prize drawing. "So," he told Shelby, "just get on the phone to all the customers whose loans you handle and see what prizes they're willing to donate for this year's drawings." Shelby asked, "Isn't it wrong for us to pressure our customers into donating prizes?" Ben replied angrily, "These prizes are not for us! The money is not for us! This is charity! What could be unethical about that?"

Shelby went home that evening to prepare for the trip to the ranch. She hadn't called any of her customers for donations, and she didn't want to go on the trip unless the bank paid. She was also $20,000 in debt from school, and it had taken her four months after graduation to find this job. "I guess this is just the way business is done," she concluded.

....

Discussion Questions

1. Is Shelby correct? Are both these issues "just the way business is done"?

2. Is the appearance of impropriety an important ethical constraint?

3. What problems arise in having the potential borrower pay for the collateral evaluation trip?

4. What problems arise in soliciting donations from loan customers?

5. How would it be different if a merchant offered to donate items without being asked?

6. If you were Shelby, would you pursue the donations issue or just follow the process the bank has always used?

Foundations of Business Ethics: What Is the Role of Business in Society? Shareholders vs. Stakeholders

3ᴬ

The Role of Business in Society

THE STUDY OF BUSINESS ETHICS is not the study of what is legal but of the application of moral standards to business decisions. Moral standards are canons of personal behavior that are neither legislated nor changed by legislation. For example, regardless of legislative and regulatory requirements, we all are committed to safety and fairness for employees in the workplace. But what happens when several moral standards conflict? A company that manufactures athletic shoes finds cheap labor in developing nations. The company pays minimum wage for that country, but those wages wouldn't bring enough in one month to allow the workers to buy a pair of the company's shoes. Factory conditions meet that nation's standards but violate nearly all U.S. minimum standards. Without the cheap labor, the shoe manufacturer can't compete. Without the jobs, the nation can't develop, but children are working 50-hour weeks in these third world countries. Fair and just treatment in the workplace is an issue the company must face in making this foreign outsourcing of labor.

Employees hold moral standards of following instructions, doing an honest day's work for a day's pay, and being loyal to their employers. But what happens when their employers are producing products that, because of inadequate testing, will be harmful to users? To whom do employees turn if employers reject them and their concerns? Other moral standards—of not intentionally harming others and adequately testing products—will present those employees with a dilemma and force them to decide an appropriate course of action.

Businesses, consumers, and employees too often subscribe to the "what's good for GM is good for the country" theory of business ethics. Jeff Dachis, the founder and former CEO of Razorfish, once said when he was questioned about the lack of independence on his board, "My partner and I control 10 percent of the company. What's good for me is good for all shareholders. Management isn't screwing up. We've created enormous shareholder value."[1] He spoke when his stock was at $56 in June 1999. In May 2001, when he added three independent directors to his board and resigned as CEO, Razorfish stock was trading at $1.11 per share. No one at Razorfish did anything illegal, but it is the presence of perspective in a company through its board and also

[1] Erick Schonfeld, "Doing Business the Dot-Com Way," Fortune, March 20, 2000, p. 116.

through the analytical framework of ethics that may save a company from its hubris. Businesses have now begun to realize that, contrary to Sir Alfred Coke's allegation that a corporation has no conscience; the corporation must develop a conscience. That conscience develops as firms and the individuals within them develop perspective on and guidelines for their respective conduct.

In defining business ethics, we are really defining the voluntary role of business: how does a business behave when the law does not dictate its conduct or the law permits conduct that might benefit shareholders but is harmful to others?

In the following readings, economist Milton Friedman and Professor Edward Freeman present different views on the role of ethics in business as well as the role of business in society. You can now add to your steps for resolving dilemmas the additional factor of your position and the position of the company and individuals involved in the role of business in society.

READING 3.1
....

The Social Responsibility of Business Is to Increase Its Profits[2]

Milton Friedman

When I hear businessmen speak eloquently about the "social responsibilities of business in a free-enterprise system," I am reminded of the wonderful line about the Frenchman who discovered at the age of 70 that he had been speaking prose all his life. The businessmen believe that they are defending free enterprise when they declaim that business is not concerned "merely" with profit but also with promoting desirable "social" ends; that business has a "social conscience" and takes seriously its responsibilities for providing employment, eliminating discrimination, avoiding pollution, and whatever else may be the catchwords of the contemporary crop of reformers. In fact they are—or would be if they or anyone else took them seriously—preaching pure and unadulterated socialism. Businessmen who talk this way are unwitting puppets of the intellectual forces that have been undermining the basis of a free society these past decades.

The discussions of the "social responsibilities of business" are notable for their analytical looseness and lack of rigor. What does it mean to say that "business" has responsibilities? Only people can have responsibilities. A corporation is an artificial person and in this sense may have artificial responsibilities, but "business" as a whole cannot be said to have responsibilities, even in this vague sense. The first step toward clarity in examining the doctrine of the social responsibility of business is to ask precisely what it implies for whom.

Presumably, the individuals who are to be responsible are businessmen, which means individual proprietors or corporate executives. Most of the discussion of social

[2] Source: The New York Times Sunday Magazine, September 13, 1970. Copyright © 1970 by The New York Times Company. Reprinted by permission.

responsibility is directed at corporations, so in what follows I shall mostly neglect the individual proprietor and speak of corporate executives.

In a free-enterprise, private-property system, a corporate executive is an employee of the owners of the business. He has direct responsibility to his employers. That responsibility is to conduct the business in accordance with their desires, which generally will be to make as much money as possible while conforming to the basic rules of the society, both those embodied in law and those embodied in ethical custom. Of course, in some cases his employers may have a different objective. A group of persons might establish a corporation for an eleemosynary purpose—for example, a hospital or a school. The manager of such a corporation will not have money profit as his objective but the rendering of certain services.

In either case, the key point is that, in his capacity as a corporate executive, the manager is the agent of the individuals who own the corporation or establish the eleemosynary institution, and his primary responsibility is to them.

Needless to say, this does not mean that it is easy to judge how well he is performing his task. But at least the criterion of performance is straightforward, and the persons among whom a voluntary contractual arrangement exists are clearly defined.

Of course, the corporate executive is also a person in his own right. As a person, he may have many other responsibilities that he recognizes or assumes voluntarily—to his family, his conscience, his feelings of charity, his church, his clubs, his city, his country. He may feel impelled by these responsibilities to devote part of his income to causes he regards as worthy, to refuse to work for particular corporations, even to leave his job, for example, to join his country's armed forces. If we wish, we may refer to some of these responsibilities as "social responsibilities." But in these respects he is acting as a principal, not an agent; he is spending his own money or time or energy, not the money of his employers or the time or energy he had contracted to devote to their purposes. If these are "social responsibilities," they are the social responsibilities of individuals, not of business.

What does it mean to say that the corporate executive has a "social responsibility" in his capacity as businessman? If this statement is not pure rhetoric, it must mean that he is to act in some way that is not in the interest of his employers. For example, that he is to refrain from increasing the price of the product in order to contribute to the social objective of preventing inflation, even though a price increase would be in the best interests of the corporation. Or that he is to make expenditures on reducing pollution beyond the amount that is in the best interests of the corporation or that is required by law in order to contribute to the social objective of improving the environment. Or that, at the expense of corporate profits, he is to hire "hard-core" unemployed instead of better-qualified available workmen to contribute to the social objective of reducing poverty.

In each of these cases, the corporate executive would be spending someone else's money for a general social interest. Insofar as his actions in accord with his "social responsibility" reduce returns to stockholders, he is spending their money. Insofar as his actions raise the price to customers, he is spending the customers' money. Insofar as his actions lower the wages of some employees, he is spending their money.

The stockholders or the customers or the employees could separately spend their own money on the particular action if they wished to do so. The executive is exercising a distinct "social responsibility," rather than serving as an agent of the stockholders or the customers or the employees, only if he spends the money in a different way than they would have spent it.

But if he does this, he is in effect imposing taxes, on the one hand, and deciding how the tax proceeds shall be spent, on the other.

This process raises political questions on two levels: principle and consequences. On the level of political principle, the imposition of taxes and the expenditure of tax proceeds are governmental functions. We have established elaborate constitutional, parliamentary, and judicial provisions to control these functions, to assure that taxes are imposed so far as possible in accordance with the preferences and desires of the public—after all, "taxation without representation" was one of the battle cries of the American Revolution. We have a system of checks and balances to separate the legislative function of imposing taxes and enacting expenditures from the executive function of collecting taxes and administering expenditure programs and from the judicial function of mediating disputes and interpreting the law.

Here the businessman—self-selected or appointed directly or indirectly by stockholders—is to be simultaneously legislator, executive, and jurist. He is to decide whom to tax by how much and for what purpose, and he is to spend the proceeds—all this guided only by general exhortations from on high to restrain inflation, improve the environment, fight poverty, and so on and on.

The whole justification for permitting the corporate executive to be selected by the stockholders is that the executive is an agent serving the interests of his principal. This justification disappears when the corporate executive imposes taxes and spends the proceeds for "social" purposes. He becomes in effect a public employee, a civil servant, even though he remains in name an employee of a private enterprise. On grounds of political principle, it is intolerable that such civil servants—insofar as their actions in the name of social responsibility are real and not just window-dressing—should be selected as they are now. If they are to be civil servants, then they must be selected through a political process. If they are to impose taxes and make expenditures to foster "social" objectives, then political machinery must be set up to guide the assessment of taxes and to determine through a political process the objectives to be served.

This is the basic reason why the doctrine of "social responsibility" involves the acceptance of the socialist view that political mechanisms, not market mechanisms, are the appropriate way to determine the allocation of scarce resources to alternative uses.

On the grounds of consequences, can the corporate executive in fact discharge his alleged "social responsibilities"? On the one hand, suppose he could get away with spending the stockholders' or customers' or employees' money. How is he to know how to spend it? He is told that he must contribute to fighting inflation. How is he to know what action of his will contribute to that end? He is presumably an expert in running his company—in producing a product or selling it or financing it. But nothing about his selection makes him an expert on inflation. Will his holding down the price of his product reduce inflationary pressure? Or, by leaving more spending power in the hands of his customers, simply divert it elsewhere? Or, by forcing him to produce less because of the lower price, will it simply contribute to shortages? Even if he could answer these questions, how much cost is he justified in imposing on his stockholders, customers, and employees for this social purpose? What is his appropriate share and what is the appropriate share of others?

And, whether he wants to or not, can he get away with spending his stockholders', customers', or employees' money? Will not the stockholders fire him? (Either the present ones or those who take over when his actions in the name of social responsibility have reduced the corporation's profits and the price of its stock.) His customers and his employees can desert him for other producers and employers less scrupulous in exercising their social responsibilities.

This facet of "social responsibility" doctrine is brought into sharp relief when the doctrine is used to justify wage restraint by trade unions. The conflict of interest is naked and clear when union officials are asked to subordinate the interest of their members to some more general social purpose. If the union officials try to enforce wage restraint, the consequence is likely to be wildcat strikes, rank-and-file revolts and the emergence of strong competitors for their jobs. We thus have the ironic phenomenon that union leaders—at least in the U.S.—have objected to government interference with the market far more consistently and courageously than have business leaders.

The difficulty of exercising "social responsibility" illustrates, of course, the great virtue of private competitive enterprise—it forces people to be responsible for their own actions and makes it difficult for them to "exploit" other people for either selfish or unselfish purposes. They can do good—but only at their own expense.

Many a reader who has followed the argument this far may be tempted to remonstrate that it is well and good to speak of government's having the responsibility to impose taxes and determine expenditures for such "social" purposes as controlling pollution or training the hard-core unemployed, but that the problems are too urgent to wait on the slow course of political processes, that the exercise of social responsibility by businessmen is a quicker and surer way to solve pressing current problems.

Aside from the question of fact—I share Adam Smith's skepticism about the benefits that can be expected from "those who affected to trade for the public good"—this argument must be rejected on grounds of principle. What it amounts to is an assertion that those who favor the taxes and expenditures in question have failed to persuade a majority of their fellow citizens to be of like mind and that they are seeking to attain by undemocratic procedures what they cannot attain by democratic procedures. In a free society, it is hard for "good" people to do "good," but that is a small price to pay for making it hard for "evil" people to do "evil," especially since one man's good is another's evil.

I have, for simplicity, concentrated on the special case of the corporate executive, except only for the brief digression on trade unions. But precisely the same argument applies to the newer phenomenon of calling upon stockholders to require corporations to exercise social responsibility (the recent GM crusade, for example). In most of these cases, what is in effect involved is some stockholders trying to get other stockholders (or customers or employees) to contribute against their will to "social" causes favored by the activists. Insofar as they succeed, they are again imposing taxes and spending the proceeds.

The situation of the individual proprietor is somewhat different. If he acts to reduce the returns of his enterprise in order to exercise his "social responsibility," he is spending his own money, not someone else's. If he wishes to spend his money on such purposes, that is his right, and I cannot see that there is any objection to his doing so. In the process, he, too, may impose costs on employees and customers. However, because he is far less likely than a large corporation or union to have monopolistic power, any such side effects will tend to be minor.

Of course, in practice the doctrine of social responsibility is frequently a cloak for actions that are justified on other grounds rather than a reason for those actions.

To illustrate, it may well be in the long-run interest of a corporation that is a major employer in a small community to devote resources to providing amenities to that community or to improving its government. That may make it easier to attract desirable employees, it may reduce the wage bill or lessen losses from pilferage and sabotage or have other worthwhile effects. Or it may be that, given the laws about the deductibility of corporate charitable contributions, the stockholders can contribute more to charities they favor by having the corporation make the gift than by doing it themselves, since they can in that way contribute an amount that would otherwise have been paid as corporate taxes.

In each of these—and many similar—cases, there is a strong temptation to rationalize these actions as an exercise of "social responsibility." In the present climate of opinion, with its widespread aversion to "capitalism," "profits," the "soulless corporation" and so on, this is one way for a corporation to generate goodwill as a by-product of expenditures that are entirely justified in its own self-interest.

It would be inconsistent of me to call on corporate executives to refrain from this hypocritical window-dressing because it harms the foundations of a free society. That would be to call on them to exercise a "social responsibility"! If our institutions, and the attitudes of the public, make it in their self-interest to cloak their actions in this way, I cannot summon much indignation to denounce them. At the same time, I can express admiration for those individual proprietors or owners of closely held corporations or stockholders of more broadly held corporations who disdain such tactics as approaching fraud.

Whether blameworthy or not, the use of the cloak of social responsibility, and the nonsense spoken in its name by influential and prestigious businessmen, does clearly harm the foundations of a free society. I have been impressed time and again by the schizophrenic character of many businessmen. They are capable of being extremely far-sighted and clear-headed in matters that are internal to their businesses. They are incredibly short-sighted and muddle-headed in matters that are outside their businesses but affect the possible survival of business in general. This short-sightedness is strikingly exemplified in the calls from many businessmen for wage and price guidelines or controls or incomes policies. There is nothing that could do more in a brief period to destroy a market system and replace it by a centrally controlled system than effective governmental control of prices and wages.

The short-sightedness is also exemplified in speeches by businessmen on social responsibility. This may gain them kudos in the short run. But it helps to strengthen the already too prevalent view that the pursuit of profits is wicked and immoral and must be curbed and controlled by external forces. Once this view is adopted, the external forces that curb the market will not be the social consciences, however highly developed, of the pontificating executives; it will be the iron fist of government bureaucrats. Here, as with price and wage controls, businessmen seem to me to reveal a suicidal impulse.

The political principle that underlies the market mechanism is unanimity. In an ideal free market resting on private property, no individual can coerce any other, all cooperation is voluntary, all parties to such cooperation benefit or they need not participate. There are no "social" values, no "social" responsibilities in any sense other than the shared values and responsibilities of individuals. Society is a collection of individuals and of the various groups they voluntarily form.

The political principle that underlies the political mechanism is conformity. The individual must serve a more general social interest—whether that be determined by a church or a dictator or a majority. The individual may have a vote and a say in what is to be done, but if he is overruled, he must conform. It is appropriate for some to require others to contribute to a general social purpose whether they wish to or not.

Unfortunately, unanimity is not always feasible. There are some respects in which conformity appears unavoidable, so I do not see how one can avoid the use of the political mechanism altogether.

But the doctrine of "social responsibility" taken seriously would extend the scope of the political mechanism to every human activity. It does not differ in philosophy from the most explicitly collectivist doctrine. It differs only by professing to believe that collectivist ends can be attained without collectivist means. That is why, in my book *Capitalism and Freedom*, I have called it a "fundamentally subversive doctrine" in a free society, and have said that in such a society, "there is one and only one social responsibility of business—to use its resources and engage in activities designed to increase its profits so long as it stays within the rules of the game, which is to say, engages in open and free competition without deception or fraud."

Discussion Questions

1. How does Dr. Friedman characterize discussions on "social responsibilities of business"? Why?

2. What is the role of a corporate executive selected by stockholders?

3. What analogy does Dr. Friedman draw between trade union wages and corporations' decisions based on social responsibilities?

4. Would Dr. Friedman ever support voluntary actions on the part of a corporation (e.g., conduct not prohibited specifically or mandated by law)?

A Stakeholder Theory of the Modern Corporation[3]

R. Edward Freeman

Corporations have ceased to be merely legal devices through which the private business transactions of individuals may be carried on. Though still much used for this purpose, the corporate form has acquired a larger significance. The corporation has, in fact, become both a method of property tenure and a means of organizing economic life. Grown to tremendous proportions, there may be said to have evolved a "corporate system"—which has attracted to itself a combination of attributes and powers, and has attained a degree of prominence entitling it to be dealt with as a major social institution.[4]

Despite these prophetic words of Berle and Means (1932), scholars and managers alike continue to hold sacred the view that managers bear a special relationship to the stockholders in the firm. Since stockholders own shares in the firm, they have certain rights and privileges, which must be granted to them by management, as well as by others. Sanctions, in the form of "the law of corporations" and other protective mechanisms in the form of social custom, accepted management practice, myth, and ritual, are thought to reinforce the assumption of the primacy of the stockholder.

The purpose of this paper is to pose several challenges to this assumption, from within the framework of managerial capitalism, and to suggest the bare bones of an alternative theory, a *stakeholder theory of the modern corporation*. I do not seek the demise of the modern corporation, either intellectually or in fact. Rather, I seek its transformation. In the words of Neurath, we shall attempt to "rebuild the ship, plank by plank, while it remains afloat."[5]

My thesis is that I can revitalize the concept of managerial capitalism by replacing the notion that managers have a duty to stockholders with the notion that managers bear a fiduciary duty to stakeholders. Stakeholders are those groups who have a stake or claim in the firm. Specifically I include suppliers, customers, employees, stockholders, and the local community, as well as management in its role as an agent for these groups. I argue that the legal, economic, political, and moral challenges to the currently received theory of the firm, as a nexus of contracts among the owners of the factors of production and customers, require us to revise this concept. That is, each of these stakeholder groups has a right not to be treated as a means to some end, and

---

[3] From William R. Evan and R. Edward Freeman, "A Stakeholder Theory of the Modern Corporation: Kantian Capitalism," and R. Edward Freeman, "The Politics of Stakeholder Theory," Business Ethics Quarterly 4 (1994) pp. 409–421.

[4] A. Berle and G. Means. The Modern Corporation and Private Property. New York: Commerce Clearing House, 1932, p. 1.

[5] The metaphor of rebuilding the ship while afloat is attributed to Neurath by W. Quine, Word and Object (Cambridge: Harvard University Press, 1960). The point is that to keep the ship afloat during repairs we must replace a plank with one that will do a better job. Our argument is that stakeholder capitalism can so replace the current version of managerial capitalism.

therefore must participate in determining the future direction of the firm in which they have a stake.

The crux of my argument is that we must reconceptualize the firm around the following question: For whose benefit and at whose expense should the firm be managed? I shall set forth such a reconceptualization in the form of a *stakeholder theory of the firm.* I shall then critically examine the stakeholder view and its implications for the future of the capitalistic system.

The Attack on Managerial Capitalism

The Legal Argument

The basic idea of managerial capitalism is that in return for controlling the firm, management vigorously pursues the interests of the stockholders. Central to the managerial view of the firm is the idea that management can pursue market transactions with suppliers and customers in an unconstrained manner.

The law of corporations gives a less clear-cut answer to the question: In whose interest and for whose benefit should the modern corporation be governed? While it says that the corporations should be run primarily in the interests of the stockholders in the firm, it further says that the corporation exists "in contemplation of the law" and has personality as a "legal person," limited liability for its actions, and immortality, since its existence transcends that of its members. Therefore, directors and other officers of the firm have a fiduciary obligation to stockholders in the sense that the "affairs of the corporation" must be conducted in the interest of the stockholders. And stockholders can theoretically bring suit against those directors and managers for doing otherwise. But since the corporation is a legal person, existing in contemplation of the law, managers of the corporation are constrained by law.

Until recently, there was no constraint at all. In this century, however, the law has evolved to effectively constrain the pursuit of stockholder interests at the expense of other claimants of the firm. It has, in effect, required that the claims of customers, suppliers, local communities, and employees be taken into consideration, though in general they are subordinated to the claims of the stockholders.

For instance, the doctrine of "privity of contract," as articulated in *Winterbottom v. Wright* in 1842, has been eroded by recent development in product liability law. . . . Caveat emptor has been replaced, in large part, with caveat venditor.

The same argument is applicable to management's dealings with employees. The National Labor Relations Act gave employees the right to unionize and bargain in good faith. It set up the National Labor Relations Board to enforce these rights with management. The Equal Pay Act of 1963 and Title VII of the Civil Rights Act of 1964 constrain management from discrimination in hiring practices; these have been followed with the Age Discrimination in Employment Act of 1967.

The law has also protected the interests of local communities. The Clean Air Act and Clean Water Act have constrained management from "spoiling the commons."

I have argued that the result of such changes in the legal system can be viewed as giving some rights to those groups that have a claim on the firm, for example, customers, suppliers, employees, local communities, stockholders, and management.

It raises the question, at the core of the theory of the firm: In whose interest and for whose benefit should the firm be managed? The answer proposed by managerial capitalism is clearly "the stockholders," but I have argued that the law has been progressively circumscribing the answer.

The Economic Argument

In its pure ideological form managerial capitalism seeks to maximize the interests of stockholders. In its perennial criticism of government regulation, management espouses the "invisible hand" doctrine. It contends that it creates the greatest good for the greatest number, and therefore government need not intervene. However, we know that externalities, moral hazards, and monopoly power exist in fact, whether or not they exist in theory. Further, some of the legal apparatus mentioned above has evolved to deal with just these issues.

The problem of the "tragedy of the commons" or the free-rider problem pervades the concept of public goods such as water and air. No one has incentive to incur the cost of clean-up or the cost of nonpollution since the marginal gain of one firm's action is small. Every firm reasons this way, and the result is pollution of water and air. Since the industrial revolution, firms have sought to internalize the benefits and externalize the costs of their actions. The cost must be born by all, through taxation and regulation; hence we have the emergence of the environmental regulations of the 1970s.

Similarly, moral hazards arise when the purchaser of a good or service can pass along the cost of that good. There is not incentive to economize, on the part of either the producer or the consumer, and there is excessive use of the resources involved. The institutionalized practice of third-party payment in health care is a prime example.

Finally, we see the avoidance of competitive behavior on the part of firms, each seeking to monopolize a small portion of the market and not compete with one another. In a number of industries, oligopolies have merged, and while there is questionable evidence that oligopolies are not the most efficient corporate form in some industries, suffice it to say that the potential for abuse of market power has again led to regulation of managerial activity. In the classic case, AT&T, arguably one of the great technological and managerial achievements of the century, was broken up into eight separate companies to prevent its abuse of monopoly power.

Externalities, moral hazards, and monopoly power have led to more external control on managerial capitalism. There are de facto constraints, due to these economic facts of life, on the ability of management to act in the interests of the stockholders.

A Stakeholder Theory of the Firm

The Stakeholder Concept

Corporations have stakeholders, that is, groups and individuals who benefit from or are harmed by, and whose rights are violated or respected by, corporate actions. The concept of stakeholders is a generalization of the notion of stockholders, who themselves have some special claim on the firm. Just as stockholders have a right to demand certain actions by management, so do other stakeholders have a right to make claims. The exact nature of these claims is a difficult question that I shall address, but the logic is identical to that of the stockholder theory. Stakes require action of a certain sort, and conflicting stakes require methods of resolution.

Freeman and Reed (1983)[6] distinguish two senses of *stakeholder*. The "narrow definition" includes those groups who are vital to the survival and success of the corporation. The "wide-definition" includes any group or individual who can affect or is affected by the corporation. I shall begin with a modest aim: to articulate a stakeholder theory using the narrow definition.

Stakeholders of the Modern Corporation

Figure 3.1 depicts the stakeholders in a typical corporation. The stakes of each are reciprocal, since each can affect the other in terms of harms and benefits as well as rights and duties. The stakes of each are not univocal and would vary by particular corporation. I merely set forth some general notions that seem to be common to many large firms.

Owners have financial stake in the corporations in the form of stocks, bonds, and so on, and they expect some kind of financial return from them. Either they have given money directly to the firm, or they have some historical claim made through a series of morally justified exchanges. The firm affects their livelihood or, if a substantial portion of their retirement income is in stocks or bonds, their ability to care for themselves when they can no longer work. Of course, the stakes of owners will differ by type of owner, preferences for money, moral preferences, and so on, as well as by type of firm. The owners of AT&T are quite different from the owners of Ford Motor Company, with stock of the former company being widely dispersed among 3 million stockholders and that of the latter being held by a small family group as well as by a large group of public stockholders.

Employees have their jobs and usually their livelihood at stake; they often have specialized skills for which there is usually no perfectly elastic market. In return for their labor, they expect security, wages, benefits, and meaningful work. In return for their loyalty, the corporation is expected to provide for them and carry them through difficult times. Employees are expected to follow the instructions of management most of the time, to speak favorably about the company, and to be responsible citizens in the local communities in which the company operates. Where they are used as a means to

FIGURE 3.1 Stakeholders in a Typical Corporation

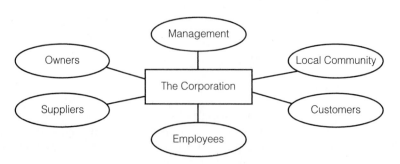

[6] E. Freeman and D. Reed, "Stockholders and Stakeholders: A New Perspective on Corporate Governance," in C. Huizinga, ed., Corporate Governance: A Definitive Exploration of the Issues (Los Angeles: UCLA Extension Press, 1983).

an end, they must participate in decisions affecting such use. The evidence that such policies and values as described here lead to productive company–employee relationships is compelling. It is equally compelling to realize that the opportunities for "bad faith" on the part of both management and employees are tremendous. "Mock participation" in quality circles, singing the company song, and wearing the company uniform solely to please management all lead to distrust and unproductive work.

Suppliers, interpreted in a stakeholder sense, are vital to the success of the firm, for raw materials will determine the final product's quality and price. In turn the firm is a customer of the supplier and is therefore vital to the success and survival of the supplier. When the firm treats the supplier as a valued member of the stakeholder network, rather than as simply a source of materials, the supplier will respond when the firm is in need. Chrysler traditionally had very close ties to its suppliers, even to the extent that led some to suspect the transfer of illegal payments. And when Chrysler was on the brink of disaster, the suppliers responded with price cuts, accepting late payments, financing, and so on. Supplier and company can rise and fall together. Of course, again, the particular supplier relationships will depend on a number of variables such as the number of suppliers and whether the supplies are finished goods or raw materials.

Customers exchange resources for the products of the firm and in return receive the benefits of the products. Customers provide the lifeblood of the firm in the form of revenue. Given the level of reinvestment of earnings in large corporations, customers indirectly pay for the development of new products and services. Peters and Waterman (1982)[7] have argued that being close to the customer leads to success with other stakeholders and that a distinguishing characteristic of some companies that have performed well is their emphasis on the customer. By paying attention to customers' needs, management automatically addresses the needs of suppliers and owners. Moreover, it seems that the ethics of customer service carries over to the community. Almost without fail the "excellent companies" in Peters and Waterman's study have good reputations in the community. I would argue that Peters and Waterman have found multiple applications of Kant's dictum, "Treat persons as ends unto themselves," and it should come as no surprise that persons respond to such respectful treatment, be they customers, suppliers, owners, employees, or members of the local community. The real surprise is the novelty of the application of Kant's rule in a theory of good management practice.

The local community grants the firm the right to build facilities and, in turn, benefits from the tax base and economic and social contribution of the firm. In return for the provision of local services, the firm is expected to be a good citizen, as is any person, either "natural or artificial." The firm cannot expose the community to unreasonable hazards in the form of pollution, toxic waste, and so on. If for some reason the firm must leave a community, it is expected to work with local leaders to make the transition as smoothly as possible. Of course, the firm does not have perfect knowledge, but when it discovers some danger or runs afoul of new competition, it is expected to inform the local community and to work with the community to overcome any problem. When the firm mismanages its relationship with the local community, it is in the same position as a citizen who commits a crime. It has violated the implicit social contract with the community and should expect to be distrusted and ostracized. It should not be surprised when punitive measures are invoked.

---

[7] T. Peters and R. Waterman, In Search of Excellence (New York: Harper and Row, 1982).

I have not included "competitors" as stakeholders in the narrow sense, since strictly speaking they are not necessary for the survival and success of the firm; the stakeholder theory works equally well in monopoly contexts. However, competitors and government would be the first to be included in an extension of this basic theory. It is simply not true that the interests of competitors in an industry are always in conflict. There is no reason why trade associations and other multi-organizational groups cannot band together to solve common problems that have little to do with how to restrain trade. Implementation of stakeholder management principles, in the long run, mitigates the need for industrial policy and an increasing role for government intervention and regulation.

The Role of Management

Management plays a special role, for it too has a stake in the modern corporation. On the one hand, management's stake is like that of employees, with some kind of explicit or implicit employment contract. But, on the other hand, management has a duty of safeguarding the welfare of the abstract entity that is the corporation. In short, management, especially top management, must look after the health of the corporation, and this involves balancing the multiple claims of conflicting stakeholders. Owners want higher financial returns, while customers want more money spent on research and development. Employees want higher wages and better benefits, while the local community wants better parks and day-care facilities.

The task of management in today's corporation is akin to that of King Solomon. The stakeholder theory does not give primacy to one stakeholder group over another, though surely there will be times when one group will benefit at the expense of others. In general, however, management must keep the relationships among stakeholders in balance. When these relationships become imbalanced, the survival of the firm is in jeopardy.

When wages are too high and product quality is too low, customers leave, suppliers suffer, and owners sell their stocks and bonds, depressing the stock price and making it difficult to raise new capital at favorable rates. Note, however, that the reason for paying returns to owners is not that they "own" the firm, but that their support is necessary for the survival of the firm, and that they have a legitimate claim on the firm. Similar reasoning applies in turn to each stakeholder group.

A stakeholder theory of the firm must redefine the purpose of the firm. The stockholder theory claims that the purpose of the firm is to maximize the welfare of the stockholders, perhaps subject to some moral or social constraints, either because such maximization leads to the greatest good or because of property rights. The purpose of the firm is quite different in my view.

Discussion Questions

1. What problems does Freeman see with having government regulation control the operation of corporations?

2. What problems does Freeman see with having the free market control the operation of corporations?

3. List the stakeholders of a corporation. Are government and competitors included? Why or why not?

4. What is the role of management in the stakeholder model?

5. Explain the references to Kant and King Solomon.

6. The city of Phoenix, because of its rapid growth, has reached a point where its airport is not large enough to accommodate all incoming and outgoing air traffic. Managers for the city indicate the airport needs two new runways as well as additional flight paths over the city in order to meet the growing demands of commercial airlines for use of Phoenix as an international hub. List all who will be affected and/or benefit from the expansion of the airport.

7. Suppose that there are objections to the airport expansion. List categories of those you believe might object. Are they stakeholders of commercial airlines? Should they have a say in whether the airlines expand service to Phoenix? Should they have a say in whether the airlines pay for the expansion of the Phoenix airport?

READING 3.3
....

Appeasing Stakeholders with Public Relations[8]

This reading provides a different perspective on the stakeholder vs. shareholder debate. The author questions its wisdom and precision.

Robert Halfon

The problem in today's era of corporate pseudo-ethics is that the pendulum has shifted too far. From genuine philanthropy, . . . 'corporate responsibility' has mutated into a dangerous form of political correctness. The enlightened, entrepreneurial philanthropy of old has, through activist agitation, become the burden of today's so-called 'corporate responsibility.' At least four distinct trends are in evidence here: the rise of single-issue activist groups; the targeting of companies with dealings in specific countries or specific industries; a rise in public sympathy for such actions; and a seal of approval guaranteed by many Western governments today.

Corporations have an obligation to anticipate and deal with these threats. This can be done in a number of ways. First, every important commercial activity should be rigorously assessed for its political risk. This means the risks or threats a business may face (from pressure groups, governments, *et al.*) in undertaking a particular activity. Business needs to inform itself at the highest level of the political environment in which it operates. As one commentator on these matters argues without hesitation:

> The lessons that need to be understood are simple. It does not matter where you are, or how big you are, if you are not prepared, pressure groups have the ability to make your company a member of the endangered species. You cannot respond effectively in six minutes to a campaign that has probably taken six months to organize. . . . Our first option

[8] *Robert Halfon*, Corporate Irresponsibility: Is Business Appeasing Anti-business Activists? *Great Britain: The Social Affairs Unit, 1998, p. 7.*

is to ignore the increasing threat of pressure groups and lose everything. Our second option is to fight back, challenge and probably win. We have the opportunity to deliver results by promoting morality; challenging credibility; setting policy and practices; offering solutions and advice.[9]

Once the political risks are evaluated, then two actions are required: first, for businesses to mount an efficient public relations campaign, arguing the case for corporate capitalism and stressing how their activities are benefiting the national—or global—economy in which they operate. All businesses, forewarned, should be proactive, not reactive. They must be prepared to fight fire with fire and, if necessary, should be prepared to take their case all the way to the courts. Secondly, companies across the spectrum must band together and act in unison to limit the unaccountable, undemocratic and often extra-legal activities of the activist groups they are up against.

....

Discussion Questions

1. What does Halfon see as the proper tools for handling stakeholder objections?

2. Can you describe a situation in which his tool may not be effective? What are the costs to the company if his tools fail to halt the opposition of stakeholders to a proposed corporate action?

READING 3.4
....

A Combination of Ethics, Law, Capitalism, and Economics: The Coase Theorem[10]

Integration of Stakeholder Theory Across Law, Business and Philosophy—The Study's Property Ownership and Economic Connection and Coase

The Coase Theorem,[11] rarely discussed and barely understood, has been too long ignored in the stakeholder debate. It is a theorem related to social costs, which are at the heart of stakeholder premises and the most contentious issue in corporate governance as groups vie for the allocation of limited resources.

Simply stated, the Coase Theorem holds that "the initial allocation of legal entitlements does not matter from an efficiency perspective so long as they can be freely exchanged. In other words, 'misallocation of legal entitlements by law will be cured in the market by free exchange.'"[12]

[9] Tony Meehan, "The Art of Media Manipulation," The Herald, May 10, 1997.

[10] Excerpted from Stephen K. Happel and Marianne M. Jennings. "The Post-Enron Era for Stakeholder Theory: A New Look at Corporate Governance and the Coase Theorem," 54 Mercer Law Review 1 (2003), pp. 873–938.

[11] Ronald Coase, "The Problem of Social Cost," 3 Journal of Law & Economics 1 (1960).

[12] This is the Coase Theorem as restated by Robert D. Cooter, "The Coase Theorem," World of Economics (1970), p. 51.

The Coase Theorem's application to stakeholderism is best understood through Coase's infamous example of the wood-and-coal-burning locomotives that emit sparks as they travel along the tracks. The sparks, from time to time, set fire to the farmers' fields that line the tracks. The railroad can reduce the farmers' damages by installing spark arresters, using different fuel to power the engines, or running fewer trains. The farmers, on the other hand, can plant crops farther back from the tracks, not store items or build facilities near the tracks.

The legal remedy for the farmers in terms of the damages to their land and crops lies within the law of nuisance. The farmers bring suit for damages as well as for an injunction enjoining the operation of the trains on the track.[13] Legal entitlements seem to govern the situation and one side will win; the railroad operates with impunity and the resulting damage to the land or the farmers enjoin the railroad operation and have flawless harvests but no transportation for those crops.[14]

But, the initial allocations, as described here, brought about through legal entitlements are not definitive or final because such allocations ignore issues of efficiency and avoid the inevitable disgruntlement that comes from allocation that is not a win-win result. Market forces still can provide a resolution:

> According to the Coase Theorem, these appearances are misleading, because while the law creates the initial allocation of entitlements, the market determines the final allocation. To illustrate, if farmers have a right to enjoin the railroad, they can sell this right. Specifically, the railroad could pay a sum of money to the farmers in exchange for a legally binding promise not to enjoin the railroad. Conversely, if the railroad has the right to emit sparks with impunity, it can sell this right. Specifically, farmers could pay a sum of money to the railroad in exchange for a legally binding promise to reduce spark emissions.
>
> Whatever the initial allocation of rights, the farmer and the railroad have an incentive to continue trading entitlements so long as there are potential gains from trade. As with ordinary goods, the gains from trading legal entitlements are not exhausted until each entitlement is held by the party who values it the most. To illustrate, if, say, farmers have a right to be free from sparks, and if the entitlement to emit sparks is worth more to the railroad than the right to be free from sparks is worth to farmers, both parties will benefit from the farmers selling their rights to the railroad. The potential gains from trade are exhausted when entitlements are allocated efficiently. Thus, when the market works, the equilibrium allocation of legal entitlements will be efficient.[15]

Stakeholder theory can be seen as a response to perceived injustices by legal entitlements. There is disgruntlement about the very creation of a legal creature known as a corporation.[16] Further, the perceived superiority of shareholders' legal entitlements has produced demands for accountability beyond that owed legally to shareholders. The

---

[13] *The legal issues are never as simplistic as assumed by economists. Whether an injunction lies for the use of the tracks is dependent upon the court's analysis of the balancing of the need for the trains, track, and transportation and the farmers' rights to the fields, flora, and fauna. For an explanation of the legal issues in nuisance, see Marianne M. Jennings,* Real Estate Law, *6th Ed. (Mason, Ohio: South-Western/West, 2002), pp. 35–37.*

[14] *In the words of Shakespeare, "All are punished," in some fashion regardless of the turn the legal system takes.* Romeo and Juliet, *Act V, Scene 3.*

[15] *Cooter, supra note 12, p. 53.*

[16] *The concerns about the corporation (along with responses to those concerns) can be found in Michael Novak,* The Fire of Invention *(Lanham, MD; Rowman & Littlefield, 1997).*

desire is to impose another legal structure over the existing one so that non-shareholders would have rights in the outcome.[17]

One critical point in the Coase theorem as well as in the equation of stakeholders with the farmers is the very heart of the theorem, which is that stakeholders already do have legal entitlements in the form of nuisance actions. Understanding that the law on nuisance can entitle a property owner to obtain an injunction means that the railroad and its shareholders must balance the interests according to their costs of fuel, costs of spark arresters, and perhaps even alternative routes. The question for corporations and shareholders, faced with their legal entitlements as well as the potential conflicting entitlements of those affected by their conduct is, once again, the economic costs of their choices. Economically speaking, the railroad's most efficient solution may very well be to provide a remedy for the stakeholder farmers.

Despite the obvious nature of the legal rights and the economic realities of balancing interests and costs, neither corporations and their shareholders nor various stakeholder groups have been particularly efficient or proficient in understanding or executing upon their positions of entitlement under law. Indeed, there appears to be evolving sympathy for *ultra vires* legal intervention atop existing legal entitlements. Stakeholders and proponents of stakeholder theory are not content to permit market efficiencies to run their course and corporations and shareholders, oddly, seem all too unwilling to recognize the economic costs of not addressing the issues and concerns of the farmer/stakeholders. The railroads are waiting too long to act and the farmers are impatient and not cognizant of their bargaining position under current legal entitlements.

There is a rogue's gallery, amply noted in the literature, of firms that have paid significantly for postponing the inevitable renegotiation of legal entitlements. Johns-Manville's asbestos product was an excellent insulator that provided the company with a near monopoly position. However, the company waited over 30 years after learning of ill health effects of asbestos to take steps to protect employees and customers. The costs of litigation forced the company into Chapter 11 bankruptcy. The alternate cost was that the firm must pay 25 percent of its net income to a trust fund used to cover damages to personnel and property caused by asbestos.

While Dow Corning's silicone implants were not the health hazard the initial litigation alleged, the bankrupting scenario could have been avoided had Dow Corning simply been more forthcoming about the risks of implants.

These firms and others pay extraordinary costs when they ignore small legal entitlements or pass on the opportunity to establish an entitlement equilibrium. Not addressing issues from the time of their revelation proves costlier for companies.

---

[17] *The Coase train example does break down a bit in drawing the analogy to stakeholder theory. For example, employees would be the victims of sparks (downsizings, safety, pensions) and may or may not be protected by legal entitlements. In an employment-at-will state, for example, employees who are terminated have little if any recourse. On safety issues, they may have the protection of both state and federal laws that could enjoin the company's unsafe activities and fine it as well. Further, in some situations, such as in international markets, the employees themselves are not objecting, but stakeholder theorists who stand on the sidelines incite the employees to demand more (when they are downsized) or less (fewer) (when there are safety violations). The equilibrium Coase describes cannot be achieved when one side does not play by rational market choices but rather by emotional and politically charged ones.*

While the Coase theorem would seem to provide a solution for the balancing of stakeholder and shareholder interests, there are several caveats. The first such caveat is that it must be permitted to work within the confines of market structure. That is, this balancing of interests and rights is dependent upon the vested interests of the parties. Legal entitlements exist because there are such rights as property ownership and free market exchanges. Many of the proposed normative contracts and stakeholder applications award rights and interests to those who are not tied to the market's efficiencies through investment, risk, and incentives.

Such a lack of a financial stake is itself a disincentive for efficient market bartering in those circumstances where the corporation's activities affect others. The farmers have the investment, risk, and incentives for disposition of the sparks issue. Farmers' rights activists do not have those financial stakes in the claim. With little downside risk, their resolution of the railroad spark problem may well be one that removes the railroad because they would fail to recognize, as farmers would, that crops need transportation to market. Bargaining cannot occur when one side has nothing to lose by demanding its resolution. In effect, stakeholder theory removes one party from the deliberations (the company). That party has its best advocacy tools removed from it.

Under circumstances in which concerned stakeholders vs. invested stakeholders are at the bargaining table, the outcomes would create uncertainty for the company and resultant uncertainty in the capital markets. Raising capital for businesses and growth would quickly turn into an unknown for which there would be few takers if the legal parameters of stakeholders and their input could not be adequately explained in investment documents.

A second caveat for reliance upon the Coase theorem is that for efficient exchanges that resolve conflicting legal entitlements to take place, there must be enforceable contracts. To the extent that stakeholder interests are given the power to override commercial and shareholder obligations, the natural market efficiencies and allocations are lost. The Coase theorem has an underlying assumption that legal entitlements exist in various settings and to various degrees. An unwillingness to recognize those contractual and other rights results in a loss of the principles of market exchange. One must explore the Coase theorem proposition convinced of the wisdom of enforceable contracts and the need for examining legal rights in the context of stakeholder interests.[18] The Coase theorem proposition thus assumes that the heart of stakeholder theory—that there should be obligations beyond law—is incorrect. While there may be efficiencies beyond the law, the creation of non-legal obligations or even legal obligations in derogation of property rights deprives companies of the opportunities for market-based realignments.

---

[18] *To understand the theorists' commitment to normative as opposed to actual contract rights, see Robert A. Phillips, "Stakeholder Theory and a Principle of Fairness,"* 7 Business Ethics Quarterly 51 *(1997) and Thomas Donaldson and Thomas Dunfee, "Toward a Unified Conception of Business Ethics: Integrative Social Contracts Theory,"* 19 Acad. Mgmt. Rev. 252 *(1994).*

Discussion Questions

1. What must be present for the Coase theorem to work?

2. Explain the example given about the negotiation of rights among stakeholders.

3. What happens when companies do not negotiate with stakeholders at the right time?

READING 3.5

Principles of Social Responsibility in Business

This reading is a summary of several of the more widely adopted voluntary codes of social responsibility that businesses have adopted as their posture on the issue of social responsibility. To assist companies in positioning their role in society, some organizations have developed standards and statements of principles. The purpose of these standards is to provide businesses with resolutions in advance of dilemmas. Those companies that adopt these types of lists of standards have already resolved certain ethical dilemmas in advance. These standards are also a means for looking at ethical dilemmas presented in this book. You can use these standards as a means of developing resolutions.

Referred to as SA 8000, the Council on Economic Priorities (CEP) models its standards after ISO (International Standards Organization) 9000 and ISO 14000—the two standards for quality control and environmental management systems.

SA 8000 is also an employment-focused stakeholder standard providing guidelines in the following areas: child labor, forced labor, health and safety, freedom of association, discrimination, disciplinary practices, working hours, compensation, and management.

The CEP does offer SA 8000 certification following a company audit for compliance. The SA 8000 guidelines are available at http://www.cepaa.org.

The Caux Round Table Principles of Business provide a broad look at stakeholder accountability, going beyond labor requirements. The general stakeholder definition in the Principles covers customers, employees, and shareholders and also lists the following as business responsibilities: accountability beyond shareholders; innovation, justice, and respect for the world community; business beyond the letter of the law; respect for rules; support for multilateral trade; respect for the environment; and avoidance of illicit operations. The principles found at http://www.cauxroundtable.org then establish stakeholder principles such as treating customers with dignity, providing customers with high-quality goods, treating customers fairly, improving living conditions for workers, ensuring health and safety of workers while at work, communicating honestly and openly with employees, not discriminating, assisting in training for employees, exercising fair pricing policies, avoiding unnecessary litigation, bringing suppliers into their processes, paying suppliers on time, conserving the environment, opening markets, promoting competition, and respecting intellectual property. The guidelines do include providing a return to shareholders.

The Interfaith Center's guidelines for business focus on 16 areas: ecosystems; national communities; local communities; indigenous communities; the employed; women in the workforce; minority groups; persons with disabilities; child labor; forced labor; suppliers; financial integrity; ethical integrity; shareholders; joint ventures and partnerships; and customers and consumers. Each area then has guidelines. The Interfaith Center also publishes an annual report on shareholder proxy proposals (which tend to focus on these 16 areas) and their fate at annual meetings. The Interfaith Principles also incorporate by reference other shareholder standards such as CERES principles, available through Interfaith Center on Corporate Responsibility, 475 Riverside Drive, Room 550, NY, NY 10015, (212) 870-2295.

The Society for International Business Ethics (IBE) focuses on 13 areas: political activities; health and safety; gifts; conflicts of interest; insider dealing; equal opportunity and discrimination; alcohol and drug abuse; sexual harassment; disclosure of company information; financial transactions; fair competition; environment; and software copying.

The IBE code is available at http://www.ibe.org.uk.

The Clarkson Principles of Stakeholder Management evolved from the intersection of these codes and can be found at http://www.rotman.utoronto.ca/ccbe/. The seven Clarkson Principles are as follows:[19]

Principle 1	Managers should acknowledge and actively monitor the concerns of all legitimate stakeholders, and should take their interests appropriately into account in decision making and operations.
Principle 2	Managers should listen to and openly communicate with stakeholders about their respective concerns and contributions, and about the risks that they assume because of their involvement with the corporation.
Principle 3	Managers should adopt processes and modes of behavior that are sensitive to the concerns and capabilities of each stakeholder constituency.
Principle 4	Managers should recognize the interdependence of efforts and rewards among stakeholders, and should attempt to achieve a fair distribution of the benefits and burdens of corporate activity among them, taking into account their respective risks and vulnerabilities.
Principle 5	Managers should work cooperatively with other entities, both public and private, to ensure that risks and harms arising from corporate activities are minimized and, where they cannot be avoided, appropriately compensated.
Principle 6	Managers should avoid altogether activities that might jeopardize inalienable human rights (e.g., the right to life) or give rise to risks which, if clearly understood, would be patently unacceptable to relevant stakeholders.
Principle 7	Managers should acknowledge the potential conflicts between (a) their own role as corporate stakeholders, and (b) their legal and moral responsibilities for the interests of stakeholders, and should address such conflicts through open communication, appropriate reporting and incentive systems and, where necessary, third-party review.

[19] *Clarkson Centre for Business Ethics*, Principles of Stakeholder Management. *Toronto: CCBE, 1999, p. 4.*

3 B

Applying Social Responsibility and Stakeholder Theory

The aim of the stakeholder literature and of the economic views on voluntary corporate conduct is to provide a framework for the social role of the corporation or, the social responsibility of business. What is the responsibility of a business when it produces a morally controversial product? What is the responsibility of a company when it has access to child labor in other countries and the tremendous cost savings it provides? And should a company do business in a country with human rights violations? These issues of social responsibility can dominate the press coverage of a corporation and infiltrate its annual meeting through shareholder proposals on social responsibility issues. This section provides background on the various theories regarding the social responsibility of corporations.

READING 3.6

Schools of Thought on Social Responsibility[20]

The following excerpt deals with the various schools of thought on social responsibility. These postures can be found across industries and can be used as a framework for analysis of dilemmas.

Ethical Postures, Social Responsibility, and Business Practice

The ethical perspective of a business often sets the tone for its operations and employees' choices. Historically, the philosophical debate over the role of business in society has evolved into four schools of thought on ethical behavior based on the responses to two questions: (1) Whose interest should a corporation serve? and (2) To whom should a corporation be responsive in order to best serve that interest? There are only two answers to these questions—"shareholders only" and "the larger society"— and the combination of those answers defines the school of thought.

[20] From Business: Its Legal, Ethical and Global Environment, *6th Ed.*, by Marianne M. Jennings, pp. 46–47. Copyright © 2003. Reprinted with permission of South-Western, a division of Thomson Learning.

Inherence

According to the inherence school of thought, managers answer only to shareholders and act only with shareholders' interests in mind. This type of manager would not become involved in any political or social issues unless it was in the shareholders' best interests to do so, and provided the involvement did not backfire and cost the firm sales. Milton Friedman's philosophy, as previously expressed, is an example of inherence. To illustrate how a business following the inherence school of thought would behave, consider the issue of a proposed increase in residential property taxes for school-funding purposes. A business that subscribes to the inherence school would support a school-tax increase only if the educational issue affected the company's performance and only if such a position did not offend those who opposed the tax increase.

Enlightened Self-Interest

According to this school of thought, the manager is responsible to the shareholders but serves them best by being responsive to the larger society. Enlightened self-interest is based on the view that, in the long run, business value is enhanced if business is responsive to the needs of society. In this school, managers are free to speak out on societal issues without the constraint of offending someone, as in inherence. Businesses would anticipate social changes and needs and be early advocates for change. For example, many corporations today have instituted job sharing, child-care facilities, and sick-child care in response to the changing structure of the American family and workforce. This responsiveness to the needs of the larger society should also be beneficial to shareholders, because it enables the business to retain a quality workforce.

The Invisible Hand

The invisible hand school of thought is the opposite of enlightened self-interest. According to this philosophy, business ought to serve the larger society and it does this best when it serves the shareholders only. Such businesses allow government to set the standards and boundaries for appropriate behavior and simply adhere to these governmental constraints as a way of maximizing benefits to their shareholders. They become involved in issues of social responsibility or in political issues only when society lacks sufficient information on an issue to make a decision. Even then, their involvement is limited to presenting data and does not extend to advocating a particular viewpoint or position. This school of thought holds that it is best for society to guide itself and that businesses work best when they serve shareholders within those constraints.

Social Responsibility

In the social responsibility school of thought, the role of business is to serve the larger society, and that is best accomplished by being responsive to the larger society. This view is simply a reflection of the idea that businesses profit by being responsive to society and its needs. A business following this school of thought would advocate full disclosure of product information to consumers in its advertising and would encourage political activism on the part of its managers and employees on all issues, not just those that affect the corporation. These businesses believe that their sense of social responsibility contributes to their long-term success.

CASE 3.7
....

SUVs, the Environment, Safety, and Stakeholders

The Evolution and Devolution of the SUV Market

In 1990, the SUV/light truck market consisted of approximately 4 million units sold out of 14 million total vehicle sales in the United States. By 1999, the percentage of the total market had increased and total sales were higher. SUVs/light truck sales were 8.2 million of 16.4 million units sold.[21] 47.6 percent of Ford Motor Company's sales are of SUVs, primarily its Ford Explorer and larger Expedition, but also of its even larger Excursion. These vehicles took the place of the truck-like Bronco and smaller Bronco II.

The largest players in the SUV market (with the number of units sold in 2000) are as follows:[22]

Ford Expedition	203,412
Jeep Grand Cherokee	181,908
Dodge Durango	139,811
Ford Explorer	93,710
Chevrolet Suburban	48,982
Chevrolet Tahoe	47,103

In 1997, most auto manufacturers expanded their SUV offerings and entered the luxury SUV market. These SUVs, with prices around $50,000, featured in-vehicle televisions and VCRs, leather interiors, and all the amenities of luxury cars. The new market entrants are listed below:

GM	Cadillac Escalade
GMC	Yukon Denali
GM	Tahoe
Lincoln	Navigator
Mercedes	M Class SUV
BMW	BMW X5
Lexus	RX300
Toyota	LandCruiser

By 2000, the U.S. segment of the luxury SUV market was 80.5 percent.[23] At that time, SUV purchases constituted one of every five auto sales in the United States and were the highest-margin products in all the automakers' lineups.[24] Profits per SUV averaged $10,000 per unit. Profits on the Ford Excursion were at the top of the field at

[21] Jerry Flint, "GM Discovers Sport Utilities," Forbes, August 7, 2000, p. 68 (citing Wards' AutoInfo Bank data).

[22] Micheline Maynard, "Plush Sport Utility Sales Soar," USA Today, December 9, 1998, p. 3B; "The History of Small Cars in America," USA Today, July 2, 1999, p. 3B.

[23] Micheline Maynard, "Plush Sport Utility Sales Soar," USA Today, December 9, 1998, p. 3B.

[24] Id.

$18,000 per unit. At that time, SUVs comprised 20 percent of all of Ford's vehicle sales and accounted for the majority of Ford's profits.[25]

By the summer of 2001, there were some indications of a slowdown in the SUV market. Many attributed the decrease in sales to the price of gasoline and its escalation. However, vehicles that are crossover SUVs, part-auto and part-truck, appeared to be enjoying an increase in sales by mid-2001.[26]

In 2002, there were 750 million cars and trucks on the road around the world; 4 million vehicles sold in 2003 were SUVs.[27] Sales of the larger SUVs dropped during 2002, about 2 percent, the same drop rate for all vehicles. Sales of the car-based SUVs were, however, up 23 percent in 2002.[28] Other figures show SUV sales up 6.9 percent for 2002. SUVs and pickups produced 90 percent of the Big Three automakers' profits in 2002.

Market data on SUV buyers indicated that the primary reason for their purchase of an SUV is safety (44 percent) followed by need (due to family size—33 percent) followed by a desire to go off-roading (10 percent) and finally by "wanted to be with the latest trend" (10 percent).[29]

The SUV has proven to be a lightning rod in public discussion in the areas of environmentalism and safety.[30] There has been intense media coverage of SUVs and a resulting emotionalism on all sides about the ethics of owning, driving, and manufacturing SUVs. These issues and attitudes are explored in the following sections.

The SUV and the Environment

Among industrialized nations, the United States emits the greatest amount of carbon dioxide, the greenhouse gas (GHG) most often mentioned in connection with the phenomenon known as global warming. As of 1998, one-third of U. S. GHGs come from motor vehicles. That figure was one-fourth in 1992 when the Framework Convention on Climate Change was agreed upon at the Earth Summit in Rio de Janeiro in 1992.[31]

Between 1992 and 1997, the nations in attendance at the Rio summit engaged in negotiations over both voluntary and binding emissions standards. Those negotiations could be charitably described as contentious. At the Kyoto meeting in 1997 and the Buenos Aires meeting in 1998, the U.S. delegation argued for developing nations to make commitments for reduction in their GHG emissions. The position of the developing nations is that GHGs have resulted from the expansion of industries in countries such as the United States and that the United States and other industrial countries should bear the greatest burden when it comes to reduction of GHGs.

---

[25] Robert H. Frank, "Feeling Crash-Resistant in an S.U.V.," The New York Times, May 16, 2000, p. A31; "The Unsung Comeback of the Large Car," The New York Times, October 3, 1999, p. MB1, 8.

[26] Joseph B. White, Stephen Power, and Milo Geyelin, "America's Love Affair with Sport's Utilities Is Now Cooling Off," The Wall Street Journal, May 30, 2001, pp. A1, A8.

[27] Jerry Flint, "The Holy War on SUVs," Forbes, March 3, 2003, p. 74.

[28] Id.

[29] Jeffrey Ball and Sholnn Freeman, "SUV Love Going Strong," The Tribune, August 27, 2000, pp. B1, B2; Jeffrey Ball and Sholnn Freeman, "Driving Sports Utility Sales," USA Today, November 18, 1998, p. 1B.

[30] Ellen Goodman, "SUV Backlash Promises to Be Big, Dirty," Arizona Republic, May 11, 1999, p. B7.

[31] Donald O. Mayer, "Greenhouse Gas Emissions and the Social Responsibility of Automakers," Business and Society Review, Vol. 105, Number 3, pp. 347–360.

Since the 1992 Earth Summit, CO_2 emissions from motor vehicles have outpaced all other U.S. sources. The largest growth in auto sales has been in sport utility vehicles (SUVs) and light trucks. Both of these vehicles are covered under more lenient government fuel efficiency standards. Trucks, buses, and vehicles in excess of 8,000 pounds are not subject to federal fuel efficiency standards at all. Sample weights of SUVs follow:[32]

Toyota LandCruiser	5,115 pounds
GM Tahoe	4,828 pounds
Lincoln Navigator	5,390 pounds
GM Suburban	4,914 pounds
Toyota 4-Runner	3,885 pounds

A Lincoln Towne Car, a four-door luxury sedan, weighs 4,156 pounds.

In 1997, *The New York Times* ran a report that concluded that because of a loophole, these vehicles, including SUVs, had emissions 20 to 100 percent higher than cars.[33] The article noted that if Americans had continued buying just cars instead of light trucks and SUVs, then CO_2 emissions would have been "down by 9.3%."

Later in 1997, California air quality officials revealed a proposal to require trucks, minivans, and most SUVs to meet the same emissions standards as passenger cars by the year 2004. That proposal is now law.

Following the Kyoto treaty of December 12, 1997, which, if ratified by the United States, would have required the United States to reduce its emissions to its 1990 levels by the year 2012, Ford and Chrysler announced on January 5, 1998, that they would cut the emissions of their SUVs and minivans. At a cost of $100 per vehicle or $100 million per year, Ford announced that its Windstar vans would immediately meet the same emissions standards as its passenger vehicles. *The New York Times* reported on the Ford decision as follows:

> . . . Jacques Nasser [Ford's president of worldwide automotive operations] made clear in an interview that Ford wanted to maintain the acceptability of sports utility vehicles as alternatives to cars, while gaining an advantage over rival automakers in catering to environmentally aware families. 'Anybody who has concerns about the environment can set them aside,' Nasser said adding that Ford was also influenced by recent articles in *The New York Times* on the environmental problems of light trucks.[34]

USA Today ran a series of articles during 1999 on the following topics: the disadvantages of driving a small car in an SUV-dominated market and road; the high center of gravity in small SUVs and the danger of rollovers; and the car makers' detours around CAFÉ rules. CAFÉ (Corporate Average Fuel Economy) rules are the mileage standards the federal government requires each automaker to attain when the fuel economies of all the vehicles they sell in a model year are averaged together. The standard for cars is 27.5 miles per gallon in combined city and highway driving and the standard for trucks and SUVs is 20.7 miles per gallon. The fine for failing to meet CAFÉ is $5.50 for each 0.1 miles

---

[32] Toyota, GM, Ford, Lincoln Web sites.
[33] Keith Bradsher, "Light Trucks Increase Profits but Foul Air More than Cars," The New York Times, November 30, 1997, p. A1.
[34] Fara Warner, "Ford's SUVs in 2000 to Meet 2004 Standards," The Wall Street Journal, May 18, 1999, p. B22.

per gallon short of the CAFÉ standard. If an automaker sells 1 million cars that average 27 miles per gallon instead of 27.5 miles per gallon, then the fine is $27.5 million.

Foreign automakers have generally ignored the CAFÉ standards and simply paid the fines, as they say, "as a cost of doing business." U.S. automakers are in compliance because criminal sanctions include prison time for officers and managers. *USA Today* concluded, however, that U.S. automaker compliance was meaningless because the automakers are permitted to carry credits forward when they exceed CAFÉ and juggling model years, by mid-year introduction of vehicles, can result in exclusion of large chunks of sales of larger vehicles that would decrease the miles per gallon.

Following the series in *The New York Times* and *USA Today*, Ford announced that it would escalate its emissions standards for its trucks and SUVs. Jacques Nasser announced on May 17, 1999, that Ford's trucks, including its Explorer and Expedition, would meet EPA (Environmental Protection Agency) emissions standards for 2004 by the year 2000. Nasser said he wants customers to have the choice of a full range of Ford products and not have to choose "between the one that is environmentally friendly and the one that isn't."[35]

In early 2000, Ford released its social responsibility report, called "Corporate Citizenship Report," and its chairman announced it to the shareholders at Ford's annual meeting in May 2000. William Clay Ford, Jr. read the Sierra Club's description of the Ford Excursion at the meeting as, "a gas-guzzling rolling monument to environmental destruction." Mr. Ford promised that his company would do better. Sales of the Excursion in 1999 were 15,838 units, in excess of the 15,000 produced. There was a waiting list for buyers.

The following day, *The Detroit Free Press* carried the story of the Ford announcement with the following headline in its business section, "Ford admits its trucks hurt the earth." The Associated Press headline was, "Ford admits dilemma: SUVs vs. environment." Environmental groups said that they would use the report for lobbying in Washington for more stringent regulations. Debbie Zemke, director of Ford's corporate governance, said Ford still stood by its decision to be forthright, "We just said: 'For heaven's sake, everybody else is talking about it, so why shouldn't we?'"[36]

While environmental groups praised the admission, others questioned the wisdom of such a step. A member of the Michigan congressional delegation said, "It does make it more difficult for us to propose reasonable standards. The company is trying to find itself right now, and we're not sure where it is."[37]

With increasing sales of SUVs, radical environmental groups that were anti-SUV began to emerge and there was a flurry of activity related to the SUVs. Law enforcement officials noted an increasing trend around the country in which SUVs on dealership lots are set afire during the night with calling cards left by environmental groups.[38] Generally, the fires are started by the Earth Liberation Front (ELF) and 30 SUVs were burned at an Oregon dealership in 2001.

---

[35] Id.

[36] Keith Bradsher, *"Ford's Admission Perplexes the Neighbors in Henry's Hometown,"* The New York Times, *April 13, 2000,* pp. B1, B4.

[37] Id.

[38] John Cloud, *"Why the SUV Is All the Rage,"* Time, *February 24, 2003, pp. 35-42.*

Emotion has surrounded the debate on SUVs. The Detroit Project announced its "What would Jesus drive?" campaign in which priests, ministers, and rabbis denounced the SUVs as evidence of an uncaring soul insensitive to God's earth.[39]

Near the end of 2000, several environmental groups began a project of tagging SUVs. The bumper stickers are placed, stealth fashion on parked SUVs, and they read, "I'm changing the environment. Ask me how!" Those participating indicated the bumper stickers are a form of public shame designed to modify behaviors. The bumper sticker includes the name of a Web site, http://www.changingtheclimate.com, which provides instructions for the removal of the bumper sticker.[40]

When the United States invaded Afghanistan, antiwar activists introduced ads, paid for by Ariana Huffington, that linked driving an SUV to funding terrorists through the use of so much oil.[41]

GM and DaimlerChrysler announced that while they would not be accelerating their emissions reductions programs, they were working on alternative fuel vehicles. "We have different objectives on how we get to lower emissions," was the DaimlerChrysler response. GM noted, "It is taking its own path to lower vehicle emissions in the U.S. and around the world."

Since 1996, the automakers have funded ($1.6 billion to date) the Partnership for a New Generation of Vehicles (PNGV). The goal is to develop an 80 miles per gallon family car. There have been alliances with fuel cell technology firms as part of the project, but there are not results as yet and there is no pledge that anything developed there will be brought to the market.

By 2001, the industry average of miles per gallon for sport utility vehicles was at 21.2 miles per gallon, which exceeds the mandatory federal standard of 20.7. Automakers point to the achievement as an indication of their good faith. Environmentalists point to the achievement as an indication that Congress needs to raise the miles per gallon standard.[42] However, by the end of 2001, executives of all of the Big Three auto manufacturers were expressing doubts about Ford's ability to meet its pledge of improving fuel economy from 20 miles per gallon to 25 miles per gallon by 2005. Dieter Zetsche, CEO of the Chrysler Group, said, "Taking 25 percent out in five years is very ambitious."[43] In 2004, Ford announced it was ending production of the Excursion.

A recent poll reveals that 66 percent of U.S. citizens believe global warming is a reality, and 72 percent support an agreement among nations to cut CO_2 emissions. Other studies show that drivers may love their SUVs, but also feel some guilt. Some have quoted the 1960's activist Eldridge Cleaver and concluded that they "are not part of the solution, but part of the problem."[44]

---

[39] Id.

[40] Karen Gaudette, "'Mad Taggers' Take Aim at SUVs," The Tribune, December 26, 2000, p. A10.

[41] Cloud, supra note 38; Karen Lundegaard, Jeffrey Ball and Gregory L. White, "Auto Makers Start to Back Away From Big SUVs," The Wall Street Journal, January 27, 2003, pp. A1, A8.

[42] James R. Healey, "Fuel Efficiency Fires Renewed Public Debate," USA Today, July 27, 2001, pp. 1B, 2B.

[43] Danny Hakim, "Fuel Targets for Sports Utilities Pose Difficulties for Automakers," The New York Times, November 23, 2001, pp. C1, C5.

[44] Matthew L. Wald, "Even S.U.V. Drivers Can Find Ways to Hug a Tree," The New York Times, January 30, 2000, p. BU12.

The Energy Department began publishing a list of the vehicles with the highest rates of gas consumption, known as the "worst gas guzzlers," with the following vehicles leading the list:[45]

Hummer H2	12 mpg
Lincoln Navigator	13.25 mpg
Mercedes-Benz G500	13.45 mpg
GMC Yukon XL, Cadillac Escalade	13.8 mpg
Land Rover Discovery Series II	13.8 mpg

The Hummer has been an unusually emotional target for environmental groups. A book by John Lamm, the editor of *Road & Track,* calls this new SUV "Satan's station wagon." Lamm documents that only 5 to 10 percent of sales of the vehicle are to ranchers and others who use the vehicle for off-road driving; 90 to 95 percent of sales are to "successful achievers" whose only brush with off-road is "with the landscape architect."[46]

SUV owners have formed their own group for advocacy. The Sport Utility Vehicle Owners Association of America, Inc. was started in 2000 and is self-described as an advocacy group for life, liberty, and the right to drive a large vehicle. The association charges $50 for membership and has not been given any funding by automakers. A spokesman for DaimlerChrysler said, "To some extent, he's [William D. Brouse, the president] got more credibility if he's not supported by the auto industry."[47] The association has taken the approach of educating policymakers and the public on the virtues of SUVs, including safety and their ability to carry significant numbers of passengers at one time.

The SUV and Safety

At the same time that the Kyoto coverage and SUV emissions issues arose, questions about SUV safety erupted. Data from the U.S. Department of Transportation showed that the death rate for accidents involving smaller cars is 3 per 10,000 registered vehicles. The death rate for SUVs is 1.3 per 10,000 registered vehicles.[48] A study of fatalities revealed that over half of the deaths of small car drivers and occupants resulted from collisions with other cars, not SUVs. SUV collisions with smaller vehicles that resulted in deaths of the occupants of smaller cars constituted 7 percent of the total vehicle fatalities.[49] The conclusion of the study by the Insurance Institute for Highway Safety was that small cars do not provide sufficient protection for their occupants. The data also show that large SUVs are three times as likely as large cars or minivans to kill occupants of the other vehicle in a crash.[50]

A 2001 study by the Insurance Institute for Highway Safety concluded that it was the height of the SUV that was a critical factor in the amount of damage and types of

[45] Karen Gaudette, "'Mad Taggers' Take Aim at SUVs," The Tribune, December 26, 2000, p. A10.

[46] David Kiley, "Book Chronicles Making of an Urban Legend," USA Today, March 10, 2003, p. 7B.

[47] Keith Bradsher, "In Proud Defense of the S.U.V.," The New York Times, March 25, 2001, p. BU2.

[48] Gary Stoller, "SUVs' Roll Risk Called Greatest," USA Today, July 17, 2000, p. 1A.

[49] Jayne O'Donnell, "Smaller Cars; Trucks Aren't Biggest Worry," USA Today, February 10, 1998, p. 1B.

[50] Laurie McGinley, "Gas Savings vs. Safety Stirs Debate," The Wall Street Journal, September 6, 1990, pp. B1, B8.

injuries in other cars struck by SUVs. This study was particularly critical of the Mercedes M-Class SUV, a product of DaimlerChrysler, which was, oddly, promoted as the first SUV to minimize damage to other vehicles in the event of a collision. Also, by lowering the vehicles the Institute found that the SUVs caused greater damage, but the damage to persons in other vehicles was to the legs and lower parts of the body. Injuries to the torso and head are more dangerous. The Institute report stressed the need for lower vehicles.[51]

Further data focused on the rollover risk of SUVs. A series in *The New York Times* on rollover risk concluded:

> The number of people in all types of vehicles dying in crashes has remained relatively steady over the last decade, as has the number dying in crashes involving rollovers. But the number of people in sports utility vehicles dying in crashes has grown almost as fast as the number of SUVs on the road, and most of the deaths have been in rollovers.[52]

Total deaths of SUV drivers per million registered vehicles in 1998 were 550 for all SUVs, 641 for small vehicles, 472 for trucks, and 348 for cars. Also, in 62 percent of the fatal accidents involving SUVs, a rollover was involved.[53]

As a result of the various reports, the National Highway Traffic Safety Administration (NHTSA) proposed requiring rollover-warning labels in all SUVs. Phil Haseltine, the president of the American Coalition for Highway Safety, a group funded by the auto industry, responded to the NHTSA proposal, "The vast majority of rollover fatalities results from high-risk behavior, not vehicle design. Colorful warning stickers aren't going to make a difference."[54] The 1998 statistics show that 62 percent of all deaths in SUVs were the result of rollovers. That rate is three times the rollover death rate for cars. Deaths in 1998 from SUV rollovers were 1,705. The 2002 safety studies indicated that there is a higher fatality rate in SUV rollover accidents, but in those accidents, nearly all drivers and passengers were not wearing their seat belts.[55]

With confusing and contradictory studies, the NHTSA still eventually mandated warning stickers that were placed in all SUVs and included the following language:

> WARNING: Higher Rollover Risk
>
> Avoid Abrupt Maneuvers and Excessive Speed
>
> See Owner's Manual for Further Information[56]

The pro- and con-SUV studies continued and a Rutgers University study concluded that since SUVs have been on the road, single-driver fatalities have decreased by 7.5 percent.[57] Overall, since the upward swing in the sale of SUVs, there has been a

---

[51] Keith Bradsher, "Study Says Height Makes S.U.V.'s Dangerous in Collisions," The New York Times, May 16, 2001, p. C4.

[52] Keith Bradsher, "Congress Appears Ready to Tackle Vehicle Rollover Problem," The New York Times, September 21, 2000, pp. C1, C12.

[53] Gregory L. White, "Auto Makers Rush to Improve Safety of SUVs," The Wall Street Journal, May 16, 2000, pp. B1, B4.

[54] Anna Wilde Mathews, "Industry Finds Devil in the Details of Plan for Bolder SUV Labels," The Wall Street Journal, February 24, 1999, pp. A1, A8.

[55] Jerry Flint, "The Holy War on SUVs," Forbes, March 3, 2003, p. 74.

[56] Jayne O'Donnell, "Rollover Rules Expected for SUVs," USA Today, May 7, 1999, p. 1A.

[57] Jayne O'Donnell, "Feds Plan New Warning on Sports Utilities," USA Today, February 17, 1999, p. 1B.

50 percent decline in traffic fatalities per vehicle.[58] The authors of the study do note other factors such as increased penalties for driving under the influence, seat belt laws, and air bags. However, even after controlling for these factors statistically, the professors believe that SUV ownership carries substantial safety benefits for both drivers and passengers. The authors refer to their results as a "net savings in lives," with this conclusion, "The increased safety to occupants of light trucks outweighs potential increases in fatalities to occupants of other vehicles."[59]

In September 2000, Congress held hearings on rollover deaths. The hearings released information indicating that of 35,806 deaths that occurred in vehicles in 1999, rollovers were a factor in 10,657. Ninety-two percent of all rollovers occurred because the vehicle was "tripped," which means that it happened because the vehicle struck another car, a curb, a guard rail, or other large object that caused it to teeter onto one side. Legislation with bipartisan support would require all vehicles to carry a rollover rating given by the National Academy of Sciences following their studies of the vehicles and attributed risk factors for rollover.[60] The insurance and auto industry support the proposed rating system. Consumers Union, publisher of *Consumer Reports*, opposes the rating system on the grounds that standards for the rating are too lax.

Running parallel to the rollover issues has been the Ford Explorer/Firestone Tire controversy (see Case 7.22). Both companies were defendants in class action lawsuits brought against them for those injured or killed in rollover accidents involving Ford Explorers equipped with certain brands of Firestone tires. The cause of the accidents and ultimate accountability remain questionable, but the accidents have been lumped together by the public with the general SUV safety concerns.[61]

The Ford Explorer/Firestone Tire issue had a dramatic impact on the sales of the Ford Explorer. Ford tried to change public perception by releasing data showing that the death rate for its Explorer is lower than the death rates for smaller SUVs of other manufacturers. The NHTSA released figures showing that the Ford Explorer had a driver death rate of 56 per million registered vehicles. But of the 89 car models for which death rates are available, 74 had higher death rates. Of 34 pickups, 32 had higher death rates, and the death rates for 7 sports cars (including the Mazda Miata and Ford Mustang) were all higher.[62]

However, Ford continued to feel the sting from the questions about SUVs, and its CEO, Jacques Nasser, resigned in October 2001 following questions by the Ford board about his management style and approach to issues and employees.

In March 2000, all the automakers announced that they would redesign their SUVs by placing steel rails two inches lower inside their underbodies to reduce the risk of their overriding cars' bumpers and doorsills in collisions.[63] The change in design came

---

[58] Brock Yates, "SUVs Mean Safer Roads," The Wall Street Journal, *April 5, 2001, p. A22.*

[59] Id.

[60] James R. Healey, "Deaths by the Gallon," USA Today, *July 2, 1999, pp. 1B, 2B.*

[61] Milo Geyelin and Timothy Aeppel, "For Firestone, Tire Trial Is Mixed Victory," The Wall Street Journal, *August 28, 2001, pp. A3, A4.*

[62] Jerry Flint, "The Holy War on SUVs," Forbes, *March 3, 2003, p. 74.*

[63] Keith Bradsher, "Automakers Modifying S.U.V.'s to Reduce Risk to Other Drivers," The New York Times, *March 21, 2000, pp. A1, C4.*

from complaints of small-car drivers who pointed to the data on SUVs actually driving over cars following collisions.

At least one class action suit is pending on SUV rollovers.[64] An appeals court has ruled that there was a sufficient basis for pursuing the plaintiffs' theory that there was a failure to warn about the rollover risk. Trial in the case is now pending. Other cases are pending and an increase in the number of suits is likely.[65]

In 2003, Jeffrey W. Runge, the new head of NHTSA, testified before Congress and indicated that SUV rollover risk was great and that consumer perceptions about increased safety in SUVs was largely misplaced.[66] He placed rollovers as 3 percent of all U.S. auto accidents in 2001 and noted that deaths in rollover accidents were most likely to occur in pickup trucks.

The rollover issue was not the only safety risk. In 1998, *The New York Times* created a new SUV concern when it ran a series on the danger of the headlights of SUVs. The series concluded:

> As sport-utility vehicles get higher, their headlights have reached the level of the side mirrors of the cars, producing a blinding glare when cars are in front of them.[67]

The head of the society for automotive engineers said of the glare problem, "My feeling is that it's debilitating; it wears you down." Robert C. Lange, vehicle safety director for GM responded, "I suspect there are very few if any collision events associated with glare."[68] Sonja L. Bultnyck, a spokeswoman for Chrysler, said that the problem is that drivers do not keep sufficient space between their vehicles when they are driving and that the headlight problem is not one of vehicle design but inconsiderate drivers.

The public reports on the headlights were largely based on a 1996 auto industry task force report recommending that the headlights on trucks and SUVs should be lower. The report from a group comprised of engineers from the major auto manufacturers recommended that the maximum allowable headlight height be reduced from 54 inches to either 36 or 40 inches. Twenty years ago the headlight height on a Jeep Wagoneer was 33 inches. Today's GM Suburban's headlights are at 39 inches.

The headlight battle took a new turn in 2001 as drivers complained about the brightness and color of headlights, and an ongoing investigation into the safety issues focuses on all headlights and not just those of SUVs.[69]

Americans and Their SUVs

Despite the intense media coverage of the safety and environmental issues, sales of SUVs indicate a strong love affair between these vehicles and the American public. Auto industry analyst Maryann Keller notes that consumers' car purchases "are dictated by their desires for performance, comfort, and safety, not by an ecological

[64] Connick v. Suzuki Motor Co., *675 N.E.2d 584 (Ill. 1997)*.

[65] Gary Stoller, "Popularity of SUVs Likely to Mean More Lawsuits," USA Today, *July 17, 2000, p. 3B.*

[66] Karen Lundegaard, "Auto-Safety Czar Warns Drivers of SUV Dangers," The Wall Street Journal, *January 15, 2003, pp. A1, A2.*

[67] Keith Bradsher, "Larger Vehicles Are Hampering Visibility," The New York Times, *November 22, 1998, p. Y17.*

[68] Id.

[69] James R. Healey, "Bright Lights, Big Controversy," USA Today, *June 7, 2001, pp. 1B, 2B.*

standard." A Detroit consultant notes that the SUV has enjoyed a particular connection with customers, "The SUV is such a close connector with their values. They're not going to give it up easily." A GM spokeswoman noted, "We're hell-bent on continuing momentum in SUVs and trucks."[70] GM did introduce a new hybrid-electric vehicle that it plans to put in 1 million vehicles to increase fuel-efficiency, from an average of 20.7 mpg to 22.2 mpg. CEO G. Richard Wagoner noted, "We have a responsibility to provide cleaner emissions and better fuel efficiency."[71]

The GM momentum has continued among other car companies as they have designed, produced, and sold a slightly different type of SUV. The new SUV is the "Family-size crossover vehicle" which includes features of a car, a minivan, and an SUV. These are vehicles with reduced rollover risk, lower headlights, and a perceived greater comfort level in the consumers who buy them. Nissan launched its Murano. Honda introduced its Element. GM introduced its Saturn Vue. Ford introduced its Freestyle in 2004. Acura has its MDX, Volvo its new XC90, Infinity its FX 45, Lexus its RX 330, Honda its Pilot, Buick its Rendezvous, and Toyota its Highlander. Women have driven the change, as it were, in the design because they did not like the truck feel of traditional SUVs and were concerned about the safety issues. Many of the new models feature air bags for knees.[72]

Discussion Questions

1. List all of the stakeholders in the SUV controversy and explain their desires and interests in whether auto manufacturers continue to produce SUVs.

2. What do you think is driving the demands for the SUV?

3. How do you resolve conflicts among the various stakeholder groups in the SUV controversy?

4. Assume the role of a senior manager at one of the major U.S. automakers. What steps would you take to resolve the controversy? Do you think the crossover vehicles were the solution?

5. How would you apply the stakeholder theory to the SUV controversy? What would Milton Friedman do if he were an auto company executive facing the SUV issues and controversies even as sales of the SUV increased?

CASE 3.8

Ice-T, the *Body Count* Album, and Shareholder Uprisings

Ice-T (Tracy Morrow), a black rap artist signed under the Time Warner label, released an album called *Body Count* in 1992 that contained a controversial song, "Cop Killer." The lyrics included: "I've got my twelve-gauge sawed-off . . . I'm 'bout to dust some cops off . . . die, pig, die."

[70] Brock Yates, "Pecksniffs Can't Stop the SUV," The Wall Street Journal, May 17, 2000, p. A26.
[71] David Welch and Kathleen Kerwin, "Detroit Is Wrecking Its SUV Edge," Business Week, March 3, 2003, p. 42.
[72] Sholnn Freeman, "SUVs for People Ashamed to Buy One," The Wall Street Journal, March 4, 2003, pp. D1, D4.

The song set off a storm of protest from law enforcement groups. At the annual meeting of Time Warner at the Beverly Wilshire Hotel, 1,100 shareholders, as well as police representatives and their spokesman, Charlton Heston, denounced Time Warner executives in a five-hour session on the album and its content. Heston noted that the compact disc had been shipped to radio stations in small replicas of body bags. One police officer said the company had "lost its moral compass, or never had it." Others said that Time Warner seemed to cultivate these types of artists. One shareholder claimed that Time Warner was always "pushing the envelope" with its artists, such as Madonna with her *Sex* book, and its products, such as the film *The Last Temptation of Christ*, which drew large protests from religious groups. Another shareholder pointed out that Gerald Levin, Time Warner president, promised a stuttering-awareness group that the cartoon character Porky Pig would be changed after they made far fewer vocal protests.

Levin responded that the album would not be pulled. He defended it as "depicting the despair and anger that hang in the air of every American inner city, not advocating attacks on police." Levin announced Time Warner would sponsor a TV forum for artists, law enforcement officials, and others to discuss such topics as racism and free speech. At the meeting, Levin also announced a four-for-one stock split and a 12 percent increase in Time Warner's dividend.

The protests continued after the meeting. Philadelphia's municipal pension fund decided to sell $1.6 million in Time Warner holdings to protest the Ice-T song. Said Louis J. Campione, a police officer and member of the city's Board of Pensions and Retirement, "It's fine that somebody would express their opinions, but we don't have to support it."

Several CEOs responded to Levin's and Time Warner's support of the song.[73] Roger Salquist, CEO of Calgene, Inc., noted:

I'm outraged. I think the concept of free speech has been perverted. It's anti-American, it's antihumanity, and there is no excuse for it.

I hope it kills them. It's certainly not something I tolerate, and I find their behavior offensive as a corporation.

If you can increase sales with controversy without harming people, that's one thing. [But Time Warner's decision to support Ice-T] is outside the bounds of what I consider acceptable behavior and decency in this country.

David Geffen, chairman of Geffen Records, who refused to release Geto Boys records because of lyrics, said:

The question is not about business, it is about responsibility. Should someone make money by advocating the murder of policemen? To say that this whole issue is not about profit is silly. It certainly is not about artistic freedom.

If the album were about language, sex, or drugs, there are people on both sides of these issues. But when it comes down to murder, I don't think there is any part of society

[73] The Wall Street Journal. *Eastern Edition (Staff Produced Copy Only)* by Wall Street Journal News Round Up. Copyright 1992 by Dow Jones & Co. Inc. Reproduced with permission of Dow Jones & Co. Inc. in the format textbook via Copyright Clearance Center.

that approves of it. . . . I wish [Time Warner] would show some sensitivity by donating the profits to a fund for wounded policemen.

Jerry Greenfield, co-founder of Ben & Jerry's Homemade, Inc., responded that "songs like 'Cop Killer' aren't constructive, but we as a society need to look at what we've created. I don't condone cop killing. [But] to reach a more just and equitable society everyone's voice must be heard."

Neal Fox, CEO of A. Sulka & Company (an apparel retailer owned by Luxco Investments), said:

As a businessperson, my inclination is to say that Time Warner management has to be consistent. Once you've decided to get behind this product and support it, you can't express feelings of censorship. They didn't have recourse.

Also, they are defending flag and country for the industry. If they bend to pressures regarding the material, it opens a Pandora's box for all creative work being done in the entertainment industry.

On a personal basis, I abhor the concept, but on a corporate basis, I understand their reasoning.

John W. Hatsopoulos, executive vice president of Thermo Electron Corporation, had this to say:

I think the fact that a major U.S. corporation would almost encourage kids to attack the police force is horrible. Time Warner is a huge corporation. That they would encourage something like this for a few bucks. . . . You know about yelling fire in a crowded theater.

I was so upset I was looking at [Thermo Electron's] pension plan to see if we owned any Time Warner stock [in order to sell it]. But we don't own any.

Bud Konheim, CEO of Nicole Miller, Ltd., weighed in with:

I don't think that people in the media can say that advertising influences consumers to buy cars or shirts, and then argue that violence on television or in music has no impact. The idea of media is to influence people's minds, and if you are inciting people to riot, it's very dangerous.

It's also disappointing that they chose to defend themselves. It was a knee-jerk reaction instead of seizing the role to assert moral leadership. They had a great opportunity. Unfortunately, I don't think they will pay for this decision because there is already so much dust in people's eyes.

George Sanborn, CEO of Sanborn, Inc., said: "Would you release the album if it said, 'Kill a Jew or bash a fag'? I think we all know what the answer would be. They're doing it to make money."

Mark Nathanson, CEO of Falcon Cable Systems Company, responded: "If you aren't happy with the product, you don't have to buy it. I might not like what [someone like Ice-T] has to say, but I would vigorously defend his right to express his viewpoint."

Stoney M. Stubbs, Jr., chairman of Frozen Food Express Industries, Inc., commented: "The more attention these types of things get, the better the products sell. I don't particularly approve of the way they play on people's emotions, but from a business standpoint [Time Warner is] probably going to make some money off it. They're protecting the people that make them the money . . . the artists."[74]

Despite the flap over the album, sales were less than spectacular. It reached number 32 on the Billboard Top 200 album chart and sold 300,000 copies.[75]

Levin had defended Time Warner's position:

Time Warner is determined to be a global force for encouraging the confrontation of ideas. We know that profits are the source of our strength and independence, of our ability to produce and distribute the work of our artists and writers, but we won't retreat in the face of threats of boycotts or political grandstanding. In the short run, cutting and running would be the surest and safest way to put this controversy behind us and get on with our business. But in the long run, it would be a destructive precedent. It would be a signal to all the artists and journalists inside and outside Time Warner that if they wish to be heard, then they must tailor their minds and souls to fit the reigning orthodoxies.

In the weeks and months ahead, Time Warner intends to use the debate engendered by the uproar over this one song to create a forum in which we can bring together the different sides in this controversy. We will invest in fostering the open discussion of the violent tensions that Ice-T's music has exposed.

We're under no illusions. We know all the wounds can't be healed by such a process or all the bitterness—on both sides—talked out of existence. But we believe that the future of our country—indeed, of our world—is contained in the commitment to truth and free expression, in the refusal to run away.[76]

By August 1992, protests against the song had grown and sales suffered. Ice-T made the decision himself to withdraw "Cop Killer" from the *Body Count* album. Time Warner asked music stores to exchange the *Body Count* CDs for ones without "Cop Killer." Some store owners refused, saying there were much worse records. Former Geto Boys member, Willie D., said Ice-T's free speech rights were violated. "We're living in a communist country and everyone's afraid to say it," he said.

Following the flap over the song, the Time Warner board met to establish general company policies to bar distribution of music deemed inappropriate. By February 1993, Time Warner and Ice-T agreed that Ice-T would leave the Time Warner label because of "creative differences." The split came after Time Warner executives objected to Ice-T's proposed cover for his new album, which showed black men attacking whites. In an ironic twist, Ice-T is now a co-star on the NBC television series *Law and Order: Special Victims Unit,* as Detective Odafin "Fin" Tutuola, partner of Richard Belzer's character, Detective John Munch.[77]

In 2004, Ice-T introduced his own line of clothing, a trend among rap music stars. He had been on a six-year hiatus from music because of the death of two of his group

---

[74] *"Time Warner's Ice-T Defense Is Assailed,"* The Wall Street Journal, July 23, 1992, pp. B1, B8.

[75] *Mark Landler, "Time Warner Seeks a Delicate Balance in Rap Music Furor,"* The New York Times, June 5, 1995, p. 1B.

[76] The Wall Street Journal. *Eastern Edition (Staff Produced Copy Only) by Holman W. Jenkins, Jr. Copyright 1996 by Dow Jones & Co. Inc. Reproduced with permission of Dow Jones & Co. Inc. in the format textbook via Copyright Clearance Center.*

[77] *http://www.nbc.com/lawandorder*

members. The drummer, Beatmaster V, died of leukemia, and Mooseman, the bass player, was killed in South Central LA, in the kind of thing "I rap about every day," Ice-T comments.[78] The album that followed *Body Count, Violent Demise, Last Days,* was barely heard and rarely sold. However, Ice-T is preparing for a *Body Count II* album, and has offered the following perspective on the first *Body Count* album and where the country is at:

"I wasn't trying to start all that drama with that [Body Count] album. On the song 'Cop Killer' I was just being honest. I never really reached for controversy. I just said what was on my mind, like I'm saying now."[79]

"Since Clinton was in the White House, everybody became very complacent, everybody kicked back," he continued. "He had sex in the White House, what's there to worry about? But now we got Bush—or son of a Bush—in there, and he's out to control the world. He's trying to be Julius Caesar and so it's time for more music about things. It's time for *Body Count.*"

Following the Ice-T issue, Time Warner's board undertook a strategy of steering the company into more family-oriented entertainment. It began its transition with the 1993 release of such movies as *Dennis the Menace, Free Willy,* and *The Secret Garden.*

However, Time Warner's reputation would continue to be a social and political lightning rod. In June 1995, presidential candidate Senator Robert Dole pointed to Time Warner's rap albums and movies as societal problems. Public outcry against Time Warner resulted.

In June 1995, C. DeLores Tucker, 67, and head of the National Political Congress of Black Women handed Chairman of Time Warner Michael J. Fuchs the following lyrics from a Time Warner label recording:

> *Her body's beautiful,*
>
> *so I'm thinkin' rape.*
>
> *Grabbed the bitch by her mouth,*
>
> *slam her down on the couch.*
>
> *She begged in a low voice:*
>
> *"Please don't kill me."*
>
> *I slit her throat*
>
> *and watch her shake like on TV.*
> > —GETO BOYS, *MIND OF A LUNATIC*

and asked Mr. Fuchs the following, "Read this out loud. I'll give you $100 to read it." Mr. Fuchs declined.

---

[78] http://www.vh1.com/artists/news/1459713/01272003/ice_t.jhtml (Accessed October 21, 2004.)
[79] Id.

Mrs. Tucker was joined by William Bennett, a GOP activist and former Education Secretary. Mrs. Tucker believes Time Warner is "pimping pornography to children for the almighty dollar. Corporations need to understand: What does it profit a corporation to gain the world but lose its soul? That's the real bottom line."

In June 1995, following Mrs. Tucker's national campaign, Time Warner fired Doug Morris, the chairman of domestic music operations. By July, Morris and Time Warner were in litigation. Morris had been a defender of gangsta rap music and had acquired the Interscope label that produced albums for Tupac Shakur and Snoop Doggy Dogg. Mr. Fuchs said the termination had nothing to do with the rap controversy.

Rap accounts for less than 10 percent of total sales in the record industry. Total sales are about $12 billion with rock music bringing in $4 billion of the sales. Some retail chains, including Wal-Mart, refuse to carry the gangsta rap albums and some radio stations refuse to play the songs. The songs cited included the following:

> *"I'd rather use my gun 'cause I get the money quicker . . . got them in the*
> *frame—Bang! Bang! . . . blowing [expletive] to the moon."*
> —TUPAC SHAKUR, "STRUGGLIN"

These lyrics contain slang expressions for using an AK-47 machine gun to murder a police officer:

> *"It's 1-8-7 on a [expletive] cop . . . so what the [expletive] does a nigger like you*
> *gotta say? Got to take trip to the MIA and serve your ass with a [expletive] AK.*
> —SNOOP DOGGY DOGG, "THA' SHIZNIT"

Discussion Questions

1. Was Ice-T's song an exercise of free speech or sensationalism for profit?

2. Would you have taken Levin's position?

3. Evaluate the First Amendment argument.

4. Does screening lyrics set a dangerous precedent?

5. Would shareholder objections influence your response to such a controversy?

6. What was Time Warner's purpose in firing Morris? By November 1995, Time Warner's Levin fired Michael Fuchs. What message is there for executives in controversial products?

7. Offer your thoughts on Ice-T's new career and role.

CASE 3.9
Guns 'n Social Responsibility

The issues of the manufacture and sale of guns continues to be an issue of social responsibility. While the issues surrounding guns are complex and are progressing through both legislatures and courts, all of the issues can be grouped into two broad categories: the issues affecting retail sales and issues affecting production and distribution.

Retail Issues, Guns, and Social Responsibility

(1) Criminal Activity Using Purchased Guns

At the retail level, there is significant activity and liability for the sale of weapons that are then used in the commission of crimes.

During the early 1990s, there was a substantial increase in the number of such cases and resulting litigation. For example, in October 1993, a court ordered Kmart Corporation to pay $12.5 million to Deborah Kitchen, who was left a quadriplegic after her boyfriend, Thomas Knapp, shot her point-blank in the neck with a rifle he purchased at Kmart. The trial records show he was so drunk at the time of purchase that he could not legibly complete the federal firearms forms, so a clerk did it for him. The family of a couple slain by their schizophrenic son with a .38 caliber handgun he had purchased at Wal-Mart sued Wal-Mart in December 1993.[80]

By the end of 1993, both Wal-Mart and Kmart announced they would no longer sell any handguns at their retail stores. Firearm sales for the two discounters totaled $158 million. A Wal-Mart spokesman said, "A majority of our customers tell us they would prefer not to shop in a retail store that sells handguns."[81]

Both retailers were the last to stop selling guns. Montgomery Ward and Sears, Roebuck and Co. stopped in 1981; Ward's felt the sales were too problematic, and Sears cited burdensome paperwork.

(2) The Toy Gun Controversy

The retail issues were not limited, however, to actual weapons. There were a number of incidents involving toy guns within the same time frame. In September 1994, a 13-year-old boy was fatally shot by a police officer in the stairwell of a New York City housing project because he was carrying a toy gun the officer assumed to be real. A similar incident occurred when another officer shot and wounded a 16-year-old youth who was also carrying a toy gun.

By October 1994, both Kay-Bee Toy Stores, now K•B Toys, and Toys 'R' Us announced that they would no longer carry realistic-looking military- or police-style weapons. They would sell only brightly colored, oversized toy guns or those with logos or decals that clearly distinguish them from real weapons.

---

[80] Robert Davis, "Gun Sales All 'Supply and Demand,'" USA Today, April 19, 1994, p. 1B.
[81] Andrea Gerlin, "Wal-Mart Stops Handgun Sales Inside Its Stores," The Wall Street Journal, December 23, 1993, pp. B1, B8.

Said Ann Iverson, president and CEO of K•B, which has a chain of 1,100 stores nationwide, "This step is just a part of K•B's strategy to re-evaluate our merchandise mix and address what families need today in terms of fun, safe, and developmentally sound toys."[82] Toy guns represent 2 percent of K•B's inventory.

CEO Michael Goldstein of Toys 'R' Us has led an industry initiative to eliminate the realistic-looking guns. He said, "The issue is the potential harm that these products pose to children and others. We believe that by taking this step we can help raise awareness and encourage manufacturers and other retailers to join us in this effort."[83]

A Toys 'R' Us shopper commented, "If it saves a couple kids' lives, I think it's a good thing. Actually, it's a courageous move. They're going to lose business."[84]

The year 2001 saw a reemergence of litigation related to how retailers conduct their sales of shotguns and their responsibility when the purchaser is not checked adequately.

Kmart was the defendant in one of the most widely publicized lawsuits. Ryan Eslinger, who was 19 at the time, bought a shotgun at a Kmart in Kimball Junction, Utah. Eslinger had been declared mentally incompetent by a court, but when he filled out the questionnaire for the Bureau of Alcohol, Tobacco and Firearms (ATF) that is required prior to gun purchases, he answered "no" to the form's question on mental illness.

The Kmart clerk accepted Eslinger's passport as identification because Eslinger did not have a driver's license. However, the passport did not have Eslinger's current address.

Eslinger returned the next day to the Kmart with the gun, which had been completely disassembled. He asked for assistance in putting the gun back together. At that point Kmart's store security pulled the ATF application that Eslinger had completed. When he saw that the application noted that there was no proof of current address, the security guard called Kmart's legal department, but no one returned the call. The security guard refused to give the gun back to Eslinger, but he was overruled by the store manager.

The gun was reassembled and Eslinger took the gun home and shot and killed himself.

In the fall of 2001, Kmart lost the lawsuit filed against it by Mr. Eslinger's parents.

The lawyer for Eslinger argued that Kmart had not adequately trained its personnel on the sale of guns. Kmart's video for training on gun sales indicates that the most important sale is the "one you don't make."[85] At the time Eslinger purchased the gun there was testimony that indicated he was drooling and that he had self-inflicted

---

[82] Joseph Pereira and Barbara Carton, "Toys 'R' Us to Banish Some 'Realistic' Toy Guns," The Wall Street Journal, October 14, 1994, pp. B1, B9.
[83] Id.
[84] Id.
[85] Margaret Cronin Fisk, "Kmart to Pay $3 Million for Selling Gun to Suicidal Teen," National Law Journal, October 1, 2001, p. B1.

injuries. Kmart argued that he looked clean cut. The jury awarded $1.5 million in damages and another $1.5 million in punitive damages in the wrongful death suit.

(3) Retail Regulatory Circumvention

As the litigation battles over purchased guns continued, more regulations were being passed, particularly at the federal level, that limited the types of guns that could be manufactured and sold in the United States. Congress placed controls on assault weapons with a resulting impact on retail gun stores that sold the weapons as part of their core business. The ban expired in 2004.

Sylvia Daniel of Ducktown, Tennessee, is known as "Machine Gun Mama" and the "First Lady of Firearms." She still sells machine guns outlawed under President Ronald Reagan in 1986 because they were made before the ban went into effect. In 1985, she sold them for $185; now, she sells them for $3,000. She and her husband specialize in selling weapons by finding loopholes in gun control laws. Wayne Daniel said, "If there is a dollar to be made, make it. It may be immoral but not illegal. The bottom line is money. This is a legal business."[86]

The Daniels sell their semiautomatic M-11/9 pistol nationwide. An agent of the Bureau of Alcohol, Tobacco and Firearms noted that this weapon is good for only two things: the firing range and killing. Sylvia Daniel agreed, but added, "It's not the gun, it's the people. We sell to federally licensed dealers. They sell it to you. Did you take it home and put it under your bed and your son got it and killed with it? Is that my fault? I know kids are killed every day. But the problem is not the gun. . . . It's not about gun control. It's about crime control."[87]

The Daniels also sell a "Mac-in-a-sack" for $160, which consists of fifty-two parts for the M-11/9. Excluded are the barrel and frame where the serial number would be, so buyers can make guns with no serial number. The Daniels also sell a briefcase that holds a Mac and has a switch to fire the pistol. The ATF labels the briefcase, one of the Daniels' best-sellers, an assassination device.

Manufacture and Distribution, Guns, and Social Responsibility

There are also several issues in the manufacture and distribution of weapons. These extend beyond the retail level and the issues related to selling guns to whether companies should manufacture guns and whether their distribution systems and types of guns exacerbate social problems.

(1) Cheap Handguns

One of the principal targets of anti-gun activists has been the so-called "Saturday Night Special," a gun that costs about $13 to make and then retails for between $59 and $70. The gun has a long history that traces back to the Jennings family of California, a family that focused on the successful sales of handguns.

Three gun manufacturers in California evolved from the Jennings family. George Jennings founded Raven Arms, Inc., in 1970 and made the Raven .25. George's son,

---

[86] Robert Davis, "Gun Sales All 'Supply and Demand,'" USA Today, April 19, 1994, p. 2A.
[87] Id.

Bruce Jennings, left Raven in 1978 to form Jennings Firearms, Inc., which manufactures another Saturday Night Special, the Jennings .22, which costs $13 to make and retails for $75 to $89.

George's son-in-law, Jim Davis, left Raven in 1982 to start Davis Industries, Inc., which makes a third Saturday Night Special, the Davis .38; this gun costs $15 to make and retails for $95 to $100.

Based on ATF data on handguns sold after 1986, the leading handguns used in crimes are the Davis, the Raven, and the Jennings.

Many criminologists, prosecutors, and gun-sale reform advocates maintain that the availability of cheap weapons escalates crime and killing. Josh Sugarmann of the Violence Policy Center, which studies violence prevention, said of the Saturday Night Specials: "We have a fire burning, and these companies are throwing gasoline on it. These people know what the inner-city gun buyer wants."[88]

Dave Brazeau, the general manager of Raven Arms, responded, "If it wasn't a gun, it would just be something else—a rock, a bow and arrow, or a baseball bat."[89]

Only a few states ban the cheap handguns. Maryland, for example, has banned the Jennings .22 and the Raven .25 as "unreliable as to safety." South Carolina and Illinois have banned the three California companies' brands because the zinc-alloy frames melt at less than 800 degrees.[90]

Smith & Wesson holds the top slot in gun sales, but the three Jennings-related companies together account for 22 percent of all handguns sold and 27 percent of all handguns used in crimes across the country.[91]

The Saturday Night Specials are often sold in bulk in states where gun laws are lax and then smuggled to urban areas for sale. An illegal gun dealer in Harlem commented, "Here, where I live, every young kid has a .22 or a .25. It's like their first Pampers."[92]

Congress passed the Brady Bill in 1991, which mandates a five-day waiting period for handgun purchases. Other proposals on gun bans have passed and some remain on the table to ban the sale of Saturday Night Specials altogether.

A number of states also proposed regulations of Saturday Night Specials. Some note that firecrackers are regulated but firearms are not.

(2) Generic Liability and Distribution

With legislation carrying political and emotional battles, many gun control advocates have used litigation as a means of controlling the number of guns available. Imposing liability is seen as a means for curbing both production as well as the number of gun manufacturers.

---

[88] Alix M. Freedman, "A Single Family Makes Many of Cheap Pistols That Saturate Cities," The Wall Street Journal, February 28, 1992, p. A1.
[89] Id.
[90] Id.
[91] Id.
[92] Id.

For example, the Department of Housing and Urban Development (HUD) long rumbled about the possibility of suing gun manufacturers in order to hold them liable for security costs at federally funded public housing complexes where shootings are common. HUD's reasoning would begin a series of cases by cities that focused not on a defect in the gun's design, but in their distribution to those who are likely to abuse them in such a way as to cause harm to others.[93]

Cities around the country adopted the HUD theory as well as one from the tobacco litigation. The cities brought suit against the gun manufacturers to seek reimbursement for the costs they incur in treating gun shot victims as well as the costs of investigation and other related expenses that come from the use of guns in the commission of crime. The suits, while filed around the country, have not done well in the courts. The city of Cincinnati had its suit against several gun manufacturers dismissed.[94] The court warned of a slippery slope, "Were we to decide otherwise, we would open a Pandora's box. For example, the city could sue the manufacturers of matches for arson, or automobile manufacturers for traffic accidents, or breweries for drunken driving."[95] Courts continue to be reluctant to hold gun manufacturers liable under theories of product liability, negligent distribution, or in a third-party sense for criminal activity with their products.[96] In one case, the manufacture of guns was held to be a public nuisance. However, the NAACP had brought the suit and the court did not find that it had any harm from that nuisance and dismissed the case.[97]

The Smith & Wesson Deal and Social Responsibility

In the meantime, Smith & Wesson, a gun manufacturer, concerned about proposed Massachusetts regulation and the pending litigation, was struggling as to how to handle all the potential liability. Additionally, its parent company, Tomkins, P.L.C., a British firm, was trying to sell the 157-year-old Massachusetts company and was not having much luck given the status of the pending litigation.

Tomkins had purchased Smith & Wesson in 1987 for $112.5 million. As a manufacturer of plumbing supplies and lawn mowers, it was unprepared for the litigation and very public controversy surrounding gun manufacturers in the United States. Further, the British attitude toward handguns (they are outlawed in Britain) created considerable controversy for Tomkins at home as it began experiencing protests and boycotts over its ownership.

To find a way out of the situation, Smith & Wesson decided to break rank with its fellow gun manufacturers and it reached a settlement with the federal government that included substantial restrictions on the production and distribution of handguns. On March 17, 2000, Smith & Wesson signed an agreement with the federal government that provided for the following:

---

[93] Paul M. Barrett, "HUD May Join Assault on Gun Makers," The Wall Street Journal, July 28, 1999, p. A3.

[94] City of Cincinnati v. Beretta U.S.A. Corp., 2000 Ohio App. Lexis 3601 at * 1 (Aug. 11, 2000).

[95] Id.

[96] Hamilton v. Beretta, 750 N.E.2d 1055 (NY 2001) and see also the federal case, Hamilton v. Beretta, 264 F.3d 21 (2d Cir. 2001).

[97] NAACP v. Acusport, 2002 WL 31811717 (D.C. 2002).

In the 21-page settlement, Smith & Wesson agreed to change the way its guns are designed, marketed, and distributed. Under the key provisions of the pact, the company agreed to:

- equip all handguns with external safety locks within 60 days;
- equip all pistols with internal locking devices within two years;
- devote 2 percent of its gross revenues to the development of "smart," personalized guns that can only be fired by an authorized user;
- design firearms so that they cannot be readily operated by a child under age six;
- include chamber-load indicators on all pistols within one year; and
- stop producing firearms that accept large-capacity ammunition magazines.

The company has also agreed to add a hidden serial number on every gun to make it easier for law enforcement authorities to trace guns used by criminals. There was an interesting development after Smith & Wesson appointed James Joseph Minder to its board in 2001. In early 2004, Mr. Minder assumed the position of chairman of the board. One month later he resigned as chair, because the local newspaper, the *Arizona Republic* (Smith & Wesson's headquarters are in Scottsdale, Arizona; see p. 105 for more details), reported that Mr. Minder had completed a 3.5- to 10-year prison sentence for a series of armed robberies and an escape from prison. He had carried a sawed-off shotgun during the string of robberies, committed while he was a student at the University of Michigan. (See Case 1.9 for more details.)

Smith & Wesson also agreed to make certain changes in its methods of distribution and to place restrictions on dealers and retail sales. Within six months of the date of the settlement, Smith & Wesson would include in the packaging of each firearm sold a warning on risks of guns in the home and information about proper home storage. In addition, the gun maker agreed not to sell firearms that are resistant to fingerprints or that can be readily converted to illegal fully automatic weapons.

Also, all authorized dealers and distributors of Smith & Wesson's products are required to abide by a "code of conduct" to eliminate the sale of firearms to criminals, unauthorized juveniles, or "straw purchasers." Specifically, dealers and distributors must agree that they will:

- deny guns to purchasers unless they have completed a background check, even if the check takes longer than the current legal standard of three business days;
- make no sales to anyone who has not passed a certified firearms safety course or exam;
- require purchasers of multiple handguns to take only one gun on the day of sale and the rest two weeks later; and
- implement a security plan to prevent gun thefts.

Under the code of conduct, dealers must also agree not to allow children under 18 access, without an adult, to gun shops or sections of stores where guns are sold.[98]

In exchange, the federal government would see that all gun litigation was dismissed. There were approximately 30 such suits pending around the country.

---

[98] Gary Fields, "For Smith & Wesson, Blanks Instead of a Magic Bullet," *The Wall Street Journal*, August 24, 2000, p. A24; Paul M. Barrett, Joe Mathews, and Vanessa O'Connell, "Arms Deal," *The Wall Street Journal*, March 21, 2000, p. A1.

The reaction to the settlement was mixed. While the British hailed the decision as brilliant and many business ethicists heralded it as a socially responsible decision, Charlton Heston, president of the National Rifle Association (NRA), said, "Smith & Wesson is a good company and a fine old American name, but they're owned by the Brits. I don't really relish the idea of the Brits telling us how to deal with one part of our Bill of Rights."[99]

There was significant customer backlash, and the CEO of Tomkins, Ed Shultz, received used tea bags in his mail from U.S. customers to remind him of the Boston Tea Party.[100] There was a boycott of Smith & Wesson guns by both customers and retailers, with many retailers refusing to carry Smith & Wesson guns in their inventory.

The result was that Smith & Wesson was forced to close plants in Maine and Massachusetts, and, by September of 2000, it was forced to lay off a substantial number of workers.

In May 2001, Tomkins sold Smith & Wesson for $15 million to an Arizona gun lock company, Saf-T-Hammer Lock Corporation of Scottsdale. As part of the sale, Saf-T-Lock got $97 million in assets, including a 660,000-square-foot plant in Springfield, Massachusetts; a production facility in Houlton, Maine; Smith & Wesson patents; trademarks; intellectual property; distribution rights; inventory; equipment; and machine drawings.

The Bush Administration announced in August 2001 that it was not bound by the Smith & Wesson agreement and considered the agreement to be only a "Memorandum of Agreement," but not a binding and final contract. However, by the time the announcement was made, Smith & Wesson's sales had fallen off by one-third and it had a loss year-to-date of $57 million.[101]

The Constitutional Issues

While the gun safety, liability, and regulation issues continue, the major opposition comes from those who are concerned about the Second Amendment to the U.S. Constitution and the right to keep and bear arms. Groups such as the National Rifle Association (NRA) and Gun Owners of America, Inc. (GOA) have engaged in extensive lobbying and worked with gun manufacturers to help them in the ongoing litigation. "To bring the right to bear firearms under consumer safety is just one more element in a scheme to destroy private ownership of firearms," was a comment by Dennis Fusaro of GOA, and he added, "Putting all these bells and whistles on firearms is . . . the first step."[102]

Those against the litigation and regulation present emotionally charged arguments to counter the safety issues and discussions about children's safety that are part of the regulation advocates' presentations.

---

[99] Christine W. Westphal and Susan M. Wheeler, "When Ethical Decisions Alienate Stakeholders: Smith & Wesson as a Case Study," Paper presented at the Academy of Legal Studies, August 8, 2001, Albuquerque, New Mexico, citing The Guardian (London), August 5, 2000, Guardian City pages, p. 24.

[100] Id.

[101] Tish Durkin, "Good Deeds Can Misfire: Consider a Gunmaker's Tumble," National Law Journal, April 28, 2001, p. 1207.

[102] Id.

The constitutional issue centers around the interpretation of the Second Amendment and whether it means that there is a right to have a militia or whether it is an individual right of each citizen to own firearms and the extent of that right as well as how much can be regulated without infringing on constitutional rights.

The nature of the constitutional argument is summarized in the following excerpt from a law review piece written by Professor Sanford Levinson for the *Yale Law Journal* entitled, "The Embarrassing Second Amendment."[103] The piece is a commentary on the unwillingness of scholars to debate the issue of the right to keep and bear arms as well as a discussion about the history of the amendment and its framers' intentions (footnotes omitted).

A standard move of those legal analysts who wish to limit the Second Amendment's force is to focus on its "preamble" as setting out a restrictive purpose. Recall Laurence Tribe's assertion that that purpose was to allow the states to keep their militias and to protect them against the possibility that the new national government will use its power to establish a powerful standing army and eliminate the state militias. This purposive reading quickly disposes of any notion that there is an "individual" right to keep and bear arms. The right, if such it be, is only a state's right. The consequence of this reading is obvious: the national government has the power to regulate—to the point of prohibition—private ownership of guns, since that has, by stipulation, nothing to do with preserving state militias. This is, indeed, the position of the ACLU, which reads the Amendment as protecting only the right of "maintaining an effective state militia. . . . [T]he individual's right to bear arms applies only to the preservation or efficiency of a well-regulated [state] militia. Except for lawful police and military purposes, the possession of weapons by individuals is not constitutionally protected."

This is not a wholly implausible reading, but one might ask why the Framers did not simply say something like "Congress shall have no power to prohibit state-organized and directed militias." Perhaps they in fact meant to do something else. Moreover, we might ask if ordinary readers of late 18th Century legal prose would have interpreted it as meaning something else. The text at best provides only a starting point for a conversation. In this specific instance, it does not come close to resolving the questions posed by federal regulation of arms. Even if we accept the preamble as significant, we must still try to figure out what might be suggested by guaranteeing to "the people the right to keep and bear arms;" moreover, as we shall see presently, even the preamble presents unexpected difficulties in interpretation.

One might argue (and some have) that the substantive right is one pertaining to a collective body—"the people"—rather than to individuals. Professor Cress, for example, argues that state constitutions regularly used the words "man" or "person" in regard to "individual rights such as freedom of conscience," whereas the use in those constitutions of the term "the people" in regard to a right to bear arms is intended to refer to the "sovereign citizenry" collectively organized. Such an argument founders, however, upon examination of the text of the federal Bill of Rights itself and the usage there of the term "the people" in the First, Fourth, Ninth, and Tenth Amendments.

---

[103] Reprinted by permission of The Yale Law Journal Company and William S. Hein Company from The Yale Law Journal, Vol. 99, pp. 637–659.

Consider that the Fourth Amendment protects "[t]he right of the people to be secure in their persons," or that the First Amendment refers to the "right of the people peaceably to assemble, and to petition the Government for a redress of grievances." It is difficult to know how one might plausibly read the Fourth Amendment as other than a protection of individual rights, and it would approach the frivolous to read the assembly and petition clause as referring only to the right of state legislatures to meet and pass a remonstrance directed to Congress or the President against some governmental act. The Tenth Amendment is trickier, though it does explicitly differentiate between "states" and "the people" in terms of retained rights. Concededly, it would be possible to read the Tenth Amendment as suggesting only an ultimate right of revolution by the collective people should the "states" stray too far from their designated role of protecting the rights of the people. This reading follows directly from the social contract theory of the state. (But, of course, many of these rights are held by individuals.)

Although the record is suitably complicated, it seems tendentious to reject out of hand the argument that one purpose of the Amendment was to recognize an individual's right to engage in armed self-defense against criminal conduct. Historian Robert E. Shalhope supports this view, arguing in his article "The Ideological Origins of the Second Amendment" that the Amendment guarantees individuals the right "to possess arms for their own personal defense." It would be especially unsurprising if this were the case, given the fact that the development of a professional police force (even within large American cities) was still at least a half century away at the end of the colonial period. I shall return later in this essay to this individualist notion of the Amendment, particularly in regard to the argument that "changing circumstances," including the development of a professional police force, have deprived it of any continuing plausibility. But I want now to explore a second possible purpose of the Amendment, which as a sometime political theorist I find considerably more interesting.

Assume, as Professor Cress has argued, that the Second Amendment refers to a communitarian, rather than an individual, right. We are still left the task of defining the relationship between the community and the state apparatus. It is this fascinating problem to which I now turn.

Consider once more the preamble and its reference to the importance of a well-regulated militia. Is the meaning of the term obvious? Perhaps we should make some effort to find out what the term "militia" meant to 18th century readers and writers, rather than assume that it refers only to Dan Quayle's Indiana National Guard and the like. By no means am I arguing that the discovery of that meaning is dispositive as to the general meaning of the Constitution for us today. But it seems foolhardy to be entirely uninterested in the historical philology behind the Second Amendment.

I, for one, have been persuaded that the term "militia" did not have the limited reference that Professor Cress and many modern legal analysts assign to it. There is strong evidence that "militia" refers to all of the people, or at least all of those treated as full citizens of the community. Consider, for example, the question asked by George Mason, one of the Virginians who refused to sign the Constitution because of its lack of a Bill of Rights: "Who are the Militia? They consist now of the whole people." Similarly, the Federal Farmer, one of the most important Anti-Federalist opponents of the Constitution, referred to a "militia, when properly formed, as in fact the people themselves." We have, of course, moved now from text to history. And this history is most interesting, especially when we look at the development of notions of popular sovereignty.

It has become almost a cliché of contemporary American historiography to link the development of American political thought, including its constitutional aspects, to republican thought in England, the "country" critique of the powerful "court" centered in London.

One of this school's important writers, of course, was James Harrington, who not only was influential at the time but also has recently been given a certain pride of place by one of the most prominent of contemporary "neo-republicans," Professor Frank Michelman. One historian describes Harrington as having made "the most significant contribution to English libertarian attitudes toward arms, the individual, and society." He was a central figure in the development of the ideas of popular sovereignty and republicanism. For Harrington, preservation of republican liberty requires independence, which rests primarily on possession of adequate property to make men free from coercion by employers or landlords. But widespread ownership of land is not sufficient. These independent yeomen should also bear arms. As Professor Morgan puts it, "[T]hese independent yeomen, armed and embodied in a militia, are also a popular government's best protection against its enemies, whether they be aggressive foreign monarchs or scheming demagogues within the nation itself."

A central fear of Harrington and of all future republicans was a standing army, composed of professional soldiers. Harrington and his fellow republicans viewed a standing army as a threat to freedom, to be avoided at almost all costs. Thus, says Morgan, militia is the only safe form of military power that a popular government can employ; and because it is composed of the armed yeomanry, it will prevail over the mercenary professionals who man the armies of neighboring monarchs."

Scholars of the First Amendment have made us aware of the importance of John Trenchard and Thomas Gordon, whose Cato's Letters were central to the formation of the American notion of freedom of the press. That notion includes what Vincent Blasi would come to call the "checking value" of a free press, which stands as a sturdy exposer of governmental misdeeds. Consider the possibility, though, that the ultimate "checking value" in a republican polity is the ability of an armed populace, resumptively motivated by a shared commitment to the common good, to resist governmental tyranny. Indeed, one of Cato's Letters refers to "the Exercise of despotick Power as the unrelenting War of an armed Tyrant upon his unarmed Subjects. . . ."

Cress persuasively shows that no one defended universal possession of arms. New Hampshire had no objection to disarming those who "are or have been in actual rebellion," just as Samuel Adams stressed that only "peaceable citizens" should be protected in their right of "keeping their own arms." All these points can be conceded, however, without conceding as well that Congress—or, for that matter, that States—had the power to disarm these "peaceable citizens." Surely one of the foundations of American political thought of the period was the well-justified concern about political corruption and consequent governmental tyranny. Even the Federalists, fending off their opponents who accused them of foisting an oppressive new scheme upon the American people, were careful to acknowledge the risks of tyranny. James Madison, for example, speaks in Federalist Number Forty-Six of "the advantage of being armed, which the Americans possess over the people of almost every other nation." The advantage in question was not merely the defense of American borders; a standing army might well accomplish that. Rather, an armed public was advantageous in protecting political liberty. It is therefore no surprise that the Federal Farmer, the nom de plume of an anti-federalist critic of the new

Constitution and its absence of a Bill of Rights, could write that "to preserve liberty, it is essential that the whole body of the people always possess arms, and be taught alike, especially when young, how to use them. . . ." On this matter, at least, there was no cleavage between the pro-ratification Madison and his opponent.

In his influential Commentaries on the Constitution, Joseph Story, certainly no friend of Anti-Federalism, emphasized the "importance" of the Second Amendment. He went on to describe the militia as "the natural defence of a free country" not only "against sudden foreign invasions" and "domestic insurrections," with which one might well expect a Federalist to be concerned, but also against "domestic usurpations of power by rulers." "The right of the citizens to keep and bear arms has justly been considered," Story wrote, "as the palladium of the liberties of a republic; since it offers a strong moral check against the usurpation and arbitrary power of rulers; and will generally, even if these are successful in the first instance, enable the people to resist and triumph over them."

We also see this blending of individualist and collective accounts of the right to bear arms in remarks by Judge Thomas Cooley, one of the most influential 19th century constitutional commentators. Noting that the state might call into its official militia only "a small number" of the eligible citizenry, Cooley wrote that "if the right [to keep and bear arms] were limited to those enrolled, the purpose of this guaranty might be defeated altogether by the action or neglect to act of the government it was meant to hold in check." Finally, it is worth noting the remarks of Theodore Schroeder, one of the most important developers of the theory of freedom of speech early in this century. "[T]he obvious import of the constitutional guarantee to carry arms," he argues, "is to promote a state of preparedness for self-defense even against the invasions of government, because only governments have ever disarmed any considerable class of people as a means toward their enslavement."

Discussion Questions

1. Would any employees or owners of the Jennings-related companies be morally responsible for crimes committed with the weapons they make?

2. Would a gun dealer be morally or legally responsible for a crime committed by someone to whom he or she sold a gun?

3. The Jennings-related companies have found a very successful market niche in selling guns at affordable prices. Is it ethical to capitalize on this market factor?

4. If the price of the weapon were increased, would the gun makers' moral responsibility be reduced?

5. If you owned a sporting goods or gun store, would you carry Saturday Night Specials?

6. Describe the Daniels' ethical standards.

7. Are the Daniels persuasive in disclaiming responsibility for what guns do?

8. Aren't the Daniels just fulfilling a market need?

9. Could you work for the Daniels?

10. Are the Kmart and Wal-Mart decisions on gun sales rooted in ethics or potential liability?

11. Do retailers have a potential liability in selling toy guns?

12. Did the ban on realistic toy weapons earn publicity for the toy store chains? Do you believe that was partially their motivation? Consider the following comment by a spokeswoman for Target, which has never carried the realistic-looking guns: "The only guns we have are neon plastic toy guns. We cater to the family, and we don't really consider realistic toy guns to be a family toy."

13. If you were a toy retailer, would you carry realistic-looking toy guns?

14. If you were a retailer, would you sell guns? If no retailers sell guns, have consumers lost a fundamental constitutional right?

15. Consider the following analysis by Professors Christine Westphal and Susan Wheeler about the Smith & Wesson experience and then evaluate the stakeholder vs. shareholder debate in that scenario:

    A number of editorial writers have characterized Smith & Wesson's agreement with the government as an ethical decision that was not necessarily good business, and certainly there is some justification for that position. The agreement might also be seen as a conflict among stakeholders where Smith & Wesson betrayed its customers in order to satisfy the demands of its financiers and community.[104]

    Did Smith & Wesson betray its employees too? Did Smith & Wesson violate trust for selfish ends, as the National Shooting Sports Foundation said?

CASE 3.10

Shock Jock: Howard Stern

"Shock Jock" Howard Stern's radio talk show, which originates at Infinity Broadcasting Corporation's flagship New York station, is number one in its time slot in New York, Philadelphia, Los Angeles, Boston, and several other cities. A total of 20 million listeners tunes in each week. Stern is known for his banter that borders on, and occasionally is, indecent.[105] His on-the-air routines involve such subjects as "Butt Bongo" and "Lesbian Dial-a-Date." Infinity has been fined $1.67 million by the Federal Communications Commission (FCC) for Stern's material that allegedly violated federal on-the-air decency standards.[106] Since the fines have not deterred the violations, one commissioner has cited ongoing complaints as the basis for conducting an FCC hearing into whether Infinity's licenses for its eleven stations should be revoked.

Stern's book, *Private Parts*, published by Simon & Schuster in October 1993, had such chapter titles as "Yes, I am Fartman"; Stern appears semi-clothed on the cover. Twelve days after its release, the book was in its seventh printing, having sold more than 1 million copies.

[104] Christine W. Westphal and Susan M. Wheeler, "When Ethical Decisions Alienate Stakeholders: Smith & Wesson as a Case Study," Paper presented at the Academy of Legal Studies, August 8, 2001, Albuquerque, New Mexico, citing The Guardian (London), August 5, 2000, Guardian City pages, p. 24.
[105] Kurt Anderson, "Big Mouths," Time, November 1, 1993, pp. 60–66.
[106] "FCC Gets Complaints on 'Shock Jock,'" Mesa Tribune, March 19, 1994, p. A3.

Stern has enjoyed continued success with his 1997 critically acclaimed movie, *Private Parts*, and a 1998 CBS television contract.[107] His radio program is syndicated by Infinity Broadcasting and is carried on 75 markets nationwide. Clear Channel Communications is the owner of six stations that carry Stern's show. In February 2004, Clear Channel pulled the Stern show off its stations because Stern was in violation of a new "zero-tolerance" policy that the company had established for its on-air talent.[108] The policy, adopted in February 2004 following the FCC's concerns about decency in broadcasting that were fueled by the Janet Jackson/Justin Timberlake exposé at the 2004 Super Bowl half-time show, prohibited indecency on the air. Under the policy, any on-air talent found to violate FCC standards of decency is pulled from Clear Channel stations with no avenue for appeal. The policy also requires that all contracts with on-air personalities be renegotiated to make them partially financially responsible for any FCC fines that result from the content of their programs.[109]

Stern, during an interview with Rick Solomon, boyfriend to Paris Hilton, discussed the sexual videotape of Solomon and Hilton that had been circulating on the Internet. The discussion used sexual terms and generated a call from a listener who used racial and sexual terms. After Clear Channel bounced Stern, his ratings went up 32 percent on other stations. Stern paid a $500,000 fine, and Clear Channel admitted to broadcasting indecent material and paid a $1.75 million fine to the FCC. Stern filed a $10 million breach of contract suit against Clear Channel, and Clear Channel countersued Stern for $3 million for his breach of the contract clause on decency. Stern has slowly returned to most of the markets from which Clear Channel eliminated his show, now carried by competitors' stations.[110] Mr. Stern announced that he would be going to satellite radio, with the Sirius Company, in January 2006 when his contract with Infinity expires. The Sirius contract is a five-year, $500 million deal for Stern from a company that has only 600,000 subscribers and has yet to show a profit.[111] Mr. Stern summarized his jump to satellite radio as follows:

> I haven't been able to communicate with my audience because of all the restrictions that the government has imposed. I am being hammered by the religious right, . . . am radio's biggest star and I have decided that satellite radio offers me more potential than terrestrial radio. I can't do the same show I did a year ago because of FCC pressure.[112]

Discussion Questions

1. Does Infinity have an obligation to monitor and control Stern?

2. Does Simon & Schuster have an obligation to establish editorial standards?

[107] Julie Tilsner, "From Radio Rage, Raging Best-Sellers," Business Week, November 1, 1993, p. 42.

[108] Peter Johnson, "Clear Channel Pulls Stern off Stations," USA Today, February 26, 2004, p. 1D.

[109] http://www.clearchannel.com—go to Investors and also Decency Policy.

[110] Sarah McBride, "He 'Is What He Is' Advertisers Stand By Howard Stern," The Wall Street Journal, March 8, 2004, pp. B1, B11.

[111] Bill Carter and Nat Ives, "Where Some See Just a Shock Jock, Sirius Sees a Top Pitchman," The New York Times, October 11, 2004, pp. C1, C2.

[112] http://www.reuters.com/aitoolkit/aitArticle.jhtml?type=hotStocksNews&storyID=6432672 (Accessed October 21, 2004.) See also, Bill Carter and Jeff Leeds, "Howard Stern Says He Plans to Jump to Satellite Radio," The New York Times, October 7, 2004, pp. A1, C4.

3. Do you think shareholders of Infinity or Simon & Schuster would be concerned about standards of decency, given Stern's success?

4. Would you publish Stern's book? Would you hire him as a radio talent? Be sure to apply the models.

5. What do you learn from the fact that Stern's listening audience increased following his termination?

6. What do you think about Mr. Stern's assessment of government and the religious right and his move to satellite radio?

CASE 3.11

Dayton-Hudson and Its Contributions to Planned Parenthood

Dayton-Hudson Corporation is a multistate department store chain. In 1990, its charitable foundation gave $18,000 to Planned Parenthood and other contributions to Children's Home Society, the Association for the Advancement of Young Women, and the Young Women's Christian Association. It had contributed to Planned Parenthood for twenty-two years.

Pro-life groups have vocally criticized corporate foundations that support Planned Parenthood and have persuaded JCPenney Company and American Telephone and Telegraph to stop their contributions to the organization. After Pioneer Hi-Bred International's foundation gave $25,000 to Planned Parenthood of Greater Iowa for rural clinics that did not perform abortions, Midwest farmers began circulating a flyer headlined, "Is Pioneer Hi-Bred Pro-Abortion?" CEO Thomas Urban canceled the donation, saying, "We were blackmailed, but you can't put the core business at risk."[113] When pro-life groups raised their objections with the Dayton-Hudson foundation, the foundation's board decided to halt its contributions to Planned Parenthood.

Pro-choice supporters responded strongly by boycotting Dayton-Hudson stores, writing letters to newspaper editors and closing charge accounts. Pickets appeared outside Dayton-Hudson stores, and picketers cut up their charge cards for media cameras.

A trustee for the New York City Employees Retirement System, which owned 438,290 Dayton shares, commented: "By antagonizing consumers, they've threatened the value of our investment."[114]

Dayton-Hudson decided to resume its funding of Planned Parenthood, even though pro-life groups announced plans to boycott the company's stores.[115]

---

[113] Richard Gibson, "Boycott Drive Against Pioneer Hi-Bred Shows Perils of Corporate Philanthropy," The Wall Street Journal, June 10, 1992, p. B1.
[114] Kevin Kelly, "Dayton-Hudson Finds There's No Graceful Way to Flip-Flop," Business Week, September 24, 1990, p. 50.
[115] Fern Portnoy, "Corporate Giving Creates Tough Decisions, Fragile Balances," Denver Business Journal, November 15, 1991, p. 15.

Discussion Questions

1. Is there any way for a corporation to meet all demands in formulating policies on philanthropic giving?

2. Should contributions be considered simply an extension of marketing and made accordingly?

3. Should contributions be consistent with the firm's culture and values?

4. Is giving in to objections to certain donations by special-interest groups ethical?

5. Currently, companies that have indicated an interest in or taken steps to conduct embryonic stem-cell research have had shareholder proposals objecting to such projects or requesting that the company adopt a policy in advance of shunning such research. The proposals, such as one for the Merck 2004 annual meeting, are often submitted by religious groups that own shares in the company. Do these companies face a different dilemma from that of Dayton-Hudson?

6. Some pharmacists have refused to fill prescriptions for RU-486 (the morning-after pill) because of their religious and moral convictions. Some pharmacies have refused to stock RU-486 because of the moral convictions of their staff. How do these companies resolve their postures on right to life, abortion, and choice?

CASE 3.12

Bayer, Anthrax, Cipro Patents, and Half-Price

Following the deadly September 11, 2001, attacks on the World Trade Center, the United States experienced the first cases of anthrax it had seen since 1978. The anthrax spores were found in letters sent to the American Media, Inc., building in Florida (publishing home of the *National Enquirer* and the *Globe*); the offices of Tom Brokaw of NBC News and Dan Rather of CBS News; and the offices of Senators Tom Daschle, Patrick Leahy, and Edward Kennedy in the United States Senate. There was a series of deaths, cutaneous infections, and hundreds of employees at these organizations who tested positive for exposure to the anthrax spores. In addition, there were at least two anthrax deaths for which the source of the anthrax was not readily located.

As a result of these exposures, from letters that were mailed on September 18, 2001, the most effective antibiotic for treating anthrax, ciprofloxacin, was in high demand. Bayer AG, a German company, owns the patent for this antibiotic, which it calls Cipro. The patent expires in December 2009.

However, executives at headquarters for the company remained silent for weeks about the company's ability to manufacture sufficient amounts of the patented antibiotic. Executives indicated that the company was concerned that if it appeared in the media it would give the appearance of taking advantage of the dire circumstances.

Bayer's history made it wary of any involvement in international battles. Bayer AG had to pay reparations following World War II and its patent for its world-famous aspirin, Bayer, was stripped from it and awarded to a U.S. company. It was not until

2000 that Bayer was once again permitted to use its name. The company's low profile during the fall 2001 anthrax scares was deliberate and explained by executives as a desire to avoid appearing "exploitive of the problem" of the infections and illnesses.[116]

Frustrated with the lack of communication from Bayer, Canada suspended Bayer's patent in Canada and ordered other drug manufacturers to begin production of their pending generic formulas for Cipro. The Canadian national health service purchased one million of the Cipro-generic from another manufacturer.[117] Other drug companies do have their own formulas developed and ready to go, but could not produce these generics so long as Bayer AG held its patent protection. One company, Apotex, indicated its production method would not infringe on Bayer's patent, but Bayer threatened litigation and indicated it would deliver all the Cipro needed and/or ordered by both the United States and Canadian governments. Health officials were skeptical and one stated, "There's no way you can tell me getting it from six companies is going to be slower than getting it from one company."[118]

There has been antitrust and patent litigation surrounding Cipro. In 1997 Bayer entered into a settlement with Barr Laboratories, Inc. in which Bayer agreed to pay Barr and another generic manufacturer of ciprofloxacin $24.55 million each to not produce the drug.[119] Barr agreed to drop its challenge to Bayer's patent to Cipro in exchange for the payment. Now there are antitrust suits against Barr, Bayer, and another drug company for this agreement, which the suits contend served to eliminate competition for the sale and production of ciprofloxacin.[120]

The production levels needed in order to supply Cipro for the anthrax cases as well as for those who had been exposed to the sources (about 20,000 Americans) required a significant ramp-up.[121] Bayer AG's United States unit went into 24-hour shifts following the anthrax breakouts.[122] Mr. Brokaw held up a bottle of Cipro on his program, "NBC Nightly News," and calmed a jittery public by saying, "In Cipro we trust." Workers at one of Bayer's U.S. plants cheered with the coverage.[123]

On October 23, 2001, the following content appeared in a full-page ad in *The New York Times*:

A Message From Bayer Corporation to the American People

Our Commitment to You

In response to the attacks on America and as part of the fight against bioterrorism, the people of Bayer are substantially increasing production of Cipro (ciprofloxacin).

[116] Edmund L. Andrews, *"Drug Makers Seem Uncertain in Response to Cipro Frenzy,"* The New York Times, October 20, 2001, pp. A1, B8.

[117] Amy Harmon and Robert Pear, *"Canada Overrides Patent for Cipro to Treat Anthrax,"* The New York Times, October 19, 2001, pp. A1, B7.

[118] Id.

[119] Margaret Cronin Fisk, *"Cipro maker fighting trust suits,"* National Law Journal, October 29, 2001, p. A11.

[120] In re Ciprofloxacin Hydrochloride Antitrust Litigation (No. MDL 001383 (E.D.N.Y.)).

[121] Melody Petersen and Robert Pear, *"Anthrax Fears Send Demand for a Drug Far beyond Output,"* The New York Times, October 16, 2001, pp. A1, B7.

[122] Keith Bradsher, *"Bayer Insists Cipro Supply Is Sufficient; Fights Generic,"* The New York Times, October 21, 2001, p. B7.

[123] Vanessa Fuhrmans and Ron Winslow, *"Its Image Under Fire, Bayer AG Scrambles To Meet Cipro Demand,"* The Wall Street Journal, October 22, 2001, pp. A1, A8.

Our commitment to the American public is clear: We will meet this threat head on. Bayer is now working 24 hours a day, seven days a week to assure that Americans are equipped to fight this threat.

In the last few weeks, we have shipped tens of millions of Cipro tablets, have tripled production and have committed to shipping 200 million tablets over the next three months.

We will continue to work with the nation's healthcare professionals to ensure appropriate use of our antibiotics. We stand ready to support the United States government in providing Cipro to meet emergency needs.

As a world leader in health care, we take seriously our responsibility to help protect and improve your welfare. We will face this latest challenge together . . . and we will succeed.

You have our commitment.

Bayer

For more information, go to www.CiproUSA.com[124]

The U.S. Congress was considering suspension of the Cipro patent in the U.S. in order to ramp-up production even more.[125] The legislation would permit federal judges to suspend patents on the basis of public health issues. Secretary of Health and Human Services Tommy Thompson also issued a public threat of suspending Bayer AG's patent in order to meet the increasing demands.[126]

In response to some panic in the United States, pharmacies in Mexico, permitted to sell Cipro without a doctor's prescription, as required in the United States, were ordering large amounts of Cipro, increasing their prices, and doing a great deal of profitable business from U.S. orders. For example, the Zipp Pharmacy, located in Ciudad Juarez, a border town, said its orders for Cipro increased 15 times what they were before the anthrax infections. A nurse buying doses of Cipro for her entire family said, "What if there are mad runs on it? It's nice to have it around just in case."[127]

The Internet business for Cipro via online prescription services was booming.[128] MedicalWeb.com is a company that was found at the root of most Web sites providing Cipro information, which included the following:

2-buy-cipro.com
Cipro-for-anthrax.com
Cipro-antibiotics-anthrax-vaccines.com
1-cipro-4-anthrax.com
Cipropharmacy.com
Ciprostockpile.com
Gas-masks-israeli-gasmasks.com
Cipro-for-less.com

---

[124] The New York Times, *October 23, 2001, p. B12.*

[125] Holman W. Jenkins, Jr., *"Of Germs and Geopolitics,"* The Wall Street Journal, *October 24, 2001, p. A23.*

[126] Julie Appleby, *"HHS Chief Wants Cipro Price Cut,"* USA Today, *October 24, 2001, p. 3B.*

[127] Greg Winter, *"Si We Have Cipro; the Panicky and Profiteers Head to Mexico,"* The New York Times, *October 20, 2001, pp. B1, B8.*

[128] *"The Cipro Circus,"* The Wall Street Journal, *October 25, 2001, p. A20.*

A subsidiary of MedicalWeb.com is MedicalGroup.com, a service that connects patients with doctors who will write prescriptions for them. MedicalGroup.com has 35 physicians with whom it works who write prescriptions for patients after interacting with the patients online. The prescription is then filled by 1stOnline-Pharmacy.com, another subsidiary of MedicalWeb.com.

The company's business jumped from filling 6 to 10 Cipro orders per day to over 100 per day. The increase in activity and national attention brought regulatory attention to MedicalWeb, a company based in North Carolina. The company had already rankled professional organizations, and the newfound earnings only exacerbated the tense relationships. CEO Tania Malik of MedicalWeb.com said, "It's almost, 'Be careful what you wish for.' We did want people to know about Virtual-MedicalGroup, but my fear is people see the press and think we're arrogant."[129]

The U.S. Government began a program for purchasing Cipro from Bayer and negotiated a price of $1.00 per tablet, a discount from the usual $1.83 per tablet. The first 100 million tablets would cost only 95 cents each.[130] The government negotiated the price by using its bargaining position of suspending the patent, as the Canadian government had done. The price Bayer charges wholesalers is $5.00 per pill.[131]

Bayer refused to grant interviews on the discount program but its CEO for American operations, Helge H. Wehmeier, said, "I was smiling going in because how often in your life do you and your company have an opportunity to make a difference?"[132] Bayer would also not respond to a question on whether it was making a profit. But drug industry analysts indicated the price was perhaps enough to cover costs but little more.

Three other drug manufacturers offered their drugs for free if the federal government would approve them for the treatment of anthrax. In addition, all of the drug manufacturers formed a task force so that they could work jointly with the federal government to provide vaccines and treatments needed because of the threats of bioterrorism.[133] There is precedent for such cooperation. During World War II the pharmaceutical companies worked together to develop both penicillin as well as drugs for the treatment of malaria that affected troops in the Pacific as well as in Africa.[134]

Physicians at the Center for Disease Control (CDC) were concerned about the Mexico purchases and use of the drug without physician prescription. They note the following problems: (1) some people are allergic to Cipro and can become quite ill with just one dose; (2) Cipro has side effects for almost everyone including nausea,

[129] Julia Angwin, "Demand for Cipro Brings Sales—and Scrutiny—to Online Supplier," The Wall Street Journal, October 22, 2001, pp. B1, B6.

[130] Keith Bradsher and Edmund L. Andrews, "U.S. Says Bayer Will Cut Costs of Its Anthrax Drug," The New York Times, October 24, 2001, p. B7.

[131] Gina Kolata, "Cipro Isn't the Only Drug That Can Be Prescribed," The New York Times, October 17, 2001, p. B7.

[132] Keith Bradsher, "Bayer Halves Price for Cipro, But Rivals Offer Drugs Free," The New York Times, October 26, 2001, pp. A1, B8.

[133] Andrew Pollack, "Drug Makers Wrestle With World's New Rules," The New York Times, October 21, 2001, Section 3-1, 3-10 (Money and Business).

[134] Chris Adams, "Drug Firms Fought Efforts for Global Pact on Bioterrorism," The Wall Street Journal, October 25, 2001, p. A22.

vomiting, and loss of appetite; (3) Cipro does have an effect on the brain including possible seizures and hallucinations or simply mood changes and insomnia; and (4) Cipro damages cartilage in the joints, especially when taken by children, and is given to children only when there is the absolute need (i.e., there is an infection ongoing). The CDC has advised use of Cipro only upon determination of exposure or infection from anthrax.

Bayer continued to struggle with its position, promises, and public perception as the anthrax infections increased. Bayer's corporate policy is as follows:

> We offer our customers a wide variety of products and services in areas ranging from health care and agriculture to plastics and specialty chemicals. Bayer is research-based and is aiming for technological leadership in its core activities.
>
> Our goals are to steadily increase corporate value and generate a high value added for the benefit of our stockholders, our employees and the community in every country in which we operate. We believe that our technical and commercial expertise involves responsibility to work for the common good and contribute to sustainable development.
>
> Bayer: Success through Expertise with Responsibility.
>
> Last updated: August 2, 2001

For more information on anthrax, Cipro, and the ethical issues, visit the following Web sites:

> http://www.bayer.com
> http://www.cdc.gov
> http://www.cptech.org

The last Web site is one for Ralph Nader's Consumer Project on Technology and provides information on the patents and sale of Cipro.

Discussion Questions

1. What decisions do you think Bayer should have made in this situation?

2. Should Bayer have suspended its patent voluntarily? Professor John W. Dienhart, a business ethics professor at Seattle University, stated that Bayer should be a "good corporate citizen." He added, "This is not breaking a patent but adjusting a patent to meet a particular need." And "We're dealing with life and death itself, not Post-it Notes."[135]

   Professor Gerald C. Meyers, formerly the chairman of American Motors, encouraged Bayer to license Cipro, "They can't do anything other than license. They'll take such a hit if they refuse."[136] Professor Thomas Donaldson of the Wharton School of the University of Pennsylvania adds that companies must see the "psychology as well as the objective facts." Professor John R. Boatright of Loyola University of Chicago suggested that if Bayer can make

---

[135] Andrew Pollack, "Drug Makers Wrestle With World's New Rules," The New York Times, October 21, 2001, Section 3-1, 3-10 (Money and Business).
[136] Id.

enough Cipro, there is no ethical issue related to the patent or licensing and that sufficient production is the key question.[137]

3. Should Bayer have suspended profits on the sale? Professor Donaldson said, "Extraordinary events sometimes call for extraordinary corporate compassion. The company cannot just look at profits but must look at the face of the victims."[138]

4. What recommendations should Bayer have made on taking Cipro? Should it have backed up the warning from the CDC?

5. What do you think of the ethics and social responsibility of the Mexican pharmacies and online pharmacies profiting from selling Cipro? Are they different from Bayer or do the same ethical issues apply?

CASE 3.13

The Chicago Inner-City School Experiment

A group of Chicago businesses pooled funds to create a privately owned and operated elementary school in a Chicago inner-city neighborhood because of their concerns about the quality of education. Observing that American businesses spend $4 to $5 billion annually in training just to bring their workers to very basic skill levels, these businesses determined that they would help improve public education. They incorporated business notions on pay and accountability in the most challenging environment—an inner-city school.[139]

The school is free for neighborhood children ages two to twelve. At the school, students get breakfast, lunch, and snacks, as well as after-school care.

Teachers in the school are paid 10 percent more than their public school counterparts. The school is run like a private corporation, and the administrators and teachers understand that a lack of improvement in the students can result in termination of employment.

If it achieves its goals, this project could be a model for other schools. The founders of this Chicago experiment believe the future success of their businesses lies in the skills of their employees.[140]

[137] Id.
[138] Id.
[139] Alex Kotlowitz, "A Businessman Turns His Skills to Aiding Inner-City Schools," The Wall Street Journal, February 25, 1992, pp. A1, A8.
[140] "Why Business Should Invest in Literacy," Business Week, July 20, 1992, p. 102.

Discussion Questions

1. Would Milton Friedman support the school founders' endeavor as a proper use of shareholder funds?

2. A shareholder of one of the businesses has protested: "Why are my funds being used for an inner-city school? We have taxes for that. I invested in a distribution firm, not an education firm. Your job is to earn my dividend, not spend it on things you think are important."

   If you were the director of shareholder relations for the firm, how would you respond to the shareholder?

Individuals, Individual Values, and the Business Organization

The conscience that is dark
   with shame for his own deeds or for another's,
   may well, indeed, feel harshness in your words;

Nevertheless, do not resort to lies,
   let what you write reveal all you have seen,
   and let those men who itch scratch where it hurts.

Though when your words are taken in at first
   they may taste bitter, but once well-digested
   they will become a vital nutrient.

— DANTE, PARADISIO XVII.124–132

AT TIMES, AN INDIVIDUAL WHO has become part of a larger organization feels that his or her personal values are in conflict with those of the organization. The types of ethical dilemmas that arise between an individual and his or her company include conflicts of interests and issues of honesty, fairness, and loyalty. One who negotiates contracts for an organization may find that contract bidders are willing to offer personally beneficial incidental benefits that would tend to cloud his or her judgment with respect to which vendor is best for the company. Elsewhere, an employee may find information indicating that the company is not addressing the correctable dangers of one of its products. The individual must confront such issues, pitting concerns about continuing employment and livelihood against moral standards and safety concerns.

These concerns represent the most common and difficult dilemmas businesspeople face. Studying them, reviewing alternatives, and carefully establishing values will prepare you for the dilemmas that we all must ultimately confront. Because so many of the cases in this unit involve individual decisions and actions, it begins with a very short reading that reminds us that we do not slip into unethical and illegal conduct suddenly. Rather, we go through a gradual process of letting our standards down and rationalizing our behavior.

Trust and Employment

No one wakes up one day and thinks, "You know what would be good? A gigantic fraud! I believe I will create a gigantic fraud and make money that way." They have to ease themselves into creating a fraud. No one wakes up one day and says, "I believe I will go to work and embezzle $100,000." They will begin by using the postage meter or copier for personal reasons and work their way up to the $100,000, perhaps even taking it in small increments in order to adjust their comfort level with their conduct. One of the tasks we have in studying, understanding, and living ethics in business is drawing lines for ourselves on what we will not do and then honoring those lines we have chosen. If we start moving the lines, we can find ourselves in complete violation of the standards and absolutes we have set for ourselves, and we got there incrementally. The following concise and insightful reading provides pithy insight into this process of moving the line.

READING 4.1
The Moving Line

George Lefcoe

George Lefcoe, former commissioner of the Los Angeles County Regional Planning Commission, on his retirement and the seduction of public office:

I really missed the cards from engineers I never met, the wine and cheese from development companies I never heard of, and the honeybaked ham from, of all places, Forest Lawn Cemetery, even though the company was never an applicant before the commission when I was there.

My first Christmas as a commissioner—when I received the ham—I tried to return it, though for the record, I did not, since no one at Forest Lawn seemed authorized to accept the ham, apparently not even for burial. My guess is that no one of the many public servants who received the ham had ever tried to return it.

When I received another ham the next Christmas, I gave it to a worthy charity. The next year, some worthy friends were having a party so I gave it to them. The next year I had a party and we enjoyed the ham.

In the fifth year, about the tenth of December, I began wondering, where is my ham?[1]

....

Discussion Questions

1. What was Mr. Lefcoe's absolute line?

2. How did he cross it?

3. How did he evolve to a position that was the exact opposite of his original absolute line?

Information is a powerful business tool and often a competitor's edge. Inside information released too early to the press can harm both a company and its personnel. Information withheld can result in liability for a company. Proprietary information taken by employees from one employer to another results in a breach of trust and creates a marketplace in which fair competition is not possible. Employees must recognize the value, ownership, and implications of the use and misuse of company information. Employers and employees both trust that company information is used and released properly. The next six cases and a reading cover many issues of trust related to company information.

CASE 4.2
....

General Motors, Volkswagen, and the Traveling Executive

Jose Ignacio Lopez de Arriortua was a vice president with General Motors Corporation's GM Espana, Opel, and GM Europe AG Division (GM). Shortly after his promotion to vice president in February 1993, Mr. Lopez resigned from GM and took a position as part of the management board of Volkswagen AG, a German corporation (VW) on March 16, 1993.[2]

Joining Mr. Lopez at VW by March 22, 1993, were GM's executive director of purchasing for GM Espana, Jorge Alvarez, a platform manager for the S-Car, O-Car and Opel; Rosario Piazza, a sourcing specialist for Opel; Hugo Van der Auwera, executive director of worldwide purchasing for GM Continental (based out of Belgium); Francisco Garcia-Sanz, executive director of worldwide purchasing for GM's electrical commodity group; Andries Versteeg, manager-European liaison for advance purchasing and global sourcing; and William Admiraal, an employee of GM who is also married to Lopez's daughter, Irene.

GM filed suit under the Lanham Act (protection against the taking of trade secrets) and alleged that Mr. Lopez, from as early as August 1992 until his departure in March 1993, secretly communicated with VW representatives about a job and promised to bring along with him to his new job at VW business plans and trade secrets.[3] Specifically, the

[1] The Wall Street Journal, "Notable, Quotable," December 18, 1998, p. A14.
[2] William M. Carley, "Secret Suit: What Did He Know?" The Wall Street Journal, January 19, 1988, pp. B1, B8.
[3] General Motors Corporation v. Ignacio Lopez de Arriortua, 948 F.Supp. 656 (E.D. Mich. 1996).

suit alleges that Mr. Lopez was to bring along confidential documents, transparencies, and computer diskettes that contained the following information:[4]

- Listings of GM and Opel components by worldwide supplier, price, terms, conditions, and delivery schedules
- A copy of GM's Product Purchasing System (PPS)
- A copy of GM Europe's European Purchasing Optimization System (EPOS)
- Plans for "Plant X," the factory of the future
- Future auto plans to the year 2003
- Future strategies for purchasing[5]

GM alleged that Lopez and those GM employees who went with him to Volkswagen took over 20 cartons of stolen documents, entered the data on computers over a month-long period at VW, and had the documents transferred to a third party for shredding in order to destroy the evidence of the documents being taken from GM. An audit by KPMG Peat Marwick, commissioned by GM, concluded that the documents had been taken.[6] Following an initial denial in which VW's CEO, Ferdinand Piech, referred to the GM charges as "mudslinging," VW admitted in August 1993 that the former GM employees had indeed taken the documents but that they were destroyed shortly after they began their work at VW and that VW never had access to the information. In a statement admitting the document theft, VW said that GM employees "destroyed documents which could possibly be attributed to GM and could contain critical information, in order to remove any danger of distribution at Volkswagen."[7] The release also added that its own internal investigation found nothing "which could warrant the accusation of industrial espionage." The statement also added that the "young men didn't act correctly toward their former employer."[8]

In June 1993, German officials discovered four boxes of trade secret documents in the home of one of the associates of Lopez, as well as others in Lopez's home.[9] Those boxes were seized and German authorities ultimately indicted Mr. Lopez and three others who transferred to VW. German authorities continued with their prosecution despite VW's press release because the destruction did not mean the information was not ultimately used and the company had not used a third party to conduct the internal investigation.

These circumstances ultimately resulted in 11 different legal proceedings, including the German charges and the suit by GM for violations of the Lanham Act as well as RICO violations. Mr. Lopez was indicted on six counts of wire fraud and interstate transportation of stolen property in May 2000. The indictment alleges that in the four months preceding his departure from GM, Mr. Lopez and his assistants made an extraordinary number of requests for confidential documents.

[4] "Judge Sets Michigan Venue for GM Suit Against VW," The Wall Street Journal, October 18, 1996, p. B5.

[5] John Templeman and Peggy Salz-Trautman, "VW Figures Its Best Defense May Be a Good Offense," Business Week, August 19, 1993, p. 29.

[6] Ferdinand Protzman, "VW Sets a Board Meeting on G.M. Dispute," The New York Times, October 5, 1993, p. C4.

[7] "VW, GM 'Spy' Feud," Arizona Republic, July 30, 1993, p. B1.

[8] Audrey Choi, "VW Discloses GM Documents Were Destroyed," The Wall Street Journal, August 9, 1993, p. A3.

[9] Ferdinand Protzman, "German Prosecutors Link Lopez to Secret GM Papers," The New York Times, July 23, 1993, pp. C1, C2.

Mr. Lopez was indicted, not under the Economic Espionage Act (EEA) because that act was passed largely because of the Lopez/VW scenario and was enacted after the fact. *Ex post facto* laws cannot be applied to conduct occurring before the passage, but under computer fraud statutes.[10] The EEA makes it a crime for employees to download, copy, e-mail, transfer, or in any way provide information about their current companies to their new companies.

VW settled the suit by GM in 1997 by agreeing to pay $100 million. VW did not, however, admit any wrongdoing as part of that settlement. Mr. Lopez settled his criminal charges by the German government by agreeing to pay $224,000 to charity. Mr. Lopez left VW in 1996, largely because the company did not fulfill what he said was its promise to him to allow him to build a "dream factory." Mr. Lopez works as an auto consultant while living in the Basque region of Spain. In 1998 he was in an auto accident and suffered brain damage which has resulted in memory lapses. Of the whole GM/VW scenario, Mr. Lopez was disappointed that VW did not build his dream factory, "If I had known that, I wouldn't have changed jobs. It was my error."[11]

Discussion Questions

1. Do you think what the GM employees did was wrong?

2. Wouldn't Mr. Lopez have most of the keys to the supply chain management system of GM in his head anyway?

3. Don't competitors hire employees from their competitors with the hope of bringing in experience? Is there a line between sharing experience and sharing systems?

4. Would you have taken the documents?

5. Does it make a difference that the documents are related to the supply chain and not new products or ideas?

CASE 4.3

Boeing and the Employees Who Brought the Documents with Them[12]

In 1996, Boeing and Lockheed Martin were in a head-to-head competition for a government multi-billion-dollar contract that would furnish the rockets that are used for launching satellites into space (a project referred to in the industry as the EELV). The satellites perform various functions and could be communication or spy satellites.

---

[10] Keith Bradsher, "Former G.M. Executive Indicted on Charges of Taking Trade Secrets," *The New York Times*, May 23, 2000, pp. C1, C2.

[11] Id.

[12] The author consulted with Boeing following the ethical scandals to help with employee ethics training. The information here was taken from public documents.

It was during this competitive time frame (1996) for the rocket launcher project that Kenneth Branch, a space engineer and manager at Lockheed facilities in Florida, traveled to McDonnell Douglas facilities at Huntington Beach, California, for a job interview. McDonnell Douglas was working on the rockets bid at the same time that it was being acquired by Boeing. Boeing's acquisition of McDonnell Douglas had been finalized at the time of the Branch interview, but the logistics of acquisition had not yet been completed (it would be completed in August 1997). Boeing's acquisition of McDonnell Douglas and the combination of Lockheed with Martin Marietta meant that in the future, the federal government would basically be dealing with two large contractors on all of its projects.

Near the end of his interview at McDonnell Douglas, Branch showed the participants in the interview process a copy of Lockheed's proposed presentation for the government project. Six months after his interview, in January 1997, Branch began work at Boeing on Boeing's rocket project, a $5 billion project. The pressure at that time became intense for Boeing to win the contract. Boeing executive Frank Slazer, the director of business development for the project, encouraged Boeing employees working on EELV to develop "an improved Lockheed Martin EELV competitive assessment." He also encouraged the employees to find former Lockheed employees to get their thoughts and impressions about the project.

Sometime during the first quarter of 1997, Lockheed sent Mr. Branch a letter reminding him of his confidentiality agreement with Lockheed and his duty not to disclose any proprietary information in his new position at Boeing. During this same period, a Boeing employee filed a report that she had seen Mr. Branch in the hallway with a notebook that had the Lockheed logo on the outside. She was reprimanded by Tom Alexiou, Mr. Branch's supervisor, for doing so, and no one took any action with regard to Mr. Branch or the notebook.

Shortly after, the project was awarded in what is called a "leader-follower" contract, in which the two companies compete for the term of the satellite launcher program. Boeing did emerge as the leader in that project and was awarded 19 of the planned 28 rocket launches, a total contract value of $1.88 billion. Shortly after, there were rumblings around the industry and government agencies about Boeing's conduct and possible possession of proprietary documents during the time of the bids. The government began an investigation into whether proprietary documents passed from Lockheed to Boeing. Boeing also launched, as it were, an internal investigation and fired Mr. Branch as well as his supervisor, William Erskine, because it found that the two were in possession of thousands of pages of proprietary documents that included Lockheed Martin information on specifications and cost. The terminations were reported to the federal government along with Boeing's assurances that it had dealt with the situation and completed its cleansing of its own house.

Mr. Branch and Mr. Erskine filed suit against Boeing for wrongful termination and document production began as part of the discovery process in the suit. While the suit was dismissed in 2002, the details of Boeing's internal investigation still made their way into the court case, including documents and a memo describing the conduct of Mr. Branch and Mr. Erskine and Boeing executives. The interest of the Justice Department was piqued and its investigation into Boeing's conduct also began in 2002. In one telling exchange, a project specialist, Steve Griffin, confronted Mr. Erskine with his conduct related to the EELV project: Mr. Erksine admitted that he had an "under the table" arrangement to get Lockheed bid documents from Mr. Branch and that he did ultimately incorporate what he learned into Boeing's bid. The internal investigation revealed this conversation between the two following that disclosure

> Griffin: We just took a Procurement Integrity Law class. I can't believe you did that.

> Erksine: I was hired to win . . . and I was going to do whatever it took to do it.

Mr. Griffin ultimately reported the information to his boss and the internal investigation resulted.

The judge in the case ordered the men to pay Boeing's legal fees, but the two men signed agreements promising not to disclose details about the case or discuss it with the media in exchange for Boeing waiving its rights to collect its legal fees. However, at the end of April 2003, Boeing shipped 11 boxes of documents to Lockheed Martin. The documents in the boxes had the Lockheed Martin logo and were stamped "Proprietary." When those documents arrived, the entire sordid history emerged in the press.[13] Boeing did not disclose the issues and investigations surrounding EELV in its SEC documents until May 2003, after a *Wall Street Journal* report on the investigations and litigation appeared. Jim Albaugh, CEO of the defense systems division, indicated that management had not really focused on the inquiries and investigations until that public disclosure.[14]

Boeing and Lockheed have been in a virtual dead heat for military contracts for some time, with Lockheed Martin slightly ahead in 2000 and 2001 and the two nearly tied at $15 billion each in 2002.

The scandal reached Congress, where it exemplified concerns about government contracts with Boeing.[15] Pending at the time of the erupting investigation into the EELVA contracts was an $18 billion contract with the Air Force for the delivery of Boeing 767 tankers, aircraft used to refuel fighter jets in midair. Congress held hearings on the Defense Department's decision to award a tanker contract to Boeing because CEO Albaugh had called Air Force Assistant Secretary Marvin Sambur for help in closing the deal. Sambur did step in to help, and Congressional wrath resulted. Senator John McCain noted, "It's astonishing. Even in light of serious allegations, they [Boeing] continued to push to railroad the [tanker]deal through, and they still are."[16]

The public relations fall-out from the tankers issue not only created negative reaction in Congress; it created public perception problems. In order to win back public favor and attempt to refute the charges, Boeing ran a series of one-page ads in newspapers around the country, including the *Wall Street Journal.*[17]

Continuing ethical lapses (See Case 2.7 on Boeing's recruitment while bids were pending of a government official who had not recused herself) forced a shake-up in

[13] Anne Marie Squeo and Andy Pasztor, "U.S. Probes Whether Boeing Misused a Rival's Documents," The Wall Street Journal, May 5, 2003, p. A1, A7.

[14] Anne Marie Squeo, J. Lynn Lunsford, and Andy Pasztor, "Boeing's Plan to Smooth Bumps of Jet Market Hits Turbulence," The Wall Street Journal, August 25, 2003, pp. A1, A6.

[15] Stanley Holmes, "Boeing: Caught In Its Own Turbulence," Business Week, December 8, 2003, p. 37.

[16] Byron Acohido, "Boeing's Call for Help from Air Force Raise More Questions," USA Today, December 8, 2003, p. 3B.

[17] See May 4, 2004, p. A7.

Boeing, with the termination of its CFO, Michael Sears.[18] The Air Force pulled $1 billion in satellite contracts (about 7 contracts) from Boeing as a penalty for its conduct with the Lockheed documents.[19] Air Force Undersecretary Peter Teets released the following statement in making the announcement:

> "We do not tolerate breaches of procurement integrity, and we hold industry accountable for the actions of their employees."[20]

Just prior to the Air Force announcement, Boeing had issued its own announcement that the expected revenues from commercial satellites and rocket launchers had been greatly overestimated by that division. Boeing took a $1.1 billion charge to reflect the fact that those revenues had already been overestimated.[21] Two of Boeing's former executives were indicted for their role in the documents scandal. Lockheed has filed suit against Boeing for the appropriation of the documents. CEO Philip Condit fired Sears, saying "Boeing must and will live by the highest standards of ethical conduct."[22] However, Condit departed abruptly on December 1, 2003.[23] When Condit resigned, analysts, observers, employees, and others took stock of Boeing and what had gone wrong. One wrote, "Under Condit, engineering skills and ethics seemed to lose sway over senior management." Condit's four marriages, two to Boeing employees, one of whom was pink-slipped during her relationship with Condit, created a culture that ran contra to the conservative traditions of the Boeing culture. When Condit moved into the Four Seasons Olympic Hotel in Seattle and had the suite remodeled at company expense, even the board members became nervous, quietly saying among themselves that they had "another Clinton" on their hands.[24] As the culture of the company deteriorated, Boeing missed strategic opportunities. Doubting the ability of Airbus to bring the A380 555-passenger jet to market, Boeing opted out of that jumbo-jet market. Airbus won 120 orders for the super jumbo jet and seized Boeing's market for large jetliners. Shareholders were in revolt.

Since the time of the management shake-up and all the fall-out from the documents and the defense employee recruitment, Boeing has repositioned itself and worked toward a culture change. However, the issues continue to arise. In April 2004, the U.S. Attorney's Office in Los Angeles expanded its investigation of the Lockheed Martin document case into Boeing work for NASA and the possibility that other Lockheed documents were used on NASA projects. The documents are different and involve different managers, but the pattern of abuse is the same.[25] Boeing has, however,

---

[18] Ironically, Mr. Sears' book Soaring Through Turbulence was scheduled for release from the publisher at the same time. Julie Creswell, "Boeing Plays Defense," Fortune, April 19, 2004, p. 91. Its publication has been delayed indefinitely. Del Jones, "Fired Boeing Executive Encounters Book Turbulence," USA Today, November 28, 2003, p. 2B. Some quotes from the book: "Corporate leaders need a model that will keep them clear of impropriety and the appearance of impropriety." "Either you are ethical or you are not. You have to make that decision; all of us do. And there is no in between."

[19] J. Lynn Lunsford and Anne Marie Squeo, "Boeing CEO Condit Resigns In Shake-Up at Areospace Titan," The Wall Street Journal, December 2, 2003, pp. A1, A12.

[20] Edward Iwata, "Air Force Punishes Boeing by Taking 7 Contracts," USA Today, July 25, 2003, p. 1B.

[21] Anne Marie Squeo, J. Lynn Lunsford, and Andy Pasztor, "Boeing's Plan to Smooth Bumps of Jet Market Hits Turbulence," The Wall Street Journal, August 25, 2003, pp. A1, A6.

[22] Gary Strauss, Byron Acohido, Elliot Blaire Smith, and Marilyn Adams, "Boeing CEO Abruptly Quits after Controversy," USA Today, December 2, 2003, p. 1B.

[23] Stanley Holmes, "Boeing: What Really Happened," Business Week, December 15, 2003. p. 33.

[24] Id.

[25] Andy Pasztor and Jonathan Karp, "Federal Officials Widen Probe into Boeing's Use of Rival's Data," The Wall Street Journal, April 27, 2004, pp. A7, A10.

repositioned itself and refocused on its private jetliner business. It already has orders for 50 of its new 7E7 aircraft from All Nippon Airways, for a total contract price of $6 billion. The first deliveries of those planes will be in 2008. As a result of these contracts and ongoing changes and reforms, Boeing has performed well. Its shares reached $42.28 by December 30, 2003, and the U.S. Navy selected Boeing to deliver up to 210 F/A 18 fighter jets for a total contract price of $9.6 billion.[26] In June 2004, the Navy awarded a $23 billion contract to Boeing to convert 737 jets into antisubmarine aircraft, a contract that replaces plans that had been supplied by Lockheed Martin originally.[27] The contract was awarded even as the government investigation on the EELV was still ongoing. When former CEO Harry Stonecipher returned from retirement to reassume his role following Mr. Condit's resignation, he told the business press, "We're cleaning up our own house."[28] When asked if he could provide assurance to investors and customers that the scandals were behind Boeing, Mr. Stonecipher said, "Well, as in definitely behind us, they'll never be definitely behind us until all the lawsuits are finished. Rather than trying to convince people that it's all behind us, I have convinced them that we have a process and a will to deal with it, vigorously and summarily.["][29]

Discussion Questions

1. What made the engineers and executives want the Lockheed documents and then use them?

2. What were the long-term costs and consequences of their use of the documents?

3. Do you think the fact that Boeing continued to receive contracts is evidence that ethics don't matter?

4. What elements of Boeing's culture lend themselves to ethical lapses?

5. One analyst has said that the problem with Boeing is that it cannot admit that the problems were internal, that it always seeks to blame the problems on a "few bad apples." Is this statement valid?

6. List the categories of ethical breaches that you see in this scenario.

CASE 4.4

The Sale of Sand to the Saudis

Joe Raymond's position as sales manager for Granite Rock and Sand was in jeopardy. His unit had been low performer in terms of sales for the last seven quarters. Joe's supervisor, vice president Tom Haws, told Joe that he had through the next quarter to pull his unit out of last place. Haws also told Joe that Joe would have to be replaced if the improvement did not occur.

Joe and his wife had just purchased their first home. With their mortgage payments totaling $2,100 per month, the loss of Joe's salary would mean the loss of their home.

[26] *"Closing Bell,"* Business Week, January 12, 2004, p. 42.
[27] Leslie Wayen, *"Boeing Wins Navy Contract to Replace Sub Chasers,"* The New York Times, June 15, 2004, pp. C1, C9.
[28] Ron Insana, *"We're Cleaning Up Our Own House,"* USA Today, January 5, 2004, p. 4B.
[29] Laura Rich, *"A Boeing Stalwart, War or Peace,"* The New York Times, July 18, 2004, p. BU4.

Following Tom's warning, Joe began interviewing candidates for a vacant sales position in his unit. Joe had conducted three interviews when the final candidate, Jessica Morris, arrived. During the interview with Morris, Joe learned that she was the victim of a layoff by a competitor, Silt, Sand, and Such. Joe was not terribly impressed with Morris, but just before she left, she opened her briefcase and offered Joe a sheet of paper bearing the name of an official in the Saudi Arabian government. Morris explained:

> When I was with Silt, Sand, and Such, we started a program for finding innovative markets for our products. You know, we wanted to tap markets no one had ever thought of. After a lot of research, we discovered that Saudi desalinization plants need a particular type of sand they don't have over there, but we have here. We're the only firm that knows about this. If you hire me, I can see the sale through for Granite.

Morris added:

> Look, I need this job. You need your sales up. Think about it and call me.

After Morris left, Joe sat in his office and felt his problems were solved. Or were they?

Discussion Questions

1. If you were Joe, would you hire Morris?

2. Would anyone be harmed if you hired Morris?

3. What long-term problems could you foresee if Morris were hired?

4. Would using the information from Morris be illegal? Would Morris be committing a crime?

5. Would you be able to trust Morris if you hired her?

CASE 4.5

The Compliance Officer Who Strayed

Marisa Baridis, 29, was the legal compliance officer at Morgan Stanley, Dean Witter, Discover and Company. Ms. Baridis was in charge of what is commonly referred to as the "Chinese wall" in brokerage houses. Her job was to be certain that sensitive information did not cross from the side of the house putting together deals to the side of the house that buys stock. Her responsibilities included making certain that confidential information about Morgan Stanley clients did not leak to the brokerage side of the business so that Morgan Stanley brokers would not use inside information for trading.

Ms. Baridis met Jeffrey Streich, 31, in the summer of 1997. Mr. Streich was a broker who specialized in speculative stocks. Over a six-month period, Ms. Baridis allegedly provided Mr. Streich with information in exchange for $2,500 for each tip. However, late in October 1997, Mr. Streich and Ms. Baridis would have their last meeting when Mr. Streich went to their meeting wearing a hidden recorder, and there was a camera across the street that videotaped them both sitting in the window of a restaurant. The tape shows Mr. Streich handing Ms. Baridis $2,500 in one-hundred-dollar bills.

Ms. Baridis, who was indicted on charges of trading on inside information to make a profit, was fired from her $70,000-a-year job. Her father posted her $250,000 bail. Her indictment included statements by her obtained on a surveillance tape. When asked if she understood the implications of the tips and their scheme to profit she said, "It's the most illegalest thing you can do."[30] Ms. Baridis received kickbacks totaling $40,000. In another segment of the tape she is asked if she understands what would happen if they were caught, "We'd be interviewed in every magazine. We'd be in like. . . we'd be, who were the people of the '80s? Boesky? Michael Milken. We'd be bigger than that."[31] She added, "It's fun. If you don't get greedy."[32]

Prior to her indictment, Ms. Baridis had an upscale Manhattan apartment with rent of $2,400 per month. The extra money from the sale of information had afforded her a comfortable New York lifestyle. Her assets were frozen and prosecutors obtained $100,000 in a seizure of those assets. Overall, the insider tips involved thirteen companies and netted those involved in the trading over $1 million.[33]

Ms. Baridis entered a guilty plea in exchange for a lighter sentence contingent upon her cooperation. A college friend of Ms. Baridis also entered a guilty plea in federal court to charges of insider trading. Mr. Mitchell Sher, 32, admitted that he made cash payments to Ms. Baridis in exchange for her furnishing confidential information about pending events such as mergers for Morgan Stanley clients.[34]

Mr. Sher admitted that he used information provided to him by Ms. Baridis to trade in shares of Georgia-Pacific Corp., Burlington Resources, and two other companies. Unlike the ten other individuals charged in the case, Mr. Sher was not a broker but rather a vice president for a book distributor. He also admitted in his plea that Ms. Baridis had fed him confidential information in exchange for cash when she worked for Smith Barney earlier in her career.

When asked to comment on the Baridis case, an executive with Smith Barney said, "We had trusted the individual with great responsibility and that trust was misplaced."[35]

Discussion Questions

1. What is troublesome about insiders using information in advance of public disclosure to make money?

2. Why do regulators police such exchanges of information?

3. What does this case say about compliance programs and officers?

[30] Dean Starkman, "Three Indicted for Insider Trading Tied to Ex-Morgan Stanley Aide," The Wall Street Journal, November 26, 1997, p. B2.
[31] Elise Ackerman, "Remember Boesky? Many Gen Xers Don't," U.S. News & World Report, November 22, 1999, p. 52.
[32] Peter Truell, "Lessons of Boesky and Milken Go Unheeded in Fraud Case," The New York Times, November 26, 1997, pp. C1, C10.
[33] Peter Truell, "Sparring for Pieces of the Wall Street Action," The New York Times, December 26, 1997, pp. C1, C2.
[34] Dean Starkman, "Five Brokers Indicted for Insider Trades Linked to Ex-Morgan Stanley Officer," The Wall Street Journal, December 23, 1997, p. B9.
[35] Peter Truell, "An Employee on Wall Street Is Arrested," The New York Times, November 7, 1997, p. C8.

CASE 4.6

Espionage and Job-Hopping

Employees throughout a company have access to proprietary information, including customer lists, management techniques, and future plans.

What happens when those employees want to leave their current employer and go to work for a competitor? Or what happens when employees use or sell proprietary information?

Steven L. Davis, a lead process control engineer with Wright Industries, Inc., was part of a team working on the development and fabrication of equipment for Gillette Co.'s secret new shaving system. The new Gillette shaving system, predicted to be revolutionary, had been kept a very closely held secret. Wright Industries had been hired by Gillette. Mr. Davis was indicted by a federal grand jury on ten counts of wire fraud and theft of trade secrets. The indictment alleged Mr. Davis sent five faxes and electronic mail messages to Gillette's competitors with language intended to solicit interest in the purchase of Gillette's new technology. The messages included Mr. Davis's complaint that he had been passed over for a promotion.[36]

One of the competitors that received the fax alerted Gillette. Gillette contacted federal authorities and after an undercover investigation, Mr. Davis was charged. Mr. Davis then sent follow-up messages to the companies he had originally contacted complaining that someone "had betrayed him."

Discussion Questions

1. Is Mr. Davis's situation different because he did not work directly for Gillette?

2. If you had been one of the competitors Mr. Davis allegedly contacted, would you have notified Gillette?

3. Is there any irony in Mr. Davis's comment about betrayal?

4. What are the pros and cons of covenants in employee contracts that prohibit them (for a period of time) from working for a competitor? Some examples of recently enforced covenants:

   • Daniel O'Neill, the former head of Campbell Soup Co.'s soup division, could go to work for H.J. Heinz Co., but not in its soup division until August 1998 (a one-year ban).
   • Kevin R. Donohue, a former executive vice president with Kodak, was prohibited from working for a competitor (Fuji had hired him and Kodak sued for breach of contract) for one year.
   • William Redmond, a soft-drink marketing executive with PepsiCo, was prohibited from going to work for the beverage division of Quaker Oats for six months.[37]

---

[36] Mark Maremont and Joseph Pereira, "Engineer Indicted on Charges He Stole Trade Secrets on Gillette Shaving System," The Wall Street Journal, *September 26, 1997, p. B2.*
[37] "Non Compete Clauses are Serious," The Wall Street Journal, *December 10, 1996, p. A1.*

5. Are employees such as the executives in Question 4 capable of working for a competitor without divulging information? Consider the perspective of one executive, "It's difficult to have a competitive advantage over other companies unless there's something that you can call sacred to your company."[38]

CASE 4.7

The Glowing Recommendation[39]

Randi W. is a 13-year-old minor who attended the Livingston Middle School where Robert Gadams served as vice principal. On February 1, 1992, while Randi was in Gadams's office, Gadams sexually molested Randi.

Gadams had previously been employed at the Mendota Unified School District (from 1985 to 1988). During his time of employment there, Gadams had been investigated and reprimanded for improper conduct with female junior high students, including giving them back massages, making sexual remarks to them, and being involved in "sexual situations" with them.

Gilbert Rossette, an official with Mendota, provided a letter of recommendation for Gadams in May 1990. The letter was part of Gadams's placement file at Fresno Pacific College, where he had received his teaching credentials. The recommendation was extensive and referred to Gadams's "genuine concern" for students, his "outstanding rapport" with everyone, and concluded, "I wouldn't hesitate to recommend Mr. Gadams for any position."

Gadams had also previously been employed at the Tranquility High School District and Golden Plains Unified District (1987–1990). Richard Cole, an administrator at Golden Plains, also provided a letter of recommendation for the Fresno placement file that listed Gadams's "favorable" qualities and concluded that he "would recommend him for almost any administrative position he wishes to pursue." Cole knew, at the time he provided the recommendation, that Gadams had been the subject of various parents' complaints, including that he "led a panty raid, made sexual overtures to students, sexual remarks to students." Cole also knew that Gadams had resigned under pressure because of these sexual misconduct charges.

Gadams's last place of employment (1990–1991) before Livingston was Muroc Unified School District, where disciplinary actions were taken against him for sexual harassment. When allegations of "sexual touching" of female students were made, Gadams was forced to resign from Muroc. Nonetheless, Gary Rice and David Malcolm, officials at Muroc, provided a letter of recommendation for Gadams that described him as "an upbeat, enthusiastic administrator who relates well to the students," and who was responsible "in large part," for making Boron Junior High School (located in Muroc) "a safe, orderly and clean environment for students and staff." The letter concluded that they recommended Gadams "for an assistant principalship or equivalent position without reservation."

[38] Id.

[39] *Adapted from* Randi W. v. Muroc Joint Unified School District, *929 P.2d 582 (Cal. 1997).*

All of the letters provided by previous administrators of Gadams were sent in on forms that included a disclosure that the information provided "will be sent to prospective employers."

Through her guardian, Randi W. filed suit against the districts, alleging that her injuries from Gadams's sexual touching were proximately caused by their failure to provide full and accurate information about Gadams to the placement service.

Discussion Questions

1. If you were a former administrator to whom Gadams reported, what kind of recommendation would you give?

2. Should the previous administrators have done something about Gadams prior to being placed in this dilemma?

3. Do administrators owe their loyalty to employees? to students? to the school district? to the parents?

4. Is this type of recommendation commonly given to get rid of employees?

5. Should friendship have a higher value than honesty?

6. Why do you think the administrators said nothing?

READING 4.8

The Ethics of Confrontation[40]

Marianne M. Jennings

I. Introduction

Studying a recent California court decision brought to mind the issue of the ethics of confrontation and the underlying question of why there is such hesitancy to confront truth at appropriate times and take the actions necessary to remedy its consequences. The California case, *Randi W. v. Muroc Unified School District*,[41] involves Robert Gadams, an educational administrator for the junior high/middle school years, who had been accused of improper touching or sexual conduct with students at four schools where he had served as an administrator.

Apparently the principals of the first three schools, the district administrators, and school boards wanted no more than to be rid of him and the confrontation that would be necessary to revoke his certification. Each passed him along to other schools, with glowing letters of recommendation. One former principal wrote that Gadams made his junior high a "safe, orderly and clean environment for students and staff." Another wrote that he would recommend Gadams "for an assistant principalship or equivalent position without reservation."

---

[40] *"The Ethics of Confrontation: The Virtues and Vice in Remaining Silent,"* Corporate Finance Review 6(4): 42–46 (2002). Reprinted from Corporate Finance Review by RIA, 395 Hudson Street, New York, NY 10014.

[41] *929 P.2d 582 (Cal. 1997).*

It was at the fourth school where this problematic administrator perpetrated real harm against a young girl that his history emerged, but only because of litigation filed by her parents.

The case raises the question that is a universal one in business: why is there such a hesitancy to bring to a head evolving problems? Why is there such a fear of confrontation? The reasons are many, as noted in the following sections, but the justifications are few and the benefits virtually nonexistent.

II. Examples in Business of Confrontation Avoidance

While the case that has piqued this discussion is one from the field of education, business with all its respect for the bottom line and performance results, certainly has no dearth of examples of avoiding confrontation until the result is the same messy litigation evident in the *Muroc* case.

One could begin with performance evaluations. Businesses have finally migrated to rankings and grades as a means of evaluating employees and sorting the wheat from the chaff because the nature of evaluation content was grounded in confrontation avoidance. Annual evaluations of marginal employees were often difficult to distinguish from those of stellar performers because managers avoided the confrontation of candid performance reviews with employees, fearing the reaction and possible process of appeals involving everything from company reviews to allegations of discrimination.

However, rather than confront the often messy issues in disparate performance, candid feedback, and justified termination or reprimand, employers have resorted to rankings as a means of annual performance evaluations. For example, Ford Motor Company has 18,000 managers who are grouped into sets of 30–50. Of each group, 10 percent must be assigned an "A" grade, 80 percent must be assigned a "B" grade, and 10 percent must be given a "C" grade. Those with the bottom grades are then eased out of the company. Those with a "C" grade cannot be given a pay raise and those with a "C" grade for two years in a row are demoted or terminated. There are no exceptions made for any of the groups, but Ford did cut back on the "C" requirement to 5 percent for 2001.

The companies hide the issues within a number system. At Sun Microsystems, employees given a "C" are given 90 days to improve. If they do not improve, they are given a chance to resign and take a severance package or risk termination. Cisco Systems has established a goal of getting rid of 1 of every 20 employees with the focus being on employees given substandard performance evaluations. GE has a 20-70-10 plan for ranking employees. GE follows a carrot approach in that it rewards the top 20 percent so well that few ever leave the company. GE uses the 10 percent group to terminate employees, and it terminates about 8,000 management and professional employees each year. Jack Welch has noted that those in the 10 percent would end up leaving the company anyway because they are unhappy in not performing and GE just makes the inevitable decision for them early.[42] While the system may ease the employee hassles, it never really confronts the issues the employees and their supervisors should be grappling with as part of the evaluation. The numbers are a substitute for analysis and feedback, the most painful aspects of performance evaluation.

[42] Del Jones, "More Firms Cut Workers Ranked at the Bottom to Make Way for Talent," *USA Today*, May 30, 2001, pp. 1B, 2B.

In financial performance, employees, managers, and auditors have all been engaged in a well-choreographed ritual of confrontation avoidance. FINOVA, the Phoenix-based company that was once a darling of Wall Street for its double-digit growth and named consistently one of the top ten companies in America to work for, had at least one year of confrontation avoidance over its accounting practices. During that time employees expressed reservations, concern, and even outrage over the company's failure to write down a $70 million loan to a California computer firm (among other issues) and both the concerns and some employees were dismissed. Their managers understood their concerns and many agreed, but they were unwilling to confront senior management over the issues. The auditors were unwilling to do the same until after the company's initial 1999 annual report had gone to press. The result was a public confrontation, a dismissal of the auditors, new auditors and the eventual disclosure of all that the employees and managers had avoided confronting senior managers about.

There are other examples of this financial avoidance that have appeared in these discussions over the past five years: the slippery slope of earnings management; Al Dunlap and the booking of a sale of parts that they are charged with knowing would be reversed once the quarterly earnings goals were met; Joseph Jett, Nick Leeson, and other rogue traders who were not confronted by their managers despite their unrealistic returns to the firms until outsiders demanded such; and the list goes on with every business sharing the common thread of avoiding or postponing confrontation.

III. Why We Avoid Confrontation

The "don't rock the boat" attitude is frequently seen as the virtuous road. Confrontation is messy—there are often hurt feelings. There are embarrassing revelations. There are destroyed careers. There are costs. Whether confrontation involves sexual misconduct by an assistant school principal or cooking the books by a manager or bond trader, the impact is the same.

Human nature flees from such situations. Further, there is within human nature that rationalization that avoiding confrontation is being "nice," and nice is associated with ethics.

There are also the harsh realities of confrontation. To confront the assistant school principal with allegations and carry through with a disciplinary process for the loss of a license to teach is time consuming and reflects on the school and administrators who hired him in the first place. There is exposure to liability.

The same is true with the business scenarios presented. A good employee evaluation means that the employee is happy, there are no reviews, no messy discussions, and no allegations of discrimination. Not confronting a rogue trader means enjoying the ride of their performance and earnings and worrying about consequences at another time when perhaps something else will come along to counterbalance any of their harmful activities. Not insisting that a loan be written down carries with it the comfort of steady growth and earnings and a hope that future financial performance can make up for the loss when it eventually must be disclosed.

There is a great deal of rationalization that goes into the avoidance of confrontation. There is a comfort in maintaining status quo. There is at least a postponement of legal issues and liabilities. Often, avoiding confrontation is a painless road that carries with it the hope that whatever lies beneath does not break through and reveal its ugliness. Often confrontation carries with it the hope that a problem will solve itself or become a moot issue.

IV. The Harms of Avoiding Confrontation

Postponing confrontation does not produce a better result when the issue at the heart of the needed confrontation inevitably emerges. Those harms include liability, individual harms, reputational damage, and the loss of income as the issue chugs along without resolution.

A. Physical Harm

In the *Muroc* case, all of the districts were liable for their failure to take action and then issuing glowing letters of recommendation. Had the issue of sexual misconduct and the assistant principal been confronted the first time there was misconduct, there would not have been the remaining three schools and victims.

B. Loss of Reputation and Income

In FINOVA's case, a $3 billion company can survive the write-down of a $70 million loan. It cannot, as FINOVA's bankruptcy has shown, survive that write-down when the investment community loses trust as the disclosure of the bad loan and its write-down are withheld until there is a confrontation that must necessarily be public because of the change in auditors.

In Joseph Jett's case, there were a number of employees who questioned the earnings Jett was posting in managing the government bonds section of Kidder Peabody. They raised the impossibility of Jett's earnings curve in the bond market. Instead of confronting Jett, the managers continued to enjoy the ride. The longer the ride, the greater the fall-out, and Kidder Peabody was destroyed as a result of the eventual confrontation with Jett's fabricated sales and revenues.[43]

C. Liability Increased

Another example is the eventual confrontation between Ford and Firestone over who and what was responsible for the Ford Explorer debacle and the accidents and deaths. The two companies' longstanding business relationship and an unwillingness to deal with data and questions accomplished little. With more information percolating on a regular basis, both companies acknowledged, even as they battled with each other in a media confrontation, that neither has emerged with its reputation intact in the public eye. Civil litigation and an investigation by the federal government as well as depositions of top executives in the companies were trickled out to the public. Those depositions have had some inconsistencies with some of the public statements by Bridgestone/Firestone.

For example, Bridgestone/Firestone has issued public statements that it was not aware of peeling issues with its tires used on the Ford Explorer. However, a deposition of Firestone's chief of quality reveals that he believes he discussed the issue of the tires with

[43] Sylvia Nasar, "Kidder Scandal Tied to Failure of Supervisors," The New York Times, July 26, 1994, pp. C1, C14.

the company's CEO in 1999, a full year before the issue became public with the resulting recall. David Laubie, who retired from the company in May 2000, said that he handled consumer claims and quality control issues for the company and had received complaints which he passed along to the CEO in memo form as well as in their regular meetings.

In testimony before Congress in September 2000, Firestone's executive vice president, Gary Crigger, testified that the company only became aware of the problem in July or August of 2000.

Another issue in the case has been Firestone's allegation that Ford did not put the proper tire pressure instructions with the Ford Explorer. Firestone said that Ford's recommendation of an unusually low tire pressure, 26 pounds per square inch, caused the sidewalls to flex and get hot, which then weakened the tires. However, both the depositions of Mr. Laubie and the current quality control chief of Firestone indicate that no one from Firestone ever discussed the low tire pressure issue with anyone at Ford.[44] The lack of confrontation before, during, and after the public revelations about some issue, whatever that may prove to be, surrounding the Ford Explorer and its tires, cost both companies in terms of reputation and perhaps liability.

V. The Deceptive Lull of "Being Nice"

One of the faulty assumptions in avoiding confrontation is that the "niceness" benefits the individuals affected. A good performance evaluation is beneficial to the employee. Not taking disciplinary action permits a teacher or administrator to continue his career and earn a living. Not raising a financial reporting issue means that shareholders can continue to enjoy returns and market value. Not questioning an employee's unusual success means that the earnings figures stand unscathed. Many are protected when confrontation is avoided.

The difficulty with the protection argument is that it presumes that the truth will not emerge. When it does, the preservation of a career in light of information introduces greater liability. Termination of an employee for cause may carry with it the difficulties of challenge and even litigation. Not terminating an employee for cause who goes on later to do more harm exposes the company to liability. The difficulty with not disclosing matters that affect earnings is that when those matters do emerge, there is not just the resulting restatement of earnings but the accompanying lack of investor trust and resulting reduction in market value. The greatest harm in avoiding confrontation is that what the confrontation could have minimized is exacerbated by the postponement.

VI. The Ethics of Confrontation

While not widely accepted as a principle of virtue, there is an ethical duty of confrontation. Edmund Burke was a proponent of such a duty with his admonition of two centuries ago, "All that is necessary for evil to triumph is for good men to do nothing." There is the more modern phraseology that holds that if there is a legal or ethical problem in a company and an employee or manager or executive says nothing, they become part of the problem.

---

[44] James R. Healey and Sara Nathan, "Depositions in Tire Lawsuits Don't Match Company's Lines," USA Today, December 11, 2000, p. 3B.

However, one of the reasons for the hesitancy in confrontation not discussed earlier is a certain degree of ineptness on the part of those who must do the confronting. If confrontation is indeed a virtue, are there guides for its exercise? The following offers a model for confrontation.

A. Determine the facts.

An underlying disdain for confrontation arises because too often those who do the confronting are wrong. Prior to confrontation, prepare as if you were working on a budget, a product launch or a financing. Know what is happening or what has happened and obtain as much background information as possible. Preparation also serves as protection for any fears of liability from taking action. Employers need to understand that well-documented personnel actions are not a basis for discrimination suits. And termination of employees who are harming others is not actionable if the harm is established.

B. If you don't know the facts, or can't know the facts, present the issue to those involved and affected.

Ford and Firestone will perhaps not know the issues of liability and accountability for years to come with regard to the Explorer and the tires. However, their lack of information should not have prevented them from confronting each other or confronting the customers and public with the information they did have.

In the case of allegations or when an employee has raised a question about how a particular matter is being carried on the books, you may only be presented with one side. That lack of information need not preclude you from raising the question. In the case of the school administrator, the students made an allegation against the assistant principal. The principal has no way of knowing whether the allegation is true or false, but he can go to the assistant principal and raise the issue and then can proceed with the types of hearings or inquiries that can provide the information or at least constitute the confrontation.

A financial officer can hear from employees a number of views on carrying certain items on the books. The very definition of materiality opens the door to that type of disagreement. But a good financial officer knows that an open discussion of the issue, and confrontation of the issue with those who tout various views, is the solution that serves the company best in the long run. Without such confrontation, the failure to listen to an employee's view exacerbates the eventual fall-out from a bad decision. The public confrontation of the issue is, in and of itself, insurance against the fall-out should that decision prove to be wrong.

C. Always give the opportunity for self-remedy.

One of the reasons confrontation enjoys such universal disdain is that very often the confrontation is done circuitously. If your attorney has done something questionable, confront him or her first and then report them to the state bar for discipline. If an employee has engaged in misconduct, tell them and don't let him or her hear it from someone else. If earnings are overstated, employees should work within the company for self-remedy before heading to the SEC.

One of the virtue constraints in the ethics of confrontation is having the courage to discuss the issues and concerns with those who are involved in creating them. An end run is not a confrontation. It is an act of cowardice that can result in the liability discussed earlier.

D. Don't fear the fall-out and hassle.

The reasons for the lack of confrontation discussed earlier included the realistic observation that many avoid confrontation because it is too much trouble. However, as also noted earlier, if there is a problem that remains unconfronted, it does not improve with age. Indeed, the failure to make a timely confrontation often proves to result in more costs in the long run. Hassles don't dissipate as confrontation is postponed or avoided.

VII. Conclusion

The ethics of confrontation are quite simply that confrontation is a necessary part of managing an honest business. Confrontation openly airs disagreement. Confrontation prevents the damage that comes from concealed truth. Confrontation preserves reputations when it produces the self-remedies that are nearly always cheaper than those imposed from the lack of confrontation. Niceness is rarely the ethical route when issues and facts need to be aired. Confrontation, while not always pleasant, is often the only resolution of a problem.

....

Discussion Questions

1. What are the consequences of the failure to raise an issue, whether legal or ethical, when it first arises?

2. What factors contribute to the failure to confront an issue?

3. What steps could a business take to encourage confrontation?

Taking Advantage

What happens when you have the upper hand when it comes to knowledge and information? Do you have an obligation to share with the other side in your negotiations that they are making incorrect assumptions? Do you let them know that there are downsides to your product? Do you use technology to circumvent privacy and property rights issues? The ethical category of taking unfair advantage is one in which one party has a superior bargaining, knowledge, information, or power position and uses it to cause the other side to lose something in the process. Sometimes parties take advantage of others just by their philanthropic position. Their goodness in cause is used to justify unfairness in treatment.

CASE 4.9
....
Napster: The Ethics of Peer-to-Peer File Sharing

Napster, Inc., a company founded by Shawn Fanning and Sean Parker, operated an online service for "peer-to-peer file sharing" (http://www.napster.com) so that users could, free of charge, download recordings via the Internet through a process known as "ripping," which is the downloading of digital MP3 files. MP3 is the abbreviated term for audio recordings in a digital format known as MPEG-3. This compressed format allows for rapid transmission of digital audio files from one computer to another.[45]

Napster's online service provided a search vehicle for files stored on others' computers and permitted the downloading of the recordings from the hard drives of other Napster users. Napster provided technical support as well as a chat room for users to exchange information. The result, at the time when Napster was originally operating, was that users who registered and had a password through Napster could download single songs and complete CDs or albums, via the peer-to-peer file sharing.

A & M Records and others, including Geffen Records, Sony Music, MCA Records, Atlantic Recording, Motown Records, and Capital Records, are in the business of the commercial recording, distribution, and sale of copyrighted musical compositions and

[45] A & M Records, Inc. v. Napster, Inc., *239 F.3d 1004 (9th Cir. 2001).*

sound recordings. They filed suit against Napster, Inc. (Napster) as a contributory and vicarious copyright infringer. Related copyright suits were filed by Metallica and Andre Young (Dr. Dre). Metallica demanded that Napster deregister its music from its file-sharing service. Dr. Dre indicated, "I don't like people stealing my music," when he was asked about his litigation.[46] Mike Stoller, a songwriter since age 17 whose portfolio includes "Hound Dog," "Jailhouse Rock," and "Love Potion No. 9," also filed suit against Napster and wrote the following in an opinion piece for *The New York Times*:

> I fear for the 17-year-old songwriter looking forward to a career in the music business today. Napster and companies like it are not only threatening my retirement, but the future of music itself. In fact, by taking the incentive out of songwriting, Napster may be pushing itself closer to a time when there won't be any songs for its users to swap.[47]

Professor Paul Kedrosky of the University of British Columbia wrote the following in his call for an injunction shutting down Napster:

> Let's be blunt: Napster-style file sharing is theft. But for some reason commentators don't see it that way. Instead we hear all sorts of tripe about waves of change, the inevitability of the Internet, and so on.
>
> Why do so-called opinion leaders so smirkingly dismiss theft? In a nutshell, it's because aging would-be hipsters are trying to demonstrate their technology bona fides to amoral technologists.
>
> Opinioneers aside, the rest of us should know better. So why don't we treat online music theft the same way we treat offline theft? In part, because it doesn't feel like theft. After all, you're just sitting at home downloading files. It's not as if you slipped a CD from Sam Goody into your coat pocket, then scrambled out the door.
>
> Napster has done little to dissuade people from thinking otherwise. After standing blithely by while millions of dollars in pirated music flowed over its servers. Napster is now insisting that it has a role to play. It has, it insists, market presence and could be a new means of distribution for music. In other words, it is saying, "Just pay us!" Sound familiar? It should. It's a classic shakedown right out of Mafia 101.[48]

The controversy over Napster created fierce media and Congressional battles among and between artists, fans, and music companies. Recording artists and record companies called peer-to-peer file sharing nothing more than copyright infringement. "It's a technology no one anticipated and the law doesn't apply," was the observation of one legal expert. Don Henley, formerly of The Eagles, and Alanis Morissette both testified before Congress that Napster deprived them of their royalty income and their rights in their intellectual property. Members of the rock group Metallica complained that fans who downloaded music via Napster exhibited a lack of morals.

Other artists were busily establishing Internet strategies. Lance Bass, of the teen band 'N Sync, developed strategies for digital music. By participating in teen chat rooms, Bass learns which songs his fans take a liking to and has been selling his songs over the Internet. He makes about $1 per CD sold because the record companies have monopolies on

---

[46] *Holman W. Jenkins, Jr., "Let's Give It Up for Metallica,"* The Wall Street Journal, *May 10, 2000, p. A27.*
[47] *Mike Stoller, "Songs That Won't Be Written,"* The New York Times, *October 7, 2000, p. A29.*
[48] *Paul Kedrosky, "Napster Should Be Playing Jailhouse Rock,"* The Wall Street Journal, *July 31, 2000, p. A32.*

distribution and spend large amounts on marketing. One of the executives for TransContinental Records, the company that has 'N Sync under contract, notes, "An awful lot of established bands out there are looking at their digital strategy and looking at record companies and saying, 'Why do I need you?'"[49]

Others noted that if Napster were liable under the law for the downloading, so also were the phone companies and cable companies that furnish the lines that permit Internet access and the resulting downloading of the music. And the Napster users' arguments could be summed up as one *Time* magazine reader wrote, "Using Napster is like inviting 100,000 friends over for *Monday Night Football*—not what the network intended, but not illegal." In an interview with *The New York Times Magazine*, Mr. Fanning said, "Thirty-seven million users can't all be criminals."[50]

The Recording Industry Association of America (RIAA) began tracing the origins of file-sharing sites and tipped off law enforcement authorities. A number of 18- and 19-year-old freshmen around the country were arrested in their dorm rooms as they facilitated music downloading.[51]

As the controversy over the file-sharing/infringement issues continued, Napster began to experience some issues with its logo. File sharers were downloading and copying the Napster logo and it was even showing up on t-shirts. Napster filed suit against those using the trademark without authorization for infringement, seeking an injunction as well as damages.

When the record companies filed suit against Napster, the district court granted a preliminary injunction to the plaintiffs enjoining Napster from "engaging in, or facilitating others in copying, downloading, uploading, transmitting, or distributing plaintiffs' copyrighted musical compositions and sound recordings, protected by either federal or state law, without express permission of the rights owner."[52]

The federal court of appeals for the ninth circuit entered a temporary stay of the injunction to review the case. Both the trial court and the appellate court struggled with the issues of what Napster was and what it actually allowed computer users to do and whether it was a violation of the law or simply a question of ethics.

The evidence at the trial showed that a majority of Napster users used the service to download and upload copyrighted music. Napster users also uploaded file names to the search index so that others could make copies of the same music once they had gone to the trouble of downloading the various songs.

Napster owner Shawn Fanning, who was 18 at the time he created the Napster technology, and his lawyer, David Boies (who represented the Justice Department in its litigation against Microsoft, and former vice president Albert Gore, Jr. in his litigation over the Florida recounts) argued that Napster users did not directly infringe plaintiffs' copyrights because the users were engaged in fair use of the material. They identified three specific alleged fair uses: sampling, where users made temporary copies of a work before purchasing (using the service to listen to a song before purchasing the CD);

---

[49] Amy Kover, "Digital Artists Want Control," Fortune, June 26, 2000, p. 134.
[50] David D. Kirkpatrick, "Napster," The New York Times Magazine, June 10, 2001, p. 73.
[51] Jenny Eliscu, "Freshman Busted for MP3 Piracy," Rolling Stone, November 9, 2000, p. 33.
[52] 114 F. Supp.2d 896 (N.D. Cal. 2000).

space-shifting, where users accessed a sound recording through the Napster system that they already owned in audio CD format (they owned the Beatles' White Album in record, tape, or CD form and wanted it in MP3 technology); and permissive distribution of recordings by both new and established artists (artists permitting the downloading of their songs and performances).

However, the evidence at the trial showed that permissive uses were the exception and not the rule and that there were repeated and exploitative unauthorized copies of copyrighted works made, for the most part, to save the expense of purchasing authorized copies.

The federal copyright laws do permit "fair use" of copyrighted materials. Fair use, when properly applied, is limited to copying by others that does not materially impair the marketability of the work which is copied. The evidence at the district court level showed that a service like Napster harms the market in "at least" two ways: it reduces audio CD sales among college students and it "raises barriers to plaintiffs' entry into the market for the digital downloading of music."[53]

However, Napster did present evidence from its own expert, Dr. Peter S. Fader, who concluded in his report that Napster was beneficial to the music industry because MP3 music file-sharing stimulated more audio CD sales than it displaced. However, the trial court judge dismissed most of Dr. Fader's report because Dr. Fader played a minimal role in overseeing the administration of the survey and there was a general lack of objective data in his report.

The district court also found that both the market for audio CDs and the market for online distribution were adversely affected by Napster's service. Once a user listed a copy of music he or she already owned on the Napster system in order to access the music from another location, the song became "available to millions of other individuals," not just the original CD owner.

Napster argued that it could not be held liable for copyright infringement because it was not participating in the downloading and could not supervise the use of its system. However, the court ruled that Napster knew how its system was being used even if it was not aware of each specific instance. In fact, Napster's founders were aware of their vulnerability. During the proceedings in district court, the music companies proffered a document authored by Napster co-founder Sean Parker that mentioned "the need to remain ignorant of users' real names and IP addresses 'since they are exchanging pirated music'"; and the RIAA had informed Napster of more than 12,000 infringing files, some of which were still available.

Napster was eventually shut down by the federal court. Several interim steps were taken as the companies tried to get their songs de-registered. Any slight difference in title spelling or phrasing meant users could circumvent the blocks. However, the German record company BMG purchased Napster and has begun doing marketing surveys of former Napster users to determine how much they would be willing to pay for subscription services to copyrighted music.

New platforms and means for sharing music have developed since the time of the Napster litigation. Grokster and Morpheus are defendants in a lawsuit that a federal

---

[53] 114 F. Supp.2d 896, 911.

appellate court recently ruled could appropriately be tried in the United States even though the two services are located outside the United States. Courts reached a similar conclusion on Kazaa.

The RIAA has begun an aggressive enforcement policy of filing suit against those who are engaged in significant amounts of downloading. These individual suits have resulted in settlements. In some cases, the RIAA is only able to track the user name of the person who is engaged in the downloading. The RIAA has gone to court to require Internet service providers to disclose the users' names. In one case, Verizon, a telecommunications company, was ordered to turn over to music companies the name of one of its customers because the customer was making copyrighted music available on the Internet to other users. Verizon had resisted turning over the name because it alleged that it was not involved in the sharing of the music, that it was peer-to-peer file sharing and not a service on its network. The RIAA indicated that the subscriber whose name it sought had shared 600 songs online with others. Attorneys for Verizon argued that there was a breach of privacy through the required release because it opened up the prospect of Internet service providers reading and reviewing private e-mails.[54]

While the litigation against the file sharers is ongoing, colleges and universities are trying to find solutions because of their potential liability when students use their Internet services to download music. Penn State University has negotiated a deal with the revised online Napster to pay for the right for its students to download music. The deal is a first and was negotiated, the president of Penn State indicates, because the students told him how important downloading music is to them.

Under the deal, students have unlimited rights to listen to music on up to three personal computers as long as they are still students at Penn State. If they want to download the songs, it will cost $0.99 per song. The university will pay for the Napster service out of the $160 technology fee the students pay each year. The university did not reveal how much it was paying per student, but indicated that it was "substantially less" than the $9.95 Napster charges for each individual subscription.

The service was made available first to 18,000 students in campus residences, followed by gradual extension to the university's 83,000 graduate and undergraduate students. All students were covered by the fall of 2004.[55]

Discussion Questions

1. Do you think that downloading the music was legal? Do you think it was ethical?

2. Why do some use the term *peer-to-peer file sharing* while others refer to the downloading as theft?

3. Congress passed the Digital Millennium Copyright Act of 1998, an act that prohibited the circumvention of encryption devices on copyrighted materials in order to make copies. The DMCA also held those who provided the means, such as software programs, for circumvention

[54] Anna Wilde Mathews, "Judge Orders Verizon to Name Song-Swapper," The Wall Street Journal, January 22, 2003, pp. B1, B5; Jefferson Graham, "Judge Orders Verizon to Name Pirate," USA Today, January 22, 2003, p. 1B.

[55] Amy Harmon, "Penn State Will Pay To Allow Students To Download Music," The New York Times, November 7, 2003, pp. A1, A16.

of encryption devices liable for copyright infringement. Further, those who provide server access, such as colleges and universities, are required to do periodic checks to verify that their systems are not being used for such circumvention. What are these complex laws attempting to do?

4. What is the difference between downloading and theft?

5. Must morals and ethics change because technology has made things so different?

6. What happens if there are no protections for intellectual property?

7. Hilary Rosen, the CEO of RIAA, said the following in an interview with *USA Today*, "The Napster battle was classic. People took their free music really seriously. It was amazing how strongly people felt about their principled right to someone else's property."[56] What does her statement reflect in terms of her ethical values? About those of the downloaders?

8. When Mr. Fanning discovered that his Napster logo had been placed on t-shirts and was being sold by another entrepreneur for a profit, he sought to stop the t-shirt sales. What ethical model from Unit 1 offers a rich irony in his actions?

9. You do not download music from the Internet unless you pay the fees for the songs. However, your roommate, child, or partner is not as committed as you are to avoiding copyright infringement. Their explanation? "It's just file sharing! A little P2P. It doesn't really hurt anyone, so could I use your computer? I know you don't do it, but there's nothing to stop me. I don't feel guilty about it." You would really like to keep the peace between you, and it seems like a small thing. What would you do? How can you approach the issue?

CASE 4.10
Nestlé Infant Formula

While the merits and problems of breast-feeding versus using infant formula are debated in the United States and other developed countries, the issue is not so balanced in third world nations. Studies have demonstrated the difficulties and risks of bottle-feeding babies in such places.

First, refrigeration is not generally available, so the formula, once it is mixed or opened (in the case of premixed types), cannot be stored properly. Second, the lack of purified water for mixing with the formula powder results in diarrhea or other diseases in formula-fed infants. Third, inadequate education and income, along with cultural differences, often lead to the dilution of formula and thus greatly reduced nutrition.

Medical studies also suggest that regardless of the mother's nourishment, sanitation, and income level, an infant can be adequately nourished through breast-feeding.

In spite of medical concerns about using their products in these countries, some infant formula manufacturers heavily promoted bottle-feeding.

These promotions, which went largely unchecked through 1970, included billboards, radio jingles, and posters of healthy, happy infants, as well as baby books and formula samples distributed through the health care systems of various countries.

[56] *"Rosen Weighs in on Napster, Lyrics—and Her CDs," USA Today, May 2, 2001, p. 3D.*

Also, some firms used "milk nurses" as part of their promotions. Dressed in nurse uniforms, "milk nurses" were assigned to maternity wards by their companies and paid commissions to get new mothers to feed their babies formula. Mothers who did so soon discovered that lactation could not be achieved and the commitment to bottle-feeding was irreversible.

In the early 1970s, physicians working in nations where milk nurses were used began vocalizing their concerns. For example, Dr. Derrick Jelliffe, the then-director of the Caribbean Food and Nutrition Institute, had the Protein-Calorie Advisory Group of the United Nations place infant formula promotion methods on its agenda for several of its meetings.

Journalist Mike Muller first brought the issue to public awareness with a series of articles in the *New Internationalist* in the 1970s. He also wrote a pamphlet on the promotion of infant formulas called "The Baby Killer," which was published by a British charity, War on Want. The same pamphlet was published in Switzerland, the headquarters of Nestlé, a major formula maker, under the title "Nestlé Kills Babies." Nestlé sued in 1975, which resulted in extensive media coverage.

In response to the bad publicity, manufacturers of infant formula representing about 75 percent of the market formed the International Council of Infant Food Industries to establish standards for infant formula marketing. The new code banned the milk nurse commissions and required the milk nurses to have identification that would eliminate confusion about their "nurse" status.

The code failed to curb advertising of formulas. In fact, distribution of samples increased. By 1977, groups in the United States began a boycott against formula makers over what Jelliffe called "comerciogenic malnutrition."

One U.S. group, Infant Formula Action Coalition (INFACT), worked with the staff of Senator Edward Kennedy of Massachusetts to have hearings on the issue by the Senate Subcommittee on Health and Human Resources, which Kennedy chaired. The hearings produced evidence that 40 percent of the worldwide market for infant formula, which totaled $1.5 billion at the time, was in third world countries. No regulations resulted, but Congress did tie certain forms of foreign aid to the development by recipient countries of programs to encourage breast-feeding.

Boycotts against Nestlé products began in Switzerland in 1975 and in the United States in 1977. The boycotts and Senator Kennedy's involvement heightened media interest in the issue and led to the World Health Organization (WHO) debating the issue of infant formula marketing in 1979 and agreeing to draft a code to govern it.

After four drafts and two presidential administrations (Carter and Reagan), the 118 member nations of WHO finally voted on a code for infant formula marketing. The United States was the only nation to vote against it; the Reagan administration opposed the code being mandatory. In the end, WHO made the code a recommendation only, but the United States still refused to support it.

The publicity on the vote fueled the boycott of Nestlé, which continued until the formula maker announced it would meet the WHO standards for infant formula marketing. Nestlé created the Nestlé Infant Formula Audit Commission (NIFAC) to demonstrate its commitment to and ensure its implementation of the WHO code.

In 1988, Nestlé introduced a new infant formula, Good Start, through its subsidiary, Carnation. The industry leader, Abbott Laboratories, which held 54 percent of the market with its Similac brand, revealed Carnation's affiliation: "They are Nestlé," said Robert A. Schoellhorn, Abbott's chairman and CEO.[57] Schoellhorn also disclosed that Nestlé was the owner of Beech-Nut Nutrition Corporation, officers of which had been indicted and convicted (later reversed) for selling adulterated apple juice for babies.[58]

Carnation advertised Good Start in magazines and on television. The American Academy of Pediatrics (AAP) objected to this direct advertising, and grocers feared boycotts.

The letters "H.A." came after the name "Good Start," indicating the formula was hypoallergenic. Touted as a medical breakthrough by Carnation, the formula was made from whey and advertised as ideal for babies who were colicky or could not tolerate milk-based formulas.

Within four months of Good Start's introduction in November 1988, the FDA was investigating the formula because of six reported cases of vomiting due to the formula. Carnation then agreed not to label the formula hypoallergenic and to include a warning that milk-allergic babies should be given Good Start only with a doctor's approval and supervision.

In 1990, with its infant formula market share at 2.8 percent, Carnation's president, Timm F. Crull, called on the AAP to "examine all marketing practices that might hinder breast-feeding."[59] Crull specifically cited manufacturers' practices of giving hospitals education and research grants, as well as free bottles, in exchange for having exclusive rights to supply the hospital with formula and to give free samples to mothers. He also called for scrutiny of the practice of paying pediatricians' expenses to attend conferences on infant formulas.

The AAP looked into prohibiting direct marketing of formula to mothers and physicians' accepting cash awards for research from formula manufacturers.

The distribution of samples in third world countries continued during this time. Studies by the United Nations Children's Fund found that a million infants were dying every year because they were not breast-fed adequately. In many cases, the infant starved because the mother used free formula samples and could not buy more, while her own milk dried up. In 1991, the International Association of Infant Food Manufacturers agreed to stop distributing infant formula samples by the end of 1992.

In the United States in 1980, the surgeon general established a goal that the nation's breast-feeding rate be 75 percent by 1990. The rate remains below 60 percent, however, despite overwhelming evidence that breast milk reduces susceptibility to illness, especially ear infections and gastrointestinal illnesses. The AAP took a strong position that infant formula makers should not advertise to the public but, as a result, new entrants into the market (such as Nestlé with its Carnation Good Start) were disadvantaged because long-time formula makers Abbott and Mead Johnson were well-established

---

[57] Rick Reiff, "Baby Bottle Battle," Forbes, November 28, 1988, pp. 222–224.
[58] For details of the apple juice case, see Case 5.16.
[59] Julia F. Siler and D. Woodruff, "The Furor over Formula Is Coming to a Boil," Business Week, April 9, 1990, pp. 52–53.

through physicians. In 1993, Nestlé filed an antitrust suit alleging a conspiracy among AAP, Abbott, and Mead Johnson.

Some 200 U.S. hospitals have voluntarily stopped distributing discharge packs from formula makers to their maternity patients because they felt it "important not to appear to be endorsing any products or acting as commercial agents."[60] A study at Boston City Hospital showed that mothers who receive discharge packs are less likely to continue nursing, if they nurse at all. UNICEF and WHO offer "Baby Friendly" certification to maternity wards that take steps to eliminate discharge packs and formula samples.

Discussion Questions

1. If you had been an executive with Nestlé, would you have changed your marketing approach after the boycotts began?

2. Did Nestlé suffer long-term damage because of its third world marketing techniques?

3. How could a marketing plan address the concerns of the AAP and WHO?

4. Is anyone in the infant formula companies morally responsible for the deaths of infants described in the United Nations study?

5. Is the moratorium on distributing free formula samples voluntary? Would your company comply?

6. If you were a hospital administrator, what policy would you adopt on discharge packs?

7. Should formula makers advertise directly to the public? What if their ads read, "Remember, breast is best"?

Sources

"Breast Milk for the World's Babies," *The New York Times*, March 12, 1992, p. A18.

Burton, Thomas B., "Methods of Marketing Infant Formula Land Abbott in Hot Water," *The Wall Street Journal*, May 25, 1993, pp. A1, A6.

Freedman, Alix M., "Nestlé's Bid to Crash Baby-Formula Market in the U.S. Stirs a Row," *The Wall Street Journal*, February 6, 1989, pp. A1, A10.

Garland, Susan B., "Are Formula Makers Putting the Squeeze on the States?" *Business Week*, June 18, 1990, p. 31.

Meier, Barry, "Battle over the Market for Baby Formula," *The New York Times*, June 15, 1993, pp. C1, C15.

"Nestlé Unit Sues Baby Formula Firms, Alleging Conspiracy with Pediatricians," *The Wall Street Journal*, June 1, 1993, p. B4.

[60] Andrea Gerlin, "Hospitals Wean from Formula Makers' Freebies," The Wall Street Journal, *December 29, 1994.*

Post, James E., "Assessing the Nestlé Boycott: Corporate Accountability and Human Rights," *California Management Review* 27, 1985, pp. 113–131.

Star, Marlene G., "Breast Is Best," *Vegetarian Times*, June 1991, pp. 25–26.

"What's in a Name?" *Time*, March 29, 1989, p. 58.

Individual Rights and the Business Organization

"Good intentions are not a substitute for good actions."
MARIANNE JENNINGS

IN THIS SECTION, THE FOCUS MOVES FROM how the individual treats the organization to how the organization treats the individual. How much privacy should employees have? What pre-employment tests and screening are appropriate? What obligations does an employer have with respect to the workplace atmosphere? Should employees have job security? The conflicts between employers and their employees' rights take many forms.

5ᴬ

Corporate Due Process

Should fairness be a criterion in employer decisions? Must employers provide a forum
for employee grievances?

CASE 5.1

Ann Hopkins, Price Waterhouse, and the Partnership

Ann Hopkins was a senior manager in the Management Advisory Services division of
the Price Waterhouse Office of Government Services in Washington, D.C. After
earning undergraduate and graduate degrees in mathematics, she taught mathematics at her alma mater, Hollins College, and worked for IBM, NASA, Touche Ross,
and American Management Systems before beginning her career with Price
Waterhouse in 1977.[1] She became the firm's specialist in large-scale computer system
design and operations for the federal government. While salaries in the accounting
profession are not published, estimates put her salary as a senior manager at about
$65,000. By 1982, she had been proposed as a candidate for partnership along with
eighty-eight other Price Waterhouse employees. Estimates of the increase in salary
were that she would earn almost double, or $125,000 annually, on average (1980
figures).

At that time, Price Waterhouse was a nationwide professional accounting partnership. A senior manager became a candidate for partnership when the partners in her
office submitted her name for partnership status.

In 1982, Price Waterhouse had 662 partners, 7 of whom were women. Hopkins was
responsible for bringing to Price Waterhouse a two-year, $25 million contract with the
Department of State.

All of the firm's partners were invited to submit written comments regarding each
candidate on either "long" or "short" evaluation forms. Partners chose a form
according to their exposure to the candidate. All partners were invited to submit

[1] There are conflicting reports on her starting date at Price Waterhouse. Some reports indicate 1977 and some indicate
1978.

comments, but not every partner did so. Of the thirty-two partners who submitted comments on Hopkins, one stated that "none of the other partnership candidates at Price Waterhouse that year [has] a comparable record in terms of successfully procuring major contracts for the partnership."[2]

Her billable hours were 2,442 in 1982 and 2,507 in 1981, amounts that none of the other partnership candidates' billable hours even approached.

After reviewing the comments, the firm's Admissions Committee made recommendations about the partnership candidates to the Price Waterhouse Policy Board. The recommendations consisted of accepting the candidate, denying the promotion, or putting the application on hold. The Policy Board then decided whether to submit the candidate to a vote, reject the candidate, or hold the candidacy.

There were no limits on the number of persons to whom partnership could be awarded and no guidelines for evaluating positive and negative comments about candidates. Price Waterhouse offered forty-seven partnerships to the eighty-eight candidates who had been nominated, another twenty-seven were denied partnerships, and twenty, including Ms. Hopkins, were put on hold. Ms. Hopkins had received more "no" votes than any other candidate for partnership, with most of those votes coming from members of the partnership committee outside the firm's government services unit.

Of the eighty-eight candidates for partnership in 1982, Hopkins was the only woman. Thirteen of the thirty-two partners who submitted comments on Hopkins supported her; three recommended putting her on hold; eight said they did not have enough information; and eight recommended denial.

The partners in Hopkins' office praised her character as well as her accomplishments, describing her in their joint statement as "an outstanding professional" who had a "deft touch," a "strong character, independence, and integrity." Clients appear to have agreed with these assessments. One official from the State Department described her as "extremely competent, intelligent," "strong and forthright, very productive, energetic, and creative." Another high-ranking official praised Hopkins' decisiveness, broadmindedness, and "intellectual clarity"; she was, in his words, "a stimulating conversationalist."[3] Hopkins "had no difficulty dealing with clients and her clients appear to have been very pleased with her work."[4] She "was generally viewed as a highly competent project leader who worked long hours, pushed vigorously to meet deadlines, and demanded much from the multidisciplinary staffs with which she worked."[5]

On too many occasions, however, Hopkins' aggressiveness apparently spilled over into abrasiveness. Staff members seem to have borne the brunt of Hopkins' brusqueness. Long before her bid for partnership, partners evaluating her work had counseled her to improve her relations with staff members. Although later evaluations indicate an improvement, Hopkins' perceived shortcomings in this important area eventually doomed her bid for partnership. Virtually all of the partners' negative remarks about Hopkins—even those of partners who supported her—concerned her "interpersonal skills." Both "[s]upporters and opponents of her candidacy indicated that she was

---

[2] Price Waterhouse v. Hopkins, *490 U.S. 228 (1989)*.

[3] Price Waterhouse v. Hopkins, *490 U.S. 228 (1989), at 234*.

[4] Id.

[5] Id.

sometimes overly aggressive, unduly harsh, difficult to work with, and impatient with staff."[6]

Another partner testified at trial that he had questioned her billing records and was left with concern because he found her answers unsatisfying:

> I was informed by Ann that the project had been completed on sked within budget. My subsequent review indicated a significant discrepancy of approximately $35,000 between the proposed fees, billed fees [and] actuals in the WIPS. I discussed this matter with Ann who attempted to try and explain away or play down the discrepancy. She insisted there had not been a discrepancy in the amount of the underrealization. Unsatisfied with her responses, I continued to question the matter until she admitted there was a problem but I should discuss it with Krulwich [A partner at OGS]. My subsequent discussion with Lew indicated that the discrepancy was a result of 500 additional hours being charged to the job (at the request of Bill Devaney . . . agreed to by Krulwich) after it was determined that Linda Pegues, a senior consultant from the Houston office working on the project had been instructed by Ann to work 12–14 hrs per day during the project but only to charge 8 hours per day. The entire incident left me questioning Ann's staff management methods and the honesty of her responses to my questions.[7]

All of the partners' comments from the partnership deliberations were attached to the parties' filings in the case.

Clear signs indicated, though, that some of the partners reacted negatively to Hopkins' personality because she was a woman. One partner described her as "macho," while another suggested that she "overcompensated for being a woman"; a third advised her to take "a course at charm school."[8] Several partners criticized her use of profanity. In response, one partner suggested that those partners objected to her swearing only "because it[']s a lady using foul language."[9] Another supporter explained that Hopkins "ha[d] matured from a tough-talking somewhat masculine hardnosed manager to an authoritative, formidable, but much more appealing lady partner candidate."[10] In order for Hopkins to improve her chances for partnership, Thomas Beyer, a partner, suggested that she "walk more femininely, talk more femininely, dress more femininely, wear make-up, have her hair styled, and wear jewelry."[11] Ms. Hopkins said she could not apply makeup because that would require removing her trifocals and she would not be able to see. Also, her allergy to cosmetics made it difficult for her to find appropriate makeup. Mr. Beyer also suggested that she should not carry a briefcase, should stop smoking, and should not drink beer at luncheon meetings.

Dr. Susan Fiske, a social psychologist and associate professor of psychology at Carnegie-Mellon University, reviewed the Price Waterhouse selection process and concluded that it was likely influenced by sex stereotyping. Dr. Fiske indicated that some of the partners' comments were gender-biased, while others that were gender-neutral were intensely critical and made by partners who barely knew Hopkins.

[6] Price Waterhouse v. Hopkins, *490 U.S. 228 (1989)*, at 235.
[7] *Appelant's brief*, Price Waterhouse v. Hopkins, *490 U.S. 228 (1989)*.
[8] Price Waterhouse v. Hopkins, *490 U.S. 228 (1989)*, at 235.
[9] Id.
[10] Id.
[11] Id.

Dr. Fiske concluded that the subjectivity of the evaluations and their sharply critical nature were probably the result of sex-stereotyping.[12]

However, there were numerous comments such as the following that voiced concerns about nongender issues:

> In July/Aug 82 Ann assisted the St. Louis MAS practice in preparing an extensive proposal to the Farmers Home Admin (the proposal inc 2800 pgs for $3.1 mil in fees/expenses & 65,000 hrs of work). The proposal was completed over a 4 wk period with approx 2000 plus staff/ptr hrs required based on my participation in the proposal effort & sub discussions with St. L MAS staff involved. Ann's mgmt style of using to trial & error techniques" (ie, sending staff assigned off to prepare portions of the proposal with little or -no guidance from her & then her subsequent rejection of the products developed) caused a complete alienation of the staff towards Ann & a fear that they would have to work with Ann if we won the project. In addition, Ann's manner of dealing with our staff & with the Houston sr consultant on the BIA project, raises questions in my mind about her ability to develop & motivate our staff as a ptr. (No) [indicates partner's vote][13]

> I worked with Ann in the early stages of the Ist State Whelan Dept proposal. I found her to be a) singularly dedicated. b) rather unpleasant. I wonder whether her 4 yrs with us have really demonstrated ptr qualities or whether we have simply taken advantage of "workaholic" tendencies. Note that she has held 6 jobs in the last 15 yrs, all with outstanding companies. I'm also troubled about her being (having been) married to a ptr of a serious competitor.[14] (Insuff—but favor hold. at a minimum)

> Ann's exposure to me was on the Farmers Home Admin Blythe proposal. Despite many negative comments from other people involved I think she did a great job and turned out a first class proposal. Great intellectual capacity but very abrasive in her dealings with staff. I suggest we hold, counsel her and if she makes progress with her interpersonal skills, then admit next year. (Hold)[15]

Although Hopkins and nineteen others were put on hold for the following year, her future looked dim. Later, two partners withdrew their support for Hopkins, and she was informed that she would not be reconsidered the following year. Hopkins then resigned.[16]

Ms. Hopkins, who litigated the Price Waterhouse denial of her partnership as a violation of Title VII of the Civil Rights Act of 1964 (which prohibits discrimination in employment practices), has stated she filed the suit to find out why Price Waterhouse made "such a bad business decision."[17] She did not learn of the partners' comments until discovery during the case. The Supreme Court found for Ms. Hopkins. In 1990, on remand, Ms. Hopkins was awarded her partnership[18] and $350,000 in damages.

---

[12] Cynthia Cohen, "Perils of Partnership Reviews: Lessons from Price Waterhouse v. Hopkins," Labor Law Journal, October 1991, pp. 677–682.

[13] Price Waterhouse v. Hopkins, 490 U.S. 228 (1989).

[14] Ms. Hopkins left Deloitte Touche when her husband was made a partner there and firm policy prohibited partners' spouses from working for the company.

[15] Price Waterhouse v. Hopkins, 490 U.S. 228 (1989).

[16] Id., p. 233.

[17] Interview with Ann Hopkins, June 18, 1993.

[18] Technically, Ms. Hopkins was made a principal, a title reserved for those reaching partner status who do not hold CPA licenses.

Today at Price Waterhouse offices in Washington, D.C., 44 percent of the professional staff are women and 22 percent are minorities.[19] In accounting firms generally, the number of female principals has grown from 1 percent in 1983 to 18 percent today. Ms. Hopkins became a partner at Price Waterhouse following her U.S. Supreme Court victory.

Discussion Questions

1. What ethical problems do you see with the Price Waterhouse partnership evaluation system?

2. Suppose that you were a partner and a member of either the Admissions Committee or the Policy Board. What objections, if any, would you have made to any of the comments by the partners? What would have made it difficult for you to object? How might your being a female partner in that position have made objection more difficult?

3. In what ways, if any, do you find the subjectivity of the evaluation troublesome? What aspects of the evaluation would you change?

4. To what extent did the partners' comments reflect mixed motives (i.e., to what extent did their points express legal factors while others expressed illegal ones)?

5. Ms. Hopkins listed three factors to help companies avoid what happened to her: (a) clear direction from the top of the enterprise, (b) diversity in management, and (c) specificity in evaluation criteria. Give examples of how a company could implement these factors.

---

[19] "More Women Become Partners in Accounting," The Wall Street Journal, August 10, 1993, p. B1.

Employee Screening

What can an employer do to check an employee's background, personality, and potential? How do we know such tests are accurate? Could they destroy opportunities?

CASE 5.2

Post-9/11 Security Screening

The post-9/11 world has had its impact on employers. Companies are now screening their current and prospective employees far more carefully, digging deep into their pasts, and virtually eliminating anyone with any type of criminal conviction.

For example, Eli Lilly terminated a 46-year-old employee when its post-terrorist-attack employment checks revealed that she had been found guilty of check deception, a misdemeanor. The employee, Kimberly Kelly, had bounced a $60 check, and when the appliance company to which she had written the check couldn't find her, it went forward with criminal charges. She was fined $179 for court costs and fees and ordered to pay the $60 plus interest.

Eli Lilly has required background checks of the 7,000 employees of its outside vendors and has refused continuing employment if the vendor employees refuse to consent to the new background checks. By March 2002, over 100 workers had been terminated, either through lack of consent or because of information uncovered in the background check.

Unions for the employees are protesting, but an Eli Lilly spokesperson says it must do the checks to protect its employees, its assets, and its products. Eli Lilly has indicated that despite union allegations, it has been consistent in its application of the checks to all employees and that it only began the checks with outside vendor employees because it saw that as a high-risk pool inasmuch as it had no hiring control over them. Most of the terminations are for crimes such as battery and assault and financial fraud, the areas security experts see as most likely to spawn terrorist participation.

There have been some mishaps, such as cases of mistaken identity. There have also been some reversals of automatic termination for criminal convictions where the employees have been able to demonstrate significant change as well as time lapsed.[20]

Discussion Questions

1. What are the rights of employers with regard to termination for cause? Without cause?

2. Could there be discrimination in such background checks?

3. Would employers be liable for the failure to conduct such background checks?

4. What values are in conflict?

5. Which value should trump the other?

---

[20] Ann Davis, "Employers Dig Deep Into Workers' Pasts, Citing Terrorism Fears," The Wall Street Journal, March 12, 2002, pp. A1, A12.

5c

Employee Privacy

Does a line separate my private life from my employment? How much can I be watched at work? Are mandatory drug tests a violation of my privacy or necessary for safety in my field?

CASE 5.3

Employee and Technology Privacy: Is the Boss Spying?

Technology has permitted employees to work more quickly, efficiently, and even from home as telecommuting has become an option for many companies and their employees. The interesting dichotomy is that while technology makes employees' work much easier, it also provides tracking for employers of virtually everything employees do while at work. One company posted this motto, "In God we trust. All others we monitor." Following are the various forms of technology and their use in the workplace. In each of these forms of technology there are issues of employees' privacy and rights as well as employers' rights with regard to business property and employees' use of time.

Surveillance by Employers

Internal theft, liability for harm to customers, the need to ensure good driving records, and customer service are a few of the reasons businesses give for keeping a secret eye on employees.[21] From the well-known secret shoppers of the retail industry to phone company monitoring of operator performance, employers gather data on employee performance and wrongdoing.

Safeway Stores, Inc., a large multistore grocery chain, has dashboard computers in its 782 delivery trucks. The computers monitor speed, oil pressure, engine RPMs and idling, and the length of stops. Safeway touts the program for its efficacy with regard to driver safety and truck maintenance.

---

[21] Christina E. Garza, "The Touchy Ethics of Corporate Anthropology," *Business Week, September 30, 1991, p. 78.*

In other businesses, high-tech developments enable employers to eavesdrop on employees' telephone and office conversations, while small cameras monitor employee work habits and behavior through pinholes in office walls.[22]

The electronic surveillance of phone conversations has increased as employers seek to monitor productivity, accuracy, and courtesy. Such monitoring is permissible if the monitored party (the employee) consents. Legislation proposed at the state level would require employers to sound a beeping tone when monitoring begins to alert the employee under observation. But an AT&T official notes that employers need the ability to monitor without notice: "Factory supervisors don't blow whistles to warn assembly-line workers they're coming."[23]

In contrast, Barbara Otto, the director of *9 to 5*, a national association of working women, maintains that monitoring affects personal calls: "Employers start catching non-work-related information. They discover that employees are spending weekends with a person of the same sex or talking about forming a union."[24]

The American Civil Liberties Union objects to monitoring because of the current lack of required notice and also because employees lack access to the information employers gather about them via electronic means.

The Internet at Work and Employee Privacy

How employees use their computers and online access at work is a subject of much study as well as surveillance by employers. Vault.com conducted a survey of workers and asked how they use the Internet at work for non-work-related activity and found the following:[25]

News reading	72%
Travel arrangements	45%
Shopping	40%
Job searching	37%
Special interests (hobbies)	37%
Stock-checking	34%
Planning social events	28%
Instant messaging	26%
Music downloads	13%
Games	11%
Chatting	9%
Pornography	4%

Employers have software that enables them to see which Web sites employees have visited, when they visited, and how long they stayed there. Many employers have been issuing reports that indicate which employees are spending large amounts of time

---

[22] Jeffrey Rothfeder, et al., "Is Your Boss Spying on You?" Business Week, January 15, 1990, pp. 74–75.

[23] Richard Lacayo, "Nowhere to Hide," Time, November 11, 1991, p. 34.

[24] Id., p. 39.

[25] Alan Cohen, "Worker Watchers," Fortune, Summer 2001 (special issue Fortune/CNET Technology Review), p. 70.

surfing the net. One employer warned an employee about too much online shopping during working hours and then blocked the sites so that the employee could not access them.

While employees are concerned about privacy, employers are concerned about productivity and the fact that downloading music, for example, can result in the employer's network jamming. Also, employers are concerned that the types of sites being visited, such as pornographic sites, may result in liability for the employer for an atmosphere of harassment.[26] A recent survey sponsored by the Ethics Officer Association provides insight into employee Internet use and employer monitoring of that use.[27] Employers have been concerned about such use because one estimate is that if 50 employees spend 3 hours per week on recreational surfing during work hours the cost per week to a company is $3,322.50.[28] And the latest survey indicates that employees spend about 2 hours per day surfing the net.

The same Vault.com survey found that 90 percent of all employees surf the net during work hours for things unrelated to their jobs and 37 percent have used their computers at work to access the Internet to look for another job. About 13 percent say that they spend two or more hours per working day surfing the net for things unrelated to their jobs. However, 53 percent say that they limit their nonwork Internet access to 30 minutes per working day.[29]

There are also companies that will police for employers new employees' use of the Internet. Websense, Inc. serves this function for 12,000 companies, including 239 of the Fortune 500. The cost is approximately $15 per employee per year.

E-Mail and Employee Privacy

Other issues of employee privacy center around electronic mail systems. Electronic mail (e-mail) systems enable employees to communicate and interact by typing messages on their personal computers. E-mail is often described as a cross between a telephone conversation and a memo. The result is a means of communication, more casual than a memo, that allows users to relax and say more. On the other hand, unlike a telephone conversation, e-mail produces a written record of often casual conversations.

E-mail use by employees is prevalent, as the following results from a United Kingdom survey indicate:

38 percent have used employer e-mail for political purposes
30 percent have sent racist, pornographic, sexist, or otherwise discriminatory e-mails while at work[30]

[26] Ann Carrns, "Those Bawdy E-Mails Were Good for a Laugh—Until the Axe Fell," The Wall Street Journal, February 4, 2000, pp. A1, A8.

[27] W. Michael Hoffman, Laura P. Hartman and Mark Rowe, "You've Got Mail . . . And the Boss Knows: A Survey by the Center for Business Ethics of Companies' Email and Internet Monitoring," 108 Business and Society 285 (2003).

[28] Elron Software, "Guide to Internet Usage and Policy," 2003, p. 12. http://www.elronsoftware.com

[29] Cohen, "Worker Watchers," p. 70.

[30] Institute for Global Ethics, "U.K. Survey Finds Many Workers Are Misusing Email," Newsline 5(10), March 11, 2002.

The survey also obtained information from 106 companies about their monitoring practices:

- 92 percent of companies engage in monitoring
- 75 percent regularly record employees' e-mail transmissions
- Most allow "reasonable personal usage of e-mail and the Internet," but only 42 percent define what constitutes "reasonable personal usage"
- Those activities considered "reasonable personal usage" are

News	84%
E-mail to family	86%
401(k) dealings	77%
Online banking	54%
Online shopping	51%
Online trading	28%
Job search	25%

- 86 percent of companies block certain Web sites
- 19 percent monitor Web site traffic by employees
- 69 percent use IT to monitor; 13 percent use the legal department; only 9 percent use the ethics office
- 80 percent notify employees of monitoring using the code of ethics, training, and policy manual

Employers have access to employee files and e-mail messages; moreover, employers can retain backup files of such messages even when users have deleted them. Courts have ruled that e-mail messages belong not to the employee but to the employer and are discoverable in litigation, whereupon they must be turned over to the opposing party. In one case an e-mail message from a corporate president to an employee's manager, deleted from the president's and manager's files but saved on the company's hard drive, read, "I don't care what it takes. Fire the _____ bitch." After the message was produced during discovery in the employee's suit, the result was an immediate $250,000 settlement.[31]

In addition to the litigation issues of e-mail, there are the employee usage issues. Employees often use company e-mail systems for sending along jokes, lists, and even electronic forms of chain letters and messages. Not only are these e-mails discoverable, employers can be held liable for their content in terms of defamation and sexual harassment if the messages serve to create an atmosphere of harassment for employees. In *Blakely v. Continental Airlines*, 751 A.2d 538 (N.J. 2000), the court held that because an employer can be held liable for a hostile environment generated by employees who use the company e-mail system to send jokes, messages, and photos, employers need to be able to monitor employees' e-mails.

A survey of 1,438 employees found the following:

78.9 percent of employees send one to ten non-work-related e-mail messages per day
37 percent of employees reported that they surf the Web constantly at work

Michelle Murphy, a former customer-service representative at The Principal Financial Group, was fired after she used company e-mail to send jokes such as "A Few

---

[31] Richard Behar, "Who's Reading Your E-Mail?" Fortune, February 3, 1997, pp. 57–70.

Good Reasons Cookie Dough Is Better Than Men" and "Top 10 Reasons Why Trick-or-Treating Is Better Than Sex." Principal Financial's employee handbook included the following:

> The corporation's electronic mail system is business property and is to be used for business purposes. The corporation reserves the right to monitor all electronic messages.[32]

Murphy has appealed her termination, but the court again made it clear that the e-mail system belongs to the employer and can be used as the employer directs and employees can be subject to disciplinary action for violation of the employer's policies on e-mail usage.[33]

Michael Smyth, a manager for Pillsbury in Pennsylvania, sent an e-mail to his supervisor complaining about company executives and threatening to "kill the backstabbing bastards."[34] Shortly after, he was fired. He sued for wrongful discharge. Again, however, the employer would have the right to terminate for the use of foul language in the e-mail along with the management issues created by such conduct and words.

Another risk for employers is their liability when employees use their work computers to download music. A company based in Tempe, Arizona, Integrated Information Systems, paid $1 million to settle a lawsuit by the Recording Music Industry Association of America because the company had permitted its employees to share thousands of downloaded MP3 files.

Because of this risk, more employers are buying filtering software to prevent employee use and access of the sites and the transfer of such files. In the past 12 months, the number of sites for obtaining and sharing MP3 files has increased by 535 percent. There are now nearly 38,000 Web pages for downloading music files.[35]

Some employees are downloading movies at work and watching them there.

The American Management Association released a survey reflecting how companies handle employee Internet use:

- 78 percent of employers record and review employees' electronic communications including e-mail, voice mail, computer files, and Internet connections
- 47 percent store and review employees' e-mail
- 63 percent monitor Internet connections by employees
- 88 percent of employers inform their employees of their e-mail and other electronic policies
- 91 percent tell employees that they are monitoring their Internet connections
- 55 percent of employers discipline their employees for violating company policy on the Internet
- 19 percent fired employees for misusing e-mail
- 20 percent fired employees for misusing Internet connections
- 39 percent gave their employees a reprimand for e-mail abuse

[32] Mark P. Couch, "E-Mail Can Return to Haunt Employers, Workers," Mesa Tribune, February 2, 1997, pp. E1, E5; David C. Jacobson, et al., "Peril of the E-Mail Trail," National Law Journal, January 16, 1995, pp. C1, C22.
[33] Lisa Guernsey, "You've Got Inappropriate Mail," The New York Times, April 5, 2000, pp. C1, C10.
[34] Brenda Sandburg, "Web Postings Not Libel," National Law Journal, March 12, 2001, pp. B1, B4.
[35] Stephanie Armour, "Workers' Downloading Puts Employers at Risk," USA Today, July 30, 2002, p. 1B.

- 34 percent gave reprimands to employees misusing Internet connections
- 25 percent gave employees reprimands for improper e-mail use
- 23 percent gave employees reprimands for improper Internet use[36]

E-Mail, Privacy, Technology, and Purging

Employers and employees are now keenly aware that the "Delete" button on an e-mail system does not delete messages completely.[37] The messages could be backed up in the employer's system and there is the possibility of key-stroking technology that can be used to reconstruct messages that employees drafted but never sent.

In response to employees' concerns about their e-mail being monitored as well as concerns of businesses regarding espionage via e-mail and the types of uses of e-mails by employees, several companies have been working to develop technology that can eliminate e-mail messages. SafeMessage has unveiled a new software product that can make e-mail messages self-destruct in as little as ten seconds. Once e-mail is sent, the sender, using the SafeMessage program, can set a time frame after the message is opened for it to self-destruct, thereby removing it from the hard drive forever. It has been referred to as a shredder for computers.[38]

There is a troublesome aspect to this technology for law enforcement because messages could be sent without a trace. Also, law enforcement officials rely on e-mail to reconstruct crimes. These types of programs eliminate the back-up as well as any copies of the messages that might be floating about because e-mail messages are forwarded so easily.

In addition to the "shredding technique," the market for privacy programs for e-mail messages has grown substantially, thanks in large part to the e-mail messages of Bill Gates and other Microsoft officers used extensively in the government's antitrust case against Microsoft.[39]

Observing that an e-mail message "is about as secure as a postcard," many companies have developed software to help companies with the lack of privacy. E-mail messages generally make about twelve stops as they journey from the sender to the recipient. One of those stops is the company server, which makes a backup copy of the message that remains on the server for anywhere from one to three years at most companies. The data from servers has been subject to discovery by the courts when e-mail messages could prove relevant in a court case.[40]

Tumbleweed Communications, Inc. offers software that handles privacy with encryption devices. Recipients are notified that there is a message for them on the company server, which they can only obtain with access codes. The encrypted document can also be placed on a Web site to which only the recipient has access.

---

[36] http://www.ama.org.

[37] Michael J. McCarthy, "You Assumed 'Erase' Wiped Out that Rant Against the Boss? Nope," The Wall Street Journal, March 7, 2000, pp. A1, A16.

[38] Jeffrey Beard, "E-Mail that Evaporates," National Law Journal, July 17, 2000, p. B11.

[39] Steve Lohr, "Antitrust Case Is Highlighting Role of E-Mail," The New York Times, November 2, 1998, pp. C1, C4.

[40] Bob Tedeschi, "E-Commerce Report: Wary of Hackers and the Courts, E-Mail Users Are Turning to Services that Keep Their Messages Secure," The New York Times, January 31, 2000, p. C11.

Hush Mail is another company with a program that is so secure that even Hush employees cannot read e-mail when it is protected by the HushMail program.

These companies had a boost in business when there was a 2000 scandal regarding the ability of the White House to archive messages. The White House revealed that it failed to turn over e-mails requested as part of the investigation into fund-raising during the 1996 election because of "a software glitch." The glitch was revealed when a contractor for Northrup Grumman who was working at the White House revealed in a civil suit that she had been threatened if she revealed the e-mails or the problem with the server. The glitch resulted in 100,000 e-mails generated by 500 computer users never being turned over to the special counsel pursuant to a federal grand jury subpoena. The employee and others from Northrup claimed that they were threatened with "jail" if they spoke about the problem to their employer or spouses.

The problem was referred to as Project X and all the e-mails not turned over were labeled as "Classified." Sheryl Hall, chief of White House Computer Operations has said that at least 4,000 of the e-mails were related to Monica Lewinsky, the White House intern who became the center of a presidential scandal.[41]

Based on past White House experience, President George W. Bush sent an e-mail to 42 of his friends on January 17, 2001, just three days before his inauguration with the following:

> My lawyers tell me that all correspondence by e-mail is subject to open record requests. Since I do not want my private conversations looked at by those out to embarrass, the only course of action is not to correspond in cyberspace. This saddens me. I have enjoyed conversing with each of you.[42]

In response to the Microsoft case and White House e-mail issues, a company called Disappearing, Inc. is working to develop an encryption system that would enable senders to control whether their e-mail can be forwarded and another encryption system that would enable senders to set a date when their mail would no longer be readable.[43]

More e-mail control is also now available on the new Microsoft software. There is now a recall feature, available on Microsoft Outlook 2002. Access code requirements are also taking hold. With this type of e-mail system, the sender can encode e-mails and anyone who wants to read the message must have a password. There are also systems that delete e-mail messages after 24 hours.[44]

Visit the following Web sites for companies offering this technology:

http://www.authentica.com
http://www.specimenbox.com/di/tm

---

[41] Joe Matthews, "Burton Seeks Special Counsel in E-Mail Probe," The Wall Street Journal, March 28, 2000, p. A6.

[42] Richard L. Berke, "The Last (E-Mail) Goodbye, From 'gwb' to His 42 Buddies," The New York Times, March 17, 2001, pp. A1, A8.

[43] Amy Harmon, "E-Mail is Treacherous. So Why Do We Keep Trusting It?" The New York Times, March 26, 2000, p. WK3; see also Jerry Seper, "Northrop Officials: White House Hid Subpoenaed E-Mail," Washington Times, March 13–19, 2000 (weekly edition), p. 22.

[44] Jon Swartz, "Software Can Make E-Mail Disappear Without a Trace," USA Today, September 20, 2000, p. 1B.

For more information on e-mail security, visit
http://www.skuz.net/potatoware/links.html
For information on an e-mail encryption software, visit
http://www.Ziplip.com

E-Mail and Theft

Yet another problem with e-mail comes from unauthorized access by hackers. Employees should exercise caution about the type of information sent via e-mail because hackers use information for corporate espionage, insider trading, and even just mischief. For a 1997 article in *Fortune*, and with the company's permission, hackers hired by the magazine were able to access the company's system within a 16-hour period. With access, the hackers obtained a $5,000 bonus authorization from the CEO for an employee. Their access allowed them to read, modify, and destroy files or plant a destructive virus.[45]

Voice Mail and Privacy

Voice mail or telephone messaging is a technological convenience used by nearly 100 percent of all companies with five or more employees. In many situations, such companies do business and enter into contracts using only voice mail. However, voice mail carries with it the same privacy issues as e-mail. Employers can review the voice mail of employees and the messages and their content is discoverable in litigation.

Fax

Faxed documents reduce mailing costs and facilitate rapid negotiations and deal refinements. However, fax technology can also facilitate dishonesty. It would be difficult, for example, to determine the lack of authenticity of a signature transferred from another document to a fax. Facsimile machine technology has not evolved to the point where we can tell whether a fax has been sent, received, or sent or received in its entirety. Finally, centrally located fax machines present privacy problems as faxed materials are pulled off the machines by others and then delivered to the intended recipient.

Discussion Questions

1. Do you think employees should be able to use the Internet for personal items while they are at work?

2. Does it perhaps save time and money to allow employees to do errands via the Internet instead of taking longer lunches and breaks?

3. Is it a breach of privacy for employers to monitor employee use?

4. Is corporate spying necessary?

5. How does secret or electronic monitoring differ from a manager's decision to, without notice, walk around an office to observe behavior and work?

6. Does privacy protection apply in the case of law enforcement? What about warrants for e-mails?

7. To what extent does an employee have a right to privacy in the workplace?

[45] Behar, "Who's Reading Your E-Mail?" pp. 57–70.

8. How would disclosure of monitoring activities lessen their invasion of employee privacy?

9. How does electronic surveillance differ from going through an employee's desk?

10. How would the nature of a given business affect your decision regarding surveillance?

11. What ethical standards should businesses adopt with respect to e-mail, voice mail, and fax technology?

12. What procedures might eliminate some of the ethical dilemmas noted here?

13. Should employers disclose to potential and current employees their ability to access e-mail and voice mail?

14. Is it fair that all e-mails and voice mail generated in the workplace belong to the employer? Why or why not?

15. What policies would you adopt with regard to subject matter in your employees' voice and e-mail?

16. How do voice mail and e-mail provide opportunities for dishonesty in contracts? How might companies guarantee the authenticity of messages that utilize these devices?

CASE 5.4

The Athlete Role Model

On August 20, 1996, the North Texas Toyota Dealers Association filed suit against Michael Irvin, the Dallas Cowboys player who entered a no contest plea to charges of cocaine possession earlier in the month. The Toyota dealers' suit alleges Mr. Irvin represented himself as a moral person when he signed an endorsement contract with the Association and that, with the drug plea, he can no longer be used as a spokesperson. The suit also asks for the return of the Toyota Land Cruiser (valued at $50,000) that Mr. Irvin was given as part of the endorsement contract.[46]

Mr. Irvin returned the car voluntarily and has received a sentence of four years, deferred adjudication, a fine of $10,000, and 800 hours of community service. He was also suspended by the NFL for the first five games of the 1996–1997 season for his involvement with drugs.[47]

The lawsuit also asks for the costs of the aborted campaign and $1.2 million in lost sales. The total damages requested are $1.4 million.[48]

Discussion Questions

1. Do you think Mr. Irvin breached his endorsement contract?

2. Is morality a condition for being a spokesperson?

[46] Randall Lane, "Nice Guys Finish First," Forbes, December 16, 1996, pp. 236–242.
[47] Christine Biederman, "Irvin Given Probation in Plea Deal," The New York Times, July 18, 1996, p. B7.
[48] "Irvin Sued by Car Dealers He Endorsed," The New York Times, August 21, 1996, p. B12.

3. Is it implied in the contract?

4. Is illegal conduct grounds for termination of an endorsement contract?

CASE 5.5

Private Parts and Public Life: Screening Out Employees Who Misbehave: Janet Jackson and CBS

Recently, the morals issue has touched more than just endorsement contracts, but actual performance contracts. For example, the following is the CNN report of the halftime show with Janet Jackson and Justin Timberlake at the 2004 Super Bowl:

"The decision to have a costume reveal at the end of my halftime show performance was made after final rehearsals," Jackson said in a statement.

"MTV was completely unaware of it. It was not my intention that it go as far as it did. I apologize to anyone offended—including the audience, MTV, CBS, and the NFL."

MTV produced the halftime show, which was broadcast by CBS. Both had issued their own apologies.

On Monday, Federal Communications Commission Chairman Michael Powell ordered an investigation of the incident.

An estimated 140 million people were watching the show when at the end, pop star Justin Timberlake popped off part of Jackson's corset, exposing her breast.

Powell told CNN he was not convinced the incident was an accident.

"Clearly somebody had knowledge of it. Clearly it was something that was planned by someone," he said. "She probably got what she was looking for."

Jackson spokesman Stephen Huvane said the incident "was a malfunction of the wardrobe; it was not intentional. . . . He was supposed to pull away the bustier and leave the red-lace bra."[49]

Powell said he "expressed my great displeasure" over the incident in a telephone call Monday with CBS President and CEO Mel Karmazin, who "promised to cooperate" with the investigation.

Although Karmazin expressed "a great deal of regret," Powell said those sentiments would not deter the investigation.

The stock price of Viacom, the parent of CBS, rose more than 1 percent Monday.

"CBS deeply regrets the incident that occurred during the Super Bowl halftime show," the network said in a statement. "We attended all rehearsals throughout the week, and there was no indication that any such thing would happen.

[49] http://www.cnn.com.

"The moment did not conform to CBS broadcast standards, and we would like to apologize to anyone who was offended."

A statement from MTV said the tearing of Jackson's costume "was unrehearsed, unplanned, completely unintentional and was inconsistent with assurances we had about the content of the performance.

"MTV regrets this incident occurred, and we apologize to anyone who was offended by it."

Despite its apology, MTV did not hesitate to promote the incident after the fact. A Web page headline said: "Janet Jackson Got Nasty at the MTV-Produced Super Bowl Halftime Show."

Performing together in a routine that had included a number of bump-and-grind moves, Timberlake reached across Jackson, flicking off the molded right cup of the bustier, leaving her breast bare except for a starburst-shaped decoration held in place by a nipple piercing.

Timberlake issued his own apology. "I am sorry if anyone was offended by the wardrobe malfunction during the halftime performance at the Super Bowl," he said. "It was not intentional and is regrettable."

The White House also weighed in on the issue. "Our view is that it's important for families to be able to expect a high standard when it comes to programming," White House spokesman Scott McClellan said.

NFL Commissioner Paul Tagliabue joined the chorus. "The show was offensive, inappropriate, and embarrassing to us and our fans. We will change our policy, our people, and our processes for managing the halftime entertainment in the future in order to deal far more effectively with the quality of this aspect of the Super Bowl."

AOL, owned by CNN parent company Time Warner, attempted to distance itself from the dispute.

"While AOL was the sponsor of the Super Bowl Halftime Show, we did not produce it. In deference to our membership and the fans, AOL and AOL.com will not be presenting the halftime show online as originally planned."

CBS canceled Ms. Jackson's appearance on the Grammy awards and introduced tape delay broadcast for that event as well as the Oscars. Ms. Jackson resigned from playing Lena Horne in a movie that had not yet gone into production following discussions with 86-year-old Ms. Horne and her daughter. The FCC proposed on July 1, 2004 that 20 CBS stations pay fines of $27,500 each for the Jackson revelation, a total fine of $550,000.

Discussion Questions

1. Is there an implied morals clause in contracts?

2. Should there be?

3. Can a company cancel one contract for misbehavior in another part of a contract?

4. How can morals clauses be important when such conduct causes the stock price to increase?

CASE 5.6

Drug Testing of Employees

John Lawn, the former director of the Drug Enforcement Administration (DEA), supported mandatory drug testing, calling it "critical [i]n those occupations where either the public trust or public safety is involved."[50] He listed doctors, lawyers, airline pilots, truck drivers, and teachers as examples and urged the professions to develop their own rules and regulations for drug testing.

The percentage of employers who test employees for drugs increased from 22 percent in 1987 to 67 percent in 2001. However, some employees have questioned the accuracy of the tests and have filed suit challenging the tests and their resulting termination. And some employers note that employees can tamper with the test results.

Because of the accusations and confusion, the Department of Health and Human Services is expected to issue its employee drug-testing guidelines by the end of the year. The guidelines will dictate certain types of jobs for which employees must always be tested (pilots, conductors) and also provide procedures for conducting the tests that will then become prima facie evidence of accuracy of the test results.[51]

The federal government has Supreme Court approval for 113 drug testing programs, but state law regulates private employers in the administration of their tests. Some states limit testing to safety-sensitive jobs; other states require probable cause as a prerequisite for testing employees. Courts continue to address issues of employer need and employee privacy, along with questions involving drug test reliability.

A Seattle equipment company worker complains: "I am so tired of hearing that I have a right to privacy. What about our right to safety?"[52]

J. F. Spencer, a production manager for Pennwalt Pharmaceutical of Rochester, New York, expresses his feelings as follows:

> People at work who are illegally using drugs are infringing on the rights of law-abiding individuals. It is an invasion of privacy, but until someone comes up with a better way to keep people on drugs out of high-risk jobs, I will put up with it.[53]

But a Boston executive maintains, "Individual rights are too precious to be compromised by this route. Other ways must be found to combat drug problems in the workplace."[54] New Jersey Superior Court Judge Donald A. Smith, Jr., wrote in a decision striking down the discharge of an employee who tested positive for marijuana and Valium, "Whether it be a private or public employer, a free-for-all approach to drug testing cannot be tolerated."[55]

---

[50] David Hess, "Drug Tests Urged in Jobs Dealing with Public Trust," Arizona Republic, August 19, 1986, p. A1.

[51] Stephanie Armour, "Accused Workers Challenge Drug-Test Results in Court," USA Today, July 16, 2001, p. 1B.

[52] "Test Workers for Drugs?" Industry Week, December 14, 1987, p. 17.

[53] Id.

[54] Id.

[55] Wayne A. Green, "Drug Testing Becomes Corporate Mine Field," The Wall Street Journal, November 21, 1989, p. B1.

Kim Haggart, a quality-assurance manager at Dragon Valves, Inc., adopts the following position: "If the job is high-risk or safety-sensitive, testing should be required because impairment can affect the health and safety of others."[56]

Discussion Questions

1. What steps do you think an employer should take to ensure the validity of the drug tests?

2. Is there a difference between drug tests for new employees and using company-wide ongoing drug testing?

3. Is ongoing drug testing necessary?

4. You are the manager of a pizzeria that operates solely as a pizza delivery business. As you contemplate drug testing for your drivers, consider the following questions.

   a. What safety issues are involved with your drivers?
   b. Will your testing be random or scheduled? Explain your choice.
   c. Will you test all employees or just your drivers? Explain.
   d. Will you test employees who are in an accident? Why? Why not?
   e. Why do you think you should—or should not—test your employees?
   f. Will you test only suspicious drivers?
   g. What penalties will you impose on employees who test positive?
   h. What opportunities for rehabilitation will you offer for employees who test positive?
   i. How will you ensure the accuracy of the tests?
   j. Will you inform drivers of your testing policy before hiring them? Why? Why not?

[56] *"Test Workers for Drugs?"* p. 18.

5 D

Sexual Harassment

Sexual harassment became the topic of the 1990s when the 1991 Senate confirmation hearings of Supreme Court Justice Clarence Thomas captured the nation's attention. While the Anita Hill accusations against Justice Thomas brought the issue to the forefront, the 1998 allegations by Paula Jones and Kathleen Willey against President Clinton caused a reexamination of what constitutes sexual harassment. Employers are responsible for eliminating not just the *quid pro quo* forms of sexual harassment but also controlling the atmosphere of their places of employment. Jokes, pictures, comments, and attitudes are all issues of sexual harassment in the workplace.

CASE 5.7

Seinfeld in the Workplace

Jerold J. Mackenzie was hired by Miller Brewing Company in 1974 as an area manager of Miller distributors with a salary grade level of 7. In 1982 he had progressed to grade level 14, and he attained the position of Sales Services and Development Manager reporting to Robert L. Smith in 1987. In late 1987 Miller undertook a corporate reorganization, which led to a transfer of many of Mackenzie's responsibilities.[57]

Concerned, Mackenzie asked Smith whether the reorganization affected his grade level. Smith responded that it did not. In 1989 Miller reevaluated the grade levels of 716 positions, including Mackenzie's. As a result, Mackenzie's position was downgraded to grade level 13. The reevaluation, however, was prospective and applied to the position, not the employee. Therefore, Mackenzie was grandfathered as a grade level 14, even though his position was a grade level 13. That same year, Mackenzie's secretary, Linda Braun, made a sexual harassment complaint against him. She made another sexual harassment complaint against him in 1990.

In August of 1992 Miller sent a memo to employees whose positions had been downgraded but who had been grandfathered to their current grade level informing them that they would be downgraded to their position grade level. Therefore, as of January 1, 1993, Mackenzie would be at grade level 13. He would receive the same salary and benefits of a grade level 14, but he would not be entitled to any future grants of stock options.

[57] James L. Graff and Andrea Sachs, "It Was a Joke!" Time, July 28, 1997, p. 62.

On March 23, 1993, Patricia Best, a Miller distributor services manager who had previously reported to Mackenzie, told her supervisor, Dave Goulet, that Mackenzie had told her about a sexually suggestive episode of the "Seinfeld" television show, which made her uncomfortable. The *Seinfeld* episode is one in which Jerry forgets the first name of a woman he is dating but does recall that her name rhymes with a part of the female anatomy (Dolores was the woman's name). Ms. Best said she didn't "get it," and Mackenzie made a photocopy of the word clitoris from the dictionary. Best reported the incident to her supervisor. Miller immediately investigated the matter, and Mackenzie denied sexually harassing Ms. Best. After concluding its investigation, Miller fired Mackenzie for "unacceptable managerial performance" and "exercising poor judgment."

Mackenzie filed suit against Miller on September 29, 1994. He alleged four causes of action in tort against Miller, Smith, and Best: (1) intentional misrepresentation against Smith and Miller, (2) tortious interference with prospective contract against Smith, (3) tortious interference with contract against Best, and (4) wrongful termination against Miller. His theory supporting the intentional misrepresentation torts against Smith and Miller was that Miller had a duty to disclose after the 1987 reorganization that his position had been grandfathered and that Smith misrepresented to Mackenzie that he would not be affected by the reorganization. In support of the tortious interference claim against Best, he contended that she improperly induced Miller to terminate Mackenzie by fraudulently misrepresenting to Miller that she felt harassed by his discussion of the *Seinfeld* program. The circuit court denied the defendants' motion to dismiss.

On June 23, 1997, a jury trial began and resulted in a verdict three weeks later. The jury awarded $6,501,500 in compensatory damages and $18,000,000 in punitive damages against Miller on the intentional misrepresentation claim. The jury also awarded $1,500 in compensatory damages and $500,000 in punitive damages against Smith on the same tort. The jury found Smith liable for tortious interference with Mackenzie's promotion and awarded him compensatory damages of $100,000. Finally, the jury failed to award Mackenzie any compensatory damages for tortious interference with contract against Best, but did award him $1.5 million in punitive damages. The jurors in the case (10 women and 2 men) said the *Seinfeld* story did not offend them and they wanted to send a message with the size of the award that "sexual harassment has to be more important" than a story from a TV show.

The circuit court reduced the punitive damages against Smith to $100,000—giving Mackenzie the option to take the reduction or risk a new trial on the issue of damages—and dismissed Mackenzie's claim against Best because the jury failed to award compensatory damages. Miller and Smith appealed.

In an exhaustive opinion, the court of appeals reversed the judgment of the circuit court.[58] Mackenzie appealed and the Wisconsin Supreme Court affirmed the appellate court's decision.[59]

---

[58] Mackenzie v. Miller Brewing Co., *2000 Wis. App 48, 234 Wis.2d 1, 608 N.W.2d 331 (2000).*
[59] Mackenzie v. Miller Brewing Co., *241 Wis.2d 700, 623 N.W.2d 739 (Wis. 2001).*

Discussion Questions

1. Do you think Mackenzie's conduct was sexual harassment?

2. Do you think Mackenzie's conduct was professional?

3. Was the award excessive? Was the court of appeals correct in reversing the decision?

4. Do you think Mackenzie was wrongfully terminated? Was he already having difficulty at work? What about the previous allegations of harassment? Should Miller have taken action then to prevent the so-called "*Seinfeld* episode"?

CASE 5.8

Hooters: More Than a Waitress?

Hooters is a successful chain of restaurants and bars that features waitresses in tight shirts and very short shorts. Hooters also markets T-shirts that bear its name as well as its slogan, "More Than a Mouthful."

Former Hooters waitresses filed a class action lawsuit, alleging that the atmosphere Hooters created in its restaurants allowed them to be sexually harassed. One waitress noted on a talk show: "We thought it was a family restaurant. [The uniforms] made us look stupid."[60] The former waitresses have noted that Hooters hired no male wait staff, and that all of the waitresses at its restaurants are very young and mostly blonde. Customers, cooks, and managers, according to the women, made lewd comments and, on occasion, touched them. The women contend that Hooters' atmosphere, their mandatory uniforms, and all-male management caused them to be sexually harassed. The EEOC and Hooters settled the litigation. Hooters' dress policy and its slogans and practices remain the same.[61] Hooters continues to enjoy great success and it recently created Hooters Airlines, a company that flies to resort destinations and features Hooters girls as flight attendants.

Discussion Questions

1. Should the women have known of the problems when they agreed to work at Hooters? What bearing should such knowledge have on their right to allege harassment?

2. What ethical obligations does an employer such as Hooters owe its employees in the creation of its atmosphere?

3. What role should managers play in minimizing customer harassment?

4. Would you work for and/or patronize Hooters?

5. Every Wednesday, the Chicago-area Hooters restaurants donate half of what they earn selling spicy chicken wings to the Holy Family Lutheran Church. Between 1993 and 1995, the

[60] Andrew Blum, "Hooter Suit Lawyer Faces Ethics Complaint," National Law Journal, November 15, 1993, p. 13.
[61] Id.

Hooters restaurant gave $15,000 to the church. On one Wednesday, Hooters brought in calendar girls and a Playboy Playmate for autographs in order to increase business. When asked about the combination of Hooters and religion, Pastor Charles Infelt responded, "We're not asking people to go there. I live in a larger Lutheran world. We try not to get into that side of life. We just accept their money. We don't evaluate. Our role is to be gracious and thankful. I don't want to get into negative thoughts." Evaluate this relationship.[62]

CASE 5.9

Navy Top Guns and Sexual Harassment

In September 1991, the Tailhook Association, a private group of retired and active-duty naval aviators, held its 35th annual convention at the Las Vegas Hilton in Las Vegas, Nevada. Over 1,500 current and former aviators attended the three-day meeting. Navy funds in excess of $190,000 were used to fly the officers on military aircraft to the Las Vegas gathering.

The Tailhook convention is known for its rowdiness. During the evenings, the officers occupied twenty hospitality suites on the third floor of the Hilton. Strippers and scantily clad bartenders worked the suites, and the alcohol bill for three days was estimated at $7,000 per suite. Pornographic films were shown in the suites, and the aviators traveled from suite to suite down a 140-foot hallway. One officer, describing the scene as a "hot, drunken, messy mass of humanity,"[63] later noted that the hallway became so crowded that going from one end to the other took twenty minutes.

It was in the hallway that a pattern of sexual harassment developed over the three days. Groups of officers in civilian clothes shoved both female officers and civilians down "the gauntlet," while grabbing at their breasts and buttocks and stripping off their clothes. Many of the women were ambushed at the elevator and shoved down the long hallway of arms. Two of the women, who were civilians, filed complaints with the Las Vegas police, but the complaints were dropped for a lack of evidence.

One of the women who were forced down the gauntlet was an aide to Admiral John W. Snyder. When she complained of the treatment to Snyder, he replied, "That's what you get for going to a hotel party with a bunch of drunk aviators."[64] However, the Admiral did report the complaint, which eventually reached then-Secretary of the Navy H. Lawrence Garrett, who launched (so to speak) an investigation.

The investigators encountered difficulties because of the officers' refusals to talk about the three-day gauntlet or identify those involved. Garrett then ordered the scope of the investigation broadened to include senior officers who did not participate in the gauntlet but who were in the nearby suites and did nothing to prevent the harassment of women. The investigation targeted seventy officers and identified harassment incidents

---

[62] Richard Gibson, "Hooters Tries to Do Good Works By Selling Lots of Chicken Wings," The Wall Street Journal, February 8, 1995, p. B1.
[63] "Top Guns Dogfight with Sex Scandal," Arizona Republic, June 14, 1992, p. A17.
[64] Id.

involving twenty-six women. A videotape of the gauntlet, discovered during the investigation, shows a seventeen-year-old girl being fondled and undressed.

In June 1992, the Navy added sexual harassment training to its "Top Gun" training program and started an awareness campaign for the prevention of sexual harassment. A poster on sexual harassment titled "Not in Our Navy" is required to be placed on all Navy base bulletin boards.

At the end of June 1992, Navy Secretary H. Lawrence Garrett resigned abruptly. In his resignation letter to President George H. W. Bush, Garrett wrote that he accepted "full responsibility" for his "leadership failure" with respect to the incidents at the Tailhook convention.[65] Admiral Frank B. Kelso 2d, Chief of Naval Operations, resigned as well, two months prior to his scheduled retirement.

The Tailhook convention for 1992 was canceled. Acting Navy Secretary Daniel Howard, vowing to purge the Navy of its "hard-drinking, skirt-chasing, anything-goes philosophy"[66] evidenced by Tailhook, imposed a requirement of one day of sexual harassment training for all naval officers and enlisted persons. Howard blamed Tailhook on a "decaying culture" and the "tolerance of Stone Age attitudes about warriors returning from the sea."[67]

Following Garrett's resignation, a party at the Miramar Naval Air Station Officers' Club in California included an annual revue known as the "Tomcat Follies." In the flyers for the revue were pictures of scantily clad women holding a poster that made reference to Colorado Representative Patricia Schroeder and oral sex. Schroeder was, at that time, a member of the House Armed Services Committee who criticized the Navy for Tailhook and demanded an investigation. Two officers involved in the Follies at Miramar were relieved of their command. Congressional hearings on the sexual harassment of women in the armed services began, and Sean O'Keefe, the Pentagon comptroller, was appointed Secretary of the Navy.

Shortly after Sean O'Keefe's appointment, Lieutenant Paula Coughlin, one of the twenty-six women sexually molested at the Tailhook Las Vegas convention, said that an agent of the Naval Investigative Service assigned to her case invited her to dinner and a drive in the country in November 1991. The agent, Laney Spigener, also called Coughlin "Sweetcakes" and pawed her as she sorted through photographs in an attempt to identify officers who took part in the Tailhook gauntlet. Spigener was removed from the case and suspended for three days.

In September 1992, four women sued both the Navy and Hilton Hotels for more than $2.5 million for their sexual assault in the hotel corridor gauntlet at the Las Vegas Hilton during the Tailhook convention. Coughlin was awarded $1.7 million by a federal jury in her suit against Hilton for the Las Vegas Hilton's failure to provide adequate security at the 1991 convention. Coughlin settled her claim against the Tailhook organization. A later hearing on punitive damages resulted in an additional $5 million award from the Las Vegas Hilton to Coughlin, who has since resigned from the Navy.

---

[65] Andy Pasztor, "Garrett's Leaving Isn't Seen Protecting Administration from Scandal Fallout," The Wall Street Journal, June 29, 1992, p. A14.

[66] "Navy Orders Training on Sex Harassment," Arizona Republic, July 3, 1992, p. A8.

[67] Id.

After the Navy investigation, 140 Navy and Marine Corps pilots were implicated in the assaults of 83 women at the Tailhook convention. There were no court-martials, but 60 officers were fined or disciplined. The charges against the remaining officers were dropped for lack of evidence. Mr. O'Keefe went on to head NASA.

Discussion Questions

1. Was the gauntlet sexual harassment or just "party fun"? How might the officers who participated in the gauntlet justify their conduct? What conditions of employment or environment might allow rationalization of such behavior in the minds of the participants?

2. Would you say that such treatment at a party in which drinking has been going on for three days is deserved, if not to be expected?

3. What action, if any, should the senior officers have taken to stop the gauntlet?

4. What action should hotel management have taken?

5. Would you be reluctant to identify your fellow officers if you had been involved in or had witnessed the Tailhook incidents? Why or why not?

6. Evaluate the conduct of Naval Investigator Laney Spigener.

7. In what ways was the "tone at the top" partially responsible for Tailhook?

8. Prior to Kelso's resignation, a military judge ruled that Admiral Kelso was present at Tailhook and did nothing to stop the conduct in the gauntlet. Further, the judge stated that Kelso's control of the investigation deflected inquiry into his presence and behavior. Why might it be said that a cover-up often is worse than the conduct it's covering?

Sources

Castaneda, Carol J., and Andrea Stone, "Girl's Ordeal Reignites Scandal," *USA Today*, July 30, 1992, p. 4A.

"Choppy Waters," *Time*, July 6, 1992, p. 17.

"Citing Scandal, Navy Chief Says He'll Quit Early," *The New York Times*, February 16, 1994, p. A16.

"Grounded," *Time*, June 29, 1992, p. 31.

"Hotel to Pay $1.7 Million in Tailhook," *Mesa Tribune*, October 29, 1994, pp. A1, A12.

Jolidon, Laurence, "Harassment Is on the Front Burner," *USA Today*, July 8, 1992, pp. 1A, 2A.

"Punitive Award in Tailhook Case—$5 M," *USA Today*, November 1, 1994, p. 3A.

Rohter, Larry, "The Navy Alters Its Training to Curb Sexual Harassment," *The New York Times*, June 22, 1992, p. A11.

Schmitt, Eric, "Officials Say Navy Balked at Report," *The New York Times*, July 8, 1992, pp. A1, A10.

Smolowe, Jill, "An Officer, Not a Gentleman," *Time*, July 13, 1992, p. 36.

Stone, Andrea, "Military Sex Harassment Charged," *USA Today*, September 11, 1992, p. 3A.

Stone, Andrea, "Scandal Could be Agent of Change," *USA Today*, July 30, 1992, p. 4A.

Stone, Andrea, and Carol J. Castaneda, "Military Brass on Hill Today," *USA Today*, July 30, 1992, p. 1A.

"Swabbing the Deck," *Time*, July 20, 1992, p. 15.

"Tailhook Victim Quitting Navy," *USA Today*, February 11, 1994, p. 2A.

"Whistleblower on Tailhook to Quit Navy," *Mesa Tribune*, February 11, 1994, p. A6.

Diversity, Equal Employment, and Affirmative Action

Diversity in the workplace continues to be a stated goal, yet we still face difficult dilemmas, such as fetal endangerment when a prospective mother takes a higher-paying but higher-risk job. When has an employer done enough in terms of employee diversity and safety? Are current goals sufficient?

READING 5.10

The Benefits of Diversity: Doug Daft, CEO of Coca-Cola, Inc.

Remarks of former CEO Douglas Daft on the Importance of Diversity at Coca-Cola

Coca-Cola, Inc. entered into a settlement with the EEOC in order to dismiss complaints of 2,000 employees for racial discrimination. The total settlement amount is $191.5 million (plus costs), the largest settlement ever in a discrimination case, topping the Texaco settlement (see Case 5.13) in 1996 of $176 million.[68]

The payments will be made to current and former African-American employees of Coke and as follows:

- $92.4 million in compensatory damages to employees
- $20.6 million in attorneys' fee
- $43.5 million to promote pay equity within the company
- $35 million invested in diversity reform programs[69]

Coke also agreed to link management pay to diversity efforts by managers and form a seven-member independent panel to oversee diversity efforts at Coke and measure progress.

---

[68] Theresa Howard, *"Coke Settles Bias Lawsuit for $192.5 Million,"* USA Today, *November 17, 2000, p. 1B.*
[69] Betsy McKay, *"Coke Settles Bias Suit for $192.5 Million,"* The Wall Street Journal, *November 17, 2000, p. A3.*

The settlement with the EEOC does not dispose of individual employee claims in a $1.5 billion racial bias class action suit still pending, which employees who benefit from this settlement may still join.

The following speech by the CEO indicates a new commitment to diversity by Coca-Cola.[70]

Good evening everyone and welcome.

Thank you, Ralph, for your kind words and thanks to everyone here at King and Spalding for inviting me to speak tonight. The link between The Coca-Cola Company and King & Spalding certainly predates my thirty-year career with Coca-Cola. A number of our Directors and General Counsels have hailed from King & Spalding, including Sam Nunn, Joe Gladden, Jimmy Sibley and his father John Sibley . . . just to name a few. I am honored to be here.

Tonight, I have been asked to share a few thoughts with you about diversity . . . diversity is a simple word, but a complex subject. Complex, in part, because it is rooted in deeply personal and emotional attitudes connected to race and gender. Complex, too, because there are so many things that come together to make every individual unique, and at the same time a part of an interdependent community.

What sort of characteristics am I talking about? Ones that go well beyond race and gender . . . characteristics like professional experiences, educational backgrounds, working styles and career aspirations. Also family values, our childhood communities and the books we have read and the people we have met.

There is a near endless list of factors that help shape our perspectives. And each individual's perspective—like every individual—is indeed unique.

But that's both the beauty and the power of diversity . . . Bringing those unique perspectives together to solve a problem or capture an opportunity is what managing diversity is all about.

And as we look at the changed world after the tragedies of September 11, we can only be reminded that diversity of different peoples, with different experiences and opinions not only made this country great, but also made it a prime target of the terrorists who seek to destroy our way of life.

These terrible events remind us of the importance of understanding and embracing diversity in our country, our communities and our companies.

The reality is that managing diversity . . . simply understanding diversity . . . requires an investment on our part. An investment of time . . . an investment of focus . . . and more than anything, an investment in people. If you take anything away from my remarks this evening, I hope it will be that such investment is well worth making.

Diversity is a subject I am continually learning more about. I have spent much of my working career in places and situations where I was one of the persons who brought diversity to the team . . . including my current role as an Australian CEO of a worldwide corporation, headquartered here in Atlanta.

[70] http://www.cocacola.com.

During my years with Coca-Cola, I have lived and worked in communities throughout Asia, Europe and the United States. Most of the time, I was a minority learning to operate with respect and consideration in a societal culture very different from my own.

These experiences have helped me to appreciate the complexity of diversity and have given me an opportunity to experience its enormous power.

My commitment to diversity is rooted in seeing how a rich mosaic of perspectives builds a brand that transcends demographics . . . A brand that makes more than a billion people feel just a little bit better, a little more refreshed, and a little more connected to one another every day . . . A brand that is as at home in Brussels, as it is in Buckhead.

I am fortunate to work for The Coca-Cola Company . . . because we have a brand that lives and breathes the paradox of diversity. It is the same simple formula all over the world. And yet each individual . . . each community . . . each culture, experiences this wonderful beverage in a unique way.

I hope the beliefs I share tonight will be useful to you in your own organizations.

For us, at Coca-Cola we have a company built on relationships.

We created the world's leading brand by establishing a deep and lasting bond with our consumers. From there, we built a global marketing and distribution system second to none. We wove a global web of interconnected relationships. But all those relationships are local.

And diversity is at the core of those relationships. When we connect with consumers locally, our brands—particularly Coca-Cola—have become significantly stronger and more relevant . . . and our business has flourished.

People like to talk about Coca-Cola as a global brand . . . But the reality is that no one drinks a Coke globally . . . Local people in every market get thirsty, go to their local retailer, and buy locally-produced Cokes.

So our communication to consumers . . . their interaction with the brand . . . has to address their local needs and wants. Only if we understand them can we address them. And that understanding comes from devoting ourselves to recognizing, respecting, and celebrating the diversity of those local needs and wants.

At one point, we struggled with our advertising in China. We just could not seem to get traction. Well, when we talked to the Chinese about our advertising, we learned that we were not connecting with them culturally. Needless to say, we changed our processes, and now we have successful advertising in China. Here's another example . . . In Japan, we have a ready-to-drink coffee brand called Georgia. I am proud to say that it is the number one coffee brand in Japan. When we talked to Japanese consumers about growing the brand, we learned that they wanted variety.

So, we responded to their needs and wants by introducing multiple flavors of Georgia Coffee. We now have Georgia original, Espresso, Cappuccino and Café au-lait . . . and we now have dramatic growth of the brand.

We would not be able to grow our business the way we have around the world if we didn't open ourselves up to the perspectives of others. Genuinely expressed interest in another's point of view in a way to build bridges and mutual respect . . . it is about the power of relationships.

One more example illustrates how one product can be viewed differently by different people in different parts of the world.

Here in the U.S., you may have noticed the relaunch of POWERade, which is producing truly spectacular results . . . our overall volume for POWERade is up 17% this year! In our home country, the brand is aimed at athletes—from the professional to the weekend warrior. We tap into the desire for a beverage that replenishes you while you are working out.

However, in Japan, sports drinks are viewed very differently. They are a component of relaxation. Japanese consumers might enjoy a sports beverage, not during their workout, but after it, while they bathe. Understanding that difference has helped us make our Aquarius brand the biggest selling sports drink in Japan.

Understanding diversity has led to innovation for our carbonated brands too. For example, I hope that all of you will try our newest brand extension, diet Coke with Lemon.

Sometime ago, some of our people came up with an idea . . . In the U.S., they said, "People sit at cafes and restaurants and enjoy diet Coke with a lemon in their drink." They asked, "Why don't we put that flavor into the beverage itself, so that consumers can enjoy the same taste while they are on the go?"

As a result, diet Coke with Lemon is currently being introduced in the Midwest to rave reviews and will be rolled out nationwide later this month.

These are all a result of listening to new and different perspectives—from inside and outside our Company—and incorporating them into our decision-making to grow our business. In short . . . diversity marketing.

Why do we talk about diversity this way? Why don't we discuss, first and foremost, zero-tolerance policies against discrimination, or how to help sensitize our workforces to respect others of different racial or ethnic backgrounds?

At Coca-Cola, we certainly do all these things. We believe that diversity is not merely about compliance . . . it is about values; it is about relationships. Taking advantage of diversity is a critical key to who we are and to our business success.

And even if you don't operate in two hundred countries around the world, any organization will be more successful if it can access a broader array of perspectives and then channel them towards the organization's mission. Those perspectives can be driven not only by race or gender, but also by functional background or professional expertise.

Put simply . . . you are not taking advantage of your diversity if, in developing a new strategy, you gather a group of people with the same perspective or business expertise, say a group of marketers, or a group of accountants, or even lawyers . . . sorry . . . You'll get limited, narrow points of view.

We all must recognize, respect, value and celebrate the uniqueness of all members of our organizations as we embrace diversity as one of our fundamental values.

At Coca-Cola, we value a workforce that mirrors the consumers we serve, and we continue to build towards that objective. And let's be clear about what that means. Yes, it is including African-Americans, Latinos, and Asian-Americans. And it is also bringing together young people with those closer to my age . . . It's single parents . . . It's liberals and conservatives. It is working diligently to maintain a workforce that possesses the experiences, backgrounds and influences that can enrich our lives and enhance our business.

How does that get translated into the workplace? Well, it means that we encourage innovative thinking, by everyone at every level, and taking calculated risks to develop our business to meet changing consumer tastes. Again, it's a role that must be embraced by senior management.

It starts with education. All of us, from myself on, have participated in strategic diversity management sessions—to educate ourselves, to understand how we can best leverage our diversity to support our business, and to apply what we learn to our operations.

But it also involves ensuring that the lessons we learn in these sessions are reinforced in the everyday life of our corporation . . . and that, of course, is the objective.

This commitment to bring diversity to the way we do business extends beyond the Company and into society at large, through the communities of which we are a part. Through our local people and those of our bottling partners, we are part of the community connecting with local residents through local marketing and local civic programs. We create opportunities for our consumers to[o]. For example, our Urban Economic Partnership in Harlem developed with our largest U.S. bottler, Coca-Cola Enterprises, has expanded to several other communities in the Northeast. Many of the people hired in those new jobs have been promoted from account managers to district managers and sales managers.

As we continue our long history of being part of the communities we serve, we are continually seeking opportunities to partner with our neighbors and use innovative diversity initiatives to help other organizations develop their own benefit from diversity.

Last fall we donated $1.5 million to the American Institute of Managing Diversity for the establishment of the Diversity Leadership Academy, right here in Atlanta.

The Diversity Leadership Academy is designed to build diversity management skills and capabilities in leaders from various sectors within the community—including government, non-profits, education and business—so they all can benefit from better diversity management.

Our grant will enable 300–400 leaders to participate in this innovative program. The first classes began on October 4.

In addition, last week, I announced that our vice president of Diversity Strategies, Juan Johnson, has become the president of the Diversity Leadership Academy. While remaining a vice president of our company, Juan will lead the Atlanta Academy to serve as a model for other communities across the nation and the world. Charlene Crusoe-Ingram will succeed him as vice president for Diversity Strategy and Culture, reporting directly to [. . .] Realizing the full potential of diversity is essential to our business . . . from the communities we serve, to the decisions we make every day about our operations. Diversity has a direct impact on The Coca-Cola Company:

- It improves our understanding of local markets;
- It makes us a better employer and business partner;
- It helps us compete more effectively;
- It makes us better neighbors in our communities; and ultimately,
- It builds value for our shareowners.

Respecting and benefiting from diversity in our businesses and in our communities is not only a guiding principle but also a core value of The Coca-Cola Company.

That's why our success demands that we continue to develop a worldwide team rich in its diversity of thinking, perspectives, backgrounds and culture.

Only when we do that can we keep developing a unique intellectual and physical system throughout the world, a system with the people and assets to refresh consumers in local communities in over 200 countries.

Enjoy tonight's dinner, and I know that the diverse perspectives that each of you will bring to your conversations will be fascinating.

Thank you.

Discussion Questions

1. Why does Mr. Daft believe diversity is important?

2. What personal experiences does he have with the issue of diversity?

3. What are the five components of Coke's diversity program?

4. Do you think the program was put into place because of the EEOC issues? Do you think the program will prevent future EEOC issues?

5. You can study Coca-Cola's actions in ginning up data in order to sell Frozen Coke to Burger King in Case 7.19. Do you think a company that adopts a good posture on diversity is immune from honesty issues and vice versa?

CASE 5.11

On-the-Job Fetal Injuries

Johnson Controls, Inc., is a battery manufacturer. In the battery manufacturing process, the primary ingredient is lead. Exposure to lead endangers health and can harm a fetus carried by a female who is exposed to lead.

Before Congress passed the Civil Rights Act of 1964, Johnson Controls did not employ any women in the battery manufacturing process. In June 1977, Johnson Controls announced its first official policy with regard to women who desired to work in battery manufacturing, which would expose them to lead:

Protection of the health of the unborn child is the immediate and direct responsibility of the prospective parents. While the medical professional and the company can support them in the exercise of this responsibility, it cannot assume it for them without simultaneously infringing their rights as persons.

Since not all women who can become mothers wish to become mothers (or will become mothers), it would appear to be illegal discrimination to treat all who are capable of pregnancy as though they will become pregnant.[71]

[71] International Union v. Johnson Controls, Inc., *499 U.S. 187, 191 (1991).*

The policy stopped short of excluding women capable of bearing children from jobs involving lead exposure but emphasized that a woman who expected to have a child should not choose a job that involved such exposure.

Johnson Controls required women who wished to be considered for employment in the lead exposure jobs to sign statements indicating that they had been told of the risks lead exposure posed to an unborn child: ". . . that women exposed to lead have a higher rate of abortion . . . not as clear as the relationship between cigarette smoking and cancer . . . but medically speaking, just good sense not to run that risk if you want children and do not want to expose the unborn child to risk, however small."

By 1982, however, the policy of warning had been changed to a policy of exclusion. Johnson Controls was responding to the fact that between 1979 and 1982, eight employees became pregnant while maintaining blood lead levels in excess of thirty micrograms per deciliter, an exposure level that OSHA categorizes as critical. The company's new policy was as follows:

> It is Johnson Controls' policy that women who are pregnant or who are capable of bearing children will not be placed into jobs involving lead exposure or which would expose them to lead through the exercise of job bidding, bumping, transfer or promotion rights.[72]

The policy defined women capable of bearing children as "all women except those whose inability to bear children is medically documented."[73] The policy defined unacceptable lead exposure as the OSHA standard of thirty micrograms per deciliter in the blood or thirty micrograms per cubic centimeter in the air.

In 1984, three Johnson Controls employees filed suit against the company on the grounds that the fetal-protection policy was a form of sex discrimination that violated Title VII of the Civil Rights Act. The three employees included Mary Craig, who had chosen to be sterilized to avoid losing a job that involved lead exposure; Elsie Nason, a fifty-year-old divorcee who experienced a wage decrease when she transferred out of a job in which she was exposed to lead; and Donald Penney, a man who was denied a leave of absence so that he could lower his lead level because he intended to become a father. The trial court certified a class action that included all past, present, and future Johnson Controls' employees who had been or would continue to be affected by the fetal-protection policy Johnson Controls implemented in 1982.

At the trial, uncontroverted evidence showed that lead exposure affects the reproductive abilities of men and women and that the effects of exposure on adults are as great as those on a fetus, although the fetus appears to be more vulnerable to exposure. Johnson Controls maintained that its policy was a product of business necessity.

The employees argued in turn that the company allowed fertile men, but not fertile women, to choose whether they wished to risk their reproductive health for a particular job. Johnson Controls responded that it had based its policy not on any intent to discriminate, but rather on its concern for the health of unborn children. Johnson Controls also pointed out that inasmuch as more than forty states recognize a parent's right to recover for a prenatal injury based on negligence or wrongful death, its policy was designed to prevent

[72] Id., p. 191.
[73] Id., p. 192.

its liability for such fetal injury or death. The company maintained that simple compliance with Title VII would not shelter it from state tort liability for injury to a parent or child.

Johnson Controls also maintained that its policy represented a bona fide occupational qualification and that it was requiring medical certification of non-childbearing status to avoid substantial liability for injuries.

Discussion Questions

1. As the director of human resources for Johnson Controls, would you support or change the policy on women performing lead-exposure tasks? Why?

2. Why should women be given—or not given—the choice to accept the risk of exposure?

3. To what extent should a woman have the right to make decisions that will affect not only her health but the health of her unborn child? To what extent should a woman's consent to or acknowledgment of danger mitigate an employer's liability? What if a child born with lead-induced birth defects sues? Should the mother's consent apply as a defense?

4. The U.S. Supreme Court eventually decided Johnson Controls' policy was discriminatory and a violation of Title VII [*International Union v. Johnson Controls, Inc.*, 499 U.S. 187 (1991)]. What steps would you take as director of human resources to create a "policy-free" work setting?

5. The fallout from the *Johnson Controls* decision has been that many women have been working in jobs that expose them to toxins. The U.S. Supreme Court did acknowledge in its holding that there might be tort liability resulting from its decision but that such liability was often used as a guise or cover for gender discrimination. However, 14 years after the decision, women who were held to be entitled to the high-risk jobs are now suing their employers for the birth defects in their children. For example, IBM has several suits from employees and their children against it for defects allegedly tied to production line toxins.[74] The position of many of the employers is that even if there were evidence linking the toxins to birth defects, the women took the jobs with knowledge about the risk and agreed to that risk. How can employers, legislators, and public policy specialists reconcile antidiscrimination laws and these risks of exposure?

6. At what times, if any, should discrimination issues be subordinate to other issues, such as the risk of danger to unborn children?

CASE 5.12

Denny's: Discriminatory Service with a Smile

On March 24, 1993, a group of minority customers filed a lawsuit in San Jose, California, against the Denny's restaurant chain. Denny's was requiring its minority customers to pay cover charges and to prepay for meals. In April, Denny's settled the charges with the Justice Department.[75]

---

[74] Stephanie Armour, "Workers Take Employers to Court over Birth Defects," USA Today, February 26, 2002, pp. 1A, 2A. For more information, go to http://www.cdc.gov/niosh.

[75] Chuck Hawkins, "Denny's: The Stain That Isn't Coming Out," Business Week, June 28, 1993, pp. 98–99.

On May 24, 1993, six African-American Secret Service agents filed suit against Denny's, claiming the wait staff at the Annapolis, Maryland, Denny's had been deliberately slow in serving them (the agents had waited 55 minutes), thereby effectively denying them service. Their white colleagues had been served in a timely fashion.[76]

Other Denny's customers who are black complained that they were told they would have to pay first if they wanted to eat at Denny's.

In July 1993, Denny's signed a $1 billion pact to settle the Secret Service case and all other claims. In the pact, Denny's agreed to:[77]

- Buy nearly $700 million in food, paper, and supplies from black-owned businesses.
- Launch a training and recruitment program to increase black representation in Flagstar's[78] management ranks from 4.4 percent to 12 percent.
- Add 53 black-run franchises. Denny's had 1,485 restaurants, only one of which was operated by a black franchisee.
- Funnel Flagstar business to black accountants, lawyers, ad agencies, and banks.[79]

Denny's also agreed to pay $46 million to black patrons and $8.7 million for legal fees. An additional $28 million was paid to California customers to settle civil rights cases there. The six agents in the Annapolis restaurant will split $17.7 million. The customers in the class action suit each received about $180 each as their part of the settlement.[80]

Denny's now buys $50 million in supplies from minority contractors and one in four of its store managers is black.[81] At the time of the settlement, Denny's had only two minority contractors. In 1997, Denny's began a $5 million ad campaign that features black families entering Denny's restaurants.[82] Denny's CEO now tells employees, "I will fire you if you discriminate."[83]

Discussion Questions

1. In what ways could you say that Denny's is an example of a firm failing to monitor its practices?

2. How costly was Denny's discrimination?

3. How effective would encouraging employees to report discrimination be as a step in changing the corporate culture at Denny's and other service organizations?

4. Denny's includes the following information on its Web site about diversity:[84]

- Forty-eight percent of parent company Advantica's more than 46,221 company employees are minorities; 11 percent are African-Americans and 31 percent are Hispanic-American.

---

[76] Anne Faircloth, "Denny's Changes Its Spots," Fortune, May 13, 1996, pp. 133–142.
[77] Blair S. Walker, "Denny's, NAACP Sign $1 Billion Pact," USA Today, July 2, 1993, pp. 1B, 2B.
[78] Flagstar is the parent company for Denny's.
[79] Id.
[80] Del Jones, "Denny's Checks Smaller than Plaintiffs Expected," USA Today, December 12, 1995, p. 1B.
[81] Eleena de Lisser and Benjamin A. Holden, "Denny's Begins Repairing Its Image—and Its Attitude," The Wall Street Journal, March 1, 1994, pp. B1, B3.
[82] Laura Bird, "Denny's TV Ad Seeks to Mend Bias Image," The Wall Street Journal, June 21, 1993, p. B6; see also Melanie Wells, "Denny's Serves Up $5M Ad Campaign to Fix Racist Image," USA Today, May 23, 1997, p. 1B.
[83] Emory Thomas, Jr., "Denny's Shines Its Bad Image with New Deal," The Wall Street Journal, November 9, 1994, pp. B1, B7.
[84] Used with permission of DFO, Inc.

Thirty-two percent of Advantica's restaurant and multi-restaurant supervisory positions are held by minorities.

- Minority employees represent 32 percent of Denny's parent company Advantica's management; African-Americans, Hispanic-Americans, and Asian-Pacific Americans account for 12 percent, 14 percent and 6 percent, respectively, of Advantica's management.
- *Working Woman* magazine ranked Advantica, Denny's parent company, 12th in its 2001 survey of the "Top 25 Companies for Women Executives."
- *Fortune* magazine ranked Advantica, Denny's parent company, number 1 in its list of "America's 50 Best Companies for Minorities" for two consecutive years—2000 and 2001.
- Advantica, Denny's parent company, received the 1997 Fair Share Corporate Award for Minority Business Development from the National Association for the Advancement of Colored People (NAACP) in June 1997.
- Jim Adamson, former chairman and CEO of Advantica, Denny's parent company, received the "CEO of the Year" Award from Kweisi Mfume, President and CEO of the National Association for the Advancement of Colored People (NAACP) in June of 1996. He also received the national "Humanitarian of the Year" Award from the prestigious American Jewish Committee in February 1997 for his work in the diversity arena.

Since October 1994, Denny's has been Save the Children's largest corporate sponsor. Through the enthusiastic support of its employees, franchisees and customers, Denny's has contributed over $2.5 million and has positively impacted the lives of more than 75,000 disadvantaged children in over 100 U.S. communities. Denny's goal continues to be to raise $1 million annually for Save the Children. Donations to Save the Children are primarily the result of in-store coin canister donations, a 10-cent donation from each All-American Slam and kids' menu Smiley-Face Hotcakes plate sold, as well as raffles, car washes, etc.

The partnership has been a win-win for both parties. As Denny's national charity, Save the Children receives annual contributions from the nation's largest family restaurant chain for its domestic Web of Support programs. Web of Support programs are committed to increasing quality, out-of-school time for children at-risk to the influence of drugs, teenage pregnancy, and dropping out of high school. In return, this initiative provides an opportunity for local restaurant employees, franchisees, and customers to get more involved with the programs in their individual communities.

Denny's commitment to Save the Children is more than just a financial relationship. In the first half of 1998, Denny's donated more than 2,700 Harlem Globetrotter basketball game tickets to Save the Children, enabling disadvantaged children nationwide to attend these entertaining events and pre-game basketball demonstrations. Additionally, more than 100 Save the Children youth received complimentary admission to a five-day Harlem Globetrotters summer basketball camp held in markets across the country.

Do you think the progress was the result of the discrimination cases? Do you think Denny's will experience discrimination cases in the future? Why or why not? Are there similarities between Denny's programs and philosophies and Coca-Cola's (see Reading 5.10)?

5. Denny's has security cameras in every restaurant. Those cameras, while intended to help deter and solve crimes, also videotape employees' interactions with customers. The cameras have proven to be a help in suits that claim discrimination. For example, in 2000, two African-American males filed suit against Denny's (Advantica Restaurant Group, Inc. is Denny's owner) for alleged discrimination in one restaurant's failure to seat them. The lawyer

for Advantica asked to see the videotape from the restaurant. The two plaintiffs were only in the Denny's waiting area for 10 minutes before leaving. And during the time they were waiting, the host had seated Hispanics, African-Americans, and others, in the order in which they entered the restaurant. The plaintiffs withdrew their suit.[85]

Is the use of these tapes and cameras ethical? Is their use for non-security reasons ethical?

CASE 5.13

Texaco: The Jelly Bean Diversity Fiasco

In November 1996, Texaco, Inc. was rocked by the disclosure of tape-recorded conversations among three executives about a racial discrimination suit pending against the company. The suit, seeking $71 million, had been brought by 6 employees, on behalf of 1,500 other employees, who alleged the following forms of discrimination:

- I have had KKK printed on my car. I have had my tires slashed and racial slurs written about me on bathroom walls. One co-worker blatantly called me a racial epithet to my face.
- Throughout my employment, three supervisors in my department openly discussed their view that African-Americans are ignorant and incompetent, and, specifically, that Thurgood Marshall was the most incompetent person they had ever seen.
- Sheryl Joseph, formerly a Texaco secretary in Harvey, Louisiana, was given a cake for her birthday which occurred shortly after she announced that she was pregnant. The cake depicted a black pregnant woman and read, "Happy Birthday, Sheryl. It must have been those watermelon seeds."[86]

The suit also included data on Texaco's workforce:

| 1989 | Minorities as a percentage of Texaco's workforce | 15.2% |
| 1994 | Minorities as a percentage of Texaco's workforce | 19.4% |

Years to Promotion by Job Classification

Minority employees	Job	Other employees
6.1	Accountant	4.6
6.4	Senior Accountant	5.4
12.5	Analyst	6.3
14.2	Financial Analyst	13.9
15.0	Assistant Accounting Supervisor	9.8

[85] David E. Rovella, "Denny's Serves Up a Winning Video," National Law Journal, August 28, 2000, p. A17.
[86] Kurt Eichenwald, "Behind the Two Faces of Texaco," The New York Times, November 10, 1996, pp. 3-1, 3-10.

Senior Managers[87]

	White	Black
1991	1,887	19
1992	2,001	21
1993	2,000	23
1994	2,029	23

Racial Composition (% of Blacks) by Pay Range[88]

Salary	Texaco	Other Oil Companies
$51,100	5.9%	7.2%
$56,900	4.7%	6.5%
$63,000	4.1%	4.7%
$69,900	2.3%	5.1%
$77,600	1.8%	3.2%
$88,100	1.9%	2.3%
$95,600	1.4%	2.6%
$106,100	1.2%	2.3%
$117,600	0.8%	2.3%
$128,800	0.4%	1.8%

(African-Americans make up 12% of the U.S. population.)

The acting head of the EEOC wrote in 1995, "Deficiencies in the affirmative-action programs suggest that Texaco is not committed to insuring comprehensive, facility by facility, compliance with the company's affirmative-action responsibilities."[89]

Faced with the lawsuit, Texaco's former treasurer, Robert Ulrich, senior assistant treasurer, J. David Keough, and senior coordinator for personnel services, Richard A. Lundwall, met and discussed the suit. A tape transcript follows:[90]

They look through evidence, deciding what to turn over to the plaintiffs.

Lundwall Here, look at this chart. You know, I'm not really quite sure what it means. This chart is not mentioned in the agency, so it's not important that we even have it in there. . . . They would never know it was here.

---

[87] Adam Bryant, "How Much Has Texaco Changed?" The New York Times, November 2, 1997, pp. 3-1, 3-16.

[88] Eichenwald, "Behind the Two Faces of Texaco," p. 3-10.

[89] Richard W. Stevenson, "Texaco Is Said to Set Payment Over Sex Bias," The New York Times, January 6, 1999, pp. C1, C4.

[90] Kurt Eichenwald, "Texaco Executives, On Tape, Discussed Impeding a Bias Suit," The New York Times, November 4, 1996, pp. A1, C4.

Keough	They'll find it when they look through it.
Lundwall	Not if I take it out they won't.

The executives decide to leave out certain pages of a document; they worry that another version will turn up.

Ulrich	We're gonna purge the [expletive deleted] out of these books, though. We're not going to have any damn thing that we don't need to be in them—
Lundwall	As a matter of fact, I just want to be reminded of what we discussed. You take your data and . . .
Keough	You look and make sure it's consistent to what we've given them already for minutes. Two versions with the restricted and that's marked clearly on top—
Ulrich	But I don't want to be caught up in a cover-up. I don't want to be my own Watergate.
Lundwall	We've been doing pretty much two versions, too. This one here, this is strictly my book, your book . . .
Ulrich	Boy, I'll tell you, that one, you would put that and you would have the only copy. Nobody else ought to have copies of that.
Lundwall	O.K.?
Ulrich	You have that someplace and it doesn't exist.
Lundwall	Yeah, O.K.
Ulrich	I just don't want anybody to have a copy of that.
Lundwall	Good. No problem.
Ulrich	You know, there is no point in even keeping the restricted version anymore. All it could do is get us in trouble. That's the way I feel. I would not keep anything.
Lundwall	Let me shred this thing and any other restricted version like it.
Ulrich	Why do we have to keep the minutes of the meeting anymore?
Lundwall	You don't, you don't.
Ulrich	We don't?
Lundwall	Because we don't, no, we don't because it comes back to haunt us like right now—
Ulrich	I mean, the pendulum is swinging the other way, guys.

The executives discuss the minority employees who brought the suit.

Lundwall	They are perpetuating an us/them atmosphere. Last week or last Friday I told . . .
Ulrich	[Inaudible.]
Lundwall	Yeah, that's what I said to you, you want to frag grenade? You know, duck, I'm going to throw one. Well, that's what I was alluding to. But the point is not, that's not bad in itself but it does perpetuate us/them. And if you're trying to get away and get to the we . . . you can't do that kind of stuff.
Ulrich	[Inaudible.] I agree. This diversity thing. You know how black jelly beans agree . . .
Lundwall	That's funny. All the black jelly beans seem to be glued to the bottom of the bag.
Ulrich	You can't have just we and them. You can't just have black jelly beans and other jelly beans. It doesn't work.
Lundwall	Yeah. But they're perpetuating the black jelly beans.
Ulrich	I'm still having trouble with Hanukkah. Now, we have Kwanza (laughter).[91]

[91] *Del Jones, "Oil Giant Argues Tapes Didn't Contain Racial Slur," November 12, 1996, p. 1B; see also Kurt Eichenwald, "Blowing the Whistle, and Now Facing the Music," The New York Times, March 16, 1997, pp. 3-1, 3-12, 3-13.*

The release of the tape prompted the Reverend Jesse Jackson to call for a nationwide boycott of Texaco.[92] Sales fell 8 percent, Texaco's stock fell 2 percent, and several institutional investors were preparing to sell their stock.[93]

Texaco did have a minority recruiting effort in place and the "jelly bean" remark was tied to a diversity trainer the company had hired.[94] The following are excerpts from Texaco's statement of vision and values:

Respect for the Individual

Our employees are our most important resource. Each person deserves to be treated with respect and dignity in appropriate work environments, without regard to race, religion, sex, age, national origin, disability or position in the company. Each employee has the responsibility to demonstrate respect for others.

The company believes that a work environment that reflects a diverse workforce, values diversity, and is free of all forms of discrimination, intimidation, and harassment is essential for a productive and efficient workforce. Accordingly, conduct directed toward any employee that is unwelcome, hostile, offensive, degrading, or abusive is unacceptable and will not be tolerated.[95]

A federal grand jury began an investigation at Texaco to determine whether there had been obstruction of justice in the withholding of documents.[96]

Within days of the release of the tape, Texaco settled its bias suit for $176.1 million, the largest sum, at that time, ever allowed in a discrimination case. The money allowed an 11 percent pay raise for blacks and other minorities who joined in the lawsuit.[97]

Texaco's chairman and CEO at that time, Peter I. Bijur, issued the following statement after agreeing to a settlement:

Texaco is facing a difficult but vital challenge. It's broader than any specific words and larger than any lawsuit. It is one we must and are attacking head-on.

We are a company of 27,000 people worldwide. In any organization of that size, unfortunately, there are bound to be people with unacceptable, biased attitudes toward race, gender and religion.

Our goal, and our responsibility, is to eradicate this kind of thinking wherever and however it is found in our company. And our challenge is to make Texaco a company of limitless opportunity for all men and women.

We are committed to begin meeting this challenge immediately through programs with concrete goals and measurable timetables.

---

[92] Kurt Eichenwald, "Rights Groups Urge Boycott of Texaco," The New York Times, November 13, 1996, pp. C1, C6.

[93] Allanna Sullivan and Peter Fritsch, "Texaco's Bijur Says Company Is Trying to Settle Bias Suit," The Wall Street Journal, November 13, 1996, p. A12; see also Del Jones, "Jackson Calls for Boycott of Texaco," USA Today, November 13, 1996, p. 1A.

[94] Kurt Eichenwald, "U.S. Inquiring Into Texaco's Actions in Suit," The New York Times, November 5, 1996, pp. C1, C2.

[95] Eichenwald, "Behind the Two Faces of Texaco," pp. 3-1, 3-10.

[96] Ellen Neubourne, "Texaco Race-Bias Tapes: Were Erasures Intended?" USA Today, July 11, 1997, p. 1B.

[97] "Texaco to Pay $176 Million to End Bias Suit," Arizona Republic, November 16, 1996, pp. A1, A15.

I've already announced certain specific steps, including a redoubling of efforts within Texaco to focus on the paramount value of respect for the individual and a comprehensive review of our diversity programs at every level of our company.

We also want to broaden economic access to Texaco for minority firms and increase the positive impact our investments can have in the minority community. This includes areas such as hiring and promotion; professional services such as advertising, banking, investment management and legal services; and wholesale and retail station ownership.

To assist us, we are reaching out to leaders of minority and religious organizations and others for ideas and perspectives that will help Texaco succeed in our mission of becoming a model of diversity and workplace equality.

It is essential to this urgent mission that Texaco and African-Americans and other minority community leaders work together to help solve the programs we face as a company—which, after all, echo the problems faced in society as a whole.

Discrimination will be extinguished only if we tackle it together, only if we join in a unified, common effort.

Working together, I believe we can take Texaco into the 21st century as a model of diversity. We can make Texaco a company of limitless opportunity. We can make Texaco a leader in according respect to every man and woman.[98]

Even after the announcement, Texaco stock was down $3 per share, a loss of $800 million total, and the boycott was continued. Texaco's proposed merger with Shell Oil began to unravel as Shell's CEO expressed concern about Texaco's integrity. However, after the settlement, additional information about the case began to emerge.[99]

Holman W. Jenkins, Jr. wrote the following piece for *The Wall Street Journal*:

Quietly, corporate America is debating whether Texaco's Peter Bijur did the right thing.

Mr. Bijur gets paid to make the hard calls, and with the airwaves aflame over "nigger" and "black jelly beans," Texaco took a battering in the stock and political markets. He had every reason for wanting to put a stop-loss on the media frenzy. "Once the taped conversations were revealed," he says, settling was "reasonable and honorable." So now Texaco is betting $176 million that paying off minority employees and their lawyers is the quickest way out of the news.

But as the company's own investigation showed, the truly inflammatory comments reported in the media never took place. They were purely a fabrication by opposing lawyers, and trumpeted by a credulous *New York Times*. And some digging would have shown this problem cropping up before in the career of Mike Hausfeld, lead attorney for the plaintiffs.

In an antitrust case years ago, he presented a secret recording that he claimed showed oil executives conspiring to threaten gasoline dealers. But a check by the same expert who handled the Nixon Watergate tapes showed no such thing. Says Larry Sharp, the Washington antitrust lawyer who opposed Mr. Hausfeld: "To put it generously, he gave himself the benefit of the doubt in making the transcript."

---

[98] Peter I. Bijur, "Texaco Will Wipe Out Bias," USA Today, November 14, 1996, p. 14A.
[99] Bari-Ellen Roberts and Jack E. White, "Portrait of a Company Behaving Badly," Time, March 16, 1998, pp. 46–51.

But this time the lie has been rewarded, and the broader public, unschooled in legal cynicism, heads home believing Texaco an admitted racist.

The catechism of corporate crisis management says you can't fight the media. Mr. Bijur had to consider that Jesse Jackson was threatening a boycott if Texaco failed to "regret, repent and seek renewal." Mr. Jackson pointedly added that "any attempt to shift to denial would add insult to injury"—a warning against trying to spread some egg to the faces of those who were fooled by the fake transcript.

There may have been wisdom, if not valor, in Mr. Bijur's decision to run up the white flag. But he also evinced symptoms of Stockholm Syndrome, telling CNN that Texaco was just the "tip of the iceberg" of corporate racism. Ducking this fight so ignominiously may yet prove a penny-wise, pound-foolish strategy. The City of Philadelphia has decided to dump its Texaco holdings anyway, partly out of fear of more litigation.

What else could Texaco have done? It could have apologized for any offense, but stuck up for its former treasurer Bob Ulrich, who was wronged by the phony transcript and stripped of his medical benefits by Texaco. And the company could have vowed to fight the lawsuit like the dickens, arguing that Texaco is not the cause of society's racial troubles but has tried to be part of the solution.

Start with the tapes: A fair listening does not necessarily reveal a "racist" conversation by executives at Texaco, but certainly a candid conversation about the problems of race at Texaco. They spoke of "jelly beans" dividing into camps of "us" and "them," an honest representation of life at many companies, not just in the oil patch.

Mr. Bijur could have made this point, starting with the *New York Times*, which has been embroiled in its own discrimination lawsuit with Angela Dodson, once its top-ranking black female. In a complaint filed with New York City's Human Rights Commission, she claims the paper was "engaged in gender-based harassment and disability-based discrimination . . . because *The Times* no longer wanted me, as a black person, to occupy a position as Senior editor."

Her deepest ire is reserved for *Times* veteran Carolyn Lee, who is white and more accustomed to being lauded as a champion of women and minorities. Ms. Dodson told the Village Voice: "It got to the point that whenever I was in her presence or earshot she made remarks [about other black people] that could only be taken as negative."

This sounds remarkably like the anecdotes filed in the Texaco complaint. All an outsider can safely conclude is that race makes everything more complicated, as sensitivity begets sensitivity. Mr. Bijur would have done more for racial understanding had he used his platform to open up this subject.

Yes, the cartoonist racists are out there, he might have said, but the *Times* coverage of Texaco only found cartoonist racists. The paper could have looked to its own experience for another story—a story about how garden-variety interpersonal conflict can land even decent people in the snares of racial mistrust.

This is what affirmative action, by throwing people together, was supposed to get us past. And it may be no accident that our most quota-ridden newspaper, *USA Today*, jumped off the bandwagon on the Texaco tapes, noting the ambiguity of whether the "jelly bean" remarks were meant to be hostile or friendly to blacks.

And McPaper kept on asking intelligent questions, like whether the *New York Times* had been "used by plaintiffs in the case to promote a faulty but more inflammatory transcript?" ("Not unless the court was used," answered *Times* Business Editor John Geddes, sounding like a lawyer himself.)

So Mr. Bijur was not facing a uniformly hopeless media torrent. The truth, even a complicated truth, catches up with the headlines eventually.

In time, he might have found surprising allies drifting to his side. The *New Republic* and the *New Yorker* have run thoughtful articles arguing that businesses should be allowed to use quotas but shouldn't be subject to harassment litigation if they don't. Right now, we do the opposite: Forbid companies to promote by quota, then sue them under federal "adverse impact" rules when they don't.

In effect, liberal voices are arguing that business could do more for minorities with less conflict if freedom of contract were restored. The world is changing, and companies have their own reasons nowadays for wanting minorities around. They need input from different kinds of people on how to deal with different kinds of people. No doubt this is why McPaper feels free to thumb its nose at the conformity crowd on stories like Texaco and church-burnings. (See September's *Harvard Business Review* for what business is thinking about diversity now.)

If companies were set free to assemble the work forces most useful to them, they could sweep away a heap of excuses for recrimination. Whites couldn't feel cheated out of jobs. Blacks wouldn't end up at companies that want them only for window-dressing. And the world could go back to feeling OK about being an interesting place. We might even allow that cultural patterns other than racism may explain why so many rednecks, and so few blacks, become petroleum engineers.

Mr. Bijur may have made the best of a bad deal for his shareholders. Whether it was best for America is a different judgment.[100]

Richard Lundwall, the executive who taped the sessions with the other executives, was charged with one count of obstruction of justice. Lundwall had turned over the tapes of the conversations to lawyers for the plaintiffs in the discrimination suit on October 25, 1996. Lundwall had been terminated.

Texaco hired attorney Michael Armstrong to investigate the underlying allegations. Mr. Armstrong found the tapes had not been transcribed correctly.

As part of its settlement, Texaco agreed to, at a cost of $55 million, assign a task force to police hiring and promotion as well as requiring mentors for black employees and sensitivity training for white employees.[101]

The following interview with CEO Bijur appeared in *Business Week*:

Q: *How did your legal strategy change once the news of the tapes was printed?*

A: When I saw [the story], I knew that this lawsuit was pending and moving forward. I made the judgment that we needed to accelerate the settlement process. And those discussions on settlement commenced almost immediately.

[100] *Wall Street Journal. Eastern Edition (Staff Produced Copy Only) by Gerald M. Levin. Copyright 1992 by Dow Jones & Co. Inc. Reproduced with permission of Dow Jones & Co. Inc. in the format textbook via Copyright Clearance Center.*
[101] *"Texaco: Lessons from a Crisis in Progress,"* Business Week, December 2, 1996, p. 44.

Q: *It has been reported that you didn't get the board of directors involved with the settlement talks and other issues. Why not?*

A: You're drawing conclusions that are erroneous. The board was fully involved throughout the entire process. I talked to numerous directors personally. We had several board and executive committee meetings. The board was fully supportive of our actions.

Q: *Have you met with shareholders?*

A: Yes, of course. I went down to [New York] and met with the Interfaith Center on Corporate Responsibility, which is a group of religious shareholders. I expressed our position on this and listened carefully to their position and got some good counsel and guidance. But I wanted to provide our side of the issue as well. I have met with [New York State Comptroller] Carl McCall and [New York City Comptroller] Alan Hevesi about concerns that they had, and I will continue to meet with other shareholders as I normally do.

Q: *Why do you think the oil industry has such a poor reputation on issues of racial diversity and gender equality? How does Texaco stack up against the others?*

A: The percentage of minorities within Texaco is just about average for the petroleum industry. We have made really significant progress in the last several years in improving the percentage. But there are some very interesting points that need to be examined to place in context what may be going on in this industry. I just read a study that showed that in 1995, there were only nine petroleum engineering minority graduates that came out of all engineering schools in the United States—only nine. That's not an excuse. But it is indicative of why it is difficult for this industry to have a lot of people in the pipeline. Now, of course, that does not apply to accountants, finance people, and anybody else. But we are a very technically oriented industry.

Q: *Have you personally witnessed discrimination at Texaco?*

A: In the nearly 31 years I have been with Texaco, I have never witnessed an incident of racial bias or prejudice. And had I seen it, I would have taken disciplinary action. I've never seen it.

Q: *Is there a widespread culture of insensitivity at Texaco?*

A: I do not think there is a culture of institutional bias within Texaco. I think we've got a great many very good and decent human beings, but that unfortunately we mirror society. There is bigotry in society. There is prejudice and injustice in society. I am sorry to say that, and I am sorry to say that probably does exist within Texaco. I can't do much about society, but I certainly can do something about Texaco.

Q: *What are your views on affirmative action?*

A: Texaco's views on affirmative action have not changed a bit. We have supported affirmative action, and we will continue to support affirmative action.

Q: *This is your first big trial since taking over. What have you learned?*

A: I've learned that as good as our programs are in the company—and they really are quite good, even in this area—there's always more we can do. We've got to really drill down into the programs. We've got to make certain that they're meeting the objectives and goals we've set for them.

Q: *Are there other lessons in terms of your style of management?*

A: I don't think I would do anything different the next time than what I did this time.

Q: *How will you make sure the spirit as well as the letter of the policy is followed at Texaco?*

A: We're going to put more and more and more emphasis on it until we get it through everybody's head: Bigotry is not going to be tolerated here.[102]

Robert W. Ulrich was indicted in 1997.[103] Mr. Lundwall entered a "not guilty" plea on July 8, 1997, and J. David Keough has sued Texaco for libel. Texaco named Mary Bush, a financial consultant, as its first black female board member.[104]

As Lundwall's prosecution has proceeded, new discoveries have been made. For example, "purposeful erasures" have been found on the tapes.[105]

In an interim report on its progress toward the settlement goals, Texaco revealed the following:

Polishing the Star

As part of its settlement of a discrimination lawsuit brought by black employees, Texaco has moved on a half-dozen fronts to alter its business practices.

Hiring Asked search firms to identify wider arrays of candidates. Expanded recruiting at historically minority colleges. Gave 50 scholarships and paid internships to minority students seeking engineering or technical degrees.

Career Advancement Wrote objective standards for promotions. Developing training program for new managers. Developing a mentoring program.

Diversity Initiatives Conducted two-day diversity training for more than 8,000 of 20,000 U.S. employees. Tied management bonuses to diversity goals. Developing alternative dispute resolution and ombudsman programs.

Purchasing Nearly doubled purchases from minority- or women-owned businesses. Asking suppliers to report their purchases from such companies.

Financial Services Substantially increased banking, investment management and insurance business with minority- and women-owned firms. A group of such firms underwrote a $150 million public financing.

Retailing Added three black independent retailers, 18 black managers of company-owned service stations, 12 minority or female wholesalers, 13 minority- or women-owned Xpress Lube outlets and 6 minority- or women-owned lubricant distributors.[106]

---

[102] Tim Smart, "Texaco: Lessons from a Crisis-in-Progress." Reprinted from December 2, 1996, issue of Business Week by special permission, © 1997 by McGraw Hill, Inc.

[103] Terzan Ewing, "Ex-Texaco Official Is Indicted in Case Tied to Bias Suit," The Wall Street Journal, June 30, 1997, p. A9.

[104] "Texaco Board Names First Black Woman," USA Today, July 8, 1997, p. 2B.

[105] Mike France and Tim Smart, "The Ugly Talk on the Texaco Tape," Business Week, November 18, 1996, p. 58.

[106] Bryant, "How Much Has Texaco Changed?" pp. BU1, BU16.

In May 1998, the Texaco executives were acquitted of all criminal charges.[107] Lawyers argued successfully that the tapes were interrupted over 500 times and were "utterly untrustworthy"[108] and that the executives had not been adequately instructed by their lawyers on document production.

Mr. Bijur's conduct in the "Jelly Bean Fiasco" was heralded by managers and academics worldwide. He was in demand at virtually all large conferences as a guest speaker. However, Texaco did not perform as well as other oil companies during his tenure. For example, Texaco and Chevron each had revenues of $50 billion in 2000, but Texaco's profits were $2.5 billion, as compared to Chevron's $5.2 billion. Near the end of 2000, the Texaco board agreed to merge the company with Chevron.

Before that merger occurred, Mr. Bijur resigned abruptly from Texaco after being summoned by the Texaco board to a meeting at which the board announced that it had lost confidence in him. There had been a series of issues such as the $2 million remodeling of the corporate suite at New York City's Carlyle Hotel, the use of the company jet, and his romance with a subordinate whom he eventually married in the summer of 2000. Texaco and Mr. Bijur have declined to discuss the issues, but an audit concludes that while there may have been bad judgment in Mr. Bijur's behavior and decisions, there was nothing illegal or even "serious."[109]

....

Discussion Questions

1. Provide a summary of the players and their concerns.

2. Discuss the ethics of the recording.

3. Why do you think the executives discussed document destruction? Why were they acquitted?

4. What ethical issues surround diversity training and affirmative action?

5. Evaluate Texaco's performance and Mr. Bijur's behavior since the time of the settlement of this case. Consider that Texaco's spending with minority firms was at $528 million, just 2 years into its 5-year-$1 billion promise.[110]

6. Read the following and discuss whether Mr. Bijur acted in the shareholders' interests.

[107] David E. Rovella, "Texaco Execs' Verdicts Roil Prosecution," National Law Journal, May 25, 1998, pp. B1, B2.
[108] Steve Liesman, "Texaco Bias Case Leads to Acquittals," The Wall Street Journal, May 13, 1998, p. A3.
[109] Thaddeus Herrick and Nikhil Deogun, "Insiders Assert Behavior an Issue with Texaco CEO," The Wall Street Journal, March 16, 2001, pp. B1, B4.
[110] "Texaco's Spending with Minority Firms Ahead of Five-Year Plan," The Wall Street Journal, March 17, 1999, p. B6.

A Texaco Chairman Who Believed the N.Y. Times[111]

Paul Craig Roberts

Texaco and its shareholders are the first victims of the 1991 Civil Rights act. This legislation permits plaintiffs in job-discrimination cases to be awarded compensatory and punitive damages in addition to back pay.

Before the 1991 act, class-action suits threatened companies that lacked race and gender proportion in their work force with having to fork over years of back pay to preferred minorities who had not been hired. Since there was seldom any evidence that the companies had actually discriminated against any of the individuals, the companies would sometimes fight these suits rather than settle them.

This rankled the sharp lawyers who make tens of millions of dollars off such lawsuits and civil rights groups that need voluntary settlements of discrimination suits as proof of institutionalized racism. They wanted a bigger club over the companies to force faster and easier settlements, and the Bush administration gave it to them by adding compensatory and punitive damages.

This tripled the cost to a company of losing a discrimination suit in court, thereby making settlement instead of trial a near certainty. Since the accused company just wants to settle, the accuser does not need evidence that would have to stand up in court.

The Texaco case illustrates this perfectly. Michael Hausfeld, the lawyer for the black employees, claimed to have an audio tape of Texaco executives using racial slurs while conspiring to hide evidence of Texaco's discrimination. He gave what he said was a transcript of the incriminating tape to Kurt Eichenwald of the *New York Times*.
Mr. Eichenwald was not sufficiently professional to recognize Mr. Hausfeld's vested interest ($38.3 million is his and co-counsel Dan Berger's share of the settlement), and he did not ask to listen to the tape and to check the transcript against it. He quoted on trust from the inflammatory transcript that was handed to him.

The next mistake in the farce was made by Texaco Chairman Peter I. Bijur. He believed the *New York Times* still had reportorial integrity and was horrified by what he read about his executives. He quickly announced a generous settlement and placed financial sanctions on the presumed guilty executives. All of this happened before anyone listened to the tapes. When the tapes were finally transcribed by disinterested professionals, it turned out that Mr. Eichenwald's report, the catalyst for the record settlement, was inaccurate. No one had used a racial epithet, and the reference to black employees as jelly beans was an innocent multicultural metaphor that diversity trainers had taught the company to use. All Texaco employees are jelly beans, and the different colors are supposed to be appropriately mixed in the jar. What the company executives are actually protesting in the taped conversation is the "us-them" attitude of black employees: "You can't have just we and them. You can't just have black jelly beans and other jelly beans. It doesn't work," said Texaco treasurer Robert Ulrich.

[111] Paul Craig Roberts, "A Texaco Chairman Who Believed The N.Y. Times," The Washington Times, December 15, 1996, p. 32. Reprinted by permission of Paul Craig Roberts and Creators Syndicate, Inc.

The outcome is that the *New York Times* reporter's predisposition to believe in a racist corporate America made it easy for a sharp lawyer to use him to win a big case and establish a precedent: Companies that established quotas for hiring now will have to establish them for promotions. If they do not, every one of the preferred minorities on their payrolls can use the club of compensatory and punitive damages to extort large settlements.

But this is the least of it. Texaco's abject surrender to a lie has cemented into the belief system the image of racist America that civil rights plaintiffs have labored to establish. Corporate America is in a dither. Quotas are not more important to success than marketing, finance, or manufacturing. There is talk of providing boards of directors with full-time staffs to implement and monitor "diversity goals."

The ultimate casualty may be California's Civil Rights Initiative (already, a federal judge temporarily has blocked its implementation). The initiative, which passed comfortably in the November elections, seeks to reestablish equality before the law in California state and local government employment and university admissions. But it will prove difficult to admit students and to hire and promote government employees by individual merit alone when group rights are the rule in corporate America.

CASE 5.14

Hunter Tylo: Pregnancy Is Not a BFOQ

Hunter Tylo was hired by Spelling Entertainment Group to play a character who would "strut in a bikini to steal actress Heather Locklear's husband" on the television show *Melrose Place*. Ms. Tylo never began work on the contract because she was fired after she disclosed to the show's executives that she was pregnant.[112]

Mr. Spelling, the owner of the Spelling Entertainment Group, explained that Ms. Tylo was fired because he did not think it was fair to have scripts rewritten around a character and actress who had not yet appeared on the show. Mr. Spelling noted that he had worked with Ms. Locklear during her pregnancy, using various camera angles to avoid revealing Ms. Locklear's pregnancy.

In a letter to Mr. Spelling from actress Gabrielle Carteris, who plays a character on Mr. Spelling's other show, *Beverly Hills 90210*, Ms. Carteris expressed support for Mr. Spelling, "I just had to let you know how sorry I am with regards to the trial. It was particularly upsetting, when for me you were so very supportive of my getting pregnant."[113]

Mr. Spelling also said that following Ms. Tylo's termination, he offered her a contract for the following season that would have paid more than her fee of $13,500 per episode that was provided on the terminated contract and that the new contract would have run for more episodes. Ms. Tylo refused the offer and filed suit. She was awarded $4 million by a jury for emotional distress and $894,601 for economic loss.[114]

[112] Maureen Dowd, "Civil Rights Siren," The New York Times, December 24, 1997, p. A13.

[113] Ann Oldenburg, "'Hurt' Spelling Says Tylo's Pregnancy Wasn't Issue," USA Today, December 26, 1997, p. 1D.

[114] Ann Oldenburg, "Actress Fired for Being Pregnant Wins Lawsuit," USA Today, December 23, 1997, p. 1D.

Discussion Questions

1. Is there a distinction between Ms. Tylo's circumstances and Ms. Locklear's?

2. Is not being pregnant a BFOQ (bona fide occupational qualification) for playing a "vixen" on a television series?

3. Did Mr. Spelling give sufficient justification for Ms. Tylo's termination?

5 F

Whistle-Blowing

In a true confrontation between personal values and company policy, employees are often faced with the knowledge that their employer is acting unethically in a way that does or could hurt someone else. How should they react? What should they do? Why do employers often ignore employees' concerns?

READING 5.15

The Options for Whistle-Blowers

Employees who are faced with a situation at work in which their values are at odds with the actions of their employers are grappling with their sense of loyalty to the company and their co-workers as well as their own value system. For example, an employee who knows that her company's product is defective is torn between her concern for customers who buy the product and her loyalty to the company and her fellow workers, who may also be her friends. She is concerned about her livelihood, her co-workers' livelihood, and the safety of others. Table 5.1 illustrates the options available to those who find their values at odds with the company's conduct.

Discussion Questions

1. What choices do whistle-blowers have?

2. As you read the following cases, decide which type of whistle-blower was involved.

CASE 5.16

Beech-Nut and the No-Apple-Juice Apple Juice

Beech-Nut was heavily in debt, had only 15 percent of the baby food market, and was operating out of a badly maintained eighty-year-old plant in Canajoharie, New York. Creditors and debt were growing. Beech-Nut needed to keep its costs down, its production

TABLE 5.1 Employee concerns and employee dissent

Nature of the perceived activity triggering the concern				
	Illegal, immoral, or illegitimate		Not illegal, immoral, or illegitimate	
Expression of the concern (voice)	**Exit dimension**			
	Stay	**Go**	**Stay**	**Go**
External dissent to someone who can take action	External whistle-blowing	Exit with public protest	Secret sharing	Exit with secret sharing
Internal dissent to someone who can take action	Internal whistle-blowing	Protest during exit interview	Employee participation, grievance	Explain reason for resignation in exit
Dissent in some other form	Discussion, confrontation with wrongdoer	Exit with notice to wrongdoer	Sabotage, strikes	Sabotage, strikes with exit
No expressed dissent	Inactive observation	Inactive departure	Silent disgruntlement	Silent departure

From: Peter B. Jubb, "Whistleblowing: A Restrictive Definition and Interpretation," 21 *Journal of Business Ethics* 77, 80 (1999). Reprinted with kind permission of Kluwer Academic Publishers.

up, and increase its market share. In 1977, Beech-Nut made a contract with Interjuice Trading Corporation (the Universal Juice Corporation) to buy its apple juice concentrate. The contract was a lifesaver for Beech-Nut because Interjuice's prices were 20 percent below market and apple concentrate was used as a base or sweetener in 30 percent of Beech-Nut's baby food products.

With this much-lower-cost key ingredient (the savings were estimated to be about $250,000 per year), Beech-Nut had reached a turnaround point. Here was a little company that could take on Gerber Baby Foods, the number-one baby food company in the United States. Nestlé Corporation, the international food producer based in Switzerland, saw potential in this little company, and bought Beech-Nut in 1979. By the early 1980s, Beech-Nut had become the number-two baby food company in the United States. However, because of its substantially increased marketing costs, Beech-Nut's money pressures remained.

Jerome J. LiCari was the director of research and development for Beech-Nut Nutrition Corporation. Beech-Nut still had the low-cost Interjuice contract, but LiCari was worried. There were rumors of adulteration (or the addition or substituted use of inferior substances in a product) flying about in the apple juice industry. Chemists in LiCari's department were suspicious, but they did not yet have tests that could prove the adulteration.

In October 1978, Dr. LiCari learned from other sources that the concentrate might be made of syrups and edible substances that are much cheaper than apples. LiCari reported what he had learned to John Lavery, Beech-Nut's vice president for operations. Lavery's job included management of the purchasing and processing of apple juice concentrates.

Concerned, Lavery sent two employees to inspect Universal's blending operation. What the employees found was only a warehouse without any blending facility. Lavery did nothing more and did not ask about where Interjuice's blending operation was or whether he could have it inspected. Instead, he had Universal officers sign a "hold harmless" agreement, an addendum to the purchase contract that was intended to protect Beech-Nut if any legal claims or suits related to the juice resulted.

Under federal law, a company can sell a product that tastes like apple juice but is not really apple juice so long as the label discloses that it is made from syrups, sweeteners, and flavors. However, Beech-Nut's labels indicated that there was apple product in its apple juice and apple sweetener in the other products in which the concentrate was used, such as the baby fruits, where it provided a sweeter taste. Selling products labeled as apple juice or as containing apple product when they are in fact made with syrups and flavorings is a federal felony. Lavery wanted the hold-harmless agreement for protection against any claims that might be filed under these laws.

During this time, LiCari and his staff were able to develop some tests that did detect the presence of corn starch and other substances in the apple concentrate that were consistent with the composition of adulterated juice. LiCari continued to tell Lavery that he was concerned about the quality of the concentrate supplied by Universal. LiCari told Lavery that if a supplier was willing to adulterate concentrate in the first place it would likely have little compunction about continuing to supply adulterated product even after signing a hold-harmless document.

Lavery reminded LiCari that Universal's price to Beech-Nut for the concentrate was 50 cents to a dollar per gallon below the price charged by Beech-Nut's previous supplier. He also reminded LiCari of the tremendous economic pressure under which the company was operating. The revenue from Beech-Nut's apple juice was $60 million between 1977 and 1982. Lavery told LiCari that he would not change suppliers unless LiCari brought him tests that would "prove in a court of law that the concentrate was adulterated." He also told Dr. LiCari that any further testing of the product was to be a low item on his list of work assignments and priorities.

In 1979, LiCari sent the concentrate to an outside laboratory for independent analysis. The test results showed that the concentrate consisted primarily of sugar syrup. LiCari told Lavery of the lab results, but Lavery did nothing. In July 1979, Lavery also received a memorandum from the company's plant manager in San Jose, California, that indicated that approximately 95,000 pounds of concentrate inventory was "funny" and "adulterated," in that it was "almost pure corn syrup." The plant manager suggested that Beech-Nut demand its money back from the supplier. Instead, Lavery told the manager to go ahead and use the tainted concentrate in the company's mixed juices. Beech-Nut continued to purchase its apple juice concentrate from Universal.

LiCari and his staff continued their efforts to communicate to Lavery and other company officials that the Interjuice concentrate was adulterated. In August 1981, LiCari sent a memorandum to Charles Jones, the company's purchasing manager, with a copy to Lavery, stating that although the scientists had not proven that the concentrate was adulterated, there was "a tremendous amount of circumstantial evidence" to that effect, "paint[ing] a grave case against the current supplier." LiCari's memorandum concluded that "[i]t is imperative that Beech-Nut establish the authenticity of the Apple Juice Concentrate used to formulate our products. If the authenticity cannot be established, I feel that we have sufficient reason to look for a new supplier."[115]

Lavery took no action to change suppliers. Rather, he instructed Jones to ignore LiCari's memorandum, criticized LiCari for not being a "team player," and called his scientists "Chicken Little." He threatened to fire LiCari.[116] In his evaluation of LiCari's performance for 1981, Lavery wrote that LiCari had great technical ability but that his judgment was "colored by naivete and impractical ideals."[117]

In late 1981, the company received, unsolicited, a report from a Swiss laboratory concluding that Beech-Nut's apple juice product was adulterated, stating, "[t]he apple juice is false, can not see any apple."[118] Lavery reviewed this report, and one of his aides sent it to Universal. Universal made no response, and Beech-Nut took no action.

Nils Hoyvald became the CEO of Beech-Nut in April 1981. Both before and after becoming president of Beech-Nut, Hoyvald was aware, from several sources, about an adulteration problem. In November 1981, Beech-Nut's purchasing manager raised the problem. Hoyvald took no action. Rather, he told Lavery that, for budgetary reasons, he would not approve a change in concentrate suppliers until 1983.[119]

In the spring of 1982, Paul Hillabush, the company's director of quality assurance, advised Hoyvald that there would be some adverse publicity about Beech-Nut's purchases of apple juice concentrate. On June 25, 1982, a detective hired by the Processed Apple Institute visited Lavery at Beech-Nut's Canajoharie, New York plant, and told him that Beech-Nut was about to be involved in a lawsuit as a result of its use of adulterated juice. The investigator showed Canajoharie plant operators documents from the Interjuice dumpster and new tests indicating that the juice was adulterated. The institute invited Beech-Nut to join its lawsuit against Interjuice (a suit that eventually closed Interjuice). Beech-Nut declined. It did cancel its future contracts with Interjuice, but it continued to use its on-hand supplies for production because of the tremendous cost pressures and competition it was facing.

LiCari also took his evidence of adulteration to Hoyvald. Hoyvald told LiCari he would take up the issue. Several months later, after no action had been taken, LiCari resigned. After leaving Beech-Nut, LiCari wrote an anonymous letter to the Food and Drug Administration (FDA) disclosing the juice adulteration at Beech-Nut. He signed

[115] Chris Welles, "What Led Beech-Nut Down the Road to Disgrace," Business Week, February 22, 1988, pp. 124–128.
[116] U.S. v. Beech-Nut, Inc., 871 F.2d 1181 (2nd Cir. 1989), at 1185; 925 F.2d 604 (2nd Cir. 1991); cert. denied, 493 U.S. 933 (1989).
[117] Welles, "What Led Beech-Nut Down the Road to Disgrace," p. 128.
[118] U.S. v. Beech-Nut, Inc., 871 F.2d 1181 (2nd Cir. 1989), at 1185; 925 F.2d 604 (2nd Cir. 1991); cert. denied, 493 U.S. 933 (1989).
[119] Id.

the letter, "Johnny Appleseed." The FDA began an investigation of Beech-Nut and its products and supplier, but Beech-Nut was not cooperative. The explanation managers offered was simple. When the FDA first notified the company of the problem, Beech-Nut had 700,000 cases of the spurious juice. By stalling, Beech-Nut was able to sell off some of those cases and ship others overseas (details follow), leaving it with the destruction of just 200,000 cases of the fake product.

An FDA investigator observed:

> They played a cat-and-mouse game with us. When FDA would identify a specific apple juice lot as tainted, Beech-Nut would quickly destroy it before the FDA could seize it, an act that would have created negative publicity.[120]

When New York state government tests first revealed that a batch of Beech-Nut's juice contained little or no apple juice, Beech-Nut had the juice moved during the night, using nine tanker trucks. CEO Hoyvald realized that not being able to sell the inventory of juice the company had on hand would be financially crippling. So, he began delaying tactics designed to give the company time to sell it.

To avoid seizure of the inventory in New York by state officials in August 1982, Hoyvald had this juice moved out of state during the night. It was transported from the New York plant to a warehouse in Secaucus, New Jersey, and the records of this shipment and others were withheld from FDA investigators until the investigators independently located the carrier Beech-Nut had used. While the FDA was searching for the adulterated products but before it had discovered the Secaucus warehouse, Hoyvald ordered virtually the entire stock in that warehouse shipped to Beech-Nut's distributor in Puerto Rico; the Puerto Rico distributor had not placed an order for the product and had twice refused to buy the product even at great discounts offered personally by Hoyvald.

In September 1982, Hoyvald ordered a rush shipment of the inventory of apple juice products held at Beech-Nut's San Jose plant, and took a number of unusual steps to get rid of the entire stock. He authorized price discounts of 50 percent; the largest discount ever offered before had been 10 percent. Hoyvald insisted that the product be shipped "fast, fast, fast," and gave a distributor in the Dominican Republic only two days, instead of the usual thirty, to respond to this product promotion. In order to get the juice out of the warehouse and out of the country as quickly as possible, Beech-Nut shipped it to the Dominican Republic on the first possible sailing date, which was from an unusually distant port, which raised the freight cost to an amount nearly equal to the value of the goods themselves. Finally, this stock was shipped before Beech-Nut had received the necessary financial documentation from the distributor, which, as one Beech-Nut employee testified, was "tantamount to giving the stuff away."[121]

Hoyvald also used Beech-Nut's lawyers to help delay the government investigation, thereby giving the company more time to sell its inventory of adulterated juice before the product could be seized or a recall could be ordered. For example, in September 1982, the FDA informed Beech-Nut that it intended to seize all of Beech-Nut's apple juice products made from Universal concentrate; in October, New York State authorities

---

[120] Welles, "What Led Beech-Nut Down the Road to Disgrace," p. 128.
[121] U.S. v. Beech-Nut, Inc., 871 F.2d, at 1186. This segment of the case was adapted from the judicial opinion.

advised the company that they planned to initiate a local recall of these products. Beech-Nut's lawyers, at Hoyvald's direction, successfully negotiated with the authorities for a limited recall, excluding products held by retailers and stocks of mixed juice products. Beech-Nut eventually agreed to conduct a nationwide recall of its apple juice, but by the time of the recall Hoyvald had sold more than 97 percent of the earlier stocks of apple juice. In December 1982, in response to Hoyvald's request, Thomas Ward, a member of a law firm retained by Beech-Nut, sent Hoyvald a letter that summarized the events surrounding the apple juice concentrate problem as follows:

From the start, we had two main objectives:

1) to minimize Beech-Nut's potential economic loss, which we understand has been conservatively estimated at $3.5 million, and
2) to minimize any damage to the company's reputation.

We determined that this could be done by delaying, for as long as possible, any market withdrawal of products produced from the Universal Juice concentrate. . . .

. . . In spite of the recognition that FDA might wish to have Beech-Nut recall some of its products, management decided to continue sales of all such products for the time being. . . . The decision to continue sales and some production of the products was based upon the recognition of the significant potential financial loss and loss of goodwill, and the fact that apple juice is a critical lead-in item for Beech-Nut.

Since the mixed fruit juices and other products constituted the bulk of the products produced with Universal concentrate, one of our main goals became to prevent the FDA and state authorities from focusing on these products, and we were in fact successful in limiting the controversy strictly to apple juice.[122]

In November 1986, Beech-Nut, Hoyvald, and Lavery, along with Universal's proprietor Zeev Kaplansky and four others ("suppliers"), were indicted on charges relating to the company's sale of adulterated and misbranded apple juice products. Hoyvald and Lavery were charged with (1) one count of conspiring with the suppliers to violate the FDCA, 21 U.S.C. §§331(a), (k), and 333(b) (1982 & Supp. IV 1986), in violation of 18 U.S.C. §371; (2) 20 counts of mail fraud, in violation of 18 U.S.C. §§1341 and 2; and (3) 429 counts of introducing adulterated and misbranded apple juice into interstate commerce, in violation of 21 U.S.C. §§331(a) and 333(b) and 18 U.S.C. §2. The suppliers were also charged with introducing adulterated concentrate into interstate commerce.

Hoyvald and Lavery pleaded not guilty to the charges against them. Eventually, Beech-Nut pleaded guilty to 215 felony violations of §§331(a) and 333(b); it received a $2 million fine and was ordered to pay $140,000 to the FDA for the expenses of its investigation. Kaplansky and the other four supplier-defendants also eventually pleaded guilty to some or all of the charges against them. Hoyvald and Lavery thus went to trial alone. LiCari testified at the trials, "I thought apple juice should be made from apples."[123]

---

[122] Id., pp. 1186–1187.
[123] Welles, "What Led Beech-Nut Down the Road to Disgrace," p. 128.

The trial began in November 1987 and continued for three months. The government's evidence included that previously discussed. Hoyvald's principal defense was that all of his acts relating to the problem of adulterated concentrate had been performed on the advice of counsel. For example, there was evidence that the Beech-Nut shipment of adulterated juices from its San Jose plant to the Dominican Republic followed the receipt by Hoyvald of a telex sent by Sheldon Klein, an associate of the law firm representing Beech-Nut, which summarized a telephone conference between Beech-Nut officials and its attorneys as follows:

> We understand that approximately 25,000 cases of apple juice manufactured from concentrate purchased from Universal Juice is [sic] currently in San Jose. It is strongly recommended that such product and all other Universal products in Beech-Nut's possession anywhere in the US be destroyed before a meeting with [the FDA] takes place.[124]

Hoyvald and Klein testified that they had a follow-up conversation in which Klein told Hoyvald that, as an alternative, it would be lawful to export the adulterated apple juice products.

The jury returned a verdict of guilty on all of the counts against Lavery. It returned a verdict of guilty against Hoyvald on 359 counts of adulterating and misbranding apple juice, all of which related to shipments after June 25, 1982. It was unable to reach a verdict on the remaining counts against Hoyvald, which related to events prior to that date.

The federal district court sentenced Hoyvald to a term of imprisonment of a year and a day, fined him $100,000, imposed a $9,000 special assessment, and ordered him to pay the costs of prosecution. In March 1989, the federal court of appeals for the second circuit reversed the conviction on the ground that venue was improperly laid in the Eastern District instead of the Northern District of New York. The case was remanded to the district court for a new trial.[125] In August 1989, Hoyvald was retried before Chief Judge Platt on 19 of the counts on which a mistrial had been declared during his first trial. After four weeks of trial, the jury was unable to agree on a verdict and a mistrial was declared.

Rather than face a third trial, Hoyvald entered into a plea agreement with the government on November 7, 1989. It was agreed that the government would recommend that the court impose a suspended sentence; five years probation, including 1,000 hours of community service; and a $100,000 fine. On November 13, 1989, the district court accepted the plea and imposed sentence. At that plea proceeding Judge Platt agreed, at Hoyvald's request, to defer the beginning of his community service to give him three weeks time to travel to Denmark to visit his 84-year-old mother.

Six months later, in May 1990, Hoyvald again requested permission from his probation officer to return to Denmark to visit his mother, and then to be permitted to visit "East and West Germany, Switzerland, Hungary, Czechoslovakia, and Greece" on business, a journey that would take slightly more than three weeks. The Probation

---

[124] U.S. v. Beech-Nut, Inc., *871 F.2d 1181, at 1194. Again, this material is adapted from the case.*
[125] United States v. Beech-Nut Nutrition Corp., *871 F.2d 1181 (2nd Cir.), cert. denied, 493 U.S. 933, 110 S.Ct. 324, 107 L.Ed.2d 314 (1989).*

Department expressed no opposition to the trip so long as he "supplies an appropriate itinerary and documentation as to the business portions of his trip." The United States Attorney did not oppose the request. On May 22, 1990, Hoyvald requested permission to travel to the other European countries to "look for a job and to investigate business opportunities" in those countries. The district court ruled that Hoyvald could visit his mother in Denmark but denied the request to travel to other countries.

Discussion Questions

1. No one was ever made ill or harmed by the fake apple juice. Was LiCari overreacting?

2. Did LiCari follow the lines of authority in his efforts? Is this important for a whistle-blower? Why?

3. What pressures contributed to Beech-Nut's unwillingness to switch suppliers?

4. Using the various models for analysis of ethical dilemmas that you have learned, point out the things that Lavery and Hoyvald and others in the company failed to consider as they refused to deal with the Interjuice problem.

5. Why did LiCari feel he had to leave Beech-Nut?

6. Why did LiCari write anonymously to the FDA?

7. Is it troublesome that Hoyvald and Lavery escaped sentences on a technicality? Is the sentence too light?

8. Why do you think Hoyvald and the others thought they could get away with the adulterated juice? Why did they play the "cat-and-mouse" game? What principles about ethics have you learned that might have helped them analyze their situation more carefully and clearly?

9. Beech-Nut's market share went from 19.1 percent of the market to 15.8 percent, where it has hovered ever since. Why? What were the costs of Beech-Nut's fake apple juice and its "cat-and-mouse game" with the FDA? Do you think consumers still remember this conduct?

CASE 5.17

NASA and the Space Shuttle Booster Rockets

Morton Thiokol, Inc., an aerospace company, manufactures the solid-propellant rocket motors for the Peacekeeper missile and the missiles on Trident nuclear submarines. Thiokol also worked closely with the National Aeronautics and Space Administration (NASA) in developing the *Challenger*, one of NASA's reusable space shuttles.

Morton Thiokol served as the manufacturer for the booster rockets used to launch the *Challenger*. NASA had scheduled a special launch of the *Challenger* for January 1986. The launch was highly publicized because NASA had conducted a nationwide search for a teacher to send on the flight. For NASA's twenty-fifth shuttle mission, teacher Christa McAuliffe would be on board.

On the scheduled launch day, January 28, 1986, the weather was cloudy and cold at the John F. Kennedy Space Center in Cape Canaveral, Florida. The launch had already been delayed several times, but NASA officials still contacted Thiokol engineers in Utah to discuss whether the shuttle should be launched in such cold weather. The temperature range for the boosters, as specified in Thiokol's contract with NASA, was between 40° F and 90° F.

The temperature at Cape Canaveral that January morning was below 30° F. The launch of the *Challenger* proceeded nevertheless. A presidential commission later concluded, "Thiokol management reversed its position and recommended the launch of [the *Challenger*] at the urging of [NASA] and contrary to the views of its engineers in order to accommodate a major customer."[126]

Two of the Thiokol engineers involved in the launch, Allan McDonald and Roger Boisjoly, later testified that they had opposed the launch. Boisjoly had done work on the shuttle's booster rockets at the Marshall Space Flight Center in Utah in February 1985, at which time he noted that at low temperatures, an O-ring assembly in the rockets eroded and, consequently, failed to seal properly. Though Boisjoly gave a presentation on the issue, little action was taken over the course of the year. Boisjoly conveyed his frustration in his activity reports. Finally, in July 1985, Boisjoly wrote a confidential memo to R. K. (Bob) Lund, Thiokol's vice president for engineering. An excerpt follows:

> This letter is written to insure that management is fully aware of the seriousness of the current O-ring erosion problem. . . . The mistakenly accepted position on the joint problem was to fly without fear of failure. . . . [This position] is now drastically changed as a result of the SRM [shuttle recovery mission] 16A nozzle joint erosion which eroded a secondary O-ring with the primary O-ring never sealing. If the same scenario should occur in a field joint (and it could), then it is a jump ball as to the success or failure of the joint. . . . The result would be a catastrophe of the highest order—loss of human life. . . .
>
> It is my honest and real fear that if we do not take immediate action to dedicate a team to solve the problem, with the field joint having the number one priority, then we stand in jeopardy of losing a flight along with all the launch pad facilities.[127]

In October 1985, Boisjoly presented the O-ring issue at a conference of the Society of Automotive Engineers and requested suggestions for resolution.[128]

On January 27, 1986, the day before the launch, Boisjoly attempted to halt the launch. Mr. McDonald also offered his insights to a group of NASA and Thiokol engineers, However, four Thiokol managers, including Lund, voted unanimously to recommend the launch. One manager had urged Lund to "take off his engineering hat and put on his management hat."[129] The managers then developed the following

---

[126] Judith Dobrzynski, "Morton Thiokol: Reflections on the Shuttle Disaster," Business Week, March 14, 1988, p. 82.

[127] Russell Boisjoly, et al., "Roger Boisjoly and the Challenger Disaster: The Ethical Dimensions," Journal of Business Ethics 8, 1989, pp. 217–230.

[128] "No. 2 Official Is Appointed at Thiokol," The New York Times, June 12, 1992, p. C3; "Whistle-blowing: Not Always a Losing Game," EE Spectrum, December 1990, pp. 49–52.

[129] Boisjoly, "Roger Boisjoly and the Challenger Disaster," pp. 217–230.

revised recommendations. Engineers were excluded from the final decision and the development of these findings.[130]

- Calculations show that SRM-25 [the designation for the Challenger's January 28 flight] O-rings will be 20° colder than SRM-15 O-rings
- Temperature data not conclusive on predicting primary O-ring blow-by
- Engineering assessment is that:

    - Colder O-rings will have increased effective durometer [that is, they will be harder]
    - "Harder" O-rings will take longer to seat
    - More gas may pass primary [SRM-25] O-ring before the primary seal seats (relative to SRM-15)
    - Demonstrated sealing threshold [on SRM-25 O-ring] is 3 times greater than 0.038" erosion experienced on SRM-15
    - If the primary seal does not seat, the secondary seal will seat
    - Pressure will get to secondary seal before the metal parts rotate
    - O-ring pressure leak check places secondary seal in outboard position which minimizes sealing time
    - MTI recommends STS-51L launch proceed on 28 January 1986
    - SRM-25 will not be significantly different from SRM-15[131]

After the decision was made, Boisjoly returned to his office and wrote in his journal:

I sincerely hope this launch does not result in a catastrophe. I personally do not agree with some of the statements made in Joe Kilminster's [Kilminster was one of the four Thiokol managers who voted to recommend the launch] written summary stating that SRM-25 is okay to fly.[132]

Seventy-four seconds into the *Challenger* launch, the low temperature caused the seals at the booster rocket joints to fail. The *Challenger* exploded, killing Christa McAuliffe and the six astronauts on board.[133]

The subsequent investigation by the presidential commission placed the blame for the faulty O-rings squarely with Thiokol. Charles S. Locke, Thiokol's CEO, maintained, "I take the position that we never agreed to the launch at the temperature at the time of the launch. The *Challenger* incident resulted more from human error than mechanical error. The decision to launch should have been referred to headquarters. If we'd been consulted here, we'd never have given clearance, because the temperature was not within the contracted specs."[134]

Both Boisjoly and McDonald testified before the presidential panel regarding their opposition to the launch and the decision of their managers (who were also engineers) to override their recommendation. Both Boisjoly and McDonald also testified that following their expressed opposition to the launch and their willingness to come forward, they had been isolated from NASA and subsequently demoted. Since testifying,

[130] Paul Hoversten, "Engineers Waver, then Decide to Launch," USA Today, January 22, 1996, p. 2A.
[131] Boisjoly, "Roger Boisjoly and the Challenger Disaster," pp. 217–230.
[132] Interview with Roger Boisjoly, June 28, 1993.
[133] Paul Hoversten, Patricia Edmonds, and Haya El Nasser, "Debate Raged Night Before Doomed Launch," USA Today, January 22, 1996, pp. A1, A2.
[134] Dobrzynski, "Morton Thiokol," p. 82.

McDonald has been assigned to "special projects." Boisjoly, who took medical leave for post-traumatic stress disorder, has left Thiokol, but receives disability pay from the company. Currently, Mr. Boisjoly operates a consulting firm in Mesa, Arizona. He speaks frequently on business ethics to professional organizations and companies.[135]

In May 1986, then-CEO Locke stated, in an interview with *The Wall Street Journal*, "This shuttle thing will cost us this year 10¢ a share."[136] Locke later protested that his statement had been taken out of context.[137]

In 1989, Morton Norwich separated from Thiokol Chemical Corporation. The two companies had previously merged to become Morton Thiokol. Following the separation, Thiokol Chemical became Thiokol Corporation. Morton returned to the salt business, and Thiokol, remaining under contract with NASA through 1999, redesigned its space shuttle rocket motor to correct the deficiencies. No one at Thiokol was fired following the *Challenger* accident. Because of this incident and defense contractor indictments, the Government Accountability Project was established in Washington, D.C. The office provides a staff, legal assistance, and pamphlets to help whistle-blowers working on government projects.

Discussion Questions

1. Who is morally responsible for the deaths that resulted from the *Challenger* explosion?

2. If you had been in Allan McDonald's or Roger Boisjoly's position on January 28, 1986, what would you have done?

3. Evaluate Locke's comment on the loss of ten cents per share.

4. Should the possibility that the booster rockets might not perform below 30° F have been a factor in the decision to allow the launch to proceed?

5. Roger Boisjoly offers the following advice on whistle-blowing:

   a. You owe your organization an opportunity to respond. Speak to them first verbally. Memos are not appropriate for the first step.
   b. Gather collegial support for your position. If you cannot get the support, then make sure you are correct.
   c. Spell out the problem in a letter.

   Mr. Boisjoly acknowledges he did not gather collegial support. How can such support be obtained? Where would you start? What would you use to persuade others?

6. Scientist William Lourance has written, ". . . a thing is safe if its attendant risks are judged to be acceptable."[138] Had everyone, including the astronauts, accepted the risks attendant to the *Challenger's* launch?

---

[135] Interview with Roger Boisjoly.
[136] Dobrzynski, "Morton Thiokol," p. 82.
[137] "No. 2 Official Is Appointed at Thiokol," p. C3; "Whistle-blowing," pp. 49–52.
[138] Joseph R. Herkert, "Management's Hat Trick: Misuse of 'Engineering Judgment' in the Challenger Incident," *Journal of Business Ethics* 10, 1991, p. 617.

7. Groupthink is defined as

> . . . a mode of thinking that people engage in when they are deeply involved in a cohesive in-group, when the members' strivings for unanimity override their motivation to realistically appraise alternative courses of action. . . . Groupthink refers to the deterioration of mental efficiency, reality testing, and moral judgment that results from in-group pressures.[139]

Is this what happened when Thiokol's management group took off its "engineering hats"?

CASE 5.18

Dow Corning and the Silicone Implants: Questions of Safety and Disclosure

The Development of the Silicone-Filled Breast Implant

In the early 1960s, Dow Corning and other manufacturers began marketing silicone-filled implants for use in breast enlargement procedures. The silicone implants are breast-shaped bags filled with silicone gel. The bag itself is made of another form of silicone that is like a heavy plastic; this latter material is the same substance used in sealant and the children's toy, Silly Putty.

The other companies that manufactured the implants included Heyer-Schulte Corporation, to which several Dow Corning scientists and salesmen had migrated along with their silicone gel implant knowledge, and McGhan Medical Corporation, an offspring corporation resulting from the subsequent departure of the Dow migrants from Heyer-Schulte. Much of the attention regarding the implants has focused on Dow Corning because the Heyer-Schulte and McGhan implants simply duplicated the Dow Corning product, and these other manufacturers relied upon Dow's implant tests.

Transfers of the ownership of implant firms have exacerbated the complexity of implant liability. That complexity is somewhat simplified in Figure 5.1.

In the mid-1970s, Dow Corning conducted animal studies regarding problems with leakage from the implants. Though Dow furnished the studies to the FDA, it did so under a confidentiality procedure that prevented their disclosure under the Freedom of Information Act.

In the course of conducting its research, Dow Corning found that laboratory animals exposed to silicone gels developed tumors. A panel of research experts examined the Dow Corning studies and concluded that 80 percent of the exposed animals had developed tumors. The figure was so high that the panel deemed the research suspect and labeled the study "inconclusive." A 1975 study eventually discovered during litigation in 1994 explained that silicone implants harmed the immune systems of mice. A lawyer representing women in a class action suit against Dow found the study among Dow documents.

---

[139] Irving L. Janis, *Victims of Groupthink*, Houghton, Mifflin, Boston, MA: 1972.

FIGURE 5.1 History and Ownership of Silicone Implant Manufacturers

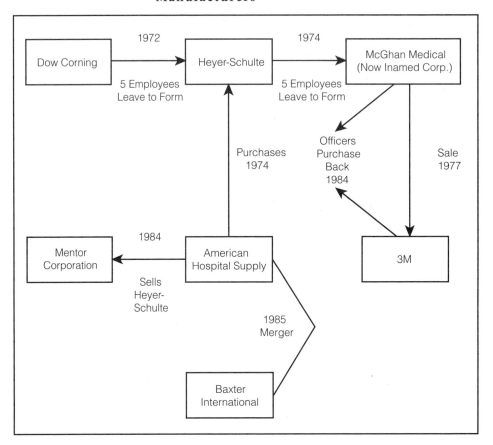

Internal Studies and Safety Questions

Thomas D. Talcott, a Dow materials engineer, disputed the panel's conclusions and resigned from the firm in 1976 after a dispute with his supervisors over the safety of the implants. Internal documents from Dow Corning, revealed later in litigation, indicate that Mr. Talcott was not a lone dissenter on the safety issue. Also in 1976, the chairman of the Dow Corning task force working on the new implants wrote, "We are engulfed in unqualified speculation. Nothing to date is truly quantitative. Is there something that migrates out or off the mammary prosthesis? Yes or no? Does it continue for the life of the implant or is it limited or controlled for a period of time? What is it?"[140] According to a Dow Corning salesperson's 1980 characterization, "[the Dow Corning decision to sell a] questionable lot of mammaries on the market has to rank right up there with the Pinto gas tank."[141] Other internal documents revealed in litigation verified that early on, the company had known that the silicone gel could "bleed" and "migrate" into women's bodies.

[140] *"Records Show Firm Delayed Breast Implant Safety Study," Mesa Tribune, January 13, 1992, p. A1.*
[141] *"Silicone Blues," Time, February 24, 1992, p. 65.*

In a deposition in an implant case against 3M, a Heyer-Schulte chemist disclosed that "[t]his phenomenon [gel bleeding] started to become of interest in the mid '70s."[142] He indicated that a breast implant placed on a blotter would leave a mark, especially if you applied pressure to the implant and allowed time to pass.

In 1983, a Dow Corning scientist, Bill Boley, wrote in an internal memo, "I want to emphasize that, to my knowledge, we have no valid long-term implant data to substantiate the safety of gel for long-term implant use."[143] There was, at that time, strong demand in the medical community for the silicone implant because of its great potential for reconstructive purposes.

Mr. Jan Varner, a former Dow Corning employee who currently is president of McGhan Medical (Inamed), maintains that very few implants leaked and any leakage was "very, very small."[144]

Other Companies' Concerns

Outside Dow Corning, other companies expressed their own concerns about silicone implants. James Rudy, then-president of Heyer-Schulte Corporation, wrote a "Dear Doctor" letter in 1976 to inform physicians about the risk of the implants rupturing. Between 1976 and 1978, Congress gave the FDA its first authority to regulate medical "devices" such as implants. Nevertheless, despite the studies and warnings, the implants continued to be sold to approximately 150,000 women per year. It was also at this time that a two-year Dow Corning study found malignant tumors in 80 percent of the laboratory animals exposed to silicone gels.

The study concluded:

As you will see, the conclusion of this report is that silicone can cause cancers in rats; there is no direct proof that silicone causes cancer in humans; however, there is considerable reason to suspect that silicone can do so.[145]

In response, the FDA noted:

The sponsor [of the study], Dow Corning, does not dispute the results of the current bioassay, i.e., Dow Corning agrees that silicone gel is sarcomagenic. However, this sponsor contends that induction of sarcoma in rats is due to solid-state carcinogenesis (Oppenheimer effect). This is uniquely a rodent phenomenon. Therefore, that it is of no human health consequence as a solid-state cancer in man has not been documented. In support of these contentions, an epidemiological study by Delpco, et. al. [sic], has been cited and shows no increased incidence of cancer in breast implant recipients.[146]

FDA staff members added the following comment in their report on the studies:

Solid-state tumor has been reported in rats, mice, chickens, rabbits and dogs. It is biologically unconvincing that man is a uniquely resistant species.[147]

[142] Thomas Burton, "Several Firms Face Breast-Implant Woes," *The Wall Street Journal, January 23, 1992, p. B1.*

[143] Judy Foreman, "Choice on Breast Implants Divide Women," *Arizona Republic, January 21, 1992, p. C1.*

[144] Burton, "Several Firms Face Breast-Implant Woes," *p. B1.*

[145] *Id.*

[146] Tim Smart, "Breast Implants: What Did the Industry Know, and When?" *Business Week, June 10, 1991, p. 94;* Tim Smart, "This Man Sounded the Silicone Alarm in 1976," *Business Week, January 27, 1992, p. 34.*

[147] *Id.*

At the time of the report, the FDA proposed reclassification of the gel implants as medical devices required to be proven safe before they could be sold. The agency imposed the stricter classification over the objections of both surgeons and sellers of the implants. Data regarding the safety of the implants was not required, however, until April 1991.

Problems with the Implants Begin

As the regulatory arena for the implants changed, product liability suits by women experiencing implant-related side effects began. Their problems included rupturing of the silicone sacs, which then spilled the silicone gel into their bodies, causing painful inflammations as their bodies' autoimmune systems tried to combat the invading foreign substance. Other autoimmune disorders appeared in women who experienced leakage or ruptures:

- scleroderma: a disorder which thickens and stiffens the skin and results in the build-up of fibrous tissue in the body's organs;
- lupus erythematosus: a disease characterized by chronic joint pain and rashes; and
- rheumatoid arthritis: a disease of stiffening of the joints.[148]

In a 1984 landmark case, a federal district court, in awarding Maria Stern of Nevada $1.5 million in punitive damages, held that Dow Corning had committed fraud in marketing the implants as safe. In ruling on a post-trial motion, U.S. District Judge Marilyn Hall Palel wrote that although Dow Corning's own studies "cast considerable doubt on the safety of the product, the company had not disclosed those studies to patients, including Stern, an act that she labeled "highly reprehensible."[149]

Following the Stern case, in 1985 Dow began to place in its implant packages inserts that mentioned the possibility of "immune system sensitivity and possible silicone migration following rupture."[150]

In a 1987 position statement, Dow Corning did not dispute the possibility of implant leakage but did discount the linkage between those leaks and immune-system problems. A 1982 medical study that the company cited in the statement supported Dow Corning's assertion that there was no connection between implants and breast cancer. Also, the statement indicated that any leaked silicone would be picked up by the lymph system and excreted or stored. The position statement discounted the immune-system problems, maintaining that only silicone of lesser purity would cause such problems.

Following Dow Corning's position statement, litigation activity increased as the FDA received 2,500 reports of illnesses or injuries associated with the implants.[151] By the end of 1991, nearly 1,000 implant lawsuits were pending against manufacturers.[152]

Early in the year, a New York jury awarded $4.5 million, nearly three times the Stern award, to a woman who alleged that her 1983 silicone implant with a polyurethane-foam covering had caused her breast cancer.

---

[148] Andrew Purvis, "A Strike Against Silicone," Time, January 20, 1992, pp. 40–41.

[149] Smart, "Breast Implants," p. 98.

[150] Id.

[151] Hal Mattern, "New Concerns About Breast Implants," Arizona Republic, January 7, 1992, pp. C1, C4.

[152] Michele Galen, John Byrne, Tim Smart, and David Woodruff, "Debacle at Dow Corning: How Bad Will It Get?" Business Week, March 2, 1992, p. 36.

Regulatory Action

While Dow Corning appealed the New York case, Bristol-Myers withdrew its implant following the FDA's confirmation of a study that linked the foam used to coat the implant with a cancer-causing agent known as 2-toluene diamine (TDA). In the 1970s, the FDA banned the foam, used primarily in air and auto filters, from use in hair dyes because of the risk of birth defects. The FDA's order requiring manufacturers to prove the safety of their implant products or withdraw them from the market became effective in May 1991 and mandated that the proof from the manufacturers be forthcoming within a decade.

At the same time, Ralph Nader's group, the Public Citizen Health Research Group, met in Washington, D.C., with trial lawyers, women who had had the implants, and others. The group called for the full release of all implant-related safety data to date.

Sybil Goldrich, one of the women leading the movement against implants, had received implants in 1983, following her bilateral mastectomy for breast cancer. Nearly a decade of medical problems, including the removal of her ovaries and uterus, resulted; her doctors attributed those problems to the implants. Ms. Goldrich has commented, "There is no way to detoxify from this chemical." Her suit was dismissed in 1994 because the statute of limitations on product liability and negligence had run out. She was unable to establish fraud.[153]

In September 1991, the FDA required implant manufacturers to provide risk information to women considering implant surgery. The agency, which specified the information required to be disclosed, issued the rule as an interim measure while it reviewed data on implant safety. These were the risks required to be disclosed:

- hardening of tissue around the implant,
- interference with mammography and tumor detection, and
- the possibility of leakage, autoimmune diseases, and cancer.

The FDA began its hearings on the silicone implants in October 1991. Speakers on both sides of the issue offered impassioned testimony. Manufacturers had boxes of data to support their claims that their products were harmless. Nearly four hundred women from thirty-seven states traveled to Washington to testify in favor of the implants. Recruited by plastic surgeons, the women testified about the importance of the implants to their physical and mental well-being and their freedom of choice. The women spoke of how the implants had helped them to recapture their self-esteem and gain psychological boosts in their battles with breast cancer.[154]

Physicians and professors of pharmacology and toxicology offered testimony to the contrary. Sybil Goldrich, by now the founder of Command Trust Network, a group advocating further study, asked of the women who testified:

> Do they know that silicone is bleeding into their bodies steadily? Do they know that implants are only good for a limited time and they will have to have surgery again and again?[155]

[153] Goldrich v. Dow Corning, *31 Cal.Rptr.2d 162 (1994).*
[154] *"Women State Case for Breast Implants,"* Mesa Tribune, *October 21, 1991, p. A3.*
[155] Id.

Speaking from a different perspective, Sharon Green, the executive director of the Y-ME National Organization for Breast Cancer Information, supported implant sales:

> Who are these women and why have so many of them rebuilt their bodies? As can be expected, many of our callers are breast cancer survivors. They have faced breast loss, a year or two of chemotherapy, and some have had their chests radiated. They face each day hoping that they have overcome cancer. Many no longer want to be reminded every morning and night of the cancer that played havoc with their bodies.
>
> It is estimated that one-third of current breast cancer patients are having reconstruction, most often with silicone implants. Saline implants can be an alternative, but they are not as aesthetically pleasing. An estimated 20% of implants are performed to reconstruct the breast; the rest, for augmentation. Y-ME's most recent survey (October 1991) of its own Hotline counselors—all breast cancer survivors—showed that among the respondents who had implants, the overwhelming majority were satisfied with their implants and 87% believed the devices helped their emotional recovery.
>
> Y-ME's position is clear and simple. If silicone breast implants can be scientifically proved dangerous, then this information should be made available to women. If the data are inconclusive, we demand full disclosure of all information so women can make decisions based on fact and not on unscientific claims and anecdotes. We also understand that no medical device can be guaranteed 100% safe and that some people are willing to take greater risks to improve the quality of their lives. However, it should be a personal choice based on all the medically verified evidence as it is known today.
>
> To ban or severely limit silicone breast implants based on inconclusive data would be one more insult to women by taking away their right to make informed decisions regarding their own bodies. For others to deny the right of a woman to implants because they fundamentally believe implants are unnecessary is arrogance in its ugliest form.[156]

After the hearings, the panel recommended unanimously that implants stay on the market but also called for continuing safety tests, concluding that the tests conducted by the four largest manufacturers had been inadequate. The panel cited the following hazards, offered during the hearings, for specific testing:

> Scarring and hardening of breast tissue,
> Implant leakage,
> Reduced effectiveness of mammograms,
> Autoimmune reactions,
> Infections, and
> Cancer.

Impact on Corning

In December 1991, another plaintiff, Mariann Hopkins, was awarded $7.3 million by a San Francisco jury that found Dow Corning had knowingly sold her a defective implant. The court of appeals for the Ninth Circuit affirmed the decision in 1994.

---

[156] *Testimony of Sharon Green, Food and Drug Administration Hearings on Silicone Breast Implants, Fall 1991.*

On December 30, 1991, the FDA sent Dow Corning a warning letter regarding the information Dow Corning was providing via a toll-free telephone number carried in ads about the safety of the implants. The FDA stated in the letter that the hotline information was used in a "confusing or misleading context."

On January 6, 1992, the FDA asked the medical device industry to halt the sale of silicone-gel implants until the agency could review new safety studies. FDA commissioner David Kessler asked all plastic surgeons to discontinue their use of the implants until the FDA could review information from Dow Corning that came to light in two product liability suits against a Dow Corning subsidiary. There was, however, no substitute in terms of natural look and texture for the silicone implants, and demand remained strong.

Following the disclosure of the information in the product liability suits, by mid-January 1992, Corning's stock had dropped $10 to $68.375 per share, while Dow Chemical's stock had fallen 87.5 cents per share. The two companies are joint venturers in manufacture and sale of breast implants. Within days of the stock price slip, investors had filed suits against the company. Ten suits were pending by March.

In February 1992, the General and Plastic Surgery Devices Panel of the FDA recommended that the use of implants for cosmetic enlargement be restricted but that implants be made available to women with breast cancer and "anatomical defects."[157]

By March, Dow Corning had announced its intent to withdraw from the implant market. Class action suits by women with immune-system disorders were pending around the country, and Ira Reiner, the Los Angeles County district attorney, began a criminal probe into whether Dow Corning concealed health risks associated with the implants. Reiner proceeded under California's new so-called "be-a-manager-go-to-jail" law, which holds executives criminally liable for product defects that cause harm to either a company's employees or its customers. Reiner has observed, "There's no deterrent like a clank of a jail cell closing behind you."[158] Mr. Reiner left office before the criminal cases were completed.

In early 1992, two women were hospitalized after using razors to remove their implants because they could not afford surgery for removal. Both were suffering from autoimmune diseases. Both had complications from the attempted self-removals and had to undergo surgery to complete the implant removals.[159] By the summer of 1992, Dow Corning reported that its second-quarter earnings had dropped 84.4 percent because of a $45 million pretax charge for eliminating its silicone gel breast-implant business. Even without the one-time charge, Dow Corning's earnings were down 19 percent.[160]

[157] Jeff Nesmith, "Scientific Panel Suggests Breast Implant Restrictions," Mesa Tribune, February 21, 1992, pp. A1, A12.
[158] Ronald Grover, "The L.A. Lawman Gunning for Dow Corning," Business Week, March 2, 1992, p. 38.
[159] "Woman Cuts Breast to Get Implant Aid," Mesa Tribune, May 15, 1992, p. A1; "Woman Claims She Removed Her Own Implants," Phoenix Gazette, April 17, 1992, p. A2.
[160] "Dow Corning's Profits Down 84.4% in Quarter," The New York Times, July 28, 1992, p. C2.

Ongoing Warnings

In mid-1992, the Department of Health and Human Services established a Breast Implant Information Service that offered information and study enrollment for women with implants. The following is an excerpt:

UPDATE ON SILICONE GEL-FILLED BREAST IMPLANTS[161]

On April 16, 1992, FDA announced that, in keeping with the recommendations of its outside advisory panel, it would allow silicone gel–filled breast implants to be available, but only under special conditions.

Since FDA continues to be concerned about the safety of these devices, all patients to receive breast implants must be enrolled in clinical studies. FDA recognizes that there is a public health need for the implants among patients who have lost a breast because of cancer or trauma, or who have a serious malformation of the breast requiring reconstruction. Thus any woman who needs the implant to reconstruct the breast will be permitted access to such studies. Implants for the purpose of augmentation (breast enlargement) will be available only to a very limited number of women who are enrolled in controlled clinical studies approved by FDA and designed to study specific safety questions relevant to the device.

The following should help to answer questions about how FDA's decision will affect women, and what they should know about the implants.

Under what circumstances will the implants be available?

Silicone gel–filled implants will be available for clinical studies in three stages.

Stage 1:

Since FDA's April 16 decision, women with an urgent need for reconstruction with the implants have been allowed access to them. This category includes:

- women with temporary tissue expanders in place for breast reconstruction following mastectomy, who need to complete their reconstruction with gel-filled implants;
- women with silicone gel-filled implants who need replacement for medical reasons, such as rupture, gel leakage or severe contracture; and
- women having mastectomies before the studies are in place and for whom immediate reconstruction at the time of mastectomy is medically and surgically more appropriate than implantation at a later time. For women in this category, physicians must document that saline-filled implants are not a satisfactory alternative.

In order for a woman to get the implants in Stage 1, her doctor must first certify that she falls into one of the above three categories. She will have to sign a special form certifying that she has been told about the risks of the implants, and agree to enroll in a registry so that she can be notified in the future, if necessary, about new information on the implants.

Stage 2:

In this stage, breast implant manufacturers will set up studies which will enroll any woman who needs the gel-filled implants for breast reconstruction. FDA must approve these studies before they can begin.

[161] *FDA's Breast Implant Information Service, issued May 25, 1992.*

Eligible women will include those who have had breast cancer surgery, severe injury to the breast, or a medical condition causing a severe breast abnormality. Women who must have an existing implant replaced for medical reasons will also be eligible.

As in Stage 1, all women will have to be told about the risks, provide informed consent, and be enrolled in a registry. It will probably take until mid-summer until plans are in place for these studies.

Stage 3:

In addition to the Stage 2 studies, FDA will require carefully controlled research studies for each model of silicone implant that manufacturers wish to continue marketing. These Stage 3 studies will include both reconstruction and augmentation patients and will be focused on specific safety questions about the implants, such as how often rupture and hardening of the scar tissue around the implants occur. They will also evaluate the psychological benefits of the implants. The studies will be limited to the number of patients required to answer the safety questions.

As in Stages 1 and 2, women will have to be told about the risks, provide informed consent, and be enrolled in a registry. In addition, women in the Stage 3 studies will be followed more extensively to check for problems related to the implants.

Designing these Stage 3 studies will take time, and so they cannot begin as quickly as the Stage 2 studies.

How can a woman get enrolled in these studies?

She should contact the doctor who would be performing the implant surgery. The doctor can then contact the manufacturer of the implants to find out which hospitals or doctors' offices are taking part in the studies in that particular area.

The Settlement

In April 1994, Dow (along with Bristol-Myers Squibb and Baxter Healthcare Corp.) reached a $4.2 billion[162] settlement with women who claimed to have health problems resulting from the implants. 3M, Union Carbide, Inamed, Wilshire Foam, and Applied Silicone, all suppliers of silicone to implant manufacturers, settled with the women for approximately $500 million.

In February 1995, a jury in Houston, Texas, held Dow Chemical Company liable in a breast implant litigation case. Dow has appealed the case, which awarded $5.2 million to two female plaintiffs. Although this case could not be traced, Dow was held liable in other cases [*Dow Chemical Co. v. Manlum*, 970 P.2d 98 (Nev. 1998) and *TMJ v. Dow*, 113 F.3d 1484 (8th Cir. 1996)].

By October 1995, the global $4.2 billion settlement had fallen apart and Bristol-Myers Squibb, Baxter, and 3M joined together to make their own settlement proposal. Since then, Bristol, Baxter, and 3M have settled with two-thirds of the women who have brought claims, paying between $10,000 and $250,000 each. Bristol also won two jury verdicts in August 1997.

---

[162] Thomas M. Burton, "Frequency of Reoperations for Woman with Breast Implants Put at Nearly 25%," *The Wall Street Journal*, March 6, 1997, p. B6.

In 1997, a Mayo Clinic study found that 25 percent of women with implants required reoperations to fix problems such as abnormal tissue growth or chronic pain. The rate for reoperation was higher (34 percent) among post-cancer patients with implants. The early science, upon which the class action suits relied, has been labeled "junk science." Most studies conclude that the reactions to implants will occur in about 5 percent of women, about the percentage of the population that will have some reaction to prescription drugs once they are on the market.

In February 1996, a Harvard medical school study of 10,830 women with silicone implants concluded that there was a "small but statistically significant increased risk" of contracting immune-system illnesses once a woman has the implants.

Dow faced 19,000 product liability lawsuits and proposed a reorganization plan for emerging from Chapter 11 bankruptcy. Under the plan, $600 million would be set aside for women to settle their lawsuits and another $1.4 billion would go to women with implants if a jury trial found causation between the presence of the implants and immune-system illnesses. About 1 million women have implants. Creditors, under the proposal, would receive $1 billion.

Also during this time, it was revealed that John E. Swanson, an executive at Dow Corning for 27 years who had helped shape its ethics program, concluded that his wife Colleen's devastating illnesses were caused by her Dow Corning implants. Colleen Swanson had sued Dow Corning in 1992.

Colleen settled her suit in 1993, and three months later Swanson left Dow Corning. Swanson then cooperated with senior writer for *Business Week*, John A. Byrne, for Byrne's book, *Informed Consent: A Story of Personal Tragedy and Corporate Betrayal . . . Inside the Silicone Breast Implant Crisis.*

In August 1997, Dow Chemical lost its first class action suit, involving 1,800 women in federal district court in New Orleans. The case held the parent responsible. Two other verdicts were rendered previously against Dow Chemical, but they were not class action suits. The verdicts were overturned by the trial judge and the appellate court.[163]

Also in 1997, a federal district judge appointed a panel of scientists to review articles and studies to assist him with evidentiary rulings. The issue the parties disputed at length was whether the cases could be consolidated for trial. The federal court of appeals consolidated 10,000 cases into one trial in federal district court in Detroit. Baxter, Bristol-Myers Squibb, and 3M were unsuccessful in getting their cases consolidated with Dow Corning's in Detroit.[164] Eventually, nearly 200,000 women filed claims. In 1999, Dow Corning received approval for the $4.5 billion settlement with what was, by then, 300,000 women. After attorneys' fees, the amount available for the women was $3.2 billion.[165] The plan provided for settlements of $10,000 to $250,000, depending upon the severity of the illnesses. However, anyone could accept a $2,000 "no-questions asked" payment.[166] During 2003 and 2004, the FDA grappled with the safety of

---

[163] Spitzfaden v. Dow Corning, *708 So.2d 777 (La. App. 1998).*
[164] Hall v. Baxter, *947 F. Supp. 1387 (D. Or. 1996).*
[165] *Thomas Burton, "Dow Corning Bankruptcy Plan Approved,"* The Wall Street Journal, *December 1, 1999, pp. A3, A16.*
[166] Id.

saline implants and held hearings on whether to allow silicone implants once again.[167] Initially, the special panel that held the hearings recommended allowing the implants back on the market.[168] However, in a rare action, the FDA commissioners rejected the panel's recommendation and voted to continue the ban but allow long-term studies before making a final determination.[169]

Discussion Questions

1. Who is morally responsible for the harms alleged from the implants? Should the information from the 1975 study have been disclosed?

2. Did Thomas Talcott act ethically in resigning in 1976?

3. If you had been Talcott, what would you have done?

4. Is the freedom of choice issue a moral standard?

5. Did members of the FDA staff have moral responsibilities with respect to the women with implants?

6. Did James Rudy relieve himself of any responsibility through his "Dear Doctor" letter?

7. What would you have done if you were Swanson?

Sources

Blakeslee, Sandra, "Lawyers Say Dow Study Saw Implant Danger," *The New York Times*, April 7, 1994, pp. A1, A9.

Burton, Thomas M., "3M, Four Others Join Implant Settlement," *The Wall Street Journal*, April 12, 1994, p. B8.

Burton, Thomas M., "Dow Chemical, for First Time, Is Found Liable in a Trial Over Breast Implant," *The Wall Street Journal*, February 16, 1995, p. B8.

"Dow Corning Prevails in Breast Implant Suit," *National Law Journal*, September 26, 1994, p. B2.

Hopkins v. Dow Corning Corp., 1994 WL 460 325 (9th Cir. 1994).

Taylor, Gary, "Implant Plaintiffs Reach Into a Deep Pocket," *National Law Journal*, January 23, 1995, p. A8.

Taylor, Gary, "Jurors Fault Dow Units on Implants," *National Law Journal*, February 27, 1995, p. A1.

---

[167] *Rita Ruben, "Saline Implants Studied for Safety," USA Today, March 1, 2000, pp. 1D, 2D.*
[168] *Gina Kolata, "F.D.A. Backs Breast Implants Made of Silicone," The New York Times, October 16, 2003, pp. A1, A26.*
[169] *Steve Sternberg, "FDA Rejects Silicone Implants," USA Today, January 9–11, 2004, p. 1A.*

CASE 5.19

....

The Teacher with Tough Standards: Honesty

Piper High School is in Piper, Kansas, a town located about twenty miles west of Kansas City, Misssouri. Christine Pelton was a high school science teacher there. Ms. Pelton, 26, had a degree in education from the University of Kansas and had been at Piper for two years.

Ms. Pelton was teaching a botany class for sophomores, a course that included a tradition of an extensive project as part of the course requirements. The project included a lengthy paper but also creative exhibits and illustrations. The project had been part of the curriculum and Piper High School tradition for ten years. The students were required to collect twenty different leaves, write one or two paragraphs about the leaves, and then do an oral presentation on their projects. When Ms. Pelton was describing the writing portion of the project and its requirements to her students, she warned them not to use papers posted on the Internet for their projects. She had her students sign contracts that indicated they would receive a "0" grade if they turned in others' work as their own. The paper counted for 50 percent of their grade in the course.

When the projects were turned in, Ms. Pelton noticed that some of the students' writing in portions of the paper was well above their usual quality and ability. Using an online service called Turnitin (http://www.turnitin.com/), she found that 28 of her 118 students had taken substantial portions of their papers from the Internet.[170] She gave the students a "0" grade on their term paper projects. The result was that many of the students would fail the semester in the course.

The students' parents protested, and both her principal, Michael Adams, and the school district superintendent, Michael Rooney, backed her decision. However, the parents appealed to the school board, and the board ordered Ms. Pelton to raise the grades. Mr. Rooney, acting at the board's direction, told Ms. Pelton that the decision of the board was that the leaf project's weight should be changed from 50 percent to 30 percent of the course's total semester grade, and that the 28 students should have only 600 points deducted from their grade rather than the full 1,800 points the project was originally worth. Ms. Pelton said, "I was really shocked at what their decision was. They didn't even talk to me or ask my side."[171] The result was that 27 of the 28 students avoided receiving an "F" grade in the course, but the changed weight also meant that 20 of the students who had not plagiarized their papers got a lower grade as a result.

She resigned in protest on the day following the board's decision. She received twenty-four job offers from around the country following her resignation. Mr. Adams, the principal, and one teacher resigned at the end of the year to protest the lack of support for Ms. Pelton. Mr. Adams cited personal reasons for his resignation, but he

---

[170] There is also another program that can be used: http://www.mydropbox.com.

[171] "School Board Undoes Teacher's F's," Wichita Eagle, January 31, 2002, http://www.kansas.com/mld/kansas/news/state/2574467.htm

added, "You can read between the lines."[172] At the time of Ms. Pelton's experience, 50 percent of the teachers had indicated they would resign. The superintendent, Michael Rooney, remained and said he stood by the teacher, but did not think that the school board was wrong: "I take orders as does everyone else, and the Board of Education is empowered with making the final decisions in the school district."[173]

The board debated the case in executive session and refused to release information, citing the privacy rights of the students. The local district attorney for Wyandotte County, Nick A. Tomasik, filed suit against the board for violating open meetings laws. The board members were deposed as part of his civil action. Citizens of Piper began a recall action against several of the school board members. The local chapter of the National Education Association, representing the eighty-five teachers in the district, has been brought into settlement negotiations on the suit because of their concerns that action that affects teachers can be taken without input and without understanding the nature of the issues and concerns.

The fallout for Piper has been national. *Education Week* reported the following as results of the actions of the students and the school board:

> All 12 deans of Kansas State University signed a letter to the Piper school board that included the statement: "We will expect Piper students . . . to buy into [the university's honor code] as a part of our culture."
>
> Angered, Piper school board member James Swanson—who is one of the targets of the recall drive—wrote the university to note that the implication that Piper students might be subject to greater scrutiny because of one controversial incident involving only 28 students was unfair. He received an apology from university officials.
>
> More troubling to the community, Piper students have also been mocked. At an inter-scholastic sporting event involving Piper, signs appeared among the spectators that read "Plagiarists."
>
> Students have reported that their academic awards, such as scholarships, have been derided by others. And one girl, wearing a Piper High sweatshirt while taking a college-entrance exam, was told pointedly by the proctor, "There will be no cheating."[174]

Several of the parents pointed to the fact that there was no explanation in the Piper High School handbook on plagiarism. They also said that the students were unclear on what could be used, when they had to reword, and when quotations marks are necessary. Other parents complained about Ms. Pelton's inexperience. One teacher said, "I would have given them a chance to rewrite the paper."

Both the school board and the principal asked Ms. Pelton to stay, but she explained, "I just couldn't. I went to my class and tried to teach the kids, but they were whooping and hollering and saying, 'We don't have to listen to you any more.'"[175] Ms. Pelton began operating a day care center out of her home.

[172] Andrew Trotter, "Plagiarism Controversy Engulfs Kansas School," Education Week, April 3, 2003. http://www.edweek.org/ew/newstory.cfm?slug=29piper.h21.
[173] Id.
[174] Andrew Trotter, "Plagiarism Controversy Engulfs School," April 3, 2002, http://www.edweek.org/ew/newstory.cfm?slug=29piper.h21.
[175] Id.

The annual Rutgers University survey on academic cheating reveals that 15 percent of college papers turned in for grades are completely copied from the Internet. In a look at Internet papers, the New Jersey Bar Foundation found the following:

> A Rutgers University survey of nearly 4,500 high school students revealed that only 46 percent of the students surveyed thought that cutting and pasting text directly from a Web site without attributing the information was cheating, while only 74 percent of those surveyed thought that copying an entire paper was cheating. Donald McCabe, the Rutgers University researcher that conducted the survey told *USA Today*, "In the students' minds what is on the Internet is public knowledge."[176]

A senior from the Piper, Kansas, school told CBS News, "It probably sounds twisted, but I would say that in this day and age, cheating is almost not wrong."[177]

Almost one year later the school board adopted guidelines on plagiarism for use in the district's school as policy. The Center for Academic Integrity gave its Champion of Integrity Award for 2002 to Ms. Pelton and Mr. Adams.

The center's criteria for this award are that the teacher or administrator took:

1. an action, speech, or demonstration that draws attention to a violation of academic integrity
2. an action that, in an attempt to promote or uphold academic integrity, may subject the nominee to reprisal or ridicule
3. an action motivated by commitment to and conviction about the importance of academic integrity and not by public acclaim or monetary gains[178]

Discussion Questions

1. Do you believe the students understood that what they did was wrong?

2. Was the penalty appropriate?

3. What do you think of the grading modifications the board required?

4. Evaluate the conduct of the parents.

5. Evaluate the statement of the senior that cheating is no longer wrong.

6. What were the consequences for Piper and the students?

7. Do you think the copying was unethical? Why do we worry about such conduct? Isn't this conduct just a function of the Internet? Isn't it accepted behavior?

For More Information

Jodi Wilgoren, "School Cheating Scandal Tests a Town's Values," *New York Times*, February 14, 2002, pp. A1, A28.

[176] *New Jersey State Bar Foundation, http://www.njsbf.com/njsbf/student/eagle/winter03-2.cfm.*
[177] *Leonard Pitts, Jr., "Your Kid's Going to Pay for Cheating—Eventually," June 21, 2002.*
http://www.jewishworldreview.com/0602/pitts062102.asp.
[178] *http://www.academicintegrity.org/cai_champ.asp.*

On Plagiarism[179]

Richard A. Posner

Recently two popular historians were discovered to have lifted passages from other historians' books. They identified the sources in footnotes, but they failed to place quotation marks around the purloined passages. Both historians were quickly buried under an avalanche of criticism. The scandal will soon be forgotten, but it leaves in its wake the questions What is "plagiarism"? and Why is it reprobated? These are important questions. The label "plagiarist" can ruin a writer, destroy a scholarly career, blast a politician's chances for election, and cause the expulsion of a student from a college or university. New computer search programs, though they may in the long run deter plagiarism, will in the short run lead to the discovery of more cases of it.

We must distinguish in the first place between a plagiarist and a copyright infringer. They are both copycats, but the latter is trying to appropriate revenues generated by property that belongs to someone else—namely, the holder of the copyright on the work that the infringer has copied. A pirated edition of a current best seller is a good example of copyright infringement. There is no copyright infringement, however, if the "stolen" intellectual property is in the public domain (in which case it is not property at all), or if the purpose is not appropriation of the copyright holder's revenue. The doctrine of "fair use" permits brief passages from a book to be quoted in a book review or a critical essay; and the parodist of a copyrighted work is permitted to copy as much of that work as is necessary to enable readers to recognize the new work as a parody. A writer may, for that matter, quote a passage from another writer just to liven up the narrative; but to do so without quotation marks—to pass off another writer's writing as one's own—is more like fraud than like fair use.

"Plagiarism," in the broadest sense of this ambiguous term, is simply unacknowledged copying, whether of copyrighted or uncopyrighted work (Indeed, it might be of uncopyrightable work for example, of an idea). If I reprint *Hamlet* under my own name, I am a plagiarist but not an infringer. Shakespeare himself was a formidable plagiarist in the broad sense in which I'm using the word. The famous description in *Antony and Cleopatra* of Cleopatra on her royal barge is taken almost verbatim from a translation of Plutarch's *Life of Mark Antony:* "on either side of her, pretty, fair boys apparelled as painters do set forth the god Cupid, with little fans in their hands, with which they fanned wind upon her" becomes "on each side her / Stood pretty dimpled boys, like smiling Cupids, / With divers-colour'd fans, whose wind did seem / To glow the delicate cheeks which they did cool." (Notice how Shakespeare improved upon the original.) In *The Waste Land,* T. S. Eliot "stole" the famous opening of Shakespeare's barge passage, "The barge she sat in, like a burnish'd throne, / Burn'd on the water" becoming "The Chair she sat in, like a burnished throne, / Glowed on the marble."

Mention of Shakespeare brings to mind that *West Side Story* is just one of the links in a chain of plagiarisms that began with Ovid's *Pyramus and Thisbe* and continued

[179] Reprinted from Richard A Posner, The Atlantic Monthly, April 2002, p. 23. Copyright © Atlantic Monthly Company, April 2002.

with the forgotten Arthur Brooke's *The Tragical History of Romeus and Juliet,* which was plundered heavily by Shakespeare. Milton in *Paradise Lost* plagiarized Genesis, as did Thomas Mann in *Joseph and His Brothers.* Examples are not limited to writing. One from painting is Edouard Manet, whose works from the 1860s "quote" extensively from Raphael, Titian, Velasquez, Rembrandt, and others, of course without express acknowledgement.

If these are examples of plagiarism, then we want more plagiarism. They show that not all unacknowledged copying is "plagiarism" in the pejorative sense. Although there is no formal acknowledgement of copying in my examples, neither is there any likelihood of deception. And the copier has added value to the original-this is not slavish copying. Plagiarism is also innocent when no value is attached to originality; so judges, who try to conceal originality and pretend that their decisions are foreordained, "steal" freely from one another without attribution or any ill will.

But all that can be said in defense of a writer who, merely to spice up his work, incorporates passages from another writer without acknowledgment is that the readability of his work might be impaired if he had to interrupt a fast-paced narrative to confess that "a predecessor of mine,__, has said what I want to say next better than I can, so rather than paraphrase him, I give you the following passage, indented and in quotation marks, from his book__." And not even that much can be said in defense of the writer who plagiarizes out of sheer laziness or forgetfulness, the latter being the standard defense when one is confronted with proof of one's plagiarism.

Because a footnote does not signal verbatim incorporation of material from the source footnoted, all that can be said in defense of the historians with whom I began is that they made it easier for their plagiarism to be discovered. This is relevant to how severely they should be criticized, because one of the reasons academic plagiarism is so strongly reprobated is that it is normally very difficult to detect. (In contrast, Eliot and Manet wanted their audience to recognize their borrowings.) This is true of the student's plagiarized term paper, and to a lesser extent of the professor's plagiarized scholarly article. These are particularly grave forms of fraud, because they may lead the reader to take steps, such as giving the student a good grade or voting to promote the professor, that he would not take if he knew the truth. But readers of popular histories are not professional historians, and most don't care a straw how original the historian is. The public wants a good read, a good show, and the fact that a book or a play may be the work of many hands—as, in truth, most art and entertainment are—is of no consequence to it. The harm is not to the reader but to those writers whose work does not glitter with stolen gold.

Discussion Questions

1. Who is harmed by plagiarism?

2. What is plagiarism?

3. Who "steals" freely without attribution?

4. Why do we care about plagiarism?

The Changing Time Cards

John Michael Gravitt was hired in 1980 at the General Electric jet engine plant as a machinist for $9.69 per hour. A Vietnam veteran, Gravitt was pleased to be among the 18,000 people working at GE's mile-long plant in Cincinnati, Ohio. The plant, which produced engines for both military and commercial aircraft, manufactured the engine for the U.S. military's B-1 bomber.

Gravitt had an excellent performance record. After eleven weeks as a machinist, he was promoted to the supervisory position of foreman. As a foreman, he was in a position to see workers' time cards. Gravitt discovered that workers' training and idle time were being charged to defense jobs. He also noticed that time cards were being altered so that work on projects that had overrun their budgets was being charged to other projects. To facilitate making the changes, the foremen received, in their mailboxes, "hot sheets" listing the projects that were in cost overruns.

Gravitt himself was encouraged to alter his workers' time cards, and during his first year as foreman, he did as he was told, charging his machinists' time to specified contracts. (For example, he was told to charge the workers' nonproductive time to expensive contracts.)[180] After the first year, however, he began to question the practice. Sometimes overruns were charged to projects that weren't even in the plant yet. Gravitt first complained to his unit manager, who sent him to a plant supervisor, who gave Gravitt a "this-happens-everywhere-in-the-real-world" speech. Concerned because GE was dealing with the federal government, Gravitt went to a private attorney. The attorney also gave him the "real world" speech. Gravitt went on with his work but ignored the "hot sheets" and refused to alter time cards. His supervisor did it for him.

John F. Tepe Jr., a foreman who worked with Gravitt, followed orders and altered 50 to 60 percent of his workers' daily time cards. When Gravitt confronted Tepe and told him he could go to jail for altering the cards, Tepe replied that he was "just carrying out orders and there wasn't any chance of getting caught."[181]

By early 1983, Gravitt had decided to gather proof of the time card alterations. For two months, on weekend shifts, he went into the office of his supervisor's secretary, Karen Kerr, who had prepared the "hot sheets," and photocopied both "hot sheets" and time cards. Gravitt also wrote an eight-page letter, which he delivered, along with his documentation, to Brian H. Rowe, a senior vice president at the Cincinnati plant, on June 29, 1983. Gravitt was fired that day.

An internal audit by GE showed that 80 percent of Gravitt's allegations were true and 20 percent could not be disproved.

Gravitt testified before the Senate Subcommittee on Administrative Practice and Procedure and filed suit against GE under the 1863 False Claims Act, which allows private citizens to bring suit against profiteers and recover part of the bounty collected.

---

[180] *Personal interview with John M. Gravitt, June 24, 1993.*
[181] *Gregory Stricharchuk, "Ex-Foreman May Win Millions for His Tale About Cheating at GE,"* The Wall Street Journal, *June 23, 1988, p. 16.*

Fines under the False Claims Act are $5,000 to $10,000 per violation, with 30 percent going to those who successfully bring the case. Gravitt felt that the fines would have an impact on future conduct at GE and at other businesses: "It's the only way people will know they can do something to correct what isn't right."[182] Others argued that the False Claims Act encourages employees not to talk first with employers about problems they spot.[183] Mr. Gravitt settled his suit with GE in 1989 for an undisclosed amount.

Discussion Questions

1. Did altering the cards harm anyone?

2. Did Mr. Gravitt make an ethical choice in reporting the time card alterations?

3. Did Mr. Gravitt have to violate Ms. Kerr's privacy to collect documentation?

4. Was Mr. Tepe correct in saying that he was not responsible because he was just following orders?

5. Mr. Gravitt commented that a GE executive who spoke at his foreman's training session explained "how to succeed at GE." The executive's advice was that if a superior asks what 2 + 2 is, your answer should be "whatever you want it to be." What effect would such a philosophy have on a firm's ethical climate?

6. Mr. Gravitt noted that foremen's bonuses at GE were tied to time cards and vouchers. Does such an incentive send the wrong signal to employees?

7. Mr. Gravitt has been unable to find work with any GE contractor in Cincinnati, but he remains proud of his actions, his suit, and the money the federal government recovered. His advice for companies: "Listen to the honest people. Protect them. Transfer them or promote them and clean up the problem."[184] What would GE need to change to implement Mr. Gravitt's ideas?

CASE 5.22

Harvard Business Review and the Welch Interview

Ms. Suzy Wetlaufer, editor of the *Harvard Business Review*, interviewed former GE CEO and business legend, Jack Welch, for a piece in the business magazine. She asked in December 2001 that the piece be withdrawn because her objectivity might have been compromised. Those at the magazine did another interview and published that interview in the February issue of the magazine.

---

[182] Id.

[183] Amal Kumar Naj, "GE's Drive to Purge Fraud Is Hampered by Workers' Mistrust," The Wall Street Journal, July 22, 1992, p. A1.

[184] Since the time of Mr. Gravitt's testimony GE has implemented a program The Wall Street Journal describes as a "remarkable effort" to encourage employees to act ethically and report any wrongdoing. For example, managers can spring pop quizzes on employees by asking questions such as "What are the three ways to report wrongdoing?" Employees who respond correctly get a gift such as a coffee mug.

Soon afterward, the editorial director of the magazine, Walter Kiechel, who supervises Ms. Wetlaufer, acknowledged that a report in the *Wall Street Journal* about an alleged affair between Ms. Wetlaufer and Mr. Welch was correct and that Mr. Welch's wife, Jane, had called to protest the article's objectivity. At that time, Mr. Welch refused to confirm or deny that there had been an affair. Ms. Wetlaufer is divorced.

Some staff members asked that Ms. Wetlaufer resign from her $277,000 per year job, but she initially survived termination.[185] Their objections were that she compromised her journalistic integrity. Mr. Kiechel, on the other hand, noted that she did "the right thing in raising her concerns."[186]

Mr. Welch's wife of thirteen years, Jane, filed for divorce soon after the article appeared. The Welches did have a prenuptial agreement, but that agreement expired after ten years, leaving Mrs. Welch entitled to one-half of what is estimated to be Welch's nearly $1 billion net worth.[187] The result was a battle over assets that spilled over into the business and popular press. The documents filed in the divorce proceedings revealed the following:

Estimated value of 6 residences in 3 states	$30.7 million
Securities accounts	$249 million
Investments in limited partnerships	$14.2 million
GE non-qualified stock options (net value)	$72.7 million
Monthly income	$1.4 million
Monthly expenses	$366,114[188]

Mr. Welch asked the judge to deduct $200 million from his assets as the amount he has pledged to his four children from his first marriage, an arrangement that was part of his divorce settlement with Carolyn B. Welch.[189] That request was refused because the pledge only takes effect at Mr. Welch's death and does not eliminate lifetime obligations to any current spouses. Mr. Welch told the judge, "This is taking up too much time. I'd like to get on with my life and have her get on with her life. These issues are all resolvable."[190]

His now ex-wife Jane earned the upper hand in the divorce proceedings by revealing Mr. Welch's retirement perks from General Electric including:

- An apartment in New York owned by GE
- Courtside seats at the U.S. Open
- Security personnel for international travel
- Satellite TV at four of their homes
- $17,307 per day in consulting fees

---

[185] James Bandler, "Harvard Editor Faces Revolt Over Welch Story," The Wall Street Journal, *March 4, 2002, pp. B1, B4.*

[186] Del Jones, "Editor Linked with Welch Finds Job at Risk," USA Today, *March 5, 2002, p. 3B.*

[187] Christine Dugas, "Some Prenups Are Set Up to Expire," USA Today, *March 15, 2002, p. 3B.*

[188] Gary Stoller, "Welch Discloses Finances in Divorce Court," USA Today, *October 31, 2002, p. 1B.*

[189] Geraldine Fabrikant, "Judge Permits a Litigator to Join the Welch Divorce Team," The New York Times, *October 31, 2002, p. C3.*

[190] Id.

- Wine
- Car and driver[191]

The revelations brought instant reactions from shareholders who felt that the extensive perks indicated a board that was either asleep at the wheel or not concerned about lavish expenses.[192] The SEC opened an investigation examining the following issues with GE:

- whether there had been adequate disclosure about the nature of Mr. Welch's retirement contract
- whether there had been adequate disclosure of Mr. Welch's perks while he was CEO
- whether all retirement benefits bestowed have been disclosed by GE[193]

Mr. Welch reached a new agreement with GE and published an op-ed piece in the Wall Street Journal, and agreed to pay for his retirement perks.[194]

In part, the *Wall Street Journal* op-ed stated:

I want to share a helluva problem that I've been dealing with recently.

Papers filed by my wife in our divorce proceeding became public and grossly misrepresented many aspects of my employment contract with General Electric. I'm not going to get into a public fight refuting every allegation in that filing. But some charges have gotten a lot of media attention. So, for the record, I've always paid for my personal meals, don't have a cook, have no personal tickets to cultural and sporting events. In fact, my favorite team, the Red Sox, has played 162 home games over the past two years, and I've attended just one.

I spent 41 years at GE, the past 21 as chairman. My respect for the company and my fondness for its employees make me hate the fact that my private life has brought unwelcome and inaccurate attention to the company.

I've debated what to do about this. In my mind, it comes down to two choices. I could keep the contract as it is, and tough-out the public attention. Or I could modify the contract and open myself to charges that the contract was unfair in the first place.

My employment contract was drawn up in 1996. GE was enjoying great results and was in the second year of a succession plan for a new CEO. The GE board knew I loved my job, and, frankly, I had no plans to leave, despite persistent rumors in the media that other companies were recruiting me.

But GE's two previous CEOs had retired at ages 62 and 63, and the board wanted to make sure I wouldn't do the same, especially in light of the quintuple bypass surgery I had undergone the year before. With these facts in mind, the board came to me and suggested

---

[191] Rachel Emma Silverman, "Here's the Retirement Jack Welch Built: $1.4 million a Month," The Wall Street Journal, October 31, 2002, pp. A1, A15.

[192] Del Jones abd garry Strauss, "Jane Welch Reveals Jack's GE Perks in Divorce Case," USA Today, September 9, 2002, p. 4B

[193] Matt Murray, "SEC Investigates GE's Retirement Deal with Jack Welch," The Wall Street Journal, September 17, 2002, pp. B1, B3.

[194] David Cay Johnston and Reed Abelson, "G.E.'s Ex-Chief to Pay for Perks, But the Question Is: How Much?" The New York Times, September 17, 2002, pp. C1, C2.

an employment contract, which offered me a special one-time payment of tens of millions of dollars to remain as CEO until December 2000, when I would be 65.

I instead suggested an employment contract that spelled out my obligations to GE, including my post-retirement obligations, and the benefits I would receive in return. For six years, the contract was disclosed to shareholders through the proxy statement, posted on the Securities and Exchange Commission website, and discussed in the media. I agreed to take the post-retirement benefits that are now being questioned instead of cash compensation—cash compensation that would have been much more expensive for the company.

Over the next five years, GE prospered and I lived up to my end of the bargain.

That said, in spite of the contract's validity and benefits to GE, a good argument can be made for modifying it today.[195]

Mr. Welch married Ms. Welaufer on April 24, 2004 in Boston's Park Street Church. The two now live in a 26,000-square-foot home on Beacon Street in Boston with Ms. Wetlaufer's four children, ages 9 to 15.[196] They co-wrote Mr. Welch's second book, which the two sold to Random House for $4 million based on a two-page proposal.[197] The book will be called *Winning* and the advance is $3.1 million less than Mr. Welch received for his first book, *Jack: Straight From the Gut*. Mr. Welch said that his wife/co-author and he make a good team, "We have a lot going on. We've got my greasy fingernails and her brains."[198]

The SEC brought charges against GE for its failure to fully disclose Mr. Welch's compensation package. Those charges were settled in September 2004 in a consent decree in which GE neither admitted nor denied the SEC's accusations but agreed to make full disclosure of Mr. Welch's compensation package. The SEC was troubled by a proxy disclosure that put the compensation at $399,925 when the real figure was $2.5 million.[199]

Discussion Questions

1. Do you think there was a conflict of interest with Ms. Wetlaufer if there was an affair between her and Mr. Welch?

2. Were the staff members correct to protest?

3. What were the consequences of Mr. Welch's affair and divorce?

4. Does Mr. Welch rationalize his post-employment perks?

5. Did the headline of the newspaper test apply to Mr. Welch's original contract terms?

[195] Jack Welch, "My Dilemma—And How I Resolved It," The Wall Street Journal, September 16, 2002, p. A14.

[196] "Jack and Suzy Wetlaufer," People, May 10, 2004, p. 215.

[197] Hugo Lindgren, "Welch Makes Another Major Book Deal," The New York Times, February 4, 2004, pp. C1, C4.

[198] Id.

[199] Geraldine Fabrikant, "G.E. Settles S.E.C. Case on Welch Retirement Perks," The New York Times, September 24, 2004, p. C2.

5 _G

Employee Rights

Compliance with labor laws. International operations and plants. These issues affect employees' attitudes at work and the reputation of a business.

CASE 5.23

Cheap Labor: Children, Sweatshops, Human Rights, and the Fifty-Hour Work Week

With the passage of GATT and NAFTA, a worldwide market has been emerging. In addition to the international market for goods, there is also an international market for labor. Many U.S. firms have subcontracted the production of their products to factories in China, Southeast Asia, and Central and South America.

The National Labor Committee (NLC), an activist group, periodically releases information on conditions in foreign factories and the companies utilizing those factories. In 1998, the NLC issued a report that Liz Claiborne, Wal-Mart, Ann Taylor, Esprit, Ralph Lauren, JCPenney, and Kmart were using subcontractors in China that use Chinese women (between the ages of 17 and 25) to work 60 to 90 hours per week for as little as 13 to 23 cents per hour. The Chinese subcontractors do not pay overtime, house the workers in crowded dormitories, feed them a poor diet, and operate unsafe factories.[200]

Levi Strauss pulled its manufacturing and sales operations out of China in 1993 because of human rights violations, but announced in 1998 that it would expand its manufacturing there and begin selling clothing there. Peter Jacobi, the president of Levi Strauss, indicated that it had the assurance of local contractors that they would adhere to Levi's guides on labor conditions. Jacobi stated, "Levi Strauss is not in the human rights business. But to the degree that human rights affect our business, we care about it."[201, 202]

---

[200] Jon Frandsen, "Chinese Labor Practices Assailed," Mesa Tribune, March 19, 1998, p. B2.

[201] Mark Landler, "Reversing Course, Levi Strauss Will Expand Its Output in China," The New York Times, April 9, 1998, p. C1.

[202] G. Pascal Zachary, "Levi Tries to Make Sure Contract Plants in Asia Treat Workers Well," The Wall Street Journal, July 28, 1994, pp. A1, A5.

The Mariana Islands is currently a site of investigation by the Department of Interior for alleged indentured servitude of children as young as 14 in factories there.[203] Wendy Doromal, a human rights activist, issued a report that workers there have tuberculosis and oozing sores. Approximately $820 million worth of clothing items are manufactured each year on the islands, which are a U.S. territory. Labels manufactured there include The Gap, Liz Claiborne, Banana Republic, JCPenney, Ralph Lauren, and Brooks Brothers.[204]

U.S. companies' investments in foreign manufacturing in major developing nations like China, Indonesia, and Mexico have tripled in 15 years to $56 billion, a figure that does not include the subcontracting work. In Hong Kong, Singapore, South Korea, and Taiwan, where plants make apparel, toys, shoes, and wigs, national incomes have risen from 10 percent to 40 percent of American incomes over the past 10 years. In Indonesia, since the introduction of U.S. plants and subcontractors, the portion of malnourished children in the country has gone from one-half to one-third.[205]

In a practice that is widely accepted in other countries, children, ages 10 to 14, labor in factories for 50 or more hours per week. Their wages enable their families to survive. School is a luxury, and a child attends only until he or she is able to work in a factory. The Gap, Levi Strauss, Esprit, and Leslie Fay have all been listed in social responsibility literature as exploiting their workers.[206] In 1994, the following appeared in a quarter-page ad in *The New York Times*:

The Price of Corporate Greed at Leslie Fay

Marie Whitt is fighting to keep the job she has held for 17 years at a Leslie Fay plant in Wilkes-Barre. Marie earns $7.80 an hour—hardly a fortune. On June 1st, she and 1,800 co-workers were forced to strike because Leslie Fay plans to dump them. Ninety percent are women whose average age is 50. They have given their whole working lives to the company and losing their jobs would be a disaster. Marie knows she will never find a comparable job in today's economy. Without her union benefits, she and her husband won't be able to pay for his anti-cancer medication. "What Leslie Fay wants to do is so rotten," she says. "You've got to draw the line somewhere and fight."

Dorka Diaz worked for Leslie Fay in Honduras, alongside 12- and 13-year-old girls locked inside a factory where the temperature often hits 100° and where there is no clean drinking water. For a 54-hour week, including forced overtime, Dorka was paid a little over $20. With food prices high—a quart of milk costs 44 cents—Dorka and her three-year-old son live at the edge of starvation. In April, Dorka was fired for trying to organize a union. "We need jobs desperate," she says, "but not under such terrible conditions."[207]

Leslie Fay executives claim they can only "compete" by producing in factories like Dorka's. But identical skirts—one made by Dorka, the other by Marie—were recently purchased at a big retail chain here. Both cost $40. Searching the world for ever-cheaper sources of labor is not the kind of competition America needs. Leslie Fay already does 75%

[203] Zachary, "Levi Tries to Make Sure Contract Plants in Asia Treat Workers Well," pp. A1, A5.

[204] John McCormick and Marc Levinson, "The Supply Police," Newsweek, February 15, 1993, pp. 48–49.

[205] Allen R. Myerson, "In Principle, a Case for More 'Sweatshops,'" The New York Times, June 22, 1997, p. E5.

[206] Dana Canedy, "Peering Into the Shadows of Corporate Dealings," The New York Times, March 25, 1997, pp. C1, C6.

[207] From Ms. Diaz's testimony before a hearing of the Subcommittee on Labor-Management Relations, Committee on Education and Labor, U.S. House of Representatives, Wilkes-Barre, Pennsylvania, June 7, 1994.

of its production overseas. If it really wants to compete successfully in the global economy, it would modernize its facilities here in the U.S. as many of its competitors have done. But Leslie Fay wants to make a fast buck by squeezing every last drop of sweat and blood out of its workers. Marie Whitt and Dorka Diaz don't think that's right. And they know it's a formula for disaster—for all of us.

You can help by not buying Leslie Fay products—until Leslie Fay lives up to its corporate responsibilities at home and overseas.

Don't buy Leslie Fay! Boycott all clothing made by Leslie Fay and sold under these labels: Leslie Fay, Joan Leslie, Albert Nipon, Theo Miles, Kasper, Le Suit, Nolan Miller, Castleberry, Castlebrook.[208]

In the United States, the issue of sweatshops came to the public's attention when it was revealed that talk-show host Kathie Lee Gifford's line of clothing at Wal-Mart had been manufactured in sweatshops in Guatemala, and CBS ran a report on conditions in Nike subcontractor factories in Vietnam and Indonesia.[209] The reports on Nike's factories issued by Vietnam Labor Watch included the following: women required to run laps around the factory for wearing non-regulation shoes to work; payment of subminimum wages; physical beatings, including with shoes, by factory supervisors; and most employees are women between the ages of 15 and 28. Philip Knight, CEO of Nike, included the following in a letter to shareholders:

Q: Why on earth did NIKE pick such a terrible place as Indonesia to have shoes made?

A: Effectively the US State Department asked us to. In 1976, when zero percent of Nike's production was in Taiwan and Korea, Secretary of State Cyrus Vance asked Charles Robinson . . . to start the US-ASEAN Business Council to fill the vacuum left by the withdrawal of the American military from that part of the world . . . Chuck Robinson accepted the challenge, put together the council and served as Chairman of the US side for three years. Mr. Robinson was a Nike Board member at that time as he is today . . . "Nike's presence in that part of the world," according to a senior state department official at that time, "is American foreign policy in action."[210]

Nike sent former U.N. Ambassador Andrew Young to its overseas factories in order to issue a report to Knight, the board, and the shareholders.[211] Young did tour factories but only with Nike staff and only for a few hours. Young issued the following findings:

- Factories that produce Nike goods are "clean, organized, adequately ventilated, and well-lit"
- No evidence of a "pattern of widespread or systematic abuse or mistreatment of workers"
- Workers don't know enough about their rights or about Nike's own code of conduct
- Few factory managers speak the local language, which inhibits workers from lodging complaints or grievances

[208] From a statement published by the International Ladies Garment Workers Union in The New York Times, June 9, 1994, p. A16.
[209] Jeff Ballinger and Claes Olsson, Beyond the Swoosh: The Struggle of Indonesians Making Nike Shoes, ICDA/Global Publications Foundations, Uppsala Sweden 1997.
[210] Sharon R. King, "Flying the Swoosh and Stripes," The New York Times, March 19, 1998, pp. C1, C6.
[211] Ellen Neuborne, "Nike to Take a Hit in Labor Report," USA Today, March 27, 1997, p. 1A.

- Independent monitoring is needed because factories are controlled by absentee owners and Nike has too few supervisors on site[212]

On October 18, 1997, there were international protests against Nike in 13 countries and 70 cities. On October 13, 1997, 6,000 Nike workers went on strike in Indonesia followed by a strike of 1,300 in Vietnam.[213]

On November 8, 1997, an Ernst & Young audit about unsafe conditions in a Nike factory in Vietnam was leaked to *The New York Times* and made front-page news.[214]

Michael Jordan, NBA and Nike's superstar endorser, agreed to tour Nike's factories in July 1998, stating, "the best thing I can do is go to Asia and see for myself. The last thing I want to do is pursue a business with a negative over my head that I don't have an understanding of. If there are issues . . . if it's an issue of slavery or sweatshops, [Nike executives] have to revise the situation."[215]

From June 1997 to January 1998, Nike distributed 100,000 plastic "code of conduct" cards to plant workers. The cards list workers' rights. Nike's performance has dropped. Its stock price has dropped from a 1996 high of $75.75 per share to a March 1998 low of $43 per share.[216] (Its share price rebounded to $62 by March 2002 and increased to $91.70 by December 2004.)

Retail order cancellations caused sales to decrease by 3 percent in 1997. Nike planned to reduce its labor force by 10 to 15 percent, or 2,100 to 3,100 positions.[217, 218]

Press for Change and Global Exchange, an activist group, made the following demands of Nike in 1998:

1. **Accept independent monitoring by local human rights groups to ensure that Nike's Code of Conduct is respected by its subcontractors.** The GAP has already accepted independent monitoring for its factories in El Salvador, setting an important precedent in the garment industry. If Nike were to accept such monitoring in Indonesia, it would set a similar positive precedent in the shoe industry, making Nike a true leader in its field.
2. **Settle disputes with workers who have been unfairly dismissed for seeking decent wages and work conditions.** There are dozens of Indonesian workers who have been fired for their organizing efforts, and thousands who have been cheated out of legally-promised wages. Nike must take responsibility for the practices of its subcontractors, and should offer to reinstate fired workers and repay unpaid wages.
3. **Improve the wages paid to Indonesian workers.** The minimum wage in Indonesia is $2.26 a day. Subsistence needs are estimated to cost at least $4 a day. While Nike claims to pay double the minimum wage, this claim includes endless hours of overtime. We call on Nike to pay a minimum of $4 a day for an eight-hour day, and to end all forced overtime.[219, 220]

[212] "Nike Tries to Quell Exploitation Charges," The Wall Street Journal, June 25, 1997, p. A16.
[213] Patricia Seller, "Four Reasons Nike's Not Cool," Fortune, March 30, 1998, pp. 26–28.
[214] Bob Herbert, "Brutality in Vietnam," The New York Times, March 28, 1997, p. A19.
[215] Bill Richards, "Tripped Up By Too Many Shoes, Nike Regroups," The Wall Street Journal, March 3, 1998, pp. B1, B15.
[216] Tom Lowry and Bill Beyers, "Earnings Woes Trip Nike; Layoffs Loom," USA Today, February 25, 1998, p. 1B.
[217] Id.
[218] "Nike Refuses to 'Just Do It,'" Business Ethics, January/February 1998, p. 8.
[219] Lowry and Beyers, "Earnings Woes Trip Nike," p. 1B.
[220] "Nike Refuses to 'Just Do It,'" p. 8.

The American Apparel Manufacturers Association (AAMA), which counts 70 percent of all U.S. garment makers in its membership, has a database for its members to check labor compliance by contractors.[221] The National Retail Federation has established the following statement of Principles on Supplier Legal Compliance (now signed by 250 retailers):

1. We are committed to legal compliance and ethical business practices in all of our operations.
2. We choose suppliers that we believe share that commitment.
3. In our purchase contracts, we require our suppliers to comply with all applicable laws and regulations.
4. If it is found that a factory used by a supplier for the production of our merchandise has committed legal violations, we will take appropriate action, which may include canceling the affected purchase contracts, terminating our relationship with the supplier, commencing legal actions against the supplier, or other actions as warranted.
5. We support law enforcement and cooperate with law enforcement authorities in the proper execution of their responsibilities.
6. We support educational efforts designed to enhance legal compliance on the part of the U.S. apparel manufacturing industry.[222]

The U.S. Department of Labor has recommended the following to improve the current situation:

1. All sectors of the apparel industry, including manufacturers, retailers, buying agents and merchandisers, should consider the adoption of a code of conduct.
2. All parties should consider whether there would be any additional benefits to adopting more standardized codes of conduct [to eliminate confusion resulting from a proliferation of different codes with varying definitions of child labor].
3. U.S. apparel importers should do more to monitor subcontractors and homeworkers [the areas where child labor violations occur].
4. U.S. garment importers—particularly retailers—should consider taking a more active and direct role in the monitoring and implementation of their codes of conduct.
5. All parties, particularly workers, should be adequately informed about codes of conduct so that the codes can fully serve their purpose.[223]

By 2000, Nike, still experiencing campus protests for its overseas plant conditions, began to experience economic impact as the students protested their colleges and universities signing licensing agreements with Nike. For example, Nike ended negotiations with the University of Michigan for a six-year multi-million dollar licensing agreement because Michigan joined the consortium. And Phil Knight withdrew a pledge to make a $30 million donation to the University of Oregon because the university joined the consortium.

Nike continues to support the Fair Labor Association, an organization backed by the White House with about 135 colleges and universities as members, but its membership there has not halted the consortium's activities.[224]

[221] "Slave Labor," Fortune, December 9, 1996, p. 12.

[222] Martha Nichols, "Third-World Families at Work: Child Labor or Child Care?" Harvard Business Review, January–February 1993, pp. 12–23.

[223] Daniela Deane, "Senators to Hear of Slave Labor on U.S. Soil," USA Today, March 31, 1998, p. 9A.

[224] Steven Greenhouse, "Anti-Sweatshop Group Invites Input by Apparel Makers," The New York Times, April 29, 2000, p. A9.

Nike continues to be a target in op-ed pieces and various magazine articles regarding its labor practices around the world. Nike CEO Phil Knight responds to these opinion pieces and articles by writing letters to the editor, citing Nike's standards and independent and outside reviews of its factories; conditions. One such letter went to the editor of the *New York Times* in response to a negative op-ed piece there on Nike's labor practices.

Marc Kasky filed suit against Nike in California alleging that the op-ed pieces and letters in response to negative op-ed pieces about Nike violated the False Advertising Act of California. The act permits state agencies to take action to fine corporate violators of the act as well as obtain remedies such as injunctions to halt the ads.

Nike challenged the suit on the grounds that such an interpretation and application of the advertising regulation violated its rights of free speech. The lower court agreed with Kasky and held that the advertising statute applied to Nike's defense of its labor practices, even on the op-ed pages of newspapers. Nike appealed to the U.S. Supreme Court. The U.S. Supreme Court held that the case could not be reviewed until Nike had actually gone through the state process for finding it in violation of the False Advertising Act.[225] The case was remanded for trial, but Nike settled the matter with the California authorities under terms that were not disclosed.

In 2004, *Business Ethics* magazine presented its Social Reporting Award to Gap, Inc. for being the first company to issue a report on vendor compliance with its factory standards. The report disclosed both positive aspects and contractor failures. For example, Gap disclosed that 25 percent of its factories in Mexico paid subminimum wages and factories in China had obstructions in the aisles. The company has been recognized for its candor and pledge to improve.[226]

....

Discussion Questions

1. One executive noted, "We're damned if we do because we exploit. We're damned if we don't because these foreign economies don't develop. Who's to know what's right?"

   Levi Strauss & Company, discovering that youngsters under the age of 14 were routinely employed in its Bangladesh factories, could either fire 40 underage youngsters and impoverish their families or allow them to continue working. Levi compromised and provided the children both access to education and full adult wages.

   Nike has shoe factories in Indonesia, and the women who work in those factories net $37.46 per month. However, as Nike points out, their wages far exceed that of other factory workers. Nike's Dusty Kidd notes, "Americans focus on wages paid, not what standard of living those wages relate to."

   Economist Jeffrey D. Sachs of Harvard has served as a consultant to developing nations such as Bolivia, Russia, Poland, and Malawi. He observes that the conditions in sweatshops are horrible, but they are an essential first step toward modern prosperity. "My concern is not that there are too many sweatshops, but that there are too few. These are precisely the jobs

---

[225] Nike v. Kasky, *539 U.S. 654 (2003). Lower court decisions at* Kasky v. Nike, *2 P.3d 1065 (2000) and* Kasky v. Nike, *45, P.3d 243 (2002).*

[226] *"Gap, Inc. Social Reporting Award,"* Business Ethics, *Fall 2004, p. 9.*

that were the stepping stone for Singapore and Hong Kong, and those are the jobs that have to come to Africa to get them out of their backbreaking rural poverty."[227]

Business executives respond as follows:

"If someone is willing to work for 31 cents an hour, so be it—that's capitalism. But throw in long hours, abusive working conditions, poor safety conditions, and no benefits, and that's slavery. It was exactly those same conditions that spawned the union movement here in the U.S." —John Waldron

"If the wages of 31 cents per hour were actually fair wages, adults would gladly do the work instead of children." —Wesley M. John

"Just when you think the vile remnants of those who would build empires on the blood and bones of those less fortunate than ourselves have slithered off into the history books, you come across this kind of tripe. For shame for rationalizing throwing crumbs to your fellow human beings so that you and your ilk can benefit at their expense." —Jose Guardiola

Discuss the economic, social and ethical issues of plants and wages in developing countries. Consider the following excerpt from *The Economist*:

If a Chinese manufacturing worker can be hired for only 25 cents an hour, compared with $17 in America or $32 in Germany, surely it makes sense for western firms to shift all their production to China? International comparisons of labour costs often provoke such a question. They also provoke protests by trade unions and others in the rich world, who fear that unless governments do something, workers there will either see their wages driven down to third-world levels too, or face a jobless future. That "something" could mean blocking cheap imports or subsidizing exports.

Some jobs are inevitably being sucked out of the rich world and into the poorer one as western firms seek to cut their costs. Yet the threat that low-wage countries pose to employment in the rich countries is greatly exaggerated. After all, if cheap labour guaranteed economic success, nations such as Bangladesh or Mozambique would dominate global output.

So why don't they? One reason is that wages largely reflect international differences in productivity: cheap labour in emerging economies goes hand in hand with lower productivity. Cassandras draw little comfort from this. As poor countries get hold of the latest production techniques, they argue, richer ones will lose their traditional advantage. Third-world producers will be able to combine low wages with first-world technology—and hence productivity levels—making themselves super-competitive. This is nonsense. In the long run, increases in productivity will be offset by higher wages or a stronger exchange rate. Witness the experience of South Korea, where wages have risen from less than one-tenth to more than two-fifths of American levels over the past ten years.[228]

2. Would you employ a twelve-year-old in one of your factories if it were legal to do so?

3. Would you limit hours and require a minimum wage even if it were not legally mandated?

---

[227] "Slave Labor," p. 12.

[228] From "Invasion of the Job Snatchers," The Economist, November 2, 1996, p. 18. © 1996 The Economist Newspaper Group Inc. Reprinted with permission. Further reproduction prohibited. http://www.economist.com

4. Would you work to provide educational opportunities for these child laborers?

5. Why do you think the public seized on the Kathie Lee Gifford and Nike issues?

....

Sources

Gibbs, Nancy, "Suffer the Little Children," *Time*, March 26, 1990, p. 18.

Mitchell, Russell, and Michael O'Neal, "Managing by Values," *Business Week*, August 1, 1994, pp. 40–52.

"Nike's Workers in Third World Abused, Report Says," *Arizona Republic*, March 28, 1997, p. A10.

"Susie Tompkins," *Business Ethics*, January/February 1995, pp. 21–23.

READING 5.24
Human Rights Declarations and Company Policies

The issue of international labor has become a focus for nongovernmental entities as well as companies with international operations. In this reading you will review the corporate human rights and labor policies of ChevronTexaco, Levi Strauss & Co., and Unocal. You will also review the Sullivan Principles and the United Nations position on human rights.

ChevronTexaco Statement on Human Rights and Labor[229]

The ChevronTexaco Way explicitly states the company's "support for universal human rights." We are proud to have been among the early endorsers of The Global Sullivan Principles, a code of corporate conduct formulated by Rev. Leon H. Sullivan in 1999. These principles set high standards that are well aligned with the values shared by all ChevronTexaco employees.

We will be transparent in our implementation of these principles and provide information which demonstrates publicly our commitment to them.

Partnerships between ChevronTexaco and the local communities in which it operates are based on more than philanthropy. Only where both the business and the community make progress through mutual understanding and respect can either side hope to succeed.

We've learned to listen to the needs of the local community first and then engage in mutually beneficial partnerships where together we can become a greater force for positive community change. This includes employment and training opportunities as well as the improvement of local facilities and care for the environment.

[229] http://www.chevrontexaco.com.

Our community involvement, always geared to local needs, has taken many different forms. For example:

- In Venezuela, we built 10 schools where 4,500 students are now receiving a higher quality education.
- In Angola, where many children have been displaced and orphaned by civil war, we support a center for the homeless that educates and trains young women for entry into the work force.
- In Kazakhstan, we've provided mobile health clinics in remote areas where local populations previously had little or no health care.
- In the United States, we've contributed to music programs that help youngsters perform better in math and the sciences.
- In Singapore, we help promising local university students through relevant work experience and assignments.

Resource: The Global Sullivan Principles[230]

Preamble

The objectives of the Global Sullivan Principles are to support economic, social and political justice by companies where they do business; to support human rights and to encourage equal opportunity at all levels of employment, including racial and gender diversity on decision making committees and boards; to train and advance disadvantaged workers for technical, supervisory and management opportunities; and to assist with greater tolerance and understanding among peoples; thereby, helping to improve the quality of life for communities, workers and children with dignity and equality. I urge companies large and small in every part of the world to support and follow the Global Sullivan Principles of corporate social responsibility wherever they have operations.

1 Feb 1999   *The Rev. Leon H. Sullivan*

Principles

As a company, which endorses the Global Sullivan Principles we will respect the law, and as a responsible member of society we will apply these Principles with integrity consistent with the legitimate role of business. We will develop and implement company policies, procedures, training and internal reporting structures to ensure commitment to these principles throughout our organization. We believe the application of these Principles will achieve greater tolerance and better understanding among peoples, and advance the culture of peace.

Accordingly, we will:

- Express our support for universal human rights and, particularly, those of our employees, the communities within which we operate, and parties with whom we do business.
- Promote equal opportunity for our employees at all levels of the company with respect to issues such as color, race, gender, age, ethnicity or religious beliefs, and

---

[230] Global Sullivan Principles, Rev. Leon H. Sullivan. http://www.globalsullivanprinciples.org.

operate without unacceptable worker treatment such as the exploitation of children, physical punishment, female abuse, involuntary servitude, or other forms of abuse.

- Respect our employees' voluntary freedom of association.
- Compensate our employees to enable them to meet at least their basic needs and provide the opportunity to improve their skill and capability in order to raise their social and economic opportunities.
- Provide a safe and healthy workplace; protect human health and the environment; and promote sustainable development.
- Promote fair competition including respect for intellectual and other property rights, and not offer, pay or accept bribes.
- Work with governments and communities in which we do business to improve the quality of life in those communities—their educational, cultural, economic and social well-being—and seek to provide training and opportunities for workers from disadvantaged backgrounds.

Promote the application of these principles by those with whom we do business.

Levi Strauss & Co. Global Sourcing and Operating Guidelines[231]

Success Stories

Inspiring Change

During a follow-up visit to a contractor in central Mexico, a Levi Strauss & Co. assessor determined that the increased size of the workforce and the changes in physical layout of the factory required additional emergency exits. The contractor, hesitant at first, made the necessary changes and conducted evacuation drills to prepare workers for various emergencies. Four months later, the area in which the factory was located suffered a massive earthquake. Because of the new exits and the emergency drills, the facility's 800 employees were able to evacuate quickly and safely.

Motivating Improvement

A supplier in India who failed Levi Strauss & Co.'s initial assessment due to wage violations and health and safety conditions that did not meet our guidelines requested a reassessment four months later. The assessor was pleased to see a dramatic improvement at the facility. Not only had the supplier corrected the violations, but there was a noticeable improvement in employee morale. The supplier noted that the changes he made in order to meet Levi Strauss & Co. guidelines contributed significantly to lower turnover, improved product quality and higher efficiency at his facility.

Protecting the Environment

Levi Strauss & Co. suppliers around the world have made efforts to improve and protect the environment in line with our Terms of Engagement and in locally appropriate ways. Contractors in Israel, Croatia and Turkey have installed innovative technologies that not only clean their wastewater, but also use less energy and reduce the amount of treatment chemicals required. Suppliers in Greece and Tunisia have received local and national prizes for their environmental improvement efforts.

---

[231] http://www.levi.com.

A Leader in Socially Responsible Worldwide Sourcing

Levi Strauss & Co. is recognized as a leader in corporate citizenship, including ethical practices in sourcing production around the world.

In 1991, we became the first multinational company to establish a comprehensive ethical code of conduct for manufacturing and finishing contractors working with the company. This code, known as the *Global Sourcing and Operating Guidelines,* directs business practices, such as fair employment, worker health and safety, and environmental standards, among others. Our groundbreaking code earned the company the America's Corporate Conscience Award for International Commitment from the Council on Economic Priorities.

Evaluation & Compliance

Levi Strauss & Co. is committed to ensuring compliance with our code of conduct at all facilities that manufacture or finish our products around the world. Our goal is to achieve positive results and effect change by working with our business partners to find long-term solutions that will benefit the individuals who make our products and will improve the quality of life in local communities. We work on-site with our contractors to develop strong alliances dedicated to responsible business practices and continuous improvement.

If Levi Strauss & Co. determines that a business partner is not complying with our Terms of Engagement, we require that the partner implement a corrective action plan within a specified time period. If a contractor fails to meet the corrective action plan commitment, Levi Strauss & Co. will terminate the business relationship.

We also work with non-governmental organizations (NGOs) for input and recommendations to improve our worldwide internal monitoring process. Levi Strauss & Co. actively participates in the *Fair Labor Association (FLA)*, a collaborative effort between the business, NGO and university communities aimed at protecting workers' rights and improving independent monitoring systems. In addition, we also participate in the *Ethical Trading Initiative (ETI)*.

Our Global Sourcing and Operating Guidelines help us to select business partners who follow workplace standards and business practices that are consistent with our company's values. These requirements are applied to every contractor who manufactures or finishes products for Levi Strauss & Co. Trained inspectors closely audit and monitor compliance among approximately 600 cutting, sewing, and finishing contractors in more than 60 countries.

The Levi Strauss & Co. Global Sourcing and Operating Guidelines include two parts:

I. The Country Assessment Guidelines, which address large, external issues beyond the control of Levi Strauss & Co.'s individual business partners. These help us assess the opportunities and risks of doing business in a particular country.

II. The Business Partner Terms of Engagement, which deal with issues that are substantially controllable by individual business partners. These Terms of Engagement are an integral part of our business relationships. Our employees and our business partners understand that complying with our Terms of Engagement is no less important than meeting our quality standards or delivery times.

Country Assessment Guidelines

The numerous countries where Levi Strauss & Co. has existing or future business interests present a variety of cultural, political, social and economic circumstances.

The Country Assessment Guidelines help us assess any issue that might present concern in light of the ethical principles we have set for ourselves. The Guidelines assist us in making practical and principled business decisions as we balance the potential risks and opportunities associated with conducting business in specific countries. Specifically, we assess whether the:

- Health and Safety Conditions would meet the expectations we have for employees and their families or our company representatives;
- Human Rights Environment would allow us to conduct business activities in a manner that is consistent with our Global Sourcing and Operating Guidelines and other company policies;
- Legal System would provide the necessary support to adequately protect our trademarks, investments or other commercial interests, or to implement the Global Sourcing and Operating Guidelines and other company policies; and
- Political, Economic and Social Environment would protect the company's commercial interests and brand/corporate image. We will not conduct business in countries prohibited by U.S. laws.

Terms of Engagement

- Ethical Standards
  We will seek to identify and utilize business partners who aspire as individuals and in the conduct of all their businesses to a set of ethical standards not incompatible with our own.
- Legal Requirements
  We expect our business partners to be law abiding as individuals and to comply with legal requirements relevant to the conduct of all their businesses.
- Environmental Requirements
  We will only do business with partners who share our commitment to the environment and who conduct their business in a way that is consistent with Levi Strauss & Co.'s Environmental Philosophy and Guiding Principles.
- Community Involvement
  We will favor business partners who share our commitment to improving community conditions.
- Employment Standards
  We will only do business with partners who adhere to the following guidelines:
  Child Labor: Use of child labor is not permissible. Workers can be no less than 15 years of age and not younger than the compulsory age to be in school. We will not utilize partners who use child labor in any of their facilities. We support the development of legitimate workplace apprenticeship programs for the educational benefit of younger people.

Prison Labor/Forced Labor: We will not utilize prison or forced labor in contracting relationships in the manufacture and finishing of our products. We will not utilize or purchase materials from a business partner utilizing prison or forced labor.

Disciplinary Practices: We will not utilize business partners who use corporal punishment or other forms of mental or physical coercion.

Working Hours: While permitting flexibility in scheduling, we will identify local legal limits on work hours and seek business partners who do not exceed them except for appropriately compensated overtime. While we favor partners who utilize less than sixty-hour workweeks, we will not use contractors who, on a regular basis, require in excess of a sixty-hour week. Employees should be allowed at least one day off in seven.

Wages and Benefits: We will only do business with partners who provide wages and benefits that comply with any applicable law and match the prevailing local manufacturing or finishing industry practices.

Freedom of Association: We respect workers' rights to form and join organizations of their choice and to bargain collectively. We expect our suppliers to respect the right to free association and the right to organize and bargain collectively without unlawful interference. Business partners should ensure that workers who make such decisions or participate in such organizations are not the object of discrimination or punitive disciplinary actions and that the representatives of such organizations have access to their members under conditions established either by local laws or mutual agreement between the employer and the worker organizations.

Discrimination: While we recognize and respect cultural differences, we believe that workers should be employed on the basis of their ability to do the job, rather than on the basis of personal characteristics or beliefs. We will favor business partners who share this value.

Health & Safety: We will only utilize business partners who provide workers with a safe and healthy work environment. Business partners who provide residential facilities for their workers must provide safe and healthy facilities.

Unocal's Policies on Human Rights[232]

Note: Unocal has had perhaps the greatest public relations challenges of the three companies because of its presence in Myanmar (Burma), its planned presence in Afghanistan, and the related human rights issues.

At Unocal, we recognize our responsibility to support fundamental human rights and to advance the development of civil society.

Human rights are not just a matter for governments. They have become business issues, in part, because advocacy groups and the media have highlighted abuses in countries where multinational corporations are operating. Today, every multinational corporation is challenged to promote human rights, including freedom from discrimination, the right to life and security, freedom of expression and religion, freedom from slavery, and the right to fair working conditions.

---

[232] Reprinted by permission of Unocal. http://www.unocal.com.

Basic human values and high standards of ethical conduct have always been a central part of Unocal's approach to business and critical to our company's success. An American company that is more than a century old, Unocal is proud of its global reputation. We deeply believe in our core values: *honesty, integrity, excellence and trust.* And we take to heart our commitment "to improve the lives of people wherever we work."

Unocal's Code of Ethics and Compliance Guidelines states: *"We are committed to meeting the highest ethical standards in all our operations, whether at home or abroad. This includes treating everyone fairly and with respect, maintaining a safe and healthful workplace, and improving the quality of life wherever we do business. It also means conducting our business in a way that engenders pride in our employees and respect from the world community."*

As a global corporation, we have a responsibility to promote and protect human rights in all of our activities. But what precisely does this responsibility entail? Should the company be expected to use its influence to address human rights issues in local communities and host countries at large? And if so—how?

What, if anything, is the role of the multinational corporation in supporting human rights?

Unocal, as a U.S. company operating in many different foreign countries, has a legal and ethical obligation to remain politically neutral. Our economic impact, however, is far from neutral. We have seen time and again how our presence has improved the quality of life for people—regardless of politics. And history suggests that economic progress typically promotes increasing respect for human rights.

Our energy development operations have clear human rights implications. We generate economic growth that gives political confidence and influence to a rising middle class. We hire, train and provide advancement opportunities for the citizens of our host countries. We introduce modern values and concepts, such as equal employment opportunity regardless of sex, race, ethnic background or religious preference. We provide a supportive working environment in which all employees may freely contribute. We introduce safety training and environmental programs into the workplace, and offer health care and educational opportunities that further empower communities. And, in keeping with our commitment to improve people's lives wherever we work, we support a wide variety of humanitarian and philanthropic initiatives.

These are not simply by-products of our commercial activities. Rather, they constitute what we see as our responsibility and commitment to the people and the countries where we work.

Moreover, the nature of our business also creates long-term relationships with host country leaders and other key decision makers. Often, in the context of discussing our energy development activities with government officials, Unocal is able to raise concerns about human rights issues and privately present our views.

We know that it is not enough to set high standards of business conduct, we must also live by them. This is especially true of our investments in developing countries. Our experiences in Southeast Asia during the past 30 years demonstrate the value of economic engagement and the important benefits to communities that come from our health care, education, sanitation and other local initiatives.

A more recent case in point is our involvement in the Yadana natural gas development project offshore Myanmar (Burma), where we have taken a leadership role in ensuring that no human rights abuses have occurred in the project's activities. The main difference between our activities in other countries decades ago and in Myanmar now, is that Myanmar has become highly politicized, even though our approach has remained the same.

Unocal has been the subject of considerable attack over alleged human rights violations in conjunction with the Yadana project. Our critics have accused us of using forced labor in building the pipeline across Myanmar to the Thai border. These accusations are absolutely false. From the onset of the project, Unocal has carefully monitored the labor practices followed by the project operator, Total, a French energy company. We have sent our own fact-finding teams to the pipeline area.

Two internationally known human rights experts visited the project and the nearby villages in January 1998. Their report stated that *"not only are [the project operators] paying fair wages, well above the market price, but they are keeping their employees happy and the inhabitants of the 13 villages near the pipeline have experienced great improvement in their lives."*

Several U.S. Embassy officials also visited the pipeline region and reported similar findings. No credible source has ever called our attention to evidence that any forced labor was used on the project.

In 1996, the U.S. State Department issued a report on human rights in Burma. The report noted that "during 1996 there were repeated allegations that forced labor was used on a project to build a pipeline across the Tenasserim Region. The preponderance of evidence indicated that the pipeline project has paid its workers at least a market wage."

In September 1998, the U.S. Department of Labor issued its "Report on Labor Practices in Burma." Although Labor Department officials did not visit Burma to prepare this report, the document discusses issues related to Unocal's investment in the Yadana Project and attempts to tie alleged labor abuses in other parts of Burma to the Yadana Project. Unocal sent a letter to the Secretary of Labor questioning the authorship and research methods of this report and requested a formal investigation into the bias reflected in the report's sections on the Yadana project.

A recently released State Department cable reported that "If charges are made that the pipeline was built with forced labor, we would find such charges very difficult to believe." The same cable further states that "It appears that the pipeline project operators have made a concerted effort to improve the living conditions of residents in the vicinity of the pipeline, and that at least for the short term, the pipeline has raised the socio-economic level in the area."

Unocal would not tolerate the use of forced labor or other human rights abuses on any of our projects. We are proud of our record of improving the lives of people wherever we work. We are equally proud of the benefits provided to the people of Myanmar through our investment in the Yadana project. The project has created high-paying jobs for thousands of workers. It has supported a wide variety of educational, medical and economic programs for nearly 35,000 villagers living near the pipeline route. The Yadana project has built roads, schools, health centers and sanitation systems, and introduced a number of successful economic development initiatives for local farmers. These include poultry, pig and cattle farming, as well as other agricultural and small enterprise activities that have made the region a thriving, inter-related area.

The impact of the various socio-economic programs on local citizens is significant and lasting. Already, babies are being born healthier, with far better life expectancy, as a direct result of the doctors, clinics and health care programs that have been introduced into a region where previously there were none. Infant mortality rate in the villages in the pipeline vicinity has dropped by more than half the national average—to 46 deaths per 1,000 live births, compared with 95 deaths per 1,000 live births for the country overall.

Another important measure of achievement is education. In the pipeline area, thanks to new (or refurbished) schools and supplies, 77 percent of children now attend and complete school. Elsewhere in Myanmar, the U.S. State Department has reported that although education is compulsory, almost 40 percent of children never enroll in school, and only 25 to 35 percent complete primary school.

For all these reasons, the Yadana energy development project is helping to promote peace and prosperity through the Myanmar-Thailand region. We offer this project as a model of corporate responsibility in a developing country.

The United Nations' Universal Declaration of Human Rights[233]

UN DECLARATION

Universal Declaration of Human Rights

Adopted and proclaimed by the United Nations General Assembly resolution 217 A (III) of 10 December 1948.

Preamble

Whereas recognition of the inherent dignity and of the equal and inalienable rights of all members of the human family is the foundation of freedom, justice and peace in the world,

Whereas disregard and contempt for human rights have resulted in barbarous acts which have outraged the conscience of mankind, and the advent of a world in which human beings shall enjoy freedom of speech and belief and freedom from fear and want has been proclaimed as the highest aspiration of the common people,

Whereas it is essential, if man is not to be compelled to have recourse, as a last resort, to rebellion against tyranny and oppression, that human rights should be protected by the rule of law,

Whereas it is essential to promote the development of friendly relations between nations,

Whereas the peoples of the United Nations have in the Charter reaffirmed their faith in fundamental human rights, in the dignity and worth of the human person and in the equal rights of men and women and have determined to promote social progress and better standards of life in larger freedom,

---

[233] *http://www.un.org.*

Whereas Member States have pledged themselves to achieve, in cooperation with the United Nations, the promotion of universal respect for and observance of human rights and fundamental freedoms,

Whereas a common understanding of these rights and freedoms is of the greatest importance for the full realization of this pledge,

Now, therefore,

The General Assembly,

Proclaims this Universal Declaration of Human Rights as a common standard of achievement for all peoples and all nations, to the end that every individual and every organ of society, keeping this Declaration constantly in mind, shall strive by teaching and education to promote respect for these rights and freedoms and by progressive measures, national and international, to secure their universal and effective recognition and observance, both among the peoples of Member States themselves and among the peoples of territories under their jurisdiction.

Article 1

All human beings are born free and equal in dignity and rights. They are endowed with reason and conscience and should act towards one another in a spirit of brotherhood.

Article 2

Everyone is entitled to all the rights and freedoms set forth in this Declaration, without distinction of any kind, such as race, color, sex, language, religion, political or other opinion, national or social origin, property, birth or other status.

Furthermore, no distinction shall be made on the basis of the political, jurisdictional or international status of the country or territory to which a person belongs, whether it be independent, trust, non-self-governing or under any other limitation of sovereignty.

Article 3

Everyone has the right to life, liberty and security of person.

Article 4

No one shall be held in slavery or servitude; slavery and the slave trade shall be prohibited in all their forms.

Article 5

No one shall be subjected to torture or to cruel, inhuman or degrading treatment or punishment.

Article 6

Everyone has the right to recognition everywhere as a person before the law.

Article 7

All are equal before the law and are entitled without any discrimination to equal protection of the law. All are entitled to equal protection against any discrimination in violation of this Declaration and against any incitement to such discrimination.

Article 8

Everyone has the right to an effective remedy by the competent national tribunals for acts violating the fundamental rights granted him by the constitution or by law.

Article 9

No one shall be subjected to arbitrary arrest, detention or exile.

Article 10

Everyone is entitled in full equality to a fair and public hearing by an independent and impartial tribunal, in the determination of his rights and obligations and of any criminal charge against him.

Article 11

Everyone charged with a penal offence has the right to be presumed innocent until proved guilty according to law in a public trial at which he has had all the guarantees necessary for his defense.

No one shall be held guilty of any penal offence on account of any act or omission which did not constitute a penal offence, under national or international law, at the time when it was committed. Nor shall a heavier penalty be imposed than the one that was applicable at the time the penal offence was committed.

Article 12

No one shall be subjected to arbitrary interference with his privacy, family, home or correspondence, nor to attacks upon his honor and reputation. Everyone has the right to the protection of the law against such interference or attacks.

Article 13

Everyone has the right to freedom of movement and residence within the borders of each State.

Everyone has the right to leave any country, including his own, and to return to his country.

Article 14

Everyone has the right to seek and to enjoy in other countries asylum from persecution.

This right may not be invoked in the case of prosecutions genuinely arising from non-political crimes or from acts contrary to the purposes and principles of the United Nations.

Article 15

Everyone has the right to a nationality.

No one shall be arbitrarily deprived of his nationality nor denied the right to change his nationality.

Article 16

Men and women of full age, without any limitation due to race, nationality or religion, have the right to marry and to found a family. They are entitled to equal rights as to marriage, during marriage and at its dissolution.

Marriage shall be entered into only with the free and full consent of the intending spouses.

The family is the natural and fundamental group unit of society and is entitled to protection by society and the State.

Article 17

Everyone has the right to own property alone as well as in association with others.

No one shall be arbitrarily deprived of his property.

Article 18

Everyone has the right to freedom of thought, conscience and religion; this right includes freedom to change his religion or belief, and freedom, either alone or in community with others and in public or private, to manifest his religion or belief in teaching, practice, worship and observance.

Article 19

Everyone has the right to freedom of opinion and expression; this right includes freedom to hold opinions without interference and to seek, receive and impart information and ideas through any media and regardless of frontiers.

Article 20

Everyone has the right to freedom of peaceful assembly and association.

No one may be compelled to belong to an association.

Article 21

Everyone has the right to take part in the government of his country, directly or through freely chosen representatives.

Everyone has the right to equal access to public service in his country.

The will of the people shall be the basis of the authority of government; this will shall be expressed in periodic and genuine elections which shall be by universal and equal suffrage and shall be held by secret vote or by equivalent free voting procedures.

Article 22

Everyone, as a member of society, has the right to social security and is entitled to realization, through national effort and international co-operation and in accordance with the organization and resources of each State, of the economic, social and cultural rights indispensable for his dignity and the free development of his personality.

Article 23

Everyone has the right to work, to free choice of employment, to just and favorable conditions of work and to protection against unemployment.

Everyone, without any discrimination, has the right to equal pay for equal work.

Everyone who works has the right to just and favorable remuneration ensuring for himself and his family an existence worthy of human dignity, and supplemented, if necessary, by other means of social protection.

Everyone has the right to form and to join trade unions for the protection of his interests.

Article 24

Everyone has the right to rest and leisure, including reasonable limitation of working hours and periodic holidays with pay.

Article 25

Everyone has the right to a standard of living adequate for the health and well-being of himself and of his family, including food, clothing, housing and medical care and necessary social services, and the right to security in the event of unemployment, sickness, disability, widowhood, old age or other lack of livelihood in circumstances beyond his control.

Motherhood and childhood are entitled to special care and assistance. All children, whether born in or out of wedlock, shall enjoy the same social protection.

Article 26

Everyone has the right to education. Education shall be free, at least in the elementary and fundamental stages. Elementary education shall be compulsory. Technical and professional education shall be made generally available and higher education shall be equally accessible to all on the basis of merit.

Education shall be directed to the full development of the human personality and to the strengthening of respect for human rights and fundamental freedoms. It shall promote understanding, tolerance and friendship among all nations, racial or religious groups, and shall further the activities of the United Nations for the maintenance of peace.

Parents have a prior right to choose the kind of education that shall be given to their children.

Article 27

Everyone has the right freely to participate in the cultural life of the community, to enjoy the arts and to share in scientific advancement and its benefits.

Everyone has the right to the protection of the moral and material interests resulting from any scientific, literary or artistic production of which he is the author.

Article 28

Everyone is entitled to a social and international order in which the rights and freedoms set forth in this Declaration can be fully realized.

Article 29

Everyone has duties to the community in which alone the free and full development of his personality is possible.

In the exercise of his rights and freedoms, everyone shall be subject only to such limitations as are determined by law solely for the purpose of securing due recognition and respect for the rights and freedoms of others and of meeting the just requirements of morality, public order and the general welfare in a democratic society.

These rights and freedoms may in no case be exercised contrary to the purposes and principles of the United Nations.

Article 30

Nothing in this Declaration may be interpreted as implying for any State, group or person any right to engage in any activity or to perform any act aimed at the destruction of any of the rights and freedoms set forth herein.

....

Discussion Questions

1. Make a list of all of the factors the statements of principles and company policies have in common.

2. What omissions are there in the company policies when compared with the principle statements?

3. If you were developing a policy for your company on human rights and international labor operations, how would you go about doing so?

4. What is the position in each of the statements on child labor?

Business Operations: Financial Issues

"If we were making that decision now in light of the press scrutiny we have been receiving, we probably would not have taken that risk."
ROBERT C. WINTERS
FORMER CHAIRMAN, PRUDENTIAL INSURANCE

"Cookies." "Cookies with raisins."
THE CODE WORDS AT PHAR-MOR FOR A SECOND SET OF BOOKS
AND FALSE ENTRIES, RESPECTIVELY.

FROM CASH AND INTERNAL CONTROLS to "grease" payments in foreign operations, businesses face continuing dilemmas about the propriety of the use and flow of funds.

From production to shutdown, everything a business does affects its workers, their well being, the environment, and the community. Decisions in these areas require a careful balancing of many interests. This unit covers the financial issues in operations and the following unit covers all other operations of a business.

Control of funds offers opportunities for misuse of funds. A lack of careful supervision can present tempting opportunities for personal and business gain that later could serve to destroy the firm. Who's in charge? How much information do they have? Can misuse be controlled? What information and numbers a company puts in its financial reports and public disclosures controls what shareholders and other investors do in the stock market. Shareholders and investors rely on honest and forthright disclosures from companies. When those disclosures comply with legal requirements but are misleading, we have ethical issues for the companies, the shareholders, and the stock market. And what if the officers and directors are not honest with each other and themselves and the company resources become their personal source of funds? In this section we study the companies that faced these ethical issues.

6A

Financial Reports: Earnings, Transparency, and Management

READING 6.1

Earnings Management: The Ethical Issues Remain[1]

Marianne M. Jennings

When Arthur Levitt was the chairman of the Securities Exchange Commission, the federal agency responsible for regulating accurate disclosures in companies' financial reports, he gave a speech at New York University that became known as the "Numbers Game" speech. He spoke about companies and their efforts to use earnings management, a process in which they use accounting rules and financial manipulations to meet goals or make their earnings seem smooth. Mr. Levitt said, "Too many corporate managers, auditors, and analysts are participants in the game of nods and winks. In the zeal to satisfy consensus earnings estimates and project a smooth earnings path, wishful thinking may be winning the day over faithful representation . . . Managing may be giving way to manipulation; integrity may be losing out to illusion."[2]

Earnings management has been business practice for so long, so often, and by so many that many business people no longer see it as an ethical issue, but an accepted business practice. *Fortune* magazine has even offered a feature piece on the "how to's" and the importance of doing it. It remains an unassailable proposition, based on the financial research, that a firm's stock price attains a quality of stability through earnings management. However, the financial issues in the decision to manage earnings are but one block in the decision tree. In focusing on that one block, firms are losing sight

[1] Adapted from an article in Corporate Finance Review 3(5): 39–41 (March/April 1999). Reprinted from Corporate Finance Review by RIA, 395 Hudson Street, New York, NY 10014.
[2] "The Numbers Game," speech of Arthur Levitt, Chairman, Securities and Exchange Commission, NYU Center for Law and Business, September 28, 1998.

of the impact such activities have on employees, employees' conduct, and eventually on the company and its shareholders.

Many experts praised Mr. Levitt's speech because they explained that the U.S. capital markets are the most successful in the world because of integrity in capital formation. Issues on financial reporting and earnings management are at the heart of that integrity-based system. Understanding the issue of earnings management is important as you begin to study the cases involving companies that used this process, perhaps to an extreme. What is earnings management? How is it done? How effective is it? How do accountants and managers perceive it from an ethical perspective?

What Is Earnings Management?

Earnings management consists of actions by managers used to increase or decrease current reported earnings so as to create a favorable picture for either short-term or long-term economic profitability. Sometimes managers want to make earnings as low as possible so that the next quarter, particularly if they are new managers, the numbers look terrific and it seems as if it is all due to their new management decisions. Earnings management consists of activities by managers to meet or exceed earnings projections in order to increase the company's stock value.

You can pick up just about any company's annual report and see how important consistent and increasing earnings are. Tenneco's 1994 annual report provides this explanation in the management discussion section, "All of our strategic actions are guided by and measured against this goal of delivering consistently high increases in earnings over the long term." Eli Lilly noted it had 33 years of earnings without a break. Bank of America's annual report notes, "Increasing earnings per share was our most important objective for the year."

How Do Firms Manage Earnings?

The methods for managing earnings are varied and limited only by manager creativity within the fluid accounting rules. The common techniques are:

- Write down inventory
- Write up inventory product development for profit target
- Record supplies or next year's expenses ahead of schedule
- Delay invoices
- Sell excess assets
- Defer expenditures

In his NYU speech, Chairman Levitt noted 5 popular methods for earnings management.

(1) Large-charge restructuring—This helps clean up the balance sheet (often referred to as the "big bath"). A company acquiring another company takes large expenses for the acquisition because the next quarter its effective management and control makes things look so much better because the expenses are way down.

(2) Creative acquisition accounting—acquisition price is designated as "in-process" research and can then be written off in a "one-time" charge to avoid future earnings drag. This is a process of taking items that should be charged to earnings over time in a one-shot deal. Again, the one-time hit to earnings makes future earnings look so much better.

(3) Cookie jar reserves—The use of unrealistic assumptions to estimate sales returns, loan losses, or warranty costs. These losses are stashed away in good times and then dipped into to make earnings look better when bad times hit.

(4) Materiality—Companies avoid recording issues because they are too small to worry about. They are, as the accounting profession calls them, *immaterial*. The problem is that hundreds of immaterial items do add up on a single financial statement. Also, these decisions not to report things seem to create a psychology in managers that finds them always avoiding reporting bad news or trying to find ways around disclosure.

(5) Revenue recognition—"Channel stuffing," or shipping inventory before orders are placed, is a means of managing earnings. Sales are recognized as final and booked as revenue before delivery or final acceptance, sometimes without the buyer even knowing.

Earnings management can also be broken down into categories. Operations earnings management would involve delaying or accelerating research and development expenses (R&D), maintenance costs, or the booking of sales (channel stuffing). Finance earnings management is the early retirement of debt. Investment earnings management consists of sales of securities or fixed assets. Accountings earnings management could include the selection of accounting methods (straight-line vs. accelerated depreciation), inventory valuation (last in first out [LIFO], or first in first out [FIFO]) and the use of reserves (the cookie jar).

How Effective Is Earnings Management?

Earnings management is effective in increasing shareholder value. A consistent pattern of earnings increases results in higher price-to-earnings ratios. That ratio is larger the longer the series of consistent earnings. Firms that break patterns of consistent earnings experience an average 14 percent decline in stock returns for the year in which the earnings pattern is broken. However, the discovery of earnings manipulation at a company results in a stock price drop of 9 percent.

How Do Accountants and Managers Perceive Earnings Management?

There are certain incentives for managers to engage in earnings management. For example, compensation contracts may provide dramatic incentives for managing earnings. Bausch & Lomb, Sears, and Cendant are all examples of companies whose managers manipulated earnings because of incentive systems and goals that brought the managers personal benefits. Incentives for earnings management can also come from sources other than compensation incentives for executives. Covenants in debt contracts, pending proxy contests, pending union negotiations, pending external financing proposals, and pending matters in the political/regulatory processes can all be motivational factors for earnings management. Many managers use earnings management as a strategic tool to have an impact on pending matters.

Research indicates that the more seasoned auditors and managers are more likely to accept earnings management in a wide variety of circumstances and will use a wide variety of methods of earnings management. They believe earnings management is necessary to increase the value of the stock of the company by influencing investors' perceptions about the company's value.

The Ethics of Earnings Management

The question that fails to arise in the context of management decisions on managing earnings is whether the practices are ethical. Managers and accountants comply with the technical rules, but technical compliance may not result in financial statements that are a full and fair picture of how the company is doing financially. In a system dependent upon reliable, known as transparent financial information, the practice of earnings management conceals relevant information. Research shows that firms that engage in earnings management are more likely to have boards with no independence and eventually higher costs of capital.

Earnings management became so much of a problem that the SEC has new rules that require companies to show a sort of "before and after" picture of their financial statements. The "before" picture is the "pro forma" or the financial statements with all the assumptions and favorable earnings management techniques. The "after" financials will show what happens if the accounting assumptions change. Accounting rules are being reviewed and studied and changed by the Financial Accounting Standards Board (FASB), the American Institute of Certified Public Accountants (AICPA), and the SEC.

The new approach to accounting rules and earnings management focuses on the ethical notion of balance: if you were the investor instead of the manager, what information about earnings management would you want disclosed? If you were on the outside looking in, how would you feel about the decision to book extra expenses this year in order to even out earnings in a year not so stellar?

Discussion Questions

1. Is there a gradual increase in the level of earnings management?

2. What are the motivations for moving expenses and revenues around in quarters and years?

3. Don't shareholders benefit by earnings management? Who is really harmed by earnings management?

4. Put earnings management into one of the ethical categories you have learned.

5. Make up a headline description of earnings management.

Bibliography

Burgstanler, David and Ilia Dichev, "Earnings Management to Avoid Earnings Decreases and Losses," *Journal of Accounting and Economics* 24, 1997, p. 99.

Dechow, Patricia M., Richard G. Sloan, and Amy P. Sweeney, "Causes and Consequences of Earnings Manipulation: An Analysis of Firms Subject to Enforcement Actions by the SEC," *Contemporary Accounting Research* 13(1), 1996, p. 1.

Jiabalbo, James, "Discussion of 'Causes and Consequences,'" *Contemporary Accounting Research* 13(1), 1996, p. 37.

Merchant, Kenneth A. and Joanne Rockness, "The Ethics of Managing Earnings: An Empirical Investigation," *Journal of Accounting and Public Policy* 13, 1994, pp. 79–94.

Remarks by Arthur Levitt, "The Numbers Game," September 28, 1998, New York University. http://www.sec.gov/news/speeches/spch220.txt

Zweig, Kenneth Rosen and Marilyn Fischer, "Is Managing Earnings Ethically Acceptable?" *Management Accounting*, March 1994, p. 31.

READING 6.2

Chainsaw Al and the Ethics of Materiality in Financial Reporting[3]

Marianne M. Jennings

I. Introduction

Al Dunlap was once Mr. Fix-it. He turned Scott Paper around and then moved on to Sunbeam. He used the same approach there that he had in the past, that approach that won him the moniker, "Chainsaw Al." He slashed employees, reduced costs, and sent the stock price soaring. He was a Wall Street darling as he slashed employee payrolls while touting the need for efficiency. His 1996 book, *Mean Business: How I Save Bad Companies and Make Good Companies Great* (with Bob Andelman) was a business favorite.[4] When business managers uttered "Chainsaw Al," they did so with a knowing smile. So renowned was his reputation that just the announcement in 1996 that he was Sunbeam's new CEO caused a 50 percent jump of the company's stock price in just one day. Sunbeam was at $12.50 per share on the day before the announcement of Mr. Dunlap's hiring and closed at over $18 by the end of day of the announcement.

Mr. Dunlap had a history of achievement; he had gone into Scott Paper and slashed its work force and size and then sold it to Kimberly-Clark for a substantial gain for the shareholders. That same strategy was planned for Sunbeam.

But Sunbeam was not as amenable to the Scott slash-and-sell format of recovery. In fact, Mr. Dunlap was dismissed as CEO of Sunbeam by 1998. The underlying reasons for that dismissal were issues related to the earnings stated for Sunbeam's 1997 financials. But it would be years before anyone understood how bad those misstatements were. In February 2001, Sunbeam filed for bankruptcy. In May 2001, the SEC announced fraud charges against Mr. Dunlap and 4 other former Sunbeam executives. The charges stem from accounting issues; the SEC takes issue with the booking of certain items and the auditors claim immateriality as a defense. At the heart of the Sunbeam accounting dispute with the SEC is a key question on financial reporting: if materiality is the standard for disclosure, when are items material? And at the heart of the issue of materiality is not the law, but ethics and the ethics of financial reporting.

---

[3] "The Ethics of Materiality in Financial Reporting," *Corporate Finance Review 6(3): 37–42 (2001). Reprinted from* Corporate Finance Review *by RIA, 395 Hudson Street, New York, NY 10014.*

[4] *There is another book that is non-autobiographical: John Byrne,* Chainsaw: The Notorious Career of Al Dunlap in the Era of Profit-at-Any-Price *(New York: Harper Business, 1999).*

II. The Sunbeam Books

Understanding what happened with Sunbeam is the first step to addressing what is not a new issue in accounting and auditing, that of materiality, but which is sure to receive continuing attention and direction because of this high-profile case.

In 1996, when Mr. Dunlap first came on board, Sunbeam took huge write-offs from the plant closings and layoffs that Mr. Dunlap ordered. However, for 1997, Sunbeam showed a profit, and Mr. Dunlap told analysts via conference call that Sunbeam had "an amazing year" and "We are winning in every aspect of our business." The Board gave Mr. Dunlap a $2 million raise in his base salary as well as stock options for his quick turnaround of their ailing company.

The result of the financial reports and Mr. Dunlap's optimistic statements was that Sunbeam's stock rose to its peak of $52 in the first quarter of 1998. With its credit riding high, Sunbeam undertook, under Mr. Dunlap's direction, the acquisition of Coleman, Inc., First Alert, Inc., and Mr. Coffee. The fits were logical because Coleman sold camping equipment, including lanterns; First Alert sold home smoke alarms; and Mr. Coffee was a premier home coffee machine producer.

However, it soon became obvious that Sunbeam did not have the funds for the acquisitions. In fact, within the first quarter of 1998, revelations about the 1997 financials began to emerge. A summary of the accounting and audit issues, which resulted in what the SEC has said was $62 million in mythical income of the $189 million reported, appears below.

- Sunbeam, Inc., a maker of home appliances such as electric blankets, the Oster line of blenders, mixers, can openers, and electric skillets, has a rather large inventory of parts it needs for the repair of these appliances when they come back while under warranty. Sunbeam used a warehouse owned by EPI Printers to store the parts, which were then shipped out as needed. Sunbeam proposed selling the parts to EPI for $11,000,000 and then booking an $8,000,000 profit. However, EPI was not game for the transaction because its appraisal of the parts came in at only $2,000,000. To overcome the EPI objection, Sunbeam let EPI enter into an agreement to agree at the end of 1997. The "agreement to agree" would have EPI buy the parts for $11,000,000, which Sunbeam would then book as a sale with the resulting profit. However, the agreement to agree allowed EPI to back out of the deal in January 1998. The deal was booked, the revenue recognized, Mr. Dunlap viewed as a recovery artist, the share price went up and all was well. And all without EPI ever spending a dime.
- The value of Sunbeam's inventory was substantially reduced in 1996 so that when sales of it were recorded in 1997, the profits were unusually high.
- Sunbeam took additional write-downs in 1996 that the SEC alleges became a "cookie jar" of reserves that then would permit the appearance of higher profits in 1997.
- Sunbeam engaged in what is known as "channel stuffing" which is when inventory is shipped out before delivery is required or, in some cases, even requested, so that it can be reflected as sales for that quarter. For example, Sunbeam shipped electric blankets to a distributor and asked it to hold the blankets until the retailer was ready for shipment and promised the distributor a portion of the profits as a reward for taking the shipment so that Sunbeam could book a sale.

- Sunbeam also shipped orders to retailers that had not actually been placed with the idea of "cleaning up" in the next quarter or year once the company was past its recovery mode.

The SEC complaint accused Sunbeam and five of its executives, including its CFO and Mr. Dunlap, of "orchestrating a fraudulent scheme to create the illusion of a successful restructuring of Sunbeam and facilitate the sale of the company at an inflated price." The SEC director of enforcement called the fraud accusations part of the SEC's ongoing efforts to prevent "fraudulent earnings-management practices."[5]

III. The Auditor's Role

With such obvious issues of accounting improprieties, where were the auditors? Arthur Andersen served as the outside auditor for Sunbeam during this time, and its managing partner, Phillip E. Harlow, did see the questions and didn't particularly care for the Sunbeam executives' responses. Mr. Harlow asked the executives to restate earnings reflecting changes he deemed necessary. Management refused and the financials were certified anyway.

Further, Mr. Harlow did not see some of the issues and changes as "material" and required no action on the part of Sunbeam executives in terms of restating earning prior to his certification. For example, the "agreement to agree" with EPI, while nothing more than a sham transaction, was not "material" with regard to Sunbeam's level of income. Mr. Harlow defined materiality only in the sense of percentage of income and did not see such a disclosure as a reflection of management integrity. The total amount of the items Mr. Harlow permitted that the SEC now challenges amounted to 16 percent of Sunbeam's profits for 1997.

Mr. Harlow hired PricewaterhouseCoopers to go over Sunbeam's books and his judgment calls, and those auditors agree that Mr. Harlow certified "materially accurate financial statements."[6]

IV. The Role of Materiality

Mr. Harlow and PricewaterhouseCoopers are correct in their interpretation of the FASB and AICPA rules. The amounts involved in many of the noted improprieties were not "material" in a percentage-of-income sense. The problem is that an individual auditor's definition of materiality is the cornerstone of a certified audit. All an auditor does is certify that the financial statements "present fairly, in all material respects, the financial position of _____, in conformity with generally accepted accounting principles."

There is no definition of materiality for the accounting profession. My research shows that most auditors use a rule of thumb of 5 to 10 percent as a threshold level of disclosure, such as 5 percent of net income or 10 percent of assets or vice versa.[7] They may also use a fixed dollar amount or an index of time and trouble in relation to the amount in question.[8]

---

[5] Jonathan Weil, "Five Sunbeam Ex-Executives Sued by SEC," The Wall Street Journal, May 16, 2001, pp. A3, A4.

[6] Andersen has settled the suit brought against it by shareholders for $110 million. Floyd Norris, "S.E.C. Accuses Former Sunbeam Official of Fraud," The New York Times, May 16, 2001, pp. A1, C2.

[7] Marianne M. Jennings, Philip M. Reckers, and Daniel C. Kneer, "A Source of Insecurity: A Discussion and an Empirical Examination of Standards of Disclosure and Levels of Materiality in Financial Statements," 10 J. Corp. L. 639 (1985).

[8] Jeffries, "Materiality as Defined by the Courts," 51 CPA J. 13 (1981).

However, it is clear just from the amount of regulatory action, shareholder litigation, and judicial definitions, that the standard for materiality employed by auditors is not the same as the standard other groups would use in deciding which information should be disclosed. Table 6.1, adapted from research previously published, shows this expectations gap.

TABLE 6.1 Reflections on the Expectations Gap

Type of event	% of judicial who would not disclose	% of CPAs who would not disclose
Inventory reduction (5%)	54.7%	80.5%
Inventory reduction (10%)	47%	63%
Lawsuit (5% of net income and 75% probability of success)	24%	63%
Lawsuit (5% of net income and 50% probability of success)	36%	77%
Lawsuit (10% of net income and 75% probability of success)	16%	25%
Lawsuit (10% of net income and 50% probability of success)	25%	54%
Bribe (5% net income)	15%	10%
Bribe (10% net income)	-0-	4%

V. The Role of Ethics in Materiality

The data and litigation demonstrate that there is something about the expectations of investors and those who ultimately determine liability for non-disclosure that differ from the standards employed by corporations and the auditing profession in making decisions on whether items must be disclosed and when they should be disclosed. Also, given that there are no definitive rules on what is and is not material and the pressures that audit firms feel, as in the Sunbeam case, to sign off on financials, the leadership role on materiality belongs to the financial executives of a company. Those who present the figures for audit and eventually disclosure should establish clear standards for what will be disclosed and when it will be disclosed.

A. Who sets the rules for materiality and disclosure and why?

The CEO and CFO, along with the support of the board, and particularly the audit committee, should establish clear rules for disclosure that reflect the values of the company. Such a collection of rules, grounded in values, is a means of not only preventing the types of poor judgment calls in the Sunbeam case, but a means of ensuring that disappointed shareholders do not take advantage of the expectations gap on disclosure and place the company and its auditors in the unforgiving and costly arena of litigation.

B. What types of materiality standards should be adopted?

The table gives a fairly clear starting point for adopting standards and rules for materiality in a company's financial reports. In the table, there is little disagreement about the need to disclose a bribe, regardless of the amount. This meeting of legal (and hence SEC) minds and accounting minds illustrates the common grounds on materiality. First, the standard is not necessarily always monetary. There are issues, such as a company engaging in bribery, that reflect the nature of management and its operations. This type of information affects the investment decision for it is a fairly accurate predictor of how a company will perform if management integrity, or in this case compliance with the law, is missing.

With that beginning, that management integrity seems universally important; we can proceed with a checklist for disclosure. There are some items that must always be disclosed: bribe, criminal conduct on the part of the company or officers, regulatory sanctions, and any other types of matters, regardless of amount, that reflect on the quality of management, although not in an income-material fashion.[9]

With that outside parameter, managers should move to the more difficult questions that surround conduct such as that in the Sunbeam case: issues of earnings management, perhaps pushed to the extreme there. The human imagination knows no limits in the methods that have and will be developed for booking or not booking items in a creative fashion. It would be impossible to develop a chart that provided a "yes, disclose" or "no, no need to disclose" on every possible nuance of earnings management. But, there can be a definitive model for getting to the heart of an accounting issue in which there is a question about its disclosure, non-disclosure, or the timing of either. As a company establishes its ethical standards for materiality and disclosure, it should adopt the following questions as a framework for resolution:

- What historically has happened in cases in which these types of items are not disclosed? In our company? In other companies?
- What are the financial implications if this item is not disclosed now?
- What are our motivations for not disclosing this item?[10]
- What are our motivations for booking this item in this way?
- What are our motivations for not booking this item?
- How do we expect this issue to be resolved?
- Are our expectations consistent with the actions we are taking vis-à-vis disclosure?
- If I were a shareholder on the outside, would this be the kind of information I would want to know?

For each of these questions, there is an illustration that can help everyone involved understand the significance of the inquiry and the decision.

1. What has happened historically?
The failure to disclose information, the overbooking of losses, and other forms of earnings management have not served any companies well. Sunbeam, Cendant, FINOVA,

[9] In fact, the SEC issued a Staff Accounting Bulletin (SAB) in August 1999 that clearly establishes some "musts" for materiality. One of those is whether there is an issue of the violation of the law, any concealment or the nondisclosure of regulatory action. And the SEC has noted, "There is effectively no safe harbor; a simple numerical test [for materiality] is not sufficient." Elizabeth MacDonald, "Accounting Gets Two-Sided Overhaul," The Wall Street Journal, September 8, 1999, p. A2.
[10] In thinking about this question, the words of outgoing SEC chairman Arthur Levitt are instructive, "In markets where missing an earnings projection by a penny can result in a loss of millions of dollars in market capitalization, I have a hard time accepting that some of these so-called nonevents simply don't matter." Id.

ConAgra, and W.R. Grace are all examples of companies that thought they could manage earnings and hang on until the next quarter brought better news. In the cases of FINOVA (a failure to write down a $70 million loan that had gone bad and challenging the auditors on its disclosure) and Sunbeam, the result was bankruptcy. Cendant, ConAgra, and W.R. Grace continue to pay the price in terms of squandered trust.

As this question is contemplated it is perhaps best to assume that the laws of probability don't apply. These matters have a way of percolating to the surface and the longer the truth percolates, it not only doesn't get any better, its fallout becomes more significant for the company.

2. *What are the financial implications if this item is not disclosed?*

If non-disclosure translates into meeting market expectations, then there is an issue of pressure. For Sunbeam, the nondisclosure of creative booking of sales meant that its stock price soared and that it was in a position to begin an acquisition program that would see its fate become that of Scott Paper with all the returns that brought to its shareholders.

It is within this question that managers and auditors feel the greatest pressure. In the case of Sunbeam, it is not difficult to imagine that those who saw the issues of non-disclosure and their relevance were thinking, "But this is Al Dunlap running the show!" There was no reason to doubt his judgment call on these accounting matters because of his track record. However, precisely because of a stellar track record, officers are subject to the temptation of excessive management of earnings.

Under this question are the close calls of accounting. For example, America Online (AOL) capitalized its advertising expenses in 1996 under an accounting rule that permitted such if the company could show, by some formula, that such an investment was necessary and would yield results. AOL had developed a formula for the customer and revenue results from advertising dollars and had capitalized its advertising costs, rather than expensed them. The SEC disputed the judgment call and AOL paid a fine. However, hindsight shows that AOL was correct in its formula and in sinking funds into advertising dollars because its heavy advertising netted it its customer base that thrives today.[11] While AOL proved to be right in hindsight on the efficacy of advertising dollars, it did release income statements that were over-inflated because they did not indicate the dollars of income being expended for advertising purposes. While AOL settled the charges with the SEC, it admitted no wrongdoing.

For those handling such close call issues, perhaps there is a non-either/or answer to the question. For example, AOL could capitalize the ad dollars but include an explanation of that approach in the financials so that investors understand the true financial picture of the company.

3. and 4. *What are our motivations for booking or not booking this item?*

As a means of checks and balances for the temptation of the moment and the process of group think in the management decision-making process, this question forces those involved to understand their motivation because that motivation may provide insight into whether the booking or non-booking of the item is ethically

---

[11] Floyd Norris, *"AOL Pays a Fine to Settle a Charge That It Inflated Profits,"* The New York Times, May 16, 2000, p. C1.

correct. Motivations that cloud judgment include bonuses tied to earnings goals, option rights, pending retirements, and other types of personal rewards that tempt the soul and strain the values. Look also to pride in achievement. Mr. Dunlap certainly had monetary motivation, but with his book and reputation, there was a certain pride in achievement that he was loathe to lose.

5. *How do we expect this issue to be resolved?*
   If your resolution is to "make it up next quarter," or "hang on until _____," then there is a problem. Timing is everything and, using the lack of presence of the laws of probability, don't count on timing to be impeccable. There are plenty of good intentions in all reporting decisions. This question asks you to focus on resolution if you decide to disclose or not disclose a particular issue or item. For example, California Micro Devices, Inc. inflated its sales and earnings figures by booking bogus sales to fake companies. Not a bad source of revenue, if you can fake it. Fully one-third of its 1994 revenue was bogus and by 2000, even the auditors were being investigated for fraud because everyone had the good intentions of keeping the company afloat and the employees working.[12]

6. *Is the resolution you anticipate consistent with the actions you are taking?*
   In the case of FINOVA, the company had no resolution for the write-down of $70 million. The decision was just to postpone it hoping that other areas of the company could make up for the loss over time. If the non-disclosure has to be resolved by something unrelated to the issue, you perhaps have a fairly good indication that you are pushing the envelope on materiality.

7. *If you were a shareholder on the outside, would you want to know what is being withheld from you?*
   This question is perhaps the most telling and the one that will give employees a clear indication of management expectations on materiality. This question asks that you put yourself in the position of someone who has invested or is about to invest in the company. Is this the type of information that investor would deem important and relevant in making that investment decision to buy, sell, or hold your stock? Campbell's Soup faced 5 class action lawsuits by shareholders for its alleged inflation of the value of its stock by reporting inflated product sales to distributors when, in reality, no product had ever been shipped to them, let alone sold.[13] In short, how would you want to be treated as a shareholder with regard to this information? Once you know the answer to that question, the issue of materiality is not as difficult as CPAs or judges make it. In fact, it is this shareholder perspective that prevents the eventual shareholder suits that follow the failure to take into account this view.

Truth doesn't get better with time. If the company has sales, performance, and write-down issues, withholding that information with the hope that things will get better seems to be the beginning of the decline. Truth withheld means reputational capital squandered when the truth is eventually revealed, as it always is under the non-probability laws of financial reporting. To avoid the fate of Sunbeam and its executives, begin with the 7-point analysis of financial reporting. The seven factors leave little doubt as to the definition of this confusing concept of materiality.

---

[12] Elizabeth MacDonald, "Auditors Miss a Fraud and SEC Tries to Put Them Out of Business," The Wall Street Journal, *January 6, 2000, pp. A1, A8.*
[13] "Campbell's in the Soup?" National Law Journal, *February 7, 2000, p. B3.*

Discussion Questions

1. Were the shareholders of Sunbeam ultimately served in the best way by the decision to enter into the sham contract?

2. Why does "making it up in the next quarter" not work?

3. Do you think there are other ways for a company to survive beyond earnings management? If you were a manager and you were not going to meet quarterly goals, what would you do and say?

CASE 6.3

Creative Medical Billing

Billie Jean Young is the administrator for Los Lomas, a private hospital located in Palm Springs, California. Los Lomas serves patients who carry insurance in 95 percent of the procedures the hospital performs. Los Lomas' noninsurance procedures tend to be plastic surgery; all plastic surgery patients pay in advance. The nature of the medical business at Los Lomas is largely the result of the hospital's location in an upper-middle class retirement/resort area.

Young has just read a recent study that shows that 98 percent of all hospital bills contain errors. Internal data for Los Lomas shows that the hospital receives complaints of errors on approximately 20 percent of the bills it issues.

The study indicates that doctors are "fudging" on insurance claims. All the players in the health care system follow a billing system based on 500 groups of 3,500 medical procedures and 12,574 diagnostic codes. How an illness is coded can make a substantial difference in the amount of reimbursement the medical provider receives for the care of the patient. For example, coding the removal of a mole as a larger procedure (known as "upcoding") will bring additional funds from an insurer. Breaking down surgeries (or "unbundling" them) into segments such as exploration, removal, and repair of scar tissue will substantially increase claims. Itemizing each test in a battery of tests ("exploding" the battery) can triple the cost of a single blood sample. Doctors accomplish all these billing strategies by savvy use of the coding process.

Insurers do have computer programs to check for "code creeps" (increased billing by coding), but often reject such claims in a report to the patient that explains how the charges exceed "usual and customary limits." The patient must then pay personally the amounts considered excessive.[14]

In many cases, miscoding is done to help provide patients with insurance coverage when coverage might not otherwise be available. For example, a patient's insurance might not cover routine tests as part of a physical but would cover those same tests if they were coded "to rule out cancer." Infertility procedures would not be covered, but diagnostic surgery to determine the presence of endometriosis would.

---

[14] Steve Marshall, "Overcharges Force New Rx in Fla. Hospitals," *USA Today*, July 6, 1992, p. 1A.

Most medical care providers hire consultants to help them with "upcoding." One consultant noted, "Every hospital does it or they die." Still another consultant noted, "Why shouldn't they go for the higher one?" But another consultant noted, "Oh, I grant you, there are shades of gray, but when hospitals cross the line, they know it." He also labeled the art of upcoding a "pathetic commentary on our times. These guys should be figuring out how to better treat patients in their hospitals."[15]

Many of these practices result from the inability to collect bills from uninsured patients who are simply unable to pay. Hospitals often use billings for insured patients to cover the costs they must absorb in providing care for uninsured patients. For example, one Florida hospital charged an insured patient $15 for one ounce of petroleum jelly. However, the five-digit CPT coding system is complex, confusing, and fraught with ambiguities. Some errors are the result of these factors.

Medicare recently announced a "bundling" payment policy for heart surgeries, under which it will pay a package price for coronary bypass procedures. The price will include all charges for both hospitals and doctors. Medicare officials maintain that "unbundled" bills encourage doctors to perform more procedures. Doctors maintain that the policy will sacrifice quality of care and their autonomy in making treatment decisions.[16]

As these issues were unfolding, Ms. Young noted the evolving story of Columbia Health Care. Columbia/HCA Healthcare Corporation, Inc., the nation's largest hospital chain (342 hospitals), was investigated by the FBI for upcoding. The investigation began with an early-morning FBI raid on Columbia offices.[17] A Columbia newsletter once noted that the difference between coding a hip vs. a femur procedure is $4,493.[18]

Columbia began its own internal probe as the FBI investigated. Three executives were indicted in July 1997 on charges of defrauding the government by overbilling. In September 1997 Columbia warned its profits would decline with earnings per share dropping from 46 cents per share to 20 or 25 cents per share. Columbia fired its top executives and began a process of downsizing that included the reduction of the number of its hospitals from 345 to 220.

By October 1997, the FBI filed an affidavit in its investigation describing the fraud at Columbia/HCA as "systemic." The FBI unearthed a system in which expenses were overstated in order to take advantage of the fact that government oversight was lax because of low staffing and sheer complexity of the accounting and billing systems. Intent was alleged because Columbia waited two to three years before counting profits from these additional expenses to be certain that there were no audits or federal disputes with the expenses booked. The usual practice if a government agent found overstated expenses was to simply repay the amount. Generally there were no fines or

[15] Rhonda Rundle, "How Doctors Boost Bills by Misrepresenting the Work They Do," The Wall Street Journal, December 6, 1989, p. A1.

[16] Ron Winslow, "Medicare Tries to Save With One-Fee Billing for Some Operations," The Wall Street Journal, June 10, 1992, pp. A1, A5.

[17] Julie Appleby, "Columbia Agrees to $745M Penalty," USA Today, May 19, 2000, p. 1B; Kurt Eichenwald, "Hospital Company Agrees to Pay $745 Million in U.S. Fraud Case," The New York Times, May 19, 2000, p. B1.

[18] In May 2000, Columbia changed its name to HCA — the Healthcare Co., as part of its effort to remove any taint from its image that resulted from the investigation, criminal charges, settlement, and criminal trials of its former executives. "Columbia/HCA Changes Name," The New York Times, May 26, 2000. New York Times Archives.

interest. The FBI alleged that Columbia established its bookkeeping and accounting procedures in order to maximize its benefits from such a system.

The three executives that had been fired, plus one additional executive who was indicted later, Jay Jarrell, Robert Whiteside, Michael Neeb, and Carl Lynn Dick, went to trial in Florida in July 1999. Both Mr. Jarrell and Mr. Whiteside were convicted of defrauding the federal government. Mr. Neeb was acquitted. The jury was unable to reach a verdict in Mr. Dick's case, and his trial ended with a hung jury. Mr. Jarrell was sentenced in December 1999 to 33 months in prison and a $10,000 fine and was ordered to pay $1.7 million in restitution to the federal government.

Shareholder lawsuits began against Columbia all around the country. Between March 1997 and August 1997, the value of Columbia's stock dropped by one third. Columbia's auditor, KPMG Peat Marwick, was also named as a defendant in the suits.[19] By 2000, Columbia had spent over $200 million in attorneys' fees and internal investigation costs.[20]

Several whistle-blowers initially filed suit against Columbia and then were joined by the Justice Department. They had been assisting the FBI. U.S. Attorney James Sheehan said that the whistle-blowers were invaluable to the investigation, "The whistle-blowers get you inside, share the company's intent and knowledge, and provide a road map for routines and systems."[21] Under federal whistle-blower protection statutes, those who report violations of federal laws by their companies are entitled to a percentage of the fine if the company settles or is found guilty of the violation and is required to pay a fine as part of either disposition. For example, for his role in reporting the billing issues at Olsten Home Health Care Service, Inc., Donald McLendon was given 24 percent of the $41 million penalty Olsten agreed to pay in order to settle the case. Olsten was once a business partner of Columbia.

One of the whistle-blowers at Columbia was James Alderson, a hospital accountant, who had been with Columbia for a number of years and at one hospital was asked to create two sets of books. At all the locations where he worked, he suspected that his employer was inflating expenses in its submissions to Medicare.[22]

By 2000, Columbia agreed to a settlement of $745 million on Medicare fraud charges, the largest settlement in the history of Medicare. The settlement covered only the criminal charges and three of the five sets of civil charges. By March of 2001, the Justice Department had filed a new set of charges against Columbia.[23] The new charges allege more inflation of Medicare cost reports as well as the payment of kickbacks to physicians. The Justice Department is asking for $400 million more in false claims reimbursements with these charges.[24]

At the same time the additional charges were filed, Michael Chertoff, the lead outside defense lawyer for Columbia HCA in these health care charges, was nominated by President George W. Bush and confirmed by the Senate to head the criminal division of

---

[19] Kurt Eichenwald, "Accounting Firm Is Named In Medicare Fraud Lawsuit," The New York Times, May 29, 1999, p. B5.

[20] Holman W. Jenkins, Jr., "A Hospital Chain's Lemonade Man," The Wall Street Journal, May 24, 2000, p. A27.

[21] Kurt Eichenwald, "He Blew the Whistle and Health Giants Quaked," The New York Times, October 18, 1998, pp. MB1, 13 (Section 3).

[22] Id.

[23] Lucette Lagnado, "HCA Faces New U.S. Filing on Medicare," The Wall Street Journal, March 19, 2001, p. B13.

[24] "U.S. to Seek $400 Million More at HCA," The New York Times, March 16, 2001, p. C5.

the Justice Department. Some analysts reacted positively to his appointment because of their belief that it was a signal that the Bush administration would not be pursuing health care providers as vigorously as the Clinton Justice Department had.[25]

Ms. Young thought of what happened to Columbia and its executives and the charges that were still pending and wondered how she could develop a policy for her hospital. She also knew that she had the same types of systemic and structural issues as Columbia. For example, her hospital had physicians working there who had an ownership interest in the hospital. She wondered if she would be able to suggest policies given their ownership and authority.

Discussion Questions

1. If everyone was doing their billing in the same fashion, why is there a concern about ethics or possible illegality?

2. If there are shades of gray in diagnosing, is there any problem with always taking the higher code?

3. Do hospitals exist to make money or treat the ill?

4. How did shades of gray turn into allegations of systemic fraud and criminal indictments?

5. Why are there whistle-blowers in this case?

6. Should Ms. Young commission a study of the billing practices at Los Lomas and implement any changes that would correct the overbilling described?

7. Will Ms. Young be able to affect physicians' conduct in coding?

8. Do fudging, upcoding, exploding, and unbundling really harm anyone? Aren't many patients helped by these practices?

9. If patients are not complaining, is it a wise use of resources to audit bills?

10. In many cases, hospitals and physicians maintain these billing practices in order to shift costs. That is, they receive payment from insured patients to make up for the lack of payment from the uninsured who are unable to pay. Is this fair? Is it honest? Should it be disclosed?

CASE 6.4
MiniScribe and the Auditors

MiniScribe, founded in 1980 and based in Longmont, Colorado, was a disk drive manufacturer. When MiniScribe hit a slump in the mid-1980s because it had lost its largest customer, IBM, the board of directors brought in Q. T. Wiles. Called the "Mr. Fix-It" of

---

[25] *Mr. Chertoff was the chief counsel for the Senate Whitewater Investigation during the Clinton years and has been the chief architect of the country's antiterrorism program, including expanding changes in the authority of federal agents for wiretaps and investigations.*

high technology industries, Wiles had turned around Adobe Systems, Granger Associates, and Silicon General, Inc.[26]

When Wiles took over at MiniScribe, he engaged the venture-capital and investment banking firm of Hambrecht & Quist to raise the capital needed for the firm's turnaround. Hambrecht & Quist raised $20 million in 1987 through the sale of debentures. Wiles was, at that time, the chairman of Hambrecht & Quist. Hambrecht & Quist purchased $7.5 million of the debentures and also purchased a 17 percent interest in MiniScribe.

With new capital and simultaneous cost cuts, MiniScribe's sales went from $113.9 million in 1985 to a projected $603 million in 1988. In 1987, MiniScribe's board asked Wiles to stay on for another three years. That year, MiniScribe's stock climbed to $14 per share.

During 1988, the computer industry underwent another slump, and by May, Wiles and other officers were selling stock. Wiles sold 150,000 shares for between $11 and $12 per share, and seven other officers sold 200,000 shares.

By the time the shares were sold, MiniScribe held the unenviable position of having high inventory and high receivables. Industry sales were down, and MiniScribe customers were not paying their bills. In early 1989, MiniScribe announced a $14.6 million loss for the final quarter of 1988. MiniScribe's ratio of inventory to sales was 33 percent (the industry average was 24 percent), and its receivables were ninety-four days behind (the industry average was seventy days). The amount of receivables went from $109 million to $173 million in the last quarter of 1988.[27]

MiniScribe's release of the new financial information resulted in an in-house audit, shareholder lawsuits, and an investigation of stock trading by the Securities and Exchange Commission (SEC).[28] Scrutiny by regulators, outside directors, and the SEC revealed that Wiles, through his unrealistic sales goals, had created a high-pressure environment for managers.[29] In interviews, managers described "dash meetings" in which Wiles spouted his management philosophies. In one such meeting, Wiles had two controllers stand as he fired them, saying, "That's just to show everyone I'm in control of the company."[30] Wiles' attorney described him as "fairly autocratic and very demanding of the people who work for him."[31]

The in-house audit uncovered that, by late 1986, financial results had become the sole criterion for performance evaluations and bonuses at MiniScribe.[32] To be sure that they hit their quotas, MiniScribe sales personnel had used creative accounting maneuvers.[33] For example, in one case a customer was shipped twice as many disk drives as had been ordered—at a value of $9 million. Although the extra drives were returned, the sale for all the drives had already been booked.[34]

[26] "ITT Qume Chief Named President at MiniScribe," Electronic News, November 5, 1984, pp. 20–21.

[27] Michelle Schneider, "Firm's Execs 'Perpetrated Mass Fraud,' Report Finds," Rocky Mountain News, December 12, 1989, pp. 1-B, 2-B.

[28] "Internal Probe Underway by Directors at MiniScribe," Electronic News, May 29, 1989, p. 19.

[29] Peter Sleeth, "Audit to Compound MiniScribe's Troubles," The Denver Post, August 6, 1989, pp. 1H–7H.

[30] Andy Zipser, "Recipe for Sales Led to Cooked Books," The Denver Post, August 14, 1989, pp. 2B–3B.

[31] Id.

[32] Stuart Zipper, "Filings Reveal MiniScribe Struggle," Electronic News, January 15, 1990, pp. 38, 40.

[33] Peter Sleeth, "MiniScribe Details 'Massive Fraud,'" The Denver Post, September 12, 1989, pp. 1C, 4C.

[34] Michelle Schneider, "MiniScribe Execs Rigged Huge Fraud, Audit Says," Rocky Mountain News, September 12, 1989, pp. 1B–2B.

The investigation also revealed that, in some orders, sales were booked at the time of shipment even though title would not pass to the customer until completion of shipment. An examination of MiniScribe's financial records showed that the company had manipulated its reserves to offset its losses.[35] MiniScribe posted only 1 percent as reserves, whereas the industry range was 4 to 10 percent. In some of the transactions the audit uncovered, shipments sent to MiniScribe warehouses were booked as sales when, in fact, customers were not even invoiced until the drives were shipped from the warehouse.[36]

Through these creative manipulations and others, MiniScribe officers kept up a rosy fiscal appearance for the firm's auditors, Coopers & Lybrand. For example, for the 1987 audited financials, company officials packaged and shipped construction bricks (pretend inventory valued at $3.66 million) so that these products would count as retail sales. When bricks were returned, the sales were reversed but inventory increased. Obsolete parts and scraps were rewrapped as products and shipped to warehouses to be counted in inventory.

It was discovered during the 1986 audit by Coopers & Lybrand that company officials broke into trunks containing the auditors' work papers and increased year-end inventory figures.[37]

With the disclosure of the internal audit and the discovery of these creative accounting practices and inventory deceptions, MiniScribe's stock continued to drop, selling for $1.31 per share by September 1989. By 1990, MiniScribe had filed for bankruptcy and was purchased by Maxtor Corporation.[38]

Lawsuits against Hambrecht & Quist, Wiles, and Coopers & Lybrand were brought by Kempner Capital Management, the U.S. National Bank of Galveston, and eleven other investors in the debentures sold by Hambrecht & Quist. In February 1992, a jury awarded the investors $28.7 million in compensatory damages and $530 million in punitive damages.[39] Coopers & Lybrand was held responsible for $200 million, Wiles for $250 million, Hambrecht & Quist for $45 million, and Mr. Hambrecht for $35 million.[40]

Discussion Questions

1. What types of pressures led managers to "cook the books" at MiniScribe?

2. Were the auditors, Coopers & Lybrand, morally responsible for the investors' losses?

3. Suppose you were a manager who was asked to wrap construction bricks in disk drive packaging. Would you ask, "Why?" Would you be able to continue your employment? Would you be morally responsible for investors' losses by wrapping the bricks?

4. Were the internal control people (internal auditors) at MiniScribe morally responsible for the investors' losses?

5. Were the auditors just duped? Should deceived auditors be held responsible for investors' losses?

[35] Id.
[36] Id.
[37] Peter Sleeth, "MiniScribe Stock Plunges 36%," *The Denver Post, September 13, 1989,* p. 1D.
[38] Stuart Zipper, "MiniScribe Seeks Chapter 11 Sale of Firm for $160M," Electronic News, *January 8, 1990, pp. 1, 54.*
[39] Andrew Pollack, "Large Award in MiniScribe Fraud Suit," The New York Times, *February 5, 1992, p. C1.*
[40] Andrew Pollack, "The $550 Million Verdict," The New York Times, *February 9, 1992, p. C2.*

FINOVA and the Loan Write-Off

The FINOVA Group, Inc. was formed as a commercial finance firm in 1992. It was created as a spin-off from the Greyhound Financial Corporation (GFC). GFC underwent a complete restructuring at that time and other spin-offs included the Dial Corporation.

FINOVA, headquartered in Phoenix, Arizona, quickly became a Wall Street darling. Its growth was ferocious. By 1993, its loan portfolio was over $1 billion both through its own loans as well as the acquisition of U.S. Bancorp Financial, Ambassador Factors, and TriCon Capital. In 1994, FINOVA had a successful $226 million stock offering. By 1995, its loan portfolio was $4.3 billion. Standard & Poors rated the company's senior debt as "A" and Duff & Phelps upgraded its rating to "A" in 1995 when FINOVA issued $115 million in convertible preferred shares and its portfolio reached $6 billion. FINOVA's income went from $30.3 million in 1991 to $117 million by 1996 to $13.12 billion in 1999. *Forbes* named FINOVA to its Platinum 400 list of the fastest-growing and most profitable companies in January 2000.

FINOVA was consistently named as one of the top companies to work for in the United States (it debuted as #12 on the list published by *Fortune* magazine in 1998 and subsequent years). Its benefits included an on-site gym for employee workouts and tuition for the children of FINOVA employees (up to $3,000 per child) who attended any one of the three Arizona state universities under what FINOVA called the "Future Leaders Grant Program."[41] FINOVA also had generous bonus and incentive plans tied to the stock price of the company. *Fortune* magazine described the 500 stock options each employee is given when hired, the free-on-site massages every Friday, concierge services, and unlimited time off with pay for volunteer work as a "breathtaking array of benefits."[42]

The name FINOVA was chosen as a combination of "financial" and "innovators." However, some with language training pointed out that FINOVA is a Celtic term that means "pig with lipstick." FINOVA took pride in its strategic distinction from other finance companies. It was able to borrow cheaply and then make loans to businesses at a premium. Its borrowers were those who were too small, too new, or too much in debt to qualify at banks.[43] Its 1997 annual report included the following language from FINOVA's CEO and chairman of the board, Sam Eichenfeld:

> FINOVA is, today, one of America's largest independent commercial finance companies. We concentrate on serving midsize business—companies with annual sales of $10 million to $300 million—with arguably the industry's broadest array of financing products and services. The goals we set forth in our first Annual Report were to:
>
> - grow our income by no less than 10% per year;
> - provide our shareholders with an overall return greater than that of the S & P 500;
> - preserve and enhance the quality of our loan portfolios;
> - continue enjoying improved credit ratings

[41] Dawn Gilbertson, "Finova's Perks Winning Notice," Arizona Republic, December 22, 1998, pp. E1, E9.

[42] "The 100 Best Companies to Work For," Fortune, January 11, 1999, p. 122.

[43] Riva D. Atlas, "Caught in a Credit Squeeze," The New York Times, November 2, 2000, pp. C1, C21.

We have met those goals and, because they remain equally valid today, we intend to continue meeting or surpassing them in the future. Many observers comment on FINOVA's thoughtfulness and discipline and, indeed, FINOVA prides itself on its focus.

FINOVA also had a reputation for its generous giving in the community. Again, from its 1997 annual report:

FINOVA believes that it has a responsibility to support the communities in which its people live and work. Only by doing so can we help guarantee the future health and vitality of our clients and prospects, and only by doing so can we assure ourselves of our continuing ability to attract the best people.

Over the years, not only have FINOVA and its people contributed monetarily to a broad range of charitable, educational and cultural causes, but FINOVA people have contributed their time and energy to a variety of volunteer efforts.

In 1996, FINOVA contributed more than $1.5 million and thousands of volunteer hours to educate and develop youth, house the homeless, feed the hungry, elevate the arts, and support many other deserving causes around the country.

FINOVA's ascent continued in the years following the 1997 report. Its stock price climbed above $50 per share and management continued to emphasize reaching the income goals and the goals for portfolio growth. Throughout the company many spoke of the unwritten goal of reaching a stock price of $60 per share. That climb in stock price was rewarded. The stock traded in the $50 range for most of 1998 and 1999, reaching a high of $54.50 in July of 1999.

At the end of 1998, FINOVA reported that Mr. Eichenfeld's compensation for the year was $6.5 million, the highest for any CEO of firms headquartered in Phoenix. More than half of the compensation consisted of bonuses. Mr. Eichenfeld and his wife purchased a $3 million home in Paradise Valley shortly following the year-end announcement in 1998 of his compensation.[44] Mr. Eichenfeld was named the 1999 Fabulous Phoenician by *Phoenix Magazine* which included the following description:

A true mensch in every sense of the word, Sam casually says, "I do what I can," referring to the community for which he has done so much. While he maintains a modest air on the outside, Sam admits, "I take a lot of pride in having created a lot of opportunity for a lot of people." As long as Sam is head of FINOVA and lives in this community, we're sure there will be many more people who will benefit from his kindness and his generosity.[45]

It was sometime during the period from 1996 through 1998 that issues regarding financial reporting arose within the company. FINOVA had a decentralized management structure that created autonomous units. There were at least sixteen different finance divisions such as Commercial Equipment Finance, Commercial Real Estate Finance, Corporate Finance, Factoring Services, Franchise Finance, Government Finance, Healthcare Finance, Inventory Finance, Transportation Finance, and Rediscount Finance. Each of these units had its own manager, credit manager, and financial manager. In many cases, the failure of one unit to meet prescribed goals resulted in another unit making up for that shortcoming through some changes in

[44] *"Finova Chief Splurges on $3 Million Mansion,"* Arizona Republic, *January 23, 1998, pp. E1, E7.*
[45] Phoenix Magazine, *1999.*

that unit's numbers that they would report for the consolidated financial statements of FINOVA.

The Resort Finance division was a particularly high-risk segment of the company. Resort Finance was the term used to describe what were time-share interests that FINOVA was financing.[46] Time-share financing is a particularly risky form of financing because lenders are loaning money to borrowers who live in France for property located in the Bahamas that has been built by a company from the Netherlands and is managed by a firm with its headquarters in Britain. The confluence of laws, jurisdiction, and rights makes it nearly impossible to collect should the borrowers default. And the default rate is high because time-sharing interests are a luxury item that are the first payments to be dropped when households experience a drop in income because of illness or the loss of a job.

Resort Finance would prove to be a particularly weak spot in the company and an area in which questions about FINOVA's financial reporting would arise. For example, FINOVA had a time-share property loan for an RV park in Arkansas that had a golf course and restaurant. The idea, when first acted on in 1992, was that folks could pay for a place to park their RV in beautiful Arkansas for a week or two in a time-share RV resort. When the loan was made in 1992, the property had a book value of $800,000. At the time of the default in 1995, the property was worth $500,000. FINOVA took back the property but did not write down the loan. It did, however, continue to report the loan as an earning asset even as it capitalized the expenses it incurred to maintain the golf course and restaurant. By 1997, FINOVA was carrying the Arkansas time-share resort on its books as a $5.5 million earning asset. One manager remarked, "You couldn't sell all of Arkansas and get $5.5 million and we were carrying a bad loan at that amount."[47]

Because of its lending strategies, FINOVA had higher risk in virtually all of its lending divisions. For example, it was highly invested in high-tech companies because they fit the category of too new and too risky for banks.

However, FINOVA edged into the *Fortune* 1000 and built new company headquarters in Scottsdale, Arizona, as part of a revitalization project there. Its headquarters housed 380 employees, cost $50 million to construct, and was located just north of the tony Scottsdale Fashion Square shopping mall. FINOVA had about 1,000 other employees at offices around the world.

In the first quarter of 1999, FINOVA again caught national attention for the cover of its annual report that would soon be released. The cover featured a robot, but the head of the robot had an underlying wheel that readers could rotate. There were six heads to the robot, all photos of FINOVA employees. The torso of the robot was a safe and the arms and legs were made of symbols of the various industries in which FINOVA had lending interests. "When you have innovators in your name, you can't do a generic annual report," was the description from a FINOVA PR spokesman.[48]

---

[46] Interviews with Jeff Dangemond, former finance/portfolio manager, FINOVA, 1996–2000.
[47] Id.
[48] "Cover of Finova's '98 Report Turns Heads," Arizona Republic, April 9, 1999, p. E1.

However, the buzz over the annual report cover was small compared to what happened when the cover, printed ten weeks in advance of the content, was to be coupled with the numbers inside the report. FINOVA announced that its annual report would be delayed. It was unclear what was happening until its longstanding auditors, Deloitte and Touche, were fired. Mr. Eichenfeld explained that FINOVA fired its auditors because they had waited so long to discuss their concerns and issues with management. He indicated that he felt they should have raised the issues much earlier than on the eve of the release of the numbers.[49]

FINOVA then hired Ernst & Young, but when the annual report was finally released the company also announced that it would be restating earnings for the year. The price of the company's stock began to decline. FINOVA worked diligently to restore credibility, with its officers noting that the auditors' disagreements with management's numbers were often because the company was too conservative in its accounting and that there were counterbalances for decisions on aggressive vs. conservative accounting practices.[50] However, with a shift in economic conditions and the end of the high-tech market run, the asset quality of FINOVA's portfolio was deteriorating. FINOVA's acquisition of the Fremont Financial Group of California for $765 million only increased investors' concerns about the direction of the company and the quality of its management. By the end of 1999, its stock price had dipped to $34 per share.

In early 2000, when it was again time for the release of the annual report, there was to be another announcement about FINOVA's financial position. FINOVA announced that it was writing down a $70 million loan to a California computer manufacturer. Ernst & Young refused to certify the financial statements until the write-off was taken and the resulting shake-up followed.[51] At the same time as the announcement of the write-off, the FINOVA board announced Sam Eichenfeld's retirement with a compensation package of $10 million.[52]

FINOVA had to take an $80 million hit, or $0.74 per share, in one day to cover the loan write-off of $70 million plus the compensation package. FINOVA's stock, which had dipped to $32 per share when the 1998 issues on the annual report delay first surfaced, dropped to $19.88 in one day of heavy trading. The 38 percent dip in stock value was the largest for any stock that day on the New York Stock Exchange, March 27, 2000.[53] As analysts noted, there was a downward spiral because the trust had been breached in 1998; confidence was not regained and this latest write-off and its delay served to shake investor confidence. Two rating agencies immediately lowered FINOVA's credit ratings and the costs of its funds jumped dramatically.[54]

Shareholder lawsuits began in May 2000 with several alleging that the $70 million loan had been in default eight months earlier but that, because of bonus and compensation packages tied to the share price, the officers and managers opted not to write the loan off in order to maximize their compensation packages, which were computed at the end of December before the write-off was taken.

---

[49] Dawn Gilbertson, "Finova Record Smudged," Arizona Republic, April 18, 1999, pp. D1, D2.

[50] Max Jarman, "Finova Group's Stock Sinks," Arizona Republic, December 10, 1999, pp. E1, E2.

[51] Anne Brady, "Shareholders Sue Finova Executives," The Tribune, May 20, 2000, p. B1.

[52] Dawn Gilbertson, "Surprises at Finova," Arizona Republic, March 28, 2000, pp. B1, B9.

[53] Id.

[54] Rhonda L. Rundle, "Finova Retains Credit Suisse Unit to Assess Operations," The Wall Street Journal, May 10, 2000, p. A12.

Also during May 2000, Credit Suisse First Boston, hired to aid the company strategically, announced that FINOVA had lost a $500 million line of credit from banks. Such a loss was seen as mandating the sale of the company because commercial loan companies must have $1 in a credit line as back-up for every $1 in commercial paper. FINOVA's stock fell to $12.62 on May 9, 2000.[55] Analysts noted that FINOVA's aggressive growth strategy placed it in a particularly vulnerable situation because, as credit lines dried up, it had more exposure on its large loan portfolios. Further, the nature of those portfolios was such that its default rate was higher than other commercial lenders. Analysts valued its loan portfolio at $0.58 on the dollar.[56]

By early 2001, FINOVA was reporting that it had lost $1 billion for the year.[57] It declared Chapter 11 bankruptcy on March 7, 2001. Its default on its bond debt was the largest since the Great Depression. Its bankruptcy is the eighth largest in history, with Enron now ranking number one (see Case 6.8). Its stock price fell to $1.64 per share on April 2, 2001. The stock would fall to $0.88 per share until Warren Buffett's Berkshire Hathaway Company and Leucadia National Corporation made a buy-out proposal for FINOVA, which caused the stock to jump to $2.13 in March 2001.[58] Berkshire Hathway owns $1.4 billion of FINOVA's debt including $300 million in bank debt and $1.1 billion in public bonds.

GE Capital and Goldman Sachs then countered the Buffett offer, but the bankruptcy court approved the Buffett offer.[59] However, pursuant to its rights under the agreement, the Buffett team backed out of the purchase and FINOVA remains in bankruptcy.

Discussion Questions

1. Why do you think the officers and managers waited until the auditors required it to write off the $70 million loan?

2. Do you think the incentive plans had any effect on the reported earnings? Why or why not?

3. Was FINOVA too generous with a resulting loyalty that was blinding? What impact would the types of perks FINOVA offered have on you as an employee?

4. Was FINOVA forthcoming about the level of risk in its business?

5. Most of the FINOVA employees are gone or have been laid off. What impression do you think their time at FINOVA makes as prospective employers read their résumés?

[55] Donna Hogan, "Finova Finances May Force Sale," The Tribune, May 9, 2000, pp. B1, B2.

[56] Atlas, "Caught in a Credit Squeeze," pp. C1, C21.

[57] Max Jarman, "Finova Posts $1 Billion Loss," Arizona Republic, April 3, 2001, p. D1.

[58] Paul M. Sherer and Devon Spurgeon, "Finova Agrees to a Bailout by Berkshire and Leucadia," The Wall Street Journal, February 28, 2001, pp. C1, C18.

[59] Edward Gately, "Bankruptcy Court OKs Finova Plan," The Tribune, August 11, 2001, p. B1.

CASE 6.6

Phar-Mor Earnings

Founded in 1982, Phar-Mor, the discount drug store chain, enjoyed a decade of phenomenal financial success. From 1982 to 1992, its sales grew to $3 billion. In that same period, Phar-Mor expanded from a single store to 305 stores in 33 states. It employed 23,000 workers in 1992. Phar-Mor's concept was to use warehouse-size-and-style stores that offered prescription drugs as well as items ranging from spaghetti sauce to videotapes.[60]

Founders Michael I. Monus and David S. Shapira utilized the concept of low margins to infiltrate even those markets where discount pharmacies were already operating. Opening nearly sixty stores each year, Phar-Mor was ranked as the forty-ninth largest privately held company in the United States in 1991.

Monus, a sports fan, started the World Basketball League (WBL) for short players (those six feet, seven inches or less in height) and also was a part owner and promoter of the Colorado Rockies. The WBL had only ten teams in midsize towns like Erie, Pennsylvania, but Mr. Monus spared no expense in running the league. League officials enjoyed limousine service, and the perks for the WBL commissioner included a Cadillac.[61]

On July 20, 1992, Phar-Mor officers were told (anonymously) of a transfer of Phar-Mor funds to the WBL in the amount of $100,000. An internal audit examination didn't find the $100,000 but did uncover several questionable transactions.[62]

By July 28, 1992, Mr. Monus, who was Phar-Mor's president, had been demoted to vice chairman. On July 31, 1992, Mr. Monus was fired, and the remaining Phar-Mor officers alerted federal authorities.[63] Additionally, Phar-Mor's chief financial officer, Patrick Finn, and its outside auditor, Coopers & Lybrand, were dismissed.[64]

David S. Shapira was appointed as Phar-Mor's chief executive officer.[65] In a statement, Mr. Shapira said that about $10 million in Phar-Mor funds had been funneled to the WBL. Mr. Shapira also stated that Mr. Finn and Mr. Monus had engaged in a "fraudulent scheme to cover up failures in the company and operating losses." As a result, Phar-Mor had had, in reality, no profits for the last three years: The company had overstated its profits by $350 million. Mr. Shapira referred to the work of Mr. Monus and Mr. Finn as "intricate criminal activity to defraud the company and its investors." Phar-Mor took a one-time reduction in earnings of $350 million in fiscal year 1993.

---

[60] Gabriella Stern, "Chicanery at Phar-Mor Ran Deep, Close Look at Discounter Shows," The Wall Street Journal, January 20, 1994, pp. A1, A4.

[61] George Anders, "Phar-Mor Scandal Clouds Corporate Partners," The Wall Street Journal, August 6, 1992, pp. C1, C19.

[62] Gabriella Stern and Clare Ansberry, "A Founder Embezzles Millions for Basketball, Phar-Mor Chain Says," The Wall Street Journal, August 5, 1992, pp. A1, A8.

[63] Calmetta Y. Coleman, "Phar-Mor's Haft Agrees to Quit His Position," The Wall Street Journal, August 25, 1997, p. B7.

[64] Gabriella Stern, "Phar-Mor Hires President, Shuffles Its Top Executives," The Wall Street Journal, February 5, 1993, p. B2.

[65] Gabriella Stern, "Phar-Mor Fiasco Puts Shapira in Hot Seat," The Wall Street Journal, August 7, 1992, p. B1.

Mr. Monus was tried for fraud and embezzlement. In an earlier trial, there was a hung jury and investigations for jury tampering. Mr. Monus was convicted of 109 felony counts of fraud and embezzlement in 1995 and was sentenced to 235 months in prison. Mr. Monus said at his sentencing,

> In the 10 years I was at Phar-Mor, Phar-Mor grew to 300 stores in some 35 states and 20,000 employees. The important thing is not the numbers to me . . . , but the employees—all those dedicated, loyal, and highly motivated people.
>
> I want them to know the sorrow and regret that I have. The sorrow and regret will live with me for the rest of my life.[66]

In response to the news of the company's problems and earnings reductions, many suppliers stopped shipping goods to Phar-Mor, except on a C.O.D. basis. Banks began filing liens on Phar-Mor properties, and the company contemplated a proposal to close 100 stores. By August 17, 1992, Phar-Mor had filed for Chapter 11 bankruptcy. The general counsel for Coopers & Lybrand issued a statement saying that Phar-Mor had showed "no remorse for the hiring, retaining, and promoting of this senior management the board now claims are 'crooks.' Responsible boards have oversight of their management and knowledge of their company's operations. Phar-Mor is a closely held non-public company in which the owners, managers, and the board are closely allied. Collusion and fraud at the senior management level did not occur in a vacuum."[67]

A lawyer of the American Institute of Certified Public Accountants (AICPA) stated that "if the fraud involves collusion among a number of people, the ordinary auditing procedures wouldn't necessarily uncover it."[68]

The final independent examiner's report on the Phar-Mor losses, completed in January 1994, revealed that those involved had kept two sets of books: the official books, which contained false entries, and a second set of records (called "cookies"), where the false entries (called "raisins") were monitored. The final loss figure due to insider fraud was $1 billion: Phar-Mor had had no earnings during the five-year period preceding the 1992 Chapter 11 filing.[69]

The court-appointed auditor discovered the following:

- a memo from general counsel warning Mr. Shapira of a lack of financial controls and conflicts of interest involving top executives;
- the back-dating of promissory notes by officers to exercise expired stock options;
- executives hiring (with company funds) cheerleaders in hot pants to escort them around Las Vegas;
- an internal memo questioning the expenditure of $30,000 for Nicole Miller neckties;
- the purchase by Phar-Mor of costume jewelry for sale in its stores from a firm in which Monus's brother was a part owner; Phar-Mor would have saved $2.1 million by purchasing the jewelry from another vendor; and

[66] "Monus, Co-Founder of Phar-Mor, Gets a 20-Year Sentence," The Wall Street Journal, December 4, 1995, p. B8.
[67] Milt Freudenheim, "Phar-Mor and Its Ex-Auditor Clash on Fraud Case," The New York Times, August 6, 1992, p. C3.
[68] Milt Freudenheim, "Phar-Mor Says Profit Was Faked," The New York Times, August 5, 1992, pp. C1, C4.
[69] Stephen D. Williger, "Phar-Mor—A Lesson in Fraud," The Wall Street Journal, March 28, 1994, p. A14.

- the fact that in 1989, Phar-Mor had adopted an essentially invisible code of ethics: officers questioned by the examiner were unaware of its existence.

Phar-Mor emerged from Chapter 11 bankruptcy in 1995 with a new CEO, David Schwartz, and board.[70] Its annual revenues were at that time $1.1 billion, down from its 1992 high of $3.1 billion. The number of employees was reduced by two-thirds and the company was closely held with Robert Haft holding a 31 percent share. Phar-Mor was to have merged with Shopko Stores in 1996, but it was acquired by Avatex in 1997.[71]

Discussion Questions

1. List the ethical violations by the various parties at Phar-Mor.

2. What elements in the company allowed such a large fraud to occur?

3. Was the company treated as a personal asset of the officers? What problems resulted from this attitude?

4. Suppose you had drafted the internal memo that expressed concerns about internal controls and conflicts of interest. What would you have done if the company took no action in response? What would you do next?

5. If you, as a Phar-Mor employee, had discovered the two sets of books, whom would you tell?

6. List those who have been harmed by the collusion at Phar-Mor.

Sources

Ansberry, Clare, "Phar-Mor's Problems May Give Boost to Rest of Drug Discount Industry," *The Wall Street Journal*, August 6, 1992, p. A4.

"Hard Pills to Swallow," *Time*, August 17, 1992, p. 16.

Murray, Matt, "Wounded Phar-Mor Found a Healer in Antonio Alvarez," *The Wall Street Journal*, May 26, 1995, p. B1.

"Phar-Mor Dismisses 2 More," *The New York Times*, August 7, 1992, p. C4.

Schiller, Zachary, "Wait a Minute—Phar-Mor Is Still Kicking," *Business Week*, March 8, 1993, pp. 60, 61.

Stern, Gabriella, "Phar-Mor, Embattled Chain, Is Trying to Stem Panic Among Vendors, Lenders," *The Wall Street Journal*, August 12, 1992, p. A3.

[70] "Phar-Mor, Inc. Plan for Reorganization Is Cleared by Judge," The Wall Street Journal, *August 30, 1995, p. A8; see also "2 New Plans for Phar-Mor in Revamping,"* The New York Times, *April 25, 1995, p. C2.*
[71] *Matt Murray, "Phar-Mor to Merge with Shopko Stores,"* The Wall Street Journal, *September 10, 1996, p. A3.*

CASE 6.7

Overstated Earnings: Bausch & Lomb

The Hong Kong division of Bausch & Lomb enjoyed double-digit growth during the 1980s and 1990s. In some years earnings increased 25 percent; by 1993, the Hong Kong operation had total revenues of $100 million.

Earnings on contact lenses sales seemed to be absolutely unbeatable with sales increasing at double-digit pace.

It was in 1994 that Bausch & Lomb's twelve continuous years of double-digit growth in both sales and earnings (excluding one-time events) came to a halt with a company announcement that excessive distributor inventories would result in a significant reduction in 1994 earnings. The final result was a decline of 54 percent in earnings to $88.5 million. Sales were down only slightly to $1.9 billion. The table on the following page reflects the shortfalls.[72]

An SEC investigation, as well as one by *Business Week*, revealed some underlying problems in operations of Ray-Ban Sunglasses. For example, the Hong Kong unit was faking sales to real customers but then dumping the glasses at discount prices to gray markets. The contact lens division shipped products that were never ordered to doctors in order to boost sales. Some distributors had up to two years of unordered inventories. The U.S., Latin American, and Asian contact lens divisions also dumped lenses on the gray market, forcing Bausch & Lomb to compete with itself.

The SEC charged Bausch & Lomb with violation of federal securities law for overstatement of earnings. Bausch & Lomb settled the charges with the SEC in 1997. Without admitting or denying the allegations, Bausch & Lomb agreed to a cease and desist order and John Logan, a regional sales director for the contact lens division, agreed to pay a $10,000 fine. The cease and desist order also named the former president of Bausch & Lomb's contact lens division, the former controller, the vice president of finance, and the former director of distributor sales.[73, 74]

Bausch & Lomb emphasized that the SEC found no evidence that top management knew of the overstatement of profits at the time it was made. However, the SEC's associate director of enforcement said, "That's precisely the point. Here is a company where there was tremendous pressure down the line to make the numbers. The commission's view is that senior management has to be especially vigilant where the pressure to make the numbers creates the risk of improper revenue recognition."[75]

Former employees testified they were given a target number each year by operating unit and no excuses were accepted. One division manager, expecting a shortfall, said he was told to make the numbers but "don't do anything stupid." The manager said, "I'd walk

---

[72] Mark Maremont, "Blind Ambition," Business Week, October 23, 1995, pp. 78–92.
[73] Mark Maremont, "Judgment Day at Bausch & Lomb," Business Week, December 25, 1995, p. 39.
[74] Floyd Norris, "Bausch & Lomb and SEC Settle Dispute on '93 Profits," The New York Times, November 18, 1997, p. C2.
[75] Id.

Division	1993	Millions of dollars Planned 1994	Actual 1994
TOTAL BAUSCH & LOMB			
Sales	1872.2	2051.9	1850.6
Operating Earnings	300.9	344.7	168.8
US EYEWEAR			
Sales	190.1	200.0	153.5
Operating Earnings	42.3	48.6	19.7
US CONTACT LENS			
Sales	151.0	176.0	85.8
Operating Earnings	16.8	20.5	−61.7
ASIA-PACIFIC			
Sales	148.9	169.7	107.8
Operating Earnings	34.6	46.8	4.0
ORAL CARE			
Sales	68.8	73.0	50.8
Operating Earnings	2.6	4.2	−10.3
MIRACLE EAR*			
Sales	—	57.9	37.3
Operating Earnings	—	2.3	−12.9
CANADA AND LATIN AMERICA			
Sales	126.1	154.0	113.4
Operating Earnings	17.8	27.3	6.4
EUROPE, MIDDLE EAST, AFRICA			
Sales	246.5	249.0	240.6
Operating Earnings	60.7	60.3	53.0

*Acquired during 1993.

away saying, 'I'd be stupid not to make the numbers.'" Another manager said that in order to meet targets they did 70% of their shipments in the last three days of the month.[76]

Bausch & Lomb also settled a shareholder lawsuit over the overstatement of earnings for $42 million.[77] Following this settlement and with the SEC charges behind it, Bausch & Lomb began its climb back from its tarnished image. It has, as the analysts prone to make puns have noted, lost its focus and has had trouble seeing the vision of the future clearly and sharpening its image. Its overseas operations have been a drain because those sales account for $1.8 billion in sales, but the devaluation of other

[76] Maremont, "Blind Ambition," Business Week, October 23, 1995, pp. 78–92.
[77] Mark Maremont, "Bausch & Lomb's Board Puts on Its Glasses," Business Week, November 6, 1995, p. 41.

currencies has been costly.[78] It tried to enter the two-week contact lens market but found that Johnson & Johnson had beat it there and had it fairly cornered.[79]

The 148-year-old company that was once synonymous with eye care and quality has had a rugged climb back up and it has not yet reached its former levels of success in sales, revenues, or earnings.[80]

Discussion Questions

1. What went wrong with the Bausch & Lomb culture?

2. How was the company affected? Financially? Competitively?

3. Why are all those named in the consent decree "former" employees?

4. What changes would you make to prevent these types of issues?

5. Why do you think Bausch & Lomb has struggled for so many years to make a recovery that seems to elude it?

CASE 6.8

Enron—The CFO, Conflicts, and Cooking the Books with Natural Gas and Electricity[81]

I. Introduction

Enron Corp. was an energy company that was incorporated in Oregon in 1985 with its principal executive offices located in Houston, Texas. By the end of 2001, Enron Corp. was the world's largest energy company, holding 25 percent of all of the world's energy trading contracts.[82] Enron's own public relations materials described it as "one of the world's leading electricity, natural gas, and communications companies" that "markets electricity and natural gas, delivers physical commodities and financial and risk management services to companies around the world, and has developed an intelligent network platform to facilitate online business."[83] Enron was also one of the world's most admired corporations, holding a consistent place in *Fortune* magazine's 100 best companies to work for. The sign in the lobby of Enron's headquarters read, WORLD'S LEADING COMPANY.[84] Employees at Enron's headquarters had access to an on-site health club, subsidized Starbucks coffee, concierge service that included massages, and

---

[78] "Bausch & Lomb to Introduce New Contacts," The Wall Street Journal, March 18, 1999, pp. B1, B9.

[79] Claudia H. Deutsch, "New Chief Inherits a Bausch & Lomb That Is Listing Badly," The New York Times, November 17, 2001, pp. C1, C2.

[80] Zina Moukheiber, "Eye Strain," Forbes, October 4, 1999, pp. 58–60; see also Erile Norton, "CEO Gill to Retire From Bausch & Lomb; Carpenter Is Seen As Possible Successor," The Wall Street Journal, December 14, 1995, p. B3.

[81] Adapted from Marianne M. Jennings, "A Primer on ENRON: Lessons from A Perfect Storm of Financial Reporting, Corporate Governance and Ethical Culture Failures," 39 California Western Law Review 163–262 (2003).

[82] Noelle Knox, "Enron to Fire 4,000 from Headquarters," USA Today, December 4, 2001, p. 1B.

[83] From the class action complaint filed in the Southern District of Texas, Kaufman v. Enron.

[84] Bethany McClean, "Why Enron Went Bust," Fortune, December 24, 2001, pp. 59–72.

car washes, all for free.[85] Those employees with Enron Broadband received free Palm Pilots, free cell phones, and free wireless laptops.[86]

In November 2001, a week following credit agencies' downgrading of its debt to "junk" grade, Enron filed for bankruptcy. At that time, it was the largest bankruptcy ($62 billion) in the history of the United States.[87] Since then, it has dropped and is now just one of the 10 largest bankruptcies in the history of the United States.

II. Background on Enron

Enron began as the merger of two gas pipelines, Houston Natural Gas and Internorth, orchestrated by Kenneth Lay, and emerged as an energy trading company. Poised to ride the wave of deregulation of electricity, Enron would be a power supplier to utilities. It would trade in energy and offer electricity for sale around the country by locking in supply contracts at fixed prices and then hedging on those contracts in other markets. There are few who dispute that its strategic plan at the beginning showed great foresight and that its timing for market entry was impeccable. It was the first mover in this market and it enjoyed phenomenal growth. It became the largest energy trader in the world, with $40 billion in revenue in 1998, $60 billion in 1999, and $101 billion in 2000. Its internal strategy was to grow revenue by 15 percent per year.[88]

When Enron rolled out its online trading of energy as a commodity, it was as if there had been a Wall Street created for energy contracts. Enron itself had 1,800 contracts in that online market. It had really created a market for weather futures so that utilities could be insulated by swings in the weather and the resulting impact on the prices of power. It virtually controlled the energy market in the United States. By December 2000 Enron's shares were selling for $85 each. Its employees had their 401(k)s heavily invested in Enron stock, and the company had a matching program in which it contributed additional shares of stock to savings and retirement plans when employees chose to fund them with Enron stock.

When competition began to heat up in energy trading, Enron began some diversification activities that proved to be disasters in terms of producing earnings. It acquired a water business that collapsed nearly instantaneously. It also had some international investments, particularly power plants in Brazil and India, that had gone south. Its $1 billion investment in a 2,184-megawatt power plant in India was in ongoing dispute as its political and regulatory relations in that country had deteriorated and the state utility stopped paying its bills for the power.[89]

In 1999, it announced its foray into fiber optics and the broadband market. Enron overanticipated the market in this area and experienced substantial losses related to the expansion of its broadband market. Like Corning and other companies that overbuilt, Enron began bleeding quickly from losses related to this diversification.[90]

---

[85] Alexei Barrionuevo, "Jobless in a Flash, Enron's Ex-employees Are Stunned, Bitter, Ashamed," The Wall Street Journal, December 11, 2001, pp. B1, B12.

[86] Id.

[87] Richard A. Oppel, Jr. and Riva D. Atlas, "Hobbled Enron Tries to Stay On Its Feet," The New York Times, December 4, 2001, pp. C1, C8.

[88] "Why John Olson Wasn't Bullish on Enron," http://knowledge.Wharton.upenn.edu/013002_ss3.

[89] Saritha Rai, "New Doubts on Enron's India Investment," The New York Times, November 21, 2001, p. W1.

[90] Proposed complaint, class action litigation, November 2001, http://www.kaplanfox.com.

III. The Financial Reporting Issues

A. Mark-to-Market Accounting

Enron followed the Financial Accounting Standards Board's (FASB's) rules for energy traders, which permit such companies to include in current earnings those profits they expect to earn on energy contracts and related derivative estimates.[91] The result is that many energy companies have been posting earnings, quite substantial, for noncash gains that they expect to realize some time in the future. Known as "mark-to-market" accounting, the earnings for a company look terrific, but those earnings are based on assumptions. An example helps to illustrate the wild differences that might occur when values are placed on these energy contracts that are marked to the market price. Suppose that an energy company has a contract to sell gas for $1.00 per gallon, with the contract to begin in 2004 and run through 2014. If the price of gas in 2002 is $0.80 per gallon, then the value of that contract can be booked accordingly and handsomely, with a showing of a 20 percent profit margin. However, suppose that the price of gasoline then climbs to $1.20 per gallon during 2003. What is the manager's resolution and reconciliation in the financial statement of this change in price? The company has a ten-year commitment to sell gas at a price that will produce losses. Likewise, suppose that the price of gas declines further to $0.50 per gallon in 2003. How is this change reflected in the financial statements, or does the company leave the value as it was originally booked in 2002? And how much of the contract is booked into the present year? And what is its value presently?

The difficulty with mark-to-market accounting is that the numbers that the energy companies carry for earnings on these future contracts are subjective. The numbers they carry depend upon assumptions about market factors. Those assumptions used in computing future earnings booked in the present are not revealed in the financial reports and investors have no way of knowing the validity of those assumptions or even whether they are conservative or aggressive assumptions about energy market expectations. It becomes difficult for investors to cross-compare financial statements of energy companies because they are unable to compare what are apples and oranges in terms of earnings because of the futuristic nature of the income and the possibility that those figures may never come to fruition.

For example, the unrealized gains portion of Enron's pretax profit for 2000 was about 50 percent of the total $1.41 billion profit originally reported. That amount was one-third in 1999.

This practice of mark-to-market accounting proved to be particularly hazardous for Enron management because their bonuses and performance ratings were tied to meeting earnings goals. The result was that their judgment on the fair value of these energy contracts, some as long as 20 years into the future, was greatly biased in favor of present recognition of substantial value.[92] The value of these contracts is dependent upon assumptions and variables, which are not discussed in the financial statements, not readily available to investors and shareholders, and include wild cards such as the weather,

---

[91] Jonathan Weil, "After Enron, 'Mark to Market' Accounting Gets Scrutiny," The Wall Street Journal, December 4, 2001, pp. C1, C2.
[92] Susan Lee, "Enron's Success Story," The Wall Street Journal, December 26, 2001, p. A11.

the price of natural gas, and market conditions in general. One analyst has noted, "Whenever there's a considerable amount of discretion that companies have in reporting their earnings, one gets concerned that some companies may overstate those earnings in certain situations where they feel pressure to make earnings goals."[93] A FASB study showed that when a hypothetical example on energy contracts was given at a conference, the valuations by managers for the contracts ranged from $40 million to $153 million.[94]

Some analysts were concerned about this method of accounting because these are noncash earnings. Some noted that Enron's noncash earnings were over 50 percent of its revenues. Others discovered the same issues when they noted that Enron's margins and cash flow did not match up with its phenomenal earnings records.[95] For example, Jim Chanos, of Kynikos Associates, noted that no one was really sure how Enron made money and that its operating margins were very low for the reported revenue. Mr. Chanos concluded that Enron was a "giant hedge fund sitting on top of a pipeline."[96] Mr. Chanos noted that Wall Street loved Enron because it consistently met targets, but he was skeptical because of off-the-balance sheet transactions.[97] Mr. Chanos and others who brought questions to Enron were readily dismissed. For example, *Fortune* reporter Bethany McClean experienced pressure in 2000 when she began asking questions about the revenues and margins and Mr. Lay called her editor to request that she be removed from the story. The Enron CEO at the time, Jeffrey Skilling, refused to answer her questions and labeled her line of inquiry as "unethical."[98] During an analysts' telephonic conference with Mr. Skilling in which Mr. Chanos asked why Enron had not provided a balance sheet, Mr. Skilling called Mr. Chanos, an "a___h____."[99] Mr. Chanos opted for selling Enron shares short and declined to disclose the amount of money he has made as a result of his position.

John Olson, an analyst with a Houston company, reflected that most analysts were unwilling to ask questions. When Mr. Olson asked Mr. Skilling questions about how Enron was making money, Mr. Skilling responded that Enron was part of the new economy and that Olson, "didn't get it."[100] Mr. Olson advised his company's clients not to invest in Enron because, as he explained to them, "Never invest in something you can't understand."[101] Mr. Olson was fired by Merrill Lynch following the publication of his skeptical analysis about Enron. Merrill Lynch continues to deny that it fired Mr. Olson for that reason. Enron was a critical client for Merrill Lynch and four former Merrill investment bankers were indicted and convicted for their role in one Enron transaction.[102]

---

[93] Id.

[94] Weil, "After Enron, 'Mark to Market' Accounting Gets Scrutiny," The Wall Street Journal, December 4, 2001, p. C2.

[95] McClean, "Why Enron Went Bust," pp. 62–63. Ms. McLean had written a story in the summer of 2001 entitled, "Is Enron Overpriced?" for Fortune. The lead line to the story was, "How exactly does Enron make its money?" The story was buried. It enjoyed little coverage or attention until November 2001. Ms. McClean is now an analyst on the Enron case for NBC and has been featured on numerous news shows. Felicity Barringer, "10 Months Ago, Questions on Enron Came and Went With Little Notice," The New York Times, January 28, 2002, p. A11. Ms. McClean wrote a book with Peter Elkind, The Smartest Guys in the Room.

[96] Id.

[97] Cassell Bryan-Low and Suzanne McGee, "Enron Short Seller Detected Red Flags in Regulatory Filings," The Wall Street Journal, November 5, 2001, pp. C1, C2.

[98] Id., p. 60.

[99] Id., p. C2.

[100] "Why John Olson Wasn't Bullish on Enron," http://www.knowledge.wharton.upenn.edu/013002_ss3.

[101] Id.

[102] Kurt Eichenwald, "Jury Convicts 5 Involved in Enron Deal with Merrill," The New York Times, November 4, 2004, pp. C1, C4.

When *U.S. News & World Report* published Mr. Olson's analysis and advice, Kenneth Lay sent Mr. Olson's boss a handwritten note with the following:

> John Olson has been wrong about Enron for over 10 years and is still wrong. But he is consistant [sic].

Upon reading the note sent to his boss, Mr. Olson responded, "You know that I'm old and I'm worthless, but at least I can spell *consistent*."[103]

B. Off-the-Books Entities

Enron's books not only suffered from the problem of mark-to-market accounting, the company also made minimal disclosures about its off-the-balance-sheet liabilities that it was carrying.[104] These problems, coupled with the mark-to-market value of the energy contracts, permitted Enron's financial statements to paint a picture that did not adequately reflect the risk investors had.

Enron had created, by the time it collapsed, about 3,000 off-the-books entities, partnerships, limited partnerships, and limited liability companies (called *special purposes entities* or SPEs in the accounting profession) that carried Enron debt and obligations that had been spun off but did not have to be disclosed in Enron's financial reports because, under an accounting rule known as FASB 125, the debt and obligations in off-the-books entities did not have to be disclosed so long as Enron's ownership interests in the entities never exceeded 49 percent. Disclosure requirements under GAAP and FASB kicked in at 50 percent ownership at that time. Under the old rules, when a company owned 50 percent or more of a company, it had to disclose transactions with that company in the financials as "related party transactions."

Enron created a complex network of these entities and some of the officers of the company even served as principals in these companies and began earning commissions for the sale of Enron assets to them. Andrew Fastow, Enron's CFO, was a principal in many of these off-the-book entities. His wife, Lea, also a senior officer at Enron, was also involved in handling many of the SPEs. In some of the SPEs, the two discussed the possibility of having some of the payments come to their two small children.

In 1999, Enron described one of these relationships in its 10K (an annual report companies must file with the SEC) as follows:

> In June 1999, Enron entered into a series of transactions involving a third party and LJM Cayman, L.P. (LJM). LJM is a private investment company, which engages in acquiring or investing in primarily energy-related investments. A senior officer of Enron is the managing member of LJM's general partner.[105]

The effect of all of these partnerships was to allow Enron to transfer an asset from its books, along with the accompanying debt, to the partnership. An outside investor would fund as little as 3 percent of the partnership, with Enron occasionally providing even the front money for the investor. Enron would then guarantee the bank loan to

---

[103] "Why John Olson Wasn't Bullish on Enron," http://www.knowledge.wharton.upenn.edu/013002_ss3.
[104] Richard A. Oppel, Jr. and Andrew Ross Sorkin, "Enron Corp. Files Largest U.S. Claim For Bankruptcy," The New York Times, December 3, 2001, pp. A1, A16.
[105] Enron Corp. 10K, Filed December 31, 1999, p. 16.

the partnership for the purchase of the asset. Enron would pledge shares as collateral for these loans it guaranteed in cases where the bank felt the asset transferred to the partnership was insufficient collateral for the loan amount.[106] By the time it collapsed, Enron had $38 billion in debt among all the various SPEs, but carried only $13 billion on its balance sheet.[107]

To add to the complexity of these off-the-books loans and the transfer of Enron debt, many of the entities formed to take the asset and debt were corporations in the Cayman Islands. Enron had 881 such corporations, with 700 formed in the Cayman Islands and, in addition to transferring the debt off its balance sheet, it enjoyed a substantial number of tax benefits because corporations operate tax-free there. The result is that Enron paid little or no federal income taxes between 1997 and 2000.[108] Comedian Robin Williams referred to Enron executives as "The Investment Pirates of the Caribbean."

IV. Relatives and Doing Business With Enron

In addition to these limited liability company and limited partnership asset transfers, there were apparently a series of transactions authorized by Mr. Lay in which Enron did business with companies owned by Mr. Lay's son, Mark, and his sister, Sharon Lay. Jeffrey Skilling had hired Mark Lay in 1989 when Mr. Lay graduated with a degree in economics from UCLA. However, Mr. Lay left Enron feeling that he needed to "stand on his own and work outside of Enron."[109] Enron eventually ended up acquiring Mr. Lay's son's company and hired him as an Enron executive with a guaranteed pay package of $1,000,000 over three years as well as 20,000 stock options for Enron shares.[110] There was a criminal investigation into the activities of one of the companies founded by Mark Lay, but he was not charged with wrongdoing. He did pay over $100,000 to settle a civil complaint in the matter, but admitted no wrongdoing. Mark Lay has entered a Baptist seminary in Houston and plans to become a minister.[111]

Sharon Lay owned a Houston travel agency and received over $10 million in revenue from Enron during the period from 1998 through 2001 years, one-half of her company's revenue during that period.[112] Both Ms. and Mr. Lay say that they made all the necessary disclosures to the board and regulators about their business with Enron.

V. Enron's Demise

Enron's slow and steady decline began in the November/December 2000 time frame when its share price was at $85. By the time Jeffrey Skilling announced his departure as CEO on August 14, 2001, with no explanation, the share price was at about $43. Mr. Skilling says that he left the company simply to spend more time with his family, but his departure raised questions among analysts even as Kenneth Lay returned as

---

[106] John R. Emshwiller and Rebecca Smith,"Murky Waters: A Primer on Enron Partnerships," The Wall Street Journal, January 21, 2002, pp. C1, C14.

[107] Bethany McLean and Peter Elkind, "Partners in Crime," Fortune, October 27, 2003, p. 79.

[108] David Gonzalez, "Enron Footprints Revive Old Image of Caymans," The New York Times, January 28, 2002, p. A10.

[109] David Barboza and Kurt Eichenwald, "Son and Sister Of Enron Chief Secured Deals," The New York Times, February 2, 2002, pp. A1, B5.

[110] Id.

[111] Id.

[112] Id.

CEO.[113] *The Wall Street Journal* raised questions about Enron's disclosures on August 28, 2001, as Enron was beginning an aggressive movement for selling off assets.[114] By October, Enron disclosed that it was reporting a third quarter loss and it took a $1.2 billion reduction in shareholder equity. Within days of those announcements, CFO Andrew Fastow was terminated and in less than 2 weeks, Enron restated its earnings dating back to 1997, a $586 million, or 20 percent, reduction.

Following these disclosures and the announcement of Enron's liability on a previously undisclosed $690 million loan, CEO Kenneth Lay left the company as CEO, but remained as chairman of the board.[115] Mr. Lay waived any rights to his parachute, reportedly worth $60 million, and also agreed to repay a $2 million loan from the company.[116] Mr. Lay's wife, Linda, appeared on NBC with correspondent Lisa Meyer on January 28, 2002, and indicated that she and Mr. Lay were "fighting for liquidity."[117] She indicated that all their property was for sale, but a follow-up check by Ms. Meyer found only one of a dozen homes owned by the Lays was for sale. Mr. Lay consulted privately with the Rev. Jesse Jackson for spiritual advice, according to Mrs. Lay.[118]

VI. The Enron Culture

Enron was a company with a swagger. It had an aggressive culture in which a rating system required that 20 percent of all employees be rated at below performance and encouraged to leave the company. As a result of this policy, no employee wanted to be the bearer of bad news.

Margaret Ceconi, an employee with Enron Energy Services, wrote a five-page memo to Kenneth Lay on August 28, 2001 stating that losses from Enron Energy Services were being moved to another sector in Enron in order to make the Energy Service arm look profitable. One line from her memo read, "Some would say the house of cards are falling."[119] Mr. Lay did not meet with Ms. Ceconi, but she was contacted by Enron Human Resources and counseled on employee morale. When she raised the accounting issues in her meeting with HR managers, she was told they would be investigated and taken very seriously, but she was never contacted by anyone about her memo. Her memo remained dormant until January 2002 when she sent it to the U.S. House of Representatives' Energy and Commerce Committee, the body conducting a series of hearings on the Enron collapse.

Ms. Ceconi's memo followed two weeks after Sherron Watkins, a former executive, wrote of her concerns about "accounting scandals" at Enron. Ms. Watkins was a former Andersen employee who had been hired into the executive ranks by Enron. Ms. Watkins

---

[113] John E. Emshwiller and Rebecca Smith, "Behind Enron's Fall, A Culture of Operating Outside Public View," The Wall Street Journal, *December 5, 2001" pp. A1, A10.*

[114] John E. Emshwiller, Rebecca Smith, Robin Sidel, and Jonathan Weil, "Enron Cuts Profit Data of 4 Years by 20%," The Wall Street Journal, *November 9, 2001, p. A3.*

[115] Id.

[116] Richard A. Oppel, Jr. and Floyd Norris, "Enron Chief Will Give Up Severance," The New York Times, *November 14, 2001,* pp. C1, C10.

[117] Alessandra Stanley and Jim Yardley, "Lay's Family Is Financially Ruined, His Wife Says," The New York Times, *January 29, 2002, pp. C1, C6.*

[118] Id.

[119] Julie Mason, "Concerned Ex-worker Was Sent to Human Resources," Houston Chronicle, *January 30, 2002,* http://www.chron.com.

wrote a letter to Kenneth Lay on August 15, 2001, that included the following, "I am incredibly nervous that we will implode in a wave of accounting scandals. I have heard from one manager-level employee from the principal investments group say, 'I know it would be devastating to all of us, but I wish we would get caught. We're such a crooked company.'"[120] She also warned that Mr. Skilling's swift departure would raise questions about accounting improprieties and that "It sure looks to the layman on the street that we are hiding losses in a related company."[121] In her memo she listed J. Clifford Baxter as someone Mr. Lay could talk to in order to verify her facts and that her concerns about the company were legitimate. Ms. Watkins wrote the memo anonymously on August 15, 2001, but by August 22, and after discussing the memo with former colleagues at Andersen, she told her bosses that she was the one who had written the memo.

In the months prior to Enron's collapse, employees became suspicious about what was called "aggressive accounting" and voiced their concerns in online chat rooms.[122] Clayton Verdon was fired in November 2001 for his comments about "overstating profits," made in an employee chat room. A second employee was fired when he revealed in the chat room that the company had paid $55 million in bonuses to executives on the eve of its bankruptcy.[123] Enron indicated that the terminations were necessary because the employees had breached company security.

VII. The Enron Board

Some institutional investors have raised questions about conflicts and the lack of independence in Enron's board.[124] Members of Enron's board were well compensated with a total of $380,619 paid to each director in cash and stock for 2001. One member of the board was Dr. Wendy L. Gramm, the former chairwoman of the Commodity Futures Trading Commission and wife of Senator Phil Gramm, the senior U.S. senator from Texas, who received campaign donations from Enron employees and its PAC. Dr. Gramm opted to own no Enron stock and accepted payment for her board service only in a deferred compensation account.

Dr. John Mendelsohn, the president of the University of Texas M.D. Anderson Cancer Center in Houston, also served on the Enron board, including its audit committee. Dr. Mendelsohn's center received $92,508 from Enron and $240,250 from Linda and Ken Lay after Dr. Mendelsohn joined the Enron board in 1999.[125]

VIII. After the Fall

Litigation is pending on all of these issues. Enron fired 5,100 of its 7,500 employees by December 3, 2001. Each employee will receive a $4,500 severance package, if the bankruptcy court approves it. However, the employees are more concerned about their financial futures. Many held Enron stock and were compensated with Enron stock options. The stock was trading at $0.40 per share on December 3, 2001. Enron employees' 401(k) plans, funded with Enron stock, lost $1.2 billion in 2001. "Almost

---

[120] Michael Duffy, "What Did They Know and When Did They Know It?" Time, January 28, 2002, pp. 16–27.
[121] Id.
[122] Alex Berenson, "Enron Fired Workers For Complaining Online," The New York Times, January 21, 2002, pp. C1, C8.
[123] Id.
[124] Reed Abelson, "Enron Board Comes Under a Storm of Criticism," The New York Times, December 16, 2001, p. BU4.
[125] Jo Thomas and Reed Abelson, "How a Top Medical Researcher Became Entangled With Enron," The New York Times, January 28, 2002, pp. C1, C2.

everyone is gone. Upper management is not talking. No managing directors are around, and police are on every floor. It's so unreal," said one departing employee.[126] One employee, George Kemper, a maintenance foreman, who is part of a suit filed against Enron related to the employees' 401(k) plans, whose plan was once worth $225,000 and is now worth less than $10,000, said, "How am I going to retire now? Everything I worked for the past 25 years has been wiped out."[127]

Just prior to declaring bankruptcy, Enron paid $55 million in bonuses to executives described as "retention executives," or those the company needs to stay on board in order to continue operations.[128]

Tragically, J. Clifford Baxter, a former Enron vice chairman, and the one officer Ms. Watkins suggested Mr. Lay talk with, took his own life in his 2002 Mercedes Benz about a mile from his $700,000 home in Sugar Land, Texas, a suburb 25 miles from Houston. Mr. Baxter, who earned his MBA at Columbia, had left Enron in May 2001, following what some employees say was his voicing of concerns over the accounting practices of Enron and its disclosures.[129] SEC records disclose that Mr. Baxter sold 577,000 shares of Enron stock for $35.2 million between October 1998 and early 2001.[130] He had been asked to appear before Congress to testify, was a defendant in all the pending litigation, and was last seen in public at his yacht club where he took his yacht out for a sail. Those who saw him indicated that his hair had become substantially grayer since October when the public disclosures about Enron's condition began. Mr. Baxter was depicted as a philanthropist in the Houston area, having raised money for charities such as Junior Achievement and other organizations to benefit children. He had created the Baxter Foundation with $200,000 from Enron and $20,000 of his own money to assist charities such as Junior Achievement, the American Cancer Society, and the American Diabetes Association.[131]

As noted, Enron had a matching plan for its employees on the 401(k). However, 60 percent of their plan was invested in Enron stock. Between October 17 and November 19, 2001, when the issues surrounding Enron's accounting practices and related transactions began to surface, the company put a lock down on the plan so that employees could not sell their shares.[132] Prior to the lockdown, most of the executives had sold off large blocks of Enron stock. For example, Jeffrey Skilling, who left the company in August 2001, sold off 500,000 shares on September 17, 2001.[133] He had sold 240,000 shares in early 2001 and at the time of Enron's bankruptcy owned 600,000 shares and an undisclosed number of options.[134] Mr. Lay also sold a substantial amount of stock in August 2001, but his lawyer had indicated the sale of the stock was necessary in order to repay loans.[135]

---

[126] Richard A. Oppel, Jr. and Riva D. Atlas, "Hobbled Enron Tries to Stay On Its Feet," The New York Times, December 4, 2001, pp. C1, C8.

[127] Christine Dugas, "Enron Workers Sue Over Retirement Plan," USA Today, November 27, 2001, p. 5B.

[128] Richard A. Oppel, Jr. and Kurt Eichenwald, "Enron Paid $55 Million for Bonuses," The New York Times, December 4, 2001, pp. C1, C4.

[129] Elissa Gootman, "Hometown Remembers Man Who Wore Success Quietly," The New York Times, January 30, 2002, p. C7.

[130] Mark Babineck, "Deceased Enron Executive Earned Respect in the Ranks," Houston Chronicle, http://www.houstonchronicle.com, January 26, 2002.

[131] Id.

[132] Id.

[133] Richard A. Oppel, Jr., "Former Head of Enron Denies Wrongdoing," The New York Times, December 22, 2001, pp. C1, C2.

[134] Id.

[135] Richard A. Oppel, Jr., "Enron Chief Says His Sale of Stock Was to Pay Loans," The New York Times, January 21, 2002, pp. A1, A13.

In addition to the impact on Enron, its employees, and Houston, there was a world-wide ripple effect. Enron has large stakes in natural gas pipelines in the United States and around the world as well as interests in power plants everywhere from Latin America to Venezuela. It is also a partial owner of utilities, including telecommunications networks. Congressional hearings were held as the House Energy and Commerce Committee investigated the company's collapse. Representative Billy Tauzin of Louisiana scheduled the investigation and noted, "How a company can sink so far, so fast, is very troubling. We need to find out if the company's accounting practices masked severe underlying financial problems."[136] Senator Jeff Bingham, chairman of the Senate Energy Committee, said, "I believe that our committee is keenly aware of the need for enhanced oversight and market monitoring."[137]

Enron's bankruptcy filing included a list of creditors 54 pages long. While the bankruptcy filing showed $24.76 billion in assets and $13.15 billion in debt, these figures do not include those off-the-balance sheet obligations, estimated to be about $27 billion.[138]

The effect also extends to Enron's energy customers, which include Pepsico, the California state university system, JCPenney, Owens-Illinois, and Starwood Hotels & Resorts. Enron had contracts with 28,500 customers. These customers are now revisiting their contracts for loopholes on both sides and ensuring that they have contingency plans in place. California's state universities were in negotiations for renewal of their 1998 contract with Enron, but those talks are now in a stalemate.[139]

Trammell Crow has halted the groundbreaking ceremony for its planned construction of new Enron headquarters; a building that would have been 50 stories high and included offices, apartments, and stores.[140]

The ripple effect even stretches into unrelated investments. Five major Japanese money market funds with heavy Enron investments fell below their face value by December 3, 2001.[141] These losses will have an impact primarily on retirees because the five funds were seen as "safe haven" funds for investors.

As the bankruptcy proceeds, the Enron board has hired Stephen F. Cooper as CEO, to replace Mr. Lay. Mr. Cooper is a specialist in leading companies through bankruptcy, including TWA and Federated Department Stores.[142]

Enron's collapse also appears to be raising concerns among state regulators about the entire deregulation issue in the utility industry. Several members of Congress have noted that lawmakers and regulators cannot leave energy products in the regulatory shadows if the companies involved in the industry are harming both consumers and investors.[143]

---

[136] Richard A. Oppel, Jr. and Andrew Ross Sorkin, "Ripples Spreading From Enron's Expected Bankruptcy," The New York Times, November 30, 2001, pp. C1, C6, C7.

[137] "Financial Threat from Enron Failure Continues to Widen," Financial Times, December 1, 2001, p.1.

[138] Rebecca Smith and Mitchell Pacelle, "Enron Files for Chapter 11 Bankruptcy, Sues Dynegy," The Wall Street Journal, December 3, 2001, p. A2.

[139] Rhonda L. Rundle, "Enron Customers Seek Backup Suppliers," The Wall Street Journal, December 3, 2001, p. A10.

[140] Allen R. Myerson, "With Enron's Fall, Many Dominoes Tremble," The New York Times, December 2, 2001, pp. 3-1, MB1.

[141] Ken Belson, "Enron Causes 5 Major Japanese Money Market Funds to Plunge," The New York Times, December 4, 2001, p. C9.

[142] Shaila K. Dewan and Jennifer 8. Lee, "Enron Names an Interim Chief to Oversee Its Bankruptcy," The New York Times, January 30, 2002, p. C7.

[143] Joseph Kahn and Jeff Gerth, "Collapse May Reshape the Battlefield of Deregulation," The New York Times, December 4, 2001, pp. C1, C8.

Other political ramifications included desperate calls from Mr. Lay to officials in the Bush administration asking for help as the company neared collapse.[144] The various media have covered all of Enron's substantial political donations to President George W. Bush ($650,000 from Enron officials and its PAC over the course of his political career), as well as governors and members of Congress, noting that Republican officials received more donations than Democrats.[145]

An ongoing question is the role Enron played in Vice President Dick Cheney's energy policy committee. Aides to Mr. Cheney indicate that they met with Enron officials six times during their policy development meetings with energy companies and officials throughout the country.[146]

The SEC has opened an investigation and a national team of lawyers is handling the Justice Department investigation.[147] In the bankruptcy, Enron's creditors received 18.3 cents on the dollar, an amount far below the normal payout in a bankruptcy.[148]

Many have noted that "evidence of fraud may well be elusive" as the SEC and prosecutors investigate.[149] Professor Douglas Carmichael, a professor of accounting at Baruch College, is one who agrees, "It's conceivable that they complied with the rules. Absent a smoking-gun e-mail or something similar, it is an issue of trying to attack the reasonableness of their assumptions."[150] One auditor said that it never occurred to him that anyone would "use models to try and forecast energy prices for 10 years, and then use those models to report profits, but that the rule had not placed a limit on such trades."[151] When asked about the accounting practices of Enron, Mr. Skilling said, "We are on the side of angels."[152]

The criminal charges and indictments of Enron's top executives that are related to Enron's collapse are summarized in the chart on the following page.

....

Discussion Questions

1. Can you see that Enron broke any laws?

2. Do you think that Enron's financial reports gave a false impression?

3. Does it matter that most investors in Enron were relatively sophisticated financial institutions? What about the employees' ownership of stock and their 401(k) plans?

4. What questions could the officers of Enron have used to evaluate the wisdom and ethics of their decisions on the off-the-book entities and mark-to-market accounting? Be sure to apply the various models you have learned.

[144] Elisabeth Bumiller, "Enron Contacted 2 Cabinet Officers Before Collapsing," The New York Times, January 11, 2002, pp. A1, C4.

[145] Jeanne Cummins and Mike Schroeder, "Enron's Lay Lobbied White House for Aid," The Wall Street Journal, January 11, 2002, p. A3.

[146] Pete Yost, "Cheney, Aides Met with Enron Officials 6 Times," The Tribune, January 9, 2002, p. A16.

[147] Jo Thomas, "A Specialist in Tough Cases Steps into the Legal Tangle," The New York Times, January 21, 2002, p. C8.

[148] Mitchell Pacelle, "Enron's Creditors to Get Peanuts," The Wall Street Journal, July 11, 2003, pp. C1, C7.

[149] Floyd Norris and Kurt Eichenwald, "Fuzzy Rules of Accounting and Enron," The New York Times, January 30, 2002, pp. C1, C6.

[150] Id.

[151] Id.

[152] Neil Weinberg and Daniel Fisher, "Power Player," Forbes, December 24, 2001, pp. 53–58.

Person	Title	Charges	Disposition
Ken Lay	Chairman, CEO	Securities fraud	Under indictment
		Wire fraud	Awaiting trial
Jeffrey Skilling	CEO	Securities fraud	Awaiting trial; ordered by judge to work for Habitat for Humanity as he awaits trial following some trouble in a NYC bar
		Wire fraud	
Andrew Fastow	CFO	Securities fraud	Guilty plea; 10 years
		Wire fraud	
		Tax evasion	
Lea Fastow	Senior Officer	Tax evasion	Guilty plea; 1 year; serving her term first so that Andrew Fastow can be at home with their 2 young children before beginning his term
David Delaney	CEO Enron North America	Insider trading	Guilty plea
Ben Glisan	Treasurer	Conspiracy	Guilty plea; 5 years
Richard Causey	Chief Accounting Officer	Insider trading	Pleaded innocent
		Fraud	Awaiting trial

Note: 22 other executives were also indicted, with 5 guilty pleas to date.

5. Do you think Enron was fair in its financial reporting and with its employees?

6. Do you think Enron did anything unethical?

7. Did Mr. Fastow have a conflict of interest?

8. How should his relationships with Enron's partially owned subsidiaries been handled in terms of disclosure?

9. Was the means of operation in compliance with accounting principles?

10. Was it ethical to not consolidate the financial statements?

11. Evaluate Enron's culture.

12. Was Ms. Watkins a whistleblower?

13. Discuss the ethics of Mr. Olson and Merrill Lynch.

WorldCom: The Little Company That Couldn't After All[153]

For a time it seemed as if the little long-distance telephone company headquartered in Hattiesburg, Mississippi, would show the world how to run a telecommunications giant. But dreams turned to dust and credits turned to debits, and WorldCom would be limited to showing the world that you cannot stretch accounting rules and hope to survive.

WorldCom: From Coffee Shop Founding to Merger Giant

It was 1983 when Bernard J. Ebbers (aka "Bernie") founded Long Distance Discount Service (LDDS), a discount long-distance telephone company.[154] Local legend has it that Mr. Ebbers, a former junior high school basketball coach from Edmonton, Alberta, launched the plan for what would become a multi-billion-dollar, international company in a diner at a Days Inn in Hattiesburg, Mississippi.[155] The telephone industry in the United States was about to be deregulated, and a new industry, telecommunications, would be born. Because competitors to the once-formidable Ma Bell, long the nation's dominant phone company, would now be welcome, Mr. Ebbers and a group of small investors saw an opportunity. They followed a basic economic model in developing their company: buy wholesale and sell retail, but cheaper than the other retailers. Their strategy was to buy long-distance phone network access wholesale from AT&T and other long-distance giants and then resell it to consumers at a discount. They were about to undercut long-distance carriers in their own markets, using their own lines. There was enough money even in the planned lower margins to make money for LDDS.[156]

By 1985, Mr. Ebbers was growing weary of the new telephone venture because LDDS was in constant need of cash infusions, and the 13-unit budget motel chain Mr. Ebbers owned was the source of the cash. Following another coffee shop meeting, Mr. Ebbers agreed to take over the management of the company.[157] Mr. Ebbers' strategy upon his ascent to management was different from and bolder than just running a Mississippi phone company. Mr. Ebbers envisioned an international phone company and undertook to grow the company through acquisition. One business writer has described the next phase of LDDS as a 15-year juggernaut of mergers.[158] LDDS began regionally, and Ebbers acquired phone companies in four neighboring states. Ebbers also expanded the core business of LDDS from cheaper long distance by expanding into local service and data interchange.

By the time LDDS went public in 1989, it was offering telephone services throughout eleven Southern states and had taken on a new name, WorldCom.[159] By

---

[153] Adapted with permission from Marianne M. Jennings, "The Yeehaw Factor," 3 Wyoming Law Review 387–511 (2003).

[154] Seth Schiesel and Simon Romero, "WorldCom: Out of Obscurity to Under Inquiry," The New York Times, March 13, 2002, pp. C1, C4 and Susan Pulliam, Jared Sandberg, and Dan Morse, "Prosecutors Gain Key Witness In Criminal Probe of WorldCom," The Wall Street Journal, July 3, 2002, pp. A1, A6.

[155] Kurt Eichenwald, "For WorldCom, Acquisitions Were Behind Its Rise and Fall," The New York Times, August 8, 2002, p. A1. Seth Schiesel and Simon Romero, "WorldCom: Out of Obscurity to Under Inquiry."

[156] Barnaby J. Feder, "An Abrupt Departure Is Seen as a Harbinger," The New York Times, May 1, 2002, p. C1.

[157] Id.

[158] Kurt Eichenwald and Simon Romero, "Inquiry Finds Effort at Delay at WorldCom," The New York Times, July 4, 2002, p. C1.

[159] Barnaby J. Feder, "An Abrupt Departure Is Seen as a Harbinger," The New York Times, May 1, 2002, p. C1. The company went public on NASDAQ.

1998, WorldCom had merged sixty-four times, including mergers with MFS Communications, Metromedia, and Resurgens Communications Group.[160] WorldCom's sixty-fifth merger was its biggest acquisition. WorldCom made a $37 billion offer to purchase MCI in a bidding war with British Telecommunications and GTE.[161] British Telecom had begun the bidding in 1997 with $19 billion, and in a bidding process that enjoyed daily international coverage, the bidding just kept going until Mr. Ebbers offered Bert C. Roberts, Jr., the CEO of MCI, the additional perk of making him chair of the newly merged WorldCom/MCI, to be known as WorldCom. WorldCom won the bidding and completed what was at that time the largest merger in history.[162] WorldCom was on a Wall Street roll, a darling of investors and investment banking firms. It was able to acquire CompuServe and ANS Communications before its merger feast ended in 2000. The ending came abruptly when the Justice Department nixed WorldCom's proposed merger with Sprint, citing a resulting lack of competition in long-distance telecommunications if the $129 billion merger were approved.[163]

Despite the Justice Department's rejection of this merger proposal, WorldCom had grown to 61,800 employees, with revenues of $35.18 billion. The bulk of its revenues came from commercial telecommunications services including data, voice, Internet, and international service, with the second largest source of revenue being the consumer services division.[164]

Mr. Ebbers was a Wall Street favorite. One analyst described Mr. Ebbers' meetings with Wall Street analysts as "prayer meetings" in which no one asked any questions or challenged any numbers.[165] Few analysts ever questioned Mr. Ebbers or WorldCom's nearly impossible financial performance.[166] Mr. Ebbers made it clear to Wall Street as well as WorldCom's employees that his goals rested in the financial end of the business, not in its fundamentals. He reiterated his lack of interest in operations, billing, and customer service and his obsession with not just being the number-one telecommunications company, but being the best on Wall Street. Mr. Ebbers described his business strategy succinctly in 1997: "Our goal is not to capture market share or be global. Our goal is to be the No. 1 stock on Wall Street."[167] In a report commissioned by the bankruptcy court on the company's downfall, former U.S. Attorney General Dick Thornburgh referred to WorldCom as a "culture of greed."[168]

---

[160] Kurt Eichenwald, "For WorldCom, Acquisitions Were Behind Its Rise and Fall," The New York Times, August 8, 2002, p. B1. The MFS merger alone carried a $12 billion price tag. Eichenwald, p. B4.

[161] Barnaby J. Feder, "An Abrupt Departure Is Seen as a Harbinger," The New York Times, May 1, 2002, p. C1.

[162] Seth Schiesel and Simon Romero, "WorldCom: Out of Obscurity to Under Inquiry," The New York Times, March 13, 2002, pp. C1, C4.

[163] Rebecca Blumenstein and Jared Sandberg, "WorldCom CEO Quits Amid Probe of Firm's Finances," The Wall Street Journal, April 30, 2002, pp. A1, A9.

[164] Barnaby J. Feder, "An Abrupt Departure Is Seen as a Harbinger," The New York Times, May 1, 2002, pp. C1, C2. The annual reports for 2000 and 2001 could be found at http://www.worldcom.com. Presently, go to http://www.sec.gov and look up WorldCom in the Edgar data base. The financial statements in those reports have been restated many times, with a resulting impact of about $9 billion less in revenue than originally reported.

[165] Barnaby J. Feder, "An Abrupt Departure Is Seen as a Harbinger," The New York Times, May 1, 2002, pp. C1, C2.

[166] Id.

[167] Id.

[168] Andrew Backover, "Report Slams Culture at WorldCom," USA Today, November 5, 2002, p. 1B.

WorldCom's revenues went from $950 million in 1992 to $4.5 billion by 1996.[169] Mr. Ebbers always promised more and better in each annual report.[170]

The WorldCom era on Wall Street has been likened by those who were competing with the company to being in a race with an athlete who is later discovered to be using steroids. In fact, at AT&T, Michael Keith, the head of the business services division, was replaced after just nine months on the job because he could not match WorldCom's profit margins. When Mr. Keith told C. Michael Armstrong, CEO of AT&T, that those margins were just not possible, he was removed from his position.[171] William T. Esrey, the CEO of Sprint said, "Our performance did not quite compare and we were blaming ourselves. We didn't understand what we were doing wrong. We were like, 'What are we missing here?'"[172]

Bernie and His Empire

WorldCom's rollicking Wall Street ride was at least partially enabled by Mr. Ebbers' personality and charisma. He was flamboyant, a 6-foot, 4-inch man who tended toward cowboy boots and blue jeans. Mr. Ebbers' charm worked as well in Jackson, Mississippi, as it did with investment bankers and analysts.[173] He was a "native boy" who was making good. Mr. Ebbers was a 1957 graduate of Mississippi College, located in Clinton, Mississippi, about 30 minutes away from Jackson, Mississippi, where Mr. Ebbers built the headquarters for WorldCom.[174] Even as the company stock was falling, few who lived in Mississippi who had invested in WorldCom would let go of their stock because of an abiding faith in Ebbers.[175] Mr. Ebbers' story was a rags-to-riches one of a Canadian high school basketball player winning a scholarship to a small Mississippi college and then growing an international megabusiness.[176]

Mr. Ebbers' personal life did take some twists and turns. He divorced his wife of 27 years while WorldCom was at its peak and married, in 1998, an executive from WorldCom's Clinton, Mississippi, headquarters who was nearly 30 years his junior. Jack Grubman, the cheerleader analyst for WorldCom who worked at Salomon Brothers, attended the wedding and expensed the trip to Salomon Brothers.[177]

Mr. Ebbers' business acumen with his personal investments presented some problems. He was very good at buying businesses, but not so good at managing them. Most outsiders believed he overpaid for his investments, and he was so distant in day-to-day management that employees referred to him as "the bank," meaning that they could simply turn to him for cash for those things they desired or when they did not operate at a profit or were just plain short of cash.[178] Still, with the value of his WorldCom hold-

[169] These numbers were all computed using the company's annual reports, found under "Investor relations" at http://www.worldcom.com. Go to http://www.sec.gov and the Edgar database and plug in WorldCom under "Company name." The numbers were computed using "Selected Financial Data" as called out in each of the annual reports.

[170] In 1998, Mr. Ebbers said that if WorldCom just grew with the market, it would meet its earning targets.

[171] Seth Schiesel, "Trying to Catch WorldCom's Mirage," The New York Times, June 30, 2002, p. BU1.

[172] Id. Sprint has had its own financial difficulties.

[173] Chris Woodyard, "Pressure to Perform Felt as Problems Hit," USA Today, July 1, 2002, p. 3A.

[174] Id.

[175] Id.

[176] Daniel Henninger, "Bye-Bye Bernie Drops the Curtain on the 1990s," The Wall Street Journal, May 3, 2002, p A10.

[177] Jayne O'Donnell, "Ebbers Acts as if Nothing Is Amiss," USA Today, September 18, 2002, pp. 1B, 2B. Jessica Sommar, "Here Comes the Bribe: Grubman Expensed Trip to Ebbers' Wedding," The New York Post, August 30, 2002, p. 39.

[178] Jayne O'Donnell and Andrew Backover, "Ebbers High-Risk Act Came Crashing Down on Him," USA Today, December 12, 2002, p. 1B.

ings alone, by 1999 Mr. Ebbers had a net worth of $1.4 billion, earning him the rank of 174 among the richest Americans. Mr. Ebbers owned a minor-league hockey team (the Mississippi Indoor Bandits), a trucking company, Canada's largest ranch (500,000 acres, 20,000 head of Hereford cattle, a fly-fishing resort, and a general store), an all-terrain cycle ATC dealership, a lumberyard, one plantation, two farms, and forest properties equivalent in acreage to half of Rhode Island.[179]

Mr. Ebbers found himself heavily in debt with his personal investments, and, in need of cash, he used his infallible charm in one more venue, that of his board of directors.[180] Mr. Ebbers was able to persuade the board to allow WorldCom to extend loans in excess of $415 million to him, with the money supposedly to be used to rescue his failing businesses.[181] The problem with the loans, among many others, was that the stock Mr. Ebbers used as security was also the stock he had pledged to WorldCom's creditors in order to obtain financing for the company.[182] The result was that WorldCom's directors were taking a subordinated security interest in stock that had already been pledged, placing it well at the end of the line in terms of creditors, and both the creditors and the board were assuming that the value of the WorldCom stock would remain at an equal or higher level.[183] While the board's loans to Mr. Ebbers put WorldCom at risk of losing $415 million, the control of the company was actually at greater risk because Mr. Ebbers had pledged about $1 billion in WorldCom stock in total to his creditors as security for loans.[184] Further, if the price of the stock declined, and Mr. Ebbers did not meet margin calls, his creditors would be forced to sell the shares. Mr. Ebbers owned 27 million shares of WorldCom stock, and the sale of such large blocks of shares would have had a devastating impact on the price of WorldCom's stock.[185]

Despite all the loans and issues with his personal investments, Mr. Ebbers was a generous philanthropist with his own money as well as with WorldCom's. Clinton Mayor Rosemary Aultman called WorldCom "a wonderful corporate citizen."[186] Ebbers served on the Board of Trustees for Mississippi College and raised $500 million for a fund drive there, more money than had ever been raised by the small college. Interns and graduates from the college worked at WorldCom.

The Burst Bubble and Accounting Myths

Once the Justice Department refused to approve the final proposed merger with Sprint, WorldCom came unraveled. The unraveling had many contributing factors, one of which was the burst in the dot-com bubble and the resulting decline in the need for broadband, Internet access, and all the growth associated with the telecommunications

---

[179] Susan Pulliam, Deborah Solomon, and Carrick Mollenkamp, "Former WorldCom CEO Built an Empire on Mountain of Debt," The Wall Street Journal, December 31, 2002, p. A1.

[180] Jared Sandberg and Susan Pulliam, "Report by WorldCom Examiner Finds New Fraudulent Activities," The Wall Street Journal, November 5, 2002, pp. A1, A11.

[181] Deborah Solomon and Jared Sandberg, "WorldCom's False Profits Climb," The Wall Street Journal, November 6, 2002, p. A3.

[182] Jared Sandberg, Deborah Solomon, and Nicole Harris, "WorldCom Investigations Shift Focus to Ousted CEO Ebbers," The Wall Street Journal, July 1, 2002, pp. A1, A8.

[183] Kurt Eichenwald, "Corporate Loans Used Personally, Report Discloses," The New York Times, November 5, 2002, p. C1.

[184] Jared Sandberg and Susan Pulliam, "Report by WorldCom Examiner Finds New Fraudulent Activities," The Wall Street Journal, November 5, 2002, p. A1.

[185] Jared Sandberg and Susan Pulliam, "Report by WorldCom Examiner Finds New Fraudulent Activities," The Wall Street Journal, November 5, 2002, A1.

[186] As noted earlier, Chris Woodyard, "Pressure to Perform Felt as Problems Hit," USA Today, July 1, 2002, p. 3A.

industry.[187] The cuts in the telecom industry began in 2000 and were industrywide. Between 2000 and 2001, Lucent reduced its employment from 106,000 to 77,000, Verizon went from 263,000 to 247,000, and there was a 52.8 percent decline in employment overall in the telecom industry from 2000 to 2002, cuts that exceeded those in any other industry.[188] When the economy took a general downturn in 2002, WorldCom could no longer sustain what had been phenomenal revenue growth. However, WorldCom's phenomenal revenue growth had not been a function of business acumen. The burst bubble would bring collapses in other industries and regulatory scrutiny of revenues and accounting practices in all industries.

When Enron collapsed, the SEC, under pressure from Congress, state regulators, and investors, announced in March 2002 investigations into the financial statements of many companies. WorldCom and Qwest, two of the country's telecommunications giants, were among the SEC's targets.[189] The SEC listed the areas to be examined at WorldCom: charges against earnings, sales commissions, accounting policies for goodwill, loans to officers or directors, integration of computer systems between WorldCom and MCI, and the company's earnings estimates.[190] The SEC inquiry was referred to as a "cloud of uncertainty" over WorldCom.[191] The announcement of the SEC investigation caused a drop of $8.39 in WorldCom's share price, a 7 percent drop.[192] WorldCom had done so well for so long that many analysts expressed doubt that the SEC would find any improprieties. One noted, "I don't think they are going to find anything that they can prosecute. But you may have people try to rewrite the accounting rules so they are not so loose."[193]

At the time that the SEC announced its investigation, Cynthia Cooper, head of WorldCom's internal audit group, was just beginning her internal investigation of the rampant allegations and rumors of creative and not-so-creative accounting practices within the company.[194] With the pressure of the external regulatory investigation and WorldCom's voluntary disclosure that it had loaned Mr. Ebbers the $415 million, WorldCom came to be called "Worldron" by its own employees.[195]

1. The Acquisitions, Expenses, and Reserves

WorldCom's acquisition strategy required that there always be a bigger and better merger if the company's numbers were going to continue their double-digit growth.[196] If the mergers stopped, so also did the benefits of the accounting rules WorldCom was using to its advantage in booking the mergers.[197]

---

[187] Louis Uchitelle, "Job Cuts Take Heavy Toll on Telecom Industry," The New York Times, June 29, 2002, p. B1.

[188] Id.

[189] Andrew Backover, "WorldCom, Qwest Face SEC Scrutiny," USA Today, March 12, 2002, p. 1B. Andrew Backover, "'Cloud of Uncertainty' Rains on WorldCom," USA Today, March 13, 2002, p. 3B.

[190] Id., Andrew Backover, "'Cloud of Uncertainty' Rains on WorldCom."

[191] Id.

[192] Id.

[193] Id.

[194] Susan Pulliam and Deborah Solomon, "How Three Unlikely Sleuths Discovered Fraud at WorldCom," The Wall Street Journal, October 30, 2002, p. A1.

[195] Andrew Backover, "Questions on Ebbers Loans May Aid Probes," USA Today, November 6, 2002, p. 3B.

[196] Andy Kessler, "Bernie Bites the Dust," The Wall Street Journal, May 1, 2002, p. A18.

[197] Shawn Tully, "Don't Get Burned," Fortune, February 18, 2002, pp. 89, 90.

The pace of the mergers was so frenetic and the accounting and financials so different because of interim mergers that even the most sophisticated analysts had trouble keeping up with the books.[198] WorldCom also benefited from the market bubble of the dot-com era, one in which investors suspended intellectual inquiry about these phenomenal performers.[199]

Accounting Professor Mike Willenborg comments on this lax attitude about the confusion and inexplicable numbers during this market era, "You wonder where some of the skepticism was."[200] It almost seemed as if the more confusing the investment, the better the investment. As late as February 2002, analysts were reassuring themselves that all would be well with WorldCom, and one analyst was on the record as telling clients that the rumor swirls surrounding WorldCom would die down.[201] Indeed, the more confusing, the higher the rate of return and even greater the stock price.[202] WorldCom's stock reached $64.50 per share in June 1999, but was at $0.83 on June 26, 2002, following the announcement of the company's accounting reversals.[203]

WorldCom's fancy merger accounting was not unusual, nor is there any allegation that its methods violated accounting rules. The fancy merger accounting goes like this: a company acquires another (as WorldCom did sixty-five times) and is permitted to take a restructuring charge against earnings, the infamous "one-time charge."[204] The restructuring charge is a management determination, and there are professional disagreements among accountants, auditors, and managers as to how much these charges should be.

The tendency for managers is to overstate the restructuring charges and toss the extra charges, over and above actual charges, into reserves, sometimes referred to as the "cookie jar."[205] For example, a company makes an acquisition and books $2 billion for restructuring charges. Its earnings picture for that year is painted to look quite awful.[206] However, the actual costs of the restructuring are spread out over the time it takes for the company to restructure, which is actually two to three years, and some of the charges booked may not ever be incurred.[207] The charges taken are often called "soft charges," or "anticipated costs," and can include items such as training, new hires, computer consulting, and so forth. It is possible that those services may be necessary, but it is literally a guess as to whether they will be needed and an even bigger guess as to how much they will be. However, the hit to earnings has already been taken all at once, with the resulting rosier picture of earnings growth in subsequent years. Also, while not entirely properly so, managers have been known to use these in a future year of

---

[198] David Rynecki, "Articles of Faith: How Investors Got Taken in by the False Profits," Fortune, April 2, 2001, p. 76.

[199] Id. Securities Exchange Commissioner Cynthia Glassman described the market phenomenon in a speech she gave to the American Society of Corporate Secretaries on September 27, 2002. http://www.sec.gov/news/speech.

[200] "'Going Concerns': Did Accountants Fail to Flag Problems at Dot-Com Casualties?" The Wall Street Journal, February 8, 2001, pp. C1, C2.

[201] E. S. Browning, "Burst Bubbles Often Expose Cooked Books and Trigger SEC Probes, Bankruptcy Filings," The Wall Street Journal, February 11, 2002, pp. C1, C4.

[202] Matt Krantz, "There's Just no Accounting for Teaching Earnings," USA Today, June 20, 2001, p. 1B.

[203] Robin Sidel, "Some Untimely Analyst Advice on WorldCom Raises Eyebrows," The Wall Street Journal, June 27, 2002, p. A12.

[204] Lee Clifford, "Is Your Stock Addicted to Write-Offs?" Fortune, April 2, 2001, p. 166.

[205] Geoffrey Colvin, "Scandal Outrage, Part III," Fortune, October 28, 2002, p. 56.

[206] "Firms' Stress on 'Operating Earnings' Muddies Efforts to Value Stocks," The Wall Street Journal, August 21, 2001, pp. A1, A8.

[207] Carol J. Loomis, "Lies, Damned Lies and Managed Earnings: The Crackdown Is Here," Fortune, August 2, 1999, pp. 75, 84.

not-so-great earnings, to create a smoother pattern of earnings and earnings growth for investors.[208] Indeed, the reserves have been used to simply meet previously announced earnings targets.[209] So, taking the example further, if the actual charges are $1.5 billion, then the company has $500 million in reserves to feed into earnings in order to demonstrate growth in earnings where there may not be actual growth or to create the appearance of a smooth and upward trend.

Scott Sullivan, the CFO of WorldCom, was able to employ reserves to keep WorldCom going for two years after the merger with Sprint failed in 2000.[210] Because there were no further mergers, the company's phenomenal earnings record would have ended in 2000 had it not been for WorldCom's rather sizeable reserves.[211] One expert estimates the WorldCom's reserves could have been as high as $10 billion.[212]

2. The Capitalization of Ordinary Expenses

As WorldCom's executive team grappled with what it believed to be strategic issues that needed attention, Ms. Cooper and her team were working nights and weekends to determine how extensive the accounting issues were. By early June 2002, Ms. Cooper went to WorldCom's CFO, Scott Sullivan, with questions about the booking of operating expenses as capital expenses. When Mr. Sullivan was not as forthcoming as she expected, Ms. Cooper became more concerned. Mr. Sullivan was the most respected person in the company, but Ms. Cooper felt that he seemed hostile, and "when someone is hostile, my instinct is to find out."[213] Mr. Sullivan told Ms. Cooper that he was planning a "write down" in the second quarter if she could just hold off on the investigation.[214]

Ms. Cooper did not feel she could hold off any further on the investigation. She and her internal audit team uncovered layers of accounting issues. With the merger reserves quickly eaten away, Mr. Sullivan had to find a means for maintaining earnings levels, including the expected growth. While the precise timing for the new accounting strategy remains unclear,[215] most experts agree that at least by the first quarter of 2001, Mr. Sullivan and staff embarked on an accounting strategy that would keep WorldCom afloat but was not in compliance with Generally Accepted Accounting Principles (GAAP).[216] According to his guilty plea and those filed by others working in WorldCom's financial areas, Mr. Sullivan and colleagues were taking ordinary expenses and booking them as capital expenditures so as to boost earnings.[217]

[208] Id., pp. 74, 84.

[209] Louis Uchitelle, "Corporate Profits Are Tasty, But Artificially Flavored," The New York Times, March 28, 1999, p. BU4.

[210] Geoffrey Colvin, "Scandal Outrage, Part III," Fortune, October 28, 2002, p. 56.

[211] The reserves and some other creative accounting were often done without the executives in charge knowing that their division's accounting figures were being changed, because the changes were made from headquarters.

[212] Henny Sender, "Call Up the Reserves: WorldCom's Disclosure Is Warning for Investors," The Wall Street Journal, July 3, 2002, pp. C1, C3.

[213] Amanda Ripley, "The Night Detective," Time, December 30, 2002–January 6, 2003, pp. 45, 47.

[214] Kurt Eichenwald and Simon Romero, "Inquiry Finds Effort at Delay at WorldCom," The New York Times, July 4, 2002, p. C1.

[215] Disclosures near the end of 2002 put the date at 1999. Stephanie N. Meta, "WorldCom's Latest Headache," Fortune, November 25, 2002, pp. 34, 35.

[216] "Big Lapse in Auditing Is Puzzling Some Accountants and Other Experts," The New York Times, June 28, 2002, p. C4.

[217] Jared Sandberg, Deborah Solomon, and Rebecca Blumenstein, "Inside WorldCom's Unearthing of a Vast Accounting Scandal," The Wall Street Journal, June 27, 2002, p. A1.

For example, in 2001, WorldCom had $3.1 billion in long-distance charges.[218] Long-distance wholesale charges are the expenses of a long-distance phone service retailer. The $3.1 billion should have been booked as an operating expense. However, $3.1 billion booked as an expense would have ended the earnings streak of WorldCom with a loss for 2001. So, Mr. Sullivan and his staff charged the $3.1 billion as a capital expense and planned to amortize this amount over 10 years, a far lesser hit to earnings. The difference was that WorldCom, by capitalizing the operating expenses, showed net income of $1.38 billion for 2001, its previously announced target.[219]

However, ordinary and capital expenses require receipts and invoices for the property. The accounting lapse began unwinding when Gene Morse, a member of WorldCom's internal audit group, found $500 million in computer expenses, but could not find any documentation or invoices.[220] Mr. Sullivan had demanded that employees keep line costs at 42 percent; anything beyond that was just shifted to capital expenditures.[221] The result was that staff members spun numbers out of whole cloth, but costs were kept down even as profits were pumped artificially high. The initial disclosure of the $3.85 billion sent shock waves through the business world,[222] but before the year was out, that number would rise to $9 billion.[223]

3. Other Accounting Issues

An investigation and report commissioned by the WorldCom board and completed by former attorney general Richard Thornburgh indicates that accounting issues extended into the reporting of revenues, not just expenses.[224] Mr. Thornburgh's report, partially excised at the time of its release in deference to the Justice Department investigation, reveals that there were eventually two sets of books prepared for David Myers and Mr. Sullivan by Buford Yates. Mr. Myers was the controller of WorldCom and Mr. Yates was the head of general accounting. Mr. Myers also held a senior vice president's position at WorldCom and was well liked by the other officers and the staff. Described as a WorldCom "cheerleader" by co-workers, Myers was referred to around the company as "Mr. GQ" because he dressed so fashionably.[225] Mr. Yates prepared two charts for Mr. Myers and Mr. Sullivan, with one chart offering the real revenues and the other chart showing the revenue numbers WorldCom needed to post in order to make the numbers the company had given to Wall Street analysts.[226]

---

[218] Id.

[219] Jared Sandberg, Deborah Solomon, and Nicole Harris, "WorldCom Investigations Shift Focus to Ousted CEO Ebbers," The Wall Street Journal, July 1, 2002, pp. A1, A8.

[220] Susan Pulliam and Deborah Solomon, "How Three Unlikely Sleuths Discovered Fraud at WorldCom," The Wall Street Journal, October 30, 2002, p. A1.

[221] Sandberg, et al., supra note 217, p. A8.

[222] WorldCom's initial $3.8 billion was six times the Enron restatement of earnings. Jared Sandberg, Deborah Solomon, and Rebecca Blumenstein, "Inside WorldCom's Unearthing of a Vast Accounting Scandal," The Wall Street Journal, June 27, 2001, p. A1.

[223] Kurt Eichenwald and Seth Schiesel, "SEC Files New Charges on WorldCom," The New York Times, November 6, 2002, pp. C1, C2.

[224] Jared Sandberg and Susan Pulliam, "Report by WorldCom Examiner Finds New Fraudulent Activities," The Wall Street Journal, November 5, 2002, p. A1.

[225] Jim Hopkins, "CFOs Join Their Bosses on the Hot Seat," USA Today, July 16, 2002, p. 3B.

[226] Andrew Backover, "Trouble May Have Started in November 2000," USA Today, July 1, 2002, p. 3A.

Because of WorldCom's international organization and worldwide offices, those at the corporate level were able to use computer access to these offices' financial records and thereby change the company's final financial statements. For example, Steven Brabbs, a WorldCom executive who was based in London and who was the director of international finance and control, raised the question of the accounting changes, which had affected his division, to David Myers. Mr. Brabbs discovered, after his division's books had been closed, that $33.6 million in line costs had been dropped from his books through a journal entry.[227] Unable to find support or explanation for the entry, Mr. Brabbs raised the question of documentation to Mr. Myers. When he had no response, he suggested that perhaps Arthur Andersen should be consulted to determine the propriety of the changes.[228] Mr. Brabbs also raised his concerns in a meeting with other internal financial executives at WorldCom. Following the meeting, Mr. Myers expressed anger at him for so doing.[229]

When the next quarter financials were due, Mr. Brabbs received instructions to make these transfers at his level rather than having them done by journal entry at the corporate level. Because he was still uncomfortable with the process, but could get no response from headquarters, he established an entity and placed the costs in there. He felt his solution at least kept his books for the international division clean.[230] He continued to raise the question about the accounting propriety, but the only response he ever received was that it was being done as a "Scott Sullivan directive."[231]

Congressional documents verify that many within the company who were concerned about the accounting changes approached Mr. Myers, from as far back as July 2000, but he apparently disregarded them and went forward with the accounting changes anyway.[232] Rep. Billy Tauzin described the congressional findings related to the culture of fear and pressure as follows: "The bottom line is people inside this company were trying to tell its leaders you can't do what you want to do, and these leaders were telling them they had to."[233] When Steven Brabbs continued to raise his concerns about the accounting practices at WorldCom, even with Arthur Andersen, he received an e-mail from David Myers ordering him to "not have any more meetings with AA for any reason."[234] While the accounting issues continued to concern employees, it would be some time before they would percolate to the board level.

It was clear that those involved were aware that they were violating accounting principles.[235] An e-mail sent on July 25, 2000 from Buford Yates, director of general accounting, to David Myers, controller, reflected his doubts about changing the operating expense of purchased wire capacity to a capital expense, "I might be narrow-minded, but I can't see a

---

[227] Kurt Eichenwald, "Auditing Woes at WorldCom Were Noted Two Years Ago," The New York Times, July 15, 2002, pp. C1, C9.

[228] Id., p. C9.

[229] Id.

[230] Id.

[231] Id.

[232] Id.

[233] Jayne O'Donnell and Andrew Backover, "WorldCom's Bad Math May Date Back to 1999," USA Today, July 16, 2002, p. 1B.

[234] Jessica Sommar, "E-Mail Blackmail — WorldCom Memo Threatened Conscience-Stricken Exec," The New York Post, August 27, 2002, p. 27.

[235] A 2001 survey of CFOs indicated that 17 percent of CFOs at public corporations feel pressure from their CEOs to misrepresent financial results. Jim Hopkins, "CFOs Join Their Bosses on the Hot Seat," USA Today, July 16, 2002, p. 3B.

logical path for capitalizing excess capacity."[236] Mr. Yates sent an e-mail to Scott Sullivan that read, "David and I have reviewed and discussed your logic of capitalizing excess capacity and can find no support within the current accounting guidelines that would allow for this accounting treatment."[237] Mr. Myers admitted to investigators that "this approach had no basis in accounting principles."[238] Nonetheless, the change from operating expenses to capitalization went forward, with Betty Vinson and Troy Normand, employees in accounting, making the adjustments in the books per orders from Mr. Myers.[239] Ms. Vinson and Mr. Normand were both fired, and Mr. Yates resigned shortly after he was indicted.

Before making the decision on the accounting changes, neither Mr. Myers nor Mr. Sullivan consulted with WorldCom's outside auditor, Arthur Andersen.[240] The criminal complaint in Mr. Myers' case, and the one to which he entered a guilty plea, included the following description of the role of financial pressures in their decisions and accounting practices: "Sullivan and Myers decided to work backward, picking the earnings numbers that they knew the analysts expected to see, and then forcing WorldCom's financials to match those numbers."[241]

Mr. Sullivan had assumed the helm of WorldCom's finances as CFO in 1994, at age 32.[242] The joke around the WorldCom offices when Mr. Sullivan assumed the CFO slot was that he was "barely shaving."[243] Arriving at WorldCom in 1992 through its merger with Advanced Telecommunications, where he had been since 1987, Mr. Sullivan and Mr. Ebbers became inseparable in the mergers and deals they put together over the next eight years.[244] He earned the nickname "whiz kid," and while Mr. Ebbers was the showman for WorldCom, Mr. Sullivan was the detail person. Mr. Ebbers frequently answered questions from analysts and others with, "We'll have to ask Scott."[245]

Mr. Ebbers praised Mr. Sullivan publicly and saw to it that he was well compensated for his efforts.[246] Mr. Ebbers rewarded Mr. Sullivan with both compensation and titles. In addition to his role as CFO, he served as the secretary for the board.[247] When

[236] Kevin Maney, Andrew Backover, and Paul Davidson, "Prosecutors Target WorldCom's Ex-CFO," USA Today, August 29, 2002, pp. 1B, 2B.
[237] Id., p. 2B.
[238] Kurt Eichenwald, "2 Ex-Officials at WorldCom Are Charged in Huge Fraud," The New York Times, August 2, 2002, pp. A1, C5.
[239] Kevin Maney, Andrew Backover, and Paul Davidson, "Prosecutors Target WorldCom's Ex-CFO," USA Today, August 29, 2002, pp. 1B, 2B. See also Simon Romero and Jonathan D. Glater, "Wider WorldCom Case Is Called Likely," The New York Times, September 5, 2002, p. C9, for background given on titles of employees noted.
[240] Kurt Eichenwald, "2 Ex-Officials at WorldCom Are Charged in Huge Fraud," The New York Times, August 2, 2002, p. C5.
[241] Id. Yochi J. Dreazen, Shawn Young, and Carrick Mollenkamp, "WorldCom Probers Say Sullivan Implicates Ebbers," The Wall Street Journal, July 12, 2002, p. A3. Andrew Backover and Paul Davidson, "WorldCom Grilling Turns Up No Definitive Answers," USA Today, July 9, 2002, pp. 1B, 2B.
[242] Shawn Young and Evan Perez, "Wall Street Thought Highly of WorldCom's Finance Chief," The Wall Street Journal, June 27, 2002, pp. B1, B3.
[243] Id.
[244] Barnaby J. Feder and David Leonhardt, "From Low Profile to No Profile," The New York Times, June 27, 2002, p. C1.
[245] Id.
[246] Id., p. C6. Sullivan still lives with his wife, who has chronic health problems, in a home in Florida that is valued at $178,000, but they were in the process of constructing a home in the Boca Raton, Florida, area at a cost estimated to be $10 million, with the lot costing $2.45 million. Because of the unlimited homestead exemption in Florida, many financially troubled executives have retained significant assets while still discharging debts in bankruptcy.
[247] WorldCom Proxy Statement, April 22, 2002, http://www.sec.gov.

Mr. Sullivan was appointed to the WorldCom board at age 34, in 1996, the company press release included this quote from Mr. Ebbers: "Over the years WorldCom, Inc. has benefited [sic] immensely from the outstanding array of talent and business acumen of our Board of Directors, and Scott Sullivan will be an excellent addition to that group. He brings to the table a proven background of expertise and dedication to the Company."[248]

According to WorldCom proxy statements, Mr. Sullivan's compensation was as follows: 1997: $500,000 salary and $3.5 million bonus; 1998: $500,000 salary and $2 million bonus; 1999: $600,000 salary and $2.76 million bonus; 2000: $700,000 salary and $10 million bonus; and for 2001, Mr. Sullivan earned a salary of $700,000 and a bonus of $10 million. These figures do not include the stock options, which for the years from 1997 to 2001 totaled $1.5 million, $900,000, $900,000, $619,140, and $928,710, respectively.[249]

Congressional documents indicate that both Mr. Myers and Mr. Sullivan met with other executives indicating the need to "do whatever necessary to get Telco/Margins back in line."[250] Mr. Myers has subsequently indicated that once they started down the road, it was tough to stop.[251]

Later discussions between Mr. Myers and the head of WorldCom's internal audit group, Cynthia Cooper, reflect that he understood "there were no specific accounting pronouncements" that would justify the changes.[252] When Ms. Cooper raised the question to Mr. Myers about how the changes could be explained to the SEC, Mr. Myers, reflecting the view that it was a temporary change to see the company through until the financial picture changed, said that "he had hoped it would not have to be explained."[253]

Corporate Governance at WorldCom

The board at WorldCom was often referred to as "Bernie's Board."[254] Carl Aycock had been a member of the board since 1983 when the original company was founded.[255] Max Bobbitt and Francesco Galesi, who were friends of Mr. Ebbers, joined the board in 1992.[256] And one board member, Stiles A. Kellett, Jr., an original board member and friend of Mr. Ebbers from the early motel-meeting days, resigned in October 2002 after revelations about his extensive use of the company jet.[257] All of the directors became millionaires after the days of their humble beginnings, when the board meetings were held at the Western Sizzlin' Steakhouse in Hattiesburg, Mississippi.[258] A former board member, Mike Lewis, said few board members would disagree with Mr. Ebbers: "Rule No. 1: Don't bet against Bernie. Rule No. 2: See Rule No. 1."[259]

[248] "WorldCom, Inc. Appoints New Board Member," press release, March 12, 1996. http://www.worldcom.com (Accessed January 22, 2003).

[249] See proxy statements, 14-A at http://www.sec.gov under WorldCom for 1997–2001.

[250] Jayne O'Donnell and Andrew Backover, "WorldCom's Bad Math May Date Back to 1999," USA Today, July 16, 2002, p. 1B.

[251] Id.

[252] Yocki J. Dreazen and Deborah Solomon, "WorldCom Aide Conceded Flaws," The Wall Street Journal, July 16, 2002, p. A3.

[253] Id.

[254] Jared Sandberg and Joann S. Lublin, "An Already Tarnished Board also Faces Tough Questions over Accounting Fiasco," The Wall Street Journal, June 28, 2002, p. A3.

[255] Seth Schiebel, "Most of Board at WorldCom Resign Post," The New York Times, December 18, 2002, p. C7.

[256] Id.

[257] Susan Pulliam, Jared Sandberg and Deborah Solomon, "WorldCom Board Will Consider Rescinding Ebbers's Severance," The Wall Street Journal, September 10, 2002, p. A1.

[258] Jared Sandberg, "Six Directors Quit as WorldCom Breaks With Past," The Wall Street Journal, December 18, 2002, p. A3.

[259] Jared Sandberg and Joann S. Lublin, "An Already Tarnished Board also Faces Tough Questions over Accounting Fiasco," The Wall Street Journal, June 28, 2002, p. A3

While board members were entitled to WorldCom or MCI stock in lieu of fees and were awarded options each year, their annual retainer was $35,000 per year, with $750 for committee meetings attended on the same day as the board meetings and $1,000 for other committee meetings.[260] But this was a generous board when it came to Mr. Ebbers. Even upon Mr. Ebbers' departure, with significant loans due and owing, the board gave Mr. Ebbers a severance package that included $1.5 million per year for the rest of his life, 30 hours of use of the company jet, full medical and life insurance coverage, and the possibility of consulting fees beyond a minimum amount required under the terms of the package.[261]

The WorldCom board was not an active or curious one. Despite experiencing a lawsuit in which employees with specific knowledge about the company's accounting practices filed affidavits, the board made no further inquiries. In fact, the company dismissed the employees and ignored their affidavits when a judge dismissed the class-action suit.[262] The board was not aware of $75 million in loans to Mr. Ebbers or a $100 million loan guarantee for Mr. Ebbers' personal loans until two months after the loans and guarantees had been signed for him. Two board meetings went by after the loan approvals before the board was informed and approval given. Further, the board's approval came without any request for advice from WorldCom's general counsel.[263]

What Went Wrong: Management and Operations

The creative and not-so-creative accounting at WorldCom may have been a symptom, and not the problem. Mr. Ebbers made no secret of the fact that he was often bored by business details, operations, and fundamentals. He far preferred the art of the deal.[264] When Mr. Ebbers did get involved in operations, his involvement was more like that of an entrepreneur or small-business person trying to micromanage details. For example, when Mr. Ebbers visited his dealerships in Mississippi, he usually went in with the idea of cutting costs and would do so by focusing on things such as the allotment of cell phones to sales personnel, eliminating the water cooler, and even requiring that the heating bills be reduced.[265] As a result, WorldCom could hardly be said to have a crackerjack management team.[266] It had an abysmal record on receivables, lax in bringing in cash from regular billings.[267] One analyst described the operations side of WorldCom as follows: "WorldCom wasn't operated at all, it was just on auto pilot, using bubble gum and Band-Aids as solutions to its problems."[268]

The constant mergers threw the billing system for WorldCom customers into turmoil.[269] WorldCom had 55 different billing systems and the litigation from

---

[260] http://www.sec.gov; WorldCom proxy for 2001, p. 6.

[261] Id.

[262] Neil Weinberg, "WorldCom's Board Alerted to Fraud in 2001," Forbes, August 12, 2002, p. 56. See also Kurt Eichenwald, "Auditing Woes at WorldCom Were Noted Two Years Ago," The New York Times, July 15, 2002, p. C1.

[263] Andrew Backover, "Questions on Ebbers Loans May Aid Probes," USA Today, November 6, 2002, p. 3B.

[264] Barnaby J. Feder, "An Abrupt Departure Is Seen as a Harbinger," The New York Times, May 1, 2002, pp. C1, C2. Kurt Eichenwald, "For WorldCom, Acquisitions Were Behind Its Rise and Fall," The New York Times, August 8, 2002, p. A1.

[265] Jayne O'Donnell and Andrew Backover, "Ebbers' High-Risk Act Came Crashing Down on Him," USA Today, December 12, 2002, pp. 1B, 2B.

[266] Barnaby J. Feder, "An Abrupt Departure Is Seen as a Harbinger," The New York Times, May 1, 2002, pp. C1, C2.

[267] Marcy Gordon, "WorldCom CEO Blames Former Execs for Woes," The Tribune, from the Associated Press, July 2, 2002, p. B1.

[268] Kurt Eichenwald, "For WorldCom, Acquisitions Were Behind Its Rise and Fall," The New York Times, August 8, 2002, p. A1.

[269] One analyst noted that Mr. Ebbers may not have even seen the importance of operations, "Bernie viewed this as a series of financial-engineering maneuvers and never truly understood the business that he was in," Id., p. C2.

customers to show that the billing systems were not studies in accuracy.[270] MCI customers would find their service disconnected for nonpayment because the WorldCom side, which did the billing, never got the payments, which went to the MCI side.[271] Even when the customer's account was located, there was a great deal of foot-dragging by WorldCom in terms of both bill payment and acknowledgment of customer corrections.[272] Cherry Communications, a large customer of WorldCom, filed suit against WorldCom for $100 million in "false and questionable" bills from 1992 to 1996.[273] Cherry went into Chapter 11 bankruptcy owing WorldCom $200 million in uncollectable revenues, less the $100 million in disputes spread across the 55 billing systems. WorldCom did get stock in a reorganized Cherry Communications—a typical result, because WorldCom extended credit to small companies that were high credit risks. On average, two to three of WorldCom's commercial customers filed for bankruptcy during any given quarter.[274]

One part of the SEC investigation of WorldCom focused on whether WorldCom capitalized on the chaotic billing system to boost revenues. One technique investigated was whether services sold to one customer were then booked twice as revenues in different divisions, all at different rates and under multiple billing systems.[275] In fact, three stellar performers at WorldCom were fired because they had used the fact that revenues could often be booked twice in the confusing systems to pump up the commission figures for their sales teams. The three simply listed sales from other divisions for their employees and were able to boost commissions substantially.[276] In September 2000, WorldCom did take a write-down of $685 million for uncollectable revenues.[277]

The rapidity of the mergers left employees and managers with the day-to-day work of trying to integrate the acquired company's technology with WorldCom's in order to create a seamless communications network. That seamless network never happened because technical problems and employees consumed with constant troubleshooting meant that customer service suffered and the overall systemic issues could not be addressed.[278]

The problems were never solved because of one additional management issue, and that was the constant merger of executives from other companies with WorldCom managers.[279] One former WorldCom employee summarized the company atmosphere: "Nobody had time to adjust. There was a [reorganization] every couple of months, so people didn't know who they were supposed to be reporting to or what they were supposed to be working on."[280] MCI had the experience, but WorldCom had

---

[270] The CEO of one WorldCom customer said, "They can't even tell you what they're owed." Scott Woolley, "Bernie At Bay," Fortune, April 15, 2002, p. 63.

[271] Kurt Eichenwald, "For WorldCom, Acquisitions Were Behind Its Rise and Fall," The New York Times, August 8, 2002, p. A1.

[272] Kevin Maney, "WorldCom Unraveled as Top Execs' Unity Crumbled," USA Today, June 28, 2002, pp. 1B, 2B.

[273] Id.

[274] Scott Woolley, "Bernie At Bay," Fortune, April 15, 2002, p. 64.

[275] Id.

[276] Yochi J. Dreazen, "WorldCom Suspends Executives in Scandal Over Order Booking," The Wall Street Journal, February 15, 2002, p. A3.

[277] Kurt Eichenwald, "For WorldCom, Acquisitions Were Behind Its Rise and Fall," The New York Times, August 8, 2002, p. A1.

[278] Id.

[279] Kevin Maney, "WorldCom Unraveled as Top Execs' Unity Unraveled," USA Today, June 28, 2002, pp. 1B, 2B.

[280] Kurt Eichenwald, "For WorldCom, Acquisitions Were Behind Its Rise and Fall," The New York Times, August 8, 2002, p. A1.

control. No one took the lead in an integration effort, and the result was that WorldCom was saddled with excess and expensive capacity from improperly integrated dual systems. Power struggles apparently contributed to a type of nepotism in which Mississippi-based executives were awarded the vice-president positions in charge of operations and billing, and they lacked the experience and expertise that was necessary to fix the problems created by the mergers and create an effective billing system and integrated technology.

WorldCom Bubble Bursts

While the operations in the company became more and more fractured, the internal auditors' work continued. However, they were forced to work secretly.[281] The internal auditors worked at night to avoid detection and, at one point, concerned that their work might be sabotaged, purchased a CD-ROM burner privately and began recording the data they were gathering and storing it elsewhere.[282] Indeed, so chilly was their reception when they met with Mr. Sullivan, that Ms. Cooper arranged to meet with Max Bobbitt, the head of the board's audit committee, in secret fashion at a local Hampton Inn so that there would be no repercussions for her or her staff as they completed their work.[283] Ms. Cooper was forced to go to the board and the audit committee because she was unable to secure an adequate explanation from Mr. Sullivan, who, as noted earlier, had even asked her to delay her audit.

At one point, while Ms. Cooper's internal audit team was conducting its investigation, Mr. Sullivan confronted one of her auditors, Gene Morse, in the cafeteria. During his five years at WorldCom, he had only spoken to Mr. Sullivan twice. Mr. Sullivan asked what he was working on, and Mr. Morse responded with information about another project, "International capital expenditures," which seemed to satisfy Mr. Sullivan.[284]

Mr. Sullivan was given an opportunity to respond at that board meeting, but could offer no explanation other than his belief that the expenses were correctly booked. He refused to resign and defended his accounting practices until that final meeting, where he was fired that day by the board.[285] David Myers, the controller for the company, resigned the following day.[286] Following sufficient review by Ms. Cooper and the company's new auditor, KPMG, WorldCom announced on June 25, 2002 that it had overstated cash flow by $3.9 billion for 2001 and the first quarter of 2002 by booking ordinary expenses as capital expenditures.[287] WorldCom's shares dropped 76 percent, to 20 cents per share.[288] Trading was halted for three sessions, and when it was reopened, more than 1.5 billion shares of WorldCom were dumped on the market, sending the share price down from 20 cents to 6 cents in what was then the highest-volume selling frenzy in the history of the

---

[281] Susan Pulliam and Deborah Solomon, "How Three Unlikely Sleuths Discovered Fraud at WorldCom," The Wall Street Journal, October 30, 2002, pp. A1, A6.

[282] Amanda Ripley, "The Night Detective," Time, December 30, 2002–January 6, 2003, pp. 45, 47.

[283] There is a certain irony here. WorldCom was hatched in a low-price motel and its unraveling began at a similar location.

[284] Susan Pulliam and Deborah Solomon, "How Three Unlikely Sleuths Discovered Fraud at WorldCom," The Wall Street Journal, October 30, 2002, pp. A1, A6.

[285] Amanda Ripley, "The Night Detective," Time, December 30, 2002–January 6, 2003, p. 49.

[286] Id.

[287] Andrew Backover, Thor Valdmanis, and Matt Krantz, "WorldCom Finds Accounting Fraud," USA Today, June 26, 2002, p. 1B.

[288] Id. This restatement remained the largest in history, more than doubling the previous record set by Rite-Aid of $1.6 billion, until Parmalat collapsed. http://www.bankruptcydata.com.

market. It was the first time in the history of the market that more than 1 billion shares had ever been traded in one day. The pace exceeded the previous record of 671 million shares sold in one day, a record WorldCom held only for a few days until this trading reopened. WorldCom was delisted from the NASDAQ on July 5, 2002.[289]

WorldCom's bonds dropped from 79 cents just before the announcement of the accounting irregularities to 13 cents just following the announcement.[290] There was a flurry of subpoenas from Congress for the officers of the company.[291] The officers all took the Fifth Amendment, and $2 billion in federal contracts held by WorldCom were under review by the General Services Administration because federal regulations prohibit federal agencies from doing business with companies under investigation for financial improprieties.[292]

The SEC filed fraud charges within three days and asked for an explanation from WorldCom about exactly what had been done in its accounting.[293] On August 8, 2002, WorldCom announced that it had found an additional $3.3 billion in earnings misstatements, from 2000, with portions from 1999.[294] WorldCom declared bankruptcy on July 22, 2002, the largest bankruptcy in the history of the United States.[295]

Shortly after WorldCom filed for bankruptcy, the federal government indicted Scott Sullivan, David Myers, Betty Vinson, Buford Yates, Troy Normand, and a host of other characters involved in developing the company's financial reports.[296] Mr. Ebbers was not indicted until after Mr. Sullivan entered a guilty plea.[297]

Mr. Sullivan was indicted on federal charges of fraud and conspiracy on August 1, 2002.[298] Mr. Myers entered a guilty plea to three felony counts of fraud on September 26, 2002.[299] Mr. Yates initially entered a not guilty plea.[300] However, just one month later, Mr. Yates entered a guilty plea to securities fraud and conspiracy and agreed to cooperate with the Justice Department.[301] Ms. Vinson and Mr. Normand also entered guilty pleas to fraud and conspiracy just three days after Mr. Yates' plea.[302]

[289] Matt Krantz, "Investors Dump WorldCom Stock at Record Pace," USA Today, July 3, 2002, p. 3B. http://www.worldcom.com, Press releases, 2001, July 29, 2002. These press releases may or may not be available at http://www.mci.com. However, they were researched when the WorldCom site was functioning.

[290] Henny Sender and Carrick Mollenkamp, "WorldCom Bondholders Study Plan," The Wall Street Journal, July 5, 2002, p. A6.

[291] Andrew Backover and Thor Valdmanis, "WorldCom Scandal Brings Subpoenas, Condemnation," USA Today, June 28, 2002, p. 1A. Michael Schroder, Jerry Markon, Tom Hamburger, and Greg Hitt, "Congress Begins WorldCom Investigation," The Wall Street Journal, June 28, 2002, p. A3.

[292] Yochi J. Dreazen, "WorldCom's Federal Contracts May Be Vital," The Wall Street Journal, July 10, 2002, p. C4. For information on the Fifth Amendment, see Andrew Backover and Paul Davidson, "WorldCom Grilling Turns Up No Definitive Answers," USA Today, July 9, 2002, p. 1B. See Cases 2.7 and 4.3.

[293] Andrew Backover and Thor Valdmanis, "WorldCom Report Will Face Scrutiny," USA Today, July 1, 2002, p. 1B.

[294] Kevin Maney and Thor Valdmanis, "WorldCom Reveals $3.3B More in Discrepancies," USA Today, August 9, 2002, p. 1B.

[295] Simon Romero and Riva D. Atlas, "WorldCom Files for Bankruptcy; Largest U.S. Case," The New York Times, July 22, 2002, p. A1. Kevin Maney and Andrew Backover, "WorldCom's Bomb," USA Today, July 22, 2002, pp. 1B, 2B.

[296] Kurt Eichenwald, "2 Ex-Officials at WorldCom Are Charged in Huge Fraud," The New York Times, August 2, 2002, p. A1. See also Deborah Solomon and Susan Pulliam, "U.S., Pushing WorldCom Case, Indicts Ex-CFO and His Aide," The Wall Street Journal, August 29, 2002, p. A1.

[297] Simon Romero and Jonathan D. Glater, "Wider WorldCom Case Is Called Likely," The New York Times, September 5, 2002, p. C9.

[298] Kurt Eichenwald, "2 Ex-Officials at WorldCom Are Charged in Huge Fraud," The New York Times, August 2, 2002, p. A1.

[299] Deborah Solomon, "WorldCom's Ex-Controller Pleads Guilty to Fraud," The Wall Street Journal, September 27, 2002, p. A3.

[300] Jerry Markon, "WorldCom's Yates Pleads Guilty," The Wall Street Journal, October 8, 2002, p. A3.

[301] Id.

[302] "2 Ex-Officials of WorldCom Plead Guilty," The New York Times, October 11, 2002, p. C10.

Before the year ended, most of the WorldCom board had resigned, Michael D. Capellas, the former CEO of Compaq Computers, replaced John Sidgmore, and there was another revision of WorldCom revenues, bringing the total revisions to $9 billion.[303] However, WorldCom did reach a settlement with the SEC on the $9 billion accounting problems. The civil fraud suit settlement did not admit any wrongdoing, and required the payment of fines totaling $500 million.[304] The consent decree required WorldCom, now MCI, to submit to oversight by a type of probation officer over the company's activities and gave the SEC discretion in terms of the amount of fines that could be assessed in the future.[305] On December 9, 2002, WorldCom ran full-page ads in the country's major newspapers with the following message: "We're changing management. We're changing business practices. We're changing WorldCom."[306]

Discussion Questions

1. Consider the following statement by a government official. Securities Exchange Commissioner Cynthia Glassman included the following in a speech she gave to the American Society of Corporate Secretaries on September 27, 2002:

   [T]he distribution of securities by companies that had not made a previous public offering reached the highest level in history. This activity in new issues took place in a climate of general optimism and speculative interest. The public eagerly sought stocks of companies in certain "glamour" industries, especially the electronics industry, in the expectation that they would rise to a substantial premium—an expectation that was often fulfilled. Within a few days or even hours after the initial distribution, these so-called hot issues would be traded at premiums of as much as 300 percent above the original offering price. In many cases the price of a "hot" issue later fell to a fraction of its original offering price.

   What impact do you think the psychology of the market had on allowing WorldCom, Mr. Ebbers, and others to engage in creative accounting?

2. Consider the following:

   This phenomenon of confusion ruling in a bullish market is not unique to the 1990s stock market. Following the 1929 stock market crash, one of the biggest collapses, and a shocker to the investment world, was the bankruptcy of Middle West Utilities. The company was run by Samuel Insull according to the prevailing, and confusing, structure of the time, "elaborate webs of holding companies, each helping hide the others' financial weaknesses, an artifice strangely similar to what Enron did with its partnerships."[307] Following the bubble burst in the early 1970s, accounting firm Peat

---

[303] Seth Schiesel, "WorldCom Sees More Revisions of Its Figures," The New York Times, November 11, 2002, p. C1. Jared Sandberg, "Six Directors Quit as WorldCom Breaks With Past," The New York Times, December 18, 2002, p. A3. Andrew Backover and Kevin Maney, "WorldCom to Replace Sidgmore," USA Today, September 11, 2002, p. 1B. Stephanie N. Mehta, "Can Mike Save WorldCom?" Fortune, December 9, 2002, p. 163.

[304] Seth Schiesel and Simon Romero, "WorldCom Strikes a Deal with S.E.C.," The New York Times, November 27, 2002, p. C1.

[305] Jon Swartz, "WorldCom Settles Big Issues with SEC," USA Today, November 27, 2002, p. 1B. SEC v. WorldCom, Inc., 2002 WL 31760246 (S.D.N.Y. 2002).

[306] The New York Times, December 9, 2002, p. C3. USA Today, December 11, 2002, p. 4A.

[307] E. S. Browning, "Burst Bubbles Often Expose Cooked Books and Trigger SEC Probes, Bankruptcy Filings," The Wall Street Journal, February 11, 2002, pp. C1, C4.

Marwick, Mitchell was censured for its failure to conduct proper audits of five companies that crashed after PMM had given the firms clean and ongoing entity opinions. After the October 1987 crash, Drexel, Burnham & Lambert, Michael Milken's junk bond firm, collapsed along with a host of other companies and the savings and loan industry.[308]

What does this market history tell you about WorldCom? What does it say about the future? How could investors use this in the future?

3. Bill Parish, investment manager for Parish & Co., explained the collapse of Enron, WorldCom, and others with this insight: "There's massive corruption of the system. Earnings are grossly overstated."[309] Accounting Professor Brent Trueman of Berkeley added, "Reported numbers may not reflect the true income from operations." The phenomenon accompanies bubbles. "It is absolutely what almost invariably happens after every bubble. You should expect them [bankruptcies, scandals, and accounting disclosures], but that doesn't mean that people who haven't been through it before aren't going to be surprised. The bigger the binge, the longer and more severe the hangover."[310]

Is he right? Is fraud inevitable in a fast-paced market? Are these just natural market corrections?

4. WorldCom was eerily meeting its earnings targets precisely. One analyst did, however, notice that WorldCom was making its targets for several quarters in a row within fractions of cents. "When you see that they're making it by one one-hundredth of a penny you know the odds of that happening twice in a row are very slim. It indicates they're willing to stretch to make the quarter."[311] Are investors to blame for relying on the precise numbers and predictions? Shouldn't they have acted with greater skepticism?

5. Mr. Ebbers' conduct shows that he still believes he has done nothing wrong. At church services in Mississippi immediately following the revelation of the WorldCom accounting impropriety, Mr. Ebbers arrived as usual to teach his Sunday school class and attend services. He addressed the congregation, "I just want you to know you aren't going to church with a crook. This has been a strange week at best . . . On Tuesday I received a call telling me what was happening at WorldCom. I don't know what the situation is with all that has been reported. I don't know what all is going to happen or what mistakes have been made . . . No one will find me to have knowingly committed fraud. More than anything else, I hope that my witness for Jesus Christ [will not be jeopardized]." The congregation gave Mr. Ebbers a standing ovation.[312] Mr. Ebbers continues to teach Sunday school each Sunday at 9:15 AM, and then stays for the 90-minute service held afterward.[313] What relationship do religious views and affiliations play in business ethics?

6. What did Scott Sullivan miss in making his analysis to capitalize ordinary expenses? What questions and models might have helped him see the decision and the impact of his decision differently? When he entered his guilty plea, Mr. Sullivan said that he understood that what he did was wrong but that he was undertaking "a misguided attempt to save the company." What made him do what he did and for so long?

[308] Id.

[309] Matt Krantz, "There's Just No Accounting for Teaching Earnings," USA Today, June 20, 2001, p. 1B.

[310] E. S. Browning, "Burst Bubbles Often Expose Cooked Books and Trigger SEC Probes, Bankruptcy Filings," The Wall Street Journal, February 11, 2002, pp. C1, C4.

[311] Jared Sandberg, Deborah Solomon, and Nicole Harris, "WorldCom Investigations Shift Focus to Ousted CEO Ebbers," The Wall Street Journal, July 1, 2002, pp. A1, A8.

[312] Id., p. A1.

[313] Jayne O'Donnell, "Ebbers Acts as if Nothing Is Amiss," USA Today, September 19, 2002, pp. 1B, 2B.

7. Even when the first multi-billion-dollar restatement came, many near Clinton, Mississippi, appeared to be more in mourning than angry. One employee, sharing the shock with bar patrons at Bravo Italian Restaurant & Bar said, "People are taking it with exceptional grace. In my experience with MCI, I have never worked for a better company."[314] Others, such as Bernie's minister, give him the benefit of the doubt, concluding that he might not have known about the distortion of the numbers: "We've kind of held judgment until we know the entire story and whether he had knowledge."[315]

Evaluate the effect of these companies on the home towns in which they operate. What role does hubris and the fear of letting the locals down play in situations such as WorldCom's?

CASE 6.10

Arthur Andersen: A Fallen Giant[316]

Arthur Andersen, once known as the "gold standard of auditing," was founded in Chicago in 1913 on a legend of integrity, as Andersen, Delaney & Co. In those early years, when the business was struggling, Arthur Andersen was approached by a well-known railway company about audit work. When the audit was complete, the company CEO was outraged over the results and asked Andersen to change the numbers or lose his only major client. A 28-year-old Andersen responded, "There's not enough money in the city of Chicago to induce me to change that report!" Months later, the railway filed for bankruptcy.[317]

Over the years Andersen evolved into a multiservice company of management consultants, audit services, information systems, and virtually all aspects of operations and financial reporting. Ultimately, Andersen would serve as auditor for Enron, WorldCom, Waste Management, Sunbeam, and the Baptist Foundation, several of the largest bankruptcies of the century as well as poster companies for the corporate governance and audit reforms of the Sarbanes-Oxley Act, federal legislation enacted in the wake of the Enron and WorldCom collapses.

Andersen and Enron

Andersen served as Enron's outside auditor, and the following information regarding various conflicts of interest became public both through journalistic investigations and via the Senate hearings held upon Enron's declaration of bankruptcy:[318]

- Andersen earned over one-half ($27 million) of its $52 million in annual fees from consulting services furnished to Enron.[319]

[314] Kelly Greene and Rick Brooks, "WorldCom Staff Now Are Saying 'Just Like Enron,'" The Wall Street Journal, June 27, 2002, p. A9.

[315] Jayne O'Donnell, "Ebbers Acts as if Nothing Is Amiss," USA Today, September 19, 2002, pp. 1B, 2B.

[316] Adapted with permission from Marianne M. Jennings, "A Primer on Enron: Lessons from A Perfect Storm of Financial Reporting, Corporate Governance, and Ethical Culture Failures," 39 California Western Law Review 163–262 (2003).

[317] Barbara Ley Toffler, Final Accounting: Ambition, Greed, and the Fall of Arthur Andersen, (New York: Broadway Books, 2003), p. 12.

[318] "The Role of the Board of Directors in Enron's Collapse," Report of the Permanent Subcommittee on Investigations of the Senate Government Affairs Committee, 107th Congress, Report 107-70, July 8, 2002, pp. 39–41; hereinafter referred to as "PSI Report."

[319] Deborah Solomon, "After Enron, a Push to Limit Accountants to . . . Accounting," The Wall Street Journal, January 25, 2002, p. C1.

- There was a fluid atmosphere of transfers back and forth between those working for Andersen doing Enron consulting or audit work and those working for Enron who went with Andersen.[320]

David Duncan, the audit partner in the Houston offices of Andersen who was in charge of the Enron account, was a close personal friend of Richard Causey, Enron's chief accounting officer, who had the ultimate responsibility for signing off on all of CFO Andrew Fastow's off-the-books entities.[321] The two men traveled, golfed, and fished together.[322] Employees of both Andersen and Enron have indicated since the time of their companies' collapses that the two firms were so closely connected that they were often not sure who worked for which firm. Many Andersen employees had permanent offices at Enron, including Mr. Duncan. Office decorum thus found Enron employees arranging in-office birthday celebrations for Andersen auditors so as to be certain not to offend anyone. In addition, there was a fluid line between Andersen employment and Enron employment, with auditors joining Enron on a regular basis. For example, in 2000, seven Andersen auditors joined Enron.[323]

Enron's executives and internal accountants and the Andersen auditors resorted to two discretionary accounting areas, special purposes entities (SPEs) and mark-to-market accounting, for booking the revenues from its substantial energy contracts, approximately 25 percent of all the existing energy contracts in the United States by 2001.[324] Their use of these discretionary areas allowed them to maintain the appearance of sustained financial performance through 2001. One observer who watched the rise and fall of Enron noted, in reference to Enron, but clearly applicable to all of the companies examined here, "If they had been going a slower speed, their results would not have been disastrous. It's a lot harder to keep it on the track at 200 miles per hour. You hit a bump and you're off the track."[325] The earnings from 1997 to 2001 were ultimately restated, with a resulting reduction of $568 million, or 20 percent of Enron's earnings for those four years.[326]

Enron's Code of Ethics had both a general and a specific policy on conflicts of interest, both of which had to be waived in order to allow its officers to function as officers of the many off-the-books entities that it was creating. The general ethical principle on conflicts is as follows:

> Employees of Enron Corp., its subsidiaries, and its affiliated companies (collectively the "Company") are charged with conducting their business affairs in accordance with the highest ethical standards. An employee shall not conduct himself or herself in a manner which directly or indirectly would be detrimental to the best interests of the Company or in a manner which would bring to the employee financial gain separately derived as a direct consequence of his or her employment with the company.[327]

[320] *Seven Andersen audit employees became Enron employees in the year 2000 alone. John Schwartz and Reed Abelson, "Auditor Struck Many as Smart and Upright," The New York Times, January 17, 2002, p. C11.*

[321] *Anita Raghavan, "How a Bright Star at Andersen Fell along with Enron," The Wall Street Journal, May 15, 2002, pp. A1, A8. See also Cathy Booth Thomas and Deborah Fowler, "Will Enron's Auditor Sing?" Time, February 11, 2002, p. 44.*

[322] *Id.*

[323] *John Schwartz and Reed Abelson, "Auditor Struck Many as Smart and Upright," The New York Times, January 17, 2002, p. C11.*

[324] *Noelle Knox, "Enron to Fire 4,000 from Headquarters," USA Today, December 4, 2001, p. 1B.*

[325] *Bob McNair, a Houston entrepreneur who sold his company to Enron in 1998, quoted in John Schwartz and Richard A. Oppel, Jr., "Risk Maker Awaits Fall of Company Built on Risk," The New York Times, November 29, 2001, p. C1.*

[326] *John R. Emshwiller, Rebecca Smith, Robin Sidel, and Jonathan Weil, "Enron Cuts Profit Data of 4 Years by 20%," The Wall Street Journal, November 9, 2001, p. A3.*

[327] *Code of Ethics, Executive and Management, Enron Corporation, July 2000, p. 12.*

Enron's code also had a specific provision on conflicts related to ownership of businesses that do business with Enron, which provides:

[t]he employer is entitled to expect of such person complete loyalty to the best interests of the Company. . . . Therefore, it follows that no full-time officer or employee should:

(c) Own an interest in or participate, directly or indirectly, in the profits of another entity which does business with or is a competitor of the Company, unless such ownership or participation has been previously disclosed in writing to the Chairman of the Board and Chief Executive Officer of Enron Corp., and such officer has determined that such interest or participation does not adversely affect the best interests of the Company.[328]

The board's minutes show that it waived this policy for Andrew Fastow on at least three different occasions.[329] In post-collapse interviews, members of the board have insisted that they were not waiving Enron's code of ethics for Mr. Fastow. Rather, they have argued, and presumably will do so in court, that in granting a waiver they were simply following the code's policies and procedures.[330] Granting the waiver was a red flag. Even the conflicted Enron board saw the issue and engaged, at least once, in what was called in the minutes "vigorous discussion."[331]

David Duncan was concerned about this conflict of interest, and when Mr. Fastow first proposed his role in the first off-the-books entity, Mr. Duncan, on May 28, 1999, e-mailed a message of inquiry about the Fastow proposal to Benjamin Neuhausen, a member of Andersen's Professional Standards Group in Chicago. Mr. Neuhausen responded, with some of the response in uppercase letters for emphasis, "Setting aside the accounting, idea of a venture entity managed by CFO is terrible from a business point of view. Conflicts galore. Why would any director in his or her right mind ever approve such a scheme?" Mr. Duncan wrote back to Mr. Neuhausen on June 1, 1999, "[O]n your point 1 (i.e., the whole thing is a bad idea), I really couldn't agree more. Rest assured that I have already communicated and it has been agreed to by Andy that CEO, General [Counsel], and Board discussion and approval will be a requirement, on our part, for acceptance of a venture similar to what we have been discussing."[332] Mr. Duncan, the Andersen audit partner responsible for the Enron account, had expressed concern about the aggressive accounting practices Enron sought to use. Attorney Rusty Hardin, who served as Andersen's lead defense lawyer in the obstruction of justice case against the company for document shredding, noted that "no question David Duncan was a client pleaser."[333] Mr. Duncan also experienced pressure from his client and even consulted his pastor about how to resolve the dilemmas he faced in terms of approval of the financial statements: "He basically said it was unrelenting. It was a constant fight. Wherever he drew that line, Enron pushed that line—he was under constant pressure from year to year to push that line."[334]

The special report commissioned by the Enron board following its collapse described Enron's culture as "a flawed idea, self-enrichment by employees, inadequately designed controls, poor implementation, inattentive oversight, simple (and not so simple) accounting mistakes, and overreaching in a culture that appears to have

---

[328] Id., p. 57.
[329] PSI Report, p. 26.
[330] PSI Report, p. 25.
[331] PSI Report, p. 28, citing the Hearing Record, p. 157.
[332] PSI Report, p. 26.
[333] Anita Raghavan, "How a Bright Star at Andersen Fell Along With Enron." The Wall Street Journal, May 15, 2002, pp. A1, A8.
[334] Id., p. A8.

encouraged pushing the limits."[335] In an interview with *CFO Magazine* in 1999, when he was named CFO of the year, Mr. Fastow explained that he was able to keep Enron's share price high because he spun debt off its books into SPEs.[336]

Sherron Watkins, who became one of *Time*'s persons of the year for her role in bringing the financial situation of Enron to public light, was the vice president for corporate development at Enron when she first expressed concerns about the company's financial health in August 2001. A former Andersen employee, she was fairly savvy about accounting rules, and with access to the financial records for purposes of her new job, she quickly realized that the large off-the-books structure that had absorbed the company's debt load was problematic.[337] Labeling the SPEs "fuzzy" accounting, she began looking for another job as she prepared her memo detailing the accounting issues, because she understood that raising those issues meant that she would lose her Enron job.[338] Ms. Watkins did write her memo, anonymously, to Kenneth Lay, then chair of Enron's board and former CEO, but she never discussed her concerns or discussed writing the memo with Jeffrey Skilling, then Enron's CEO, or Andrew Fastow, its CFO, because "It would have been a job-terminating move."[339] She did eventually confess to writing the memo when word of its existence permeated the executive suite. Mr. Fastow reacted by noting that Ms. Watkins wrote the memo because she was seeking his job.[340]

Andersen recognized the focus on numbers in an internal memo as it evaluated its exposure in continuing to have Enron as a client. What follows is an excerpt from a 2000 memo that David Duncan and four other Andersen partners prepared as they evaluated what they called the "risk drivers" at Enron. Following a discussion of "Management Pressures" and "Accounting and Financial Management Reporting Risks," the following drivers were listed:

- Enron has aggressive earnings targets and enters into numerous complex transactions to achieve those targets
- The Company's personnel are very sophisticated and enter into numerous complex transactions and are often aggressive in restructuring transactions to achieve derived financial reporting objectives
- Form over substance transactions.[341]

Mr. Duncan presented the board with a one-page summary of Enron's accounting practices.[342] The summary, called "Selected Observations 1998 Financial Reporting," highlighted Mr. Duncan's areas of concern, and it was presented to the board in 1999, a full two years prior to Enron's collapse. Called "key accounting issues" by Mr. Duncan, the areas of concern included "Highly Structured Transactions," "Commodity and Equity Portfolio," "Purchase Accounting," and "Balance Sheet Issues." Mr. Duncan had assigned three categories of risk for these accounting areas, which included "Accounting

---

[335] Kurt Eichenwald, "Enron Panel Finds Inflated Profits and Few Controls," The New York Times, February 3, 2002, p. A1.

[336] David Barboza and John Schwartz, "The Finance Wizard Behind Enron's Deals," The New York Times, February 6, 2002, pp. A1, C9.

[337] Jodie Morse and Amanda Bower, "The Party Crasher," Time, January 6, 2003, pp. 53–55.

[338] Id.

[339] Rebecca Smith, "Fastow Memo Defends Enron Partnerships and Sees Criticism as Ploy to Get His Job," The Wall Street Journal, February 20, 2002, p. A3.

[340] Id.

[341] PSI Report, Hearing Exhibit 2b, Audit Committee Minutes of 2/7/99, p. 18.

[342] PSI Report, Hearing Exhibit 2b, Audit Committee Minutes of 2/7/99, p. 16.

Judgments," "Disclosure Judgements" [sic], and "Rule Changes," and he then assigned letters to each of these three categories: "H" for high risk, "M" for medium risk, and "L" for low risk.[343] Each accounting issue had at least two "H" grades in the three risk categories.

Shortly after the SEC announced its investigation of Enron, there was a great deal of document shredding at Andersen's Houston and Chicago offices. Andersen maintained that the shredding was routine, but the federal government indicted the company and Mr. Duncan. Mr. Duncan entered a guilty plea to obstruction of justice and ultimately testified against Andersen in court. Andersen was convicted of obstruction of justice. Its felony conviction meant that it could no longer conduct audits, and those clients that remained were now required to hire other auditors. Within a period of two years, Andersen went from an international firm of 36,000 employees to nonexistence.

David Duncan was active in his church, a father of three young daughters, and a respected alum of Texas A&M. Mr. Duncan's pastor talked with the *New York Times* following Enron's collapse and Duncan's indictment, and discussed with the reporter what a truly decent human being Duncan was.[344]

....

Discussion Questions

1. With the continuing revelations about the accounting practices, restatements of earnings, and regulatory investigations surrounding Andersen's other clients, including Global Crossing, WorldCom, Qwest, Waste Management, Baptist Foundation of Arizona, and Sunbeam, there was impetus for mandatory restrictions on conflicts of interest in auditing. Further, studies by various shareholder activist groups and pension plans indicated that the ratios of consulting to audit fees among the Big Five accounting firms were similar to or higher than that of Andersen. The following list of companies and their ratios of nonaudit fees to audit fees was published in 2002:[345]

   Allegheny Energy (3:1), Ameren (2:3), American Power Conversion (5:1), Apple Computer (12:6), Avon (2:9), Best Buy (4:4), Boston Properties (4:8), Bristol Myers Squibb (4:5), Constellation Energy Group (4:1), Delphi Automotive Systems (7:7), Dominion Resources (1:2), Duke Energy (3:5), Equitable Resources (3:9), First Energy (5:9), Gap (13:5), Halliburton (1:1), John Hancock Financial (9:7), Johnson & Johnson (4:6), Kmart (10:4), Lafarge North America (3:1), Liz Claiborne (2:2), Manpower (3:6), Marriott International (4:7), McGraw-Hill (2:2), PG&E (3:6), Reliant (5:1), VF (5:2), and Walt Disney (4:1).[346]

   Was the consulting by the same firm that conducted a company's audit a conflict of interest?

2. In 2000, a full two years before WorldCom's collapse, Steven Brabbs, WorldCom's director of international finance and control, who was based in London, raised objections when he discovered after he had completed his division's books for the year that $33.6 million in line

---

[343] PSI Report, Hearing Exhibit 2a, p.16.

[344] Anita Raghavan, "How a Bright Star at Andersen Fell Along With Enron," The Wall Street Journal, May 15, 2002, pp. A1, A8.

[345] Deborah Solomon, "After Enron, a Push to Limit Accountants to . . . Accounting," The Wall Street Journal, January 25, 2002, p. C1.

[346] Prior to the Sarbanes-Oxley requirements, some companies, such as Disney, opted to halt the dual role of their audit firms and barred consulting and auditing services from the same firm. Gary Strauss, "Companies Take Action to Regain Investor Trust," USA Today, July 17, 2002, p. 1B. Jonathon Weil and Jeffrey Tannenbaum, "Big Companies Pay Audit Firms More for Other Services," The Wall Street Journal, April 10, 2001, p. C1.

costs had been dropped from his books through a journal entry.[347] He was told that the changes were made pursuant to orders from CFO Scott Sullivan. He next suggested that the treatment be cleared with Arthur Andersen.[348] When there was no response to his suggestion that the external auditor be consulted, Mr. Brabbs again raised his objections in a meeting with internal financial executives a few months later. Following the meeting, Mr. Brabbs was chastised by WorldCom's controller for raising the issue again.[349]

The following quarter, Mr. Brabbs received orders from WorldCom headquarters to make another similar change, but to do so at his level rather than having it done from corporate headquarters via journal entry. Unwilling to have the entries generate from his division, he created another entity and transferred the costs to it.[350] He voiced his concerns again and was told that there was no choice because the accounting was a "Scott Sullivan directive."[351] Mr. Brabbs also had a meeting with Arthur Andersen auditors to discuss his concerns. Following the meeting he received an e-mail from WorldCom's controller, David Myers, which directed that Mr. Brabbs was "not [to] have any more meetings with AA for any reason."[352]

When WorldCom's internal audit staff began to raise questions about the reserves and the capitalization of ordinary expenses, they were prohibited from doing further work and, for the most part, worked nights and weekends to untangle the accounting nightmare they had first discovered with a simple question about receipts for some capitalized expenses. CFO Scott Sullivan asked the audit staff to wait at least another quarter before continuing with their investigation. Andersen auditors reported any internal audit inquiries to Sullivan and did not follow through on questions and concerns raised.[353]

What controls were missing? Why the reporting lines to Sullivan?

3. One of the tragic ironies to emerge from the collapse of Arthur Andersen, following its audit work for Sunbeam, WorldCom, and Enron, was that it had survived the 1980s savings-and-loan scandals unscathed. In *Final Accounting: Ambition, Greed and the Fall of Arthur Andersen,* the following poignant description appears:

> The savings-and-loan crisis, when it came, ensnared almost every one of the Big 8. But Arthur Andersen skated away virtually clean, because it had made the decision, years earlier to resign all of its clients in the industry. S&Ls for years had taken advantage of a loophole that allowed them to boost earnings by recording the value of deferred taxes. Arthur Andersen accountants thought the rule was misleading and tried to convince their clients to change their accounting. When they refused, Andersen did what it felt it had to: It resigned all of its accounts rather than stand behind accounting that it felt to be wrong.[354]

What takes a company from the gold standard to indictment and conviction?

---

[347] Kurt Eichenwald, "Auditing Woes at WorldCom Were Noted Two Years Ago," The New York Times, *July 15, 2002, pp. C1, C9.*

[348] Id., p. C9. *The information was taken from Mr. Brabbs' statement to the government during its initial investigation of WorldCom.*

[349] Id.

[350] Id.

[351] Id.

[352] Jessica Sommar, "E-Mail Blackmail — WorldCom Memo Threatened Conscience-Stricken Exec," The New York Post, *August 27, 2002, p. 27.*

[353] Susan Pulliam and Deborah Solomon, "How Three Unlikely Sleuths Discovered Fraud at WorldCom," The Wall Street Journal, *October 30, 2002, pp. A1, A6.*

[354] Barbara Ley Toffler, Final Accounting: Ambition, Greed and the Fall of Arthur Andersen *(2003), p. 19.*

Personal Ambition and Hubris

Jonathan Lebed: The Middle School Tycoon

Jonathan Lebed, a 15-year-old New Jersey middle-school student, shocked the investment world when the Securities and Exchange Commission (SEC) came knocking at his parents' door with a charge of securities fraud. It seems that Jonathan had turned his $8,000 in savings and gifts from family members into nearly $900,000 in gains on stocks traded using a pump-and-dump strategy. Jonathan did so without ever missing a day of school.

Master Jonathan, using over 20 screen names on a computer his parents had given him as a gift, would buy shares of stock and then post positive information about the stock around the Internet in various chat rooms. When the price of his chosen stock would rise, he would then sell it and move on to another stock. He did the bulk of his "pump-and-dump" trading between September 1999 and February 2000. During that time he traded, on average, 60,000 shares per day; his smallest gain in a day was $12,000 and his largest was $74,000.

Mrs. Lebed said that Jonathan had always been fascinated with the market and would often sit by the TV and watch the stock prices go across the screen on MSNBC and CNN. His mother also indicated he was not a bad stock picker, having given some of her friends and family members some good investment advice on stock.

When the SEC stepped in to halt his trading and take his computer, Jonathan became the first minor ever prosecuted by the SEC for securities fraud. His father noted that his son did nothing more than what others in the market do and yet the SEC chose to come after "a kid." Mr. Lebed stated during a *60 Minutes* interview, "I'm proud of my son. It's not like he was out stealing the hubcaps off cars or peddling drugs to the neighbors."[355] Mr. Lebed also noted that analysts behaved in the same fashion and that his son had been singled out for prosecution.

---

[355] Michael Lewis, "Jonathan Lebed: Stock Manipulator, S.E.C. Nemesis—and 15," The New York Times, *February 25, 2001,* pp. 1–18.

Michael Lewis, who conducted an investigation into the case, interviewed Richard Walker, the head of enforcement for the SEC, and asked what was different about Master Lebed's conduct from that of analysts. The following is their exchange:

> "Jonathan Lebed was seeking to manipulate the market," said Walker.
>
> But that only begs the question. If Wall Street analysts and fund managers and corporate CEOs who appear on CNBC and CNNfn to plug stocks are not guilty of seeking to manipulate the market, what on earth does it mean to manipulate the market?
>
> "It's when you promote a stock for the purpose of artificially raising its price."
>
> But when a Wall Street analyst can send the price of a stock of a company that is losing billions of dollars up 50 points in a day, what does it mean to "artificially raise" the price of a stock? The law sounded perfectly circular.[356]

The Lebeds entered into a consent decree.[357] They repaid all of the money Jonathan had made except for $273,000, a sum equal to about what is no doubt owed by his parents as taxes on the gains Jonathan made in his trading activity.[358]

Following his high school graduation, Master Lebed launched a Web site where he again touts stocks (http://lebed.biz), but now he does not take positions in the stocks he is advancing. And he adds, "I never thought there was anything wrong with what I did."[359]

He also has an investor-relations firm, Lebed & Lara, that now has about 100 clients who pay $200 per year for access to stock information.

He is running for city council in Cedar Grove, New Jersey, and he is in negotiations for a movie deal for his story.

Discussion Questions

1. Do you think Master Lebed violated the law? Why or why not?

2. Can you distinguish his conduct from a CEO or analyst plugging a particular stock?

3. Did Master Lebed take unfair advantage or should investors be more wary of information they get over the Internet?

4. Do you think Master Lebed's conduct was ethical? Why or why not? Was it honest? Was it fair?

5. Does his apparent success following the pump-and-dump scheme show that being honest and fair doesn't really matter? Why or why not?

[356] Id.
[357] Noelle Knox, "Teen Settles Stock-Manipulation Case for $285,000," USA Today, September 21, 2000, p. 1B.
[358] Gretchen Morgenson, "S.E.C. Says Teenager Had After-School Hobby: Online Stock Fraud," The New York Times, September 21, 2000, pp. A1, C10.
[359] Gary Weiss, "The Kid Stays in the Picture," Business Week, April 7, 2003, pp. 70–72.

CASE 6.12
The Inside Tract: Dan Dorfman

Late in 1995 and early in 1996, reports about Dan Dorfman, a markets expert who then did commentary for CNBC, emerged in the business press regarding Mr. Dorfman's relationship with a stock trader and the possibility of insider trading. The reports included statements that Mr. Dorfman was under investigation by the Securities and Exchange Commission (SEC), a statement the SEC and Justice Department officials neither confirmed nor denied.

The reports alleged that Mr. Dorfman moved particular stocks for friends and then profited by trading in those stocks. After the business press reported the allegations, *Money* magazine terminated Mr. Dorfman but noted that the termination was because Mr. Dorfman was hired to increase subscriptions and those numbers had, in fact, not improved. CNBC's parent company hired a law firm to conduct an investigation into the allegations.[360]

Mr. Dorfman was famous for his saying, "I own three stocks—AT&T, Boeing, and Gannett—and I never write about them."[361]

On May 7, 1996, Mr. Dorfman suffered a mild stroke and his reports could not be aired on CNBC. On August 30, 1996, CNBC announced that its internal investigation was complete, that Mr. Dorfman had cooperated fully, and that the law firm could find no evidence of illegal activity. The law firm did note, however, that it did not have the power of subpoena available to the U.S. government and that it had not examined records beyond what was publicly available and what Mr. Dorfman could furnish. According to the law firm's analysis, Mr. Dorfman's relationship with the stock promoter did not include any illegal activity.[362]

CNBC developed new conflicts of interest guidelines for its analysts in 1998. Concerned about "pump and dump," the network felt clear rules and guidelines were needed.[363] "Pump and dump" is the practice of a Wall Street professional appearing on a CNBC business show and touting a particular stock as being a potential good buy. Often unbeknownst to the viewing audience, the analyst promoting a particular stock has a large holding in the stock. After promoting the stock and the resulting price increase, the analyst sells his or her stock at a substantial gain.

Under the new rules, analysts must disclose any trading they have done in the stock prior to touting it. Analysts may not purchase stock, appear on the air to promote it, and then sell it after the price has increased.

In 2000, Arthur Levitt, the chairman of the SEC, asked that the National Association of Securities Dealers (NASD) and the New York Stock Exchange work with the SEC to develop rules to require analysts and money managers to make disclosures about potential conflicts of interest.

---

[360] Patrick M. Reilly, "Money Fires Dan Dorfman for Not Divulging Sources," The Wall Street Journal, January 4, 1996, pp. B1, B6.
[361] Laurie P. Cohen and Amy Stevens, "Dan Dorfman's Woes Mount as Investigators Widen Criminal Probe," The Wall Street Journal, February 16, 1996, pp. A1, A7.
[362] Michal Schroeder, "Losing Money," Business Week, January 15, 1996, p. 40.
[363] AP Wire Reports, December 23 and 24, 1998.

Levitt's immediate concerns focused on radio and television commentators who recommend stocks or offer highly favorable information about stock without disclosing their holdings or recent purchases in the stock. Currently, analysts who furnish reports must make disclosures in their reports about their holdings.[364]

While CNBC, Dorfman's network, investigated and found no violation of the law, Levitt pointed to Dorfman as an example of nondisclosures by media market commentators. In 2003, reporter and anchorwoman Maria Bartiromo conducted an interview of then-CEO Sanford Weil of Citigroup. The one-hour interview on CNBC began with Ms. Baritromo disclosing that she owned 1,000 shares of Citigroup stock, worth, at that time, about $45,000.[365]

Many broadcasters allege the disclosures and restrictions would make for boring radio and television programs. They have also claimed that such restrictions run contrary to First Amendment protections.

Discussion Questions

1. What are the ethical issues in this scenario?

2. Are there any ethical breaches that you can see?

3. CNBC and *Money* were placed in difficult situations that many employers must confront. What happens when allegations are made against an employee or a contractor who works for your company? What steps should the employer take? The mere suspension of an employee, even with pay, can harm the employee's reputation. However, an employer, particularly one whose own reputation is tied to the work of the employee, is at issue and it is often not possible to simply wait for the government to take action, if such action is planned. In Mr. Dorfman's case, the dilemma of the employer was compounded because Mr. Dorfman's health prevented his continuing appearances. Did CNBC act responsibly? Could they have done anything differently? What can an employer do to protect both its reputation and that of its employee?

4. Can you apply the principles of the regulatory cycle to this case? Did the networks wait too long? Should they have taken voluntary action?

5. Do you think Maria should have done the interview? What is the ethical issue?

6. CNN does not allow its reporters to cover companies or conduct interviews at companies in which they hold a substantial block of stock. Fox News takes the position that the disclosure solves the conflict of interest. However, several ethics organizations maintain that disclosure does not resolve the conflict. Fox vice president for business news Neil Cavuto says that ownership in a company sharpens his ability to cover it. CNBC prohibits all managers and news staff and their families from owning individual stocks except those of their employer company (mutual fund interests are allowed). *The Wall Street Journal* and *Business Week* prohibit employees from writing about stocks they own. Discuss these positions as well.

[364] Noelle Knox, *"TV Stock Analysts May Soon Need Disclaimer,"* USA Today, December 8, 2000, p. 3B.
[365] Patrick McGeehan, *"CNBC Disclosure Stirs Ethics Debate in Business Media,"* The New York Times, July 28, 2003, pp. C1, C6.

Martha Stewart: Not Such a Good Thing

Martha Helen Kostyra was born in 1941 in Jersey City, New Jersey, and worked her way through Barnard College with the money she earned working as both a fashion model and a maid. She was married to Andy Stewart, a graduate of Yale Law School, in 1961, during her sophomore year. As Andy became a Manhattan lawyer, Martha completed her degree in Art History at Barnard. In 1965, she had her only child, a daughter, Alexis.

In 1968, she became a licensed securities broker and a member of the New York Stock Exchange. She had a successful five-year stint on Wall Street until she and Andy purchased a home in Westport, Connecticut, a home that would become known as Turkey Hill. Martha left Wall Street to become a full-time mother and homemaker in the quintessential suburban haven.

During this time, Martha became well known for her skills as a hostess, and friends began to ask her to handle their parties and receptions. Martha began a catering business, A Catered Affair, that continued to expand and grow. By the time she published her first book in the early 1980s, her now-diverse business, known as Martha Stewart, Inc., included a retail store with prepared foods, a catering business, and endorsements for a line of products at Kmart.

In 1991, Martha ventured into both magazine publishing and television. *Martha Stewart Living* became a highly successful monthly magazine, and she had one of the most successful syndicated television shows. Martha took her company public on the New York Stock Exchange in 1999, and it was one of the hottest IPOs of the decade. The value of her interest in her company doubled in just the opening minutes as the shares sold.

By 2001, she had four magazines, thirty-four books, a newspaper column, a radio show, a catalogue sales company, and a weekly spot on *CBS This Morning*. A business icon, she was elected to the board of the New York Stock Exchange in June 2001. There seemed to be no end to the talent and success of Ms. Stewart. Everything she touched brought returns. Some speculated that association with her name enabled Kmart to survive bankruptcy.

However, it was Ms. Stewart's investment in a friend's biotech company that would cause her empire to crash. Ms. Stewart's troubles began with her ownership of 5,000 ImClone shares.[366] ImClone Systems, Inc., a pharmaceutical company, was poised in December 2001 to market Erbitux, an anticancer drug, pending FDA approval. Oddly, Erbitux was developed at the Anderson Cancer Research Institute in Houston, Texas, headed by Dr. John Mendelsohn, who served on the Enron board and its audit

---

[366] Alessandra Stanley and Constance L. Hays, "Martha Stewart's To-Do List May Include Image Polishing," The New York Times, June 23, 2003, pp. A1, A24.

committee.[367] Enron, and its chair, Kenneth Lay, were significant donors to the center. Dr. Mendelsohn also served on ImClone's board.[368] (See Case 6.9.)

Ms. Stewart was a friend of Dr. Samuel D. Waksal, the CEO of ImClone. She had invested in ImClone based upon his recommendation.[369] However, there were rumblings during the fall of 2001 that FDA approval might not be forthcoming. There were some indications during this period that both Dr. Waksal and Ms. Stewart were becoming anxious about their investment. Dr. Waksal owned 79,797 shares of ImClone stock, but, like so many other CEOs of the era, he had pledged the shares as collateral for loans, and he was deeply in debt.

When Bristol-Myers Squibb made a tender offer for ImClone shares in October 2001, at a price of $70 per share, Ms. Stewart had instructed her broker at Merrill Lynch, Peter Bacanovic, and his assistant, Douglas Faneuil, to accept the tender offer.[370] However, so many shareholders took the offer that Ms. Stewart was able to sell only about 1,000 of her shares. Her remaining interest was 3,928 shares, and the rumblings about ImClone and FDA approval only continued.

Employees at ImClone were aware, by early December 2001, that FDA approval was not likely. In fact, there was an internal memo outlining the issues and suggesting that FDA approval would not be forthcoming.[371] Harlan Waksal, Sam's brother, and also an officer of ImClone, sold $50 million worth of ImClone shares shortly after the memo was written.[372]

The share price for ImClone was over $70 in December 2001, but by December 26, 2001, the executive team at ImClone was "99 percent certain" that FDA approval would not be forthcoming. Their plan was to announce what would be the inevitable denial of approval on December 28, 2001, a Friday, after the markets had closed.[373] Dr. Waksal returned from a Caribbean vacation to sell his shares and also tipped family members to do the same. Using the same broker, Mr. Bacanovic, Dr. Waksal tried to sell his shares but was told that he would need approval from ImClone's general counsel to do so. Dr. Waksal then transferred his shares to his daughter and tried the sale through Bank of America, but was given the same requirement. Dr. Waksal forged the approval of the ImClone general counsel and the shares were sold, but Dr. Waksal eventually entered a guilty plea to

---

[367] Andrew Pollack and David Cay Johnston, "Former Chief of ImClone Systems Is Charged with Insider Trading," The New York Times, June 13, 2002, pp. B1, B6. Jerry Markon, "Active Inquiry Is Underway on Ms. Stewart," The Wall Street Journal, June 14, 2002, pp. C1, C10.

[368] Jo Thomas and Reed Abelson, "How a Top Medical Researcher Became Entangled With Enron," The New York Times, January 28, 2002, pp. C1, C2.

[369] Andrew Pollack and David Cay Johnston, "Former Chief of ImClone Systems Is Charged with Insider Trading," The New York Times, June 13, 2002, pp. C1, C6. Constance L. Hays, "Prosecutor Says Martha Stewart Spun Web of Lies About Shares," The New York Times, January 28, 2004, pp. C1, C11. Leslie Eaton, "The Ghost of Waksal Past Hovers Over the Stewart Trial," The New York Times, February 17, 2004, pp. C1, C6.

[370] Constance L. Hays and Patrick McGeehan, "A Closer Look at Martha Stewart's Trade," The New York Times, Monday, July 15, 2002, pp. C1, C9.

[371] Constance L. Hays and Patrick McGeehan, "A Closer Look at Martha Stewart's Trade," The New York Times, Monday, July 15, 2002, pp. C1, C9.

[372] Id. Andrew Pollack, "ImClone's Cancer Drug Is Back, and U.S. Approval Is Expected," The New York Times, February 11, 2004, pp. C1, C2.

[373] Riva D. Atlas, "ImClone Sues Former Chief to Recover $7 Million", The New York Times, Thursday, August 15, 2002, p. C3.

bank fraud and conspiracy and is now serving seven years in federal prison.[374] Waksal's daughters were also attempting to sell their 40,000 shares of ImClone.[375]

Douglas Faneuil became concerned when Dr. Waksal was trying to transfer shares to his daughter in order to sell them, so he sought approval from a Merrill Lynch accountant, who indicated it was illegal.[376] At that point, Mr. Faneuil contacted Peter Bacanovic, who was on vacation in Florida, and explained the rapid series of trading by the Waksal family. Mr. Bacanovic responded, "Oh my God, get Martha on the phone,"[377] When Mr. Faneuil questioned whether telling Ms. Stewart was legal, Mr. Bacanovic responded, "Of course. You must. You've got to. That's the whole point."[378] Mr. Faneuil eventually reached Martha, who was on her way to a vacation in San Jose del Cabo, Mexico, and who called from the Houston airport. The conversation was as follows:

Ms. Stewart:	Hi, This is Martha.
Mr. Faneuil:	Peter thought you'd like to act on the information that Sam is selling all his shares.
Ms. Stewart:	All of his shares?
Mr. Faneuil:	What he does have here, he's trying to sell.
Ms. Stewart (later in the call): I want to sell.	

The 3,928 shares were sold at approximately $58 per share on December 27, 2001, for a total of $229,002 If Ms. Stewart had waited until the next day, December 28, 2001, when ImClone made the announcement about the FDA's lack of approval, she could have sold the shares for a total of $189,495. The savings: $39,507.

When Dr. Waksal's illegal sales were uncovered and he entered his guilty plea, the federal government turned its attention to sales of the stock by others, including Ms. Stewart. Ms. Stewart was questioned by agents and attorneys and was ultimately charged not with stock fraud but with lying to federal investigators. When Mr. Bacanovic and Mr. Faneuil were confronted initially by an in-house investigation at Merrill with questions about Mr. Waksal's and Ms. Stewart's sale of ImClone stock, they offered their first explanation: "It was a tax-loss selling."[379] Mr. Faneuil told SEC investigators that Ms. Stewart had called for the price of the stock and then indicated to him to go ahead and sell it.

In early January 2002, one of Ms. Stewart's employees called Mr. Faneuil to complain that the sale of the ImClone stock "completely screws up our tax-loss selling plan."[380]

At that point, Mr. Bacanovic and Mr. Faneuil changed their story on the tax-planning sale: They were following orders on a $60 stop-loss agreement that Ms. Stewart already had in place. By late January, Mr. Bacanovic was giving Mr. Faneuil instructions: "Listen, I've spoken to Martha. I've met with her. And everyone's telling the same

---

[374] Andrew Pollack and David Cay Johnston, "Former Chief of ImClone Systems Is Charged with Insider Trading," The New York Times, June 13, 2002, pp. C1, C6. Andrew Pollack, "ImClone's Cancer Drug Is Back, and U.S. Approval Is Expected," The New York Times, February 11, 2004, pp. C1, C2.

[375] Constance L. Hays, "Setback for Prosecutors in Martha Stewart Trial," The New York Times, January 30, 2004, pp. C1, C4.

[376] Greg Farrell, "Faneuil Describes ImClone Stock Sales," USA Today, February 4, 2004, p. 1B.

[377] Matthew Rose and Kara Scannell, "Stewart Trial Hears Key Witness," The Wall Street Journal, February 4, 2004, pp. C1, C2.

[378] Id.

[379] Greg Farrell, "Faneuil: Broker Changed Stories," USA Today, February 5, 2004, p. 1B.

[380] Id.

story. Everyone's telling the same story. This was a $60 stop-loss order. That was the reason for her sale. We're all on the same page, and it's the truth. It's the true story. Everyone's telling the same story."[381]

However, paperwork was not on the same page. If a stop-loss order existed, it dated from October 2001 and related to Omnimedia's holdings of stock, not Ms. Stewart's personal holdings. The worksheet that Mr. Bacanovic produced also told a different story. The sheet detailed Ms. Stewart's stock holdings and had the notation "@ 60" next to ImClone, written in what prosecution evidence showed was "scientifically distinguishable ink" compared with all the other notes on the worksheet.[382] The jury found the different ink to be proof of the charges of obstruction and conspiracy to obstruct the government's investigation.[383] As a result the second story, on the stop-loss order, did not fly. Now they are all faced with not just one false story, but two false stories among them. As even Martha Stewart's lawyer noted, with the hope that the brokers would be blamed and not his client, "[Their] cover story has as many holes in it as a Swiss cheese."[384]

On March 5, 2004, a Manhattan jury found Martha Stewart guilty of four felony counts, including conspiracy, obstruction of an investigation, and two counts of making false statements to federal investigators. Meg Crane, a graphic designer, one of the jurors in the case, summed up the feelings of her fellow panelists after the verdicts were announced: "We all felt terrible about it at the end. It felt like such a foolish mistake that was increased as it went along."[385] The foreperson of the jury, Rosemary McMahon, a schoolteacher, cried and lost sleep before the jury rendered its verdict, and she noted, "We thought of everything to try to find them not guilty of these charges. We just couldn't."[386]

Ms. Stewart was a billionaire at the time she sold the ImClone shares. The amount she saved seems insignificant, immaterial, and irrelevant in the grand scheme of her investment portfolio, including substantial holdings of stock in her own company, Martha Stewart Omnimedia, Inc., which was selling for $70 per share on December 27, 2001. On December 19, 2003, just weeks before the start of her trial, Omnimedia was at $9.11. Trading in Omnimedia had to be halted when the Stewart verdict was announced, and it would fall to $7.10 in the week following. The share price as of March 12, 2004, was $10.13. For every $1 drop in the price of Omnimedia shares, Ms. Stewart has lost $30 million.[387]

Following revelations about the investigation into the sale of the ImClone stock, Ms. Stewart resigned from her position on the board of the New York Stock Exchange as well as from her position as chair of the board of Omnimedia. Following her conviction, she resigned from her position on the board of Revlon, a position she had held for

---

[381] Id.

[382] Kara Scannell and Matthew Rose, "Worksheet's Importance Grows in Stewart Case," The Wall Street Journal, February 17, 2004, pp. C1, C2.

[383] Kara Scannell and Matthew Rose, "In Stewart Case, Reluctant Jurors Found Guilt after Foolish Mistake," The Wall Street Journal, March 8, 2004, pp. A1, A6.

[384] Constance L. Hays and Jonathan D. Glater, "More Tactics Than Theatrics at the Stewart Trial," The New York Times, February 10, 2004, pp. A1, C9.

[385] Kara Scannell and Matthew Rose, "In Stewart Case, Reluctant Jurors Found Guilt after Foolish Mistake," The Wall Street Journal, March 8, 2004, pp. A1, A6.

[386] Id.

[387] Karla Scannell and Matthew Rose, "Stewart Trial Gets Under Way," The New York Times, January 28, 2004, pp. C1, C5.

eight years. The New York Times Syndication services dropped her "askMartha" column, a loss of 200 papers. Westwood One, the radio syndicator for the "askMartha" audio segments, lost affiliates immediately upon her conviction. Viacom pulled *Martha Stewart Living* from its CBS and UPN stations, and the show will have to be individually sold to independent stations.[388] Ad revenues for her publications, the single largest source of revenue for Omnimedia, began a steady decline when the investigation of the sale of the shares became public.[389] From 2002 to 2003, ad revenues dropped 25.6 percent.[390] Ms. Stewart was forced to resign as CEO of the company she built from her home in Connecticut.

On July 16, 2004, Ms. Stewart was sentenced to five months in federal prison and five months of house arrest, something she has indicated she will do at her 150-acre Bedford, New York, farm. On October 8, 2004, Ms. Stewart reported to a minimum security prison in West Virginia to serve her five-month sentence. She stated that she was abandoning the appeal of her case because "closure" was important, and she wanted to complete her sentence in time to plant her spring garden. Others felt that she wanted to be free by March because filming for the fall season of her television show would begin in March 2005.[391] The price of her company's stock when she reported to prison was $12.03. The price of ImClone stock on that same day was $54.10 per share.

Discussion Questions

1. What issues did Stewart, Bacanovic, and Faneuil miss in making their decisions about selling the ImClone stock and in their conduct following the sales? Apply the models and make a list of suggested questions they could have asked that might have affected their decisions.

2. Was it selling the shares that was illegal? If selling the shares was not illegal, was it unethical?

3. What do we learn about long-term consequences from Ms. Stewart's conduct and case?

4. What advice can you offer someone who has engaged in trading similar to Ms. Stewart's?

5. Make a list of all the costs of Ms. Stewart's sale of the stock and compare it with the losses she avoided by selling the day before the public announcement.

CASE 6.14

Dennis Kozlowski: Tyco and the $6,000 Shower Curtain[392]

Tyco International began as a research laboratory, founded in 1960 by Arthur Rosenburg, with the idea of doing contract research work for the government. By 1962, Rosenburg had incorporated and begun doing work for companies in the areas of

[388] Theresa Howard, "Business Partners Shy from Stewart," USA Today, March 9, 2004, p. 1B.

[389] Gregory Zuckerman, "Martha: The Doyenne of Dilemmas," The Wall Street Journal, March 8, 2004, pp. C1, C2.

[390] Suzanne Vranica, Matthew Rose, and Janet Adamy, "Living — Without Martha," The Wall Street Journal, March 8, 2004, pp. B1, B11.

[391] Patricia Sellers, "Why Martha Really Chose Jail," Fortune, October 4, 2004, p. 34.

[392] Adapted from Marianne M. Jennings, "The Yeehaw Factor," 3 Wyoming Law Review 387–511 (2003).

high-tech materials and energy conversion, with two divisions of the holding company, Tyco Semiconductor and Materials Research Laboratory. By 1964, the company went public and became primarily a manufacturer of products for commercial use. Today, Tyco is a conglomerate with a presence in over 100 countries and over 250,000 employees. Between 1991 and 2001, CEO Dennis Kozlowski took Tyco from $3 billion in annual sales to $36 billion in 2001 by paying $60 billion for more than 200 acquisitions.[393] In a move to reduce its U.S. tax bills, Tyco is based out of Bermuda, despite having its headquarters in Exeter, New Hampshire.[394] Tyco, with a stake in telecommunications as well, is the parent company to Grinnell Security Systems, health care products companies, and many other acquired firms, which has been its strategy for growth.[395] In fact, the troubles that Tyco experienced initially were often attributed to a skittish market reacting to the falls of Enron and WorldCom as well as problems with Global Crossing and Kmart.[396]

Shortly after Enron's bankruptcy, Tyco began to experience a decline in its share price. From December 2001 through the middle of January 2002, Tyco's shares lost 20 percent of their value.[397] In fact, following a conference in which then-CEO Dennis Kozlowski tried to reassure the public and analysts that Tyco's accounting was sound, the shares were the most heavily traded of the day (68 million on January 15, 2002), and the price dropped $4.45, to $47.95 per share.[398] However, at the same time as the loss of investor confidence in the accounting of public corporations came Tyco's announcement that its earnings had dropped 24 percent for fiscal year 2001.[399] By February, the share price had tumbled to $29.90, a drop of 50 percent from January 1, 2002.[400] Tyco was forced to borrow funds as it experienced what one analyst called a "crisis in confidence," noting, "The lack of confidence in the company by the capital markets to a degree becomes a self-fulfilling prophecy."[401]

Then there was another problem that emerged on January 28, 2002. Tyco announced that it had paid $20 million to one of its outside directors, Frank E. Walsh, and a charity of which he was the head, for him to broker a deal for one of Tyco's acquisitions.[402] The acquisition was CIT Group Finance, and Tyco acquired it for $9.5 billion.[403] Mr. Walsh, who would later plead guilty to a violation of a New York statute

[393] Daniel Eisenberg, "Dennis the Menace," Time, June 17, 2002, p. 47. Mark Maremont, John Hechinger, Jerry Markon, and Gregory Zuckerman, "Kozlowski Quits Under a Cloud, Worsening Worries About Tyco," The Wall Street Journal, June 4, 2002, pp. A1, A10.

[394] Information from http://www.tyco.com; see Investor Relations, Tyco History. Alex Berenson, "Tyco Shares Fall as Investors Show Concern on Accounting," The New York Times, January 16, 2002, p. C1.

[395] Id. Tyco bought Grinnell, the security-system and fire-alarm company; Ludlow, the packaging company, and a host of others during its especially aggressive expansion period from 1973 to 1982.

[396] Kopin Tan, "Tyco's Options Soar, While Volatility Spikes on Concerns over U.S. Accounting Practices," The Wall Street Journal, January 30, 2002, p. C14.

[397] Alex Berenson, "Tyco Shares Fall as Investors Show Concern on Accounting," The New York Times, January 16, 2002, p. C1.

[398] Id.

[399] John Hechinger, "Tyco to Lay Off 44% of Its Workers At Telecom Unit," The Wall Street Journal, February 8, 2002, p. A5.

[400] Alex Berenson and Andrew Ross Sorkin, "Tyco Shares Tumble on Growing Worries of a Cash Squeeze," The New York Times, February 5, 2002, p. C1.

[401] Id.

[402] Kate Kelly and Gregory Zuckerman, "Tyco Worries Send Stock Prices Lower Again," The Wall Street Journal, February 5, 2002, p. C1.

[403] Laurie P. Cohen and Mark Maremont, "Tyco Ex-Director Pleads Guilty," The Wall Street Journal, December 18, 2002, p. C1.

as well as a violation of federal securities laws, withheld information about the brokerage fee from the Tyco board and did not disclose the information as required in the company's SEC filings.[404] Once the SEC moved in to investigate, the company's stock continued its decline.[405] From January 2002 to August 2002, Tyco's stock price declined 80 percent.[406]

What Went Wrong: The Accounting Issues

Investors and markets are not always jittery for no reason. There were some Tyco accounting issues that centered around its acquisitions and its accounting for those acquisitions.[407] What caused investors to seize upon Tyco's financials was that it seemed to be heavily in debt despite the fact that it was reporting oodles of cash flow.[408] This financial picture resulted because of Tyco's accounting for its "good-will."[409] When one company acquires another company, it must include the assets acquired in its balance sheet. The acquirer is in charge of establishing the value for the assets acquired. From 1998 to 2001, Tyco spent $30 billion on acquisitions and attributed $30 billion to goodwill.

The problem lies in the fact that the assets that are acquired are not carried on Tyco's books with any significant value. Assets, under accounting rules, lose their value over time. Goodwill stays the same in perpetuity. However, if Tyco turns around and sells the assets it has acquired and booked at virtually zero value, the profit that it makes is reflected in the income of the company. The only way an investor in Tyco would be able to tell what has really happened in the accounting for an acquisition would be for the investor to have access to the balance sheets of the acquired companies, so that he or she could see the value of the assets as they were carried on the books of the acquired company. The bump to earnings from the sale of the assets is lovely, but the bump to profits, with no offsetting costs, is tremendous.

There were additional accounting issues related to the Tyco acquisitions. One big one was that despite having made 700 acquisitions between 1998 and 2001 for about $8 billion, Tyco never disclosed the acquisitions to the public.[410] The eventual disclosure of the phenomenal number of acquisitions did explain the lack of cash, but also deprived investors of the chance to determine how much of Tyco's growth was due to acquisitions versus running existing businesses.

---

[404] Andrew Ross Sorkin, "Tyco Figure Pays $22.5 Million in Guilty Plea," The New York Times, December 18, 2002, pp. C1, C2. E. S. Browning, "Stocks Slump in Late-Day Selloff on Round of Ugly Corporate News," The Wall Street Journal, June 4, 2002, pp. A3, A8.

[405] Michael Schroeder and John Hechinger, "SEC Reopens Tyco Investigation," The Wall Street Journal, June 13, 2002, p. A2.

[406] Kevin McCoy, "Authorities Widen Tyco Case, Look at Other Officials' Actions," USA Today, August 13, 2003, p. 1A.

[407] Floyd Norris, "Now Will Come the Sorting Out of the Chief Executive's Legacy," The New York Times, June 4, 2002, pp. C1, C10.

[408] Mark Maremont, "Tyco Made $8 Billion of Acquisitions Over 3 Years but Didn't Disclose Them," The Wall Street Journal, February 4, 2002, p. A3.

[409] "Goodwill" is an asset under accounting rules that takes into account the sort of customer value a business has. For example, if you buy a dry-cleaning business, you are not only paying for the hangers and the pressers and racks, you are paying for that dry cleaner's reputation in the community, the tendency of customers to return, and their willingness to bring their dry cleaning to this establishment—goodwill.

[410] Mark Maremont, "Tyco Made $8 Billion of Acquisitions Over 3 Years but Didn't Disclose Them," The Wall Street Journal, February 4, 2002, p. A3.

The nondisclosure of the acquisitions also helped with another accounting strategy. When Tyco made acquisitions, its goal was always to make the company acquired look as much like a dog as possible. Referred to as "spring-loading," this process makes the company look worse in terms of earnings than it really is, and when it just continues as normal the following year, the company enjoys a boost in terms of growth and respect for its management acumen. Spring-loading is easily accomplished by having the company being acquired pay everything for which it has a bill, whether that bill is due or not. When Tyco acquired Raychem, its treasurer sent out the following e-mail:

> At Tyco's request, all major Raychem sites will pay all pending payables, whether they are due or not . . . I understand from Ray [Raychem's CFO] that we have agreed to do this, even though we will be spending the money for no tangible benefit either to Raychem or Tyco."[411]

Tyco employees, when working with a company to be acquired, would also pump up the reserves, with one employee of Tyco asking an employee of an acquired firm, "How high can we get these things. How can we justify getting this higher?"[412] The final report of a team led by attorney David Boies (the lawyer who represented Napster, and also the government in its case against Microsoft, and also Al Gore in the Florida ballot dispute), retained by the Tyco board to determine what was going on with the company, indicates that Tyco executives used both incentives and pressure on executives in order to get them to push the envelope on accounting rules to maximize results.[413] Mr. Boies referred to the accounting practices of the executives as "financial engineering."

What Went Wrong—A Profligate Spender as CEO

Tyco was graced with a CEO whose profligate spending cost the company dearly, in dollars and reputation, and whose tight fist with his own money got him indicted. Dennis Kozlowski was a scary CEO whose philosophy was, "Money is the only way to keep score."[414] Mr. Kozlowski was one of the country's highest-paid CEOs. In 2001, his compensation package of $411.8 million put him at number two among the CEOs of the Fortune 500 companies."[415] Mr. Kozlowski was featured on the cover of *Business Week* and called "the most aggressive dealmaker in Corporate America."[416] He was included in the magazine's top twenty-five managers of the year. Indeed, when Tyco's problems and accounting issues emerged, many of Wall Street's "superstar" money managers were stunned.[417]

Before Tyco took its dive, Mr. Kozlowski had accumulated three Harleys; a 130-foot sailing yacht; a private plane; four homes in New York City (including a 13-room Fifth Avenue apartment, purchased in 2000),[418] New Hampshire, Nantucket, and Boca Raton

---

[411] *Herb Greenberg, "Does Tyco Play Accounting Games?"* Fortune, April 1, 2002, pp. 83, 86.

[412] Id.

[413] *Kurt Eicehnwald, "Pushing Accounting Rules to the Edge of the Envelope,"* The New York Times, December 31, 2002, pp. C1, C2.

[414] *Daniel Eisenberg, "Dennis the Menace,"* Time, June 17, 2002, p. 47.

[415] *Jonathan D. Glater, "A Star Lawyer Finds Himself The Target of a Peer,"* The New York Times, September 24, 2002, pp. C1, C8.

[416] Business Week Online, January 14, 2002, http://www.businessweek.com.

[417] *Gregory Zuckerman, "Heralded Investors Suffer Huge Losses with Tyco Meltdown,"* The Wall Street Journal, June 10, 2002, p. C1.

[418] *Theresa Howard, "Tyco Puts Kozlowski's $16.8M NYC Digs on Market,"* USA Today, September 19, 2002, p. 3B.

(15,000 square feet, purchased in 2001); and was a part-owner of the New Jersey Nets and the New Jersey Devils.[419] His Fifth Avenue apartment cost $16.8 million to buy, $3 million in renovations, and he spent $11 million on furnishings.[420] The items were delineated in the press, and the following purchases for the apartment were charged to Tyco: $6,000 for a shower curtain, $15,000 for a dog umbrella stand; $6,300 for a sewing basket, $17,100 for a traveling toilette box, $2,200 for a gilt metal wastebasket, $2,900 for coat hangers, $5,960 for two sets of sheets, $1,650 for a notebook, and $445 for a pincushion.[421]

For his new wife, Karen Mayo's, fortieth birthday, Kozlowski flew Jimmy Buffet and dozens of Karen's friends to a villa outside Sardinia for a multiday birthday celebration.[422] A memo on the party was attached as an exhibit to Tyco's 8-K, filed on September 17, 2002. The process for receiving the guests and the party schedule are described in detail, right down to what type of music was playing and at what level. The waiters were dressed in Roman togas, and there was an ice sculpture of David through which the vodka flowed. The memo includes a guest list and space for the crew of the yacht that the Kozlowskis sailed to Sardinia.[423] The total cost for the party was $2.1 million.[424] Tyco also paid Mr. Kozlowski's American Express bill, which was $80,000 for one month. A later report uncovered a $110,000 bill Tyco paid for a 13-day stay by Mr. Kozlowski at a London hotel.[425] Ironically, Mr. Kozlowski told a *Business Week* reporter in 2001, on a tour of Tyco's humble Exeter, New Hampshire, offices, "We don't believe in perks, not even executive parking spots."[426]

He appeared to be financing the lifestyle through Tyco's Key Employee Corporate Loan Program ("the KELP") and relocation loan programs (see following pages for details). According to SEC documents, Mr. Kozlowski borrowed more than $270 million from the KELP "but us[ed] only about $29 million to cover intended uses for the loans. He used the remaining $242 million of supposed KELP loans for personal expenses, including yachts, fine art, estate jewelry, luxury apartments and vacation estates, personal business ventures, and investments, all unrelated to Tyco."[427]

---

[419] Laurie P. Cohen and Mark Maremont, "Tyco Relocations to Florida Are Probed," The Wall Street Journal, June 10, 2002, p. A3. Alex Berenson and William K. Rashbaum, "Tyco Ex-Chief Is Said to Face Wider Inquiry Into Finances," The New York Times, June 7, 2002, p. C1. Kris Maher, "Scandal and Excess Make It Hard to Sell Mr. Kozlowski's Boat," The New York Times, September 23, 2002, p. A1.

[420] Andrew Ross Sorkin, "Tyco Details Lavish Lives of Executives," The New York Times, September 19, 2002, p. C1. The NYC apartment was sold for $21.8 million in October 2004. William Neuman, "Tyco to Sell Ex-Chief's Apartment for $21 Million," The New York Times, October 9, 2004, pp. B1, B4.

[421] Kevin McCoy, "Directors' Firms on Payroll at Tyco," USA Today, September 18, 2002, p. 1B. These items are also listed in the 8-K for September 17, 2002.

[422] Don Halasy, "Why Tyco Boss Fell," The New York Post, June 9, 2002, http://www.nypost.com. Laurie P. Cohen, "Ex-Tyco CEO's Ex To Post $10 Million For His Bail Bond," The Wall Street Journal, September 20, 2002, p. A5.

[423] Tyco 8-K filing, September 17, 2002, http://www.sec.gov/edgar.

[424] Mark Maremont and Laurie P. Cohen, "How Tyco's CEO Enriched Himself," The Wall Street Journal, August 7, 2002, p. A1.

[425] Mark Maremont and Laurie P. Cohen, "Tyco's Internal Inquiry Concludes Questionable Accounting Was Used," The Wall Street Journal, December 31, 2002, pp. A1, A4. Alex Berenson, "Changing the Definition of Cash Flow Helped Tyco," The New York Times, December 31, 2002, pp. C1, C2.

[426] Anthony Bianco, William Symonds, Nanette Byrnes, and David Polek, "The Rise and Fall of Dennis Kozlowski," Business Week Online, December 23, 2002, http://www.businessweek.com.

[427] http://www.sec.gov/releases/litigation. Kevin McCoy, "Directors' Firms on Payroll at Tyco," USA Today, September 18, 2002, p. 1B. These items are also listed in Tyco's 8-K filed on September 17, 2002, http://www.sec.gov/edgar. Theresa Howard, "Tyco Puts Kozlowski's $16.8M NYC Digs on Market," USA Today, September 19, 2002, p. 3B. Andrew Ross Sorkin, "Tyco Details Lavish Lives of Executives," The New York Times, September 18, 2002, p. C1. See also Tyco's 8-K filed on September 17, 2002.

Mr. Kozlowski was on the board of the Whitney Museum of Art and had Tyco donate $4.5 million to the traveling museum shows that the Whitney sponsored.[428] He was an avid fund-raiser for various philanthropic endeavors. In fact, he was at a fundraiser for the New York Botanical Garden when the news of his possible indictment (see following pages) first spread.[429] Tyco donated $1.7 million for the construction of the Kozlowski Athletic Complex at the private school, Berwick Academy, which one of his daughters attended and where he served as trustee, and $5 million to Seton Hall, his alma mater, for a building that was called the Koz Plex.[430]

Mr. Kozlowski also donated personally, particularly to charities in the Boca Raton area, where he had retained a public relations executive and where he had been given a fair amount of coverage in the *Palm Beach Post* for his contributions to local charities.[431] There is even some confusion about who was donating how much and from which tills. Kozlowski had pledged $106 million in Tyco funds to charity, but $43 million of that was given in his own name.[432] He had donated $1.3 million to the Nantucket Conservation Foundation in his own name with the express desire that the land next to his property there not be developed.[433] Tyco gave $3 million to a hospital in Boca Raton and $500,000 to an arts center there. United Way of America gave Mr. Kozlowski its "million-dollar giver" award.[434]

Mr. Kozlowski saw to it that friends were awarded contracts that Tyco paid. For example, Wendy Valliere was a personal friend of the Kozlowskis and was hired to decorate the New York City apartment. Her firm's bill was $7.5 million.[435] However, Ms. Valliere was not alone as a personal employee.[436] In 1996, Mr. Kozlowski also hired Michael Castania, a consultant who had helped him with his yacht, as an executive who was housed at Boca Raton. He was an Australian yachting expert who went on to lead Team Tyco, a corporate yachting racing team, to fourth place in the Volvo Challenge Race in June 2002.[437] Tyco also hired Ms. Mayos' personal trainer from the days when she was still married to her ex-husband and Mr. Kozlowski was still married to his ex-wife, but Mr. Kozlowski was supporting Ms. Mayo in a beach condo in Nantucket.[438]

Mr. Kozlowski was also an active player in Manhattan's art market. In June 2002 the *New York Times* reported that Mr. Kozlowski was being investigated by the district attorney's office in Manhattan for evasion of $1 million in sales tax on $13 million in

[428] Don Halasy, "Why Tyco Boss Fell," The New York Post, June 9, 2002, http://www.nypost.com.

[429] Id. Carol Vogel, "Kozlowski's Quest for Entrée into the Art World," The New York Times, June 6, 2002, pp. C1, C5.

[430] Mark Maremont and Laurie P. Cohen, How Tyco's CEO Enriched Himself, The Wall Street Journal, Aug. 7, 2002, p. A1. John Byrne, Seton Hall of Shame, Business Week Online, Sept. 20, 2002, http://www.businessweek.com.

[431] Id., p. A6. Barry Epstein, a Palm Beach PR executive said, "I represented Dennis personally. I reported to him and guided him on community involvement." Mr. Epstein has conceded that most of the money was Tyco's, not Mr. Kozlowski's.

[432] Kevin McCoy and Gary Strauss, "Kozlowski, Others Accused of Using Tyco as 'Piggy Bank,'" USA Today, September 13, 2002, pp. 1B, 2B.

[433] Mark Maremont and Laurie P. Cohen, "How Tyco's CEO Enriched Himself," The Wall Street Journal, August 7, 2002, pp. A1, A6.

[434] Id.

[435] Id.

[436] Mark Maremont and Laurie P. Cohen, "Interior Design on a Budget — the Tyco Way," The Wall Street Journal, September 18, 2002, pp. B1–B5.

[437] Mark Maremont and Laurie P. Cohen, "How Tyco's CEO Enriched Himself," The Wall Street Journal, August 7, 2002, pp. A1, A6.

[438] Anthony Bianco, William Symonds, Nanette Byrnes, and David Polek, "The Rise and Fall of Dennis Kozlowski," Business Week Online, December 23, 2002, http://www.businessweek.com.

art sales over a ten-month period.[439] Mr. Kozlowski resigned from Tyco immediately following the emergence of the report and before an indictment was handed down. A market that was already reeling from Enron and WorldCom dropped 215 points in one day, and Tyco's stock fell 27 percent that same day.[440] In fact, the indictment was handed down the following day.[441]

Tyco's Culture

Mr. Kozlowski had a strategy for getting the type of people he needed to succumb to the pressure for numbers achievement. He told *Business Week* that he chooses managers from the "same model as himself. Smart, poor, and wants to be rich."[442] Meeting numbers meant bonuses; exceeding those numbers meant, "the sky was the limit." The CEO of one of Tyco's subsidiaries had a salary of $625,000, but when he boosted sales by 62 percent, his bonus was $13 million.[443]

Mr. Kozlowski was known for being autocratic and prone to temper flare-ups.[444] When he was CEO of Tyco's Grinnell Fire Protection Systems Co., Mr. Kozlowski had an annual awards banquet where he presented awards to the best warehouse manager as well as the worst warehouse manager. The worst manager would have to walk to the front of the room in what other managers described as a "death sentence."[445]

The Loans

Tyco's Key Employee Corporate Loan Program (the "KELP") was established to encourage employees to own Tyco shares by offering dedicated loans to pay the taxes due when shares granted under Tyco's restricted share ownership plan became vested. There was no way to pay the taxes except to sell some of the shares for cash, and the loan program permitted the officers to pledge their shares in exchange for cash that was then used to pay the income tax that was due on this employee benefit.[446] Mr. Kozlowski made it clear that the loan program was available to all of his new hires,

---

[439] Alex Berenson, "Investigation Is Said to Focus on Tyco Chief over Sales Tax," The New York Times, June 3, 2002, p. C1. Laurie P. Cohen and Mark Maremont, "Expanding Tyco Inquiry Focuses on Firm's Spending on Executives," The Wall Street Journal, June 7, 2002, pp. A1, A5. Nanette Byrnes, "Online Extra: The Hunch That Led to Tyco's Tumble," Business Week Online, December 23, 2002, http://www.businessweek.com.

[440] Mark Maremont, John Hechinger, Jerry Markon, and Gregory Zuckerman, "Kozlowski Quits under a Cloud, Worsening Worries about Tyco," The Wall Street Journal, June 4, 2002, p. A1. Adam Shell, "Markets Fall as Tyco CEO's Resignation Adds to Woes," USA Today, June 4, 2002, p. 1B.

[441] Thor Valdmanis, "Art Purchases Put Ex-Tyco Chief in Hot Water," USA Today, June 5, 2002, p. 1B. Mark Maremont and Jerry Markon, "Former Tyco Chief Is Indicted for Avoiding Sales Tax on Art," The Wall Street Journal, June 5, 2002, p. A1. Alex Berenson and Carol Vogel, "Ex-Tyco Chief Is Indicted in Tax Case," The New York Times, June 5, 2002, p. C1. David Cay Johnston, "A Tax That's Often Ignored Suddenly Attracts Attention," The New York Times, June 5, 2002, p, C1. Brooks Barnes and Alexandra Peers, "Sales-Tax Probe Puts Art World In Harsh Light," The Wall Street Journal, June 5, 2002, pp. B1, B3. Susan Saulny, "Tyco's Ex-Chief to Seek Dismissal of Indictments," August 15, 2002, p. C3. Mark Maremont and Laurie P. Cohen, "Former Tyco CEO Is Charged With Two New Felony Counts," The Wall Street Journal, June 27, 2002, p. A3. Andrew Ross Sorkin and Susan Saulny, "Former Tyco Chief Faces New Charges," The New York Times, June 27, 2002, p. C1.

[442] William C. Symonds and Pamela L. Moore, "The Most Aggressive CEO," Business Week Online, May 28, 2001, http://www.businessweek.com.

[443] Id.

[444] Anthony Bianco, William Symonds, Nanette Byrnes, and David Poleck, "The Rise and Fall of Dennis Kozlowski," Business Week Online, December 23, 2002, http://www.businessweek.com.

[445] Id.

[446] This information was obtained from the press release the SEC issued when it filed suit against Mark Swartz, Dennis Kozlowski, and Mark Belnick for the return of the loan amounts. http://www.sec.gov/releases/litigation.

including Mark Swartz, the CFO, and Mark Belnick, Tyco's general counsel and executive vice president.[447]

The second loan program was a relocation program, which was established to help employees who had to move from New Hampshire to New York. The idea was to provide low-interest loans for employees who had to relocate from one set of company offices to another in order to lessen the impact of moving to a much costlier housing market.[448] One of the requirements of the relocation program was the employee's certification that he or she was indeed moving from New Hampshire to New York, or, in some cases, to Boca Raton.

Mr. Belnick has explained through his lawyer that he was entitled to the loans from the "relocation program" because he had such in writing from Mr. Kozlowski. Mr. Kozlowski offered this perk to Mr. Belnick despite the fact that Mr. Belnick was a partner in a New York City law firm and would be working in New York City for Tyco. He received the relocation fee for a difference of 25 miles between his home and Tyco's New York offices, and despite the fact that he had never lived in New Hampshire as the relocation loan program required. Although he actually didn't need to move, Mr. Belnick borrowed $4 million anyway and used it to buy and renovate an apartment in New York City. Later, he borrowed another $10 million to construct a home in Park City, Utah, because he was moving his family there and would divide his time between the two locations and the extensive international travel his job required.[449] Mr. Belnick got Mr. Kozlowski's approval for both loans, but he didn't do the corporate paperwork for relocation.

Mr. Belnick told friends from the time that he began his work with Tyco that he was uncomfortable because he was not in the loop with information from either Mr. Kozlowski or the board. However, Mr. Kozlowski offered him more lucrative contracts and additional loans, and Mr. Belnick remained on board.[450] However, there are e-mails from Tyco's outside counsel, the Wilmer Cutler firm, that indicate some information was seeping through to Mr. Belnick, and that outside counsel had concerns that were kept silent once transmitted to Mr. Belnick. For example, on March 23, 2000, partner Lewis Liman at Wilmer Cutler sent an e-mail to Mr. Belnick that read, "There are payments to a woman whom the folks in finance describe as Dennis's girlfriend. I do not know Dennis's situation, but this is an embarrassing fact."[451]

During the same period, CFO Swartz availed himself of $85 million of KELP loans. However, he used only $13 million for payment of taxes and spent the remaining

---

[447] In an 8-K filed with the SEC on September 17, 2002, Tyco outlined the loans, the spending, and its plans for the future. The 8-K is available at http://www.sec.gov/edgar. A synopsis of the information filed in the 8-K is available at http://www.tyco.com under "press releases."

[448] The rate as disclosed in the 2002 proxy was 6.24 percent.

[449] Nicholas Varchaver, "Fall from Grace, Fortune, October 28, 2002, pp. 112, 115. Amy Borrus, Mike McNamee, Williams Symonds, Nanette Byrnes, and Andrew Park, "Reform: Business Gets Religion," Business Week Online, February 3, 2003, http://www.businessweek.com. Jonathan D. Glater, "A Star Lawyer Finds Himself the Target of a Peer," The New York Times, September 24, 2002, p. C1.

[450] Jonathan D. Glater, "A Star Lawyer Finds Himself the Target of a Peer," The New York Times, September 24, 2002, pp. C1, C8.

[451] Laurie P. Cohen and Mark Maremont, "E-Mails Show Tyco's Lawyers Had Concerns," The Wall Street Journal, December 27, 2002, p. C1.

$72 million for personal investments, business ventures, real estate holdings, and trusts.[452] Mr. Swartz used more than $32 million of interest-free relocation loans, and, according to SEC documents, used almost $9 million of those relocation loans for purposes not authorized under the program, including purchasing a yacht and investing in real estate.[453]

Patricia Prue, the vice president for HR at Tyco and the one responsible for processing the paperwork for the forgiveness of the officers' loans, and who had bene-fitted from the loan forgiveness program herself, approached Mr. Kozlowski in September 2000 and asked for documentation that the board had indeed approved all the loan forgiveness for which she was doing the paperwork. Mr. Kozlowski, without ever producing board minutes, wrote a memo to Ms. Prue: "A decision has been made to forgive the relocation loans for those individuals whose efforts were instrumental to successfully completing the TyCom I.P.O."[454] Ms. Prue had received a loan of $748,309, had the loan forgiven, and then was given $521,087 to pay the taxes on the loan forgiveness.[455] Ms. Prue's bonuses totaled $13,534,523, and she was given $9,424,815 to pay the taxes on the bonuses.[456]

The issue of board approval on the loans remains a question, but compensation committee minutes from February 21, 2002, show that the committee was given a list of loans to officers and also approved Mr. Belnick's new compensation package. There was no public disclosure of these developments or the committee's review.[457] In grand jury testimony, Patricia Prue, who testified in exchange for immunity from prosecu-tion, indicated that board member Joshua Berman pressured her in June 2002 to change the minutes from that February compensation committee meeting.[458] Mr. Berman denies the allegation. However, Ms. Prue did send a memo on June 7, 2002, to John Fort, Mr. Swartz, and the board's governance committee with the following included: "As a result of the fact that I was recently pressured by Josh Berman to engage in conduct which I regarded as dishonest—and which I have refused to do—I will decline to have any personal contact with him in the future. In addition, I ask that Josh not go to my staff with any requests for information or directions."[459]

Mr. Kozlowski paid $56 million in bonuses to executives eligible for the KELP program, then gave them $39 million to pay the taxes on the bonuses, and then forgave the KELP loans given to pay taxes on the shares awarded in addition to the bonuses.

[452] http://www.sec.gov/releases/litigation. The SEC has also filed suit against Mr. Swartz, seeking the return of these funds. Mr. Swartz was also indicted by the state of New York and spent some time in jail as his family scrambled to post his bail.

[453] http://www.sec.gov/releases/litigation. These exhibits and lists are found in the 8-K for September 17, 2002, at http://www.sec.gov/edgar. Andrew Ross Sorkin and Jonathan D. Glater, "Tyco Planning to Disclose Making Loans to Employees," The New York Times, September 16, 2002, p. C1; "Ex-Chief of Tyco Posts $10 Million in Bail," The New York Times, September 21, 2002, p. B14.

[454] Id. Kevin McCoy, "Kozlowski's Statement in Question," USA Today, January 9, 2002, p. 1B.

[455] Andrew Ross Sorkin, "Tyco Details Lavish Lives of Executives," The New York Times, September 18, 2002, pp. C1, C6.

[456] "Helping Fatcats Dodge the Taxman," Business Week Online, June 20, 2002. http://www.businessweek.com.

[457] Andrew Ross Sorkin and Jonathan D. Glater, "Some Tyco Board Members Knew of Pay Packages, Records Show," The New York Times, September 23, 2002, p. A1. Mr. Belnick was fired before he was indicted on felony charges. Laurie P. Cohen, "Tyco Ex-Counsel Claims Auditors Knew of Loans," The Wall Street Journal, October 22, 2002, p. A6.

[458] Id., p. A22.

[459] Id., p. A22. Both sides acknowledge the authenticity of the memo from Ms. Prue.

A report commissioned by the Tyco board following the Kozlowski departure refers to the Tyco culture as one of greed and deception designed to ensure personal enrichment.[460]

The relocation loan program was a source of $46 million for Mr. Kozlowksi, and SEC documents allege that he "used at least $28 million of those relocation loans to purchase, among other things, luxury properties in New Hampshire, Nantucket, and Connecticut as well as a $7 million Park Avenue apartment for his then (now former) wife."[461]

Mr. Kozlowski's officer team was small and obedient.[462] Tyco had only 400 employees at its central offices and Kozlowksi only interacted with a few, a means of keeping information close to the vest.[463] Mark Swartz, Tyco's former CFO, was 40 years old at the time of Tyco's fall and his indictment on 38 counts of grand larceny, conspiracy, and falsifying business records.[464] Tyco hired him in 1991, away from Deloitte & Touche's due diligence team. By 1993, he was head of Tyco's acquisitions team, and by 1995, he was Tyco's CFO, at age 33. Mr. Kozlowski nominated Mr. Swartz for a CFO award that year, and *CFO Magazine* honored Mr. Swartz with its 2000 Excellence Award.[465] Indeed, Mr. Kozlowski and Mr. Swartz were inextricably intertwined, with Mr. Swartz even serving as trustee for one of Mr. Kozlowski's trusts for holding title to real property.[466] Both men also used a loophole in securities law to sell millions of shares of Tyco stock even as they declared publicly that they were not selling their shares in the company.[467]

Tyco's Fall

Mr. Kozlowski and Mr. Swartz were indicted under New York state laws for stealing $170 million from the company and for profiting $430 million by selling off their shares while withholding information from the public about the true financial condition of Tyco.[468] The charges against the two were based on a state law that prohibits a criminal enterprise, a type of crime generally associated with organized crime. Their joint trial began in October 2003 and ran until April 2004, when the case ended in a bizarre mistrial. When the jury began deliberations, one juror, Ruth Jordan, was labeled by some of her fellow jurors as a holdout who refused to deliberate the case. Some courtroom observers felt that Ms. Jordan had flashed an "OK" hand signal to the defendants and their counsel.[469] The judge urged the jurors to continue deliberating despite obvious rancor. Ms. Jordan came to be labeled "holdout granny" and "batty

---

[460] Andrew Ross Sorkin, "Tyco Details Lavish Lives of Executives," The New York Times, September 18, 2002, p. C1. These bonuses are from the year 2000. Kevin McCoy, "Tyco Spent Millions on Exec Perks, Records Say," USA Today, September 17, 2002, p. 1B.

[461] Id. Laurie P. Cohen, "Ex-Tyco CEO's Ex to Post $10 Million for His Bail Bond," The Wall Street Journal, September 20, 2002, p. A5.

[462] Alex Berenson, "Ex-Tyco Chief, a Big Risk Taker, Now Confronts the Legal System," The New York Times, June 10, 2002, p. B1.

[463] Anthony Bianco, William Symonds, Nanette Byrnes, and David Polek, "The Rise and Fall of Dennis Kozlowski," Business Week Online, December 23, 2002, http://www.businessweek.com.

[464] Nicholas Varchaver, "Fall from Grace," Fortune, October 28, 2002, pp. 112, 114. Andrew Ross Sorkin, "2 Top Tyco Executives Charged with $600 Million Fraud Scheme," The New York Times, September 13, 2002, pp. A1, C3.

[465] Id.

[466] Alex Berenson, "From Dream Team at Tyco to a Refrain of Dennis Who?" The New York Times, June 6, 2002, p. C1.

[467] Id., pp. C1, C5.

[468] Andrew Ross Sorkin, "Ex-Tyco Chief, Free Spender, Going to Court," The New York Times, September 29, 2003, pp. A1, A15.

[469] David Carr and Adam Liptak, "In Tyco Trial, an Apparent Gesture Has Many Meanings," The New York Times, March 29, 2004, pp. C1, C6.

blueblood" in the media.[470] However, several media outlets published her name (one with a photo), and when she reported to the judge that she had received a threat, the judge declared a mistrial.[471] The thrust of the defense was that everything Mr. Kozlowski and Mr. Swartz did was in the open, with board approval, and therefore did not fit the requirements for a criminal enterprise.[472]

Mr. Belnick was also indicted and tried, and was acquitted of all charges.[473]

....

Discussion Questions

1. Recall your readings from Unit 2 on the relationship between ethics and economics. How did Tyco's initial problems establish this connection as a very real one for the U.S. markets? What made Tyco's stock price fall initially? Evaluate this comment from a market observer: "When a CEO steps down for (alleged) tax evasion, it sends the message that all of Corporate America is crooked."[474] "It makes you think, 'Why did he do it? Is there another shoe to drop?'"[475]

2. Warren Rudman, former U.S. Senator and a member of the board at Raytheon, who knew and worked with Mark Belnick, was astonished at Mr. Belnick's indictment when it was issued. Mr. Rudman said, when told of Mr. Belnick's fall from grace: "I don't understand. Ethical, straight, cross the t's, dot the I's—that's my experience with Mark Belnick."[476] Mr. Belnick was acquitted of all charges after a jury trial in the summer of 2004. Does his acquittal mean that he acted ethically? What ethical breaches can you find in his behavior at Tyco?

3. What do you think of the ethics of Ms. Prue?

4. How do you think the spending and the loans were able to go on for so long?

5. What questions could Mr. Kozlowski and Mr. Swartz have asked themselves to better evaluate their conduct?

6. What do you think of the mistrials and acquittal? Do these show that the defendants did nothing unethical? Why or why not?

....
CASE 6.15
....

Nortel: Restatements during Restatements of Earnings

Nortel, a Canadian telecommunications firm, has the unique status of being a company involved in restating its current earnings while in the process of restating its past earnings. Nortel had to restate its 2004 earnings in the midst of ongoing restatement activity

---

[470] Id.

[471] Andrew Ross Sorkin, "Judge Ends Trial When Tyco Juror Reports Threat," The New York Times, April 3, 2004, pp. A1, B4. "Mistrials and Tribulations," Fortune, April 19, 2004, p. 42.

[472] Jonathan D. Glater, "Tyco Case Shows Difficulty of Deciding Criminal Intent," The New York Times, April 8, 2004, pp. C1, C4.

[473] "Ex-Tyco Official Says Actions Were Proper," The New York Times, June 26, 2004, p. B14.

[474] Id.

[475] Adam Shell, "Markets Fall as Tyco CEO's Resignation Adds to Woes," USA Today, June 4, 2002, p. 1B.

[476] Joanthan D. Glater, "A Star Lawyer Finds Himself the Target of a Peer," The New York Times, September 24, 2002, pp. C1, C8.

for 2001, 2002, and 2003.[477] Nortel had 95,000 workers in 2001, and would have 30,000 workers after completing its latest 10 percent downsizing, which was announced along with an admission that 2004 results would need to be restated. These announcements followed the April 2004 announcement of earnings restatements for 2003, which would cut half of the company's $732 million (U.S. dollars) profits.[478] The final numbers were to be released no later than October 31, 2004, although there were indications the company might beat that deadline. New officers explained that the accounting issues related "release to income of certain accruals and provisions in prior periods."[479] There was also ongoing assurance that the company was taking its time to be certain it explored all the details and got the numbers right.

Discussion Questions

1. How does a company, already chastised by markets and auditors, for its inflated numbers, manage to do the same thing even as it is completing the correction and repentance for the earlier offenses?

2. If you were put in charge of the company, what would you do? How would you make sure the financial reports were accurate and complete?

CASE 6.16

Compensation-Fueled Dishonesty: Fraud to Get Results

Joseph Jett earned his Harvard master's degree in business administration in 1987.[480] Dismissed from his first post-degree job at CS First Boston, he then worked for Morgan Stanley but was laid off in the post-1980s Wall Street cutbacks. Despite his lack of experience in government securities, Jett was hired in 1991 by Kidder Peabody & Company to work in the government bonds section of its fixed-income department.

The fixed-income department was headed by Edward A. Cerullo, an exceptionally bright, hands-off manager who emphasized profits and was credited with turning Kidder around following the late-1980s insider trading scandals. Some fixed-income traders so feared telling Cerullo of losses that they underreported their profits at certain times so that they would have reserves to cover any future losses.

At the time of Cerullo's tenure and Jett's employment, Kidder Peabody was owned by General Electric (GE), which had purchased it in 1986 for $602 million. To establish Kidder as a Wall Street force, GE poured $1 billion into the firm and had begun to see a return only from 1991 to 1994. In 1992, GE had tried to sell Kidder to Smith Barney,

---

[477] Simon Avery, "Nortel Fires 7, Slashes Jobs as It Refocuses Its Operations," The Globe and Mail, August 20, 2004, pp. B1, B4.
[478] Simon Avery, "Restated 2004 Nortel Results Set for Release," The Globe and Mail, August 19, 2004, p. B3.
[479] Roma Luciv, "Nortel May Beat Deadline," The Globe and Mail, September 13, 2004, p. B1.
[480] Because of a balance on his tuition bill, he did not receive his degree until 1994. In June 1994, he paid the balance due on his tuition, and Harvard processed his degree.

Harris Upham & Company, but the sale fell through when Smith Barney learned of the extent of Kidder's mortgage-backed bond inventory.

Jett's initial performance in the bonds section was poor: he lost money. Fellow traders recalled Jett's first months on the job as demonstrating his lack of knowledge; some questioned whether Jett should have been hired at all. Even when Jett began earning profits, his reputation remained mediocre. "I don't think he knew the market. He made mistakes a rookie would make," said a former Kidder trader who worked in the 750-member fixed-income section with Jett.

Hugh Bush, a trader at Kidder, raised questions when he examined Jett's trades. In April 1992, Bush accused Jett of "mismarking" or misrecording trading positions, an illegal practice. Bush's allegations were never investigated, and he was fired within a month.

In 1991, Linda LaPrade sued Kidder, claiming that she was terminated as a vice president when she brought illegal trading to the attention of Cerullo. She also claimed she was told to increase allotments from government agency security issuers by "any means necessary."

Also in 1991, the National Association of Securities Dealers (NASD) fined Kidder and Cerullo $5,000 for conduct by one of Kidder's bond traders, Ira Saferstein, who profited from a customer error.[481]

During this same period, Jett's profits bulged to 20 percent of the fixed-income group's total, and he was made head of the government bond department. Jett's profits, however, did not exist. Jett had taken advantage of an accounting loophole at Kidder that enabled him to earn a $9 million bonus for 1993 alone. The fictitious profits were posted through an accounting system that separated out the interest portion of the bond. Jett captured the profit on the "strip" (the interest portion of the bond) before it was reconstituted or turned back into the original bond. Kidder's system recognized profits on the date that the reconstituted bond was entered into the system. The result was that over two and one-half years, Jett generated $350 million in fictitious profits. When the scheme was uncovered by auditors in April 1994, GE had to take a $210 million write-off in its second quarter.

On April 17, 1994, Jett was fired, his bonus and accounts frozen, and the SEC began an investigation. Kidder hired Gary G. Lynch, a lawyer and former head of enforcement at the SEC, to conduct an inquiry into the losses and Jett's conduct.

As Lynch's inquiry progressed and the SEC stepped in, the casualties at Kidder began and continued in a steady stream:

- June 22, 1994: GE fired Kidder CEO Michael Carpenter.
- July 14, 1994: Kidder's brokerage chief, Michael Kechner, quit.
- July 22, 1994: Cerullo quit.
- August 4, 1994: Kidder fired three additional trading managers.

In December 1994, GE sold Kidder to Paine Webber for $670 million. The sale required GE to take a $917 million loss on the value of Kidder's assets and a $500 million

---

[481] Cerullo said of the Saferstein incident, "The guy did something we told him not to. He did it again, and we fired him on the spot. He did the trade, and I got smacked."

write-off for the fourth quarter of 1994. GE's income dropped 48 percent for the quarter or about 45 cents per share. About half of Kidder Peabody's 5,000 employees would be laid off following completion of the deal.

A group of GE shareholders sued GE for the loss in share value resulting from the Kidder problems, the write-off, and the subsequent sale of Kidder for a loss.

Lynch determined that Jett acted alone: "The obvious motive for this effort was to achieve a degree of recognition and compensation that had previously eluded Jett in his professional career." Lynch added that the fraud was not detected because Jett's immediate supervisors did not understand the nature of his trading activities. Their failure to review trade tickets allowed Jett to perpetrate his fraud. Lynch concluded with what he called a simple message: "You have to understand how people are making money."

When the logistics of the fraud were explained, GE Chairman John F. (Jack)Welch, Jr., said, "It's a pity that this ever happened. Jett could have made $2 to 3 million honestly."

Mr. Jett did file a $25 million libel suit against Kidder, Peabody, and its lawyers and officers. However, the papers were not served on any of the defendants perhaps because such litigation would permit unlimited discovery and questioning of Mr. Jett.

In early January 1996, the SEC filed civil administrative charges against Jett. Mr. Jett responded by saying, "I am completely innocent of these charges against me—I will not allow people to condemn me wrongly."

Edward Cerullo was charged with the failure to supervise. Mr. Cerullo settled and agreed to a one-year suspension as well as a fine of $50,000.

Mr. Jett decided to fight the charges and said, "Kidder and GE have taken my name and dragged it through the mud. They have robbed me of two of the most productive years of my life." Mr. Jett gave up his apartment and has lived with friends. Kidder permitted him to take $150,000 he had in his retirement account, and he has worked hauling furniture for $8 per hour. Mr. Jett says he gave $2 million of the money to his parents. In late 1996, a panel of NASD arbitrators agreed to release $1 million from Jett's brokerage account that had been frozen.

In a 1996 interview on CBS's *60 Minutes*, Gary Lynch was asked if there was any chance Mr. Jett was innocent. Mr. Lynch responded, "There's no chance." However, *Business Week* did produce an opinion piece on Joseph Jett and referred to the SEC case as "flimsy."

At Mr. Jett's June 1996 hearing, he testified, using his computer diary, that management knew about his bond-trading strategy. The alleged scheme was one of using government strips or securities that were created by peeling away and repackaging the interest payments on 30-year government bonds. One expert explained it as changing $1 into four quarters. There is a change in structure, but there are no revenues, and Mr. Jett was booking the changes as revenues.

Following Mr. Jett's hearing, the SEC filed a brief in the matter accusing Mr. Jett of introducing "bogus diary entries" from his computer. Mr. Jett had introduced twenty diary entries at his hearing to show management knowledge. However, only five of those entries matched entries retrieved from the master computer files of

Kidder and obtained by the SEC. A federal judge found Mr. Jett more credible than many of the GE witnesses who testified against him, and the National Association of Securities Dealers (NASD) ordered GE to return nearly $6 million in bonuses that GE had confiscated from Mr. Jett when the SEC investigation began. The U.S. Attorney's office did not indict Mr. Jett for any crimes. He represented himself before the SEC at the agency's hearing on his request for reinstatement in February 2004. However, the SEC fined Mr. Jett for records violations. Mr. Jett has appealed those sanctions as well as his banishment by the SEC from the securities industry. On March 5, 2004, the SEC upheld its banishment of Mr. Jett and ordered him to pay back $8,210,000 in profits and $200,000 in civil penalties.[482] An excerpt of the decision follows:

> We find that Jett's purported trading strategy deceived Kidder about the profitability of his securities trading. Jett created and implemented a scheme that exploited an anomaly in Kidder's computer system. The scheme generated "profits" on the firm's books that transformed Jett's failed securities trading into an apparent success. As a result, Kidder doubled Jett's salary, promoted him, and paid him multi-million-dollar bonuses. These "profits" misrepresented Kidder's financial condition on firm books, records, and regulatory filings, and would have to be written off, at firm expense. When inventory constraints during the balance sheet reduction effort impinged on his scheme, Jett himself claims he adapted it by developing and implementing the idea of "offsetting" recons, which allowed him to continue to book illusory profits. This was a scheme devised and orchestrated by Jett for his benefit.

> Jett argues that he disclosed the facts about his "trading strategy" to Mullin, Cerullo, some of their subordinates, such as Bernstein, and an internal auditor, that they could have learned the facts from various firm documents or reports, and that they benefitted from the profits Jett booked. Mullin, Cerullo, Bernstein, and the auditor testified that they did not know about Jett's scheme. The Division argues that Jett's representations to others constituted more deception and that the documents and reports did not alert others to the nature and source of Jett's "profits."

> The law judge found the Division's witnesses to be more credible than Jett's contrary claims. Specifically, the judge found that neither Jett's supervisors nor the firm understood the source of Jett's "profits." Further, the judge found that "Jett knew that Kidder had not approved and did not know the source of his profits."

> Based on our own de novo review, we find that Jett deceived the firm. In making this finding, we by no means suggest that others at Kidder are without blame with respect to Jett's activities. As noted at the outset of this opinion, the Commission found in separate settled orders imposing sanctions that Jett's supervisors, Mullin and Cerullo, failed reasonably to supervise Jett with a view to preventing his securities law violations. Nor do we suggest that Kidder, which had ceased to exist by the time of those sanctions, acted in an exemplary fashion. Rather, our finding concerns Jett's own culpability and is that Jett defrauded the firm.

> Like the law judge, we think that on these facts it is highly implausible that numerous Kidder personnel fully understood Jett's strategy, as he asserts, but let hundreds of millions

---

[482] http://www.sec.gov/litigation/opinions/33-8395.htm. Accessed October 21, 2004.

of dollars in imaginary profits build up and continue to grow over time until, inevitably, they were revealed, with predictably negative consequences for Kidder's (and its parent GE's) balance sheet. Moreover, we have exhaustively examined the record and the Division's and Jett's conflicting claims regarding what Jett told others, what his statements meant, what various documents or data conveyed, and what the others at the firm understood. We give considerable weight to the law judge's credibility determinations, which are based on hearing the witnesses' testimonies and observing their demeanor.

The evidence shows that Jett claimed to others that his huge profits derived from various forms of legitimate trading, including "making [the] bid/offer spread," "making markets for customers," increasing "the volume of customer business," trading in the long (30-year) bond, basis and yield curve trading, and strip/recon "arbitrage." Jett even asserted that "every which way in which the [yield] curve could move, we're on the right side of the spread relations." Jett never mentioned that GT recorded profits automatically on the trade date when he entered a forward recon, or otherwise identified the so-called "time-related" component of his purported arbitrage trading strategy. Nor did Jett ever, until the investigation of his activities in late March 1994, adequately explain his "three-part strategy."[483]

Mr. Jett's latest book, *Broken Bonds: My Immoderate Life of Love, Passion, War on Affirmative Action and Jack Welch's GE*, was released two weeks after his SEC hearing on his reinstatement.[484] Ironically, his book was released on the same day as Mr. Welch's second book on effective management.

....

Discussion Questions

1. An executive noted that Wall Street firms "have become victims of compensation schemes resulting in outrageously high salaries and bonuses. It brings out the worst in people who have any worst in them." Are compensation schemes responsible for poor ethical choices? Does a firm establish an ethical tone or culture with its compensation system? Should the jump in revenues from Jett's unit from 6 percent to 27 percent have triggered an investigation?

2. Cerullo earned an estimated $20 million in compensation during the time of Jett's alleged scam. In other words, he enjoyed increased compensation if Jett did well.

   Consider this rap song, "Requiem Rap at Kidder P Blow," that circulated around Kidder during its final pre-sale days:

   Big Boss and Joe went skiing in the snow:

   He said, Joe, what you're doing, don't wanna know;

   But, keep on doing it, doing it though,

   'Cause I am the Main Man at Kidder P Blow.

   . . . Then one month Kidder P took a double blow;

   Joe's profits were phony, the Man said so;

---

[483] Id.

[484] Mr. Jett's first book was Black and White on Wall Street, *published in 1999.*

And the Fed jacked rates so the economy'd slow;

April was the cruelest month at Kidder P Blow.

. . . GE aimed all the blame at Ed Curello [sic]

He was the man who'd let the boys go.

To Joe and the V-Man he never said no.

'Twas the worst of times at Kidder P Blow.

   Jett maintains his supervisors knew what he was doing, directed his trading, and used the profits to deflect scrutiny from Kidder's mortgage bond problems. Even if his supervisors did not know, did they not want to know? Is it an ethical violation to ignore signals?

3. What parts of the GE-Kidder culture and circumstances contributed to the "do what is necessary" ethical posture?

4. Why were Bush's and LaPrade's allegations so readily dismissed? Why were they fired?

5. Lynch's report concluded that the attitude in the Kidder bond department was "never question success," and that no one was willing to ask hard questions about Jett's ever-increasing profits. Were other employees enjoying the success too much? What ethical breaches did they commit by ignoring the implausibility of the success?

6. Lynch's report noted that some Kidder employees had questions about Jett's trading but "were reluctant or unsure how to report their concerns despite the existence of legal and compliance departments and an ombudsman." What could Kidder Peabody have done to eliminate such hesitancy?

7. List all the lives affected and harm resulting from Jett's conduct.

8. Mr. Jett is now an off-shore hedge-fund trader. Does he violate the spirit of the SEC sanctions against him?

CASE 6.17

The Ethics of Bankruptcy

In 1980, there were 287,570 personal bankruptcies filed in the United States. In 1996, the number of personal bankruptcies topped 1 million for the first time in history. In 2001, the number of bankruptcies reached 1.5 million.[485] That number translates to a bankruptcy for 1 of every 100 households in the United States. The rate of bankruptcy filing in the United States for 1996 was eight times higher than the bankruptcy rate during the Great Depression.[486]

---

[485] http://www.abiworld.org/research/yearreview
[486] Christine Dugas, "Credit Card Delinquencies Near Record," USA Today, September 18, 1997, p. B1.

The federal judiciary has issued its annual report on bankruptcy in the United States. The following data provide indications of trends in filings for bankruptcy:

Year	Total bankruptcy filings	
	Total business	**Total nonbusiness**
2004 (through June)	35,739	1,599,986
2003	36,183	1,625,813
2002	39,091	1,508,578
2001	29,872	1,117,216
2000	35,472	1,217,972
1999	44,367	1,281,581
1998	44,367	1,398,182
1997	54,027	1,350,118
1996	53,549	1,124,006
1995	51,959	874,642

http://www.uscourts.gov/bankruptcy

The number-one reason for bankruptcy declaration for the past three years was not loss of job or health problems or divorce.[487] Nearly 30 percent of all bankruptcy filings were attributed by the petitioner to simply being "overextended."[488] Over 70 percent of those filing for personal bankruptcy chose Chapter 7, or full bankruptcy, as opposed to Chapter 13 for a consumer debt adjustment plan.[489]

Most consumer debt is owed by those who earn between $50,000 and $100,000 a year. As one lender remarked, "These are people who could afford to save and buy later." (Consumer installment debt is at 85 percent of disposable income—an increase of 23 percent in the past decade.)[490]

Current laws are perhaps too permissive and make the declaration of bankruptcy very easy and very tempting. Changing the laws and requiring different standards could hamper investment, yet the average loss of $11,000 in debt write-off per bankruptcy costs each family in the United States $100 in higher prices as creditors try to cover the losses of bankruptcy.[491]

Bankruptcy declarations became a sore spot and a source of congressional hearings and proposed bankruptcy reforms in 1999, with legislation still pending as of March 2002. By 2001, the average amount of total debt for those consumers declaring bankruptcy was $82,852. The amount of debt that was not secured by collateral was $40,654

[487] Damon Darlin, "The Newest American Entitlement," Forbes, September 8, 1997, p. 113.
[488] Christine Dugas, "Non-Mortgage Debts Top Income for Millions," USA Today, October 2, 1997, p. B1.
[489] Fred Waddell, "Easy Credit: A Wall Around the Poor," The New York Times, February 15, 1998, p. BU12.
[490] Timothy L. O'Brien, "Giving Credit Where Debt is Due," The New York Times, December 14, 1997, p. 14.
[491] Gregory Zuckerman, "Borrowing Levels Reach Record High," The Tribune, July 9, 2000, pp. B1, B2.

(includes credit card and medical debt). Other information about the average consumer bankruptcy declarant:

- Owes $2,528 in back child support
- Owes $38,760 on car loans and mortgage
- Has net income of $21,444
- Has total annual expenses of $24,324[492]

An issue that attracted Congressional attention was the homestead exemption in bankruptcy. Under this exemption, those who declare bankruptcy are able, under federal and state laws, to keep a portion or all of the equity in their home after emerging from bankruptcy. The examples that emerged during the hearings were that of corporate raider Paul A. Bilzerian being able to emerge from bankruptcy in Florida with his $5 million home because of Florida's rather generous homestead exemption. He had over $300 million in debts. Mr. Bilzerian served 20 months in federal prison following his conviction for securities crimes. Mr. Bilzerian graduated from Harvard Business School and was best known for his hostile takeover of Singer, the sewing machine company.[493]

Actor Burt Reynolds also emerged as an example because he was able to keep his $2.5 million home and estate, called Valhalla. After he declared bankruptcy in 1996, Mr. Reynolds had $10 million in debts.[494]

As noted in Case 6.10, Scott Sullivan also used Florida's protections. Some experts have noted that the bankruptcy process is being used for strategic planning and a way to avoid contracts.[495] The following examples illustrate:

TLC was an Atlanta rhythm, blues, and hip-hop band that performed at clubs in 1991. The three-woman group signed a recording contract with LaFace Records. The group's first album that LaFace produced—"Oooooooohhh . . . on the TLC Tip" in 1992—sold almost three million albums. The group's second album, "Crazysexycool," also produced by LaFace, sold five million albums through June 1996. The two albums together had six top-of-the-chart singles.

LaFace had the right to renew TLC's contract in 1996 following renegotiation of the contract terms. Royalty rates in the industry for unknown groups, as TLC was in 1991, are generally 7 percent of the revenues for the first 500,000 albums, and 8 percent for sales on platinum albums (albums that sell over one million copies). The royalty rate increases to 9.5 percent for all sales on an eighth album.

Established artists in the industry who renegotiate often have royalty rates of 13 percent, and artists with two platinum albums can command an even higher royalty.

The three women in TLC, Tionne Watkins (T-Boz), Lisa Lopes (Left-Eye), and Romanda Thomas (Chili), declared bankruptcy in July 1995. All three listed debts that exceeded their assets, which included sums owed to creditors for their cars and to Zale's and The Limited for credit purchases. Lopes was sued by Lloyd's of London, which claimed Lopes owed

---

[492] Peter T. Kilborn, "Mired in Debt and Seeking a Path Out," *The New York Times*, April 1, 2001, pp. A1, A16.
[493] Philip Shenon, "Home Exemptions Snag Bankruptcy Bill," *The New York Times*, April 6, 2001, pp. A1, A15.
[494] Id.
[495] Jeff Bailey and Scott Kilman, "Here's What's Driving Some Lenders Crazy: Borrowers Who Think," *The Wall Street Journal*, February 20, 1998, p. A1.

was it $1.3 million it paid on a policy held by her boyfriend on his home. Lopes pleaded guilty to one count of arson in the destruction of the home but denied that she intended to destroy the house.

Lopes asked that the Lloyd's claim be discharged in her bankruptcy. All three members of TLC asked that their contract with LaFace be discharged in bankruptcy because being bound to their old contract could impede their fresh financial starts. The issue for Ms. Lopes became moot when she was killed in a car accident in 2002.

During 1996 the members of three music groups declared bankruptcy just before their contracts were due for renegotiation. One record company executive has noted that record company owners are frightened by the trend: "You invest all the money and time in making them stars. Then they leave for the bigger companies and a higher take on sales. It has all of us scared."[496]

Pop singer Billy Joel also had a record contract with a small company during the initial stages of his career. When the company refused, during renegotiations, to increase his royalty rate, Joel did not produce another album during the period of the contract renewal option. Instead, he used a clause in the contract that limited him to night club and "piano bar" appearances in the event another album was not produced. For three years, Joel played small clubs and restaurants and did not produce an album. At the end of that period when his contract had expired, he negotiated a contract with Columbia. His first album with Columbia was "Piano Man," a multi-platinum album.[497]

Discussion Questions

1. Do the three women meet the standards for declaring bankruptcy? Evaluate whether Lopes's Lloyd's claim should have been discharged. Determine whether the record contract should have been discharged.

2. Is declaring bankruptcy by the members of these musical groups legal? Is it ethical? Are the musicians using bankruptcy as a way to avoid contract obligations? Are the musicians using bankruptcy as a way to maximize their income?

3. Did Joel take an ethical route? Is his solution more ethical than bankruptcy?

4. Is there a presumption of good faith built into the bankruptcy code?

5. What about millionaires who declare bankruptcy and keep their homes? Is their conduct ethical?

[496] Laura M. Holson, "Music Stars Complain About Stringent Contracts," The New York Times, September 6, 2001, pp. C1, C12.

[497] Reprinted from Anderson's Business Law: The Regulatory Environment, 14th ed., 2001, p. 658.

Business Operations: Workplace Safety Risks, Systems, and International Operations

THIS SEGMENT OF THE BOOK COVERS ISSUES that involve something other than financial reports, accounting, or planning. This unit deals with safety risks and systems in the workplace as well as the implications of international operations.

7^A

Conflicts between the Corporation's Ethics and Business Practices in Foreign Countries

Although we have a global market, we do not have global safety laws, ethical standards, or cultural customs. Businesses face many dilemmas as they decide whether to conform to the varying standards of their host nations or to attempt to operate with universal (global) standards. What we would call a bribe and illegal activity in the United States may be culturally acceptable and necessary in another country. Could you participate in such a practice?

READING 7.1
....
Why an International Code of Ethics Would Be Good for Business[1]

The global market presents firms with more complex ethical issues than they would experience if operations were limited to one country and one culture. Moral standards vary across cultures. In some cases, cultures change and evolve to accept conduct that was not previously acceptable. For example, it is permissible in India for donors to sell body organs for transplantation. Residents of India have sold their kidneys to buy televisions or just to improve their standard of living. In the United States, the buying and selling of organs by individuals is not permitted, but recently experts have called for such a system as a means of resolving the supply-and-demand dilemma that exists because of limited availability of donors and a relative excess of needy recipients.

In many executive training seminars for international business, executives are taught to honor customs in other countries and to "Do as the Romans do." Employees are often

---

[1] *This material was adapted from Larry Smeltzer and Marianne M. Jennings, "Why an International Code of Business Ethics Would Be Good for Business," Journal of Business Ethics 17: 57 (1998).*

confused by this direction. A manager for a U.S. title insurer provides a typical example. He complained that if he tipped employees in the U.S. public-recording agencies for expediting property filings, the manager would not only be violating the company's code of ethics but could also be charged with violations of the Real Estate Settlement Procedures Act and state and federal antibribery provisions. Yet, that same type of practice is permitted, recognized, and encouraged in other countries as a cost of doing business. Paying a regulatory agency in the United States to expedite a licensing process would be considered bribery of a public official. Yet, many businesses maintain that they cannot obtain such authorizations to do business in other countries unless such payments are made. So-called grease or facilitation payments are permitted under the Foreign Corrupt Practices Act, but legality does not necessarily make such payments ethical.

An inevitable question arises when custom and culture clash with ethical standards and moral values adopted by a firm. Should the national culture or the company code of ethics be the controlling factor?

Typical business responses to the question of whether cultural norms or company codes of ethics should take precedence in international business operations are the following: Who am I to question the culture of another country? Who am I to impose U.S. standards on all the other nations of the world? Isn't legality the equivalent of ethical behavior? The attitude of businesses is one that permits ethical deviations in the name of cultural sensitivity. Many businesses fear that the risk of offending is far too high to impose U.S. ethical standards on the conduct of business in other countries.

Tip: One of the misunderstandings of U.S.-based businesses is that ethical standards in the United States vary significantly from the ethical standards in other countries. Operating under this misconception can create a great deal of ethical confusion among employees. What is known as the "Golden Rule" in the United States actually has existed for some time in other religions and cultures and among philosophers. Following is a list of how this simple rule is phrased in different writings. The principle is the same even if the words vary slightly. Strategically, businesses and their employees are more comfortable when they operate under uniform standards. This simple rule may provide them with that standard.

Categorical Imperative: How would you want to be treated?

Would you be comfortable with a world in which your standards were followed?

Christian Principle: The Golden Rule

> *And as ye would that men should do to you, do ye also to them likewise.*
> —LUKE 6:31

> *Thou shalt love . . . thy neighbor as thyself.*
> —LUKE 10:27

Confucius:

> *What you do not want done to yourself, do not do to others.*

Aristotle:

We should behave to our friends as we wish our friends to behave to us.

Judaism:

What you hate, do not do to anyone.

Buddhism:

Hurt not others with that which pains thyself.

Islam:

No one of you is a believer until he loves for his brother what he loves for himself.

Hinduism:

Do nothing to thy neighbor which thou wouldst not have him do to thee.

Sikhism:

Treat others as you would be treated yourself.

Plato:

May I do to others as I would that they should do unto me.

The successful operation of commerce is dependent on an ethical business foundation. A look at the three major parties in business explains this point. These parties are the risk-takers, the employees, and the customers. Risk-takers—those furnishing the capital necessary for production—are willing to take risks on the assumption that their products will be judged by customers' assessment of their value. Employees are willing to offer production input, skills, and ideas in exchange for wages, rewards, and other incentives. Consumers and customers are willing to purchase products and services so long as they receive value in exchange for their furnishing, through payment, income and profits to the risk-takers and employers. To the extent that the interdependency of the parties in the system is affected by factors outside of their perceived roles and control, the intended business system does not function on its underlying assumptions.

The business system is, in short, an economic system endorsed by society that allows risk-takers, employees, and customers to allocate scarce resources to competing ends. Although the roots of business have been described as primarily economic, this economic system cannot survive without recognition of some fundamental values. Some of the inherent—indeed, universal—values built into our capitalistic economic system, as described here, are as follows: (1) the consumer is given value in exchange for the funds expended; (2) employees are rewarded according to their contribution to production; and (3) the risk-takers are rewarded for their investment in the form of a return on that investment. This relationship is depicted in Figure 7.1.

Everyone in the system must be ethical. An economic system can be thought of as a four-legged stool. If corruption seeps into one leg, the economic system becomes unbalanced. In international business, very often the government slips into corruption with bribes controlling which businesses are permitted to enter the country and who is awarded contracts in that country. In the United States, the current wave of reforms at the federal level is the result of perceived corruption by business in their operations in the economic system.

To a large extent, all business is based on trust. The tenets for doing business are dissolved as an economy moves toward a system in which one individual can control the market in order to maximize personal income.

Suppose, for example, that the sale of a firm's product is determined not by perceived consumer value but rather by access to consumers, which is controlled by government officials. That is, your company's product cannot be sold to consumers in a particular country unless and until you are licensed within that country. Suppose further that the licensing procedures are controlled by government officials and that those officials

FIGURE 7.1 Interdependence of Trust, Business, and Government demand personal payment in exchange for your company's right to even apply for a business license. Payment size may be arbitrarily determined by officials who withhold portions for themselves. The basic values of the system have been changed. Consumers no longer directly determine the demand.

Beyond just the impact on the basic economic system, ethical breaches involving grease payments introduce an element beyond a now-recognized component in economic performance: consumer confidence in long-term economic performance. Economist Douglas Brown has described the differences between the United States and other countries in explaining why capitalism works here and not in all nations. His theory is that capitalism is dependent on an interdependent system of production. For economic growth to be possible, consumers, risk-takers, and employees must all feel confident about the future, about the concept of a level playing field, and about the absence of corruption. To the extent that consumers, risk-takers, and employees feel comfortable about a market driven by the basic assumptions, the investment and commitments necessary for economic growth via capitalism will be made. Significant monetary costs are incurred by business systems based on factors other than customer value, as discussed earlier.

In developing countries where there are "speed" or grease payments and resulting corruption by government officials, the actual money involved may not be significant in terms of the nation's culture. Such activities and payments introduce an element of demoralization and cynicism that thwart entrepreneurial activity when these nations most need risk-takers to step forward.

Bribes and *guanxi* (gifts) in China given to establish connections with the Chinese government are estimated at 3 to 5 percent of operating costs for companies, totaling $3 billion to $5 billion of foreign investment in 1993. But China incurs costs from the choices government officials make in return for payments. For example, *guanxi* are often used to persuade government officials to transfer government assets to foreign investors for substantially less than their value. Chinese government assets have fallen over $50 billion in value over the same period of economic growth, primarily because of the large undervaluation by government officials in these transactions with foreign companies. China's economy is adrift because of this underlying corruption.

Perhaps Italy and Brazil provide the best examples of the long-term impact of foreign business corruption. Although the United States, Japan, and Great Britain have scandals such as the savings and loan failures, political corruption, and insurance regulation, these forms of misconduct are not indicative of corruption that pervades entire economic systems. The same cannot be said about Italy. Elaborate connections between government officials, the Mafia, and business executives have been unearthed. As a result, half of Italy's cabinet has resigned, and hundreds of business executives have been indicted. It has been estimated that the interconnections of these three groups have cost the Italian government $200 billion, as well as compromising the completion of government projects.

In Brazil, the level of corruption has led to a climate of murder and espionage. Many foreign firms have elected not to do business in Brazil because of so much uncertainty and risk—beyond the normal financial risks of international investment. Why send an executive to a country where officials may use force when soliciting huge bribes?

The Wall Street Journal offered an example of how Brazil's corruption has damaged the country's economy despite growth and opportunity in surrounding nations. The governor of the northeastern state of Paraiba in Brazil, Ronaldo Cunha Lima, was angry because his predecessor, Tarcisio Burity, had accused Lima's son of corruption. Lima shot Burity twice in the chest while Burity was having lunch at a restaurant. The speaker of Brazil's Senate praised Lima for his courage in doing the shooting himself as opposed to sending someone else. Lima was given a medal by the local city council and granted immunity from prosecution by Paraiba's state legislature. No one spoke for the victim, and the lack of support was reflective of a culture controlled by self-interest that benefits those in control. Unfortunately, these self-interests preclude economic development.

Economists in Brazil document hyperinflation and systemic corruption. A São Paulo businessman observed, "The fundamental reason we can't get our act together is we're an amoral society." This businessperson probably understands capitalism. Privatization that has helped the economies of Chile, Argentina, and Mexico cannot take hold in Brazil because government officials enjoy the benefits of generous wages and returns from the businesses they control. The result is that workers are unable to earn enough even to clothe their families, 20 percent of the Brazilian population lives below the poverty line, and crime has reached levels of nightly firefights. Brazil's predicament has occurred over time, as graft, collusion, and fraud have become entrenched in the government-controlled economy.[2]

Discussion Questions

1. What did you learn about universal values and ethics from the categorical imperative list?

2. What happens when a society does not have ethical standards? Be sure to discuss the example of the situation in Brazil.

3. Who are the victims of corruption and graft?

4. Do you think following U.S. ethical standards in other countries is wise? Would it be unethical not to follow those standards? Explain your answer.

CASE 7.2

Product Dumping

Once the Consumer Product Safety Commission prohibits the sale of a particular product in the United States, a manufacturer can no longer sell the product to U.S. wholesalers or retailers. However, the product can be sold in other countries that have not prohibited its sale. The same is true of other countries' sales to the United States. For example, Great Britain outlawed the sale of the prescription sleeping pill Halcion but sales of the drug continue in the United States.[3] The British medical community

---

[2] Thomas Kamm, "Why Does Brazil Face Such Woes? Some See A Basic Ethical Lapse," The Wall Street Journal, February 4, 1994, p A1.
[3] "The Price of a Good Night's Sleep," The New York Times, January 26, 1992, p. E9.

reached conclusions regarding the pill's safety that differed from the conclusions reached by the medical community and the Food and Drug Administration here. Some researchers who conducted studies on the drug in the United States simply concluded that stronger warning labels were needed.

The Consumer Product Safety Commission outlawed the sale of three-wheel all-terrain cycles in the United States in 1988.[4] Although some manufacturers had already turned to four-wheel models, other manufacturers still had inventories of three-wheel cycles. Testimony on the cycles ranged from contentions that although the vehicles themselves were safe the drivers were too young, too inexperienced, and more inclined to take risks (i.e., to "hot dog"). However, even after the three-wheel product was banned here, outlawed vehicles could still be sold outside the United States.

For many companies, chaos follows a product recall because inventory of the recalled product may be high. Often, firms must decide whether to "dump" the product in other countries or to take a write-off that could damage earnings, stock prices, and employment stability.

Discussion Questions

1. If you were a manufacturer holding a substantial inventory of a product that has been outlawed in the United States, would you have any ethical concerns about selling the product in countries that do not prohibit its sale?

2. Suppose the inventory write-down that you will be forced to take because of the regulatory obsolescence is material—nearly a 20 percent reduction in income will result. If you can sell the inventory in a foreign market, legally, there will be no write-down and no income reduction. A reduction of that magnitude would substantially lower share market price, which in turn would lead your large, institutional shareholders to demand explanations and possibly seek changes in your company's board of directors. In short, the write-down would set off a wave of events that would change the structure and stability of your firm. Do you now feel justified in selling the product legally in another country?

3. Is selling the product in another country simply a matter of believing one aspect of the evidence—that the product is safe?

4. Would you include any warnings with the product?

CASE 7.3

The Taboo of Women in Management

International management consulting firm Burns & McCallister is listed by *Working Mother* magazine as one of the top fifty firms in the United States for employment of working mothers and by *Working Woman* magazine as one of the top ten firms for

---

[4] "Outlawing a Three-Wheeler," *Time*, January 11, 1988, p. 59.

women. The firm has earned this reputation for several reasons. First, nearly 50 percent of its partners are women. Second, it has a menu of employee benefits that includes such things as flex hours, sabbaticals, family leave, home-based work, and part-time partner-track positions.

However, Burns & McCallister recently has been the subject of a series of reports by both the *Los Angeles Times* and *The New York Times* that scrutinize its policy on female executives in certain nations. Burns & McCallister has learned, through fifty years of consulting, that certain countries in which it negotiates for contracts prohibit the inclusion of women in the negotiation process. The cultures of many of these countries do not permit women to speak in a meeting of men. Consequently, Burns & McCallister has implemented a policy prohibiting women partners from being assigned these potential account negotiations and later the accounts themselves. Clerical help in the offices can be female, but any contact with the client must be through a male partner or account executive.

For example, Japan still has a two-track hiring system, with only 3 percent of professional positions open to women.[5] The remainder of the women in the Japanese corporate workforce become office ladies who file, wear uniforms, and serve tea. Dentsu, Inc., a large Japanese ad firm, had a picture of the typical Dentsu "Working Girl" in its recruiting brochure. Surrounding the photo are comments primarily about her physical appearance: (1) Her breasts are "pretty large." (2) Her bottom is "rather soft."

In response to criticism regarding Burns & McCallister's posture, the head of the firm's New York office has explained:

> Look, we're about as progressive a firm as you'll find. But the reality of international business is that if we try to use women, we don't get the job. It's not a policy on all foreign accounts. We've just identified certain cultures in which women will not be able to successfully land or work on accounts. This restriction does not interfere with their career track. It does not apply in all countries.

The National Organization for Women (NOW) would like Burns & McCallister to apply to all its operations the standards that it employs in the United States. No restrictions are placed on women here, the organization argues, and other cultures should adapt to our standards; we should not change U.S. standards to adapt to their culture. NOW maintains that without such a posture, change can never come about.

Discussion Questions

1. Do you agree with Burns & McCallister's policy for certain cultures with regard to women partners?

2. Is Burns & McCallister doing anything that violates federal employment discrimination laws?

3. Given Burns & McCallister's record with regard to women, is the issue really relevant to women's advancement in the firm?

---

[5] Ted Holden and Jennifer Wiener, "Revenge of the 'Office Ladies,'" *Business Week*, July 13, 1992, pp. 42–43.

4. What if the cultures in which the prohibition of women applied traditionally bring in the highest dollar accounts? Would your opinion regarding the posture be different?

5. Do you agree with the position that change can never come about if Burns & McCallister does not take a stand?

6. Would Burns & McCallister be sacrificing revenues in changing its policies? Is this an appropriate sacrifice?

READING 7.4

The Ethics of Business in China and Business Ethics in China[6]

Marianne M. Jennings

I. Introduction

It isn't often that company officers examine an untapped market of nearly a billion consumers and then take a pass on having their company be the first-mover in that market. Yet more companies have made that decision than not with respect to doing business in China. Perhaps they have seen too much investment with too little returns for too long. Or perhaps they have reached a far more sophisticated conclusion about new markets in this global economy. That sophisticated conclusion comes from the realization that the presence of bribery and its resulting corruption in any country is a real risk.[7] Indeed, businesses have come to understand that the ethical issue in moving into a market fraught with bribery and corruption is not whether they would engage in bribery to do business in that country. The real ethical issue is whether you do business in the country at all.

It cannot be easy for companies and their officers to remain committed to the principle of "we don't bribe" when new markets and opportunities are so extensive. However, the decision "we don't bribe" is not just one of principle. This is a decision grounded in economics, and as companies and officers consider their strategic global moves, the internal moral wrestling match over entering markets should be brief for the moral and financial decisions on those markets and the issues of corruption and bribery are one and the same.

In the following sections are shown the reminders of why bribery and corruption, an ongoing problem in China, are such detrimental forces in economic and social progress in the untapped markets that await the advances global business can bring. Finally, a conclusion provides direction to businesses in moving forward a global economy free from the self-imposed restraints of corruption.

---

[6] Corporate Finance Review 5(6): 42–45 (2001). Reprinted from Corporate Finance Review by RIA, 395 Hudson Street, New York, NY 10014.

[7] The New York Times noted in March 1999 that the number one complaint of the Chinese is "All this corruption." The report noted, "Yet corruption is now virtually built into the middle levels of China's vast authoritarian apparatus, under an ideology that has become a hollow shell while the new market economy swells around it." Seth Faison, "No. 1 Complaint of Chinese: All This Corruption," The New York Times, March 11, 1999, p. A3.

II. Don't Lose Sight of the Bottom Line

It is nothing less than a fascinating exercise when teaching MBA students ethics to come to the point in the semester where we discuss what I have come to call the role of "stuff" in doing business. In China, it is referred to as "guanxi." In Mexico, it is called "mordida." "Stuff" is comprised of the gifts and perks we take and spread in the hope of landing a sale, closing a deal, or doing business in a country. Businesses give away everything from Super Bowl tickets to lunches to embroidered logo shirts in the hope of gaining more business.

MBA students, experienced in the ways of business prior to returning to school, cite the benefits of stuff as follows: good will, loyalty, advertising, and a host of other nonquantifiable benefits that accrue because of the gifts, token and otherwise, of business. However, what they cannot give to me in any of the cases we study or from their experiences is a formula correlation between the amount spent on "stuff" and increases in revenues. In other words, "stuff" is a business custom in the United States and the degree of "stuff" exchanged is often greater in other countries such as China, but there is little analytical evidence to show that the expense of "stuff" actually produces a return on the investment.

During a seminar for regional sales reps, I raised the issue of "stuff" and was met with understandable discomfort. The reason they were in Phoenix was to entertain potential buyers they were flying in for the Phoenix Open Golf Tournament. They explained the thousands of dollars they were spending on each potential client. I asked them how many clients they had gained when they had done the same thing last year for the Phoenix Open. Their response was, "None." In fact, one regional manager pointed out that the company executive he had flown in took the trip and then negotiated a deal with a competitor.

The panic of "this is the way it has always been done," or "everybody does this"[8] often overtakes the usual business analysis of, "How much is this costing me?" and "What will I get in return?"

In forgetting to perform that simple financial analysis, companies also fail to recognize that those businesses that are contracting with them must also perform a similar analysis, "What do they propose for the cost?" "Is there someone who is cheaper?" "Is their service or product better?" In other words, "stuff" does not make accounting and revenue principles disappear. And decision-makers are always accountable for the purchasing contracts they make. "Stuff" is really a superficial fix for what should be the real foundation of a long-term business relationship: service, quality, reliability, promptness, and accuracy. In short, what keeps business is working long and hard at business, not "stuff."

The principles of business do not change across international boundary lines. The exchange of gifts may be customary in a country but should always be undertaken with the same quantitative analysis as other business expenditures: Why am I spending this

---

[8] Professor Henri-Claude de Bettignes has provided the following descriptions of bribery or "extensive stuff" in international business: "(1) Refusal to bribe is a Western hang-up. (2) Bribery is a parallel distribution system. Everyone does it. (3) It is the traditional way of doing business in this culture." Ron Berenbeim, "Cutting Off the Supply Side of Bribes," Vital Speeches of the Day, Vol. LXV, April 15, 1999, p. 409.

money? What do I expect in return? Over the long term, what will be the return on this expenditure?

Businesses too often retreat to the facile position that there can be no success in a country that has a culture in which gifts and even bribes are "the way business is done." They not only abandon sound decision-making tools in retreating to such a rationalization, but they also shortchange their earnings and their shareholders as they adopt a quick-fix solution rather than a strategy of a long-term presence and continuing and stable returns.

III. Don't Forget the Need for Trust in Business

Free trade is not possible in an atmosphere of bribery, graft, and corruption. In the 1996 Congressional hearings on international corruption, Robert S. Lieken testified, "Reducing bribery, smuggling and kickbacks is part and parcel of free trade; anti-corruption is part and parcel of democracy. Today's decisive battles for free trade, development and democracy may well be fought on the terrain of corrupt practices."[9]

While urban legend holds that bribery is an inevitable part of international business, business transactions and the nature of doing business in any particular country are becoming more and more transparent.[10] Most countries are moving in the direction of full disclosure among their government officials, as in the case of Tanzania, where the president now makes his assets public.[11] This slow but certain movement is the result of leaders in these countries being trained in U.S. universities and returning to their countries with the principles and requirements for free trade. Some countries even ban companies from doing business within their borders when they discover that the company has engaged in bribery.[12] *The Wall Street Journal* notes that there are not more European scandals, there are simply "a more assertive judiciary, a more aggressive press, and a more inquisitive citizenry."[13]

Significant costs are associated with the presence of corruption. There is the political unrest caused by the prosecution and conviction of government officials engaged in bribery, but there is the resulting reluctance for businesses to initiate either new business or new contracts in a country where there is unrest and the stigma of corruption. There is also the impact of a market operating with prices being set artificially so that the few can command the fees they deem appropriate. Hong Kong has established its Independent Commission Against Corruption and its studies estimate the guanxi constitutes 3 to 5 percent of companies' operating costs or between $3 and $5 billion

---

[9] Hearings of the Senate Caucus on Int'l Narcotics Control & the Senate Finance Comm. Subcomm. On Int'l Crime, *104th Cong. (1996)*. Leiken is the president of New Moment, a nonprofit organization dedicated to fostering democracy internationally.

[10] Transparency International, a nonprofit devoted to creating international disclosure standards for business, has written, "major multi-nationals have not understood that the whole value system of dealing with developing countries is changing radically and rapidly . . . The colonial mind-set of 'bribery as usual' is coming under greater risk for bribers." See http://www.transparency.org.

[11] Michael A. Almond and Scott D. Syfert document a number of changes in countries' leaders in "Beyond Compliance: Corruption, Corporate Responsibility and Ethical Standards in the New Global Economy," 22 N.C. J. Int'l L. & Com. Reg. 389, 431 (1997).

[12] Mark J. Murphy, "International Bribery: An Example of an Unfair Trade Practice?" 21 Brooklyn J. Int'l L. 385, 391 (1995).

[13] Thomas Kamm et al., "Europe Can't Decide Whether Dirty Money In Politics Is a Problem," The New York Times, January 9, 2000, p. A1.

each year.[14] The list of cost reductions when bribery was eliminated includes: Russia, where food prices dropped nearly 20 percent when vendors were protected from extortion by government officials and Italy, where freeway construction costs dropped 50 percent when government officials responsible for that contracting were indicted and convicted for bribery.

The final impact of corruption is on the perceptions of all those potential consumers in these untapped markets. The presence of bribery and corruption is more than just demoralizing; the presence of bribery deprives a market of its central characteristic of trust. Free markets are markets of honesty and independence, not dependence and a veil of secrecy. Hayek noted that the greatest impact of governmental actions that run contra to free market concepts is the psychological change or the alteration in the character of the people.[15] In China, a businessman noted that other businesspeople were paying to become their own regulators or even decision-makers on contracts they could award themselves when he noted, "An official job is like a piece of fruit. You pay the money and it is yours."[16] Such cynicism is not conducive to the entrepreneurial spirit needed for economic progress.

IV. What Business Is Doing About Corruption

The Conference Board's Working Group on Global Business Ethics is but one of many organizations working to halt corruption, particularly in China. Their proposal is one to "cut off the supply side of bribes."[17] In doing so, the group asks that its members make two firm commitments, the first to quality and the second to a resolve not to engage in bribery no matter how justified they may feel in taking such actions. The quality commitment is at the heart of business longevity and customer trust and represents a reaffirmation of Friedman's notion that ethical behavior leads to successful performance over the long term. Just U.S. business devotion to the theories of Deming's total quality management makes the first commitment relatively easy.

It is, however, the second area of commitment, which requires a pledge not to engage in bribery that the Conference Board emphasizes as it notes how easily firms can waver without such an absolute standard. An example illustrates the level of justification or rationalization that can arise when utilitarianism rather than absolutism becomes a company's standard of conduct. Suppose that a foreign government is about to award a contract for the construction of a bridge in that country. A U.S. firm wishes to bid for the project but knows that the other firms' bids will be lower and that they will pay bribes to the government officials making the decision. The executives of the U.S. firm are also relatively confident that the firms engaged in bribery for the bridge contract will cut corners, provide a lower quality bridge, and perhaps sacrifice safety in the process. Those executives might feel comfortable, under a standard of utilitarianism, in engaging in bribery to get the contract because they would, after all, be saving lives by building a higher quality bridge.

The firm is rationalizing. It is impossible for that firm to draw knowledgeable conclusions on the other firms' quality levels. The firm is simply using its perceived

[14] Karen Pennar, "The Destructive Cost of Greasing Palms," Business Week, December 6, 1993, p. 133.
[15] F. A. Hayek, The Road to Serfdom, University of Chicago Press, 1994, p. xxxix.
[16] Seth Faison, "No. 1 Complaint of Chinese: All This Corruption," The New York Times, March 11, 1999, p. A3.
[17] Berenbeim, "Cutting Off the Supply Side of Bribes," p. 408.

superior quality to justify bribery. The firm has fallen victim to the "everyone else does it" syndrome. While the question seems to become gray as the issue of quality is factored in, it is important to understand that the market is capable of screening quality. For the country's future, the best solution is for the company to bid, not pay the bribes and then disclose the practices publicly. There is a cleansing process that immediately follows such a disclosure and the company with the winning bid may find itself banned from doing business. This cleansing, as noted earlier, is becoming more common because freedom from corruption is inextricably intertwined with economic progress.

The Conference Board solution is the correct one. It is incumbent on businesses to eliminate the supply side of corruption so that in a true utilitarian sense those countries in which they choose to do business can have the benefits and growth of free trade in a transparent economy.

Discussion Questions

1. Why do companies pay bribes in other countries?

2. What are the short-term implications of bribes?

3. What are the long-term implications of bribes?

4. What impact do bribes have on economic systems?

CASE 7.5

The Adoption Agency and Señor Jose's Fees

Ninos and Ninas, Inc. is an adoption agency located in El Paso, Texas, that focuses on international adoptions. Most of the infants Ninos and Ninas places are from South American countries.

Couples, primarily from the United States, work with Ninos and Ninas to adopt children. The fee for Ninos and Ninas' work ranges from $15,000 to $20,000. Couples pay the fee willingly because of the agency's twenty-year history of excellent work and its extensive knowledge of adoption requirements in South American countries.

Joan and David Ryan have applied with Ninos and Ninas to adopt a child. Their U.S. certification is complete, and they have submitted their application along with a $10,000 deposit to Ninos and Ninas.

After their application is processed, the Ryans receive a notice from Esther Tomkin, Ninos and Ninas' director of adoption services, that a baby girl is now available. Ms. Tomkin instructs them that she will need an additional $5,000 as well as $5,000 in cash in unmarked bills in an envelope to be placed in a postal box located in El Paso. Ms. Tomkin's letter explains:

You should bring the $5,000 with you when you come to El Paso to pick up your new daughter. Once you have paid the $5,000 to Ninos and Ninas and deposited the $5,000 in cash, you will have your little girl within 24 hours. You should be prepared to come to El Paso on April 10. The envelope with the cash should be marked for "Señor Jose."

Joan is concerned about the odd cash payment and phones Ms. Tomkin to discuss it. Ms. Tomkin assures Joan that "the payment is just the way adoption works in these countries. It is not a bribe; it is not a violation of the Foreign Corrupt Practices Act; it is simply a requirement to get the adoption paperwork through. Your adoption just can't get through the system without it. This is the way we've been doing business for twenty years." Joan asks, "Who is Señor Jose?" Ms. Tomkin responds, "He's just an official in the social agency who handles adoptions. He isn't even the judge who approves the adoption. Without this money, your little girl ends up a street child or malnourished in an orphanage."

Discussion Questions

1. Would the payment to Señor Jose violate U.S. laws? Does the international nature of the adoption agency's operations affect its operational standards?

2. Is the payment a bribe or a facilitating "grease" payment? Is there a difference? Does the fact that the payment is legal control the determination of whether it is ethical?

3. Does the benefit to the infant girl justify the method for accomplishing that benefit?

4. Would you go forward with the adoption?

5. Would you feel comfortable working for or adopting from Ninos and Ninas?

CASE 7.6

Salt Lake City, the Olympics, and Bribery

Officials in Salt Lake City had been trying to win the International Olympic Committee (IOC) nod for the Winter Olympics since 1966. For the IOC meeting in Rome at which the 1966 decision would be made, the Salt Lake City Olympic Committee raised $24,000 by selling Olympic pins for $1 each. Following a trip to Rome, there was $10,305 left and a two-page audit documented all the expenses for the failed try.

Business and government leaders kept trying to win over the IOC, but continued to do so on a spartan budget. For example, in 1989 the Salt Lake leaders journeyed to Greece to meet with the IOC and noted that other cities were giving the IOC members jewelry and crystal vases. Atlanta had created "The Atlanta House" and had furniture shipped from Atlanta to create an authentic Southern home. Other cities had created rooms for breakfast and lunch buffets for the IOC members. That year, Salt Lake City leaders, concerned about their lack of gifts, had some letter openers flown in to give to the IOC members.

When Salt Lake City was trying for the 1998 Winter Games, they were told in a letter from the head of Ireland's Olympic Committee that some of the IOC members were selling their votes for $100,000 in exchange for a vote for Nagano, Japan (the site eventually chosen). One of the children of a member of the IOC approached Thomas Welch, the head of the Salt Lake City Olympic Committee, and said that he could help get Salt Lake City the votes in exchange for $35,000. Mr. Welch and the members of the Salt Lake City Olympic Committee (SLCOC) refused to pay the money, although many have said it was only because they could not raise the $35,000 at the last minute. The SLCOC had simply paid for travel expenses for IOC members. For example, an audit of the 1991 expenses for the unsuccessful bid for the 1998 Winter Olympics revealed that Mr. David R. Johnson was reimbursed $2.73 for a receipt from a 7-Eleven convenience store near Utah's ski areas and an accompanying note that read, "juice for Prince Albert." Prince Albert of Monaco was an IOC member at the time and had traveled to Utah to view the sites for events. Prince Albert refused any special treatment, including limousines and any types of events or dinners in his honor. Such simplicity from a member of a royal family and also an IOC member perhaps also convinced the SLCOC members that the exchange of cash was unnecessary.

However, when SLCOC lost its bid to Nagano, despite its hopes that the issues of cash payments were not effective, its members began to talk openly about "what it took to win the Olympics" for their city. When the SLCOC began its planning in 1991 for its bid for the 2002 Winter Olympics, even the minutes from the meetings make it clear that committee members were single minded in doing all it took to get the Olympics. Mr. Johnson, a continuing and prominent member of the 2002 SLCOC, said, "Everything we had was about getting the bid. All our money was to get votes." Others have described the attitude of "doing whatever it takes" to get the Winter Olympics because the cause was a good one and it seemed that Salt Lake City was losing "for not playing the game," and "doing what everyone else was doing." There was an attitude of "if we don't do it, someone else will" and "this is the way it's always been done—we just didn't understand that."

Beginning in 1991, on the heels of their loss to Nagano, the SLCOC began its new style of garnering votes, particularly, as they thought through their strategy, the African votes. From 1991 through 1995, the SLCOC gave an estimated $1.2 million to members of the IOC or their families. Nearly $100,000 in scholarships went to children of members of the IOC. Other children of IOC members stopped by the SLCOC offices on a regular basis and picked up checks for themselves. Sibo Sibandze, son of an IOC member from Swaziland, picked up weekly checks from the SLCOC offices that ranged from $250 to $590.

A volunteer staff member described the situation on the payments and checks as follows:

> You knew these guys, they came in weekly. You saw them pick up their checks. You took them places. You didn't have to be a brain surgeon to know what was going on. It was always whispered, "Whose son is he? How much of a scholarship is he getting? How does that work?" People freaked out the first time they heard about it. Then it became second nature.[18]

[18] Jo Thomas, Kirk Johnson, and Jere Longman, "From an Innocent Bid to Olympic Scandal," The New York Times, March 11, 1999, pp. A1, A14, A15.

Audits of the SLCOC's books from this time period reveal a dramatic drop-off in documentation for payments, with many never explained. There were a series of payments to Raouf Scally totaling $14,500 in $500 installments with a notation that Mr. Scally was a son of a member of the IOC. No one has ever been able to tie him to any IOC member and subsequent investigations have not determined who he is and what role he played in the SLCOC's successful bid.

An examination of the records also revealed that the members of the SLCOC had done their homework in terms of vulnerability. Some of the dossiers on IOC members made reference to those who had complained about financial difficulties, including issues of making their mortgage payments. While IOC members are prohibited from accepting gifts valued over $150, the following are documented benefits to IOC members from the SLCOC:

- Lawn equipment, $268
- Violin, $524
- Doorknobs, $673 (one of the IOC members, Jean-Claude Ganga, an IOC member from Congo Republic, was remodeling his home)
- Jean-Claude Ganga received more than $200,000 in cash and medical treatment.
- Ganga's wife used a SLCOC member's credit card at Wal-Mart for various items and reached the maximum credit limit on the member's card.
- Bathroom fixtures, $1,488 (the same)
- Draperies, $3,117 (the same)
- Dogs, $1,010
- Letterhead stationery for one of the IOC member countries, $6,934
- Super Bowl trip for Mr. Welch and IOC members Philip Coles of Australia and Willi Kaltschmitt of Guatemala, $19,991. These two IOC members never visited Salt Lake City.
- Two-week Park City condominium rental for a vacation for Agustin Arroyo, the ICO member from Ecuador, $10,000
- The daughter of Kim Un Yung, an IOC member from South Korea, was given a contract playing with the Utah Symphony.
- English language training, $1,390
- Disneyland trip, $1,202
- Yellowstone trip, $926
- Ski lessons for a child, $414
- Furniture rental for a child, $250

Ernst & Young, the auditors for the SLCOC, uncovered most of the questionable items during a 1995 audit. The auditors' work papers indicate that they talked to SLCOC members about the scholarship programs, the amounts, and the purposes. These committee members deny that they were informed of these issues by the auditors. However, the auditors did not uncover any evidence that any of the checks that were issued were unauthorized.

What happened following the audit and the eventual public disclosure of these payments was a complex tale of several individuals trying to have someone review what the SLCOC was doing. Mr. Ken Bullock, a member of the SLCOC Board of Trustees, talked with both Governor Michael O. Leavitt's staff and members of the Salt Lake City city council. In many cases, he was dismissed as being "a little out there."

Friends said that Mr. Bullock was frustrated, bloodied, and bruised as he tried to bring the matters to someone's attention. One city council member did have a meeting with Rod Decker, a television reporter, about the scholarship issues on June 3, 1997. However, Mr. Decker accepted Mr. Johnson's explanation that children of members of the IOC had simply toured the University of Utah and that there were no scholarships. It was during this time that the law firm housing the records of the SLCOC meetings ordered the destruction of firm documents with no indication of who had given the order for their destruction. The destruction was accomplished at a time when the time frame for retention of the client's documents would not have provided for their destruction.

The story finally came to public light when a staff member from the SLCOC offices sent an anonymous letter reflecting the payment of scholarship monies to one of the children of an IOC member to a different television station from Mr. Decker's that did not run the story. On November 4, 1998, the first television story ran about possible scholarship and other payments to IOC members and their children. Both local and national news outlets descended on Salt Lake City to investigate the full extent of the payments. When a high-ranking member of the IOC used the word "bribes" in connection with the SLCOC bid, government agencies began investigations. Mr. Welch resigned from his $10,000-per-month job as head of the SLCOC, and Mitt Romney, former candidate for the U.S. Senate in Massachusetts, the owner of Staples, Inc., and candidate for Massachusetts governor in 2002, took over as head of SLCOC.

Once the news stories began, the following investigations and their outcomes resulted:

- Ethics Investigation by Gordon R. Hall, former chief justice of the Utah Supreme Court—issued a 300-page report in February 1999 that concluded no criminal activity but a host of ethical issues and violations of trust in the SLCOC's bid for the 2002 games; 24 members of the IOC are mentioned by name in the report as having received gifts and other items from the SLCOC.
- United States Olympic Committee investigation by George Mitchell (former U.S. Senator, ambassador to Ireland and head of the USOC Ethics Committee)— recommends processes, procedures, checks, and balances for future bids for games from the United States.
- U.S. Justice Department—investigation of SLCOC activities that resulted in indictments. David Simmons entered a guilty plea to charges of tax evasion after admitting that he set up a sham job for John Kim, the son of Yong Kim, an IOC member from Korea (in response to a request from Mr. Welch); John Kim is charged with lying to the FBI about his job and lying to obtain a green card. David Simmons was the head of Keystone Communications. He set up a job for John Kim that paid between $75,000 and $100,000; Keystone was then reimbursed by the SLCOC for the salary. The investigation was referred to the Reno Justice Department after the U.S. Attorney for Utah, Paul Warner, recused himself and his office from any SLCOC investigations and related matters. Justice Department investigators zeroed in on violations of the Foreign Corrupt Practices Act and tax fraud. Mr. Johnson and Mr. Welch were charged with RICO (racketeering) violations, bribery, and conspiracy in a grand jury indictment handed down in July 2000. Both rejected plea bargain agreements from the Justice

Department.[19] Their trial was scheduled to begin on July 16, 2001, however, the federal district judge dismissed the charges, noting that the state of Utah had declined to prosecute. The U.S. Attorney filed an appeal of the dismissal.[20] The Tenth Circuit Court of Appeals held that the Utah antibribery statute was constitutional and that the two men could be tried for RICO violations under federal law.[21]

- IOC internal investigation—resulted in the expulsion of six IOC members; a reprimand to Phillip Coles of Australia, who also resigned his position as a member of the Sydney Olympics Board; and revisions in rules on choosing an Olympic site. A new code of ethics was also adopted. The final years of IOC President Juan Antonio Samaranch's tenure were rocky because of the SLCOC scandal. Many had called for his resignation, but he stayed until July 2001 when his tenure expired, promising ethics reform during those final years.

- U.S. Congress—conducted hearings on IOC reforms with a stern admonition to IOC members that there would be continuing oversight on the gifts aspects of the IOC's code of ethics and that reforms were not yet complete. Congressional budget committees also examined the award of federal funds to Utah and Salt Lake City for Olympics-related transit and highway improvements.

Salt Lake City was permitted to keep the 2002 Winter Olympics after the news of the "gifts" broke, but it had trouble with corporate sponsorships and raising funds during 1999–2000 because confidence in the games was so shaken.[22] It was not until the announcement in November 1999 that Gateway Computer would be a $20 million sponsor that the tide on fund-raising was turned.[23] Visa followed later in November.[24] Further, the Sydney Summer Olympics in 2000 experienced many sponsorship withdrawals because of the Salt Lake City bid scandal.[25] Although John Hancock Mutual Life Insurance Company criticized the IOC for the scandal[26] and initially indicated it would withdraw its support, it re-upped as a sponsor for $55 million.[27]

Discussion Questions

1. Tom Schaffer, the attorney for Mr. Welch, said that his client and Mr. Johnson did "what they had to do" to win a bid in a system that "stinks."[28] Are the flaws in a system a justification for the payments? Ken Bullock has noted, "The Games are an aphrodisiac. If you want something bad enough, you stretch the boundaries. The IOC allowed this sucking up."[29]

2. In one discussion of exchanges with IOC committee members, SLCOC members brought athletes from the Sudan to the United States for training as part of an exchange for Sudan

[19] Vicki Michaelis, "Salt Lake Bid Leaders Spurn Deal," USA Today, July 14, 2000, p. 1C.

[20] Patrick O'Driscoll, "U.S. Appeals in Olympics Bribery Case," USA Today, January 24, 2002, p. 2A.

[21] U.S. v. Welch, 327 F.3d 1081(10th Cir. 2003).

[22] For example, Johnson & Johnson withdrew its sponsorship. "Johnson & Johnson Decides Against Olympic Scholarship," Arizona Republic, April 19, 1999, p. A5.

[23] Bruce Horovitz, "Gateway Logs On As Salt Lake Olympics Sponsor," USA Today, November 3, 1999, p. 1B.

[24] Bruce Horovitz, "Visa Reviews Support for Olympic Games," USA Today, November 12, 1999, p. 1B.

[25] A. Craig Copetas, "After Scandal, Local Sponsors Shun Olympics," The Wall Street Journal, April 4, 2000, pp. B1, B4.

[26] Joseph B. Treaster, "Monitor of the Olympic Mettle," The New York Times, March 28, 1999, p. BU2.

[27] Bruce Horovitz, "Reaching for Rings," USA Today, March 16, 2000, p. 1B.

[28] Kirk Johnson, "E-Mail Trail Adds Details to U.S.O.C.'s Role," The New York Times, February 10, 1999, pp. C1, C25.

[29] Nadya Labi, "The Olympics Turn into a Five-Ring Circus," Time, January 11, 1999, p. 33.

members' votes. One person associated with the exchange has said, "In our minds, we distinguished the transactions in which Sudanese athletes were brought to the United States, apparently with some understanding that we would receive Sudanese votes, from an example in which an IOC member sells their vote. It's a different thing. A distinction needs to be made."[30] Do you agree? However, another e-mail exchange raises some concerns about the funding being taken from U.S. athletes. One U.S. Olympic Committee member (USOC) wrote, "Should I take financial support away from American athletes? Or does your budget cover these international political initiatives?" A response from another USOC member was, "You can take it away from the additional revenue we will ALL benefit from after having won the 2002 Games for SLC."[31] Was there harm in this benefit to the athletes?

Dick Schultz, the executive director of the USOC, said of the e-mail exchanges that they were "unfortunate," and "People make flippant remarks on E-mails that aren't always accurate. It seems like it was handled appropriately. 'If you do this they'll vote for us'—I don't see that in any records we've turned up."[32] Do you think that the statement must be made expressly for exchanges for votes to take place?

3. Richard Pound, an IOC member and a lawyer from Montreal, was the lead investigator for the IOC report. His 24-page summary indicated, "inappropriate activities of certain members of the IOC did not commence with the candidacy of Salt Lake City." The report also notes, "It is clear the matter of gifts is going to be troublesome. In some cases, the value of the gifts was . . . not reasonably perceived as ordinary or routine."[33] How does one define appropriate gifts? What are ordinary and routine gifts? Does it make a difference that Salt Lake City was not the first site bidder to give these types of gifts?

4. When Pound issued his report and recommended a reprimand for Phil Coles, *USA Today* columnist Christine Brennan wrote the following:

This reminds me of the fabulous way the IOC handled a messy gift-taking situation involving member Phil Coles earlier this year. The IOC refused to use an independent investigator and instead let vice president Dick Pound handle the case. First Pound interrogated Coles, then he went to dinner with him. The two men, it turns out, are good friends. When the investigation was completed do you think the IOC expelled Coles? Heavens no.[34]

Why does Brennan make this point?

5. Why do you think the expelled members were from third world nations (Togo, India, Mauritius, Nigeria, Mongolia, and Algeria)?

6. One member of the SLCOC noted that a shopping trip to Wal-Mart was a "good value" and could not be corruption. Do you agree?

7. A lawyer representing the SLCOC in the Justice Department probe has stated, "There were a lot of things that were unethical, but that's a long way from being criminal."[35] Do you agree with her assessment?

---

[30] Id.

[31] Id.

[32] Id.

[33] A. Craig Copetas and Roger Thurow, "A Preliminary Report on Salt Lake Scandal Certain to Rile the IOC," The Wall Street Journal, January 20, 1999, pp. A1, A8.

[34] Christine Brennan, "Some IOC Fixes Sound Like Trouble," USA Today, December 16, 1999, p. 3C.

[35] Laurie P. Cohen and David S. Cloud, "U.S. Probe Into Salt Lake Bid Scandal To Explore Possible Federal Violations," The Wall Street Journal, February 18, 1999, p. A6.

8. Tom Welch sent a fax to his friends and copied reporters. The note contained the following language:

   I am saddened and dismayed that so many feel the need to isolate responsibility for what—at the time—were cooperative decisions. Had our agreed course of action been questioned at the time by those to whom we reported, no doubt we would have been pleased to pursue other avenues. It is ironic that those who were so supportive of our efforts to secure the Games now feel the need to distance themselves.[36]

   Do you think others knew and abandoned him once the information was public?

9. A letter to the editor of the Salt Lake City paper, *The Deseret News*, read as follows:

   Instead of pursuing legal proceedings, we should be erecting a statue of Tom Welch in Washington Square and put a canopy to keep the pigeons, vultures, the Chris Vancours, and the Steve Paces off of him. It is people like Tom, with deep passions, who accomplish much and who almost single-handedly brought the Olympics to Salt Lake and Utah.

   There is a lot of truth in the adage, no good deed goes unpunished. I know to be politically correct we had to dump him but only because he played the age-old game of favor for favor, something everyone of us plays daily. Good luck, Tom and Dave. I wish I could be on the jury.[37]

   Is the writer correct? Was it a favor-for-favor game that all of us play every day?

....

Sources

"A Time of Turmoil," *USA Today*, December 8, 1999, p. 10C.

Caldwell, Christopher, "Pillars of Salt Lake," *National Review*, March 8, 1999, pp. 35–36.

Copetas, Craig, and Roger Thurow, "Closing Ceremony: The Olympics Say Farewell to Samaranch," *The Wall Street Journal*, August 12, 2001, pp. A1, A10.

Dodd, Mike, "10 More Are Cited for Misconduct," *USA Today*, February 10, 1999, p. 4C.

Fatis, Stefan, "Olympic Broadcaster's IOC Ties Raise Questions," *The Wall Street Journal*, January 19, 1999, pp. B1, B6.

Longman, Jere, and Jo Thomas, "Report Details Lavish Spending in Salt Lake's Bid to Win Games," *The New York Times*, February 10, 1999, pp. A1, C25.

"Probe Won't Have Salt Lake Federal Prosecutor," *USA Today*, December 22, 1998, p. 3C.

Raboin, Sharon, and Kevin Johnson, "Salt Lake Fund-Raising Slowed," *USA Today*, January 14, 1999, p. 2C.

Titze, Maria, "Bid-Scandal Lawyers File Objection," *The Deseret News*, June 26, 2001, http://www.desnews.com.

---

[36] *Kristen Moulton, "Welch Defends Actions in Olympics," LA Times.com, http://www.latimes.com, Thursday, February 4, 1999.*

[37] The Deseret News, *June 24, 2001, http://www.desnews.com.*

7B

Workplace Safety

Certain safety issues continue to evolve. While given hazards await regulation, workers eventually will experience harm. How much responsibility does an employer have? Is an employer required to be proactive?

READING 7.7

The Regulatory Cycle

Marianne M. Jennings

Some years ago, when he was serving as the CEO for Motorola, before going on to become Kodak's CEO, George Fisher spoke to a group of our masters students from both engineering and business. One of the questions the students asked after he had given his thoughts on success in life and business was, "How do you become a leader in business?" His response was that those in business should take an evolving problem in their business units, their companies, their industries, or their communities and fix it before the problem was regulated or litigated. He assured the students that business people who voluntarily undertake self-correction are always ahead of the game.

There is a diagram I use to teach students this Fisher principle of leadership that shows how its best execution is found in focusing on ethics (see Figure 7.2).

Every area that is now the subject of regulation or litigation began at the left side of the scale, in the latency stage, with plenty of options for how to handle a gray area. For example, prior to the savings and loan crisis of the 1980s, appraisers were not regulated. The qualifications for an appraiser were limited and issues such as conflicts of interest were not controlled. In an area in which there are few legal guidelines, businesses have leeway in terms of their decisions. However, should those decisions violate usual ethical notions, the courts and/or the legislatures will step in to legislate ethics. In the case of appraisers there are now complete federal and state regulations on qualifications, licensing, and issues of conflicts of interest.

The regulatory cycle moves, not by data, but by public perception. Public perception changes through examples and anecdotes. We are witnessing a regulatory cycle with regard to cell phone use in cars. On the list of causes of accidents, cell phones are

FIGURE 7.2 Leadership and Ethics: Making Choices before Liability

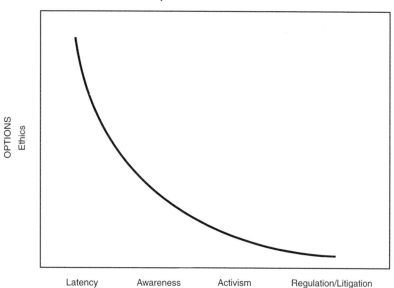

Source: Adapted from James Frierson's "Public Policy Forecasting: A New Approach," *SAM Advanced Management Journal*, Spring 1985, pp. 18–23.

at the very bottom—eating, reaching, and talking to another passenger are more frequent causes of accidents than cell phone use. Nonetheless, New York and other states have already moved to regulate cell phone use by drivers. We were living in an area untouched by regulation. We could use our cell phones when and how we wanted. However, there were safety issues, in terms of distraction, associated with the use of cell phones while driving. We could have voluntarily abstained but were unwilling to exercise that self-restraint. The result is that the law will do it for us both through attributing accident liability to us when we have an accident while using cell phones and through legislation that will permit tickets for using them while driving.

The ethical issue we are trying to solve with such regulation is whether drivers were behaving in a fashion that would be comfortable for them if other drivers behaved in the same way. In other words, would we want to be on the same road with us when we are trying to do cell phone business and drive at the same time? Probably not, but we could not voluntarily constrain ourselves and regulation stepped in to mandate such constraints.

There are businesses that do seize the moment. There is little question that the electric utility industry would look a great deal different today if it had not handled the issue of EMFs (electromagnetic fields) as effectively and openly as it did.

During the late 1970s, a scientist released a study showing that children in the Denver area who lived near transmission wires and poles were more likely to develop leukemia. Whether the study was correct or had the wrong causation was impossible to know. The electric utility industry was under no legal obligation to change anything in terms of its transmission wires and their location. Nor were they obligated to the public to research the issue or even disclose the research. Nonetheless, the industry was very aggressive and included information in customer bills about EMF: what it is, how to measure, and how to obtain help on evaluating your risk and exposure. At the same time, the utilities sponsored research on the issue to determine whether the studies were accurate.

The information in the study might have been true or false, but leaders in the industry were not going to allow the issue to be shaped by others; they took the initiative to manage an issue from an ethical perspective. If the study conclusion was correct, then the utilities had to take action to stop any further injury to those living near power lines. However, if the study conclusion was incorrect, the utilities had an issue to manage and a study to refute.

The results of that initiative on the part of the utilities were that the public was informed, the studies were conducted, and we now have data from all types of studies. The original study conclusion was correct in the sense that there were pockets of childhood leukemia, but the pockets were better explained by socioeconomic factors and not the presence of power lines. In fact, the studies seem to show that there is no connection between cancer rates and proximity to EMFs. Without these voluntary steps on the part of the utilities, I am convinced that utilities today would be managing a crisis similar to the asbestos litigation and regulation.

Those in the asbestos industry were selling an effective and unregulated product. They also had information about negative health effects from exposure to asbestos. Those effects were documented in board meeting minutes as early as 1933. However, those in the asbestos industry declined to take any steps with regard to those health studies. So long as the law permitted asbestos, they would sell it. In fact, they even tried to conceal the studies. By 1976, the industry was experiencing litigation that forced many of them into bankruptcy because the public was driving the issue, not the companies that had neglected to acknowledge and take action when they had options and opportunities. The demise of their product was managed for them by crippling litigation.

No one required action on the part of the utilities, but they made their decision from an ethical perspective. The result is that they did not see the cycle evolve to the point where they had no choices in terms of wire placement and had tremendous liability exposure because of public perception regarding EMF.

There are ethical issues that are now in the latency stage—that stage where the public is not aware of a problem and no one is filing suit or demanding regulation. Leaders take voluntary steps while there are options and emerge not only ahead in terms of financial performance, but also as individuals with foresight who recognize issues and solve them before any harm has occurred.

Discussion Questions

1. Name several issues you can think of regarding the latency stage.

2. What types of voluntary actions can businesses take?

3. What happens with regulation and litigation?

CASE 7.8

Electromagnetic Fields: Exposure for Workers and Customers

EMFs Are Discovered

Technology has brought us the phenomenon of electromagnetic fields (EMFs)—magnetic fields that result from electrical current. These fields can be found around transmission lines, home appliances, and video display terminals for computers. Wherever there is electric power, there are electric and magnetic fields that result from the charge in the electric power system. The amount of the charge produces the electric field, and the motion of the charge produces the magnetic field. Together, these two types of fields are often called an electromagnetic field (EMF).[38] Much has been written recently about the health hazards of EMFs, but the controversy has in fact been developing for over forty years.

In 1950, following its first study of EMFs, the U.S. Public Health Service reported that workers who were exposed to alternating EMFs developed cancer at a rate significantly higher than that of the population as a whole. Following this first study, public concerns about EMFs arose as utilities turned more and more to extra high voltage (EHV) transmission lines to handle increases in electrical demand. The public first noticed EHV lines as nuisances; the lines impaired TV and radio reception.

During the 1960s, Dr. Robert O. Becker found, in experiments conducted with salamanders, that the electric current associated with the animals' nervous systems triggered their regenerative process. Later Dr. Becker, working with Dr. Howard Friedman, discovered that exposing human volunteers to pulsed magnetic fields of similar frequency and considerably greater strength than those associated with magnetic storms significantly reduced the volunteers' ability to react to the appearance of light.

While EMF research continued, U.S. military projects spurred the first public involvement in the EMF issue. A Navy and GTE Sylvania project for an extra-low-frequency (ELF) test facility in Wisconsin (called Project Sanguine) met with powerful objections in 1968 from environmental groups. Neighbors of the Navy's test facility at Clam Lake reported that they were receiving electrical shocks when they turned on water faucets.[39] Environmentalists claimed that alternating magnetic fields generated by the ELF antennas could produce dangerously high voltages in power and telephone lines.[40] The Navy responded to the objections in an environmental impact statement by demonstrating that household appliances give off stronger magnetic fields than the ELF facility.

Concerns about EMF were initially minimal for two reasons. First, no transfer of energy occurs, as in X-rays, where chemical bonds are broken, or microwaves, where

---

[38] "Biological Effects of Power Frequency Electric and Magnetic Fields," Congressional Background Paper, Office of Technology Assessment, 1989.
[39] Paul Brodeur, "Annals of Radiation: The Hazards of Electromagnetic Fields," New Yorker, June 12, 1989, pp. 51–58, 62.
[40] Id.

tissue is heated. Second, all cells in the body have natural electric fields that are at least one hundred times more intense than any induced by exposure to common power-frequency fields.[41]

Dr. Becker strongly urged the Institute of Electrical and Electronic Engineers at its summer 1972 meeting to begin a program to study human exposure to electromagnetic fields. In 1973, Dr. Becker was asked to serve on the Navy's Bureau of Medicine and Surgery to review the Navy's research on the biological and ecological effects of ELF radiation. Though Dr. Becker and other members of the advisory committee recommended that the Navy further study the effects of Project Sanguine on human beings and animals, the Navy proceeded with the project. The advisory committee's warnings were never made public.[42]

Power Line Placement Becomes an Issue

During the time of the initial EMF research and the military controversies, the siting of power lines became an issue as the public became more aware of EMF. In 1973, the Power Authority of the State of New York (PASNY) was considering the construction and placement of a 765-kilovolt power line in upstate New York. Dr. Becker wrote to the PASNY and urged it to delay its decision on placement until the Project Sanguine experiments were completed. The Public Service Commission of New York (PSC) began hearings on the 765-kilovolt line in 1973.

The hearings were long and complicated, with utility experts testifying that the line's placement would present no biological hazard to citizens. Andrew Marino, a colleague of Dr. Becker, testified about his work in exposing rats to 60-hertz ELF electric fields. The exposed rats gained less weight, drank less water, and showed altered levels of blood proteins and enzymes compared to control rats. After Dr. Marino testified that ELF radiation could biologically affect humans, the utilities involved requested and received a postponement of the PSC hearings for a year. The hearings resumed in late 1975, and after pressure from Governor Hugh Carey, the PSC authorized construction of the line in 1976 but left open the issue of the required right-of-way width.

Both Drs. Becker and Marino were strongly attacked following their testimony at the PSC hearing. The chair of the National Academy of Sciences Committee told the *Saturday Review*:

> The judges threw out the case with prejudice. They ruled that Marino's not a believable witness, that he's evasive and deceitful. Here we were, being attacked by people who ultimately were thrown out of a court of justice in that way. They've all been thrown out. These guys are all a bunch of quacks.[43]

At the same time, politically based environmental opposition drove Project Sanguine from Wisconsin. The Navy's advisory committee report with Dr. Becker's recommendation to study the effects of Project Sanguine on residents near Clam Lake

---

[41] *"Biological Effects of Power Frequency Electric and Magnetic Fields,"* p. 1.

[42] Brodeur, *"Annals of Radiation,"* p. 67.

[43] Id., p. 76

finally was made public after Senator Gaylord Nelson of Wisconsin received a copy of it. In a press release, Senator Nelson accused the Navy of suppressing evidence and failing to follow through on the effects of radiation.[44]

The Werthemeier Seminal Study on EMFs

In the spring of 1974, epidemiologist Nancy Werthemeier began to study children who had died from leukemia in the Denver area. The results suggested a connection between the proximity of the children's homes to transmission lines and the incidence of leukemia. The studies, published in the *American Journal of Epidemiology*, concluded that the cancer rate of children from homes located near high-current configurations (HCC) was two to three times the normal rate of cancer. That is, if one child in a thousand gets cancer in the general population, two to three children living near HCCs would be expected to get it.[45] The homes affected included those that were less than:

1. Forty meters from large-gauge primary wires or arrays of six or more thin primary wires;
2. Twenty meters from an array of thirty-five thin primary wires or high-tension (50,230-kilovolt) wires; and
3. Fifteen meters from 240-volt wires.[46]

Dr. David Savitz repeated a Werthemeier-type study in Denver and released his results in 1986. Dr. Savitz agreed with the Werthemeier conclusion that exposure to EMF may increase the risk of developing cancer in children. However, Dr. Savitz also suggested that simple reconfiguration of the wires on transmission lines could reduce that risk substantially.

Cape Cod's PAVE PAWS

In 1976, the Air Force proposed installing a PAVE PAWS radar facility at Cape Cod, Massachusetts. No environmental impact statement was prepared, and installation began with no public input. PAVE PAWS is an acronym for Precision Acquisition of Vehicle Entry Phased Array Warning System. PAVE PAWS differs from regular radar in that instead of a rotating antenna, it has solid-state components that are controlled by computer and steered electronically; it emits ELF radiation. PAVE PAWS was used to detect sea-launched ballistic missiles.[47] The Air Force issued a 250-page report on environmental issues surrounding ELF that mentioned PAVE PAWS might cause cardiac pacemakers to skip a beat. However, construction of the project was approved and work began.

As construction began on the PAVE PAWS facility, local residents sought help from their congressman, Gerry E. Studds, who asked the Air Force for the research supporting its conclusion that PAVE PAWS presented no long-term danger to human health. At a town meeting, an Air Force official told residents that he could not guarantee that they would be safe from the effects of PAVE PAWS radiation.[48]

---

[44] Id., p. 63.

[45] Nancy Werthemeier and Ed Leeper, "Electrical Wiring Configuration and Childhood Cancer," American Journal of Epidemiology 109, 1979, p. 273.

[46] Id., p. 277.

[47] Paul Brodeur, "Annals of Radiation: The Hazards of Electromagnetic Fields Part II," New Yorker, June 19, 1989, p. 47.

[48] Id., p. 48.

Following these public meetings, the Cape Cod Environmental Coalition sued the Air Force for violating the National Environmental Policy Act by not issuing an environmental impact statement (EIS) before constructing PAVE PAWS. As a result of the suit, the Air Force agreed to study the radiation from facility towers and do an EIS.

In January 1980, Dr. Adey denounced the Air Force for its unwillingness to study PAVE PAWS and its effects on residents before building the towers. Reports of Dr. Adey's denunciation appeared in newspapers across the country.

At about the same time that the issue of ELF impact was gaining national momentum, the New York PSC issued its final decision on the 765-kilovolt line. The PSC reached the conclusion that ELF fields could have effects on humans, yet still authorized the line provided the right of way was widened to 350 feet.

Corroboration of Werthemeier's Work

Scientific studies about ELF and EMF continued. Dr. Adey released the results of his studies that showed weak ELF fields could alter the flow of calcium from brain cells and thereby alter the chemistry of the brain. Dr. Adey had used brain tissue from chicks in his studies and had also observed the behaviors of monkeys and cats. In 1976 and 1979, Carl F. Blackman, an Environmental Protection Agency (EPA) scientist, duplicated Dr. Adey's work and reached the same conclusions.[49]

In June 1982, a preliminary report of a Swedish study of childhood leukemia by Dr. Lennart Tomenius corroborated Werthemeier's results. Also in 1982, Drs. Werthemeier and Leeper published the results of their adult cancer study that indicated a correlation between transmission lines and the incidence of cancer in adults. At nearly the same time, Dr. Samuel Milham's study correlating leukemia to occupational exposure to electric and magnetic fields was published in *The New England Journal of Medicine*. Later that year, studies from the University of Southern California School of Medicine confirmed Dr. Milham's findings.[50]

Late in 1982, an article in the *Cape Cod Times* about the possible health effects of PAVE PAWS revealed that Arthur Guy was conducting a study for the Air Force of the long-term effects of low-level microwave radiation. The article entitled "PAVE PAWS: Where Has the Controversy Gone?" discussed the studies to date and questioned the Air Force figures.

In 1983, Drs. Adey and Daniel B. Lyle published the results of their further studies in *Bioelectromagnetics*. They concluded that a PAVE PAWS carrier frequency could significantly suppress the ability of cultured T-lymphocyte cells in mice to kill cultured cancer cells.

At the same time, the first studies of electrical workers appeared when Michael McDowell released the results of his studies that showed an increased risk of leukemia among workers in all electrical occupations. A 1984 study of white males in Maryland who had died of brain tumors revealed that a significantly higher than expected number had been employed in electrical occupations. Leading electronics and communications firms formed the Electromagnetic Energy Policy Alliance in 1984 to

[49] Id., p. 47.
[50] Id.

downplay the hazards of radiation. That same year, the Illinois Institute of Technology Research prepared a report for the Navy that showed that the strength of magnetic fields from household appliances dropped off so quickly with distance that such devices could not be considered major sources of indoor exposure.

In 1985, Dr. Guy released the results of his study for the Air Force, which found higher incidences of cancer in rats exposed to microwave radiation. A study done by Stanislaw Szmigielski and published that same year indicated that Polish military personnel who worked with or near radiation-emitting devices were more than three times as likely to develop cancer as unexposed personnel.

Houston Lighting Case and Public Knowledge of EMF

The first court case involving power lines was brought in 1985 by Houston Lighting & Power Company against the Klein Independent School District for the district's refusal to grant right-of-way access for the construction of power lines. The jury found for the school district and awarded compensatory and punitive damages. An appellate court later reversed the punitive damages but upheld the right of the school district to refuse the right-of-way on the grounds that the EMFs of the lines presented potential health hazards.

Following the Houston case, studies on EMF and health hazards were conducted and reported in a nearly continuous stream. In 1986, Drs. Werthemeier and Leeper released another study that demonstrated a direct connection between fetal development and the use of electric blankets and water beds. Electromagnetic fields from the water bed heaters and the blankets sent pulses that resulted in a significantly higher rate of defects in exposed fetuses. Also in 1986, the utility-funded Electric Power Research Institute (EPRI) released results of a study that indicated lower birth weights and a significant increase in the number of birth defects among swine exposed to electromagnetic radiation.

As these study results were being released, the impact of operating projects was assessable based on epidemiological studies. In March 1986, the Massachusetts Department of Health reported that women living near the Cape Cod PAVE PAWS facility had a significantly higher rate of cancer than the general population.

By 1987, Congress and state legislatures and agencies began to conduct both generic and specific-issue hearings on the placement of power lines. With all the public attention, the issue of overhead power lines near property became a discussion topic in seminars for real estate developers and agents.

The first lawsuits alleging declines in property value because of power line location and public fear began in 1988, when New York landowners sued the New York Power Authority alleging that the 345-kilovolt line, the subject of the landmark hearings in the 1970s, created a "cancer corridor" and had destroyed the market value of their properties.

The Follow-Up Studies

Studies continued to indicate the dangers of EMFs. A study of Texas utility workers showed that they had a cancer rate thirteen times greater than that of workers who were not exposed to EMFs. A later study by the University of Southern California established that electrical workers with ten years on the job had a higher risk for certain forms of brain tumors than those with five years' experience. By 1990, many counties had approved measures limiting construction of power lines. School boards, following the lead of the Houston case, closed off buildings near power lines to protect their children.[51]

A Congressional Office of Technology Assessment report on EMFs concluded: "The emerging evidence no longer allows one to categorically assert that there are no risks."[52] Department of Energy researchers noted, "There is clearly cause for concern but not for alarm."[53] Dr. David Carpenter, Dean of the School of Public Health at the State University of New York, Albany observed, "This is really harming people. In my judgment the present state of affairs is like the correlation between smoking and lung cancer 30 years ago."[54]

Utilities, through EPRI, had quadrupled spending on EMF research since 1986. But public concern continued to build. Some environmental consultants predicted that EMFs would become the biggest environmental challenge electric utilities face.

Cyrus Noe, editor of *Clearing Up*, a utility newsletter, says that electricity is a necessity of modern life and "no one is going to say that we have to turn off the lights. But utilities cannot simply gin up a plan, award a bunch of contracts and spend the EMF dilemma away. We just don't know the answers."[55]

A 1993 study conducted by Dr. David Savitz, reported in *Epidemiology* and based on his examination of 36,221 Southern California Edison workers, concluded there was no evidence of increased levels of leukemia, brain cancer, or lymphoma from EMF exposure. Savitz commented on the study's credibility and indicated that workplace EMF exposure probably could not be linked to cancer. However, he noted that further research is needed on childhood exposure to EMF and the incidence of leukemia.

In 1995, the *American Journal of Epidemiology* reported the largest study of utility workers to date. The EPRI-funded study looked at 138,905 men who worked for power companies between 1950 and 1986, including 20,733 who had died. It was the first study to take actual measurements of exposure levels.

Overall, the workers' death risk was lower than that of the general population. However, the brain cancer risk was 50 percent higher for men who worked more than five years as linemen or electricians. Further, those who were exposed to the highest levels of EMFs had more than double the risk of brain cancer. The study found that brain cancer is so rare that electrocution and work accidents should be the focus of safety measures. Further, it found no association between EMF exposure and leukemia.

Where EMFs Stand Today

In 1996, the National Research Council (NRC) issued its report on EMFs after examining 500 studies over 17 years. The NRC study was sponsored by the U.S. Department of Energy. The NRC is a private, nonprofit institution that provides research and

---

[51] David Kirkpatrick, "Can Power Lines Give You Cancer?" Fortune, December 31, 1990, pp. 80–85.
[52] Id.
[53] Id.
[54] Id.
[55] Keith Schneider, "Electricity and Cancer? The Mystery Increases," The New York Times, February 3, 1991, p. E3.

technological advice to Congress. The NRC issued the following observations about the Werthemeier and Savitz studies:

> The weak link shown between proximity to power lines and childhood leukemia may be the result of factors other than magnetic fields that are common to houses with the types of external wiring identified with the disease. These include: a home's proximity to high traffic density, local air quality, and construction features of older homes that fall into this category.[56]

The NRC report also concluded that only at levels between 1,000 and 100,000 times stronger than residential fields do cells show reaction to EMF exposure, and there is no evidence that such reactions produce adverse health effects.[57] Finally, the NRC review concluded that even high exposure to EMF does not affect the DNA of the cell, it does not act as a carcinogen, and also does not affect reproduction, development, or behavior in animals.

Several recommendations for future research were offered by the NRC:

1. Further research on occupational exposure because its efforts focused on low-frequency electric and magnetic fields in homes; and
2. Determining the reason(s) for the small increase in childhood leukemia (rare) among children in homes near power lines.[58]

In 1997, the National Cancer Institute reported its findings on children living near high voltage power lines and cancer in *The New England Journal of Medicine*. The study's authors concluded "that exposure to electromagnetic fields does not increase a child's risk of leukemia" after reviewing the health records and EMF levels in the homes of 629 children with leukemia and 619 healthy children in a nine-state area. The study found that children without cancer were exposed to the same levels of EMF energy as those with cancer.[59]

Lawsuits against utilities began with the Houston case and have continued. In one action over the leukemia death of a child whose home was near a transformer, the jury found for the utility. Still pending are economic-loss lawsuits in which homeowners are seeking recovery for property value losses resulting from their homes' locations next to transformers or wires and public fears about such proximity and EMFs. The Office of Technology and Assessment estimates that the cost of EMF litigation is between $1 billion and $3 billion per year. To date, no utility has lost a case in which there has been health-related litigation. However, utilities have settled a number of cases brought by property owners for the decline in value of their homes or the so-called psychological impact on property values. Those suits are expected to dwindle as utilities engage in the process of "prudent placement," which is the placement of power lines in areas away from private landowners and residences.

---

[56] *NRC Report on EMF (1996), p. ii (Executive summary).*

[57] *In fact, several studies showed that the exposure helped by speeding up the healing process after a bone is broken.* National Research Council News, *October 31, 1996, p. 2 as excerpted from* Possible Health Effects of Exposure to Residential Electric and Magnetic Fields, *National Academy Press, 1996.*

[58] Id.

[59] *Steve Sternberg, "Power Lines Not a Cancer Risk for Kids," USA Today, July 3–6, 1997, p. 1A.*

Discussion Questions

1. Does a clear causal connection exist between EMFs and cancer?

2. What companies should be concerned about liability for exposure to EMFs?

3. What regulations do you foresee being enacted to address the EMF issue?

4. What problems do you see for owners of land located near power lines?

5. If you were a human resources officer in an electric utility, what, if any, action would you take to protect your company's workers?

6. If you were a manufacturer or seller of electric blankets or water beds, would you warn purchasers of your products about the possible dangers of EMFs?

7. Should electric utilities make any workplace changes for safety because of EMFs?

8. Should electric utilities reconfigure wiring to minimize EMF exposure of residents near power lines?

CASE 7.9

Johns-Manville and the Asbestos Exposure

Although the public gained much of its knowledge regarding the dangers of asbestos after the litigation against asbestos manufacturers began, the information and dangers related to asbestos had been building for some time. Retracing the historical, scientific, medical, legislative, and litigation events that led to the bankruptcy of Johns-Manville offers insight into the steady progression of this business crisis.

Early History of Asbestos

Asbestos is a gray-white fibrous mineral that is heat resistant and possesses great strength. It was mined in Canada and South Africa and processed at plants throughout the world. The largest processors were Johns-Manville, Raybestos-Manhattan, Pittsburgh-Corning, Owens-Corning, GAF, UNR, AMATEX, Owens-Illinois, Nicolet, Celotex, Eagle-Picher, Keene, Fibreboard, Standard Asbestos, and Armstrong Cork. The qualities of asbestos made it seem unique and irreplaceable. At the height of its use in the United States, it could be found in everything from hair dryers to potholders to brake drums.

As early as 1 A.D., Strabo and Pliny the Elder mentioned a sickness of the lungs in slaves who wove asbestos into cloth. Hippocrates (460–377 B.C.) described silicosis in a metal digger and noted that the man "breathes with great difficulty." Marco Polo even learned of the "mineral in the mountain" that contained threads like those of wool. Autopsies performed on stonecutters in 1672 by Ijsbrand van Diemerbroech, a professor of medicine at the University of Utrecht in the Netherlands, revealed that the vesicles of their lungs were so clogged with fine dust that dissecting them was like cutting through sand. In 1700, Bernardino Ramazzini, a professor of medicine at the

University of Padua, suggested that stonecutters perform their work with their backs to the wind, so as to avoid inhaling.

In the late eighteenth century, Western technology began to use asbestos as an insulator for boilers, steampipes, turbines, ovens, kilns, and other high-temperature equipment. In England in 1819, workers who ground dry stones suffered such a high rate of silicosis (called "grinders asthma") that businesses proposed that criminals be used for the task.[60]

The Connection between Industrial Dust and Lung Disease

The problem of lung-dust infestation came to light in the United States in 1887 when an autopsy was performed on a stove-foundry worker from Poughkeepsie, New York, whose lungs showed the presence of silicosis. In 1898, when Henry Ward Johns, the founder of H. W. Johns Manufacturing (the forerunner of Johns-Manville), died, his death certificate listed the cause of death as "dust phthisis pneumonia," or what appeared to be a description of asbestosis.

Dr. Montague Murray, a London physician, established the first connection between asbestos-textile factory work and severe pulmonary fibrosis. During the course of an autopsy in 1900, Dr. Murray found spicules of asbestos in the lungs of a 33-year-old man who had died from the disease.

After Dr. Murray made his finding, other physicians reported connections between asbestos workers' occupations and their deaths by lung disease. By 1918, the U.S. government had become involved in the health issues surrounding asbestos workers, and the Bureau of Labor Statistics published a report by statistician Frederick L. Hoffman that established that asbestos workers had an unusually high death rate at an unusually early age. The report noted, moreover, that many American and Canadian insurance companies were no longer issuing policies to asbestos workers because of the "health-injurious conditions" assumed to exist in the asbestos industry.

The first asbestosis death described in medical literature appeared in the *British Medical Journal* in 1924 in an article by Dr. W. E. Cooke, who named the disease asbestosis. Shortly after, state governments began to note workers' compensation claims being filed by asbestos workers. As early as 1928, Johns-Manville sponsored studies by Dr. Leroy U. Gardner, who produced asbestosis in test animals by allowing them to inhale asbestos fibers. These studies, which were not released, were uncovered during litigation in 1971.

The Medical Inspector of Factories for the British Home Office conducted an epidemiological study of asbestos workers in 1928 that showed, among other things, an 81 percent rate of fibrosis in workers who had been in the industry twenty years or more. Based on the study findings, Parliament in 1931 enacted legislation designed to provide protection for asbestos workers. Subsequently, Dr. Anthony Lanza found, in a study he conducted for Metropolitan Life Insurance, that, based on X-ray results of long-term asbestos workers, 106 of 126 of them had already developed asbestosis.

---

[60] Most of the material in the historical section of the case, while corroborated in later litigation, was taken from what remains the authoritative work in this field: Paul Brodeur, "The Asbestos Industry on Trial," New Yorker. Mr. Brodeur's four-part series appeared in the issues of June 10, 1985, p. 64; June 17, 1985, p. 69; June 24, 1985; and July 1, 1985. The historical discussion here draws only on the June 10 and June 17 pieces.

During this period of medical discovery in the asbestos industry, so-called "silicosis" suits" began to appear around the country. Damages in these suits, which were brought by workers who alleged harmful exposure to silica dust and resulting lung problems, totaled $300 million by 1934. Alarmed by the increasing numbers of suits, several insurance companies recommended that silicosis and other pulmonary dust diseases be taken out of the courts and covered under workers' compensation.

Johns-Manville's Initial Approach to Liability

It was also during this period of medical discovery and silicosis suits that Johns-Manville experienced its first asbestos litigation. In 1933, the board of directors of Johns-Manville directed the company's CEO and president to settle asbestosis lawsuits that had been brought against Johns-Manville in New Jersey courts by Samuel Greenstone, an attorney, on behalf of eleven workers. The company made a $30,000 settlement payment in exchange for Greenstone's promise that he would not "directly or indirectly participate in the bringing of new actions against the Corporation."[61] The settlement terms, documented in the board's minutes, were not revealed until discovery during litigation some forty-five years later. They read as follows:

> The President advised the meeting that Messrs. Hobart & Minard of Newark had been approached by the attorney for the plaintiffs in the eleven pending "asbestosis" cases with an offer to settle all the cases upon a much lower basis than had ever been previously discussed. He further stated that our general counsel, Messrs. Davis Polk Wardell Gardiner & Reed, as well as Messrs. Hobart & Minard, had recommended that we settle for approximately $30,000 provided written assurances were obtained from the attorney for the various plaintiffs that he would not directly or indirectly participate in the bringing of new actions against the corporation.[62]

Johns-Manville was then the largest producer of asbestos in the United States. The company also sold asbestos to many other firms for use in other products. Manville had great liability exposure not only through its own sales, but also through its sales to other companies and eventually to third-party buyers.

When Dr. Lanza was to submit his X-ray study results to the U.S. Public Health Service, George S. Hobart, a Johns-Manville attorney, and Vandiver Brown, a corporate attorney for Johns-Manville, asked him to soften the description of asbestosis in his report. Hobart remarked:

> It is only within a comparatively recent time that asbestosis has been recognized by the medical and scientific professions as a disease. One of our principal defenses in actions against the company on the common law theory of negligence has been that the scientific and medical knowledge has been insufficient until a very recent period to place upon the owners of plants or factories the burden of taking special precautions against the possible onset of the disease to their employees.[63]

Brown added the following when he forwarded Hobart's remarks to Dr. Lanza:

> I am sure that you understand fully that no one in our organization is suggesting for a moment that you alter by one jot or tittle any scientific facts or inevitable conclusions

[61] Id.
[62] Id.
[63] Id., p. 63.

revealed or justified by your preliminary survey. All we ask is that all of the favorable aspects of the survey be included and that none of the unfavorable be unintentionally pictured in darker tones than the circumstances justify. I feel confident we can depend upon you . . . to give us this "break" and mine and Mr. Hobart's suggestions are presented in this spirit.[64]

By 1935, asbestosis was widely discussed at medical meetings, and research into the disease was ongoing. During that year, Vandiver Brown wrote to Sumner Simpson, the president of Raybestos-Manhattan. Through a series of letters, both agreed that asbestosis should not be mentioned in industry trade journals. Raybestos-Manhattan did join, however, with other asbestos product manufacturers in sponsoring long-range research programs on the biological effects of asbestos. On October 1, 1935, Sumner Simpson wrote the following in a letter to Vandiver Brown about possible publication of survey results in *Asbestos*, a trade magazine:

As I see it personally, we would be just as well off to say nothing about [asbestosis] until our survey is complete. I think the less said about asbestos, the better off we are, but at the same time, we cannot lose track of the fact that there have been a number of articles on asbestos dust control and asbestosis in the British trade magazines. The magazine Asbestos is in business to publish articles affecting the trade and they have been very decent about not re-printing the English articles.[65]

Vandiver Brown replied to Simpson's letter as follows:

I quite agree with you that our interests are best served by having asbestosis receive a minimum of publicity.[66]

Widespread Medical Evidence of Asbestosis and Asbestos as a Carcinogen

Eventually, medical research identified two major diseases that could result from exposure to asbestos dust. The first, the focus of the research, was asbestosis, which is a scarring of the lung tissue. Asbestosis does not appear immediately and may not manifest itself for ten to thirty years after initial exposure. During this time, the inhaler will appear healthy and normal and will experience no symptoms of the disease. However, inhaled asbestos fibers that remain in the lungs cause a tissue reaction that is progressive and, apparently, irreversible. The result is a slow buildup of problems, such as breathing difficulties that eventually become severe enough to make any physical exertion impossible. The second disease, mesothelioma, is a malignant and extremely painful cancer of the chest lining. This cancer has been associated only with asbestos exposure; it usually is fatal within one year after symptoms appear. Like asbestosis, this disease may not appear for twenty years after initial exposure to asbestos. For example, the mother of an asbestos worker, whose only exposure to asbestos came through washing his factory clothes in the 1960s, died of mesothelioma in 1983.

In 1936, Vandiver Brown and Sumner Simpson informed Dr. Leroy Gardner of their willingness to fund his asbestosis research, but a condition of the funding was a "bargain of silence." Gardner would be unable to publish the results of his work. In

[64] Id.
[65] Id.
[66] Id.

1977, attorney Karl Asch discovered the agreement and the results of Gardner's work, which indicated a connection between exposure to asbestos and pulmonary dust disease. Asch used the so-called "Sumner Simpson papers" as a smoking gun to show that Raybestos-Manhattan not only knew of the disease dangers but also attempted to suppress the information.

The U.S. Public Health Service recommended in 1938 an average dust level of five million particles per cubic foot to be the acceptable level of exposure for American asbestos workers. However, research into asbestosis continued to produce hundreds of medical journal articles on the disease. Theories regarding appropriate levels of exposure conflicted with each other; some research suggested that no level was appropriate.

In 1948, Dr. Kenneth Smith, the medical director for Canadian Johns-Manville, conducted an industrial hygiene survey of 708 men working at an asbestos plant in Quebec and discovered that only four of them had X-rays that showed normal, healthy lungs. The findings, which at the time were neither published nor revealed to the workers, first became public in 1976, when litigation discovery revealed the study and its results.

Because of the mounting research findings, some workers began wearing respirators to block their inhalation of asbestos dust. Finally, in the early 1950s, the information on asbestosis and asbestosis research made its way into the popular press. In 1952, the January issue of *Search*, a monthly journal of the California Tuberculosis Association, printed a picture of Johns-Manville's Lompac, California, plant with a caption that read, "Death by Dust." The articles in the journal described poor working conditions at the plant. In that same year, a week-long symposium on the subject of asbestos-related lung cancer was held, but its results were never published and, again, were discovered only during later litigation.

By 1955, unions for asbestos workers and miners had begun to raise the issue of asbestosis. Also at this time, the general counsel for the Quebec Asbestos Mining Association (Johns-Manville was a leading member of this trade group) warned the association's members that asbestos exposure posed a serious health problem for the industry.

Shortly thereafter, Johns-Manville experienced an unprecedented third-party lawsuit for negligence and breach of warranty brought by Frederick LeGrand, a New Jersey asbestos insulator who had developed asbestosis. Another New Jersey insulator filed a similar suit in 1961. These suits were the beginning of the third-party liability suits that Manville would experience over the next thirty years.

Product purchasers, installers, ship builders, and even those who occupied buildings insulated with asbestos would file suits against Manville as the ultimate supplier and responsible party for the lung disease not limited to actual asbestos purchasers and users.

The Beginning of the End: Manville's Litigation Crisis

In 1966, attorney Ward Stephenson filed suit against eleven asbestos manufacturers on behalf of his client, Claude Tomplait, an insulator who had developed asbestosis. Stephenson also litigated on behalf of Clarence Borel, another insulator who sued several asbestos manufacturers. The trial court found for Borel and more significantly, its verdict was upheld by the Fifth Circuit Court of Appeals. The appellate decision triggered 25,000 third-party asbestos lawsuits that would be brought against asbestos manufacturers over the next decade. The 1973 *Borel*[67] decision marked the beginning of the end for the asbestos industry. Between 1974 and 1988, asbestos litigation increased tenfold.

At this time, Congress had just created OSHA, and numerous recommendations for lowering the exposure levels of asbestos workers were being made. Raybestos-Manhattan shut down its New Jersey plant in 1973, and Pittsburgh-Corning, facing multimillion-dollar claims, shut down its Tyler, Texas, asbestos plant in 1974.

The 1974 annual report for Raybestos-Manhattan included the following language:

> For many years it has been known that prolonged inhalation of asbestos dust by factory workers could lead to disease. As early as 1930, Raybestos-Manhattan commissioned the Metropolitan Life Insurance Company to survey all of its factories and to make recommendations for the elimination of conditions which might present health hazards. Following presentations of the reports and recommendations, extensive long-range engineering programs were instituted at all plants to develop effective dust control systems.

Raybestos-Manhattan joined with other asbestos products manufacturers in the mid-1930s in funding long-range research programs on the biological effects of asbestos.

Because of the long latent period of asbestos-related disease, the disease being found today among some industry employees is a result of conditions existing decades ago when little was known about the health effects of asbestos or proper means of control.[68]

In 1976, 159 cases had been filed against Johns-Manville; in 1978, 792 suits were filed; and by 1982, suits were being filed at a rate of 6,000 per year. Manville settled asbestos-related suits for an average of $21,000, but by 1982 this settlement amount doubled.

Manville's Chapter 11 Resolution

A congressional bail-out on behalf of Manville and the others failed, and the lawsuits against the asbestos manufacturers continued and increased. Ultimately, it was an accounting rule, FASB-5, that led Manville into Chapter 11 bankruptcy. Coopers & Lybrand had taken the position in the previous eight SEC filings that, under FASB-5, it could not reliably estimate the costs of disposition of the suits and therefore need not make any disclosures about them before certifying the financial statements. However, before the ninth SEC filing, Litigation Analysis Group (LAG), a litigation consultant for Manville's cases, gave Manville an estimate that the cost of disposition of all future suits would be 1 billion, 900 million dollars. With this expert opinion in place, Coopers & Lybrand could no longer take its "no estimate possible" position under FASB-5. When Coopers & Lybrand refused to sign off on the financial statements needed for the SEC filing without a disclosure of the litigation liability, Manville dismissed them and hired Price Waterhouse. But, after reviewing the LAG report, Price Waterhouse reached the same conclusion and refused to certify the financial statements without a disclosure on the litigation. Unable to issue financial statements, Manville filed for Chapter 11 bankruptcy protection on August 26, 1982.

---

[67] Borel v. Fibreboard Paper Products Corp., *493 F.2d 1076 (5th Cir. 1973).*
[68] Paul Brodeur, *"The Asbestos Industry on Trial,"* New Yorker, *June 17, 1985, p. 69.*

The big problem in the Manville Chapter 11 proceedings was all the actual and pending suits against the company. The bankruptcy proceedings continued through 1989, when Manville and others agreed to the Manville Personal Injury Settlement Trust. Under the agreement, Manville was required to give $2.5 billion in assets (mostly stock) to the trust. Manville was also required, beginning in 1991, to pay annually to the trust $75 million and 20 percent of its annual net income.[69] So far, 152,000 claims have been filed and 3,000 more are expected. The average settlement has been $42,000. The approval for paying claims came in December 1994, and the resulting payment settlement gives claimants ten cents on the dollar. Also, $55.7 million of the trust funds were awarded to co-defendants who had paid Manville's share of the liability while the trust payments were in litigation.[70]

In 1976, asbestos sales accounted for 31 percent of Manville's business, or $1.6 billion. Today, 42 percent, or $2.2 billion, of the company's sales comes from fiberglass insulation.

The asbestos saga continues throughout the country and across government agencies. For example, the cleanup of asbestos in Chicago school districts has had an estimated cost of $500 million, and the Illinois Supreme Court has ruled that the school districts can proceed to recover property damages from asbestos manufacturers. The EPA, in turn, has begun issuing complaints against school districts that do not act quickly enough to replace asbestos insulation; those districts that fail to clean up their asbestos problems face a $25,000 fine.[71] Even the replacement has now produced litigation. Those who have been exposed during the replacement process now have suits pending against installers, contractors, and the original asbestos companies.

Many asbestos cases are still not settled and there are continuing claims. Late-night television includes ads from law firms seeking workers who have mesothelioma. Two-hundred thousand pending claims remain.[72] Twenty former asbestos manufacturers have settled potential future claims for $1 billion. In early 1995, OSHA issued new regulations requiring employer disclosure of the presence of asbestos in the workplace. The impact of exposure remains an issue for regulators as well as a potential source of liability. In 2000, Merrill Lynch estimated outstanding liability to be between $20 and $30 billion.[73] That estimate still remains valid today.

....

Discussion Questions

1. Suppose that you had been attorney Samuel Greenstone. Would you have agreed to no further lawsuits in exchange for the Manville settlement?

2. Suppose that you had been Dr. Anthony Lanza. Would you have taken any action with respect to the actions of George Hobart and Vandiver Brown?

[69] "Manville Trust Gets Clearance to Begin Asbestos Payments," The Wall Street Journal, December 16, 1994, p. B3.

[70] Marj Charlier, "Manville Trust, Victims' Lawyers Plan Payment Pact," The Wall Street Journal, November 19, 1990, p. B5.

[71] Barnaby Feder, "Asbestos: The Saga Drags On," The New York Times, April 2, 1989, pp. 1, 11.

[72] Gregory Zuckerman, "Specter of Costly Asbestos Litigation Haunts Companies," The Wall Street Journal, December 27, 2000, pp. C1, C15.

[73] Id.

3. In deciding on the "bargain of silence," what questions in the ethical models did the officers and directors of Johns-Manville fail to consider? Be sure to list the long-term costs and consequences of their decision.

4. If you had been Dr. Leroy Gardner, would you have accepted Manville's funding under the conditions required?

5. Should Dr. Kenneth Smith have disclosed the findings in his X-ray study to the workers involved?

6. Could Johns-Manville have taken alternative steps that would have prevented the injuries?

7. Was asbestos a needed commodity?

8. Was Johns-Manville rewarded for ignoring the asbestos problem for so long? Should Manville (as it exists today) be required to liquidate its assets to pay all the claims?

....

Sources

"A Big Win for Asbestos Workers," *Time*, July 27, 1992, p. 17.

"Asbestos Defendants Must Pay Punitive Damages," *The Wall Street Journal*, July 31, 1992, p. B6.

Lambert, Wade, and Ellen Joan Pollock, "Manville to Add Funds to Asbestos Trust," *The Wall Street Journal*, September 10, 1990, p. B11.

Lambert, Wade, and Ellen Joan Pollock, "Owen-Illinois's Insurers Receive Setback in Asbestos Case Ruling," *The Wall Street Journal*, April 10, 1990, p. B11.

Moses, Jonathan M., "Former Asbestos Makers, 2 Law Firms Map $1 Billion Pact to Curb Litigation," *The Wall Street Journal*, January 18, 1993, p. A14.

Oberkfell, Sandra L., "New OSHA Regulations Significantly Increase the Obligation of Building and Facility Owners to Protect Employees and Other Workers from Asbestos Hazards," *National Law Journal*, January 30, 1995, p. B5.

Sanchez, Sandra, "Asbestos Firms Ruled Negligent," *USA Today*, July 14, 1992, p. 1A.

Whitaker, Leslie, "Monster in the Closet," *Time*, February 6, 1989, p. 53.

Wingo v. Celotex Corp., 834 F.2d 375 (4th Cir. 1987).

CASE 7.10

Domino's Pizza Delivers

Thomas S. Monaghan invented today's pizza delivery system when, in 1960, he opened the first Domino's in Ypsilanti, Michigan. By 1993, the company had grown to 5,300 U.S. franchises. Part of Domino's success came from its 30-minute guarantee: the pizza is delivered in 30 minutes or it's free.[74]

[74] Michael Clements, "Domino's Detours 30-Minute Guarantee," *USA Today*, December 22, 1993, p. 1A.

Domino's fleet of drivers across the United States ranges from 75,000 to 80,000. Because of the time pressure, some drivers were speeding and breaking the law. In 1990, 20 traffic fatalities in the United States involved Domino's drivers.

In 1985, Frank Kranack and his wife, Mary Jean, were struck by a Domino's delivery car while driving in their station wagon just outside a suburban Pittsburgh Domino's store. Frank suffered whiplash, and Mary Jean had neck and back injuries plus permanent disability in her right arm, the area of her body nearest the impact. When the accident occurred, the manager of the Domino's store rushed out to the wreckage and told the driver, "Let's get this pizza on the road." The Kranacks filed suit seeking damages and a halt to Domino's 30-minute policy.[75]

In 1991, Domino's changed the on-time policy to a $3 refund if delivery is late to curb fraud by college students who gave incorrect directions to slow their deliveries.

In December 1992, a St. Louis jury awarded $78 million to Jean Kinder, who had been hit by an 18-year-old Domino's delivery driver in 1989. Within one week of that award, Domino's dropped its 30-minute guarantee. Monaghan noted:

> I believe we are the safest delivery company in the world. But there continues to be a perception that the guarantee is unsafe.[76]

Some franchisees had already abandoned the 30-minute guarantee. A marketing strategist commented on the decision:

> The critical issue to them is still home delivery. It's their franchise. Abandoning a time limit isn't necessarily "mortally wounding" if they can come up with another way of talking about how terrific they deliver to the home.[77]

Discussion Questions

1. Even with monitoring, screening, and training of its drivers, could Domino's guarantee that all of them would drive safely? Was the risk too great?

2. Was the public perception of safety issues hurting Domino's more than the 30-minute guarantee helped it?

3. Did the $78 million jury verdict punish Domino's for its focus on the 30-minute delivery time?

4. Would you have made the same decision as Domino's?

5. How would you characterize the ethics of the college students who purposely gave incorrect directions to get their pizzas free?

[75] Peter Mattiace, "Suit Asks Domino's Pizza Be Pulled from Fast Lane," Arizona Republic, December 1, 1990, pp. A1, A7.
[76] Krystal Miller and Richard Gibson, "Domino's Stops Promising Pizza in 30 Minutes," The Wall Street Journal, December 22, 1993, pp. B1, B3.
[77] Clements, "Domino's Detours 30-Minute Guarantee," p. 1A.

CASE 7.11
Cell Phones

The ubiquitous cell phone has come to be a lightning rod for all manner of criticism. There are now 120 million cell phone subscribers in the United States, a figure that has increased 20 times since 1990. The annoyances range from users talking too loudly to the interruption of cell phones ringing in restaurants, during concerts, and in the middle of meetings and speeches.

Jacqueline Whitmore, an expert on business manners, has been teaching the etiquette of cell phones, which includes the following rules:

1. If you must talk on the cell phone while using the restroom, wait until the conversation has ended to flush.
2. Turn cell phones off at weddings, funerals, church services, and movies. An alternative is to switch the phone to vibrate rather than ring.
3. Respect rules established for cell phones such as Amtrak's quiet car (cars designated on their trains as being free from cell phone conversation) and at opera houses in Europe where cell phones must be checked in the cloakroom.
4. Use an appropriate level of voice. Avoid "cell phone voice," which is a tendency to talk louder than normal because of surrounding activity and noise.
5. Don't discuss personal matters on a cell phone while in public.
6. It may be easier to move away than to ask the person to stop talking on a cell phone.[78]

However, these daily annoyances and frustrations with cell phones have come to a head on an issue of safety related to cell phone use. Several accidents also brought the issue to the forefront in 2000. Jason Jones, a 19-year-old midshipman at the United States Naval Academy, was charged with vehicular manslaughter in November 1999 when he veered off the highway and ran into John and Carole Hall, who were in their car which was parked alongside the road. Mr. and Mrs. Hall were both killed instantly. Jones was charged with manslaughter because prosecutors alleged that he was driving at speeds ranging from 80 to 105 miles per hour while talking on the cell phone. Jones did not deny using the cell phone, but indicated he was not speeding. The jury refused to convict him of manslaughter but did find him guilty of reckless driving.

Also during 2000, several studies were published indicating the risks associated with cell phone usage while driving. Prior to this time there had been only the study published in *The New England Journal of Medicine* that concluded a driver using a cell phone is four times as likely to be involved in an accident. According to the study, the accident rate for cell phone users while driving is higher than that for those who drive while above the legal limit for intoxication.[79] Dr. Frances Bent co-authored one study that indicated the laws for reckless driving do not carry sufficiently severe penalties for the level of distraction and carelessness resulting from cell phone use while driving. "There are no appropriate penalties for the tragedies that can result from using a cell-phone while driving. Many people are in denial that the distraction they are suffering

[78] Deborah Sharp, "Cellphones Reveal Screaming Lack of Courtesy," USA Today, September 4, 2001, p. 4A.
[79] Jeffrey Ball, "Safety Risk of Letting Drivers Use Cell Phones to Get Federal Scrutiny," The Wall Street Journal, July 14, 2000, pp. B1, B4.

while talking on a cellphone is dangerous. Drunks drive for a long time too—until the day they get in a crash."[80] A study by the Center for Urban Transportation at the University of South Florida indicates that cell phone use during driving increases the accident rate anywhere from 34 to 300 percent.

Statistically, cell phone usage is not the most common cause of driver distraction, as noted below.

What distracts drivers	
Something outside the vehicle	29.4%
Adjusting the radio	11.4%
Other occupants of vehicles	10.9%
A moving object in the car	4.3%
Other device or object	2.9%
Adjusting vehicle climate	2.9%
Eating, drinking	1.7%
Using cell phone	1.5%
Smoking	0.9%[81]

During 2001, forty-three states had some form of legislation proposed to prohibit or limit the use of cell phones while driving. Most of the legislation died in legislative committees because of the powerful lobbying by cell phone companies and also because legislators themselves are dependent on cell phone usage in their cars. The Cellular Telecommunications Industry Association supports strict enforcement of existing laws for reckless driving as applied to cell phone use while driving, but it does not support legislative bans on their use while driving. However, New Jersey has legislation that prohibits those who are driving with learner's permits from using the cell phone. Massachusetts prohibits bus drivers from using cell phones while on duty unless there is an emergency. On the other hand, Oregon and Oklahoma passed laws that prohibit cities and towns from passing ordinances that prohibit cell phone use while driving.[82] Italy and Japan prohibit cell phone use in cars unless the driver is using hands-free technology.[83]

The drive for banning cell phones while driving is largely spearheaded by Patricia Pena, a mother whose 2-year-old daughter was killed when a driver talking on a cell phone ran a stop sign and hit the Pena vehicle. Mrs. Pena began the "Advocates for Cell Phone Safety," a group that has been lobbying for laws limiting cell phone use while driving.

[80] Jessie Halladay, "Driver Wins Cellphone-Crash Verdict," USA Today, December 7, 2000, p. 10A.

[81] Gregory L. White and Andrea Peterson, "Cell Phone Firms Make Adjustments," The Wall Street Journal, July 4, 2001, p. B1.

[82] Same Howe Verhovek, "Drive Talking: Cell Phone Debate Set to Heat Up," The New York Times, September 2, 2001, p. A14.

[83] Ball, "Safety Risk of Letting Drivers Use Cell Phones to Get Federal Scrutiny," pp. B1, B4.

New York became the first state to pass restrictions on cell phone use in cars. Except for emergencies, and effective December 1, 2001, New York drivers are not permitted to use a cell phone with it next to their ears. Dialing a phone that is in a cradle or attached to a headset will be legal. Following the passage of the New York law, similar bills were introduced in 35 other states, even in those states that had declined to act on some form of legislation on driving and cell phones earlier in the year.

In response to the growing legislative trend, cellular phone companies are scrambling to develop technology to permit continued use of cell phones even when regulations are imposed. The companies fear a decline in business of the $53 billion per year cell phone industry sales. They are developing voice dialing and other hands-free technology for cell phone users. For a New York-type statute, cell phone users need only use a headset; Sprint in New York is already offering customers such a headset at a discount. Sprint also offers voice command dialing for an extra $10 per month and about 10 percent of its customers have signed on for the technology.

In addition, automakers are working to develop in-auto systems with phone companies. Ford has a joint venture with one cellular phone company in an attempt to develop a cell phone system that will meet the most stringent forms of proposed cell phone legislation.

Cell phone manufacturers continue to face one additional issue—a health concern related to the use of cell phones. The controversy centers on whether the cell phones cause cancer.

Some studies conclude that they do not, but the Wireless Technology Research program, a program funded by the cellular phone industry, has concluded that there are enough questions about their safety that no one should assure users that the phones are absolutely safe.[84]

The FDA's Center for Devices and Radiological Health has concluded that there are no adverse health effects from cell phones and that no additional warnings are needed. Following a lawsuit filed by a cell phone user in 1993 alleging that the cell phone caused his cancer, the industry placed $27 million into a blind trust for research projects supported by the funding. The Wireless Technology Research program was one of the beneficiaries of the trust.[85]

Two additional studies, one by the National Cancer Institute, indicate that cell phone users are no more likely than others to develop benign tumors or malignant brain cancers. The studies, published in *The New England Journal of Medicine* and *Journal of the American Medical Association*, indicate that exposure to radiofrequency (RF) through use of the phones is safe.

The researchers conducting the study indicated that cell phone use at the time of the studies was not as extensive or widespread and that those involved in the study had used the cell phones for only three years. Their advice is to repeat the studies in a few years to determine whether there might be some long-term impact from cell phone

---

[84] John Tuohy, "Cell Phone Researcher's Call: Be Cautious," *USA Today*, August 1, 2000, p. 1D.
[85] Review the findings on cell phone safety at http://www.medscape.com.

use. Dr. Mark Malkin, the author of the second study by the American Health Foundation, says that he does indeed use a cell phone.[86]

There are suits pending by cell phone users who allege that the phones do cause brain cancer.

....

Discussion Questions

1. If you were a cell phone manufacturer, would you take any steps to change your product?

2. Would you participate in the political and legislative processes, and if so, what position would you take?

3. Should the cell phone manufacturers undertake a vehicle safety campaign?

4. Why do you think the cell phone manufacturers' association opposes cell phone use restrictions? Do you think it will hamper sales? Do they believe so?

5. Is it ethical to use a cell phone while driving?

[86] Gina Rolata, "Cell Phone Studies See No Link to Brain Cancer," The New York Times, December 20, 2000, pp. A1, A21.

7c

Plant Closures and Downsizing

Economic downturns, intense competition, and the need to cut costs often force employers to close facilities and lay off workers. What obligations do businesses have to their employees? To the communities where their facilities are located? The dilemma of employer loyalty versus shareholder profit is a difficult one to resolve.

CASE 7.12

Aaron Feuerstein and Malden Mills[87]

Aaron Feuerstein is the chief executive officer and chairman of the board of Malden Mills, a 93-year-old privately held company that manufactures Polartec and is located in Mathuen, Massachusetts. Polartec is a fabric made from recycled plastic that stays dry and provides warmth. It is used in everything from ski parkas to blankets by companies such as L.L. Bean, Patagonia, Lands' End, and Eddie Bauer. Malden employs 2,400 locals, and Mr. Feuerstein and his family have steadfastly refused to move production overseas. Their labor costs are the highest in the industry—an average of $12.50 per hour. Malden Mills is the largest employer in what is one of Massachusetts' poorest towns.

On December 11, 1995, a boiler explosion at Malden Mills resulted in a fire that injured 27 people and destroyed three of the buildings at Malden Mills' factory site. With only one building left in functioning order, many employees assumed they would be laid off temporarily. Other employees worried that Mr. Feuerstein, then 70 years old, would simply take the insurance money and retire. Mr. Feuerstein could have retired with about $300 million in insurance proceeds from the fire.

Instead, Mr. Feuerstein announced on December 14, 1995, that he would pay the employees their salaries for at least thirty days. He continued that promise for six months, when 90 percent of the employees were back to work. The cost of covering the

[87] Adapted from Marianne M. Jennings, "Aaron Feuerstein—An Odd CEO," Business: Its Legal, Ethical and Global Environment, 6th ed., 2002, pp. 767–768.

wages was approximately $25 million to the company. During that time, Malden ran its Polartec through its one working facility as it began and completed the reconstruction of the plant, at a cost of $430 million. Interestingly, production output during this time was nine times what it had been before the fire. One worker noted, "I owe him every-thing. I'm paying him back."[88] After the fire and Feuerstein's announcement, customers pledged their support with one customer, Dakotah, sending in $30,000 to help. Within the first month following the fire, $1 million in donations was received.[89]

Malden Mills was rededicated in September 1997 with new buildings and tech-nology. About 10 percent of the 2,400 employees were displaced by the upgraded facilities and equipment, but Feuerstein created a job training and placement center on site in order to ease these employees' transition.

By the end of 2001, six years after the fire, Malden Mills had debts of $140 million and was teetering near bankruptcy. However, Malden Mills has been through bank-ruptcy before, in the 1980s, and emerged very strongly with its then new product, Polartec, developed through the company's R&D program.

Some have suggested that Mr. Feuerstein's generosity during that time is respon-sible for the present financial crisis. However, the fire destroyed the company's furniture upholstery division and customers were impatient at that time. They were not inclined to wait for production to ramp up, and Malden Mills lost most of those customers. It closed the upholstery division in 1996.

Also, there was the threat of inexpensive fleece from the Asian markets that was ignored largely because of the plant rebuilding and the efforts focused there. Finally, in 2000, the company had a shakeup in its marketing team just as it was launching its electric fabrics—fabrics with heatable wires that are powered by batteries embedded in the fleece.

Once again, however, the goodwill from 1995 remains. Residents of the town have been sending in checks to help the company, some as small as $10. An Internet campaign was begun by town residents to "Buy Fleece." The campaign is enjoying some success as Patagonia, Lands' End, and L.L. Bean report increased demand. In addition, the U.S. military placed large orders for fleece jackets for soldiers fighting in Operation Enduring Freedom in Afghanistan.

Senators Ted Kennedy and John Kerry have been lobbying GE not to involuntarily petition Malden Mills into bankruptcy. GE Capital holds one fourth of Malden Mills' debts. Its other creditors include Finova Capital, SAI Investment, Pilgrim Investment, LaSalle Bank, and PNC Bank.

The union, about to begin contract negotiations, has spoken through its leader, "We're ready to make sacrifices for a little while. Whatever he asks us to do to keep the place going."[90]

By 2002, Malden Mills was in bankruptcy. Feuerstein labored to raise the money to pay off creditors and buy his company back, but he was unable to meet the bankruptcy deadline. Malden Mills emerged from bankruptcy on September 30, 2003, but under

---

[88] "Malden Mills," Dateline NBC, August 9, 1996.
[89] Steve Wulf, "The Glow From a Fire," Time, January 8, 1996, p. 49.
[90] Lynnley Browning, "Fire Could Not Stop a Mill, but Debts May," The New York Times, November 28, 2001, pp. C1, C5.

management other than Mr. Feuerstein. He still hopes to buy the company back, but the price, originally $93 million, has increased to $120 million. Feuerstein is the president of Malden Mills, serves on its board, and earns a salary of $425,000 per year, but he is no longer in charge and cannot be until the creditors are repaid. In January 2004, members of the U.S. House and Senate were lobbying to convince the Export-Import Bank to loan Mr. Feuerstein the money he needed to buy back his company. The Ex-Im Bank, swayed by Mr. Feuerstein's commitment to keep Malden's production in the United States, increased the loan amount from the $20 million it had originally pledged, to the $35 million Mr. Feuerstein needed.

By the end of January 2004, Malden Mills had three new strategies: Mr. Feuerstein was selling Polarfleece blankets on QVC, the company would be in partnership in China with Shanghai Mills, and the company announced it would expand its military contracts. Mr. Feuerstein remains as president and chairman of the board.

As for Mr. Feuerstein, his view is simple, "There are times in business when you don't think of the financial consequences, but of the human consequences. There is no doubt this company will survive."[91]

Discussion Questions

1. Mr. Feuerstein has stated, "I don't deserve credit. Corporate America has made it so that when you behave the way I did, it's abnormal." Is he right? Was he right in continuing the salaries?

2. What impact would a closure of Malden Mills have had on Mathuen?

3. Did the fact that Malden Mills is privately held make a difference in Mr. Feuerstein's flexibility?

4. Did Mr. Feuerstein focus too much on benevolence and not enough on business? Did he rely only on goodwill to survive and did he neglect the basics of strategy, marketing, and addressing the competition?

CASE 7.13

GM Plant Closings and Efforts at Outplacement

Bleeding from losses of $4.45 billion for 1991, General Motors (GM) announced on February 24, 1992, that it would close twenty-one plants over the next few years, with twelve to be shut down in 1992, affecting more than 16,300 workers.[92]

GM is the nation's largest manufacturer, and the $4.45 billion loss was the largest ever in American corporate history.[93] Robert C. Stempel, then-GM chairman, said the United States was in an unusually deep automotive slump: "The rate of change during

---

[91] Id., p. C1.

[92] James B. Treece, "The Plants That GM Will Probably Padlock," Business Week, December 14, 1992, pp. 34–35.

[93] Doron P. Levin, "Court Backs G.M. on Plant Closing," The New York Times, August 5, 1993, p. C4.

the past year was unprecedented. And no one was immune to the extraordinary events which affected our lives and the way in which we do business."[94]

More than 3,400 workers at GM's North Tarrytown, New York, plant were to be laid off by 1995. The plant manufactured GM mini-vans: the Chevrolet Lumina, the Pontiac Trans Sports, and the Oldsmobile Silhouette. The mini-van, originally designed in the United States, was executed by GM with a wide stance and a sloping, futuristic nose. From 150,000 to 200,000 of the vans were expected to be sold annually, but sales reached only 100,000 per year—one-half of the Tarrytown plant's capacity.[95] Dealers maintained the shape of the van was too avant-garde for significant sales. "It looks like a Dustbuster," noted a GM manager anonymously.[96]

GM executives acknowledged that building one model per plant was a sloppy and expensive way to do business.[97]

The Tarrytown UAW local had negotiated with GM in 1987 to bring the mini-van production to the plant. The union members voted to accept innovative and cooperative work rules to replace expensive practices under the old contract. Also, state and local governments contributed job training funds, gave tax breaks, and began reconstructing railroad bridges to win the mini-van production plant.[98]

Dan Luria, automotive analyst for the Industrial Technology Institute, a nonprofit institute in Ann Arbor, Michigan, said "The workers did all the right things to get the mini-van but GM was just too optimistic about how many it could sell."[99]

In his speech announcing the closures, Stempel said, "We are asking you to help remake the world's largest automobile company. We can't wait."[100]

Tarrytown was only the beginning of the GM closures. In February 1993, GM announced the closure of 21 plants, with resulting layoffs of 16,300 workers. Another closure was the Willow Run plant in Ypsilanti Township, Michigan, a loss of 2,200 jobs. However, Ypsilanti Township and Washtenaw County filed suit challenging the closure because GM had promised to build cars at Willow Run through the late 1990s in exchange for tax abatements.[101] The suit alleged $13.5 million was owed in back taxes by GM for reneging on its promise to operate the plant. The suit was settled in 1994 with GM agreeing to pay half the abated taxes.[102]

---

[94] Doron P. Levin, "GM Picks 21 Plants to Be Shut as It Reports a Record U.S. Loss," The New York Times, February 25, 1992, p. A1.

[95] Adam Bryant, "Swinging the G.M. Ax: Which Plants Are Next?" The New York Times, November 10, 1992, p. C1.

[96] Doron P. Levin, "Vehicle's Design Dooms Van Plant," The New York Times, February 26, 1992, p. C4.

[97] David Woodruff and Zachary Schiller, "Smart Step for a Wobbly Giant," Business Week, December 7, 1992, p. 38.

[98] Arthur S. Hayes, "Concerns Find It Harder to Leave Town after Receiving Tax Breaks," The Wall Street Journal, March 1, 1993, p. B10.

[99] Levin, "Vehicle's Design Dooms Van Plant," p. C4.

[100] William McWhirter, "Major Overhaul," Time, December 30, 1991, p. 56.

[101] Doron P. Levin, "Judge Blocks Plan by G.M. to Close a Plant in Michigan," The New York Times, February 10, 1993, pp. C1, C5.

[102] James Bennet, "G.M. Settles Suit over Plant Closing," The New York Times, April 15, 1994, p. C3.

Discussion Questions

1. When unions and governments provide financial assistance in exchange for promises from a manufacturer to locate a plant in a particular area, should the plant owner have an obligation to continue operations?

2. Did GM just make a business decision to stop losses?

3. Should workers and governments absorb the cost of business risks, such as a poor-selling mini-van?

4. Did GM renege on its promise to Ypsilanti Township and Washtenaw County? Should business setbacks excuse plant closures? Should tax abatements be repaid?

7D

Environmental Issues

The quality of the environment has become a personal issue. Many consumers base their buying decisions on the commitment of manufacturers and other businesses to protect the environment. The environment has become a stakeholder in business operations.

CASE 7.14

Herman Miller and Its Rain Forest Chairs

In March 1990, Bill Foley, research manager for Herman Miller, Inc., began a routine evaluation of new woods to use in the firm's signature piece—the $2,277 Eames chair. The Eames chair is a distinctive office chair with a rosewood exterior finish and a leather seat and was sold in Sharper Image stores and catalog.

At that time, the chair was made of two species of trees: rosewood and Honduran mahogany. Foley realized that Miller's use of the tropical hardwoods was helping destroy rain forests. Foley banned the use of the woods in the chairs once existing supplies were exhausted. The Eames chair would no longer have its traditional rosewood finish.

Foley's decision prompted former CEO Richard H. Ruch to react: "That's going to kill that [chair]."[103] Effects on sales could not be quantified.

Herman Miller, based in Zeeland, Michigan, and founded in 1923 by D. J. DePree, a devout Baptist, manufactures office furniture and partitions. The corporation follows a participatory-management tradition and takes environmentally friendly actions. The vice president of the Michigan Audubon Society noted that Miller has cut the trash it hauls to landfills by 90 percent since 1982: "Herman Miller has been doing a super job."[104]

---

[103] David Woodruff, "Herman Miller: How Green Is My Factory?" Business Week, September 16, 1991, pp. 54–55.
[104] Id.

Herman Miller built an $11 million waste-to-energy heating and cooling plant. The plant saves $750,000 per year in fuel and landfill costs. In 1991, the company found a buyer for the 800,000 pounds of scrap fabric it had been dumping in landfills. A North Carolina firm shreds it for insulation for automobile roof linings and dashboards. Selling the scrap fabric saves Miller $50,000 per year in dumping fees.

Herman Miller employees once used 800,000 styrofoam cups a year. But in 1991, the company passed out 5,000 mugs to its employees and banished styrofoam. The mugs carry the following admonition: "On spaceship earth there are no passengers . . . only crew." Styrofoam in packaging was also reduced 70 percent for a cost savings of $1.4 million.

Herman Miller also spent $800,000 for two incinerators that burn 98 percent of the toxic solvents that escape from booths where wood is stained and varnished. These furnaces exceeded the 1990 Clean Air Act requirements. It was likely that the incinerators would be obsolete within three years, when nontoxic products became available for staining and finishing wood, but having the furnaces was "ethically correct," former CEO Ruch said in response to questions from the board of directors.[105]

Herman Miller keeps pursuing environmentally safe processes, including finding a use for its sawdust by-product. However, for the fiscal year ended May 31, 1991, its net profit had fallen 70 percent from 1990 to $14 million on total sales of $878 million.

In 1992, Herman Miller's board hired J. Kermit Campbell as CEO. Mr. Campbell continued in the Ruch tradition and wrote essays for employees on risk-taking and for managers on "staying out of the way." From 1992 to 1995, sales growth at Herman Miller was explosive, but as one analyst described it, "expenses exploded." Despite sales growth during this time, profits dropped 89 percent to a mere $4.3 million.

Miller's board, concerned about Campbell's lack of expedience, announced Campbell's resignation and began an aggressive program of downsizing. Between May and July 1995, 130 jobs were eliminated. Also in 1995, sales dropped from $879 to $804 million. The board promoted Michael Volkema, then 39 and head of Miller's file cabinet division, to CEO.[106]

Volkema refocused Herman Miller's name with a line of well-made, lower-priced office furniture using a strategy and division called SQA (Simple, Quick, and Affordable). The dealers for SQA work with customers to configure office furniture plans, and Miller ships all the pieces ordered in less than two weeks.

Revenues in 1997 were $200 million with record earnings of $78 million. In 1998, Miller acquired dealerships around the country and downsized from its then 1,500 employees.[107]

Volkema notes that staying too long with an "outdated strategy and marketing" nearly cost the company. By 1999, Herman Miller was giving Steelcase, the country's number one office furniture manufacturer, stiff competition with its Aeron chair. The

[105] Id.

[106] Susan Chandler, "An Empty Chair at Herman Miller," Business Week, July 24, 1996, p. 44.

[107] Bruce Upjohn, "A Touch of Schizophrenia," Forbes, July 7, 1997, pp. 57–59.

Aeron chair, which comes in hundreds of versions, has lumbar adjustments, varying types of arms, different upholstery colors, and a mesh back. Its price is $765 to $1,190, and it is said to be capitalizing on its "Austin Powers-like" look. The chair has thirty-five patents and is the result of $35 million in R&D expenditures and cooperation with researchers at Michigan State, the University of Vermont, and Cornell who specialize in ergonomics. The seat features a sort of spine imprimatur. That is, the chair almost conforms to its user's spine.[108]

Discussion Questions

1. Evaluate Foley's decision on changing the Eames chair woods. Consider the moral standards at issue for various stakeholders.

2. Is it troublesome that Miller's profits were off when Foley made the decision?

3. Is Herman Miller bluffing with "green marketing"? Would Albert Carr support Herman Miller's actions for different reasons?

4. Why would Herman Miller decide to buy equipment that exceeded the 1990 Clean Air Act standards when it would not be needed in three years?

5. Would you be less comfortable with Herman Miller's environmental decisions if it advertised them?

6. Has Herman Miller changed its focus? Why? Was the change in focus a chance to compete more effectively?

CASE 7.15

Exxon and Alaska

On March 24, 1989, the Exxon *Valdez* ran aground on Bligh Reef, south of Valdez, Alaska, and spilled nearly 11 million gallons of oil into Prince William Sound. The captain of the tanker was Joseph Hazelwood.

The Ninth Circuit Court of Appeals offered the following description of the accident in its review of the federal district court's award of damages against Exxon:

The vessel left the port of Valdez at night. In March, it is still dark at night in Valdez, the white nights of the summer solstice being three months away. There is an established sea lane that takes vessels well to the west of Bligh Reef, but Captain Hazelwood prudently took the vessel east of the shipping lanes to avoid a heavy concentration of ice in the shipping lane, which is a serious hazard. Plaintiffs have not claimed that Captain Hazelwood violated any law or regulation by traveling outside the sea lane. The problem with being outside the sea lane was that the ship's course was directly toward Bligh Reef.

Bligh Reef was not hard to avoid. All that needed to be done was to bear west about the time the ship got abeam of the navigation light at Busby Island, which is visible even at

---

[108] Terril Yue Jones, "Sit on It," *Forbes*, July 5, 1999, pp. 53–54.

night, some distance north of the reef. The real puzzle of this case was how the ship managed to run aground on this known and foreseen hazard.

There was less than a mile between the ice in the water, visible at night only on radar, and the reef. Captain Michael Clark, an expert witness for the plaintiffs, testified that an oil tanker is hard to turn, more like a car on glare ice than a car on asphalt:

Q: Let's talk a minute about how you turn one of these vessels. Now, this we're talking about a vessel here that's in excess of 900 feet long, all right? Over three football fields. What's it like to turn one of these?

A: Well, it's not like turning a car or a fishing boat or something. There is a—as you are traveling in one direction and you put the rudder over, even though the head of the vessel will turn, your actual direction of travel keeps going in the old direction. Sort of like you're steering a car on ice; you turn the wheel and you just keep going in the same direction. Eventually you'll start to turn and move in the direction you're headed for.

Q: Okay. Is it just as easy as turning a car?

A: No.

Q: And does it make any sense to try to compare changing course in one of these vessels fully laden to that of turning a corner with a car?

A: No.

Q: To make it turn on a vessel, there has to be a rudder command given?

A: Yes.

Q: And once you give that rudder command, is that the end of the turn?

A: No. No, you have to watch and make sure that the rudder command is made as you ordered it and to make sure that it's having the desired effect.

Q: Is there anything else that has to be done in order to put it on the course that you want it on?

A: Yes, you usually have to give counter rudder to slow the turn down.

Considering the ice in the water, the darkness, the importance of turning the vessel away from Bligh Reef before hitting it, and the tricky nature of turning this behemoth, one would expect an experienced captain of the ship to manage this critical turn.

But Captain Hazelwood left the bridge. He went downstairs to his cabin, he said, to do some paperwork. A special license is needed to navigate the oil tanker in this part of Prince William Sound, and Captain Hazelwood was the only person on board with the license. There was testimony that captains simply do not leave the bridge during maneuvers such as this one and that there is no good reason for the captain to go to his cabin to do paperwork at such a time. Captain Hazelwood left the bridge just two minutes before the turn needed to be commenced, which makes it all the more strange that he left at all.

Before leaving, Captain Hazelwood added to the complexity of the maneuver that needed to be made: he put the vessel on autopilot, which is not usually done when a vessel is out of the shipping lanes, and the autopilot program sped the vessel up, making it approach the reef faster and reducing the time during which error could be corrected. As

Captain Hazelwood left, he told Cousins, the third mate, to turn back into the shipping lane once the ship was abeam of Busby Light. Though this sounds plain enough, expert witnesses testified that it was a great deal less clear and precise than it sounds.

There are supposed to be two officers on the bridge, but after Hazelwood left, there was only one. The bridge was left to the fatigued third mate, Gregory Cousins, a man in the habit of drinking sixteen cups of coffee per day to keep awake. Cousins was not supposed to be on watch—his watch was ending and he was supposed to be able to go to sleep—but his relief had not shown up, and Cousins felt that it was his responsibility not to abandon the bridge. He was assisted only by the helmsman, Robert Kagan. Kagan, meanwhile, had forgotten his jacket, ran back to his cabin for it, and returned to the bridge a couple of minutes before the time the turn had to be initiated. Cousins and Kagan thought they had conducted the maneuver, but evidently they had not. When Cousins realized that the vessel was not turning, he directed an emergency maneuver that did not work. [From *In re Exxon Valdez*, 270 F.3d 1215 (9th Cir. 2002)]

Hazelwood had a history of drinking problems and had lost his New York driver's license after two drunken-driving convictions. The court described the problem as follows:

Captain Hazelwood's departure from the bridge, though unusual, was not inexplicable. The explanation put before the jury was that his judgment was impaired by alcohol. He was an alcoholic. He had been treated medically, in a 28 day residential program, but had dropped out of the rehabilitation program and fallen off the wagon. He had joined Alcoholics Anonymous, but had quit going to meetings and resumed drinking. Testimony established that prior to boarding his ship, he drank at least five doubles (about fifteen ounces of 80 proof alcohol) in waterfront bars in Valdez. The jury could have concluded from the evidence before them that leaving the bridge was an extraordinary lapse of judgment caused by Captain Hazelwood's intoxication. There was also testimony that the highest executives in Exxon Shipping knew Hazelwood had an alcohol problem, knew he had been treated for it, and knew that he had fallen off the wagon and was drinking on board their ships and in waterfront bars (270 F.3d 1222).

Hazelwood had joined a twenty-eight-day alcohol rehabilitation program mentioned in 1985. Almost a week after the Prince William Sound accident, Exxon revealed that Hazelwood's blood-alcohol reading was 0.061 in a test taken ten and one-half hours after the spill occurred—a level that would indicate intoxication. Exxon also announced it had fired Hazelwood.

The magnitude of the spill seemed almost incomprehensible. U.S. Interior Secretary Manual Lujan called the spill the oil industry's "Three Mile Island." After ten days, the spill covered 1,000 square miles and leaked out of Prince William Sound onto beaches along the Gulf of Alaska and Cook Inlet. A cleanup army of 12,000 was sent in with hot water and oil-eating microbes. The workers found more than 1,000 dead otters, 34,400 dead sea birds, and 151 bald eagles that had died from eating the oil-contaminated remains of sea birds.

By September 15, Exxon pulled out of the cleanup efforts after having spent $2 billion but recovering only 5 to 9 percent of the oil spilled. Alaskan officials said about 20 to 40 percent of the oil had evaporated. This meant that 50 to 75 percent of the oil was either on the ocean floor or on the beaches.

Hazelwood was indicted by the state of Alaska on several charges, including criminal mischief, operating a watercraft while intoxicated, reckless endangerment, and negligent discharge of oil. He was found innocent of all charges except the negligent discharge of oil, fined $50,000, and required to spend 1,000 hours helping with the cleanup of the beaches. Exxon paid Hazelwood's legal fees. Hazelwood now works as a maritime consultant for a New York City law firm and still holds a valid sea license.

When the *Valdez* was being repaired, shipworkers observed that Hazelwood and his crew had kept the tanker from sinking by quickly sealing off the hatches to the ship's tank, thus making a bubble that helped stabilize the ship. Citing incredible seamanship, the workers noted that an 11-million-gallon spill was preferable to a 60-million one—the tanker's load.

Following the spill, critics of Exxon maintained that the company's huge personnel cutbacks during the 1980s affected the safety and maintenance levels aboard its tankers. Later hearings revealed that the crew of the *Valdez* was overburdened with demands for speed and efficiency. The crew worked ten- to twelve-hour days and often had their sleep interrupted. Lookouts frequently were not properly posted, and junior officers were permitted to control the bridge without the required supervision. Robert LeResche, oil-spill coordinator for Alaska, said, "It wasn't Captain Ahab on the bridge. It was Larry and Curly in the Exxon boardroom."[109] In response to critics, Exxon's CEO Lawrence Rawl stated:

> And we say, "We're sorry, and we're doing all we can." There were 30 million birds that went through the sound last summer, and only 30,000 carcasses have been recovered. Just look at how many ducks were killed in the Mississippi Delta in one hunting day in December! People have come up to me and said, "This is worse than Bhopal." I say, "Hell, Bhopal killed more than 3,000 people and injured 200,000 others!" Then they say, "Well, if you leave the people out, it was worse than Bhopal."[110]

On January 1, 1990, a second Exxon oil spill occurred when a pipeline under the Arthur Kill waterway between Staten Island and New Jersey burst and spilled 567,000 gallons of heating oil. New York and New Jersey officials criticized Exxon, citing shoddy equipment and poor maintenance. It was six hours after an alarm from the pipeline safety system went off before Exxon workers shut down the pipeline. Albert Appleton, New York City commissioner on the environment, said, "Exxon has a corporate philosophy that the environment is some kind of nuisance problem and a distraction from the real business of moving oil around."[111]

Late in February 1990, Exxon was indicted on federal felony charges of violating maritime safety and antipollution laws in the *Valdez* spill. The charges were brought after Exxon and the Justice Department failed to reach a settlement. The oil company also faced state criminal charges. Alaska and the Justice Department also brought civil suits against Exxon for the costs of cleaning up the spill. Approximately 150 other civil suits were filed by fishing and tour boat operators whose incomes were eliminated by the spill. At the time of the federal indictment, Exxon had paid out $180 million to 13,000 fishermen and other claimants.

[109] In re Exxon Valdez, *296 F.Supp.2d 1071 (D. Alask. 2004)*.
[110] Jay Mathews, "Problems Preceded Oil Spill," *Washington Post, May 18, 1989, pp. A1, A18.*
[111] Chris Welles, "Exxon's Future: What Has Larry Rawl Wrought?" *Business Week, April 2, 1990, pp. 72–76.*

By May 1990, Exxon had renewed its cleanup efforts at targeted sites with 110 employees. Twice during 1991, Exxon reached a plea agreement with the federal government and the state on the criminal charges. After Alaska disagreed with the terms of the first, a second agreement was reached in which Exxon consented to plead guilty to three misdemeanors and pay a $1.15 billion fine. The civil litigation was settled when Exxon agreed to pay $900 million to both Alaska and the federal government over ten years.

The plea agreement with the governments did not address the civil suits pending against Exxon. At the end of 1991, an Alaska jury awarded sixteen fishers more than $2.5 million in damages and established a payout formula for similar plaintiffs in future litigation against Exxon. As of September 1994, Exxon had spent $2 billion to clean up shores in Alaska.

Exxon has had a stream of payouts since 1991—a total of $3.4 billion of its $5.7 billion in profits for that period. Payouts included:

- $20 million to 3,500 native Alaskans for damages to their villages;
- $287 million to 10,000 fishers;
- $1.5 billion for damages to wildlife; and
- $9.7 million for damages to Native American land.

In September 1994, a federal jury awarded an additional $5 billion in punitive damages against Exxon for the suits filed since 1991. The original verdict of Exxon's recklessness and the resulting damage awards were made by a jury following a trial that ended in 1994. The damage award was the largest in history at that time. Exxon's stock fell two and five-eighths points following the verdict. Exxon appealed the verdict to the 9th Circuit.

In 1996, during a court review of the distribution of an award in an Alaskan case, a *Wall Street Journal* article revealed that Exxon had reached secret agreements with fish processors that would require them to refund the punitive damages awarded by juries. Apparently, some type of high/low settlement was reached with the plaintiffs prior to trial, but the jury trial proceeded without disclosure of the settlement and potential refund by the plaintiffs. Under a high/low settlement, the parties agree to a ceiling and a floor on the amount of damages that can be awarded. If the parties reach a $1 million/ $5 million high/low agreement, they mean that $5 million will be the maximum damage award (including punitive damages and lawyers' fees) and $1 million will be the minimum award, regardless of the jury's actual verdict. The parties are guaranteed an outcome they can live with regardless of what the jury comes back with as a verdict. Often companies reach high/low verdicts because they need a court decision in order to take issues up on appeal, but they are concerned about their exposure in allowing a jury carte blanche on their liability. Further, even without an appeal, a verdict can bring a certain finality as well as precedent to what could be a number of cases or cases that will be brought in the future. Some believe that in the Exxon high/low agreement, there was a refund provision that required the plaintiffs to return or refund part of the settlement if the verdict came in at a lower range.

U.S. District Judge H. Russel Holland learned of the high/low agreements and called them an "astonishing ruse" to "mislead" the jury. Judge Holland set aside the agreements and allowed punitive damages to stand.

By November 1, 1996, Exxon had settled all of the *Valdez* cases and settled with its insurers for its claims. Exxon recovered $780 million of its $2.5 billion in costs, including attorney fees, from its insurers. Exxon had been in litigation with its insurers over coverage. Eugene Anderson, a lawyer who represents corporations in insurance actions, noted that insurance companies virtually always deny all large claims because "they pay lawyers much less each year in these cases than they earn in interest."[112]

In November 2001, the U.S. Court of Appeals for the 9th Circuit ruled that the $5 billion verdict in the Exxon *Valdez* case for punitive damages was excessive. The case was remanded to the federal district court for a redetermination of that damage figure.[113] On remand, the verdict was reduced to $4 billion and appealed again. It was remanded again for damage redetermination because of new U.S. Supreme case law on damages, and the last amount entered on record in 2004 was $4.5 billion.[114]

Exxon has since publicly admitted responsibility for the spill and has paid in excess of $3 billion to clean up the area along the Alaska coastline that has been a prime fishing area and an economic base for people of the area.[115]

The $287 million verdict for the fishermen, awarded as compensatory damages for the loss of their fishing rights during the cleanup, was upheld by the 9th Circuit.

Congress passed the Oil Spill Act in response to the *Valdez* disaster as well as other provisions that effectively preclude the *Valdez* from ever entering Prince William Sound again.[116]

After the 10-year marking point of the spill, many scientists undertook studies of Prince William Sound and reached conclusions along the lines of the following, from a Web site that archives summaries of all the papers presented at the conference on the 10-year anniversary of the *Valdez* spill (http://www.valdezscience.com/page/index.html):

> Natural interannual variability in the structure of the biological infaunal communities is the largest and most consistent signal observed in this study, not any residual effects of the oil spill. The results of statistical analyses of the data (ANCOVA) showed no indication of continuing oiling effects in 1998.

The scientists also noted a natural weathering process that appears to dissipate the oil and diminish its toxicity through the effects of weather and water, even before the oil disappears.

---

[112] Barbara Rudolph, "Exxon's Attitude Problem," Time, January 22, 1990, p. 51.

[113] Joseph B. Treaster, "With Insurers' Payment, Exxon Says Valdez Case Is Ended," The New York Times, November 1, 1996, p. C3.

[114] In re Exxon, 270 F.3d 1215 (9th Cir. 2001).

[115] "$5 B Exxon Verdict Is Tossed Out," National Law Journal, November 19, 2001–November 26, 2001, p. A6. See also http://www.exxon.com.

[116] 33 U.S.C. § 2732 (2001).

Discussion Questions

1. Evaluate Exxon's "attitude" with regard to the spill.

2. Why did the company cut back on staff and maintenance expenditures?

3. Was Hazelwood morally responsible for the spill?

4. Was Exxon management morally responsible for the spill?

5. What changes in Exxon's ethical environment would you make?

6. Would Exxon make the same decisions about Hazelwood and cost-cutting given the costs of the spill?

7. Evaluate the ethics in Exxon's secret deal on punitive damages.

8. Evaluate the ethics of the insurers in denying large claims in order to earn the interest while litigation over the claim is pending.

9. Why do you think the court held that the punitive damage verdict was excessive? Is there another social issue regarding litigation here?

Sources

Dietrich, Bill, "Is Oil-Spill Skipper a Fall Guy?" *Arizona Republic*, January 28, 1990, p. A2.

"Exxon Labeled No. 1 in Bungling a Crisis," *Arizona Republic*, March 24, 1990, p. A8.

"Exxon, Lloyd's Agree to Valdez Settlement," *The Wall Street Journal*, November 1, 1996, p. B2.

"Exxon Stops the Flow," *Time*, March 25, 1992, p. 51.

"Exxon to Pay $1.1 Billion in Spill," *Arizona Republic*, March 13, 1991, p. A3.

Foster, David, "Oily Legacy," *Mesa Tribune*, March 18, 1990, p. D1.

Galen, Michele, and Vicky Cahan, "Getting Ready for Exxon vs. Practically Everybody," *Business Week*, September 25, 1989, pp. 190–192.

Galen, Michele, and Vicky Cahan, "The Legal Reef Ahead for Exxon," *Business Week*, March 12, 1990, p. 39.

Hayes, Arthur S., and Milo Geyelin, "Oil Spill Trial Yields $2.5 Million," *The Wall Street Journal*, September 11, 1991, p. B2.

Kangmine, Linda, and Carol Castaneda, "For Alaska, Tide Has Changed," *USA Today*, June 14, 1994, p. 3A.

"Like Punch in Gut: Exxon Skipper Talks," *Arizona Republic*, March 25, 1990, pp. A1, A12.

Marshall, Steve, "Jury Rules Exxon Must Pay $287 Million to Alaska Fishermen," *USA Today*, August 12, 1994, p. 3A.

McCoy, Charles, "Exxon Reaches $1.15 Billion Spill Pact That Resembles Earlier Failed Accord," *The Wall Street Journal*, October 1, 1991, p. A3.

McCoy, Charles, and Peter Fritsch, "Legal Experts Surprised by Exxon Deals With Fish Processors in Valdez Case," *The Wall Street Journal*, June 14, 1996, p. B5.

"Native Americans Awarded $9.7 Million from Exxon," *National Law Journal*, October 10, 1994, p. A19.

"Nice Work, Joe," *Time*, December 4, 1989, p. 48.

"Paying up for the Exxon Valdez," *Time*, August 8, 1994, p. 18.

Rempel, William C., "Exxon Captain Acquitted," *Arizona Republic*, March 23, 1990, p. A1.

Rubin, Julia, "Exxon Submits Final Oil-Spill Cleanup Plan," *Burlington Vermont Free Press*, April 28, 1990, p. 2A.

Satchell, Michael, and Betsy Carpenter, "A Disaster That Wasn't," *U.S. News & World Report*, September 18, 1989, pp. 60–69.

Schneider, Keith, "Jury Finds Exxon Acted Recklessly in Valdez Oil Spill," *The New York Times*, June 14, 1994, pp. A1, A8.

Schneider, Keith, "$20 Million Settlement in Exxon Case," *The New York Times*, July 26, 1994, p. A8.

Solomon, Caleb, "Exxon Attacks Scientific Views of Valdez Spill," *The Wall Street Journal*, April 15, 1993, pp. B1, B10.

Solomon, Caleb, "Exxon's Real Problem: Many of Its Oil Fields Are Old and Declining," *The Wall Street Journal*, September 19, 1994, pp. A1, A6.

Solomon, Caleb, "Jury to Weigh Exxon's Actions in Spill," *The Wall Street Journal*, June 7, 1994, p. B5.

Sullivan, Allanna, "Exxon Begins Final Defense in Valdez Spill," *The Wall Street Journal*, May 2, 1994, pp. B1, B3.

Sullivan, Allanna, and Arthur S. Hayes, "Exxon's Plea Bargaining," *The Wall Street Journal*, February 21, 1990, p. B8.

Tyson, Rae, "Valdez Cleanup Is Skin Deep," *USA Today*, March 22, 1994, p. 3A.

CASE 7.16

The Death of the Great Disposable Diaper Debate

In the late 1980s, environmentalists raised concerns about the disposal of diapers in municipal landfills, space for which is scarce and becoming more so. The average infant uses 7,800 diapers in the first 130 weeks of life.

The debate over disposable diapers was complex. Disposable diapers account for just 2 percent of municipal solid waste. The time required for plastic to break down is 200 to 500 years. Eighteen billion disposable diapers go into landfills each year. An

Arthur D. Little study comparing the environmental impact of cloth and disposable diapers over the products' lifetimes found cloth diapers consume more energy and water than disposables. Cloth diapers also cost more (not counting diaper-service fees) and create more air and water pollution through washing. Critics point out that the study was commissioned by Procter & Gamble, the largest maker of disposable diapers, with 50 percent of the market. However, the study was a sophisticated "life-cycle analysis" that used elaborate computer models, and Arthur D. Little is considered an eminent research firm.[117]

In surveys in the early 1990s, four of five American parents preferred disposables. Most hospital staffs and day care centers favor using disposables even though many personally use cloth diapers. Switching from disposable to cloth diapers costs about 2.5 percent more. The disposability of the diapers was also improving with companies devoting significant R&D dollars to reducing the time for biodegradation. Procter & Gamble created advanced techniques for industrial composting of solid waste and spent $20 million to develop diapers that break down into humus.[118]

Environmentalists, however, were quite successful in obtaining regulation of disposables. Twenty states considered taxes or complete bans on disposables. Nebraska banned nondegradable disposables, with a law that took effect in October 1993. Maine required day-care centers to accept children who wear cloth diapers. New York considered requiring that new mothers be given information explaining the environmental threat of disposables. In 1990, the Wisconsin legislature barely defeated a measure to tax disposables.

Alternatives to disposables were being developed. R Med International distributes Tender Care, a disposable diaper that degrades in two to five years because its outer lining is made of cornstarch. However, the price of these diapers was substantially higher than that of other disposables and made mass market appeal impossible.

The great disposable diaper debate peaked on Earth Day in 1990. After the Little study appeared, parents' guilt about rain forests and landfills was relieved and by 1997, 80 percent of all babies were wearing disposables. Many attribute the change in attitude as well as the halt in legislative and regulatory action to Procter & Gamble's effective public relations using the Little study results. Also, Allen Hershkowitz, a senior scientist at the Natural Resources Defense Council, said, "The pediatric dermatology clearly seemed to favor disposables, while the environmental issues were murky." Environmentalists referred to Mr. Hershkowitz as "the skipper of the *Exxon Valdez*."[119]

During the 1990s, all disposable diaper manufacturers were able to develop materials that were much thinner and lighter than their predecessors. Not only were the diapers decomposing faster, but they also took up less room in the landfills.

By 1997, the National Association of Diaper Services (NADS) reported its membership at an all-time low, with closings of cloth diaper services even in ecologically conscious Boston. There are no diaper services located in any of New York City's five

---

[117] *Arthur Little declared bankruptcy in January 2002. Jonathan D. Glater, "Arthur D. Little Plans Bankruptcy Filing," The New York Times, February 6, 2002, p. C4.*
[118] *Zachary Schiller, "Turning Pampers Into Plant Food?" Business Week, October 22, 1990, p. 38.*
[119] *Kathleen Deveny, "States Mull Rash of Diaper Regulations," The Wall Street Journal, June 15, 1990, p. B1.*

boroughs. Their current marketing campaign emphasizes a two-year guarantee for potty-training with diapers free after that. Babies, the NADS says, can't feel the wetness in disposables.

The Internet has created a new submarket for cloth diapers because the network of parents who prefer cloth diapers is so easily connected. The two national companies remain Mother-ease of New York and Kooshies Baby Products of Ontario, Canada, but there are several small companies, including Darla's Place, based in Imlay City, Michigan. Founded by Darla Sowders because of her frustration with the national brands, the company uses at-home mothers to sew its product, which captures the "brown market," or the market for used diapers. The diapers are sewn a certain way that customers say prevents leaks. The brand is regarded as the "champagne" of diapers and sells at a premium above other diapers in the submarket. Despite this activity, Kimberly-Clark indicates there is no change in the demand for cloth diapers or any reduction in the use of disposables.[120] P&G reports sagging diaper sales and is competing with a new premium brand marketed as an item of clothing.[121]

Discussion Questions

1. Did Arthur D. Little have a conflict of interest with Procter & Gamble's sponsorship of its work?

2. Would it be a breach of duty to the hospital's patients and shareholders to adopt a position (that is, using cloth diapers) that increases costs?

3. Do people ignore environmental issues for the sake of convenience? Do your arguments depend on whether you must change diapers?

4. What lessons are learned from this case for applicability in other industries?

5. Did environmentalists exaggerate?

[120] Lisa Moricoli Latham, "The Diaper Rush of 1999: Cloth Makes a Comeback on the Net," The New York Times, September 19, 1999, p. BU6.
[121] Emily Nelson, "Diaper Sales Sagging, P&G Thinks Young to Reposition Pampers," The Wall Street Journal, December 27, 2001, pp. A1, A2.

7E

Purchasing: Conflicts and Bribery

Purchasing agents hold powerful positions. They make the choices to award business to other companies. Often, contractors employ tools of influence to gain favor. When are such tools unethical? Can an agent accept gifts for the award of business?

CASE 7.17

JCPenney and Its Wealthy Buyer

Purchasing agent Jim G. Locklear began his career as a retail buyer with Federated Department Stores in Dallas, where he became known for his eye for fashion and ability to negotiate low prices. After ten years with Federated, he went to work for Jordan Marsh in Boston in 1987 with an annual salary of $96,000. But three months later, Locklear quit that job to take a position as a housewares buyer with JCPenney so he could return to Dallas. His salary was $56,000 per year, he was 38 years old, he owed support payments totaling $900 per month for four children from four marriages, and the bank was threatening to foreclose on his $500,000 mortgage.[122]

Locklear was a good performer for Penney. His products sold well, and he was responsible for the very successful JCPenney Home Collection, a color-coordinated line of dinnerware, flatware, and glasses that was eventually copied by most other tabletop retailers. Locklear took sales of Penney's tabletop line from $25 million to $45 million per year and was named the company's "Buyer of the Year" several times.

However, Locklear was taking payments from Penney's vendors directly and through front companies. Some paid him to get information about bids or to obtain contracts, while others paid what they believed to be advertising fees to various companies that were fronts owned by Locklear. Between 1987 and 1992, Locklear took in $1.5 million in "fees" from Penney's vendors.

[122] Andrea Gerlin, "How a Penney Buyer Made Up to $1.5 Million on Vendors' Kickbacks," *The Wall Street Journal*, February 7, 1995, pp. A1, A18.

Penney hired an investigator in 1989 to look into Locklear's activities, but the investigator uncovered only Mr. Locklear's personal financial difficulties.

During his time as a buyer, Locklear was able to afford a country club membership, resort vacations, luxury vehicles, and large securities accounts. Although his lifestyle was known to those who worked with him, no questions were asked again until 1992, when Penney received an anonymous letter about Locklear and his relationship with a Dallas manufacturer's representative. Penney investigated and uncovered sufficient evidence of payments to file a civil suit to recover those payments and referred the case to the U.S. attorney in Dallas for criminal prosecution.

Mr. Locklear was charged by the U.S. attorney with mail and wire fraud. Mr. Locklear entered a guilty plea and provided information to the U.S. attorney on suppliers, agents, and manufacturers' reps who had paid him "fees." Mr. Locklear was sentenced to eighteen months in prison and fined $50,000. Penney won a $789,000 judgment against him and Mr. Locklear's assets have been attached for collection purposes.[123]

....

Discussion Questions

1. What ethical violations did Locklear commit?

2. Was anyone really harmed by Locklear's conduct? List the stakeholders who were affected.

3. Given Locklear's lifestyle, why did it take so long for Penney to take action? Do you see any red flags in the facts given?

4. A vendor who paid Locklear $25,000 in exchange for a Penney order stated, "It was either pay it or go out of business." Evaluate the ethics of this seller.

5. Do you agree that both the buyer and the seller are guilty in commercial bribery cases? Is the purchasing agent "more" wrong?

6. Many companies provide guidelines for their purchasing agents on accepting gifts, samples, and favors. For example, under Wal-Mart's "no coffee" policy, its buyers cannot accept even a cup of coffee from a vendor. Any samples or models must be returned to vendors once a sales demonstration is complete. Other companies allow buyers to accept items of minimal value. Still others place a specific dollar limit on the value, such as $25. What problems do you see with any of these policies? What advantages do you see?

7. Describe the problems that can result when buyers accept gifts from vendors and manufacturer's representatives.

8. Mr. Locklear said at his sentencing, "I became captive to greed. Once it was discovered, I felt tremendous relief." Mr. Locklear's pastor said Locklear coached little league and added, "Our country needs more role models like Jim Locklear."[124] Evaluate these two quotes from an ethical perspective.

---

[123] Andrea Gerlin, "J. C. Penney Ex-Employee Sentenced to Jail," The Wall Street Journal, August 28, 1995, p. A9.
[124] Id.

Cars for Cars: Honda Executives' Allocation System

From 1978 through early 1992, the amazing popularity of Honda cars, including its luxury car Acura, created excessive demand for both the cars and the franchises (dealerships). Dealers were able to sell the vehicles at thousands of dollars above the sticker price, virtually guaranteeing high profits. This intense demand and resulting guaranteed success led to American Honda Motor Co. executives getting cash and gifts from dealers and potential dealers in exchange for auto delivery allocations and the award of franchises. One man who was eventually awarded a dealership presented a Honda executive with a Mercedes-Benz. Some Honda executives accepted cash payments of up to $1 million in exchange for a franchise. Others received such gifts as swimming pools, paintings (one worth $50,000), Rolex watches, and laser karaoke machines.[125]

Honda officials in Japan were unaware of this activity by American Honda executives. Meanwhile, one person, Joseph R. Hendrick, was awarded twenty-eight dealerships during this time. An assistant U.S. attorney in New Hampshire, Michael J. Conolly, presented evidence in court that Hendrick sent payments to Stanley James Cardiges, senior vice president of sales for Honda America. Cardiges and sixteen other Honda executives pleaded guilty to federal charges of racketeering, mail fraud, and conspiracy to commit mail fraud and have forfeited $10 million to the U.S. government. Two other Honda executives were found guilty of accepting more than $15 million in kickbacks from auto dealers that were the basis of federal fraud charges in a scheme that involved dealers in thirty states.[126] In the trial of these two executives, Cardiges testified that the practice of accepting gifts was widespread in the executive suite.[127]

The total of former Honda executives and employees to plead guilty or be convicted reached twenty in 1995. Cardiges was sentenced to five years and fined $364,000.[128]

In 1996, a federal judge ruled that Honda dealers who claimed injury from the company-wide bribery scheme could file suit against Honda for racketeering and antitrust violations. The judge also ruled that high-ranking Honda Japanese executives could be named in the suit.[129]

The dealers who have brought suit claim that they lost millions in business because they refused to pay bribes and that they were not given car allocations at a time when Hondas could be sold at thousands above the sticker price. Honda settled the suit for $316 million in 1998.[130]

Throughout the country, indictments of dealers who paid bribes to the American Honda executives resulted in charges and convictions for conspiracy, money

---

[125] James Bennet, "Corruption Called Broad in Honda Case," The New York Times, April 4, 1995, pp. C1, C6.

[126] "Honda Sentence," USA Today, August 28, 1995, p. 1B.

[127] "A Big Honda Dealer Is Indicted in Federal Bribery Case," The New York Times, December 5, 1996, p. C4.

[128] James Bennet, "Guilty Plea in Honda Bribery Case," The New York Times, February 8, 1995, pp. C1, C8.

[129] "Dealers Given Right to Sue Honda Over Bribery Scheme," Arizona Republic, August 31, 1996, p. A8.

[130] "Honda Dealers Said to Settle Suit," The New York Times, July 29, 1998, p. C1.

laundering, and mail fraud. Mr. Hendrick was indicted on thirteen counts of money laundering, one count of conspiracy, and one count of mail fraud. Mr. Hendrick's brother, John, was also indicted. Mr. Hendrick stated that he gave Mr. Cardiges gifts, but called them gifts to a friend, not for influence.[131] Mr. Hendrick entered a guilty plea to a charge of mail fraud.[132]

Discussion Questions

1. What type of atmosphere did Honda America have to have for this scheme to go on for so long?

2. To whom did the money and goods paid to the executives actually belong? Were the Honda executives collecting economic rents that belonged to Honda because of the high demand for its cars?

3. Why does it matter that these executives enjoyed some extra money from Honda's success? Are these economic rents that belong to Honda?

4. If you were an executive, how would you confront your fellow officers about such payments and your unwillingness to accept them? Could you lose your job for taking such a position?

5. A defense lawyer in the trial of two executives said that Honda's top management "turned a blind eye to the kick backs and that bribe-taking was implicit, though unofficial, company policy, and therefore did not constitute a crime."[133] Evaluate his statement.

CASE 7.19

Frozen Coke and Burger King and the Richmond Rigging

Tom Moore, president of Coca-Cola's Foodservice and Hospitality Division, was looking at sales in the fountain division, a division responsible for one third of all of Coke's revenues. The fountain division sells fountain-dispensed soda to restaurants, convenience marts, and theaters. Sales were flat and he knew from feedback from the salespeople that Pepsi was moving aggressively in the area. In 1999, Pepsi had waged a bidding war to try and seize Coke's customers. Coke held about 66 percent of the fountain drink business and 44.3 percent of the soda market overall. Pepsi held 22 percent of the fountain market and 31.4 percent of the overall soda market. The war between the two giants had been reduced to a price war.

However, Moore noted that there was a potential new product line as he looked at the Frozen Coke products. At that time, Frozen Coke was a convenience store item only. Frozen Coke was still a little-known product and Moore's team at Coke pitched the idea of having Frozen Coke at Burger King along with a national advertising push

---

[131] "Honda Execs Guilty in Bribery Scheme," USA Today, June 2, 1995, p. 1B.
[132] "Auto Dealer Pleads Guilty in Honda Bribery Inquiry," The New York Times, August 15, 1997, p. C1.
[133] Bennet, "Corruption Called Broad in Honda Case," pp. C1, C6.

that would push Coke's fountain sales but also increase food sales at Burger King as customers came in to try the newly available product. Their pitch to Burger King was that Frozen Coke would draw customers and that the sales of all menu items would increase as a result.

Burger King was not ready for a marketing push because it had just lived through two marketing disasters. The first was the failure of the introduction of its new fries and another was a costly ad campaign to boost sales of the Whopper, with no impact but a great many angry franchise owners who had been required to help pay for the ads. Before Burger King would invest in another ad campaign, it wanted to see some test marketing results. Burger King asked Coke to do a promotion of Frozen Coke in a test market. Burger King chose the Richmond, Virginia area as a good test market.

If the Richmond market did not show sales during the marketing test, Moore knew that Coke risked not only no more growth in fountain sales, but also loss of Burger King's confidence and perhaps an open door for Pepsi to win Burger King over.

Promotions and the marketing test in Richmond began in February 2000. Initial sales were not good. Burger King executives made what Coke employees called "excoriating" calls to Coke team members about the poor performance. Coke pulled out all the stops and hired mystery shoppers to make sure that Burger King employees were offering the Frozen Coke to customers as had been directed during the promotion. Coke gave T-shirts and other promotional items to Burger King managers to encourage them to promote Coke sales. John Fisher, the Coke executive who had just been given the Burger King account to manage, was getting more nervous the closer Coke got to the end of the Richmond promotion time frame.

The Coke team told its own employees to buy more value meals at Burger King, the menu item that was being promoted with the Frozen Coke. Finally, Robert Bader, the Coke marketing manager who was in charge of the Richmond test, decided to hire a marketing consultant, Ronald Berryman, to get more purchases at Burger King. Mr. Berryman, who had worked with Coke in the past, developed a plan that included working with the Boys & Girls Clubs in the area. Using $9,000 wired to him by Mr. Bader from Mr. Bader's personal Visa card, Berryman gave cash to directors of these clubs and developed a homework reward program: if the kids came to the clubs and did their homework, they could go and buy a value meal at Burger King. The directors at the clubs assumed that the money for the value meals was a donation from either Burger King or Coke.

The result of the Berryman plan was that the Richmond area Burger Kings had a 6 percent increase in sales during the Frozen Coke promotion. Other Burger King stores had only 0 to 2 percent growth during the same period. As a result, Burger King agreed to invest $10 million in an ad program to promote Frozen Coke. Burger King also invested $37 million in equipment, training, and distribution in order to carry the Frozen Coke in its franchises, but sales did not follow the Richmond pattern. Estimates are that Burger King's total investment in the Frozen Coke promotion was $65 million.

Matthew Whitley, who had been with Coke since 1992, was its finance director in 2000. During some routine audit work at Coke, he ran across an expenses claim from Mr. Berryman in the amount of $4,432.01, a claim that was labeled as expenses for the "mystery shop." Mr. Whitley questioned Mr. Bader about this amount and others, what the funds were for, who Mr. Berryman was, and what the "mystery shop" submission label represented. Mr. Bader responded that the methods might be "unconventional," but they were "entrepreneurial." Mr. Fisher wrote in a memo in response:

"I would never have agreed to move forward if I believed I was being asked to commit an ethics code or legal transgression. . . We had to deseasonalize the data in order to have an accurate measure. I am not completely aware of the details of how the shops were executed but take full responsibility for the decision to execute the program."[134]

Mr. Whitley recommended that Mr. Fisher be fired because of the excessive expense and his authorization for it. Coke did not fire Mr. Fisher but Mr. Moore took away one half of his bonus for the year, saying in his memo of explanation to Mr. Fisher, "These actions exposed the Coca-Cola Co. to a risk of damage to its reputation as well as to the relationship with a major customer."[135]

However, Coke did fire Mr. Whitley, who then filed suit for wrongful termination. Coke first told Burger King of the issues the day before Mr. Whitley filed his suit. Mr. Whitley's lawyer had contacted Coke and offered to not file the suit if Coke would pay Mr. Whitley $44.4 million within one week. Coke declined the offer and disclosed the Whitley and Frozen Coke issues to Burger King. The Coca-Cola board hired the law firm of Gibson, Dunn & Crutcher and auditors Deloitte & Touche to investigate Whitley's claim.

Mr. Whitley then filed his suit. *The Wall Street Journal* uncovered the lawsuit in court documents when a reporter was doing some routine checking on Coke and ran a story on August 20, 2003 describing Mr. Whitley's experience and suit.

The reports of the law and audit firms concluded that the employees had acted improperly on the Richmond marketing test. Also, as a result, Coca-Cola issued an earnings restatement of $9 million in its fountain sales.

Burger King's CEO, Brad Blum, was informed of the report following the investigation and calling the actions of the Coke employees "unacceptable," issued the following statement:

"We are very disappointed in the actions . . . confirmed today by the Coca-Cola audit committee. We expect and demand the highest standards of conduct and integrity in all our vendor relationships, and will not tolerate any deviation from these standards."

Coke's president and chief operating officer, Steve Heyer, sent an apology to Mr. Blum:

"These actions were wrong and inconsistent with values of the Coca-Cola Co. Our relationships with Burger King and all our customers are of the utmost importance to us and should be firmly grounded in only the highest-integrity actions."[136]

Coke had to scramble to retain Burger King's business because Burger King threatened to withdraw Coca-Cola products from its restaurants. Burger King is Coke's second largest fountain customer (McDonald's is its largest). The settlement requires Coke to

---

[134] Chad Terhune, "How Coke Officials Beefed Up Results of Marketing Test," The Wall Street Journal, August 20, 2003, pp. A1, A6.
[135] Id.
[136] Chad Terhune, "Coke Employees Acted Improperly in Marketing Test," The Wall Street Journal, June 18, 2003, pp. A3, A6.

pay $10 million to Burger King and up to $21.2 million to franchisees who will still have the right to determine whether they will continue to carry the Frozen Coke products.

Coke continued with its litigation against Whitley, maintaining that he was "separated" from the company because of a restructuring and that his "separation" had nothing to do with his raising the allegations. However, in October 2003, Coke settled the lawsuit for $540,000: $100,000 in cash, $140,000 in benefits including health insurance, and $300,000 in lawyer's fees. Mr. Whitley said when the settlement was reached, "Over the past several weeks I have reflected on my relationship with Coca-Cola, a company I still respect and love. It's become increasingly clear to me that the company has taken seriously the issues I raised. That's all I ever wanted."[137]

Deval Patrick, executive vice president and Coke's general counsel, also issued the following statement when the settlement was reached, "Mr. Whitley was a diligent employee with a solid record. It is disappointing that he felt he needed to file a lawsuit in order to be heard. We want everyone in this company to bring their issues to the attention of management through appropriate channels, and every manager to take them seriously, investigate them, and make necessary changes."[138]

Mr. Fisher was promoted to a top marketing position in the fountain division at Coke in 2003. However, In April 2003, Coke's internal auditors raised questions with Mr. Fisher about why he exchanged two Disney theme park tickets that had been purchased by the company for Notre Dame football tickets. Mr. Fisher resigned shortly after, but no one at Coke has offered an explanation.

Mr. Bader is still a marketing manager in the fountain division but he does not work on the Burger King account.

Tom Moore resigned following both the settlements. A spokesperson for Coca-Cola said, "As he reflected on the events, he felt that change was necessary to avoid distractions and move the business forward."[139] Sales of Frozen Coke at Burger King have fallen to half of Coke's original estimates. Burger King has proposed changing the name to Icee.[140] Coke did sign the Subway chain for its fountain beverages, a contract that gave Coke the three largest fountain drink contracts in the country: McDonald's, Burger King, and Subway.[141] Pepsi had previously held the Subway contract.

As a result of the Whitley lawsuit, the SEC and the FBI began investigating Coke for "channel stuffing," a practice of shipping out products without orders in order to increase revenues. Coke has pledged full cooperation with the government investigations. A private suit is also pending regarding the channel stuffing.[142] Federal prosecutors are still investigating the Frozen Coke marketing tests for possible fraud charges.[143]

---

[137] Sherri Day, "Coca-Cola Settles Whistle-Blower Suit for $540,000," The New York Times, October 8, 2003, p. C1.
[138] Id.
[139] Sherri Day, "Coke Executive to Leave His Job after Rigged Test at Burger King," The New York Times, August 26, 2003, pp. C1, C2.
[140] Chad Terhune, "How Coke Officials Beefed Up Results of Marketing Test," The Wall Street Journal, August 20, 2003, pp. A1, A6.
[141] Sherri Day, "Subway Chain Chooses Coke, Displacing Pepsi," The New York Times, November 27, 2003, pp. C1, C2.
[142] Sherri Day, "Coke Employees Are Questioned In Fraud Inquiry," The New York Times, January 31, 2004, pp. B1, B14.
[143] Kenneth N. Gilpin, "Prosecutors Investigating Suit's Claims Against Coke," The New York Times, July 13, 2003, pp. B1, B4; Chad Terhune, "Coca-Cola Says U.S. Is Probing Fraud Allegations," The Wall Street Journal, July 14, 2003, p. B3.

Discussion Questions

1. Why did the executives at Coke decide to go forward with the marketing studies? What questions from the models you have studied could they have asked themselves in order to avoid the problems that resulted?

2. Make a list of everyone who was affected by the decision to fix the numbers in the Richmond test market.

3. Make a list of all of the consequences Coke experienced as a result of the Richmond rigging.

4. List the total costs to Coke of the Richmond rigging. Be sure to list any costs that you don't have figures for but that Coke would have to pay. Do you think those costs are done and over?

5. What lessons should companies learn from the Whitley firing and lawsuit?

CASE 7.20

Perks for the Good Doctors

Pharmaceutical companies, faced with the uphill battle of getting doctors to take a look at their new products, have created complex systems and programs for enticing doctors to come, sit, and absorb information about the new products. Below is a list of the various types of benefits and gifts drug companies have given doctors over the past few years to try and get them to consider prescribing their new offerings:

- An event called "Why Cook?" in which doctors are given the chance to review drug studies and product information at a restaurant as their meals are being prepared—they can leave as soon as their meals are ready and they are treated to appetizers and drinks as they wait.
- An event at Christmas tree lots at which doctors can come and review materials and pick up free Christmas trees
- Flowers sent to the doctors' offices on Valentine's Day with materials attached
- Manicures as they study materials on new drugs
- Pedicures as they study materials on new drugs
- Free car washes during which they can study materials
- Free books with materials enclosed
- Free CDs with materials attached
- Bottles of wine sent with materials attached
- Events at Barnes & Noble where doctors can browse and pick out a book for themselves for free so long as they take along some materials on a new drug.

Some doctors say that they can often enjoy dinner on a drug company as often as five times per week.

The American Medical Association frowns on the "dine and dash" format because its rules provide that dinners are acceptable so long as the doctors sit and learn something from a featured speaker. The AMA also limits gifts to those of a "minimal value" that should be related to their patients, such as note pads and pens with the new drug's name imprinted on them. The chairman of the AMA Committee says the following about the gifts, "There are doctors who say, 'I always do what's best for my patients, and these gifts and dinners and trips do not influence me. They are wrong.'"[144]

Experts estimate that drug companies spend about $1,500 per physician per year in trying to attract the physicians' attention to particular drugs in order to have the doctors prescribe them. Those figures come from the $15.7 billion drug companies spent on marketing in 2000. That figure for marketing was $9 billion in 1996.

The AMA has created a $1 million educational campaign to discourage doctors from accepting even the smallest of gifts from pharmaceuticals because of the reality and perception that these gifts influence doctors' decisions on which drugs to prescribe. Interestingly, the pharmaceutical companies themselves donated $675,000 of the $1 million.

At the same time of the announcement of the AMA campaign, Dr. Joseph Bailey proposed that the physicians in his specialty practice group simply charge pharmaceutical company representatives $65 in order to make a 10-minute pitch to a doctor about their drug(s). One doctor describes the proposal as follows, "There are some doctors who would like to have access to that information who don't want to give up two hours of their time to go to dinner. Rather than getting a free ham or a free turkey from a pharmaceutical rep, I would rather see that money put to use to directly benefit the patient."[145] The reps sign up through a separate for-profit corporation and the corporation then distributes its funds to the physicians so that there is no taint or influence from a particular company.

Discussion Questions

1. What category of ethical issue are these gifts?

2. Do you think the doctors act ethically in accepting the gifts, meals, and favors?

3. Do you think the conflict of interest is resolved?

For a look at more information on this issue and various policies relating to it, visit:

http://www.ama.org

http://www.kaisernetwork.org

CASE 7.21

The Analyst Who Needed a Preschool

The stock market of the late 1990s and early 2000s represented a period of irrational exuberance. Investors invested as they never had, but they were egged on by analysts who could say no evil of the companies they were to evaluate. For example, Citigroup is the parent company of Salomon Smith Barney, an investment banker and broker

---

[144] Chris Adams, "Doctors on the Run Can 'Dine'n'Dash' in Style in New Orleans," The Wall Street Journal, May 14, 2001, pp. A1, A6.
[145] Cheryl Jackson, "Ohio Group Tells Drug Reps: We'll Listen—If You Pay," American Medical News, August 20, 2001, pp. 1, 4.

whose star telecommunications analyst, Jack Grubman, was perhaps WorldCom's biggest cheerleader.[146] Jack Grubman's calls on WorldCom were so positive that the company came to be known as "his beloved WorldCom." For example, WorldCom had the following quote from Mr. Grubman that was included in WorldCom's 1997 annual report that was still posted on its Web site through July 2002, "If one were to find comparables to WorldCom . . . the list would be very short and would include the likes of Merck, Home Depot, Wal-Mart, Coke, Microsoft, Gillette and Disney."[147] The sycophantism of Mr. Grubman is difficult to describe because it seems almost parody, as the WorldCom ending is now known. Mr. Grubman introduced Mr. Ebbers at analyst meetings as "the smartest guy in the industry."[148] It was not until the stock had lost 90 percent of its value, and just six weeks before its collapse that Mr. Grubman issued a negative recommendation on WorldCom.[149] Mr. Grubman was free with his negative recommendations on other telecom companies. And Salomon would earn $21 million in fees if the WorldCom–Sprint merger was approved in 1999. He wrote, "We do not think any other telco will be as fully integrated and growth-oriented as this combination,"[150] Mr. Grubman attended WorldCom board meetings and offered advice.[151]

Citicorp was WorldCom's biggest lender as well as a personal lender for Bernie Ebbers, WorldCom's CEO (see Case 6.9). Mr. Ebbers' personal loans are reflected in the following chart:

Lender	Amount	Status[152]
Citigroup	$552 million	$88 million repaid
WorldCom	$415 million	Collateral seized
Bank of America	$253 million	Repaid
UBS Paine Webber	$ 51 million	Repaid
Toronto-Dominion	$ 40 million	Repaid
Morgan Keegan	$ 11.6 million	Repaid
J.P. Morgan Chase	$ 10.8 million	Repaid
Bank of North Georgia	$ 10.8 million	Repaid

The personal loans to Ebbers brought results for the banks in terms of WorldCom business.[153] Mr. Grubman's continuing positive reports on WorldCom, despite the slide of the company's stock and the clear signals from the market, earned him a subpoena to

[146] Neil Weinberg, "Wal-Mart Could Sue for Libel," Forbes, August 12, 2002, p. 56.

[147] Id.

[148] Randall Smith and Deborah Solomon, "Ebbers's Exit Hurts WorldCom's Biggest Fan," The Wall Street Journal, May 3, 2002, p. C1.

[149] Id.

[150] Id., p. C3.

[151] Id.

[152] Susan Pulliam, Deborah Solomon, and Carrick Mollenkamp, "Former WorldCom CEO Built an Empire on Mountain of Debt," The Wall Street Journal, December 31, 2002, p. A1.

[153] At least one lawsuit by a shareholder alleges that the loans were made in exchange for business with WorldCom. Andrew Backover, "Suit Links Loans, WorldCom Stock," USA Today, October 15, 2002, p. 3B.

the Congressional hearings, alongside Mssrs. Ebbers and CFO Scott Sullivan.[154] Former WorldCom employees who were directed to a special number when they wished to exercise their options and were discouraged from doing so by Salomon brokers who handled the WorldCom employee options program have filed a lawsuit.[155]

Mr. Grubman's relationship with WorldCom's senior management continues to be a target of investigation at the Congressional level and elsewhere for reasons other than the personal loan relationships and the glowing reports from Mr. Grubman.[156] WorldCom gave the bulk of its investment banking business to Salomon Smith Barney and it gave Mr. Ebbers and others the first shot at hot IPO stocks.[157] The figures in congressional records indicate that Mr. Ebbers made $11 million in profits from investments in 21 IPOs recommended to him by Salomon Smith Barney, and, more particularly, Mr. Grubman.[158] Apparently, there were plenty of games going on in terms of how those shares were allocated initially and Ebbers was one of the players let in on the best IPOs by Salomon Smith Barney. One expert described the allocation system as follows, "Looking back, it looks more and more like a pyramid scheme. The deals explain why people weren't more diligent in making decisions about funding these small companies. If the money was spread all over the place and everyone who participated early was almost guaranteed a return because of the hype, they had no incentive to try and differentiate the technology. And in the end, all the technology turned out to be identical and commodity-like."[159]

Mr. Grubman continued to issue nothing but positive reports on WorldCom as he became completely intertwined with the company, Mr. Ebbers, and the company's success.[160] In e-mails uncovered by an investigation of analysts conducted by New York Attorney General Eliot Spitzer, Mr. Grubman had complained privately that he was forced to continue his "buy" ratings on stocks that he considered "dogs." Mr. Spitzer filed suit against the analysts for "profiteering" in IPOs.[161]

Further, Mr. Ebbers was not the sole beneficiary of the Salomon Smith Barney IPO allocations, although he was the largest beneficiary.[162] Stiles A. Kellett Jr. (director, 31,500 shares), Scott Sullivan (CFO, 32,300 shares), Francesco Galesi (director), John

---

[154] Susan Pulliam, Deborah Solomon, and Randall Smith, "WorldCom Is Denounced at Hearing," The Wall Street Journal, July 9, 2002, p. A3; Gretchen Morgenson, "Salomon Under Inquiry on WorldCom Options," The New York Times, March 13, 2002, p. C9.

[155] Gretchen Morgenson, "Outrage Is Rising as Options Turn to Dust," The New York Times, March 11, 2002, p. BU1.

[156] Charles Gasparino, Tom Hamburger, and Deborah Solomon, "Salomon Made IPO Allocations Available to Ebbers, Others," The Wall Street Journal, August 28, 2002, p. A1.

[157] Gretchen Morgenson, "Ebbers Made $11 Million on 21 Stock Offerings," The New York Times, August 31, 2002, p. B1; Gretchen Morgenson, "Ebbers Got Million Shares in Hot Deals," The New York Times, August 28, 2002, p. C1; Gretchen Morgenson, "Deals Within Telecom Deals," The New York Times, August 28, 2002, pp. BU1, BU10.

[158] Id., Morgenson, "Ebbers Got Million Shares in Hot Deals" for Ebbers information and Andrew Backover, "WorldCom, Qwest Face SEC Scrutiny," USA Today, March 12, 2002, p. 1B for information on Qwest inquiry; Thor Valdmanis and Andrew Backover, "Lawsuit Targets Telecom Execs' Stock Windfalls, USA Today, October 1, 2002, p. 1B.

[159] Andrew Backover, "WorldCom, Qwest Face SEC Scrutiny," USA Today, March 12, 2002, p. 1B; Thor Valdmanis and Andrew Backover, "Lawsuit Targets Telecom Execs' Stock Windfalls, USA Today, October 1, 2002, p. 1B.

[160] Randall Smith and Deborah Solomon, "Ebbers's Exit Hurts WorldCom's Biggest Fan," The Wall Street Journal, May 3, 2002, p. C1; Andrew Backover and Jayne O'Donnell, "WorldCom Scrutiny Touches on E-mail," USA Today, July 8, 2002, p. 1B.

[161] Thor Valdmanis and Andrew Backover, "Lawsuit Targets Telecom Execs' Stock Windfalls," USA Today, October 1, 2002, p. 1B.

[162] Charles Gasparino, Tom Hamburger, and Deborah Solomon, "Salomon Made IPO Allocations Available to Ebbers, Others," The Wall Street Journal, August 28, 2002, p. A1.

Sidgmore (officer, director, and CEO after Ebbers' ouster), and James Crowe (former director of WorldCom) were also beneficiaries of the IPO allocations.[163] Apparently, those who enjoyed the benefits of Salomon's allocations also stuck with Mr. Grubman in terms of his advice once the shares were allocated, often keeping the shares for too long because of Mr. Grubman's overly optimistic views on telecommunications-related companies' stock. However, Citigroup and Salomon both denied that there was any quid pro quo between Ebbers, WorldCom, and the companies for WorldCom's investment banking business.[164]

E-mails once again reveal interesting relationships in the Wall Street scandals surrounding analysts' behaviors. Jack Grubman, an analyst with Salomon Smith Barney, was the father of twins whom he wanted to see admitted to one of Manhattan's most prestigious preschools—92nd Street Y.

Mr. Grubman wrote a memo to Sanford Weill, the chairman of Citigroup, with the following language:

> On another matter, as I alluded to you the other day, we are going through the ridiculous but necessary process of pre-school applications in Manhattan. For someone who grew up in a household with a father making $8,000 a year and for someone who attended public schools, I do find this process a bit strange, but there are no bounds for what you do for your children.
>
> Anything, anything you could do Sandy would be greatly appreciated. As I mentioned, I will keep you posted on the progress with AT&T which I think is going well.
>
> Thank you.

The backdrop for the memo is important. Citigroup pledged $1 million to the school at about the same time Grubman's children were admitted.

Mr. Weill, Mr. Grubman's CEO, asked Mr. Grubman to "take a fresh look" at AT&T, a major corporate client of Citigroup.

Mr. Weill served on the board of AT&T and AT&T's CEO, C. Michael Armstrong, served as a Citigroup director and Mr. Weill was courting Armstrong's vote for the ouster of his co-chairman at Citigroup, John Reed.

A follow-up e-mail from Mr. Grubman to Carol Cutler, another New York analyst, connected the dots:

> I used Sandy to get my kids in the 92nd Street Y pre-school (which is harder than Harvard) and Sandy needed Armstrong's vote on our board to nuke Reed in showdown. Once the coast was clear for both of us (ie Sandy clear victor and my kids confirmed) I went back to my normal self on AT&T.

At the same time as all the other movements, Mr. Grubman upgraded AT&T from a "hold" to a "strong buy." After Mr. Reed was ousted, Mr. Grubman downgraded AT&T again.

[163] Gretchen Morgenson, "Deals Within Telecom Deals," The New York Times, August 28, 2002, pp. BU1, BU10.
[164] Gretchen Morgenson, "Ebbers Got Million Shares in Hot Deal," The New York Times, August 28, 2002, p. C15.

Mr. Grubman said that he sent the e-mail "in an effort to inflate my professional importance."

In another e-mail, Mr. Grubman wrote, "I have always viewed [AT&T] as a business deal between me and Sandy."

Mr. Grubman prevented a complete retreat from WorldCom following the failed Sprint merger; there were analysts who predicted the fall of WorldCom when the merger failed. Scott Cleland, founder of Precursor Group, a Washington, D.C.–based investment research firm, predicted that the WorldCom/Sprint merger would fail, and, that if the merger failed, WorldCom would be a "dead model walking."[165] Mr. Ebbers promptly called Mr. Cleland an "idiot." Mr. Cleland does not own any individual stocks and is a stickler for conflicts of interest. Indeed, in his interview for *Fortune* magazine on his prescient call on WorldCom he said, "I should tell you I'm a Republican."[166]

Discussion Questions

1. Were there conflicts of interest?

2. Do you think any laws were violated?

3. All analysts were participating in the same types of favors and quid pro quo as Grubman. Does industry practice control ethics?

4. Attorney General Eliot Spitzer pursued the analysts and the investment houses for their lack of independence. Although they all settled the cases brought against them, what types of criminal conduct could they be charged with?

5. Mr. Spitzer found the bulk of his evidence for his cases in candid e-mails the analysts sent describing the eventual collapse of these companies even as their face-to-face evaluations of companies were most positive. Does he have the right to view their e-mails?

6. Why do you think Mr. Cleland's view of WorldCom was different from Jack Grubman's?

CASE 7.22

Ford, Firestone, and the Rolling Explorer

Firestone ATX, ATX II, and Wilderness tires came under fire in the media because of complaints about the failure of those tires being linked to so many accidents. In May 2000, following a report by a Houston television station on a correlation between the tires and accidents in that area, the National Highway Traffic Safety Administration (NHTSA) received a flurry of complaints about the tires.

[165] Stephanie N. Mehta, "Calling WorldCom's Woes," Fortune, *July 22, 2002, p. 30.*
[166] Charles Gasparino, "Ghosts of E-Mails Continue to Haunt Wall Street," The Wall Street Journal, *November 18, 2002, pp. C1, C13.*

The following is a summary from one of the many court opinions in the litigation related to the issues surrounding the Firestone tires and Ford Explorers:

In May 2000, the National Highway Traffic Safety Administration ("NHTSA") began an investigation into certain ATX and Wilderness brand tires made by Bridgestone/Firestone, Inc. That investigation was very broad, including about 60 million tires made in 41 different sizes and 53 different lines, to scores of different design specifications, at seven plants, over a decade.

On August 9, 2000, during the course of the NHTSA inquiry and with that agency's oversight, Firestone began a recall of about 14 million P235/75R15-sized ATX and Wilderness AT tires that had been sold, beginning in 1991, primarily to Ford Motor Company for use as original equipment on Explorer vehicles. Different tires are identified by brand or tire line and by alphanumeric indicators that detail certain features of the tire. For example "P235/75R15" conveys the following information: the "P" ordinarily indicates a passenger tire; "235" is the tire's section width (from sidewall to sidewall) in millimeters; "75" is the tire's aspect ratio (i.e., the tire's section height expressed as a percentage of the tire's section width); "R" denotes a radial tire; and "15" is the rim diameter in inches. Although Firestone was unable to identify any defect in the recalled tires, a tiny fraction of them—fewer than 1%—had experienced tread separation failures.

Under the Motor Vehicle Safety Act, 49 U.S.C. § 30101 *et seq.*, a "determination of 'defect' may be based exclusively on the performance record of the vehicle or component (*United States v. Gen. Motors Corp.*, 518 F.2d 420, 432 (D.C. Cir. 1975)), and NHTSA need only establish a "non–de minimus number of failures" to order a product recall. Thus, "[d]eterminations of fault or liability relevant to the award of damages at common law" do not enter into the defect inquiry under the Safety Act.

When Firestone announced the August 2000 recall, it estimated that about 6.5 million of these tires were still on the road—the others having been worn out and replaced after regular use. To expedite the recall, Firestone replaced recalled tires with new Firestone tires, and also reimbursed tire owners up to $100 per tire if they replaced recalled tires with competitive brands. By December 2000, the recall was essentially complete.

In October 2001, NHTSA determined that approximately 3.5 million Wilderness AT P235/75R15 and P255/70R16-sized tires that had been manufactured prior to May 1998 and used on sport utility vehicles should be recalled. Firestone estimated that about 768,000 of those tires might still be on the road; it agreed to replace those tires as well. NHTSA subsequently closed its investigation as to all other tires. When all was said and done, less than a third of the tires in the NHTSA investigation were subject to recall.

In May 2001, Ford separately announced that it would provide free replacement of all Wilderness AT tires on Ford vehicles, regardless of whether those tires were subject to any NHTSA order or had been recalled by Firestone.[167]

No one yet understands what went wrong with the tires. One theory is heat and poor tire maintenance. A former Firestone tire engineer, however, theorizes that these particular tires lacked nylon caps between their steel belts and the rubber to keep the

[167] In re Bridgestone/Firestone, Inc., Tires Products Liability Litigation, *287 F.Supp.2d 943 (S.D. Ind. 2002)*; In re Bridgestone/ Firestone, Inc., Tires Products Liability Litigation, *cert. denied, 537 U.S. 1105 (2002)*.

belts from sawing through the tread. Such caps are common in other tires and cost about $1.

About 100 lawsuits have been filed in courts around the country that involve accidents resulting from the tires separating. NHSTA records reveal that it has four deaths documented as well as 193 accidents from the tires. Reports of tread failure have been documented at speeds of 20 mph and the vehicle appearing most often in the reported crashes is the Ford Explorer. Many of the tire failures have occurred in vehicles with less than 2,000 odometer miles.

The NHTSA has known of the Firestone tire issues since at least 1992. At least six other nations have issued product recall notices on the tires. Ford has replaced tires in Venezuela, Ecuador, Thailand, Malaysia, Colombia, and Saudi Arabia. Ford referred to the replacements in those nations as a "customer satisfaction issue."[168]

As the Ford/Firestone tire issue has continued to evolve with both civil litigation and an investigation by the federal government, depositions of top executives in the companies have been made public. Those depositions revealed some inconsistencies, further adding to the public's confusion and resulting in protracted litigation.

For example, Bridgestone/Firestone issued public statements that it was not aware of peeling issues with the tires used on the Ford Explorer. However, a deposition of Firestone's chief of quality revealed that he believed he discussed the issue of the tires with the company's CEO in 1999, a full year before the issue became public with the resulting recall. David Laubie, who retired from the company in May 2000, said that he handled consumer claims and quality control issues for the company and had received complaints that he passed along to the CEO in memo form as well as in their regular meetings.

In testimony before Congress in September 2000, Firestone's executive vice president, Gary Crigger, testified that the company became aware of the problem only in July or August of 2000.

Firestone had raised the issue of whether Ford put proper tire pressure instructions with the Ford Explorer in incidents in Saudi Arabia.[169] Firestone maintained that Ford's recommendation of an unusually low tire pressure, 26 pounds per square inch, caused the sidewalls to flex and get hot, which then weakened the tires. However, both the depositions of Mr. Laubie and the current quality control chief of Firestone indicate that no one from Firestone ever discussed the low tire pressure issue with anyone at Ford.[170]

When Bridgestone/Firestone, Inc. issued a recall of defective tires in August 2000, for a total for a 6.5 million tires, it was the largest ever in the United States. However, the company simply did not have the inventory to replace all the tires at one time and many drivers and car owners were required to wait. The company ramped up production to 500,000 per month but, even at that rate, the replacements were not done within one year. Bridgestone/Firestone also instructed its dealers that it could offer

---

[168] James R. Healey and Sara Nathan, "More Deaths Linked to Tires," USA Today, August 2, 2000, p. 1A; James R. Healey and Sara Nathan, "Officials Have Known SUV Tire Suspicions for Decade," USA Today, August 2, 2000, p. 1B.

[169] http://www.pbs.org/newshour/bb/transportation/july-dec00/tires.

[170] James R. Healey and Sara Nathan, " Depositions in Tire Lawsuits Don't Match Company's Lines," USA Today, December 11, 2000, p. 3B.

customers any of ten acceptable substitutes for the tires, including tires from other manufacturers who would be reimbursed by the Bridgestone/Firestone dealers.[171]

Ford, after performing its own analysis of its data, including warranty claims, issued its recall because of fears that the problem was more widespread. Ford said that there was "a higher than acceptable rate of defect." The recall involved about 13 million tires. The result of the announced Ford recall was that Firestone ended its 95-year contractual relationship with Ford. There were acrimonious exchanges between the companies about responsibility, liability, and who told what to whom. The announcement from Bridgestone/Firestone appeared on its Web site, but it is no longer available. The company refused to grant permission for its reproduction here.

Ford posted the following press release on its Explorers:[172]

Myths & Facts About the Explorer

Myth: SUVs are unsafe because they roll over. SUV owners would be better off driving cars.

Fact: That's false. Advances in safety technology have made all types of passenger vehicles safer than the vehicles on the road a generation ago. And Ford's analysis of federal and state government safety data shows that, overall, SUVs are even safer than passenger cars. That's because SUVs are involved in fewer accidents—SUV drivers often have better lines of sight and SUVs are more visible to other drivers. Also, SUV occupants are often better protected when they are involved in collisions.

Although SUVs are involved in more rollover crashes than passenger cars, there is a greater risk of fatality in a passenger car in frontal, side, and rear impacts. As a result, SUVs are safer overall.

SUVs do handle differently. That is a key reason that the different handling characteristics are printed on a label appearing on the visor of every SUV all automakers build.

Leading edge safety technology available later this year on the 2002 Ford Explorer—including AdvanceTrac™ electronic stability control and Ford's new Safety Canopy™—will further reduce the risk of a rollover and serious injury or death if a rollover accident occurs. But a buckled safety belt is still the best and primary line of defense for any adult occupant in a serious accident. Children should of course be in the proper restraint system (child seat, booster seat, etc.) until they are large enough to use adult safety belts.

Myth: The Ford Explorer is more prone to roll over than other SUVs.

Fact: Not true. Ford's analysis of safety data from the U.S. Department of Transportation confirms that over the past 10 years Explorer consistently ranks among the safest vehicles in its class. The fatality rate for passenger cars is 1.5 per 100 million miles of vehicle travel. The rate for compact SUVs is lower—1.3. And the Explorer is even lower at 1.1.

Focusing on rollover accidents alone, the Explorer is safer than competitive SUVs. Ford analysis of government safety data reveals that the Explorer line is involved in 19 percent

---

[171] Norihiko Shirouzu and Timothy Aeppel, "Firestone Says It Acted to Improve Problem Tires," The Wall Street Journal, August 18, 2000, p. A3; David Kiley, "Ford Chief Wants to Speed Tire Recall," USA Today, August 17, 2000, p. 1A.
[172] http://www.ford.com.

fewer fatal rollovers than other similar SUVs. And, state safety data, which covers fatal and non-fatal rollovers, show that Explorers are involved in 16 percent fewer rollovers than competitive SUVs.

Myth: Ford launched this tire replacement effort to shift blame away from the Explorer. Something is wrong with the Explorer, but Ford wants people to think it's just a tire issue.

Fact: Not true. Ford Motor Company is replacing these tires because its number one priority is to ensure the safety of our customers and their families. Ford's concern is the Wilderness AT tire. The facts are as follows:

First, Ford fitted both Firestone tires and Goodyear tires on Explorers beginning in 1995 and through the 1997 model year. And the difference in performance is dramatic. For the roughly 3 million Firestone tires equipped on about 500,000 Explorers, Firestone's own claims database shows that there have been *1,183* claims of tread separation. For the 3 million Goodyear tires on another 500,000 Explorers (that have traveled more than 25 *billion* miles), there have been only *two* minor claims of tread separation according to claims information supplied by Goodyear. The performance on the Firestone AT tires on Explorer is 600 times worse than Goodyear tires on Explorer. *This remains the only apples-to-apples comparison in this issue.* If the vehicle was the issue, or at the very least a contributing factor, the tread separations between the Firestone and Goodyear tires would be in the same ballpark. They are not even close. That's why Ford is replacing the Firestone Wilderness AT tires.

Second, when Ford engineers tested the Wilderness AT tires over the past nine months, they found that the tires were more sensitive to stresses and consistently failed at higher rates, at lower speeds and lighter loads than other tires tested, including the Goodyear tires used on Explorer.

Third, the failure rates of Firestone Wilderness AT tires differ dramatically based on the plant in which they were made. If the vehicle were the cause of these separations, the tire plant location would not make a difference in rate of tread separations reported.

Finally, Firestone CEO John Lampe testified last year before Congress under oath and said the following: "We made some bad tires and we take full responsibility for those." When a Senator asked, "Are bad tires equated to be tires that have defects of some kind," Mr. Lampe responded, "Yes, sir."

Myth: The Firestone tires performed far better on the Ranger than the Explorer. That's proof that the Explorer is part of the reason for these tire failures.

Fact: The tires have performed better on Ranger; however, the Firestone tread separation claims on Ranger are still higher than average. And, importantly, the Firestone tread separation claims on Ranger are higher than Goodyear claims on Explorer.

In the June 11, 2001-dated issue of Business Week, Brian O'Neill, president of the Insurance Institute for Highway Safety, was asked about the Explorer-Ranger comparison. He said, "It's an apples-to-oranges comparison that has no validity in my opinion."

Ford agrees with Mr. O'Neill. Tires used on any SUV perform differently compared with tires installed on a pickup. The two vehicles are used differently. SUVs typically weigh more, and frequently are more heavily loaded, putting more stress on the tires. A sensitive tire, like we have discovered with the Wilderness AT, will not perform as well under these conditions.

Nevertheless, the larger-than-average numbers of tread separation claims for Firestone tires on Rangers *are* proof—proof that these tires should be replaced. This is why Wilderness AT tires on Ranger are part of Ford's replacement campaign.

Myth: Even if the Explorer does not cause the tread separation, it certainly is more likely to roll over as a result of the tread separation.

Fact: Not true. Ford has conducted many tests comparing Explorer with competitive SUVs and we have shared our findings with the National Highway Traffic Safety Administration. By inducing a tread separation at speeds approaching 70 mph on Explorer and competitive vehicles, with various load conditions, the Explorer's performance before, during and after a tread separation was found to be typical of other SUVs. This exhaustive study was shared with NHTSA *and* Firestone in March 2001.

The real-world accident experience shows when a Firestone tire separated on an Explorer, a rollover accident occurred on average less than 7 percent of the time. This information is based on Firestone's own claims data. Government data show Explorer and competitive SUVs have similar rollover experience in tire-related accidents. Unfortunately, Firestone tires on Explorer have separated with far greater frequency than tires on other SUVs and, of course, Goodyear tires on Explorer. *The two known Goodyear tire separations, out of about 3 million Goodyear tires in service on Explorers over the last six years, did not result in any accidents, rollovers or injuries.*

Myth: Safetyforum says that when tires fail on Explorers the results are four times more likely to produce catastrophic rollover than when they fail on other SUVs.

Fact: Ford's analysis of government data show that the Explorer has a considerably better safety record than other SUVs both in terms of fatal crashes and fatal rollover crashes. Safetyforum is misinterpreting data by using unverified reports for a variety of manufacturers. It's also misleading because it compares the Explorer to all light trucks and not just competitive SUVs.

Ford and the U.S. government use tire makers' claims data, not this collection of unverified reports. Even Safetyforum, which is a plaintiff's attorney resource organization, says they do not take into account the tire model in their analysis. The fact is that Ford's testing shows Explorers perform like other SUVs before, during, and after a tire tread separation, and real world safety data show that Explorer is among the safest vehicles on the road year after year.

Myth: Internal memos show that Ford knew about the instability of the Explorer years ago and did nothing.

Fact: That's just plain wrong. The Explorer team sought to develop a safe vehicle, recognizing that safety performance among the leaders in its class would help it to become the sales leader. And that's just what they accomplished—over the past 10 years Explorer consistently has ranked among the safest vehicles in its class based on Ford's analysis of the Federal government's real world database of crash statistics. And Explorer has been the best-selling SUV in the world each year.

Memos from engineers working on the original Explorer show them working hard to make it a safety leader, and sweating over small changes necessary for prototype vehicles to pass Ford's stringent internal safety tests that ensure safe, predictable vehicle responses in severe "limit handling" maneuvers. And yes, from time to time, they debated among themselves in their search for the optimum solutions. That is what our engineers get paid to do. If any version of those prototypes didn't pass every stringent test, changes were made until they did. That's exactly why prototypes are built. By the time the first Explorer was driven by the first customer on a real road, the vehicle had passed all of Ford's internal safety tests.

Myth: Ford has spent a lot of time looking at tires as the root cause of the problem and has done little to evaluate Explorer handling due to tire separation and rollover. It seems odd that Ford has relied solely on government data for its analysis.

Fact: While important, government data is not the only part of the evaluation of the Explorer. On March 28 and 29, 2001, Ford presented NHTSA with an exhaustive analysis of Explorer. (This technical analysis is available from NHTSA.) The analysis included stringent on-road and computer-aided testing of the Explorer and comparative SUVs in its class. The analysis dissected the performance of every major component of the Explorer that has anything to do with ride and handling, including emergency handling maneuvers and tread separation of the tires. Contrary to recent Firestone charges, it is a fact that Firestone received this thorough analysis from Ford on March 30, 2001.

The conclusion: Before, during and after a tread separation the Explorer controllability is typical of comparative SUVs. Bring in the government's data and these conclusions are consistent in the real world where analysis of statistics from the U.S. Department of Transportation shows that over the past 10 years Explorer consistently ranks among the safest vehicles in its class. The fatality rate for passenger cars is 1.5 per 100 million miles of vehicle travel. The rate for compact SUVs is lower—1.3. And the Explorer is even lower at 1.1. Likewise, focusing solely on rollover accidents, the Explorer is safer than its competition. Government figures reveal that Explorers are involved in 19 percent fewer fatal rollovers than other competitive SUVs. The same is true for single-vehicle rollover accidents—Explorer is safer than other similar-sized SUVs.

Myths & Facts About the Firestone Tires

Myth: Explorer's 26 psi recommended tire pressure is too low. That's why the tires failed.

Fact: Not true. The 2.9 million Goodyear tires performing at world-class levels on Ford Explorers convincingly disprove this myth. The recommended tire pressure for the Goodyear tires also was and, importantly, still is 26 psi. Yet the Goodyear tires are not showing the same tread separation problems. If tire pressure were really the issue, why isn't it an issue for the Goodyear tires? In addition, the extensive analyses by Ford and Firestone's independent experts show that inflation pressure generally does not cause tread separations on robust tires unless the tire is operated substantially below 26 psi.

Incidentally, the 16-inch Wilderness AT tires in the replacement program have a recommended pressure of 30 psi. Ford's analysis of Firestone's latest claims data (May 2001) showed increasing failure rates for the 16-inch tires similar to the failure rates of the 15-inch tires made in the same plant.

Myth: Ford told Firestone to decrease tire pressure to 26 psi so the vehicle could pass Ford's handling exercises and/or reduce the center of gravity. That increased the heat of the tire and caused these tread separations.

Fact: Not true. Working with Firestone, Ford engineers selected the recommended tire pressure for Explorer to optimize numerous vehicle and tire characteristics including ride quality and handling. The tire pressure selected—26 psi—is not unusual. Dozens of other competitive light trucks, SUVs, and passenger cars run on similar sized (15-inch) tires specified at 26 psi. Ford did not recommend 26 psi to lower the Explorer's center of gravity, since tire pressure has nothing to do with a vehicle's center of gravity. A 4 psi decrease (30 psi to 26 psi) lowers the center of gravity by 90 thousands of an inch (about the thickness of a nickel).

As was said earlier, the 16-inch Wilderness AT tires in the replacement program have a recommended pressure of 30 psi. Ford's analysis of Firestone's latest claims data (May 2001) showed increasing failure rates for the 16-inch tires similar to the failure rates of the 15-inch tires made in the same plant.

Myth: Firestone never agreed with Ford's recommended 26 psi tire pressure.

Fact: Firestone consistently supported Ford's recommended inflation pressure, at least until NHTSA opened its investigation in May 2000. In fact, Firestone delivered tires and paid warranty claims on those tires, year after year, under the 26 psi specification. In addition, the catalogs that Firestone issued to its dealers and customers from 1993 through 2000 state that Firestone, not just Ford, recommended 26 psi on the 15-inch tires. Furthermore, Firestone CEO Masatoshi Ono told the Wall Street Journal on August 18, 2000, that "we do not believe Ford's recommendation of 26 psi [pounds per square inch] for our tires was a mistake." Firestone approved the 26 psi recommendation in December 1989, prior to Explorer production. Goodyear also concurred in the recommendation when Ford bought Goodyear tires for Explorer.

Myth: Tires cannot tell where they have been placed on a vehicle. Yet most of the Firestone tread separations on Explorer occurred on the left rear tire. That's a sign it's the vehicle that is causing this.

Fact: False. Firestone claim data shows the same pattern for nearly all trucks and SUVs. It's consistent for GM and Daimler-Chrysler vehicles as well as Ford vehicles—the rear tires have more tread separation claims for property damage or injury than the front tires and the left rear tire tread separation claims outnumber the right rear tire tread separation claims.

Myth: Ford knew, or should have known, last summer that the recall should have been wider and are only now reluctantly replacing all the Wilderness AT tires.

Fact: Not true. Ford didn't have all the information last summer that it has today. Last summer, Ford's review of the Firestone claims data showed alarming failure rates for Firestone 15-inch ATX and Decatur-built 15-inch Wilderness AT tires. And so Ford urged Firestone to recall those tires. The Firestone claims data available to Ford *at the time* showed other Firestone Wilderness AT tires performing at world-class levels with no crashes, no rollovers, no injuries, and no fatalities.

Since last August, Ford has invested nearly 100,000 people-hours studying tires, testing tires on rigs, poring over field analysis, and conducting tire design case studies.

Then, after repeated requests, Ford obtained on May 11, 2001, additional claims data from Firestone—another piece of the puzzle that confirmed Ford's research and analysis. That data showed significantly increasing failure rates for some Wilderness AT tires and raised serious questions about the long-term durability of all of the non-recalled Wilderness AT tires. Once it obtained this information, Ford did not wait and took this preventive action to protect its customers.

Myth: Ford replaced the 16-inch Wilderness ATs overseas more than a year ago. That's proof Ford knew about the problem before last summer.

Fact: False. Ford had not, in fact, found the same failure pattern in the U.S. as it had in the overseas locations where unique usage and environmental conditions existed. Nor did Ford see the same failure pattern in the U.S. that it saw overseas. However, more recently we have seen warning signs in the U.S. that led Ford to take this action as a precautionary measure.

Myth: Ford should not have accepted "C" temperature-rated tires from Firestone. They are only tested to 85 mph.

Fact: The Firestone Wilderness AT tires are, in fact, certified to 112 mph at full vehicle loads.

The confusion is that there are two different tests used to rate tire characteristics. One test, for temperature rating, is run on a test drum with huge loads placed on the tire—far greater than the tires experience in the real world even when the vehicle is fully loaded. The 85-mph threshold a tire must pass on the test drum to be certified actually translates to speeds significantly higher in on-road usage by our customers.

A "C" temperature-rated tire is an appropriate tire for a vehicle if the tire is well manufactured and meets the performance criteria set by the automaker. Tires certified with a "C" temperature label have passed a stringent government standard, and are therefore determined to be fully acceptable. In fact, there are millions of "C" tires on some GM, Toyota and Nissan SUVs and light trucks and these tires appear to have performed well.

There is a separate test that certifies tires for a speed rating. This test is run at higher speeds and full vehicle loads. All Wilderness AT tires are speed rated "S" and are certified to 112 mph, substantially higher than the top speed of an Explorer.

Myth: The other companies are not replacing Firestone Wilderness AT tires on their vehicles. That means the tires are fine.

Fact: That is a decision that the other automakers have to make. Ford conducted extensive vehicle and tire testing, analyzed Firestone field data, and discussed findings with NHTSA. Ford concluded that there was a growing risk of additional tire failures in the future and decided to replace all Wilderness AT tires on Ford vehicles as a precautionary measure.

Other auto companies may be using different types of Firestone Wilderness tires having different specifications. It is interesting to note that days after supporting their use of Firestone tires, some of these manufacturers acknowledged that they are replacing Firestone tires on future vehicle production.

Myths & Facts About Actions in Venezuela

Myth: The Explorer is still rolling over at high rates in Venezuela. And they now have Goodyear tires. That's more proof that it's not the tire.

Fact: Absolutely false. For one thing, there has been no attempt to make any connection between these accident reports and tire failures. For another, many of these reports of "Explorer rollovers" have actually been other vehicles misreported as Ford Explorers. Other accidents mentioned include an Explorer in heavy traffic that was rear-ended by a large truck and then sandwiched between two heavy vehicles. The vehicle did not roll over, it was not in any way a tire-related incident and, thankfully, the occupants walked away with only scratches. No one, including Firestone, should make claims or allegations based on this data that is, at best, clearly flawed.

Newly obtained data from the Venezuelan transportation authority, SETRA, show that most SUV accidents in Venezuela involve vehicles other than Explorers. In the period 2000 to 2001, there were 701 accidents reported involving SUVs, but only 9 percent involved Explorers.

This data involves both fatal and non-fatal accidents in ten Venezuelan states. Two other competitors' SUVs had more fatal accidents than Explorers in Venezuela. The data was gathered and analyzed from traffic reports in the SETRA records.

The fact is Explorer, in addition to being a very popular SUV in Venezuela, has one of the safest records of any SUV in the country. Explorer's safety record in Venezuela is consistent with its performance in the U.S. where the DOT accident data confirms that Explorer is among the safest vehicles in its class.

Myth: Venezuela may ban the sale of Explorer and that's more proof that it is a dangerous vehicle.

Fact: The misinformed accusations by one Venezuelan investigator, acting on the flawed data mentioned above, does not change the fact that Explorer is a safe vehicle. The investigator has failed to substantiate any of his theories, which do not withstand any serious technical review. The Venezuelan National Assembly established an independent Technical Commission to review the investigator's allegations. Ford has been working closely with the Technical Commission and has shared its testing and analysis with them. This data and analysis disproves the investigator's allegations, including suggestions that electromagnetic interference or aerodynamic turbulence were causing vehicle rollovers.

We would expect the Venezuelan governmental agencies to act responsibly, not on a misrepresentation of hearsay.

Discussion Questions

1. Do you think it will ever be clear what happened here?

2. Who do you think will bear liability for the accidents and injuries that have resulted?

3. What conflict existed between the parties? Do you think the 95-year relationship affected the ability of both parties to see the evolving issues with the tires and the Explorer?

4. Can relationships be too long and too comfortable for the parties to confront each other?

5. What would have made the departure less acrimonious?

Sources

Bradsher, Keith, "Firestone to Stop Sales to Ford Saying It Was Used as a Scapegoat," *The New York Times*, May 22, 2001, pp. A1, C4.

Bridgestone/Firestone Web site: http://www.bridgestone-firestone.com

Kiley, David, "Ford to Replace up to 13 Million Firestone Tires," *USA Today*, May 22, 2001, p. 1A.

"Firestone Quits as Tire Supplier to Ford," *The Wall Street Journal*, May 22, 2001, pp. A3, A12.

Firestone's Web site: http://www.firestone.com

Ford's Web site: http://www.ford.com

Business and Its Competition

A BUSINESS'S RELATIONS WITH ITS COMPETITORS are evidenced in its advertising, product similarity, and pricing. The heat of competition often creates dilemmas on what to say in ads or how similar to make a product.

8^A

Advertising Content

Ads sell products. But how much can the truth be stretched? Are ads ever irresponsible by encouraging harmful behavior?

CASE 8.1
....
Joe Camel: The Cartoon Character Who Sold Cigarettes and Nearly Felled an Industry

Old Joe Camel, originally a member of a circus that passed through Winston-Salem, North Carolina, each year, was adopted by R.J. Reynolds (RJR) marketers in 1913 as the symbol for a brand being changed from "Red Kamel" to "Camel." In the late 1980s, RJR revived Old Joe with a new look in the form of a cartoon. He became the camel with a "Top Gun" flier jacket, sunglasses, a smirk, and a lot of appeal to young people.

In December 1991, the *Journal of the American Medical Association (JAMA)* published three surveys that found that the cartoon character Joe Camel reached children very effectively. Of children between the ages of 3 and 6 who were surveyed, 51.1 percent recognized Joe Camel as being associated with Camel cigarettes.[1] The 6-year-olds were as familiar with Joe Camel as they were with the Mickey Mouse logo for the Disney Channel. The surveys also established that 97.7 percent of students between the ages of 12 and 19 had seen Old Joe and 58 percent thought the ads he was used in were cool. Camel was identified by 33 percent of the students who smoke as their favorite brand.[2]

Before the survey results appeared in *JAMA*, the American Cancer Society, the American Heart Association, and the American Lung Association had petitioned the FTC to ban the ads as "one of the most egregious examples in recent history of tobacco advertising that targets children."[3]

---

[1] Kathleen Deveny, "Joe Camel Ads Reach Children, Research Finds," The Wall Street Journal, December 11, 1991, p. B1.
[2] Walecia Konrad, "I'd Toddle a Mile for a Camel," Business Week, December 23, 1991, p. 34. While the studies and their methodology have been questioned, their impact was made before the challenges and questions were raised.
[3] Deveny, "Joe Camel Ads Reach Children," p. B1.

In 1990, Camel shipments rose 11.3 percent. Joe Camel helped RJR take its Camel cigarettes from 2.7 to 3.1 percent of the market.[4]

Michael Pertschuk, former FTC head and co-director of the Advocacy Institute, an antismoking group, said, "These are the first studies to give us hard evidence, proving what everybody already knows is true: These ads target kids. I think this will add impetus to the movement to further limit tobacco advertising.[5] Joe Tye, founder of Stop Teenage Addictions to Tobacco, stated, "There is a growing body of evidence that teen smoking is increasing. And it's 100 percent related to Camel."[6]

A researcher who worked on the December 1991 *JAMA* study, Dr. Joseph R. DiFranza, stated, "We're hoping this information leads to a complete ban of cigarette advertising."[7] Dr. John Richards summarized the study as follows, "The fact is that the ad is reaching kids, and it is changing their behavior."[8]

RJR spokesman David Fishel responded to the allegations with sales evidence: "We can track 98 percent of Camel sales; and they're not going to youngsters. It's simply not in our best interest for young people to smoke, because that opens the door for the government to interfere with our product."[9] At the time the survey results were published, RJR, along with other manufacturers and the Tobacco Institute, began a multimillion-dollar campaign with billboards and bumper stickers to discourage children from smoking but announced it had no intention of abandoning Joe Camel. The Tobacco Institute publishes a free popular pamphlet called "Tobacco: Helping Youth Say No."

Former U.S. Surgeon General Antonia Novello was very vocal in her desire to change alcohol and cigarette advertising. In March 1992, she called for the withdrawal of the Joe Camel ad campaign: "In years past, R.J. Reynolds would have us walk a mile for a Camel. Today it's time that we invite old Joe Camel himself to take a hike."[10] The AMA's executive vice president, Dr. James S. Todd, concurred:

> This is an industry that kills 400,000 per year, and they have got to pick up new customers. We believe the company is directing its ads to the children who are 3, 6 and 9 years old.[11]

Cigarette sales are, in fact, declining 3 percent per year in the United States.

The average Camel smoker is 35 years old, responded an RJR spokeswoman: "Just because children can identify our logo doesn't mean they will use our product."[12] Since the introduction of Joe Camel, however, Camel's share of the under-eighteen market has climbed to 33 percent from 5 percent. Among 18- to 25-year-olds, Camel's market share has climbed to 7.9 percent from 4.4 percent.

---

[4] Konrad, "I'd Toddle a Mile for a Camel," p. 34.
[5] Deveny, "Joe Camel Ads Reach Children," p. B6.
[6] Laura Bird, "Joe Smooth for President," Adweek's Marketing Week, May 20, 1991, p. 21.
[7] Konrad, "I'd Toddle a Mile for a Camel," p. 34.
[8] "Camels for Kids," Time, December 23, 1991, p. 52.
[9] Id.
[10] William Chesire, "Don't Shoot: It's Only Joe Camel," Arizona Republic, March 15, 1992, p. C1.
[11] Id.
[12] Konrad, "I'd Toddle a Mile for a Camel," p. 34.

The Centers for Disease Control reported in March 1992 that smokers between the ages of 12 and 18 prefer Marlboro, Newport, or Camel cigarettes, the three brands with the most extensive advertising.[13]

Teenagers throughout the country were wearing Joe Camel T-shirts. Brown & Williamson, the producer of Kool cigarettes, began testing a cartoon character for its ads, a penguin wearing sunglasses and Day-Glo sneakers. Company spokesman Joseph Helewicz stated that the ads are geared to smokers between 21 and 35 years old. Helewicz added that cartoon advertisements for adults are not new and cited the Pillsbury Doughboy and the Pink Panther as effective advertising images.

In mid-1992, then-Surgeon General Novello, along with the American Medical Association, began a campaign called "Dump the Hump" to pressure the tobacco industry to stop ad campaigns that teach kids to smoke. In 1993, the FTC staff recommended a ban on the Joe Camel ads. In 1994, then-Surgeon General Joycelyn Elders blamed the tobacco industry's $4 billion in ads for increased smoking rates among teens. RJR's tobacco division chief, James W. Johnston, responded, "I'll be damned if I'll pull the ads."[14] RJR put together a team of lawyers and others it referred to as in-house censors to control Joe's influence. A campaign to have Joe wear a bandana was nixed, as was one for a punker Joe with pink hair.[15]

In 1994, RJR CEO James Johnston testified before a Congressional panel on the Joe Camel controversy and stated, "We do not market to children and will not," and added, "We do not survey anyone under the age of 18."[16]

As health issues related to smokers continued to expand, along with product liability litigation and state attorneys' general pursuit of compensation for their states' health system costs of smokers, more information about the Joe Camel campaign was discovered. Lawyers in a California suit against RJR discovered charts from a presentation at a September 30, 1974 Hilton Head, South Carolina, retreat of RJR top executives and board.[17] The charts offered the following information:

Company	Brand	Share of 14- to 24-year-old market
Philip Morris	Marlboro	33%
Brown & Williamson	Kool	17%
Reynolds	Winston	14%
Reynolds	Salem	9%[18]

[13] "Selling Death," Mesa Tribune, March 16, 1992, p. A8.

[14] Anna White, "Joe Camel's World Tour," The New York Times, April 23, 1997, p. A21.

[15] Melanie Wells and Chris Woodyard, "FTC Says Joe Camel Tobacco Icon Targeted Young," USA Today, May 29, 1991, p. 1A.

[16] Milo Geyelin, "Reynolds Aimed Specifically to Lure Young Smokers Years Ago, Data Suggest," The Wall Street Journal, January 15, 1998, p. A4.

[17] Doug Levy and Melanie Wells, "Papers: RJR Did Court Teens," USA Today, January 15, 1998, pp. 1A, 1B.

[18] Eben Shapiro, "FTC Staff Recommends Ban of Joe Camel Campaign," The Wall Street Journal, August 11, 1994, pp. B1, B8.

RJR's then-vice president of marketing, C.A. Tucker, said, "As this 14–24 age group matures, they will account for a key share of total cigarette volume for at least the next 25 years."[19] The meeting then produced a plan for increasing RJR's presence among the under-35 age group which included sponsoring NASCAR auto racing. Another memo described plans to study "the demographics and smoking behavior of 14- to 17-year-olds."[20]

Internal documents about targeting young people were damaging. A 1981 RJR internal memo on marketing surveys cautioned research personnel to tally underage smokers as "age 18."[21] A 1981 Philip Morris internal document indicated information about smoking habits in children as young as 15 was important because "today's teenager is tomorrow's potential regular customer."[22] Other Philip Morris documents from the 1980s expressed concerns that Marlboro sales would soon decline because teenage smoking rates were falling.[23]

A 1987 marketing survey in France and Canada by RJR before it launched the Joe Camel campaign showed that the cartoon image with its fun and humor attracted attention. One 1987 internal document uses the phrase "young adult smokers"[24] and notes a target campaign to the competition's "male Marlboro smokers ages 13–24."[25]

A 1997 survey of 534 teens by *USA Today* revealed the following:

Ad	Have seen ad	Liked ad
Joe Camel	95%	65%
Marlboro Man	94%	44%[26]
Budweiser Frogs	99%	92%

Marlboro was the brand smoked by most teens in the survey. The survey found 28 percent of teens between the ages of 13 and 18 smoke—an increase of 4 percent since 1991.[27] In 1987, Camels were the cigarette of choice for 3 percent of teenagers when Joe Camel debuted. By 1993, the figure had climbed to 16 percent.[28]

In early 1990, the Federal Trade Commission (FTC) began an investigation of RJR and its Joe Camel ads to determine whether underage smokers were illegally targeted

[19] Bruce Horovitz and Doug Levy, "Tobacco Firms Try to Sow Seeds of Self-Regulation," USA Today, May 16, 1996, pp. 1B, 2B.

[20] Bruce Ingersoll, "Joe Camel Ads Illegally Target Kids, FTC Says," The Wall Street Journal, May 29, 1997, pp. B1, B8.

[21] Geyelin, "Reynolds Aimed Specifically to Lure Young Smokers Years Ago," p. A4.

[22] Suein L. Hwang, Timothy Noah, and Laurie McGinley, "Philip Morris Has Its Own Youth-Smoking Plan," The Wall Street Journal, May 16, 1996, pp. B1, B4.

[23] Barry Meier, "Tobacco Executives Wax Penitent Before House Panel in Hopes of Preserving Accord," The New York Times, January 30, 1998, p. A15.

[24] Wells and Woodyard, "FTC Says Joe Camel Tobacco Icon Targeted Young," p. 1A.

[25] Id.

[26] "Joe Camel Shills to Kids," USA Today, June 2, 1997, p. 12A.

[27] Id.

[28] Alan Kline, "Joe Camel is One Species the Government Wants Extinct," Washington Times, June 8, 1997, p. 10.

by the ten-year Joe Camel Campaign.[29] The FTC had dismissed a complaint in 1994, but did not have the benefits of the newly discovered internal memos.[30]

By late 1997, RJR began phasing out Joe Camel.[31] New Camel ads feature men and women in their 20s, with a healthy look, in clubs and swimming pools with just a dromedary logo somewhere in the ad. Joe continued as a youth icon. A "Save Joe Camel" Web site developed and Joe Camel paraphernalia brought top dollar. A Joe Camel shower curtain sold for $200. RJR also vowed not to feature the Joe Camel character on non-tobacco items such as T-shirts. The cost of the abandonment was estimated at $250 million.[32]

Philip Morris proposed its own plan to halt youth smoking in 1996, which includes no vending machine ads, no billboard ads, no tobacco ads in magazines with 15 percent or more of youth subscribers, and limits on sponsorships to events (rodeos, motor sports) where 75 percent or more of attendees are adults.[33, 34]

It was also in 1997 that the combined pressure from Congress, the state attorneys general, and ongoing class action suits produced what came to be known as "the tobacco settlement." The tobacco settlement in all of its various forms bars outdoor advertising, the use of human images (Marlboro man) and cartoon characters, and vending-machine sales. This portion of the settlement was advocated by those who were concerned that teenagers would be attracted to cigarette smoking via these ads and that cigarettes were readily available in machines.[35]

While the governmental suits were settled, those suits focused simply on reimbursement for government program costs in treating smokers for their health issues related to smoking. The private litigation has not ended. A Florida jury, after finding tobacco companies guilty of fraud and conspiracy, issued a damage award of $144 billion against several companies. The bulk of the award consisted of punitive damages. The total losses to date are as follows:

$144 billion—verdict in Florida class action suit

$40 billion—settlement of Florida, Texas, and Minnesota suits

$206 billion—settlement of suits by 46 states and 5 territories

$3.4 billion—settlement of Mississippi Medicaid suit

The Florida judgment would be allocated among the tobacco companies as follows:

Phillip Morris—50%, or $73.96 billion

Lorillard—10%, or $16.25 billion

Brown & Williamson—13%, or $17.59 billion

[29] Doug Levy, "Blowing Smoke?" USA Today, January 15, 1998, pp. 1B, 2B.
[30] Shapiro, "FTC Staff Recommends Ban of Joe Camel Campaign," pp. B1, B8.
[31] "Smokin' Joe Camel Near His Last Gasp," Time, June 9, 1997, p. 47.
[32] Maria Mallory, "That's One Angry Camel," Business Week, March 7, 1994, pp. 94, 95.
[33] Horovitz and Levy, "Tobacco Firms Try to Sow Seeds of Self-Regulation," pp. 1B, 2B.
[34] Gary Rausch, "Tobacco Firms Unite to Curb Teen Smoking," Mesa Tribune, June 24, 1991, pp. B1, B6.
[35] Meier, "Tobacco Executives Wax Penitent Before House Panel," p. A15.

R.J. Reynolds—24%, or $36.28 billion

The annual sales of the companies are as follows:

Phillip Morris—$19.6 billion

R.J. Reynolds—$7.5 billion

Brown & Williamson—not available

Lorillard—$4.0 billion

Liggett—$423 million[36]

Since the time of the tobacco settlement and the Joe Camel ad campaign, the industry has changed in some ways, but in other ways remains unbowed by the events described here. For example, in 2002, Philip Morris was poised to introduce a new cigarette that was designed to save lives. If left unattended, the cigarette would extinguish itself, thus eliminating the tremendous fire risk that results from smokers falling asleep while their cigarettes are still burning. Nonextinguished cigarettes are the leading cause of fire fatalities in the United States. The cigarette was to be released under the company's Merit brand.

However, a company scientist, Michael Lee Watkins, told his superiors that the cigarettes were, in fact, a greater fire risk than conventional cigarettes, because chunks of them fell off onto smokers and nearby objects. He was fired, and Philip Morris released the Merit cigarette with special advertising emphasizing its safety. The Justice Department got wind, as it were, of the problem from Dr. Watkins, and has filed suit against Morris and other tobacco companies for deception as well as for the safety issues related to the cigarettes. Dr. Watkins has agreed to serve as a witness for the government.

Philip Morris indicates that Dr. Watkins was fired for failing to attend meetings, for speaking negatively of his colleagues, and for failing to document his research.

Philip Morris says that Dr. Watkins was correct in that chunks of the Merit safety cigarette did tend to fall off, thereby creating a different fire hazard, but the company fixed that problem by substituting a different paper before Merit was released to the market.

The suit is but one part of the legal and regulatory quagmire the tobacco companies once again find themselves in. New York passed a statute, soon to take effect, which requires that cigarettes sold in the state be "self-extinguishing" according to rules and guidelines contained in the statute. At least seven other states have similar legislation pending. Canadian health authorities are also working on fire-safe cigarette requirements.

Customers have complained about being burned when chunks of the new cigarettes fall off onto them and their clothing. The test cigarettes appeared in New York in June 2004, and the problems with them continue. The Justice Department litigation also continues, with depositions and document production.

---

[36] Rick Bragg and Sarah Kershaw, "Juror Says a 'Sense of Mission' Led to Huge Tobacco Damages," The New York Times, July 16, 2000, pp. A1, A16.

However, there are positive signs from the industry. In the summer of 2004, Philip Morris launched a massive ad campaign directed at children and teens, warning them not to begin smoking. The company ran radio and television ads directing kids and parents to a Web site for help on peer pressure, smoking, and talking about the dangers of smoking. The company also inserted multipage glossy pamphlet inserts, titled "Raising Kids Who Don't Smoke: Peer Pressure & Smoking," in major magazines. The pamphlets tell parents, "Talk to your kids about not smoking. They'll listen."

Discussion Questions

1. Suppose you were the executive in charge of marketing for R.J. Reynolds. Would you have recommended an alternative to the Joe Camel character? What if RJR insisted on the Joe Camel ad?

2. Suppose you work with a pension fund that has a large investment in RJR. Would you consider selling your RJR holdings?

3. Do you agree with the statement that identification of the logo does not equate with smoking or with smoking Camels? Do regulators agree? Did the Joe Camel ads generate market growth?

4. What effect will RJR's voluntary action have on the regulatory trend?

5. Anti-tobacco activist Alan Blum said, "This business of saying 'Oh, my God, they went after kids' is ex post facto rationalization for not having done anything. It's not as if we on the do-good side didn't know that." Is he right?

6. What do you make of Philip Morris's problems with the fire-safe cigarette? What do you make of its new antismoking ad campaign targeted at children and teens? Is it significant that the company with the highest percentage of the youth market undertook the campaign to prevent kids from smoking?

Sources

Beatty, Sally Goll, "Marlboro's Billboard Man May Soon Ride into the Sunset," *The Wall Street Journal*, July 1, 1997, pp. B1, B6.

Boot, Max, "Turning a Camel into a Scapegoat," *The Wall Street Journal*, June 4, 1997, p. A19.

Burger, Katrina, "Joe Cashes In," *Forbes*, August 11, 1997, p. 39.

Dagnoli, Judann, "RJR Aims New Ads at Young Smokers," *Advertising Age*, July 11, 1988, pp. 2–3.

Horovitz, Bruce, and Melanie Wells, "How Ad Images Shape Habits," *USA Today*, January 31–February 2, 1997, pp. 1A, 2A.

Lippert, Barbara, "Camel's Old Joe Poses the Question: What Is Sexy?" *Adweek's Marketing Week*, October 3, 1988, p. 55.

"March against Smoking Joe," *Arizona Republic*, June 22, 1992, p. A3.

Martinez, Barbara, "Antismoking Ads Aim to Gross Out Teens," *The Wall Street Journal*, March 31, 1997, pp. B1, B5.

O'Connell, Vanessa, "U.S. Suit Alleges Philip Morris Hid Cigarette-Fire Risk," *The Wall Street Journal*, April 23, 2004, pp. A1, A8.

CASE 8.2
. . . .

Alcohol Advertising: The College Focus

The mix is unquestionably there. Alcohol ads mix youth, fun, and enticing activities like scuba diving and skiing. Anheuser-Busch's Bud Light ads have Spuds MacKenzie, the "Party Animal" dog. Stroh's has its Swedish Bikini Team. Beer companies sponsor large promotions of their products on the beaches during college spring break weeks.[37]

In 1991, then-U.S. Surgeon General Antonia Novello asked the industry to voluntarily cut ads that attract minors. Novello stated, "I must call for industry's voluntary elimination of the types of alcohol advertising that appeal to youth on the bases of certain life-style appeals, sexual appeals, sports appeal, or risky activities, as well as advertising with the more blatant youth appeals of cartoon characters and youth slang."[38] A 1991 survey revealed that 10.6 million of the 20.7 million students in grades seven through twelve had had at least one drink in the last year.[39] Of the drinking group, 8 million drank weekly, 5.4 million had drinking binges, and one-half million had five or more drinks in a row at least once a week.[40]

Industry officials maintain that they are very active in and financially supportive of programs for alcohol-use education, including Mothers against Drunk Driving.

Anheuser-Busch spends $20 million of its $260 million ad budget on a campaign that features the slogan "Know when to say when." Miller Brewing Company runs a thirty-second television ad with the slogan "Think when you drink" as part of the $8 million per year that it spends to promote responsible drinking.

During spring breaks in 1991 and 1992, Miller and Anheuser-Busch did not use their multistory inflatable beer cans on popular beaches in Florida, Texas, and Mexico. In Daytona Beach, Florida, Miller put billboards along the highways with the slogan "Good beer is properly aged. You should be too." Miller's manager for alcohol and consumer issues, John Shafer, explained, "It's just good business sense to make sure we're on the right side of these issues."[41]

Patricia Taylor, a director at the Center for Science in the Public Interest, responded to the efforts by saying: "The beer companies are spending hundreds of millions every

---

[37] *The industry promoted products with multi-story inflatable beer cans. Jeffrey Zbar, "Spring Break, Inflatable Beer Bottles Gone but Other Marketers Move In,"* Advertising Age, *April 1, 1991, p. 16.*

[38] *Hilary Sout, "Surgeon General Wants to Age Alcohol Ads,"* The Wall Street Journal, *November 5, 1991, p. B1.*

[39] *Julia Flynn Siler, "It Isn't Miller Time Yet, and This Bud's Not for You,"* Business Week, *June 24, 1991, p. 52.*

[40] Id.

[41] Id.

year to present a very positive image of drinking. That overwhelms all attempts to talk about the other side of the issue."[42]

Novello ordered new studies of the link between alcohol advertising and underage drinking. She also urged the industry to drop advertising meant to appeal to young people.[43] Anheuser-Busch created a campaign with ads in trade magazines and posters for stores to remind retailers not to sell beer to underage buyers. Novello responded, "These ads may be a stronger influence on students than they realize."[44]

Late in 1996, Anheuser-Busch announced that it would stop advertising its beer on MTV. Anheuser-Busch spent $534 million on advertising in 1995, with MTV spending equaling $2 million of that total budget. However, television is known as the best method for reaching Generation X buyers. The ads were shifted to VH1. Coors has never advertised on MTV, stating, "We don't like to walk the fine line." Miller Brewing Company continues its MTV ads.

In 1998, the American Academy of Pediatrics and the American Public Health Association joined together to launch a campaign to ask Anheuser-Busch to stop using frogs, lizards, and other amphibians in its ads. The posters for these two groups trace beer ads from Spuds MacKenzie to Frank and Louis, the lizards, and ask, "Fed up with beer ads that look like cartoons?" The posters liken the animals to Joe Camel. The two groups also ran a presentation to shareholders at Anheuser-Busch's 1998 annual meeting. They were joined by Mothers Against Drunk Driving, the Marin Institute, and the Center on Alcohol Advertising.

Anheuser-Busch issued a response to the campaign noting that drunk-driving fatalities involving teens and underage drinking have both declined since 1982, and that Anheuser-Busch has spent $200 million since that time on education programs designed to halt underage drinking. Also, Anheuser-Busch did voluntarily abandon, in 1997, the frogs that refrained "Bud-weis-er."

Because of concerns about liability as well as concerns about image, the notion of college-student spring break marketing has been downplayed during the past five years by U.S. businesses. Many U.S. businesses, for reasons of costs springing from damages to property and others from liability for alcohol-induced accidents, have declined to market their products or facilities to the spring-break crowd.

To fill the void, U.S. companies have begun to use Mexico, Amsterdam, and the Caribbean as liability-free spring-break areas and are intensely marketing these sites to college students. StudentSpringBreak.com encourages students to take a trip to Amsterdam, a "pot-smoker's paradise." It also notes, "Your yearly intake of alcohol could happen in one small week in Cancun, Mexico, on spring break." Hotels and travel agencies sell $179 passes for seven bars with one all-you-can-drink-night in each one.[45]

Cancun, Jamaica, Mazatlan, Acapulco, the Bahamas, Cabo San Lucas, and Amsterdam now top Miami, Fort Lauderdale, Daytona Beach, and South Padre Island. The drinking age in the U.S. locations is 21, but it is only 18 in the travel destinations abroad.

---

[42] Id.

[43] Stuart Elliott, "A Rising Tide of Rhetoric over Warnings on Alcohol," *The New York Times*, April 2, 1991, p. D18.

[44] Id.

[45] Donna Leinwand, "Alcohol-Soaked Spring Break Lures Students Abroad," *USA Today*, January 6, 2003, pp. 1A, 2A.

Discussion Questions

1. Suppose you were an officer of a brewery whose advertising campaign targets young adults (18–21). Would you change the campaign?

2. Wouldn't your ads appeal to various groups regardless of their focus?

3. Would it be censorship for the government to control the content of your ads?

4. Are campaigns on responsible drinking sufficient?

5. Do beer companies' ads attempt to encourage underage people to drink?

6. Is the international strategy a means of circumventing the law? Is it a means of avoiding social responsibility as well as liability?

Sources

Balu, Rekha, "Anheuser-Busch Amphibian Ads Called Cold-Blooded by Doctors," *The Wall Street Journal*, April 10, 1998, p. B6.

Buck, Rinker, "Ode to Miller Beer," *Adweek's Marketing Week*, May 27, 1991, p. 16.

Colford, Steven W., "FTC May Crash Beer Promos' Campus Party," *Advertising Age*, March 25, 1991, pp. 3–4.

Horovitz, Bruce, "Brewer to Stop Ads on MTV," *USA Today*, December 23, 1996, p. 1A.

Wells, Melanie, "Budweiser Frogs Will be Put Out to Pasture," *USA Today*, January 14, 1997, pp. 1B, 8B.

Yang, Catherine, and Stan Crock, "The Spirited Brawl Ahead Over Liquor Ads on TV," *Business Week*, December 16, 1996, p. 47.

CASE 8.3

The Obligation to Screen? The Obligation to Reject: *Soldier of Fortune* Classifieds[46]

Soldier of Fortune (SOF) is a national magazine focused on guns and military clothing and aimed at "professional adventurers." In its large classified advertising section, individuals and companies offer guns, gun-related products, gun and equipment repairs, employment opportunities, and personal services.

Some of the classified ads printed between 1975, the magazine's debut, and 1984 offered services under such titles as "Mercenary for Hire," "Bounty Hunter," "High-Risk Contracts," "Dirty Work," "Mechanic," and "Do Anything, Anywhere at the Right

[46] Adapted from M. Jennings, Legal Environment of Business, 2d ed., PWS Kent, Boston, 1991, pp. 229–231.

Price." During this period, *SOF* ran 2,000 classified ads, about three dozen of which had titles like these.

Various media, including the Associated Press, United Press International, *Rocky Mountain News*, *Denver Post*, *Time*, and *Newsweek*, reported links between *SOF* classified ads and crimes or criminal plots. These connections were made directly to five specific *SOF* ads and alleged with four others. Law enforcement officials contacted *SOF* staffers in investigating two crimes linked to personal service ads in the magazine.

Nature of *SOF* Ads

Dr. Park Dietz, a forensic psychiatrist, concluded from his study of the ads that the average *SOF* subscriber—a male who owns camouflage clothing and more than one gun—would understand some phrases in *SOF's* classified ads as solicitations for illegal activity given the ads' context. At that time, *SOF* contained display ads for semi-automatic rifles and books with titles such as *How to Kill*, along with articles on "Harassing the Bear, New Afghan Tactics Stall Soviet Victory," "Pipestone Canyon, Summertime in 'Nam and the Dyin' Was Easy," and "Night Raiders on Russia's Border."

Dietz suggested that the *SOF* personal service ads carry the connotation of criminal activity because of the nature of the magazine. He noted that the same ads would not carry that connotation if they appeared in *Esquire* or *Vanity Fair*.

The Hearn Ad

In September, October, and November of 1984, *SOF* ran the following ad:

EX-MARINES-67–69 'Nam Vets, Ex-DI, weapons specialist—jungle warfare, pilot, M.E., high risk assignments, U.S. or overseas. [Phone number]

"Ex-DI" means ex-drill instructor; "M.E." means multiengine planes; and "high risk assignments" means work as a bodyguard or security specialist.

The ad was placed by John Wayne Hearn, who said he wanted to recruit Vietnam veterans for work as bodyguards and security men for executives. Hearn's partner said they also hoped to train troops for South American countries. Hearn said he did not place the ad with an intent to solicit criminal employment but that 90 percent of the responses to the ad sought his participation in illegal activities, such as beatings, kidnappings, jailbreaks, bombings, and murders. His only lawful inquiry was from a Lebanese oil conglomerate seeking bodyguards; Hearn received a commission to place seven men with it.

Robert Black contacted Hearn through the *SOF* ad. Between 1982 and 1984, Black had asked at least four friends or coworkers in Bryan, Texas, to kill his wife, Sandra Black, or help him kill her. Initially, Black discussed bodyguard work with Hearn, and then their conversations focused on Black's gun collection. In October 1984, Hearn traveled to Texas from his Atlanta home to see Black's collection. During the visit, Black told Hearn his plans for murdering his wife. After Hearn returned to Atlanta, Black repeatedly called him. In a conversation with Debbie Bannister, Hearn's girlfriend, Black offered Hearn $10,000 to kill Black's wife. Bannister then communicated the offer to Hearn.

Hearn had no previous criminal record, but on January 6, 1985, he killed Bannister's sister. On February 2, he murdered Bannister's husband, and nineteen days later, he killed Sandra Black. He was convicted of the murders and sentenced to concurrent life terms.

The Victims' Suit against *SOF*

Sandra Black's mother, Marjorie Eimann, and her son, Gary Wayne Black, sued *SOF* for negligence in publishing Hearn's ad. The trial court awarded Eimann and Black $9.4 million in damages.

An appellate court reversed the decision, saying:

> Given the pervasiveness of advertising in our society and the important role it plays, we decline to impose on publishers the obligation to reject all ambiguous advertisements for products or services that might pose a threat of harm. The burden on a publisher to avoid liability from suits of this type is too great.[47]

Other Cases of Ad Liability

SOF was sued again over a classified ad after Douglas Norwood was ambushed, assaulted, shot, and finally killed by a car bomb late in 1985. Each of his assailants had been hired through the following *SOF* ads:

> GUN FOR HIRE: 37-year-old professional mercenary desires jobs. Vietnam Veteran. Discreet and very private. Bodyguard, courier, and other special skills. All jobs considered. [Phone number]

> GUN FOR HIRE: Nam sniper instructor. SWAT. Pistol, rifle, security specialist, bodyguard, courier plus. All jobs considered. Privacy guaranteed. Mike [Phone number].[48]

The case was settled out of court in 1987.

In another case, Richard Braun was shot and killed outside his Atlanta home by an experienced mercenary, Richard Savage, who had been hired by Braun's business associate, Bruce Gastwirth, through an ad in *Soldier of Fortune*. Savage's ad began with the words "Gun for Hire." Braun's sons sued the magazine and were awarded $4.3 million. The amount was later reduced in a settlement of the case.[49]

The Association of Newspaper Classified Advertising Managers, Inc. (ANCAM) has the following policy:

> Advertisements containing statements that injure the health of readers, directly or indirectly, are not acceptable.

Another ANCAM section provides:

> Any advertisement fostering the evasion or violation of any law or making a direct or indirect offer of any article or service that violates a city, state or federal statute is unacceptable.[50]

[47] Eimann v. Soldier of Fortune Magazine, Inc., *880 F.2d 830 (5th Cir. 1989), cert. denied, 493 U.S. 1024 (1990).*
[48] Norwood v. Soldier of Fortune Magazine, *651 F.Supp 1397 (W.D. Anc. 1987).*
[49] *"Military Magazine Gets Jury Judgment Reduced,"* The Wall Street Journal, *March 1, 1993, p. B3.*
[50] *Don Tomlinson, "Choosing Social Responsibility Over Law: The Soldier of Fortune Classified Advertising Cases,"* Business & Professional Ethics Journal 9, *1990, pp. 79–96.*

Discussion Questions

1. Assume that you are *SOF's* new director of display and classified advertising. You know *SOF* was relieved of any liability for Sandra Black's death, so it is not obligated to check or reject ads. Your conscience, however, remains troubled as you review ads with such language as "high-risk assignment" and "bounty hunter." As you think about the Black case, you rationalize that Hearn was on a murder spree and Black was simply a victim of his sudden violence. On the other hand, Hearn would never have known Black if his classified ad had not brought a call from Robert Black. Further, only five to ten ads of over a total of 2,000 classifieds have resulted in crimes or criminal plots. You discuss this dilemma over lunch with your senior staff member, who responds: "Yes, but we could have prevented those crimes by not running the ads."

   Screening the ads will take time, private detectives, and an assumption of liability the law does not require you to make. Will you change *SOF's* ad policy? Will you conduct ad background checks?

2. Does this dilemma present conflicting moral standards?

3. To whom do you owe your loyalty in making your decision?

4. Should *SOF* feel morally responsible for Sandra Black's death?

5. Is the appellate court's decision not to impose liability on *SOF* an application of utilitarianism?

6. Should the decision on advertising policy be different following Sandra Black's murder?

7. William L. Prosser, a legal scholar, has stated, "Nearly all human acts . . . carry some recognizable possibility of harm to another." Why do we allow recovery for some of those harmful acts and not others?

8. *Soldier of Fortune* stopped accepting personal service ads in 1986. Is that an appropriate and ethical resolution?

CASE 8.4

Hollywood Ads

Actress Demi Moore starred in the 1995 movie entitled *The Scarlet Letter*, which was based on Nathaniel Hawthorne's book of the same name. Hollywood Pictures ran the following quote from a *Time* magazine review: "'Scarlet Letter' Gets What It Always Needed: Demi Moore." The actual review by *Time* magazine read: "Stuffy old *Scarlet Letter* gets what it always needed: Demi Moore and a happier ending." A *Time* spokesman noted that the statement was clearly ironic. In the same review, the *Time* critic, Richard Corliss, referred to the movie as "revisionist slog" and gave it an "F."

An ad for the 1995 movie *Seven* quoted *Entertainment Weekly* as calling it a "masterpiece." The actual review read, "The credits sequence . . . is a small masterpiece of dementia."

A movie industry observer stated in response to these examples, "The practice of fudging critics' quotes [in ads] is common." However, there is more than simple "fudging." Ads for the movie *Thirteen Days* included the descriptive phrases "by-the-numbers recreation" and "close to perfect" in order to reflect what producers touted as the strength of the film—its historical accuracy. But the ads also included pictures of the Spruance-class destroyer and F-15 jet fighters. Neither of these defense systems was available in 1962, the time of the movie, which is a depiction of the 13-day Cuban missile crisis during the Kennedy administration. These systems were not developed until the 1970s.

The movie studios pulled the ads after they had run for one weekend. They also pulled those ads that showed the movie's star, Kevin Costner, walking with the actors who played John and Robert Kennedy because that scene was not a part of the movie.

In 2001, ads by Sony Studios had theater critic David Manning proclaiming that *The Animal*, starring Rob Schneider and ex-"Survivor" Colleen Haskell, was "another winner." Mr. Manning also gave a favorable review of Sony's *A Knight's Tale*. However, David Manning is fictitious. He is a critic created out of whole cloth by young marketing staff members at Sony.[51]

....

Discussion Questions

1. Is the practice of fudging quotes ethical? Should Hollywood Pictures have pulled the *Scarlet Letter* ads?

2. How accurate should movie ads be? How historically authentic?

3. Is the practice of making up critics to provide quotes on movies ethical?

[51] *"Ads for Missile Crisis Movie Are Pulled Because of Errors,"* The New York Times, *January 13, 2001, p. A8.*

8 B

Appropriation of Others' Ideas

When does an idea belong to someone else? Laws on patents and copyrights afford protection in some cases, but other situations are too close to call—or are they?

CASE 8.5
Ragu Thick and Zesty

Ragu Foods, Inc., has been the leading seller of prepared spaghetti sauce in the United States since 1972. By 1973, Ragu held more than 60 percent of the market. Late in that year, Hunt-Wesson Foods, Inc., decided to enter the market with "Prima Salsa" spaghetti sauce. After extensive marketing and taste studies, Hunt-Wesson introduced its sauce in 1976 using the slogan "Extra Thick and Zesty."

Just before Hunt launched "Prima Salsa," Ragu introduced a new sauce called "Ragu Extra Thick and Zesty." Ragu's advertising campaign used a photo similar to Hunt's of a ladle of sauce being poured over noodles. Ragu's sauce was thickened with starch, whereas Hunt's used a longer cooking process. The label on the Ragu sauce did not make this distinction clear.

Hunt-Wesson executives claimed the introduction of the Ragu sauce appropriated all their work and research and created product confusion in consumers' minds.[52]

Ragu maintained that its product was simply a response to competition and good business strategy. Hunt-Wesson claimed there can be no competition because of Ragu's domination of the market, which was 65 percent in 1975, and felt Ragu's methods were unfair.

In 1990, Ragu introduced a sauce called "Ragu Fresh Italian." The Food and Drug Administration (FDA) cited Ragu for six violations of federal labeling law that centered on the word *fresh*. FDA regulations prohibit the use of "fresh" if chemical or heat processing is used. Ragu acknowledged using heat processing but maintained "fresh" is part of a trademark, not a description.[53]

---

[52] *"Critics Take Apart Label of Ragu a Word at a Time,"* Arizona Republic, May 2, 1990, p. A7.
[53] Hunt-Wesson Foods, Inc. v. Ragu Foods, Inc., *627 F.2d 919 (9th Cir. 1980)*.

In 1993, Campbell Soup introduced its Prego sauce with comparison ads that depicted Ragu as runny. Ragu sued Campbell for these "misleading ads" since Campbell did not use Ragu's Thick & Chunky sauce to do the ad comparisons.[54]

At the end of 1993, Ragu sauces had 36.2 percent of this $1.1 billion market (down from 50 percent in 1992), while Prego had 26.3 percent (up from 20 percent).

Discussion Questions

1. Was Ragu just an aggressive competitor, or did it appropriate ideas or mislead?

2. Are any moral standards violated by Ragu's conduct in these campaigns?

3. Would you feel comfortable with the "Prima Salsa" name if you were a marketing executive with Ragu? Or with the use of the term "fresh"?

4. Is product confusion a fair method of competition?

5. Aren't companies free to meet the market with their product lines?

CASE 8.6

The Little Intermittent Windshield Wiper and Its Little Inventor

Robert W. Kearns, a Maryland inventor and former engineering professor at Wayne State University in Detroit, Michigan, obtained a patent for his first intermittent car windshield wiper system in 1967. *People* magazine described the genesis of Kearns' invention as follows:

> When Robert Kearns popped open a champagne bottle on his wedding night in August 1953, he couldn't have seen that it might one day make him rich. At first he couldn't see much of anything; the cork hit him in the face, virtually blinding him in his right eye. But the accident got the homegrown inventor to thinking—about his eyes, the way they blink and, improbably, about how difficult it is to drive in a drizzling rain.
>
> Kearns's musings led to a basement invention, a windshield wiper that automatically blinks on and off in light rain.[55]

He installed it in a 1962 Ford Galaxie, then demonstrated it for Ford. Ford installed the wiper system in its cars beginning in 1969 and did so under its own patents for such a system. During the 1970s, intermittent wiper systems began appearing on the cars of major U.S. and Japanese automakers. Kearns received no money for the use of these systems. The automakers maintained that the idea was an obvious one and it was only a matter of time before their engineers developed the same type of system. They also claimed that their systems differed from Kearns's in design and function.

[54] Jack Rejtman, "Spaghetti Sauce Spat between Prego, Ragu Is Set to Thicken," The Wall Street Journal, August 4, 1993, p. B5.
[55] Ken Gross, "Wiper Man Robert Kearns Won His Patent Fight with Ford, But That Didn't Mean He Was Out of the Wood," People, August 6, 1990.

Kearns filed suit against Ford, General Motors, Chrysler, Fiat, Toyota, Ferrari, Volvo, Alfa-Romeo, Citroen, Honda, Isuzu, Mitsubishi, Nissan, Maserati, Peugeot, Renault, Rolls Royce, Saab, Toyota, and other Japanese auto manufacturers for a total of 19 different defendants. He had planned to open his own firm to supply the intermittent windshield wiper systems to all automakers but was unable to do so after the companies manufactured the systems in-house. Dr. Kearns represented himself in the cases that ran through 1995 until final resolution or settlement. In fact, Kearns set up Kearns and Associates in a building across the street from the federal court house in Detroit in order to battle the auto manufacturers. His children worked for the company formed to litigate and, at one point, Kearns was ordered to pay sanctions because his son had obtained confidential documents by dating a paralegal who worked at a law firm that was representing one of the auto manufacturers.[56]

In November 1990, Kearns settled his case with Ford Motor Company for $10.2 million, which amounted to 30 cents per car Ford sold with the intermittent wiper systems. He had turned down a $30 million offer from Ford and proceeded with litigation. In June 1992, a jury awarded Kearns $11.3 million in damages from Chrysler, or about 90 cents per car, for Chrysler's infringement of Kearns's patent. Chrysler had sold 12,564,107 vehicles with the device. Kearns had originally asked for damages ranging from $3 to $30 per car, or $37.7 to $377 million, based on the treble damage provisions of the patent infringement laws.[57] Chrysler appealed what it called the "unreasonable and excessive" verdict; however, the appeal was dismissed by the U.S. Supreme Court.[58] The amount Kearns received from Chrysler, $18.7 million, was far less than he had requested as damages.

Kearns continued to pursue his cases against the other car companies until the U.S. Supreme Court refused to reverse the dismissal of his case. He spent $4 million in legal fees in the Ford case and about $5.5 million on the case against Chrysler. He was represented by four law firms during the course of all the litigation. Dr. Kearns was a colorful figure who wrote an angry letter to the federal judge handling his first trial when the jury was unable to reach a verdict. After having the letter delivered to the judge, Dr. Kearns disappeared for several days. The jury could not reach a verdict and the judge declared a mistrial. That case, the Ford case, was eventually settled.

Kearns said his success should be an inspiration for other inventors because it proves they can win against large corporations that have used others' ideas without reimbursement. Others say that Kearns' failed marriage and his near breakdown demonstrate that a refusal to negotiate can be harmful and that most of his money went to paying lawyers in the decades-long litigation.

Discussion Questions

1. Is it ethical to use an idea based on the risk analysis that the owner of that idea simply cannot afford to litigate the matter?

---

[56] Mike Hoffman, "Fighting Knockoff Artists Is Easy. If You've Got a Lifetime to Devote to It," Inc., Dec. 1997, http://www.inc.com/magazine/19971201/1374.html.
[57] Kearns v. Ford Motor Co., 726 F.Supp 159 (E.D. Mich. 1989); see also "Chrysler Told to Pay Inventor $11.3 Million," The New York Times, June 12, 1992, p. C3.
[58] Kearns v. Chrysler Motor Corp., 62 F.3d 1430 (C.A.F.C. 1995), cert. denied, 516 U.S. 989 (1995).

2. Why was the intermittent wiper system so important to the automakers?

3. Could Kearns have done anything further to protect himself?

4. If you were an executive with one of the companies still in litigation with Kearns, would you settle the case? Why or why not?

5. Why do you think the auto manufacturers fought Kearns so extensively? Is it possible that their engineers had been working simultaneously on the idea?

CASE 8.7
V-A-N-N-A: It Belongs to Me

Samsung Electronics ran an advertising campaign that had a letter-turning blonde robot dressed in a red evening dress, complete with diamond bracelet and necklace. The ad was a takeoff on Vanna White's role of turning letters for contestants on the television game show *Wheel of Fortune*. White filed suit alleging that Samsung's use of the "Robo Vanna" was an appropriation of her image and a taking of her creative output. Samsung maintained there was no appropriation because the ads were a takeoff on *Wheel of Fortune*. The court found for Ms. White.[59]

Discussion Questions

1. Has something been taken without compensation in this case?

2. Did Samsung take advantage of *Wheel of Fortune* and Vanna White?

3. One advertising law expert has stated, "I wish these people would take a joke." Is the takeoff satire or appropriation?[60]

4. Should Samsung have sought permission to run its ads?

CASE 8.8
Copyrights, Songs, and Charity

Children at camps around the country in the summer of 1996 were not able to dance the "Macarena" except in utter silence. Their usual oldies dances were halted in 1996. The American Society of Composers, Authors & Publishers (ASCAP) notified camps and the organizations that sponsor camps (such as the Boy Scouts of America and the Girls Scouts USA) that they would be required to pay the licensing fees if they used any of the 4 million copyrighted songs written or published by any of the 68,000 members of ASCAP.

The fees for use of the songs have exceeded the budgets of many of the camps. One camp that operates only during the day charges its campers $44 per week. ASCAP

---

[59] White v. Samsung Elect. Am., Inc., *971 F.2d 1395 (9th Cir. 1992)*.
[60] *"Do You Vanna Dance with Lawyer?"* Business Week, *October 18, 1993, p. 8.*

wanted $591 for the season for the camp's use of songs such as "Edelweiss" (from *The Sound of Music*) and "This Land is Your Land." ASCAP demanded fees for even singing the songs around the campfire. ASCAP's letters to the camps reminded the directors of the possible penalties of $5,000 and up to six days in jail and threatened lawsuits for any infringement of the rights of ASCAP members. Luckily, "Kumbaya" is not owned by an ASCAP member.

Several camp directors wrote and asked for a special program that would allow their camps a discount for the use of the songs. Many of the camps are not run as for-profit businesses but rather include camps such as those for children with cancer and AIDS. ASCAP now includes the following frequently asked question on its Web site (http://www.ascap.com):

Do I need permission to perform music as part of a presentation in class or at a training seminar?

If the performance is part of face to face teaching activity at a non-profit educational institution, permission is not required. Permission is required when music is used as part of training seminars, conventions, or other commercial or business presentations.

ASCAP has over 100 licensing fee arrangements. The fees range from $200 per $700 per year, but some organizations have negotiated lower fees. The Radio Music License Committee negotiated a $1.7 billion fee arrangement with ASCAP to cover its members through 2009.

In 1999, Congress passed the Fairness in Music Licensing Amendment [17 U.S.C. 110(5)] to provide an exemption for restaurants (such as sports bars) that play radio music or television programs over speakers in their facilities. The law provides that because the radio and television rights have been acquired, restaurants and bars need not pay ASCAP additional fees. ASCAP opposed this change to the copyright laws and has proposed changes to it since 1999. Currently, ASCAP is providing testimony before Congress on the use of music over the Internet and the rights of its members.

The issue of public use of popular songs and copyrights surfaced after the September 11, 2001, attacks when Congress stood on the steps of the Capitol on the evening of September 11, 2001, and sang, "God Bless America." It was a spontaneous moment and from that time, the song became an integral part of all public functions, including the seventh inning stretch during the World Series.

Irving Berlin wrote "God Bless America" in 1940. When he did, he pledged all the royalties from the song to benefit youth organizations in the United States, specifically the Girl Scouts and Boy Scouts.

Each time there is a performance of the song, royalties are paid to the trust fund Berlin established for the administration of the royalties for the Scouts. Since that time, just the groups in New York City have received over $6 million from song performances. The annual income from "God Bless America" public performances has been about $200,000. However, the song has become a sort of second national anthem since the time of the September 11, 2001, attacks and the predictions are that the royalties from public performances will generate triple that income for this year.

Mr. Berlin died in 1989 at the age of 101 and his daughter, Mrs. Linda Emmett, administers the trust fund. Mrs. Emmett, who shares her father's commitment to the children of the United States, says that nothing would have pleased her father more than the song's newfound popularity and the resulting benefits to the Scouts.[61]

Discussion Questions

1. Why does ASCAP work so diligently to enforce its rights and collect the fees for its members' songs?

2. What risks does ASCAP run if the camps continue to use the songs without payment of the licensing fees?

3. What ethical and social responsibility issues do you see with respect to those camps that are strictly nonprofit operations?

4. Can you think of a compromise that would protect ASCAP members' rights but still offer the camps a reasonable chance to use the songs?

5. What would you do if you were an ASCAP member and owned the rights to a song a camp wished to use? Do you think Mr. Berlin's trust has the correct approach? Could his trust not simply donate the use of the song? What problems do you see with that practice?

Sources

Elisabeth Bumiller, *The New York Times,* December 17, 1996, p. B1.

Ken Ringle, *The Washington Post,* August 24, 1996, p. B1, and August 28, 1996, p. C3.

[61] *William Glaberson, "Irving Berlin Gave the Scouts a Gift of Song," The New York Times, October 14, 2001, p. A21.*

8c

Pricing

What price is fair? Is a fair price always the most customers are willing to pay? Should businesses give special discounts to nonprofit buyers?

CASE 8.9

Archer Daniels Midland: A Giant in Grain

When the Justice Department raided the offices of Archer Daniels Midland (ADM) on June 26, 1995, to search for records related to its investigation of ADM and its competitors for possible violations of federal antitrust laws, an employee in a photo store in Decatur, Illinois (the home of ADM) said, "ADM will probably get a slap on the wrist and that will be the end of it. If I got caught doing that, I'd go to jail. It is scary to think of a company being that powerful."[62]

Between that June day and October 20, 1995, ADM's stock price fell 6.5 percent. ADM, a grain-processing company, was eventually charged with price fixing for two corn-derived products: lysine, a feed supplement for cattle, and citric acid. The Justice Department was tipped off to the ADM conduct in 1992 by an ADM executive, Mark E. Whitacre. Whitacre continued to work for ADM while serving as a government informant. Mr. Whitacre's undercover work resulted in guilty pleas by three Asian companies in 1995. It was revealed during evidentiary hearings that Mr. Whitacre "selectively recorded" the conversations. Whitacre eventually agreed to plead guilty to two felonies in August 1995. The felonies were evasion of income tax and failure to disclose compensation to shareholders. When Mr. Whitacre's role with federal investigators was disclosed, ADM charged that the conspiracy was Whitacre's doing and that he had embezzled the gains from the conspiracy from ADM.

On Wednesday, October 16, 1996, ADM pleaded guilty to charges that it had fixed prices. As part of the plea agreement, ADM agreed to pay $100 million in fines and to cooperate with the government in its continuing investigation. Outraged shareholders staged a revolt at the October 17, 1996, shareholder meeting. James E. Burton, chief

---

[62] Kurt Eichenwald, "Archer Daniels Midland to Pay a $100 Million Fine in Pricing Case," The New York Times, October 15, 1996, pp. A1, C3.

executive officer of the California Public Employees Retirement System, stated, "The $100 million fine is shareholder assets that are being squandered to pay for criminal activity that never should have occurred. Where was the board of directors?"[63]

Two days after the board meeting, the ADM board accepted the resignation of Michael D. Andreas, the vice chairman of ADM and son of ADM's chairman, and Terrance Wilson, the head of ADM's corn-processing division. ADM board member Brian Mulroney, the former Prime Minister of Canada, stated upon departure from the meeting, "They no longer work here."[64]

On December 3, 1996, three officers of ADM were indicted for conspiracy in fixing prices on lysine, including Terrance Wilson and Michael Andreas. Two Japanese executives were also indicted on conspiracy charges. The ADM executives were found guilty of price fixing in 1998.[65] They were sentenced in 1999 to between 20 months and 2.5 years with fines of $350,000 each.[66]

....

Discussion Questions

1. What criminal violations do you think occurred? What ethical violations occurred?

2. Do you agree with Mr. Burton's statement?

3. Who is responsible for the conduct that led to the guilty plea? Was it best for ADM to plead guilty?

4. What do you think of Mr. Whitacre's undercover work? Would you have done the same thing and worked for the government?

5. Do you agree with the photo employee's statement? Did ADM get just a slap on the wrist? Visit http://www.admworld.com for an update on ADM's policies.

....

Sources

Armstrong, Larry, "All Roads Lead to ADM," *Business Week*, September 23, 1996, pp. 42–43.

Burton, Thomas M., "Former ADM Executive Mark Whitacre Pleads Guilty to Embezzling $9 Million," *The Wall Street Journal*, October 13, 1997, p. B12.

Eichenwald, Kurt, "Informant Said to Agree to Plea Deal," *The New York Times*, September 27, 1995, pp. C1, C3.

Eichenwald, Kurt, "Judge Lets Archer Tapes Be Admitted," *The New York Times*, April 17, 1998, p. C6.

Kilman, Scott, "Ajinomoto Pleads Guilty to Conspiring With ADM, Others to Fix Lysine Price," *The Wall Street Journal*, November 15, 1996, p. A18.

---

[63] *"ADM Still Doesn't Get It," Fortune, November 11, 1996, pp. 30–31.*
[64] *Kurt Eichenwald, "2 Executives Step Down at Archer Daniels," The New York Times, October 18, 1996, pp. C1, C4.*
[65] *Kurt Eichenwald, "Former Archer Daniels Executives Are Found Guilty of Price Fixing," The New York Times, September 18, 1998, p. C1.*
[66] *Kurt Eichenwald, "Three Sentenced in Archer Daniels Midland Case," The New York Times, July 10, 1999, pp. B1, B14.*

CASE 8.10

Sotheby's and Christie's: The No-Auction Prices

Christie's International and Sotheby's—international auction houses for art and estate items and known for their handling of the estates and property of the rich and famous such as the estate of Jaqueline Kennedy Onassis; the gowns of Diana, Princess of Wales; and the effects of Marilyn Monroe—became the subject of a price fixing investigation by the Federal Trade Commission and Justice Department. Together, the two firms controlled 95 percent of the international auction market.

The price fixing charges have their origins in "conscious parallelism." That is, the two federal agencies focused on why the two auction houses raised their commissions in lock step over the years with virtually no price competition in auction commissions. The information against Sotheby's included the following activities as evidence of the price fixing:

a. participating in meetings and conversations in the United States and elsewhere to discuss sellers' commissions;

b. agreeing to raise pricing by fixing sellers' commissions;

c. agreeing to publish nonnegotiable sellers' commission schedules;

d. agreeing to the order in which each co-conspirator would publish its nonnegotiable sellers' commission schedule;

e. issuing sellers' commission schedules in accordance with the agreements reached;

f. exchanging customer information for the purpose of monitoring and enforcing adherence to the nonnegotiable sellers' commission schedules;

g. agreeing not to make interest-free loans on consignments from sellers; and

h. not making charitable contributions as part of the pricing to sellers.[67]

The drama surrounding the Christie's and Sotheby's antitrust investigation and trial captured the interest of all levels of society in New York City and elsewhere because of the high-society status of Sotheby's and its officers. Diana D. (Dede) Brooks, the CEO of Sotheby's, was married to Michael Brooks, a prominent venture capitalist. She was a 1972 Yale graduate and had been a member of the Yale Corporation, the board of trustees of Yale University, since 1990. Her daughter graduated from Yale in 1999. Ms. Brooks resigned her position there in June 2000. Ms. Brooks resigned her position as a board member with Morgan Stanley Dean Witter when she was charged by the federal government and resigned from the boards of the Memorial Sloan-Kettering Cancer Center and the Central Park Conservancy at the same time she left the Yale Corporation.

The auction antitrust case began in December 1999, when Christopher M. Davidge, the CEO of Christie's, was terminated. Upset about what he called his "paltry" severance package and others say was his concern that he might have been set up to take the blame for any antitrust charges, Davidge demanded all of his business records from Christie's. He took everything from his files, including handwritten notes he had sent to Sotheby's CEO, Ms. Brooks. Also implicated in his files was the chair of Sotheby's, A. Alfred Taubman.

[67] *http://www.usdoj.gov/atr/cases/f6600/6656.htm.*

Mr. Davidge had initially denied, when questioned by the Justice Department, that he had any inappropriate communications with Sotheby's and Ms. Brooks. However, Mr. Davidge's former assistant, Irmgrad Pickering, told the Justice Department that she believed Mr. Davidge and Ms. Brooks had held meetings.

He turned the records over to his lawyer who, in turn, turned them over to the Justice Department. The records have been described as establishing "classic cartel behavior—price fixing pure and simple" between Christie's and Sotheby's.[68] The correspondence in his files was between him and Ms. Brooks. The correspondence reflects a pattern of the two auction houses matching their commission rates. For example, in March 1995, Christie's announced it was increasing its sellers' fees from a flat rate to a sliding scale ranging from 2 to 20 percent. Sotheby's made an announcement of the same change in sellers' rates one month later.[69]

Soon after Christie's became aware of the documents and correspondence in the hands of the Justice Department, it announced its cooperation with the federal government and was given amnesty. At the same time, Christie's announced that it was raising its buyer's commission from 17.5 to 18 percent (for buyers spending up to $80,000 and 10 percent for buyers above that amount) and charging its sellers less, taking its commission for sales down 1 to 5 percent and as low as 1.25 percent for amounts greater than $1,000.[70]

Both changes placed Sotheby's, Christie's prime competitor, in the position of charging higher commissions. The disparity in commission was the first time there was any difference in the competitors' prices in over a decade.

Mr. Taubman denied any involvement in the price fixing and offered a lie detector test conducted by a former FBI agent to establish that he did not know of the arrangements and communications between Ms. Brooks and Mr. Davidge. The two key questions in the polygraph exam, which Mr. Taubman passed, were:

> Did you tell Dede Brooks to try and reach an agreement with Davidge regarding amounts to be charged to buyers or sellers?

> Did Dede Brooks ever tell you that she had reached an agreement with Davidge about amounts to be charged to buyers and sellers?[71]

Mr. Taubman's answers of "no" to each of these questions were found to be truthful by the examiner for the polygraph. The test was conducted without any law enforcement agents present.

At nearly the same time, Christie's agreed to pay $256 million, one-half of a $512 million civil suit brought against the company, and settled a shareholder lawsuit for $30 million. Sotheby's also agreed to pay its $256 million share of the suit amount to settle civil claims. Mr. Taubman agreed to be responsible for paying $156 million of

[68] Shawn Tully, "A House Divided," Fortune, December 18, 2000, pp. 264–275.

[69] Douglas Frantz, with Carol Vogel and Ralph Blumenthal, "Files of Ex-Christie's Chief Fuel Inquiry Into Art Auction," The New York Times, October 8, 2000, pp. A1, A28.

[70] Alexandria Peers and Ann Davis, "Christie's Overhauls Commissions," The Wall Street Journal, February 8, 2000, pp. A3, A10.

[71] Frantz, Vogel, and Blumenthal, "Files of Ex-Christie's Chief," pp. A1, A28.

that corporate obligation. Representing the plaintiffs in the antitrust suit against the two auction houses was David Boies, the lawyer who represented Al Gore in the 2000 presidential election litigation, Shawn Fanning and Napster in their copyright litigation, and the federal government in the Microsoft antitrust case.

Mr. Davidge got immunity in exchange for his cooperation. Ms. Brooks entered a guilty plea on October 5, 2000, and declined all of her stock options. The 2.5 million stock options were worth $10 million, and she also waived all of her salary from Sotheby's for the period during which she was CEO, a total of $3.25 million. Her friends say she refused the options so as to put the case behind her. Others say she declined them so that she would not be held responsible for any of the costs the company incurred related to the antitrust activities. In exchange for favorable sentencing , Ms. Brooks, Mr. Taubman's one-time protégé, turned state's evidence and cooperated with the Justice Department in its investigation. Her sentence consisted of six months of house arrest, a fine of $350,000, three years' probation, and 1,000 hours of community service. At her sentencing, U.S. District Judge George Daniels said, "Diana Brooks . . . you traded your title as CEO for the title of thief and common criminal. The notoriety of your crimes will outlive you. Your decision to cooperate was self-serving, not self-saving. Your words are the all-too-familiar refrain of the white collar criminal." The judge also noted that her crimes were no less serious simply "because they are committed while wearing a business suit."[72] Ms. Brooks had already begun her community service prior to the sentencing, electing to tutor grade school children in Harlem.

In May 2001, four years after the investigation began, the Justice Department announced the indictment of Mr. Taubman as well as his counterpart at Christie's, Sir Anthony Tennant. The indictment charges price fixing over a six-year period involving over 13,000 customers. Mr. Taubman requested a separate trial from his British counterpart and his trial began in New York in November 2001. Sir Anthony was never tried because as a British subject he could not be extradited to come to the United States to defend the antitrust charges against him.

Seven days into the trial, Ms. Brooks, who worked for Sotheby's for more than twenty years, testified that Mr. Taubman had twelve meetings with Sir Anthony from 1993 through 1996, at which Mr. Taubman told her he had indicated that the two houses were killing each other and that they needed to take action. Mr. Taubman had reached a general agreement with Sir Anthony and gave Ms. Brooks a list of issues on which they had general agreement and told her to work out the details with Mr. Davidge.

Ms. Brooks did meet with Mr. Davidge on a number of occasions. She described in some detail their meetings at which they agreed mutually, sometimes simply in the back seat of her car after she picked him up at the airport, when they would raise prices and by how much. She testified that Mr. Taubman congratulated her when she advised him that she had completed the details and reached an agreement.

However, when the agreement collapsed, she refused to meet with Mr. Taubman unless Sotheby's lawyer was present. She testified that Mr. Taubman told her two things

---

[72] Dan Ackman, "Sotheby's Brooks Sent to Her Room, But No Prison," Forbes Online, April 29, 2002, http://www.forbes.com/2002/04/29/0429brooks.html.

at that time (January 2000), "Just don't act like a girl," and "You'll look good in stripes."[73]

Mr. Davidge followed Ms. Brooks to the witness stand at the trial and largely corroborated her testimony. Mr. Davidge also testified that Sir Anthony Tennant gave him a memo that outlined the agreement he had reached with Mr. Taubman to change the way the auction houses did business.[74]

Some called the trial a "he said, she said" battle.[75] Mr. Taubman was found guilty and sentenced to one year and one day in prison and a fine of $7.5 million.

Both Christie's and Davidge are immune from prosecution for antitrust violations because of their cooperation.

Following the settlements by the companies, Sotheby's, a 256-year-old company, hired Michael I. Sovern, the former president of Columbia University, as chairman of the board.

Sotheby's stock suffered during the time of the daily disclosures about the investigations, the evidence, and the resulting litigation. At the beginning of the investigation, Sotheby's stock was trading in March 1999 at $42 per share. By March 2000, it was down to $15 per share. In November 2001, as the trial unfolded, the share price was $16.24.

Discussion Questions

1. Why do we worry that two auction houses were agreeing on increases in their commission rates?

2. What do you think of Mr. Davidge's ethics? Did his intent to sue Christie's for terminating him turn out to provide Christie's with a break in the antitrust case?

3. What do you think of Ms. Brooks providing evidence on her former mentor?

4. Who is harmed if the two auction houses agree on their commissions and follow common business practices?

5. The two auction houses, by the testimony of Ms. Brooks and Mr. Davidge, also shared client lists. Is there a problem with this practice?

6. Do you think the shareholders were served well by the conduct of Sotheby's and Christie's?

7. What do you make of all of Ms. Brooks' philanthropic work?

---

[73] Ralph Blumenthal and Carol Vogel, "Chief Witness Accuses Former Boss at Sotheby's," The New York Times, November 20, 2001, pp. A1, A16.

[74] Kathryn Kranhold, "Former Christie's CEO Testifies on Key Memo in Taubman Trial," The Wall Street Journal, November 15, 2001, p. B2.

[75] Kathryn Kranhold, "Likely Evidence at Taubman Trial Boils Down to 'He Said, She Said,'" The Wall Street Journal, November 8, 2001, pp. B1, B12.

8 D

Competitors, the Playing Field, and Competition

When is it a fair fight? When has competition moved into the illegal and unethical?

CASE 8.11

Slotting: Facilitation, Costs, or Bribery?[76]

Finding "Bearwiches" on the cookie shelf in your grocery store will be a daunting task. Locating some "Frookies," a new line of fat-free, sugarless cookies, will take you on a journey through various aisles in the store, and you may find them at knee level in the health foods section. You can find packaged Lee's Ice Cream from Baltimore in Saudi Arabia and South Korea, but it will not be found on the grocery store shelves in Baltimore. The difficulty with finding these items is not that they are not good products. The manufacturers of these products cannot afford to buy shelf space. The shelf space in grocery stores is not awarded on the basis of consumer demand for Bearwiches or Frookies. Shelf space in grocery stores is awarded on the basis of the manufacturer's willingness to pay "slotting" fees. If manufacturers pay, they are given a space on the grocer's shelf. If the slotting fees are not paid, the product is not sold by the grocer.

Slotting fees are fees manufacturers pay to retailers in order to obtain retail shelf space.[77] The practice has been common in the retail grocery industry since 1987. The origins of slotting fees are unclear with different parties in the food chain offering various explanations. Retailers claim slotting was started by manufacturers with the fees paid to retailers as an inducement to secure shelf space. Another theory of origin offered by retailers is that manufacturers use slotting fees to curtail market entrants. If a manufacturer buys more space with additional fees, the market can be controlled by existing manufacturers. Manufacturers claim slotting was started by retail grocers as a means of

[76] Portions adapted from Robert J. Aalberts and Marianne M. Jennings, "The Ethics of Slotting: Is This Bribery, Facilitation, Marketing or Just Plain Compensation?" Journal of Business Ethics 20:207–215 (1999). Reprinted with kind permission of Kluwer Academic Publishers.
[77] "Slotting fees" actually pertain to obtaining space in the grocer's warehouse. "Shelf fees," which are fees for placement on the shelf are also charged by some grocery retailers.

covering the bookkeeping and warehousing costs of the introduction of a new product. However, two things are clear. First, the practice of affiliated fees for sale has expanded to other industries. The retail book industry, particularly the large chains, now demands fees from publishers for shelf slots and displays for their books. In malls, developers/landlords now demand sums as large as $50,000 from tenants or prospective tenants before a lease can be negotiated or renegotiated. These fees for a position in the mall are referred to as "key money" or "negative allowances." In certain areas, home builders are demanding "access fees" or "marketing premiums" from appliance makers and other residential construction suppliers for use of their products in the builders' developments. In the computer software industry, the packaging of software programs with computers ensures sales and requires a fee. Even the display of programs in electronic stores is subject to a fee. The second clearly evolving trend in affiliated fees is that the practice is inconsistent and the purposes of the fees are unknown. Fees differ from manufacturer to manufacturer, from product to product, and from retailer to retailer.

How Slotting Works

Food manufacturers produce more than 10,000 new products each year. However, store shelf space remains fixed. Because profit margins at grocery stores hover at very narrow levels of only 1 to 2 percent of sales,[78] additional shelf space would not increase profits or produce guaranteed returns from the new products displayed there. In addition, grocers must assume the risk of allocating shelf space to a new product that would not sell at a level sufficient to provide even the narrow margins. Retail grocers must absorb the cost of warehousing the product, accounting for it in inventory, barcoding it, and eventually stocking the shelves with it.[79] In many cases, particularly where the manufacturer is a small company, there has been little or no advertising of the product and the retail grocer must also incur the cost of advertising the product in some way or offer in-store coupons to entice customer purchases. To the retail grocer, the introduction of a new product and the allocation of precious shelf space is a high-cost risk. There are no guarantees that a new product will garner sales, and there is the downside of the loss of revenue from whatever product is displaced by the new product. To retail grocers, a slotting fee is a means of insulation from the risk of new product introduction and a means of advance recoupment of costs.

Within some retail grocery chains, slotting fees represent the net profits for the organization. Similar to the rental car industry in which earnings come from renters' fees for insurance, car seats, and additional driver coverage, some retail grocers' profits come not from the sales of food but from the fees manufacturers pay for access.

The level and nature of slotting fees vary significantly. Some retailers have a flat fee of $5,000 per product for introduction. Other retailers have a graduated fee schedule tied to the shelf space location. Eye-level slots cost more than the knee or ground level slots. The prime spaces at the ends of grocery aisles bring premium slotting fees since those spaces virtually ensure customer attention.[80] Other stores require that a "kill fee"

---

[78] Costs in the retail grocery industry are relatively fixed and cannot be readily reduced. Union wages and other unmanageable cost elements preclude effective efforts at increasing profit margins. Further, competition from the "club" stores (Costco's, Sam's Club, Price Club) is intense.

[79] The cost of shelving is that of the labor and materials involved in simply changing the shelf sign. Shelf fees are typically a minimal amount such as $50.

[80] Referred to as "prime real estate" in the industry, slotting fees follow a graduated schedule for the locations. Amounts vary according to aisle space. Bread slotting fees are $500–$1,000 per bread-type. Ice cream, with one small segment in frozen foods brings $25,000 per flavor.

be paid when a product does not sell. One supermarket chain requires $500 just for a manufacturer to make an appointment to present a new product. Some retailers will not accept a new product even with a slotting fee. Small businesses often incur the cost of product development only to be unable to place the product with grocery stores.

Some stores charge a slotting fee, an additional fee if the product is new, and a "failure fee" on new products to cover the losses if the product fails to sell. A new fee, called the "staying fee," has also developed. A staying fee is an annual rent fee that prevents the retailer from giving a manufacturer's product slot to someone else. Some manufacturers offer to buy out the product in existing space in order to make room for their product. A 1988 survey found that 70 percent of all grocery retailers charge slotting fees, with one retail store disclosing that its $15-per-store per-product slotting fees bring in an additional $50 million in revenue each year.[81] Examples of various slotting fees paid and documented

TABLE 8.1 Slotting Fees: Amounts and Terms[82]

Payer	Amount	Terms	Payee
Truzzolino Pizza Roll	$25,000	Chain-wide	Safeway
Old Capital Microwave Popcorn	$86,000	Chain-wide for $172,000	ShopRite stores
United Brands	$375,000	Frozen fruit juice bar	New York City area stores
Apple & Eve	$150,000	Fruit punch product	Limited stores in Northeast
Frookies	50¢ per box (Increased price from $1.79 to $2.29)	Sugar-free cookies	100 stores various
Frito-Lay	$100,000	New product	Each grocery store chain
Lee's Ice Cream Bread	$25,000 per flavor $1,500 per store per bread	Ice cream Chain-wide cost is $100,000	Each grocery Chains
General/manu-facturers/producers	$15,000–$30,000 per SKU (item)	New products— chain-wide	Chains

[81] No convenience store chains charge slotting fees. However, convenience stores do not warehouse inventory. Manufacturers deliver directly to the convenience stores (Gibson).

[82] Updated from Robert J. Aalberts and Marianne M. Jennings, "The Ethics of Slotting: Is This Bribery, Facilitation, Marketing or Just Plain Compensation?" Journal of Business Ethics, 20:207–215. (1999). A 1997 survey indicates the following:

Usual slotting fees:

Retailers	Varies from free to $20,000 per SKU (product)
Wholesalers	$500–$10,000 per SKU
Manufacturers	$500–$10,000 per SKU

The figures in the chart were updated through May 2001.

are found in Table 8.1. The most typical slotting fee for a new product to be placed with a grocery retailer was $10,000. Slotting fees do not typically come down over time, even if the product sells well. At the retail level for CD-ROM sales, the producers pay a 20 percent fee per shipment, regardless of whether their product is in demand.

The Legal Issues Surrounding Slotting

The chairman of the board of a small food manufacturer in Ohio wrote to his Congressman and described slotting fees in this way: "This is nothing but a device to extort money from packers and squeeze all the independent and smaller processors off the shelves and out of business. We believe this is the most flagrant restraint of trade device yet conceived."[83] The Senate Small Business Committee's investigation included a report on an interview with one small manufacturer who said, "I know for a fact that my competition is paying the lease on the buyer's BMW."[84] When the Senate hearings were held, many of the manufacturers appeared behind a screen at the hearing and used voice-altering technology because of their expressed fear of retaliation from distributors and stores for speaking out on the extent of the fees and the problems of under-the-table payments that have sprung from the practice. One manufacturer testified with a grocery bag on his head.

The Federal Trade Commission is investigating both slotting and rebate fees for possible antitrust implications. The American Antitrust Institute notes that there is an "absence of reliable industry-wide information" on slotting fees and a "pervasive secrecy surrounding what actually occurs among the major players. . . ."[85] It is possible that a slotting fee might fall under the legally prohibited conduct of commercial bribery. However, for a successful prosecution for payment of a bribe, the conduct required must be that in which funds are paid by a seller to a buyer solely for the purpose of acquiring a contract or business opportunity (in the case of slotting, a space on the shelf). As noted earlier, however, the reality is that there are costs associated with awarding an item shelf space. If the funds are simply received by the retailer and used for general operating expenses that include advertising, bookkeeping, and ware-housing, then the notion that a slotting fee is commercial bribery does not fit within the actus reus, or the required conduct, for criminal prosecution.[86]

Regardless of legalities, the use of slotting fees creates an atmosphere of confusion. It is unclear how slotting payments are made and where the payments are reported. Many small business owners report that the payments they make to grocery retailers must be made in cash. Some owners report that payments are made in cash to both the chain and to individual store managers. The atmospheric result is that there are large amounts of cash changing hands among sellers, managers, and purchasers. The former CEO of Harvest Foods, a food retailer in the South, has been indicted on charges of bribery and other related offenses for the alleged receipt of hundreds of thousands of dollars in cash for slotting fees.

---

[83] Slotting: Fair for Small Business and Consumers? *Hearing before the Committee on Small Business, United States Senate, 106th Congress, 1999.*

[84] Roger K. Lowe, "Stores Demanding Pay to Display Products on Shelves, Panel Told," Columbus Dispatch, September 15, 1999, p. 1H.

[85] Robert J. Aalberts & Marianne M. Jennings, "The Ethics of Slotting: Is This Bribery, Facilitation Marketing or Just Plain Competition?" Journal of Business Ethics 20:207 (1999).

[86] Again, it is important to note that a retailer may also charge an "advertising fee."

Because slotting fees are nonuniform and even nonuniversal, it is impossible to understand how the fee structure works, how much the fees should be, and whether the fees are actually related to the costs incurred by retailers in getting a new product to the shelf. The secretive and inconsistent nature of slotting fees and their payment in cash creates an atmosphere similar to that in drug trade.[87] Market entry rights are unclear, fees change, not everyone is permitted to buy into the system, and the use and declaration of revenues are unknown. In at least four reports on the practice of slotting fees, parties on both sides referred to slotting as the grocery industry's "dirty little secret:" Cost recoupment, the public airing of the fees, and public accounting disclosures are nonexistent for slotting fees. The secrecy of the fees and the industry's unwillingness to discuss or disclose them is problematic for manufacturers.

From the cost figures offered in Table 8.1, it is safe to conclude that slotting fees could make market entry prohibitive for many small companies. In some instances, fees have gone beyond the initial slotting costs, with some grocery chains now demanding up to $40,000 per year for a company to maintain just a square foot of retail space for its product. Even some of the larger companies have difficulty competing because of the large fees. Frito-Lay recently purchased Anheuser Busch's Eagle Snacks after Anheuser had spent over $500 million trying to increase its 17 percent market share. Frito-Lay now holds 55 percent of the snack market and pays the largest slotting fees in the grocery industry. Borden ended its foray into the snack market in 1995, and barely survived before it did so. Nearly 30 regional snack companies have gone out of business in the last three years. A vice president of Clover Club Foods, a Utah-based snack company, believes Frito-Lay's goal is to be the only salted-snack food company in the country. The Independent Baker's Association has described the current situation with slotting fees as being "out of control."

The following questions and results reflect the attitudes of those in the retail food business toward slotting:

Slotting allowances are a way of penalizing manufacturers for inadequate market tests.

52% of retailers, 72% of wholesalers, and 77% of manufacturers said they disagreed or disagreed strongly.

If a supplier can demonstrate adequate market testing of a new product, slotting fees should not be charged.

54% of retailers, 50% of wholesalers, and 0% of manufacturers said they disagreed or disagreed strongly.

Slotting fees hamper a retailer's ability to maximize the effectiveness of his product assortment.

58% of retailers, 54% of wholesalers, and 94% of manufacturers agreed strongly or agreed somewhat.[88]

---

[87] The authors could find only three manufacturers willing to discuss their personal experiences with slotting fees or industry practices. Retribution (i.e., denial of retail access) was cited as the reason for their reluctance. These three manufacturers spoke on condition of anonymity. Two other manufacturers, Richard Worth (Frookies) and Scott Garfield (Lee's Ice Cream) have been public in their discussion of slotting fees. Grocery retailers referred all questions to legal counsel or corporate officers who declined to be interviewed.

[88] Adapted from Robert Aalberts, Marianne Jennings, and Stephen Happel, "The Economics, Legalities and Ethics of Slotting Fees," Journal of Law and Commerce 21:1 (2001).

A 1997 survey by *Supermarket Business* found the following:

At present, some slotting fees are an "under the table" form of payment.	83% of retailers, 85% of wholesalers, and 79% of manufacturers strongly agreed or agreed somewhat with the statement.

Slotting and Accounting Issues

Slotting has received additional attention since 2003 because of questions and confusion surrounding the accounting for such fees. For example, if promotional fees are to be paid as part of an arrangement between a manufacturer and a retailer, how are those fees to be carried on the retailer's financial statements? Promotional fees may be paid over time, may be tied to the amount sold, or may be conditioned on certain forms of advertising and results. The flexibility in booking those promotional fees revenues has brought attention to several major retailers including Royal Ahold and its U.S. subsidiary, U.S. Food Services. *The New York Times* ran the following description of the activities and issues that resulted in the U.S. Food Services investigation and accounting restatement:

> [r]epresentatives of U.S. Foodservice are rewarded regularly with goodies like Palm hand-held computers, fax machines, vacation travel and even help with college tuition. All they have to do is earn points by persuading their customers to buy more crackers, coffeecake, plastic forks or other products that have made the company's list for intense promotion.
>
> Under the program, known as Points of Focus, U.S. Foodservice sales representatives amass points if they increase their sales of certain brands, which include the company's own labels as well as brands from nationally known "preferred vendors."
>
> Preferred-vendor status may have more to do with cash than cachet. The companies that get it have been willing to pay U.S. Foodservice for special treatment, former executives of the company say. Such payments are not illegal, and many other food companies have similar programs. But the former executives and others say that the passion with which U.S. Foodservice managers chased those payments shaped the culture of the company, the second-largest food service supplier in the country.
>
> The parent company of U.S. Foodservice, Royal Ahold N.V., one of the biggest supermarket operators in the world, is under investigation in the United States after acknowledging that it overstated earnings by at least $500 million over the last two years. The problem, which Ahold disclosed last month, involved U.S. Foodservice inflating promotional payments from its suppliers, falsely increasing its profit. Two top Ahold executives have quit, and others from U.S. Foodservice have been suspended. The Justice Department and the Securities and Exchange Commission are now investigating the company's accounting.[89]

Every major food distributor, with the exception of Sysco, has been the subject of accounting restatements or SEC investigation for issues related to the booking of revenues.[90]

---

[89] Constance Hays, "At a Food Distributor, Vendors Often Pay to Play," The New York Times, *March 30, 2003, p. C1.*
[90] Constance Hays, ""Rules Are Loosely Defined in the Food Service Industry," The New York Times, *March 5, 2003, p. C1.*

Two former vice presidents of Kmart were indicted on federal charges that they lied to accountants about a payment from a supplier and that they used that payment to supplement earnings for the company. Joseph Hofmeister was a divisional vice president of merchandising in Kmart's drugstore division. Enio Montini was a senior vice president and general manager of the same division.

The charges center on a payment of $42.4 million from American Greetings in 2001. The payment was called an "allowance" or "rebate" and covers joint advertising as well as rebates and markdowns.[91] The payment was fully booked for that quarter despite accounting rules that require an examination of possible refunds for those fees. Many argue that the accounting there is a gray area on which experts disagree and that there was no criminal intent. In fact, the area of allowances between manufacturers and retailers is one in which many stores are under SEC investigation. Kmart purchased Sears in November 2004 under new ownership.[92]

Discussion Questions

1. Are slotting fees a means of allocating risk?

2. What possible employee temptations exist?

3. Would a schedule of fees help?

4. Are slotting fees ethical?

5. Are the perceptions of the industry participants a reflection of their questions about the ethics of slotting?

6. Are the accounting issues the result of the secretive nature of the payments?

CASE 8.12

Mr. Gates: Genius and Fierce Competitor

The profit for Microsoft Corporation was $3.5 billion for fiscal 1997. Founder Bill Gates was able to capture approximately 90 percent of the personal computer (PC) market. While many argue Mr. Gates' market share is primarily the result of building a better mouse trap, Compaq Computer Co. sees Microsoft's market conquest slightly differently. In the spring of 1996, Compaq notified Microsoft that it intended to replace Microsoft's Internet access program, Explorer, with Microsoft's chief competitor's program, Netscape.

Shortly after the notification, Compaq was notified by Microsoft that its Windows 95 licensing agreement was terminated. A follow-up letter offered restoration of

[91] Lorrie Grant, "Former Kmart Executives Face 3-Count Federal Indictment," USA Today, February 27, 2003, p. 1B; Amy Merrick, "U.S. Indicts 2 Ex-Executives of Kmart Corp.," The Wall Street Journal, February 27, 2003, pp. A3, A14; Constance L. Hays, "2 Ex-Officials At Kmart Face Fraud Charges," The New York Times, February 27, 2003, pp. C1, C7.
[92] Robert Berner, "The Next Warren Buffett?" Business Week, November 22, 2004.

licensing if Compaq restored the Explorer program to its Presarios within 60 days. Compaq did so and got the licensing back.

The U.S. Justice Department brought an action seeking to hold Microsoft in contempt for violating an earlier order on "coercion by a dominant company in a way that distorts competition."[93] The 1995 order prohibited Microsoft from tying the sale of one product to the sale of another, as was proposed to Compaq.

Microsoft maintains Explorer is part of an integrated product that it can force buyers to take. However, Netscape maintains that Explorer is produced, advertised, and sold separately as a stand-alone product.

A judge issued a $1 million per day fine after a hearing on the alleged violation of tying by Microsoft. A second hearing produced an order precluding Microsoft from forcing PC makers to install Explorer.

Microsoft continued its sales practices, pointing to language in the consent decree that reads Microsoft "shall not be construed to prohibit Microsoft from developing integrated products." Microsoft endured the fines until January 1998, when Microsoft agreed to a settlement under which it will not require PC makers to take Explorer. Shortly after the settlement, the Justice Department announced a new antitrust investigation based on allegations of collusion.

Microsoft was concerned about its strategic position with respect to the Internet, a global electronic network consisting of smaller interconnected networks, which allows millions of computers to exchange information over telephone wires, dedicated data cables, and wireless links.

The United States Justice Department had an ongoing inquiry into the market shares and practices of Microsoft and twenty-three state attorneys general were also looking into the company's practices. The concerns of the Justice Department and attorneys general include:

1. Microsoft's position in the market as a monopolist (90 percent market share for operating systems).
2. Microsoft's barriers to entry for other operating systems and Web browsers. Microsoft has refused to sell its software operating system to computer companies that installed Microsoft's competitive browser, Netscape, which was gaining popularity as Microsoft's Explorer struggled.
3. Microsoft worked to inhibit the efforts of Netscape with its browser by first trying to acquire Netscape and then working to "cut off [its] air supply" by retarding Sun Corporation's development and implementation of the Java program. When Microsoft altered the portions of Sun's Java program that allowed it to work without Windows, Sun notified Microsoft that such was a violation of its licensing agreement. Microsoft's response was, "Sue us." Sun sued Microsoft one week before the Justice Department brought its suit against Microsoft. Sun's suit then ran parallel with the Justice Department's.

In issuing a three-part opinion, Judge Thomas Penfield Jackson of the district court found that Microsoft had violated the antitrust laws and ordered a remedy of breaking

---

[93] http://www.justice.gov. See complaint.

up the company. Microsoft appealed the decision. The federal appeals court upheld the finding that Microsoft violated the antitrust laws but remanded the case for a new remedy. While the remedy retrial was pending, Microsoft and the Justice Department settled the case with Microsoft agreeing to contribute $800 million in software to schools around the country.[94] State antitrust litigation is still pending.

Discussion Questions

1. Is Microsoft just competing? Would you call them a fair competitor?

2. Is there anything unethical about tying product sales?

3. What free market issues exist here?

4. Do you think that Microsoft has behaved differently following the court case?

5. Does the settlement provide for sufficient damages?

Sources

Bank, David, and John R. Wilke, "Microsoft and Justice End a Skirmish, Yet War Could Escalate," *The Wall Street Journal*, January 23, 1998, pp. A1, A6.

Krantz, Michael, "Will Reno Brake Windows?" *Time*, November 3, 1997, pp. 76–78.

Lohr, Steve, "Court Is Not Where They'd Like to Go Today," *The New York Times*, January 18, 1998, p. WK5.

Wilke, John R., "Microsoft Subject of New Antitrust Probe," *The Wall Street Journal*, April 24, 1998, p. A2.

[94] U.S. v. Microsoft, *253 F.3d 34 (C.A. D.C. 2001)*.

8 E

Business and Its Shareholders

Businesses also compete for shareholders. With so many possible investments and companies to choose from, what affects shareholders' decisions to invest and what rights do they have once they have made an investment in a company? Should shareholders have the right to control the amount paid to executives and the conduct of the company in which they have an ownership interest?

CASE 8.13

Executive Compensation

Pay levels for executives have been increasing rapidly since 1980. Sibson & Company data show that between 1980 and 1990, the average cash compensation for CEOs grew over 160 percent.[95] At the same time, the average hourly wage paid to nonsupervisory manufacturing employees did not keep pace with inflation. CEOs in United States-based companies earn 363 times more than the average employee, while Japanese CEOs earn only 16 times more.[96] Since 1990, the pay levels have more than doubled when stock options are included.

Graef Crystal conducts an annual study of CEO pay packages with an analysis of 850 CEOs of publicly-traded companies. Crystal provides the data for the best CEO performers, in terms of stock and company performance, as well as the worst performers. The 2001 study includes the following conclusions:

- The most over-compensated CEO in America is Linda Wachner, CEO of Warnaco Group. From 1991 to 1998, shares of Warnaco gave investors a total return of 10.4

[95] Jeffrey Birnbaum, "From Quayle to Clinton, Politicians Are Pouncing on the Hot Issue of Top Executives' Hefty Salaries," The Wall Street Journal, January 15, 1991, p. A16.
[96] Jill Abramson and Christopher J. Chipello, "High Pay of CEOs Traveling with Bush Touches a Nerve in Asia," The Wall Street Journal, December 30, 1991, p. A1.

percent, as compared to the 21 percent for the S&P 500. Yet during 1998, Wachner was compensated as follows:

$2.7 million	Salary
$6.0 million	Bonus
$6.5 million	Restricted stock
$73.5 million	Options
$75.6 million	Gain from exercised options

- Other CEOs on the worst performer list include Sanford Weill and John Reed, the co-CEOs for Citigroup (the merger of Citibank and Travelers), who were each paid $176 million even though there was a 2 percent drop of Citigroup's share price in 1998.

The "compensation heroes," as Crystal calls them, or those CEOs delivering the most for their salaries, are:

- Bernard Marcus and Arthur Blank—Home Depot, who each had pay of $3 million but who delivered an average annual return of 45 percent.
- Herb Kelleher—Southwest Airlines, who was paid only $674,000 despite the fact that Southwest's stock was up 38.4 percent in 2000.

Crystal presents his report to the Council of Institutional Investors, a group of portfolio managers with over $1 trillion in assets. Members of this group use the list as a starting point in making decisions as to where and when to invest their funds.

Michael S. Kesner, National Director of Compensation and Benefits Consulting for Arthur Andersen Company, notes:

> With restructuring, cost-cutting, and consolidation the order of the day, the actual impact of, say, a $5 million CEO pay package on the bottom line of a $2 billion sales company is not clearly the issue. People are now saying, to paraphrase the sound advice of late Illinois Senator Everett Dirksen, "Hey, a percent of a billion here and a percent of a billion there adds up to real money." In light of widespread plant closings, layoffs, and long lines of unemployed workers seeking limited jobs, "pay for performance" has simply taken a backseat to what the general public considers "fair."[97]

Warren Buffett, the chief executive officer of Berkshire Hathaway, disclosed that his salary of $100,000 remained the same in 1998 but that his fees for being a director fell about 11 percent to $176,600. Some of the salary and fees are taken in cash and some in equity securities.

Mr. Buffett does not use a compensation committee or consultant to determine the salaries of his officers. He alone makes the recommendations to the board on what he believes the officers should be paid. Prior to the imposition of SEC requirements, the proxy materials for Berkshire Hathaway do not include any information on how salaries are determined or whether they are competitive.

Berkshire Hathaway permits bonuses for officers but none have been paid in a number of years. The highest paid officer for Berkshire Hathaway, earned more than Mr. Buffett, and was paid $412,500 in 2001 with $31,500 additional compensation from subsidiaries.[98]

---

[97] Gary Strauss, "Study: Some CEO Salaries Don't Compete," USA Today, September 28, 1999, p. 3B.
[98] Form 14 found in the SEC filings for the company under edgar at: http://www.sec.gov/edgar/searchedgar/webusers.htm

The following CEO compensation figures are included (these figures appeared in 2001 reflecting the compensation paid in 2000) to demonstrate a correlation between the cases in the previous sections on honesty in managers and corporate accounting and compensation.

Name	Company	Compensation
Sanford Weill	Citigroup, Inc.	$224.4 million
John T. Chambers	Cisco Systems, Inc.	$157.3 million
Kenneth L. Lay	Enron Corp.	$140.4 million
L. Dennis Kozlowski	Tyco International	$125.3 million
John F. Welch	General Electric Co.	$122.5 million
Joseph P. Nacchio	Qwest Communications	$ 96.6 million
W.J. Sanders III	Advanced Micro Devices	$ 92.4 million[99]

Citigroup settled charges for its role in the Enron scandal. Mr. Nacchio left Qwest and investigations and charges are pending against executives there. Mr. Welch had to agree to relinquish some of the benefits GE was paying for in his retirement compensation, embarrassing information that emerged during his divorce proceedings (see Case 5.22).

The following are the figures for 2003 (as reported in 2004).

Company	CEO	Total compensation
MBNA	Charles M. Cawley	$46,285,747
Bear Stearns	James E. Cayne	$39,533,712
Occidental Petroleum	Ray R. Irani	$29,470,293
SBC	Edward Whitacre	$28,894,652
Merrill Lynch	E. Stanley O'Neal	$28,097,489
Sprint	Gary D. Forsee	$27,157,374
KB Home	Bruce Karatz	$26,858,373
Altria Group	Louis C. Camilleri	$23,936,679
Cendant	Henry R. Silverman	$22,813,045
Goldman Sachs	Henry M. Paulson, Jr.	$21,400,579
Lehman Brothers	Richard S. Fuld, Jr.	$20,878,386
Lockheed Martin	Vance D. Coffman	$20,260,325

Warren Buffett's total compensation for 2003 was $308,000.[100]

[99] From Business: Its Legal, Ethical and Global Environment, 6th Ed., by Marianne M. Jennings, p. 46. Copyright © 2003. Reprinted with permission of South-Western, a division of Thomson Learning.
[100] Go to the companies' 10-Ks at www.sec.gov Click on Edgar. Patrick McGeehanm, "Is C.E.O. Pay Up or Down? Both," The New York Times, April 4, 2004, Section 3. Gretchen Morgenson, "Two Packages, Two Different Galaxies," The New York Times, April 4, 2004, Section 3-1.

The *New York Times* offered a comparison of the compensation packages of Costco's CEO and that of Cendant as a means of evaluating pay versus performance.

CEO	Operating income % change	Market value % change	Salary	Bonus	Options
Cendant	36%	–29%	$3,125,000	$7,054,000	$19,158,000
Costco	28%	–18%	$ 351,000	$ 75,000	$ 2,187,000

The levels of CEO compensation have outraged large institutional investors and small shareholders. Shareholder proposals calling for reform in the setting of executive pay were submitted at the 1997 annual meetings of forty-three companies, and the trend has continued to increase, with such proposals at 324 meetings in the 2003–2004 period. Three-fourths of the 1,082 proposals in 2004 dealt with corporate governance.[101] Said Elizabeth Holtzman, a trustee of the New York City Employees Retirement System, "It is unconscionable to have sky-high executive compensation that is not related to long-term corporate performance."[102]

The California Public Employee Retirement System (CalPERS) released a list of executives and their pay in twelve high-profile companies for 1991 in an attempt to pressure management of the firms into reform. CalPERS had tried to negotiate privately with the firms but was rebuffed in some cases. CalPERS spokesman Richard H. Koppes stated "This year, the kinder and gentler approach doesn't seem to be working. That's why we released the names."[103]

Some shareholders pointed to conflicts of interest in board compensation committees: CEOs from other firms are members of the board, and lawyers whose firms furnish the bulk of the company's legal services sit on the committee that determines the compensation of the CEO. These practices were eliminated by the Sarbanes-Oxley Act, but friendly CEOs often sit on each other's boards and compensation committees.

Stanley C. Gault, chairman of Goodyear Tire & Rubber Company, has joined with the shareholders in their complaints: "The American public is tired of seeing executives make many, many millions of dollars a year when the stock price goes down, the dividends are cut, and the book value is reduced."[104] Some executives have initiated reform in their compensation system out of fear of new federal regulations. On the other hand, others, such as the late Roberto C. Goizueta of Coca-Cola, have defended their compensation: "Our stock outperformed the other twenty-nine stocks in the Dow industrial average in the past decade. The end result has been the creation of $50 billion of additional wealth for the share owners of our company in

[101] http://www.securities.stanford.edu.

[102] "Reebok Comes under Fire for Executive Pay," The Wall Street Journal, March 21, 1991, p. G1.

[103] Id.

[104] John Byrne, Dean Foust, and Lois Therriem, "Executive Pay," Business Week, March 30, 1992, p. 52.

the same time period."[105] Goizueta's defense of his compensation at the annual shareholders' meeting met with applause. However, by 1998, Coke was in turmoil after Goizueta's passing, and this continues today.[106] (see Case 7.19 for Coke's difficulties with Burger King.)

Ben & Jerry's Homemade, Inc., the Vermont ice cream manufacturer, once limited its CEO pay to seven times the average worker's salary. Herman Miller, a Fortune 500 company, limits its CEO's pay—salary and bonus—to twenty times the average employee paycheck, which was $28,000 in 1991. The average CEO compensation in the other Fortune 500 companies is 117 times the salary of the average worker. Max DePress, a member of Herman Miller's founding family and chairman of the company's board, said, "People have to think about the common good. Our CEO and senior officers make good competitive salaries when the performance is there."[107] Miller's nonunionized plant workers support the plan. He said: "This is a fair and equitable way to pay. . . . If they tried to revoke it, people would speak out."[108]

James O'Toole, executive director of the leadership institute at the University of Southern California, said the Herman Miller plan should be the model others follow, "instead of the bad examples of the 1980s. The purpose of the corporation is much broader than meeting the needs of stock speculators or the power needs of top managers."[109]

In 1992, Congress limited the ability of companies to deduct CEO compensation from their taxes as a means of controlling increases. The law puts an upper limit of $1 million on such tax deductions. At the same time, the SEC passed new rules and formats for disclosing executive compensation in annual proxy materials. Boards have also begun to act on the issue. Compensation committees comprised only of outside directors are now required, because of scandals such as those at Tyco and WorldCom (see Cases 6.9 and 6.14). These committees must hire independent consultants to advise them on compensation issues.

A new question that arises is whether the additional perks provided to executives are counted as part of the compensation package for tax purposes or reflected in the total benefits paid reports to shareholders. The types of perks many CEOs enjoy (in order of the number of corporations offering them) are:

- Annual physical
- Company car
- Financial planning
- Car phone
- Car allowance
- Tax planning/tax return preparation
- Country club membership
- First class air travel
- Company airplane usage

---

[105] *Jerry Schwartz, "Coke's Chairman Defends $86 Million Pay and Bonus,"* The New York Times, *April 16, 1992, p. C1.*
[106] *Betsey Morris, "The Real Story,"* Fortune, *May 31, 2004, p. 85.*
[107] *Jacqueline Mitchell, "Herman Miller Links Worker-CEO Pay,"* The Wall Street Journal, *May 7, 1992, p. B1.*
[108] Id.
[109] Id.

- Health club membership
- Luncheon club membership
- Legal counseling
- No-/low-interest loans

That last category has seen increasing attention because of the amounts involved. The practice of corporations loaning money to executives for their mortgages and other purposes has been largely prohibited under federal law by the Sarbanes-Oxley Act.

There appears to be no limit to the types of perks executives receive. For example, Vince McMahon, head of WWF, receives up to $50,000 per year for cleaning expenses. Macy's, Bloomingdale's, and other department stores offer up to 38 percent discounts to their executives. Avon's Andrea Jung had a $19,000 security system installed in her home at company expense.

Discussion Questions

1. So long as a company is performing and providing a return to investors and growth in the value of their investment, should executive compensation be an issue?

2. The compensation of executives is largely a deductible business expense. Are U.S. taxpayers subsidizing the large CEO salaries?

3. Should CEO pay be tied to workers' compensation?

4. Should CEO pay be tied to company performance?

5. Who should establish executive pay rates?

6. Should institutional investors and other shareholders have input on executive compensation?

7. Would government regulation of executive pay interfere with the free enterprise system?

8. How can executive compensation have an impact on company performance as well as share performance? How do you think Milton Friedman would react to controls on levels of compensation? How do you think he would react to this type of compensation program?

9. Do you see any additional conflict issues with the perks? Do you see any issues that are prevented because executives are given these perks?

CASE 8.14
Shareholder Proposals and Corporate Governance

Shareholders can submit proposals to be included in proxy solicitation materials. If the company does not oppose what is being proposed, the proposition is included as part of the proxy materials. If management is opposed, the proposing shareholder has the right of a 200-word statement on the proposal in the materials. These proposals are not permitted along with their 200-word statements unless they propose conduct that is legal and related to business operations, as opposed to social, moral, religious, and political views. During the Vietnam era, many shareholders wanted to include proposals in proxy materials for companies that were war suppliers. Their proposals centered on the political opposition to the war and not the business practices of the company.

The proposals have become an area of contention among and between management, the Securities and Exchange Commission (SEC), and shareholders because of the difficulty in defining what constitutes a business issue and what is a political issue. Shareholders argue that the company's position on social issues can be costly in terms of customer boycotts and PR backlash.

For example, Iroquois Brands, Ltd., a food company that imports French foie gras, a pâté made from the enlarged livers of force-fed geese, faced shareholder litigation over this French practice in raising the geese. The practice involves funneling corn down the geese's throats and gagging them with rubber bands to keep them from regurgitating. A shareholder asked to have a proposal included in the proxy materials that proposes that the company study the practice as an unethical business practice (cruelty to animals).[110]

Another example involved Steve Hindi, an animal rights activist who owns $5,000 in Pepsi stock. He discovered that Pepsi advertises in bull rings in Spain and Mexico and has attended annual shareholder meetings and put forward shareholder proposals to have the company halt the practice. His proposal has not yet passed, but he has started a Web site (http://www.pepsibloodbath.com) to increase pressure on the company. Pepsi has withdrawn from bullfighting ads in Mexico, but continues with them in Spain. Mr. Hindi continues his quest.[111]

The SEC and other organizations provide a tally of the types of shareholder proposals included in the proxies for publicly held companies during the 2003–2004 annual meeting season. The tally is as follows:

Limits on executive compensation	458
International operations	44
Political action committees	37
Environment	34
Consumer and health issues	34
Diversity	14

In 1999, the average shareholder support for the measures was 15 percent of all voting shares. By the 2003–2004 season, that number had grown to 52 percent. In 2003, 161 shareholder proposals won majority support. However, in several companies shareholders dropped proposals after management agreed to comply with the demands in the proposal. For example, Paychex agreed to seek out more

---

[110] Lovenheim v. Iroquois Brands, Ltd., *618 F.Supp. 554 (D.C. 1985).*

[111] Constance L. Hays, "A PepsiCo Shareholder Meeting and a Very Unhappy Shareholder," The New York Times, *April 22, 2000, pp. B1, B4.*

women and minorities for its board and the Calvert Group dropped its diversity proxy proposal. McDonald's agreed to ban workplace discrimination based on sexual orientation.

In 1998, Unocal pulled out of Afghanistan following a shareholder proposal relating to human rights issues there. The proposal was withdrawn because Unocal had withdrawn from doing business there.

The *National Law Journal* reports shareholder activism is on the increase. In 1971, a proposal by GM shareholders, including the Episcopal Church, to halt GM business in South Africa barely got 2 percent of the votes cast at the annual meeting. However, some activists have been successful in recent years with their shareholder proposals. For example:

- A Home Depot shareholder proposal to phase out sales of lumber from old forests passed and is in effect;
- A GE shareholder proposal for the company to clean up the Housatonic River in Massachusetts also passed and the company spent nearly $250 million doing so; and
- RJR split its food division from its tobacco division in response to shareholder activism.

The shareholder proposals for 2000 focused on opposition to genetically engineered food and Northern Ireland employment policies. Generic types of shareholder proposals include staggered terms for directors, independent board members, human rights issues, and diversity in boards and the company.[112] In 2004, the 1,080 shareholder proposals focused on corporate governance. For example, the 3M company had a proposal that would require an independent director who had not served as CEO to serve as chairman of the board of the company.[113] The following chart provides a look at the types of proposals filed by various companies and shareholders. Many other companies have similar proposals. The sample was chosen for its representative nature of the types of shareholder proposals filed in 2004. For example, nearly all clothing companies have a human rights proposal. Companies with operations in Africa had proposals related to the HIV/AIDS/TB and malaria health crises there. Most companies had a proposal on executive compensation, corporate governance, options, or shareholder rights. It is interesting to note that many of the same shareholder names will appear across companies with the same proposals. There are individuals, unions, and retirement funds that repeat as shareholders making proposals.

Company	**Shareholder**	**Nature of proposal**
Abbott Labs	Catholic Healthcare West	Have the company study the evolving issues of cost and access to prescription drugs in the United States

---

[112] Richard H. Koppes, "Future Governance and Activism Trends," National Law Journal, July 3, 2000, pp. B1, B14.
[113] http://www.thecorporatelibrary.com/Research/shareholder-proposals/FullText.asp?Company_ID=13838&Resolution_ID=2342&Proxy_Season=2004. At this Web site, you can view all of the shareholder proposals filed from 2001 forward. Also see http://www.sec.gov.

Company	Shareholder	Nature of proposal
Adobe Systems	Carpenters Union	Expensing of stock options
Adobe Systems	AFSCME	Requirement of mandatory share ownership by executive officers
99 Cents Stores Only	Aaron Merle Epstein	Requirement of human rights/labor/wages clauses in vendor and supplier contracts prohibiting low wages and abusive conditions
Alaska Air	John Chevedden	Eliminate supermajority requirement on shareholder votes; return to simple majority
Albertson's	Trowel Trades	Executive severance package cannot exceed 2.99 times annual compensation
Allegheny Energy	Undisclosed	Accounting firm that does audits for the company cannot perform consulting services also
Alltel	Undisclosed	Prohibition against discrimination by the company on the basis of sexual orientation
American Eagle Outfitters	New York City employees/teachers retirement funds	No child labor or sweat shop in suppliers or factories
Bristol-Myers Squibb	Evelyn Y. Davis	Political contributions
Chevron Texaco	Undisclosed	Study by management of effect of HIV/TB/malaria on company's operations and bottom line
Dow Chemical	Undisclosed	Appear in India to answer the criminal charges for Bhopal
Eastman Kodak	Donna Colavito	Elimination of biopollutants in company processing and production
Ford	Interfaith Center on Corporate Responsibility	Greenhouse gases and auto emissions
General Electric	Sisters of St. Dominic of Caldwell	Clean-up of Hudson River

Company	Shareholder	Nature of proposal
Goodyear Tire & Rubber	Undisclosed	Poison pill
Halliburton	NYC Police Pension Fund	Doing business in Iran and other countries with terrorist connections
Kellogg's	Sisters of Mercy of Detroit	Genetically engineered food products
Lockheed Martin	Evelyn Y. Davis	List of all those employed as lobbyists for the company
Loew's	Congregation of Sisters of St. Agnes	Eliminating smoking in company facilities
Merck	Human Life International	Linking executive performance and compensation to respect for human life and not engaging in embryonic stem-cell research
Northrup Grumman	School Sisters of Notre Dame Cooperative Investment Funds	Weapons production and contract bids for producing weapons
Petco	PETA	Ending the sale of animals
Pinnacle West Capital	Arizona Safe Energy Coalition	Spent nuclear fuel disposal
Rite Aid	Pension Board— United Methodist Church	Diversity in employees
Sprint	Communications Workers Pension Funds	No call centers in India
Swift Transportation	Calvert Asset Management	Diversity on the board

Corporate secretaries who handle proposals and shareholders have their own organization. Their Web site (http://www.ascs.org) includes information on shareholder proposals and shareholder activism.

Institutional investors can also be very active in shareholder proposals, and the California Public Employee Retirement Service is one of the country's most active institutional shareholders. (See http://www.calpers-governance.org.)

Discussion Questions

1. Are shareholder proposals an effective means for getting corporations to take action?

2. Are shareholders who bring these proposals acting as advocates for various stakeholders?

3. Are shareholders a means of encouraging social responsibility?

4. Are these proposals always in the best interests of the shareholders? Why do you think management opposes almost all shareholder proposals?

Business and Its Product

*"A bad reputation is like a hangover. It takes a while to get
rid of and it makes everything else hurt."*

—JAMES PRESTON, FORMER CEO, AVON

QUALITY, SAFETY, SERVICE, AND SOCIAL RESPONSIBILITY—customers want
these elements in a product and a company. Does the profit motive interfere with these
traits?

9^A

Contract Relations

The law of contracts is detailed, but ethical discussions center on the fairness of treatment and the balance of the agreement.

CASE 9.1

Intel and Pentium: What to Do When the Chips Are Down

Intel, which makes components used in 80 percent of all personal computers sold, introduced the powerful Pentium chip in 1993. Intel had spent $1 billion developing the chip and the cost of producing it was estimated to be between $50 and $150 each. When the Pentium chip was finally rolled out, Intel shipped 4 million of the chips to computer manufacturers, including IBM.

In July 1994, Intel discovered a flaw in the "floating-point unit" of the chip, which is the section that completes complex calculations quickly.[1]

The flaw caused errors in division calculations involving numbers with more than eight digits to the right of the decimal, such as in this type of equation:[2]

$$\frac{4,195,835}{3,145,727} \times 3,145,727 = 4,195,835$$

Pentium-equipped computers computed the answer, in error, as 4,195,579. Before introducing the Pentium chip, Intel had run 1 trillion tests on it. Those tests showed that the Pentium chip would produce an error once every 27,000 years, making the chance of an average user getting an error one in 9 billion.

In November, Thomas Nicely, a mathematician at Lynchburg College in Virginia, discovered the Pentium calculations flaw described above. On Thanksgiving Day 1994, Intel publicly acknowledged the flaw in the Pentium chip, and the next day its stock fell from 65⅛ to 63⅞. Intel stated that the problem had been corrected but flawed chips were still being shipped because a three-month production schedule was just ending.

[1] Evan Ramstad, "Pentium: a Cautionary Tale," Arizona Republic, December 21, 1994, p. C1.
[2] Janice Castro, "When the Chips Are Down," Time, December 26, 1994, p. 126.

Intel initially offered to replace the chips but only for users who ran complicated calculations as part of their jobs. The replacement offer carried numerous conditions.[3]

On December 12, 1994, IBM announced that it would stop all shipments of its personal computers because its own tests indicated that the Pentium flaw was far more frequent than Intel had indicated.[4] IBM's tests concluded that computer users working on spreadsheets for as little as fifteen minutes per day could produce a mistake every twenty-four days. Intel's then-CEO Andrew Grove called IBM's reaction "unwarranted." No other computer manufacturer adopted IBM's position. IBM's chief of its personal computing division, G. Richard Thoman, emphasized that IBM had little choice: "It is absolutely critical for this industry to grow, that people trust that our products work right."[5] Following the IBM announcement, Intel's stock price dropped 6.5 percent, and trading had to be halted temporarily.

On December 20, 1994, CEO Grove announced that Intel would replace all Pentium chips:

> We were dealing with a consumer community that was upset with us. That they were upset with us—it has finally dawned on us—is because we were telling them what's good for them. . . . I think we insulted them.[6]

Replacing the chips could have cost up to $360 million. Intel offered to send owners a new chip that they could install or to have service firms replace chips for customers who were uncomfortable doing it themselves.

Robert Sombric, the data processing manager for the city of Portsmouth, New Hampshire, found Intel's decision to continue selling flawed chips for months inexcusable: "I treat the city's money just as if it were my own. And I'm telling you: I wouldn't buy one of these things right now until we really know the truth about it."[7, 8]

Following the replacement announcement, Intel's stock rose $3.44 to $61.25. One market strategist praised the replacement program: "It's about time. It's very clear they were fighting a losing battle, both in public relations as well as user confidence."[9–11]

Grove responded that Intel's delay in offering replacements was based on concerns about precedent. "If we live by an uncompromising standard that demands perfection, it will be bad for everybody,"[12] he said. He also acknowledged that Intel had agreed to sell the flawed Pentium chips to a jewelry manufacturer.[13]

---

[3] James Overstreet, "Pentium Jokes Fly, but Sales Stay Strong," USA Today, December 7, 1994, p. 1B.

[4] Ira Sager and Robert D. Hof, "Bare Knuckles at Big Blue," Business Week, December 26, 1994, pp. 60–62.

[5] Bart Ziegler and Don Clark, "Computer Giants' War over Flaw in Pentium Jolts the PC Industry," The Wall Street Journal, December 13, 1994, pp. A1, A11.

[6] Jim Carlton and Stephen Kreider Yoder, "Humble Pie: Intel to Replace Its Pentium Chips," The Wall Street Journal, December 21, 1994, pp. B1, B9.

[7] Jim Carlton and Scott McCartney, "Corporations Await More Information; Will Consumers Balk?" The Wall Street Journal, December 14, 1994, pp. B1, B5.

[8] Stephen Kreider Yoder, "The Pentium Proposition: To Buy or Not to Buy," The Wall Street Journal, December 14, 1994, p. B1.

[9] Carlton and Kreider Yoder, "Humble Pie: Intel to Replace Its Pentium Chips," pp. B1, B9.

[10] "Intel Eats Crow, Replaces Pentiums," Mesa Tribune, December 21, 1994, p. F1.

[11] Catalina Ortiz, "Intel to Replace Flawed Pentium Chips," Arizona Republic, December 21, 1994, pp. A1, A8.

[12] Ziegler and Clark, "Computer Giants' War over Flaw in Pentium Jolts the PC Industry," pp. A1, A11.

[13] Otis Port, "A Chip on Your Shoulder—or Your Cuffs," Business Week, January 23, 1995, p. 8.

By December 16, 1994, ten lawsuits in three states involving eighteen law firms had been filed against Intel for the faulty chips. Chip replacement demands by customers, however, were minimal.

Intel's internal employee newsletter had an April 1, 1995 edition that spoofed the infamous chip.[14] A spoof form provided in the newsletter required customers with Pentium chips to submit a 5,000-word essay on "Why My Pentium Should Be Replaced."

In 1997, Intel launched two new products: Pentium Pro and Pentium II. A new potential bug, again affecting only intensive engineering and scientific mathematical operations, was uncovered. Intel, however, published the list of bugs with technical information and remedies for both of the new processors. One analyst commented on the new approach, "They have learned a lot since then. You can't approach the consumer market with an engineering mindset."[15]

Discussion Questions

1. Should Intel have disclosed the flaw in the Pentium chip when it first discovered it in July 1994?

2. Should Intel have issued an immediate recall? Why do you think the company didn't do that? Discuss what analysis their executives missed by applying the models you learned in Unit 1.

3. Was it ethical to offer limited replacement of the chip?

4. A joke about Intel's Pentium chip (source unknown) circulated on the Internet:

Top Ten Reasons to Buy a Pentium-Equipped Computer

10. Your current computer is too accurate.

9. You want to get into the Guinness Book of World Records as "owner of most expensive paperweight."

8. Math errors add zest to life.

7. You need an alibi for the IRS.

6. You want to see what all the fuss is about.

5. You've always wondered what it would be like to be a plaintiff.

4. The "Intel Inside" logo matches your decor perfectly.

3. You no longer have to worry about CPU overheating.

2. You got a great deal from the Jet Propulsion Laboratory.

And, the number one reason to buy a Pentium-equipped computer: It'll probably work.[16]

Based on this circulating joke, discuss the long-term impact of this chip and Intel's decisions on how to handle it on Intel.

---

[14] Richard B. Schmitt, "Flurry of Lawsuits Filed against Intel over Pentium Flaw," The Wall Street Journal, December 16, 1994, p. B3.

[15] James Kim, "Intel Proactive With Potential Buy," USA Today, May 6, 1997, p. 1B.

[16] From memo furnished to author by Intel employee at the time of the Intel chip problems.

5. Assume that you are an Intel manager invited to the 1994 post-Thanksgiving meeting on how to respond to the public revelation of the flawed chips. You believe the failure to offer replacements will damage the company over the long term. Further, you feel strongly that providing a replacement is a balanced and ethical thing to do. However, CEO Grove disagrees. How would you persuade him to offer replacements to all purchasers?

6. If you could not persuade Grove to replace the chips, would you stay at the company?

7. Has the Pentium incident caused long-term damage to the computer industry?

8. Consider the following analysis (from "Intel Eats Crow, Replaces Pentium," *Mesa Tribune*, December 21, 1994, p. F1):

   Regarding your article "Bare Knuckles at Big Blue" (News: Analysis & Commentary, Dec. 26), future generations of business school students will study Intel Corp.'s response to the problems with the Pentium chip as a classic case study in how to transform a technical problem into a public-relations nightmare.

   Intel's five-point plan consisted of:

   1) Initially deny that the problem exists;

   2) When irrefutable evidence is presented that the problem exists, downplay its significance;

   3) Agree to only replace items for people who can demonstrate extreme hardship;

   4) Continue running your current ad campaign extolling the virtues of the product as if nothing has happened;

   5) Count the short-term profits.[17]

   List other companies discussed in this book or in other readings that followed this same five-point pattern.

CASE 9.2

Hidden Car Rental Fees

During the 1980s, there were six major players in the global rental car market with the following dollar amounts of market share:

Share	**(in billions)**
Hertz	$4.0
Avis	3.2
Budget	2.5
National	2.5
Alamo	0.6
Dollar	0.5
Other	2.5[18]

[17] "Intel Eats Crow, Replaces Pentiums," p. F1.

[18] Matthew L. Wald, "Hertz to New York: Pay More," The New York Times, *January 19, 1992, p. F10.*

The competition in the industry was fierce. The companies offered customers various promotions, discounts, special rates, and other offers and the result was that customers were often confused by the variety of rates and rental plans. All the national firms have daily, weekend, and weekly rates. Some firms offer unlimited free mileage, while others offer 100 free miles with a charge for each additional mile.[19] The rates were almost impossible to compare.

When customers finally did decide on a company and rent cars, they were surprised by the additional charges that seemed to mount at the counter as they signed the paperwork for the car rental. The rental companies added extra charges for a second driver; a child seat; remote dropoff; and insurance, including collision/damage waiver (CDW), liability, personal effects, and personal accident coverage. CDW is the money-maker for the smaller rental agencies, which offer lower base rental rates and make their profits through extras such as CDW. These companies maintain that without CDW, which 90 percent of their customers take, they could not compete or survive, and prices would have to go up. Indeed, by 1992, prices at all car rental companies had risen an average of 12 percent.[20]

The CDW fees were expensive but consumers often paid the fees because of fears about what would happen if they had an accident in a rental car. A National Car Rental customer in Boston who paid nine dollars a day on top of the sixty-dollar-per-day rental fee in 1987 said, "It's expensive, but I figure you get in a crack-up and you're going to get nailed if you don't have it."[21] Nearly all insured drivers are covered by their own auto policies when they rent cars and the CDW is often double coverage but the pitch by rental agents at the counters did produce the 90 percent customer buy-in to CDW.

In 1988, regulatory and legislative bodies began investigating and challenging car rental practices.[22] Various types of regulations and challenges to the rental car industry practices popped up around the country. Some states took the position that because there was so much insurance coverage being sold at rental car counters that rental car agents should be licensed as insurance agents. Investigations found that some renters who refused CDW had been told no cars were available. Others had $1,000 to $3,000 frozen on their credit cards because they did not take CDW.[23] In 1989, several states considered legislation to ban CDWs. California passed a law that limited the waiver fee to nine dollars per day and required disclosure to the customer about its purposes (including disclosure in ads). New York and Illinois limited charges for car damage to $100 and $200, respectively, which effectively eliminated the need for most renters to buy CDW. In August 1988, a U.S. district court in New York ordered Hertz Corporation to refund $13 million to customers after the company pleaded guilty to criminal charges in connection with overcharging customers to repair vehicles that had been damaged but for which there was no CDW.[24] On September 4, 1988, the National

---

[19] Michael Katz, "FTC Forces Car Rental Firms to Reveal All," The Wall Street Journal, August 14, 1992, pp. B1, B2.

[20] James S. Hirsch, "Rental Car Firms Jack up Their Prices," The Wall Street Journal, November 4, 1992, pp. B1, B13.

[21] Corie Brown, "Cracking Down on a Costly Car-Rental Option," Business Week, November 30, 1987, p. 135.

[22] Jonathan Dahl and Christopher Winans, "States, Car-Rental Firms Collide over Damage Waivers," The Wall Street Journal, August 14, 1989, p. B1.

[23] Taylor, "Why Car Rentals Drive You Nuts," p. 74.

[24] Wald, "Hertz to New York," p. F10.

Association of Attorneys General appointed a task force headed by Kansas Attorney General Bob Stephan to study deceptive and unfair practices in the car rental industry.[25]

In August 1988, the Federal Trade Commission (FTC) cited both large and small companies for using deceptive practices in advertising. Clinton Krislov, a Chicago lawyer who represented consumers in class action lawsuits against rental agencies in Chicago and Des Moines, observed:

> This is sort of like trying to judge an ugly contest among frogs. There are, I suppose, some pockets of honesty in this business, but. . . .[26]

The FTC also proposed a regulation that would require the use of a standard rental contract and disclosure in all ads of full rental charges, including those for gas, collision protection, and repairs. The regulation would also limit charges for collisions and theft to $100.[27] The regulation did not pass, but the FTC focus on car rental industry practices continued.

In 1992, the FTC charged Dollar Rent-A-Car Systems, Inc., and Value Rent-A-Car, Inc., with failure to fully disclose information on charges to customers. Both Dollar and Value settled with the FTC in 1993 by agreeing to disclose more information in their ads.[28]

Under greater scrutiny and regulatory supervision, the companies began implementing new strategies to compensate for the lost earnings from the add-ons that were now either prohibited or declined as consumers began to understand their rights. They also began to rent to customers who were less likely to have an accident and started screening processes and restrictions on rentals. For example, during the late 1980s and early 1990s, companies refused to rent to or added a surcharge of ten to fifteen dollars a day on drivers between the ages of 21 and 25.[29-31] National began screening renters in New York City and Florida for driving-while-intoxicated (DWI) convictions or suspended or revoked licenses. Some firms charge an additional twenty-five dollars for more than one driver and have raised dropoff and refueling fees.[32-35] In 1995, Avis and Hertz reinstated mileage charges for certain renters in certain areas.[36] In 1997, Budget began charging $30–$100 for no-shows on their reservations.[37] A ban on under-age 25

---

[25] David Jones, "Illinois Moves to Ban Rental Car Waivers," National Underwriter, July 11, 1988, pp. 3, 79.

[26] Alex Taylor, III, "Why Car Rentals Drive You Nuts," Fortune, August 31, 1987, p. 74.

[27] Earl Golz, "Hidden Auto Rental Charges, Fees Can Take You for a Ride," Mesa Tribune, February 21, 1989, p. D1.

[28] Katz, "FTC Forces Car Rental Firms to Reveal All," pp. B1, B2.

[29] Susan Brink, Edward C. Baig, Steven D. Kaye, and Margaret Mannix, "A Pox on Young Drivers," U.S. News & World Report, March 29, 1993, p. 63.

[30] James S. Hirsch, "Auto Renters Hit the Brakes on Under-25s," The Wall Street Journal, March 16, 1993, p. B1.

[31] Lisa Miller, "Young Drivers Can Rent Cars, New York Rules," The Wall Street Journal, March 28, 1997, pp. B1, B2.

[32] "Car-Rental Firms Make Extra Drivers Costly," The Wall Street Journal, November 10, 1992, p. B1.

[33] Jonathan Dahl, "Rental Counters Reject Drivers without Good Records," The Wall Street Journal, October 23, 1992, p. B1.

[34] James S. Hirsch, "'Do-Not-Rent' Lists Tag Bad Drivers," The Wall Street Journal, September 15, 1993, p. B1.

[35] Matthew L. Wald, "Car-Rental Computers Rejecting High-Risk Drivers," The New York Times, September 9, 1993, pp. A1, A9.

[36] Lisa Miller, "Car Rental Industry Promises That Things Will Improve. Really," The Wall Street Journal, July 17, 1997, pp. A1, A8.

[37] Donna Rosato, "Budget Rent-A-Car to Charge No-Shows," USA Today, July 3, 1997, p. 1B.

drivers is in effect in the industry, with the exception of New York, where a judge has ruled such age-based distinctions to be a form of discrimination.[38, 39]

Competition became even more intense and the industry restructured. Dollar and Thrifty combined into one publicly held company, Dollar Thrifty. National and Alamo are now owned by Republic Industries.

In 1996, a new car rental company, Enterprise Rent-A-Car, became the nation's largest rental car company, focusing not on airports but on small towns and the need for rentals when the family car is in the shop. Enterprise holds 20 percent of the $15 billion U.S. market.[40] The price of an Enterprise rental is 30 percent below Avis or Hertz, and most of the company's fees are paid by warranty policies or insurance coverage (in the case of an accident).[41]

Discussion Questions

1. Assume you are the public affairs vice president for one of the top six rental car companies. Would you change any of your policies with respect to CDW?

2. Would you change your advertising to disclose CDW charges?

3. Would you instruct your counter agents to explain that the CDW coverage may be duplicative?

4. Would you change any of the other extra charges typical in the industry (that is, would you revamp your pricing policy)? Would such a change hurt or help your ability to compete? What do you think car rental executives missed in analyzing their contract charges, disclosures, and advertising? Apply the ethical models and determine whether the practices they were using were ethical.

5. Do you see practices in this industry that regulators may tackle in the future? Would you voluntarily change any of these practices? Recall the regulatory cycle that you studied in Unit 7 and apply it and the George Fisher guidelines on leadership to this case.

6. Is it significant that Enterprise, with its different charges, captured the market?

Sources

Bryant, Adam, "GM Agrees to Sell Car Rental Unit," *The New York Times*, April 5, 1995, pp. C1, C2.

Jacobson, Gianna, "Enterprise's Unconventional Path," *The New York Times*, January 23, 1997, pp. C1, C6.

---

[38] *Miller, "Young Drivers Can Rent Cars, New York Rules," pp. B1, B2.*
[39] *Noelle Knox, "Cars Available! But With More Strings Attached," The New York Times, January 11, 1998, p. BU6.*
[40] *Brian O'Reilly, "The Rent-A-Car Jocks Who Made Enterprise #1," Fortune, October 28, 1996, pp. 126–128.*
[41] *Matthew L. Wald, "Hertz Ends 'Drop Charges' on One-Way Rentals," The New York Times, October 15, 1992, pp. C1, C10.*

Thinning Diet Industry

Oprah Winfrey started a diet craze when she appeared on her television show in 1988 in her size-ten Calvin Klein jeans and boasted of losing sixty-seven pounds by using Sandoz Nutrition Corporation's Optifast Program. The preventive medicine center at Philadelphia's Graduate Hospital got 500 calls about Optifast on the day of Oprah's announcement. Since then, the diet industry has grown 15 percent per year with total annual revenues topping $3 billion. The major competitors in 1992, at the height of the diet market, were:

Weight Watchers International	$1.3 billion
Nutri/System, Inc.	$764 million
Diet Center, Inc.	$275 million
Thompson Medical Company (Slim-Fast)	$260 million
Sandoz Nutrition (Optifast)	$120 million[42]

Diet programs are sold through celebrity endorsements and before-and-after ads. Lynn Redgrave has represented Weight Watchers; Susan Saint James has appeared for Diet Center; and Christina Ferrara, Tommy Lasorda, Kathie Lee Gifford, Whoopie Goldberg, and others have endorsed Slim-Fast and Ultra Slim-Fast. Nutri/System has relied on radio disc jockeys to use its programs and then tell listeners about their weight losses.

The CEO of Weight Watchers likened the diet craze to the excesses of the 1980s on Wall Street: everything is more and more extreme.[43] By mid-year 1990, Representative Ron Wyden of Oregon, chair of the House Small Business Subcommittee, asked industry representatives to explain their hard-sell tactics. Wyden's hearings revealed that fully 90 percent of those who lose weight rapidly on the quick-loss programs regain the lost weight and often more within two years. Wyden asked why employees of these programs were referred to as weight loss specialists when in fact they had no expertise and were really sales personnel. Weight Watchers CEO Charles Berger testified:

> Without touching on the issue of greed, some companies in our field have overpromised quick weight loss. And the promises have grown increasingly excessive.[44]

Just before the House hearings, nineteen women sued Nutri/System and Jenny Craig, Inc., in Dade County (Miami), Florida, for gallbladder damage allegedly caused by the programs' diets. Seventeen of the women had had their gallbladders removed after participating in the Nutri/System program, even though they had no previous diagnosis of gallbladder difficulties.

In response to the suits and in the hearings, Nutri/System stated that obese people are vulnerable to a variety of ailments, including gallbladder disease. The company

---

[42] Kathleen Deveny, "Blame It on Dashed Hopes (and Oprah): Disillusioned Dieters Shun Liquid Meals," The Wall Street Journal, October 13, 1992, pp. B1, B11.
[43] Julie Johnson, "Bringing Sanity to the Diet Craze," Time, May 21, 1990, p. 74.
[44] Id.

labeled the suits "without merit" and "a carefully orchestrated" campaign by the lawyers for the nineteen women.

Nutri/System was forced into Chapter 11 bankruptcy but emerged in 1993 under new ownership and a new weight loss philosophy that included encouraging the use of exercise equipment in its facilities.

A marketing consultant has observed about the diet industry:

> There is such a market for faddish nutritional services that even if you lose some customers you'll get new ones. To some extent in this industry, a lot more depends on how good your marketing is than your product.[45]

In 1991, the Federal Trade Commission (FTC) charged Optifast 70, Medifast 70, and Ultrafast with making marketing claims that were deceptive and "unsubstantiated hype."[46] The agency called the statement "you'll have all you need to control your weight for the rest of your life" unsubstantiated.[47] The FTC also announced it was investigating other diet programs. Representative Wyden said the FTC's complaints against the three companies were only "the tail of the elephant; the real test is whether these standards will be applied throughout the industry."[48]

By mid-1992, the FTC completed its investigation of misleading advertising by more than a dozen diet chains and promulgated guidelines for such advertising.[49] Before-and-after testimonials must include pictures of typical clients, not just the most successful ones, and claims of keeping the weight off must be documented. The FTC's guidelines were the result of the National Institutes of Health's findings that virtually all dieters regain two thirds of their weight within a year and all of it within five years.[50]

As the FTC was promulgating these rules, the Food and Drug Administration (FDA) announced that it would decide whether phenylpropanolamine, an amphetamine-like stimulant, could continue to be used in appetite-suppressant products, such as Acutrim and Dexatrim. Further, lawsuits based in product liability on the inherent dangers of these diet pills (including wrongful death actions) are pending around the country.[51]

Meanwhile, Oprah Winfrey announced that she would never again use a liquid diet, and an Alabama jury awarded $15 million to the mother of a 23-year-old bride-to-be who died of heart failure after losing twenty-one pounds in six weeks under the supervision of the Physicians' Weight Loss Center.

Several sociological issues surround weight loss. Susie Orbach, author of *Fat Is a Feminist Issue*, observes that 50 million Americans begin diets every year: "When I started working in this field 22 years ago, eating problems affected a limited group,

[45] Alix Freedman and Udayan Gupta, "Lawsuits May Trim Diet Firms," The Wall Street Journal, March 23, 1990, p. B1.

[46] Jeanne Saddler, "Three Diet Firms Settle False Ad Case; Two Others Vow to Fight FTC Charges," The Wall Street Journal, October 1, 1993, p. B8.

[47] Molly O'Neill, "Five Diet Companies Ask U.S. for Uniform Rules on Ads," The New York Times, August 25, 1992, pp. C1, C2.

[48] Jeanne Saddler, "FTC Targets Thin Claims of Liquid Diets," The Wall Street Journal, October 17, 1991, pp. B1, B6.

[49] Mike Snider, "FTC Weighs Claims of Diet Program Ads," USA Today, March 26, 1993, p. 1D.

[50] Mike Snider, "FTC Cites Diet Firms for False Claims," USA Today, October 1, 1993, p. 1D.

[51] Joseph Weber, "The Diet Business Takes It on the Chin," Business Week, April 16, 1990, pp. 86–87.

women in their 30s and 40s. Now, we know from studies that girls of 9 and women of 60 are all obsessed with the way they look."[52]

The top two companies in the diet industry—Jenny Craig and Weight Watchers—were cited by the FTC in October 1993 for falsely advertising the success of their programs.[53] Three other companies (Diet Center, Nutri/System, and Physicians' Weight Loss Centers of America) settled with the FTC by agreeing to (1) not misrepresent program performance in ads, (2) gather and make available supporting data, and (3) include disclosures that most weight loss is temporary and say whether a testimonial is typical or not.[54]

The New York City Department of Consumer Affairs was the first in the nation to issue "truth-in-dieting" regulations for diet centers, violations of which carry a $500 fine:

1. Centers must post a prominent Weight-Loss Consumer Bill of Rights sign in every room where a sales presentation is made. The sign informs consumers there may be serious health problems associated with rapid weight loss and that only lifestyle changes, such as healthy eating and exercise, promote permanent weight loss.
2. All centers must also give every potential client a palm-size Consumer Bill of Rights card.
3. All centers must inform potential clients of hidden costs of products or laboratory tests that may be part of the program.
4. All centers must tell dieters the expected duration of the program.

The FTC actions against false advertising led to a 15 percent reduction in diet industry revenues in 1994.[55, 56]

In 1997, just as the industry was recovering, the American Society of Bariatric Physicians released a list of its concerns about the industry's usage of obesity drugs such as Redux and fen-Phen along with promises of permanent weight loss.[57] The presence of the new prescription obesity drugs produced new weight-loss clinics focusing entirely on the pills and prescriptions, with a total of 18 million monthly prescriptions in 1996 given, in many cases, not to the clinically obese but to those seeking to lose five to ten pounds.[58, 59]

A 1997 study found the presence of heart valve damage among users of fen-Phen and the FDA withdrew the diet drugs from the market.[60] Those who had been using the diet drugs began litigation. By 2000, American Home Products had agreed to a $4.8 billion settlement with 11,000 class action litigants.[61] Since the time of the FDA ban on

[52] Larry Armstrong and Maria Mallory, "The Diet Business Starts Sweating," Business Week, June 22, 1992, pp. 32–33.
[53] Amy Barrett, "How Can Jenny Craig Keep on Gaining?" Business Week, April 12, 1993, pp. 52–53.
[54] Keith L. Alexander, "A Health Kick at Weight Watchers," Business Week, January 16, 1995, p. 36.
[55] Weber, "The Diet Business Takes It on the Chin," pp. 86–87.
[56] Ellen Neuborne, "Weight-Loss Programs Going Hungry," USA Today, July 28, 1994, pp. 1C, 2C.
[57] Laura Johannes, "New Diet-Drug Data Spark More Controversy," The Wall Street Journal, October 1, 1997, pp. B1, B12.
[58] Robert Langreth and Laura Johannes, "Redux Diet Pill Receives a Boost in New Study," The Wall Street Journal, April 1, 1998, pp. B1, B4.
[59] Gina Kolata, "Companies Recall 2 Top Diet Drugs at F.D.A.'s Urging," The Wall Street Journal, September 16, 1997, p. A1.
[60] Jeanne Saddler, "Diet Firms' Weight-Loss Claims Are Being Investigated by FTC," The Wall Street Journal, March 26, 1993, pp. B1, B5.
[61] Steve Sternberg, "Lawsuits: Drug Development's Big Side Effect," USA Today, January 12, 2000, p. 10D.

the drugs, those companies with alternative diet drugs without as much risk have had a difficult time selling even prescription drugs. Sales of anti-obesity drugs reached almost $500 million in 1996, but by 1998 had fallen to $28.8 million, a level at which they remain.[62] There are still cases pending involving those who did not settle with the class as part of the nationwide litigation. For example, a jury awarded Gloria Lopez, a cafeteria supervisor who took Pondimin, the fenfluramine portion of fen-Phen, for five months and lost ten pounds, $54 million because her aortic valve was damaged and will eventually require replacement.[63]

Diet centers relying on the two drugs have also been named in the litigation and many, based solely on the prescription approach, have closed.[64, 65] Customers who have become plaintiffs are complaining about the lack of warnings given to them by these diet centers.

In early 1998, a study of 1,072 people, sponsored by the parent company of the manufacturers of Redux and Pondimin, found only a 6.5 to 7.3 percent rate of heart valve problems in patients who took the drugs, as opposed to a 4.5 percent rate in patients who took the dummy pill. A cardiologist labeled the difference in rates "not statistically significant." However, the FDA ban remained and the litigation continued.[66]

New products for weight reduction that speed up metabolism and suppress appetite continue to come to market. Metabolife International, Inc., ran an aggressive Web-based campaign to counter negative media reports about side effects for its Metabolife dietary supplement that the company says speeds up metabolism and reduces the appetite.[67] In 2002, the FDA began an investigation of Metabolife and other products with the ingredient called Ephedra, also known as ma huang, an herbal supplement, which is very common in many weight-loss products. Metabolife sales peaked at $1 billion in the late 1990s. In 1999, more than 12 million people used products containing Ephedra, but the FDA became concerned when at least 70 deaths and more than 1,400 adverse events were linked to Ephedra. Adverse effects included high blood pressure, insomnia, nervousness, tremors, headaches, seizures, heart attacks, and strokes.[68] Baltimore Orioles pitcher, Steve Bechler, 23, died in 2003, a death rumored to be caused by his taking Ephedra. The Ephedra Industry Council (created by Metabolife) released information indicating that in many of these cases the problem was not Ephedra but rather the poor-quality manufacturing and production involved in cheap dietary pills and products. The Rand Institute conducted a study of Ephedra to determine whether these effects are caused by Ephedra and, if so, how extensive they are.

In the meantime, the FDA discovered that Metabolife failed to turn over 13,000 health complaints about Ephedra products and the lawsuits began to erupt all over the country. In 2004, the largest jury verdict to date of $7.4 million was awarded by a Texas jury to a woman who suffered a stroke and brain damage after taking Metabolife. The

---

[62] Dana Canedy, "Predecessors' Woes Make Diet Drug a Tough Sell," The New York Times, April 11, 1998, p. B1.

[63] Margaret Cronin Fisk, "Fen-Phen Jury Awards $56 Million," National Law Journal, April 23, 2001, p. A10.

[64] "A Bill of Rights for Dieters," Shape, November 1993, p. 30.

[65] Freedman and Gupta, "Lawsuits May Trim Diet Firms," pp. B1, B2.

[66] Kolata, "Companies Recall 2 Top Diet Drugs at F.D.A.'s Urging," p. A1.

[67] Bruce Orwall, "Diet-Pill Maker Battles a Report Before It Airs," The Wall Street Journal, October 6, 1999, pp. B1, B4.

[68] http://www.cnn.com/2002/HEALTH/diet.fitness/08/15/ephedra.investigatio/.

herbal stimulant is now banned by the FDA. Michael Ellis, the founder and CEO of Metabolife, was indicted in July 2004 for lying to the FDA and also for income tax evasion.[69] The indictment charges Ellis and Metabolife, Inc. with six counts of making false, fictitious, and fraudulent representations to the FDA and two counts of corruptly endeavoring to influence, obstruct, and impede proceedings being conducted by the FDA concerning the regulation of dietary supplements containing Ephedra.

Ellis, who is a former police officer, was convicted of a misdemeanor drug charge related to the production of methamphetamine. Metabolife founder Michael Blevins was charged at the same time when the two were working out of a home to produce at least 50 pounds of methamphetamine. Ellis served probation for his guilty plea, but Blevins did prison time. Through his lawyer, Ellis responded to the FDA's criminal charges, "The government has concocted a hypertechnical violation by taking statements to a regulatory agency out of context."[70]

Discussion Questions

1. Assume that you get a part-time job as a "weight counselor" with a quick-weight-loss program. Would you have any ethical constraints in performing your job?

2. Don't people just want to lose weight quickly? What if you told them they would gain it back and face health risks but they decided to go forward anyway? Would you and your product be adhering to a proper moral standard of full disclosure and freedom of choice?

3. Does the diet industry make money from temporary motivation? Or does the diet industry provide only temporary motivation?

4. Are the weight-loss ads misleading?

5. Weight Watchers, which posted a $50 million loss in 1994, has begun a new program emphasizing health foods, heart disease prevention, and exercise. Will this type of program avoid the ethical issues of rapid-weight-loss programs?

6. Given the Redux and fen-Phen problems, what can be safely concluded about the diet industry? What would be an ethical approach to running a weight-loss clinic?

7. Do you think there is a conflict with the 1998 study's sponsorship? What precautions should those professors conducting the study take?

8. What do you learn about the industry from Metabolife, the ban, the suits, and the indictment?

Sources

Hellmich, Nanci, "Heart Valve Damage Prompts Withdrawal," *USA Today*, September 16, 1997, p. 1A.

Hellmich, Nanci, "Withdrawal of Drugs Leaves Dieters in Quandary," *USA Today*, September 22, 1997, p. 6D.

[69] http://www.cbsnews.com/stories/2004/07/23/health/main631424.shtml.
[70] http://story.news.yahoo.com/news?tmpl=story&u=/ap/20040723/ap_on_he_me/metabolife&e=1&ncid=.

Hilts, Philip J., "Medicine Remains as Much Art as Science," *The New York Times*, September 21, 1997, p. WK5.

Janofsky, Michael, "Hearing for Franchisees in Nutri/System Buyout," *The New York Times*, May 11, 1993, p. C6.

Johannes, Laura, and Steve Secklow, "Heart-Valve Problem That Felled Diet Pills Had Arisen Previously," *The Wall Street Journal,* December 11, 1997, p. A1.

Schroder, Michael, "The Diet Business Is Getting a Lot Skinnier," *Business Week*, June 24, 1991, pp. 132–134.

Sternberg, Steve, "Study: No Heart Damage From Diet Drug," *USA Today*, April 1, 1998, p. 1A.

CASE 9.4

Sears and High-Cost Auto Repairs

In 1991, the California Department of Consumer Affairs began investigating Sears Auto Repair Centers. Sears' automotive unit, with 850 repair shops nationwide, generated 9 percent of the merchandise group's $19.4 billion in revenues. It was one of the fastest growing and most profitable divisions of Sears over the previous two years.

In the California investigation, agents posed as customers at thirty-three of the seventy-two Sears automotive repair shops located from Los Angeles to Sacramento. They found that they were overcharged 90 percent of the time by an average of $223. In the first phase of the investigation, the agents took thirty-eight cars with worn-out brakes but no other mechanical problems to twenty-seven Sears shops between December 1990 and December 1991. In thirty-four of the cases, the agents were told that their cars needed additional work. At the Sears shop in Concord, a San Francisco suburb, the agent was overcharged $585 to replace the front brake pads, front and rear springs, and control-arm bushings. Sears advertised brake jobs at prices of $48 and $58.[71]

In the second phase of the investigation, Sears was notified of the investigation and ten shops were targeted. In seven of those cases, the agents were overcharged. No springs and shocks were sold in these cases, but the average overcharge was $100 per agent.

Up until 1990, Sears had paid its repair center service advisors by the hour rather than by the amount of work.[72] But in February 1990, Sears instituted an incentive compensation policy under which employees were paid based on the amount of repairs customers authorized.[73] Service advisors also had to meet sales quotas on specific auto parts; those who did not meet the quotas often had their hours reduced or were assigned to work in other departments in the Sears stores. California regulators

---

[71] James R. Healey, "Shops under Pressure to Boost Profits," USA Today, July 14, 1992, p. 1A.
[72] Gregory A. Patterson, "Distressed Shoppers, Disaffected Workers Prompt Stores to Alter Sales Commissions," The Wall Street Journal, July 1, 1992, pp. B1, B4.
[73] James R. Healey, "Sears Auto Cuts Commissions," USA Today, June 23, 1992, p. 2B.

said the number of consumer complaints they received about Sears shops increased dramatically after the commission structure was implemented.

The California Department of Consumer Affairs charged all seventy-two Sears automotive shops in the state with fraud, false advertising, and failure to clearly state parts and labor on invoices.

Jim Conran, the director of the consumer affairs department, stated:

This is a flagrant breach of the trust and confidence the people of California have placed in Sears for generations. Sears has used trust as a marketing tool, and we don't believe they've lived up to that trust. The violation of the faith that was placed in Sears cannot be allowed to continue, and for past violations of law, a penalty must be paid.[74]

Dick Schenkkan, a San Francisco lawyer representing Sears, charged that Conran issued the complaint in response to bipartisan legislative efforts to cut his agency's funding because of a state budget crunch and claimed, "He is garnering as much publicity as he can as quickly as he can. If you wanted to embark on a massive publicity campaign to demonstrate how aggressive you are and how much need there is for your services in the state, what better target than a big, respected business that would guarantee massive press coverage?"[75]

Richard Kessel, the executive director of the New York State Consumer Protection Board, stated that he also had "some real problems" with Sears' policy of paying people by commission. "If that's the policy," Kessel said, "that in my mind could certainly lead to abuses in car repairs."[76]

Immediately following the issuing of the California complaint, Sears said that the state's investigation was "very seriously flawed and simply does not support the allegations. The service we recommend and the work we perform are in accordance with the highest industry standards."[77]

It then ran the following ad:

With over two million automotive customers serviced last year in California alone, mistakes may have occurred. However, Sears wants you to know that we would never intentionally violate the trust customers have shown in our company for 105 years.

Ten days after the complaint was announced, the chairman of Sears, Edward A. Brennan, announced that Sears was eliminating the commission-based pay structure for employees who propose auto repairs.[78] He conceded that the pay structure may have created an environment in which mistakes were made because of rigid attention to goals. Brennan announced the compensation system would be replaced with one in which customer satisfaction would now be the primary factor in determining service personnel rewards, shifting the emphasis away from quantity to quality. An outside firm would be hired to conduct unannounced shopping audits of Sears auto centers to be certain the hard sells were eliminated. Further, Brennan said, the sales quotas on

---

[74] Lawrence M. Fisher, "Accusation of Fraud at Sears," *The New York Times,* June 12, 1992, pp. C2, C12.
[75] Id.
[76] Id.
[77] Tung Yin, "Sears Is Accused of Billing Fraud at Auto Centers," *The Wall Street Journal,* June 12, 1992, p. B1.
[78] Lawrence M. Fisher, "Sears' Auto Centers to Halt Commissions," *The New York Times,* June 23, 1992, p. C1.

parts would be discontinued. While he did not admit to any scheme to recommend unnecessary repairs, he emphasized that the system encouraged mistakes and he accepted full responsibility for the policies. "The buck stops with me," he said.[79]

Sears auto repair customers filed class action lawsuits in California, and a New Jersey undercover investigation produced similar findings of overcharging. New Jersey officials found that 100 percent of the Sears stores in its investigation recommended unneeded work compared to 16 percent of stores not owned by Sears.[80] On June 25, 1992, Sears ran a full-page ad in all major newspapers throughout the country. The ad, a letter signed by Brennan, had the following text:

An Open Letter to Sears Customers:

You may have heard recent allegations that some Sears Auto Centers in California and New Jersey have sold customers parts and services they didn't need. We take such charges very seriously, because they strike at the core of our company—our reputation for trust and integrity.

We are confident that our Auto Center customers' satisfaction rate is among the highest in the industry. But after an extensive review, we have concluded that our incentive compensation and goal-setting program inadvertently created an environment in which mistakes have occurred. We are moving quickly and aggressively to eliminate that environment.

To guard against such things happening in the future, we're taking significant action:

We have eliminated incentive compensation and goal-setting systems for automotive service advisors—the folks who diagnose problems and recommend repairs to you. We have replaced these practices with a new non-commission program designed to achieve even higher levels of customer satisfaction. Rewards will now be based on customer satisfaction.

We're augmenting our own quality control efforts by retaining an independent organization to conduct ongoing, unannounced "shopping audits" of our automotive services to ensure that company policies are being met.

We have written to all state attorneys general, inviting them to compare our auto repair standards and practices with those of their states in order to determine whether differences exist.

And we are helping to organize and fund a joint industry-consumer-government effort to review current auto repair practices and recommend uniform industry standards.

We're taking these actions so you'll continue to come to Sears with complete confidence. However, one thing we will never change is our commitment to customer safety. Our policy of preventive maintenance—recommending replacement of worn parts before they fail—has been criticized by the California Bureau of Automotive Repair as constituting unneeded repairs. We don't see it that way. We recommend preventive maintenance because that's what our customers want, and because it makes for safer cars on the road. In fact, 75 percent of the consumers we talked to in a nationwide survey last weekend told us that auto repair centers should recommend replacement parts for preventive maintenance. As always, no work will ever be performed without your approval.

[79] Gregory A. Patterson, "Sears' Brennan Accepts Blame for Auto Flap," The Wall Street Journal, June 23, 1992, p. B1.
[80] Jennifer Steinhauer, "Time to Call a Sears Repairman," The New York Times, January 15, 1998, pp. B1, B2.

We understand that when your car needs service, you look for, above all, someone you can trust. And when trust is at stake, you can't merely react, we must overreact.

We at Sears are totally committed to maintaining your confidence. You have my word on it.

Ed Brennan
Chairman and Chief Executive Officer
Sears, Roebuck and Co.[81]

On September 2, 1992, Sears agreed to pay $8 million to resolve the consumer affairs agency claims on overcharging in California. The $8 million included reimbursement costs, new employee training, and coupons for discounts at the service center. Another $15 million in fines was paid in 41 other states to settle class action suits.[82, 83]

In December 1992, Sears fired John T. Lundegard, the director of its automotive operations. Sears indicated that Lundegard's termination was not related to the controversy surrounding the auto centers.

Sears recorded a net loss of $3.9 billion despite $52.3 billion in sales in 1992—the worst performance ever by the retailer in its 108-year history and its first loss since 1933. Its Allstate Insurance division was reeling from damage claims for Hurricane Andrew in the Gulf Coast and Hurricane Iniki in Hawaii ($1.25 billion). Auto center revenue dropped $80 million in the last quarter of 1992, and Sears paid out a total of $27 million to settle state overcharging claims. Moody's downgraded Sears debt following the loss announcement.

In 1994, Sears partially reinstated its sales-incentive practices in its auto centers. Service advisors must earn at least 40 percent of their total pay in commissions on the sale and installation of tires, batteries, shock absorbers, and struts. Not included on commission scales are brakes and front-end alignments (the core of the 1992 problems). Earnings in auto centers have not yet returned to pre-1992 levels.

Discussion Questions

1. What temptations did the employee compensation system present?

2. If you had been a service advisor, would you have felt comfortable recommending repairs that were not immediately necessary but would be eventually?

3. What will the complaints cost Sears, regardless of their eventual disposition?

4. Did Brennan acknowledge moral responsibility for the overcharges?

5. Does it matter whether the overcharges were intentional or part of business incentives?

[81] "Open Letter," Arizona Republic, June 25, 1992, p. A9.
[82] Barnaby J. Feder, "Sears Post First Loss Since 1933," The New York Times, October 23, 1992, p. C1.
[83] "Sears Gets Handed a Huge Repair Bill," Business Week, September 14, 1992, p. 38.

6. A public relations expert has said of the Sears debacle: "Don't make the Sears mistake. When responding to a crisis, tell the public what happened and why. Apologize with no crossed fingers. Then say what you're going to do to make sure it doesn't happen again."[84] What are the ethical standards in this public relations formula?

7. What will be the likely results of the incentive reinstatement?

8. There are some who have expressed concerns about the ethical culture at Sears. While incentive systems may have created the auto center fraud problems, consider the following dilemmas involving Sears since the time of its auto center fraud cases:

- Montgomery Ward obtained an order from a federal court prohibiting Sears from hiring employees away from Wards as it works its way through Chapter 11 bankruptcy. The order was based on an e-mail sent from Sears' regional vice president, Mary Conway, in which Sears managers are instructed to "be predatory" about hiring away Montgomery Ward managers.

- A class action civil suit was filed in Atlanta against Sears by consumers who allege that Sears sold them used batteries as new. One of the plaintiffs in the suit alleges that an investigator purchased one hundred "new" batteries from Sears in 1995 (in thirty-two states) and that seventy-eight of them showed signs of previous usage. A Sears internal auto-center document explains that the high allowances the centers must give customers on returns of batteries cuts into profits and induces the sale of used batteries to compensate. (Sears denies the allegation and attributes it to disgruntled former employees and not understanding that a nick does not necessarily mean a battery is used.)[85]

- Sears admitted to "flawed legal judgment" when it made repayment agreements with its credit card customers who were already in bankruptcy, a practice in violation of creditors' rights and priorities. Sears agreed to refund the amounts collected from the 2,700 customers who were put into the program. Sears warned the refunds could have a "material effect" on earnings. The announcement caused a drop in Sears' stock price of 3⅞. Sears included the following notice to its credit card customers:

NOTICE: If you previously filed for personal bankruptcy under Chapter 7 and entered into a reaffirmation agreement with Sears, you may be a member of a Settlement Class in a proposed class action settlement. For information, please call 1-800-529-4500. There are deadlines as early as October 8, 1997 applicable to the settlement.

Sears entered a guilty plea to criminal fraud charges in connection with the bankruptcy issues and agreed to pay a $60 million fine, the largest in the history of bankruptcy fraud cases.[86] The company also settled with the fifty state attorneys general, which included $40 million in state fines, $12 million for state shareholder suits, and a write-off of the $126 million owed by the cardholders involved which was forgiven as part of the settlement.[87]

---

[84] Nat B. Read, "Sears PR Debacle Shows How Not to Handle a Crisis," The Wall Street Journal, January 11, 1993, p. A14.

[85] There were questions and investigations surrounding Exide Corporation, Sears battery supplier. The questions related to the quality of the batteries and Exide at one point announced that it expected to face criminal indictment for certain of its business practices. Keith Bradsher, "Exide Says Indictment Is Likely Over Its Car Battery Sales to Sears," The New York Times, January 11, 2001, pp. B1, B7.

[86] Joseph B. Cahill, "Sears Agrees to Plead Guilty to Charges of Criminal Fraud in Credit-Card Case," The Wall Street Journal, February 10, 1999, p. B2.

[87] Id.

Sears also settled the class action suit on the bankruptcy issue by agreeing to pay $36 million in cash and issuing $118 million in coupons to those cardholders affected by its conduct with regard to bankruptcy customers. Sears did not admit any wrongdoing as part of the settlement but indicated the action was taken "to avoid the litigation."[88] Sears spent $56 million in legal and administrative costs in handling the bankruptcy cases.

Sears has been struggling to find its market niche for some time. In 2001, it was forced to close eighty-nine stores as it watched its competitor, Montgomery Ward, close its doors for good.[89] In 2004, Kmart purchased Sears.

Discussion Questions

1. What do you believe creates Sears' culture?

2. Sears' stock price and earnings fell. What lesson is there in these consequences?

3. Compute the total costs of the bankruptcy cases to Sears.

Sources

Berner, Robert, "Sears Faces Controversy Over Car Batteries," *The Wall Street Journal*, August 26, 1997, p. B2.

Berner, Robert, and JoAnn S. Lublin, "Sears Is Told It Can't Shop for Ward Brass," *The Wall Street Journal*, August 13, 1997, pp. B1, B6.

Conlin, Michelle, "Sears: The Turnaround Is For Real," *Forbes*, December 15, 1997.

Flynn, Julia, Christina Del Valle, and Russell Mitchell, "Did Sears Take Other Customers for a Ride?" *Business Week*, August 3, 1992, pp. 24–25.

Fuchsberg, Gilbert, "Sears Reinstates Sales Incentives in Some Centers," *The Wall Street Journal*, March 7, 1994, p. B1.

Miller, James, "Sears Roebuck Expects Loss in Third Period," *The Wall Street Journal*, September 8, 1992, p. A3.

Patterson, Gregory A., "Sears Debt of $11 Billion Is Downgraded," *The Wall Street Journal*, December 11, 1992, p. A3.

"Sears Roebuck Fires Head of Its Auto Unit," *The Wall Street Journal*, December 21, 1992, p. B6.

Stevenson, Richard W., "Sears' Crisis: How Did It Do?" *The New York Times*, June 17, 1992, p. C1.

Woodyard, Chris, "Sears to Refund Millions to Bankrupt Customers," *USA Today*, April 11–13, 1997, p. 1A.

---

[88] Leslie Kaufman, "Sears Settles Suit on Raising of Its Credit Card Rates," The New York Times, *March 11, 1999, p. C2.*
[89] Amy Merrick, "Sears to Shut 89 Stores and Report Big Changes," The Wall Street Journal, *January 5, 2001, p. A4.*

Magazine Contests: The Disclosure of Odds

Investigations of American Family Publishers and Publishers Clearing House centered on the mailings sent by the companies that included the term "finalist" on the envelope and whether the materials stated clearly enough that "no purchase is required." The "finalist" notification is mailed with subscription information for the purchase of subscriptions to magazines. Most people (99 percent) who send in their entries do order magazines.

Twenty-four states investigated Publishers Clearing House and American Family Publishers in twenty-one states. The Florida Attorney General filed suit against Publishers Clearing House as well as Ed McMahon and Dick Clark, their celebrity spokespersons, for deceptive practices.

One mailing from American Family Publishers includes the following:[90]

So please accept our invitation as soon as you receive it. Once you do, you'll experience the thrill of winning—and that's guaranteed.

The investigation in the various states revealed that many senior citizens were subscribing to between twenty and thirty magazines with the hope of collecting prizes they believed were theirs. Some of the language used in the 200 million mailings included the following:

John Doe, it's down to a 2 person race for $11,000,000—you and one other person in— (state's name placed here) were issued one of two winning numbers.

We have reserved an $11,000,000 sum in your name.

Are you willing to risk letting your alternative take it all?

These statements were in bold while disclaimers establishing that the win was not all that certain were in fine print. The language printed in bold caused many to buy yet another subscription with the hope of winning.

American Family Publishers (the company with the mailings that read "YOU MAY ALREADY BE A WINNER" on the outside of the envelope) agreed to pay $1.25 million to settle allegations in thirty-two states plus the District of Columbia regarding deceptive sales practices. Lawsuits against Dick Clark and Ed McMahon, the spokesmen for the company, were settled.

The settlement requires American Family to establish a toll-free telephone number for information requests as well as a Web site. Consumers must also be given information about getting off American Family mailing lists. Finally, American Family must stop using two mail addresses for the entries. Those who were simply entering the contest were instructed to use one address, while those who were subscribing and entering were told to send their envelope to another address. The two-address system

---

[90] Tom Loury, "Settlement Won't End American Family Woes," USA Today, March 20, 1998, pp. 1B, 2B.

led many to believe that an accompanying subscription was a key in collecting the prize described in the bold print.

....

Discussion Questions

1. Do you think there was deception in any of the practices?

2. What is the role of regulators in this situation?

3. Have the companies taken advantage of potential customers?

CASE 9.6
....

McDonald's and the Disappearing Dodge Viper Game Pieces

Jerome P. Jacobson was the marketing mastermind who managed McDonald's customer games such as Monopoly and Who Wants to Be a Millionaire. Though not an employee of McDonald's, Mr. Jacobson was a principal at Simon Marketing, which made and handled the distribution of the game materials and pieces.

Being in a position of security and trust, Mr. Jacobson was able to skim off winning game pieces before they were distributed to McDonald's and then to the customers. Beginning in 1995, Mr. Jacobson, or "Uncle Jerry," as he was known, operated a ring of at least eight people who conspired to take the trips, cars, and large prizes McDonald's games offered. They are alleged to have netted $13 million from obtaining the winning game pieces.

The FBI uncovered the prize network when it began working on an anonymous tip from someone who indicated that "Uncle Jerry" might be fixing the McDonald's games. The FBI tracked closely those who were claiming the prizes and then set up a series of wiretaps that eventually led to the disclosure of the ring. The agents were able to follow members of the ring to their clandestine meetings, one of which was held in, ironically, Fair Play, South Carolina.[91] In some of the wiretaps the agents listened as the participants argued over how to split the proceeds. In other meetings they simply discussed ways to push McDonald's to pay their prizes more quickly.[92] With McDonald's cooperation in providing the names of winners for all their contests, the FBI was able to uncover the network of Uncle Jerry. McDonald's cooperated with the FBI in what would eventually become a sting operation.

What the FBI uncovered with this information and cooperation was a complex organizational structure headed by Uncle Jerry, who was based out of Lawrenceville, Georgia. Jacobson would embezzle the game pieces and then sell them to individuals around the country. These individuals would become recruiters who would ask friends

---

[91] David Stout, "8 Charged with Rigging McDonald's Promotional Games," The New York Times, August 22, 2001, p. A14.
[92] Gary Fields and Shirley Leung, "Eight People Arrested, Charged with Bilking McDonald's Contests," The Wall Street Journal, August 22, 2001, pp. A3, A8.

....

and relatives to buy pieces and claim the prizes. Some of these individuals actually mortgaged their homes in order to be able to buy the winning pieces from the recruiters. When they claimed their prizes, and they were mostly the big prizes such as a Dodge Viper and the millionaire tickets, they would pay a portion to the recruiters. The recruiters would then give a portion of their proceeds to Uncle Jerry. No one is certain where the informant fits in the organization, but he was able to supply the FBI with several names of those who were eventually arrested.

In order to right the wrong to its customers, McDonald's ran a $10 million prize giveaway weekend over the Labor Day weekend from August 30 through September 2, 2001.[93] McDonald's ended its contract with Simon Marketing at the same time. It was a 25-year relationship and McDonald's was responsible for 77 percent of Simon's revenues.[94]

Discussion Questions

1. Although an accounting firm was hired to supervise Jacobson and his distribution, apparently Jacobson operated without any checks. What does this factor and the case teach about internal controls?

2. What is the significance of the informant's work and tip?

3. When the FBI approached McDonald's, it knew that its games and image would be tarnished. Why do you think McDonald's cooperated?

4. Why did McDonald's run the $10 million Labor Day weekend game?

5. Mr. Jacobson met some of his recruiters when he worked as a police officer. Do you think their skills in law enforcement helped them evade authorities and detection for as long as they did?

[93] Bruce Horovitz, "Games Scandal Tarnishes Golden Arches," USA Today, August 22, 2001, p. 1B.
[94] Gary Strauss, "Informant Key to Unlocking Scam Behind the Golden Arches," USA Today, August 24, 2001, pp. 1B, 2B.

9 B

Product Safety

Only a manufacturer knows the results of its safety tests on a product. Only the manufacturer can correct defects or recall dangerous products. The decision to act on safety tests or recall a product is costly. The only "earnings" on recalls are the preservation of the company's reputation.

CASE 9.7
Tylenol: The Product and Its Packaging Safety

In 1982, 23-year-old Diane Elsroth died after taking a Tylenol capsule laced with cyanide. Within five days of her death, seven more people died from taking tainted Tylenol purchased from stores in the Chicago area.

Tylenol generated $525 million per year for McNeil Consumer Products, Inc., a subsidiary of Johnson & Johnson. The capsule form of the pain reliever represented 30 percent of Tylenol sales. McNeil's marketing studies indicated that consumers found the capsules easy to swallow and believed, without substantiation, that Tylenol in capsule form worked faster than Tylenol tablets.

The capsules' design, however, meant they could be taken apart, tainted, and then restored to the packaging without evidence of tampering. After the Chicago poisonings, which were never solved, McNeil and Johnson & Johnson executives were told at a meeting that processes for sealing the capsules had been greatly improved, but no one could give the assurance that they were tamperproof.

The executives realized that abandoning the capsule would give their competitors, Bristol-Myers (Excedrin) and American Home Products (Anacin), a market advantage, plus the cost would be $150 million just for 1982. Jim Burke, CEO of Johnson & Johnson, told the others that without a tamperproof package for the capsules, they would risk the survival of not only Tylenol but Johnson & Johnson. The executives decided to abandon the capsule.

Frank Young, a Food and Drug Administration commissioner, stated at the time, "This is a matter of Johnson & Johnson's own business judgment, and represents a responsible action under tough circumstances."[95]

Johnson & Johnson quickly developed "caplets"—tablets in the shape of a capsule—then offered consumers a coupon for a bottle of the new caplets if they turned in their capsules. Within five days of the announcement of the capsule recall and caplets offer, 200,000 consumers had responded. Johnson & Johnson had eliminated a key product in its line—one that customers clearly preferred—in the interest of safety. Otto Lerbinger of Boston University's College of Communication cited Johnson & Johnson as a "model of corporate social responsibility for its actions."[96]

President Ronald Reagan, addressing a group of business executives, said, "Jim Burke, of Johnson & Johnson, you have our deepest admiration. In recent days you have lived up to the very highest ideals of corporate responsibility and grace under pressure."[97]

Within one year of the Tylenol poisonings, Johnson & Johnson regained its 40 percent market share for Tylenol. While many attribute the regain of market share to tamperproof packaging, the other companies had moved to that form as well. However, it is interesting to note that McNeil was able to have its new product and packaging on the shelves within weeks of the fatal incidents. There had been some preparation for the change prior to the fatalities, but the tragedy was the motivation for the change to safer packaging and product forms.

McNeil continues to enjoy the goodwill from the rapid response to the poisonings. Even as new issues with Tylenol have developed, McNeil seems to be given the benefit of the doubt because of the goodwill and reputational capital it purchased with the capsule recalls.[98]

On December 21, 1994, the *Journal of the American Medical Association* published the results of a five-and-one-half-year study showing that moderate overdoses of acetaminophen (known most widely by the brand name Tylenol) led to liver damage in ten patients.[99, 100] The damage occurred even in patients who did not drink and was most pronounced in those who did drink or had not been eating. Further, the study by Dr. David Whitcomb at the University of Pittsburgh medical school found that taking one pill of acetaminophen per day for a year may double the risk of kidney failure.[101]

The American Association of Poison Control Centers for 1996 shows 31,511 cases of inappropriate exposure to pediatric acetaminophen products.[102] There were minor effects in 631 children and life-threatening permanent effects in six. Adult deaths from overexposure are put at 100, more than cocaine deaths (hospital statistics are not included).

Tylenol is a stunning source of revenue for McNeil and Johnson & Johnson, with revenue of $1.3 billion per year. In 1993, acetaminophen accounted for 48 percent of

[95] "Drug Firm Pulls All Its Capsules off the Market," Arizona Republic, February 18, 1986, p. A2.

[96] Pat Guy and Clifford Glickman, "J & J Uses Candor in Crisis," USA Today, February 12, 1986, p. 2B.

[97] "The Tylenol Rescue," Newsweek, March 3, 1986, p. 52.

[98] "Legacy of Tampering," Arizona Republic, September 29, 1992, p. A1.

[99] "Acetaminophen Overdoses Linked to Liver Damage," Mesa Tribune, December 21, 1994, p. A12.

[100] Doug Levy, "Acetaminophen Overuse Can Lead to Liver Damage," USA Today, December 22, 1994, p. 1D.

[101] "Second Tylenol Study Links Heavy Use to Kidney Risk," Arizona Republic, December 22, 1994, p. A6.

[102] Thomas Easton and Stephan Herrera, "J & J's Dirty Little Secret," Forbes, January 12, 1998, pp. 42–44.

the total $2.9 billion in sales of all over-the-counter drugs. Tylenol made up 70 percent of all acetaminophen sales. Advil's total sales, the next highest amount, trailed at less than $400,000,000.

Plaintiffs who claimed they were victims of overdose and the lack of effective warnings have not been successful against Johnson & Johnson.[103] The product labels before current modification read "Gentle on an infant's stomach," and Tylenol's ad slogan was, "Nothing's safer."

Patients combining Tylenol with alcohol have produced 200 cases of liver damage in the past twenty years, with fatality in 20 percent of those cases. The level of alcohol among these cases was multiple drinks every day.

In 1997, Tylenol added a new label to its infant Tylenol, "Taking more than the recommended dose . . . could cause serious health risks," because of liver damage in children.[104]

Discussion Questions

1. Was the risk small that there would be other poisonings of Tylenol capsules?

2. Were the shareholders' interests ignored in the decision to take a $150 million dollar write-off and a possible loss of $525 million in annual sales by abandoning the capsules?

3. Suppose that you were a Tylenol competitor. Would you have continued selling your capsules?

4. Was Burke's action a long-term decision? Did it take into account the interests of all stakeholders?

5. What financial arguments could be made against the decision to abandon the capsule?

6. Were the risks appropriately balanced in this case?

7. Following the poisonings, the federal government developed packaging regulations for nonprescription drugs. Should manufacturers have developed the tamperproof packaging on their own?

8. General Robert Wood Johnson, the CEO of Johnson & Johnson from 1932 to 1963, wrote a credo for his company that states the company's first responsibility is to the people who use its products and services; the second responsibility is to its employees; the third to the community and its environment; and the fourth to the stockholders.[105] Johnson and his successors have believed that if the credo's first three responsibilities are met, the stockholders will be well served. Does Johnson & Johnson follow its credo?

9. If you were a manufacturer of acetaminophen, how would you respond to the study results published in 1994? What action would you take?

10. How would you handle the resulting litigation?

11. Did the warning take too long?

[103] Deborah Sharp, "Alcohol-Tylenol Death Goes to Trial in Florida," USA Today, March 24, 1997, p. 3A.
[104] Richard Cole, "Tylenol Agrees to Warning on Labels of Risk to Children," Arizona Republic, October 19, 1997, p. A5.
[105] Brief History of Johnson & Johnson, 1992 (company pamphlet).

.... CASE 9.8
....

Ford and Its Pinto and GM and Its Malibu: The Repeating Exploding Gas Tank Problem

The Ford Pinto

In 1968, Ford began designing a subcompact automobile that ultimately became the Pinto. Lee Iacocca, then a Ford vice president, conceived the idea of a subcompact car and was its moving force. Ford's objective was to build a car weighing 2,000 pounds or less to sell for no more than $2,000. At that time, prices for gasoline were increasing, and the American auto industry was losing competitive ground to the small vehicles of Japanese and German manufacturers.

The Pinto was a rush project. Ordinarily, auto manufacturers work to blend the engineering concerns with the style preferences of consumers that they determine from marketing surveys. As a result, the placement of the Pinto fuel tank was dictated by style, not engineering. The preferred practice in Europe and Japan was to locate the gas tank over the rear axle in subcompacts because a small vehicle has less "crush space" between the rear axle and the bumper than larger cars.[106] The Pinto's styling, however, required the tank to be placed behind the rear axle, leaving only nine to ten inches of "crush space"—far less than in any other American automobile or Ford over-seas subcompact. In addition, the Pinto's bumper was little more than a chrome strip, less substantial than the bumper of any other American car produced then or later. The Pinto's rear structure also lacked reinforcing longitudinal side members, known as "hat sections," and horizontal cross members running between them, such as those in larger cars produced by Ford. The result of these style-driven changes was that the Pinto was less crush resistant than other vehicles. But, there was one more problem, which was that the Pinto's differential housing had an exposed flange and bolt heads. These resulting protrusions meant that a gas tank driven forward against the differential by a rear impact would be punctured.[107]

Pinto prototypes were built and tested. Ford tested these prototypes, as well as two production Pintos, to determine the integrity of the fuel system in rear-end accidents. It also tested to see if the Pinto would meet a proposed federal regulation requiring all automobiles manufactured in 1972 to be able to withstand a twenty-mile-per-hour fixed-barrier impact and those made after January 1, 1973, to withstand a thirty-mile-per-hour fixed-barrier impact without significant fuel spillage.[108]

The crash tests revealed that the Pinto's fuel system as designed could not meet the proposed twenty-mile-per-hour standard. When mechanical prototypes were struck from the rear with a moving barrier at twenty-one miles per hour, the fuel tanks were driven forward and punctured, causing fuel leakage in excess of the proposed

---

[106] Rachel Dardis and Claudia Zent, "The Economics of the Pinto Recall," *Journal of Consumer Affairs*, Winter 1982, pp. 261–277.
[107] Id.
[108] Id.

regulation standard. A production Pinto crashing at twenty-one miles per hour into a fixed barrier resulted in the fuel neck being torn from the gas tank and the tank being punctured by a bolt head on the differential housing. In at least one test, spilled fuel entered the driver's compartment through gaps resulting from the separation of the seams joining the rear wheel wells to the floor pan.

Ford tested other vehicles, including modified or reinforced mechanical Pinto prototypes, that proved safe at speeds at which the Pinto failed. Vehicles in which rubber bladders had been installed in the tank and were then crashed into fixed barriers at twenty-one miles per hour had no leakage from punctures in the gas tank. Vehicles with fuel tanks installed above rather than behind the rear axle passed the fuel system integrity test at thirty-one miles per hour against a fixed barrier. A Pinto with two longitudinal hat sections added to firm up the rear structure passed a twenty-mile-per-hour fixed-barrier test with no fuel leakage.[109]

The vulnerability of the Pinto's fuel tank at speeds of twenty and thirty miles per hour in fixed-barrier tests could have been remedied inexpensively, but Ford produced and sold the Pinto without doing anything to fix the defects. Among the design changes that could have been made were side and cross members at $2.40 and $1.80 per car, respectively; a shock-absorbent "flak suit" to protect the tank at $4; a tank within a tank and placement of the tank over the axle at $5.08 to $5.79; a nylon bladder within the tank at $5.25 to $8; placement of the tank over the axle surrounded with a protective barrier at $9.59 per car; imposition of a protective shield between the differential housing and the tank at $2.35; improvement and reinforcement of the bumper at $2.60; and addition of eight inches of crush space at a cost of $6.40. Equipping the car with a reinforced rear structure, smooth axle, improved bumper, and additional crush space at a total of $15.30 would have made the fuel tank safe when hit from the rear by a vehicle the size of a Ford Galaxie. If, in addition, a bladder or tank within a tank had been used or if the tank had been protected with a shield, the tank would have been safe in a rear-end collision of forty to forty-five miles per hour. If the tank had been located over the rear axle, it would have been safe in a rear impact at fifty miles per hour or more.[110]

As the Pinto approached actual production, the engineers responsible for the components of the project "signed off" to their immediate supervisors, who in turn "signed off" to their superiors, and so on up the chain of command until the entire project was approved for release by the lead engineers, and ultimately, Iacocca. The Pinto crash tests results were known to these decision makers when they decided to go forward with production.

At an April 1971 product review meeting, a report by Ford engineers on the financial impact of a proposed federal standard on fuel system integrity and the cost savings that would accrue from deferring even minimal "fixes" of the Pinto was discussed.

In 1969, the chief assistant research engineer in charge of cost-weight evaluation of the Pinto and the chief chassis engineer in charge of crash testing the early prototype both expressed concern about the integrity of the Pinto's fuel system and complained about management's unwillingness to deviate from the design if the change would cost money.

---

[109] Grimshaw v. Ford Motor Co., *174 Cal. Rptr. 378 (1981).*
[110] Id.

J. C. Echold, Ford's director of automotive safety, studied the issue of gas tank design in anticipation of government regulations requiring modification. His study, "Fatalities Associated with Crash Induced Fuel Leakage and Fires," included the following cost–benefit analysis:

> The total benefit is shown to be just under $50 million, while the associated cost is $137 million. Thus, the cost is almost three times the benefits, even using a number of highly favorable benefit assumptions.[111]

Benefits

Savings—180 burn deaths, 180 serious burn injuries, 2,100 burned vehicles

Unit cost—$200,000 per death, $67,000 per injury, $700 per vehicle

Total benefits—(180 × $200,000) + (180 × $67,000) + (2,100 × $700) = $49.15 million

Costs

Sales—11 million cars, 1.5 million light trucks

Unit cost—$11 per car, $11 per truck

Total costs—(11,000,000 × $11) + (1,500,000 × $11) = $137 million

Ford's unit cost of $200,000 for one life was based on a National Highway Traffic Safety Administration calculation developed as shown in Table 9.1.

Despite the concerns of the engineers and the above report, Ford went forward with production of the Pinto without any design change or any of the proposed modifications. Shortly after the release of the car, significant mechanical issues were recurring, with complaints by vehicle owners as well as a number of fiery rear-end collisions. One of the most public cases happened in 1971 when the Gray family purchased a 1972 Pinto hatchback (the 1972 models were made available in the Fall of 1971) manufactured by Ford in October 1971. The Grays had trouble with the car from the outset. During the first few months of ownership, they had to return the car to the dealer for repairs a number of times. The problems included excessive gas and oil consumption, down-shifting of the automatic transmission, lack of power, and occasional stalling. It was later learned that the stalling and excessive fuel consumption were caused by a heavy carburetor float.

On May 28, 1972, Mrs. Gray, accompanied by 13-year-old Richard Grimshaw, set out in the Pinto from Anaheim for Barstow to meet Mr. Gray. The Pinto was then six months old and had been driven approximately 3,000 miles. Mrs. Gray stopped in San Bernardino for gasoline, then got back onto Interstate 15 and proceeded toward Barstow at sixty to sixty-five miles per hour. As she approached the Route 30 off ramp where traffic was congested, she moved from the outside fast lane into the middle lane. The Pinto then suddenly stalled and coasted to a halt. It was later established that the carburetor float had become so saturated with gasoline that it sank, opening the float chamber and causing the engine to flood. The driver of the vehicle immediately behind

---

[111] Ralph Drayton, "One Manufacturer's Approach to Automobile Safety Standards," CTLA News, February 8, 1968, p. 11.

TABLE 9.1 Ford's Unit Cost of $200,000 for One Life

Component	1971 costs
Future productivity losses	
Direct	$132,000
Indirect	41,300
Medical costs	
Hospital	700
Other	425
Property damage	1,500
Insurance administration	4,700
Legal and court	3,000
Employer losses	1,000
Victim's pain and suffering	10,000
Funeral	900
Assets (lost consumption)	5,000
Miscellaneous accident cost	200
Total per family	$200,725[112]

Mrs. Gray's car was able to swerve and pass it, but the driver of a 1962 Ford Galaxie was unable to avoid hitting the Pinto. The Galaxie had been traveling from fifty to fifty-five miles per hour but had slowed to between twenty-eight and thirty-seven miles per hour at the time of impact.[113]

The Pinto burst into flames that engulfed its interior. According to one expert, the impact of the Galaxie had driven the Pinto's gas tank forward and caused it to be punctured by the flange or one of the bolts on the differential housing so that fuel sprayed from the punctured tank and entered the passenger compartment through gaps opening between the rear wheel well sections and the floor pan. By the time the Pinto came to rest after the collision, both occupants had been seriously burned. When they emerged from the vehicle, their clothing was almost completely burned off. Mrs. Gray died a few days later of congestive heart failure as a result of the burns. Grimshaw survived, only through heroic medical measures. He underwent numerous and extensive surgeries and skin grafts, some occurring over the ten years after the collision. He lost parts of several fingers on his left hand and his left ear, and his face required many skin grafts.[114]

As Ford continued to litigate Mrs. Gray's lawsuit and thousands of other rear-impact Pinto suits, damages reaching $6 million had been awarded to plaintiffs by 1980. In 1979, Indiana filed criminal charges against Ford for reckless homicide.

[112] Mark Dowie, "Pinto Madness," Mother Jones, September/October 1977, p. 28.
[113] "Who Pays for the Damage?" Time, January 21, 1980, p. 61.
[114] Adapted from Grimshaw v. Ford Motor Co., 174 Cal. Rptr. 348 (1981).

Discussion Questions

1. Calculate the total cost if all the "fixes" for the Pinto gas tank problem had been done.

2. What was management's position on the fixes?

3. Using the decision models you have learned, list some of the analysis questions and issues management missed in making its decision to go forward with production without any design changes.

4. Did the Pinto design violate any laws?

5. Was Ford simply answering a public demand for a small, fuel-efficient, and inexpensive auto?

6. Don't all automobiles present the potential for injuries? Do we assume risks in driving and buying an automobile?

7. If you had been one of the engineers who was concerned, what would you have done differently? Do you think there was anything you could do? What if you resigned as Dr. LiCari at Beech-Nut did (Case 5.16)? Could you then notify a government agency?

8. In 1996, Ford issued a recall on 8.7 million vehicles because a joint investigation with NHTSA revealed the ignition in certain cars could short circuit and cause a fire. Ford ran full-page ads in major newspapers. The ad from *The Wall Street Journal*, May 8, 1996, p. B7, is reproduced below:

T.J. Wagner   Ford Motor Company
Vice President   Dearborn, MI 48121

Customer Communication & Satisfaction

To Our Ford, Lincoln and Mercury Owners:

As I am sure you have read, Ford Motor Company recently announced a program to voluntarily recall 8.7 million vehicles to replace ignition switches. You should know that at the time we announced the recall, the actual number of complaints which may be related to the ignition switch in question was less than two hundredths of one percent of that total. We regret the inconvenience this has caused the customers who have placed their trust in our products.

Q: *What happened?*

A: Following an intensive investigation in cooperation with the U.S. National Highway Traffic Safety Administration and Transport Canada, we determined that the ignition switch in a very small percentage of certain models could develop a short circuit—creating the potential for overheating, smoke, and possibly fire in the steering column of the vehicle. The factors that contribute to this are a manufacturing process change to the ignition switch in combination with the electrical load through the switch.

Q: *What vehicles are affected by this voluntary recall?*

A: The following model year vehicles are affected:

- 1988 Ford EXP.
- 1988–1990 Ford Escort.

- 1988–1992 Ford Mustang, Thunderbird, Tempo, and Mercury Cougar and Topaz.
- 1993 Ford Mustang, Thunderbird, Tempo, and Mercury Cougar and Topaz models built prior to October 1992.
- 1988–1989 Ford Crown Victoria, Mercury Grand Marquis and Lincoln Town Car.
- 1988–1991 Ford Aerostar, Ford Bronco full-size sport utility and Ford F-Series light truck.

Q: *What should I do?*

A: If you own one of these vehicles, you will receive a letter from us instructing you to take your vehicle to the Ford or Lincoln/Mercury dealer of your choice and have the switch replaced free of charge. However, you do not have to wait for our letter. You may contact your dealer and arrange to have the switch replaced immediately if you choose, free of charge.

Q: *How long will it take?*

A: The repair procedure should take about one hour. But please contact your dealer in advance to schedule a time that is convenient for you.

Q: *What if I need additional help?*

A: You may contact your dealer anytime, or call our Ford Ignition Switch Recall Customer Information Line at 1-800-323-8400.

We're in business because people believe in our products. We make improvements because we believe we can make our products better. And at times we'll take a major step like this to make sure that people who buy a Ford, Lincoln or Mercury vehicle know that they bought more than a vehicle, they bought a company and a dealer organization that stands behind the cars and trucks they build and sell. This is our *Quality is Job 1* promise to you. Thank you for your patience and support.

What was different about Ford's conduct in this case? Has Ford had an ethical cultural change on product safety? Why did Ford voluntarily agree to fix almost 9 million vehicles?

The Chevrolet (GM) Malibu

On July 9, 1999, a Los Angeles jury awarded Patricia Anderson, her four children, and friend, Jo Tigner, $107 million in actual damages and $4.8 billion in punitive damages from General Motors in a lawsuit the six brought against GM because they were trapped and burned in their Chevrolet Malibu when it exploded on impact following a rear-end collision.[115]

Coleman Thorton, the jury foreman, explaining the large verdict said, "GM has no regard for the people in their cars, and they should be held responsible for it." Richard Shapiro, an attorney for GM said, "We're very disappointed. This was a very sympathetic case. The people who were injured were innocent in this matter. They were the victims of a drunk driver."[116]

---

[115] Ann W. O'Neill, Henry Weinstein, and Eric Malnic, "Jury Orders GM to Pay Record Sum," Arizona Republic, *July 10, 1999*, pp. A1, A2.
[116] Id.

The accident occurred on Christmas Eve 1993 and was the result of a drunk driver striking the Anderson Malibu at 70 mph. The driver's blood alcohol level was .20, but the defense lawyers noted they were not permitted to disclose to the jury that the driver of the auto that struck the Malibu was drunk.

The discovery process in the case uncovered a 1973 internal "value analysis" memo on "post-collision fuel-tank fires" written by a low-level GM engineer, Edward C. Ivey, in which he calculated the value of preventing fuel-fed fires. Mr. Ivey used a figure of $200,000 for the cost of a fatality and noted that there are 500 fatalities per year in GM auto fuel fire accidents. The memo also stated that his analysis must be read in the context of "it is really impossible to put a value on human life." Mr. Ivey wrote, using an estimate of $200,000 as the value of human life, that the cost of these explosions to GM would be $2.40 per car. After an in-house lawyer discovered the memo in 1981, he wrote:

> Obviously Ivey is not an individual whom we would ever, in any conceivable situation, want identified to the plaintiffs in a post-collision fuel-fed fire case, and the documents he generated are undoubtedly some of the potentially most harmful and most damaging were they ever to be produced.[117]

In the initial cases brought against GM, the company's defense was that the engineer's thinking was his own and did not reflect company policy. However, when the 1981 lawyer commentary was found as part of discovery in a Florida case in 1998, GM lost that line of defense. In the Florida case in which a 13-year-old boy was burned to death in a 1983 Oldsmobile Cutlass station wagon, the jury awarded his family $33 million.

The two documents have become the center of each case. Judge Ernest G. Williams of Los Angeles Superior Court, who upheld the verdict in the $4.9 billion LA case but reduced the damages, wrote in his opinion:

> The court finds that clear and convincing evidence demonstrated that defendants' fuel tank was placed behind the axle of the automobiles of the make and model here in order to maximize profits—to the disregard of public safety.[118]

Currently, there are 100 such cases pending around the country. The suits center around GM's mid-size "A-cars," which include the Malibu, Buick Century, Oldsmobile Cutlass, and Pontiac Grand Prix. Approximately 7.5 million cars are equipped with this gas tank design. On appeal, the Los Angeles verdict was reduced from $4.9 billion (total) to $1.2 billion.[119]

....

Discussion Questions

1. Why do you think the drunk driver was not held responsible for the Los Angeles accident?

2. If you had found the 1973 memo, what would you have done with it?

3. If you had read the 1973 memo prior to the time the Malibu was released for production and to the market, what would you have done with it?

[117] Milo Geyelin, "How an Internal Memo Written 26 Years Ago Is Costing GM Dearly," The Wall Street Journal, September 29, 1999, pp. A1, A6.
[118] Id.
[119] Margaret A. Jacobs, "BMW Decision Used to Whittle Punitive Awards," The Wall Street Journal, September 13, 1999, p. B2.

4. What happens over time when memos such as this engineer's discussion are concealed?

5. What did the GM managers miss in ignoring the engineer's concerns? Why do you think they said he was acting on his own? If an employee writes a memo about the company's product is the employee ever acting on his or her own?

6. Offer some general lessons from these two cases for business managers and for yourself when you enter the business world.

CASE 9.9

ATVs: Danger on Wheels

Honda Motor Company, Ltd.; Yamaha Motor Company, Ltd.; Suzuki Motors Company, Ltd.; Kawasaki Heavy Industries, Ltd.; and Polaris Industries all made various types of motorcycles and all-terrain vehicles (ATVs) during the late 1970s and 1980s. Honda was the leading seller of ATVs, offering a full range of three-wheel models. It even made a very small three-wheel ATV for children ages four through ten that it advertised at the height of the market in the mid-1980s. The fat-wheeled vehicles that look like large tricycles were advertised as able to conquer all land surfaces with great ease. Suzuki's ads said its ATV would "embarrass the wind."[120]

The ATV was introduced in 1977 by Honda; several other manufacturers entered the market in the following year. Yamaha and Kawasaki ATVs were larger in size and motor capacity and carried higher price tags than Honda's.

In 1978, based on a complaint from the National Association of Emergency Room Physicians (NAERP) and the American Neurological Society (ANS), the Consumer Product Safety Commission began investigating ATVs and their use and misuse. The commission's reports, which incorporated information from NAERP and ANS, found that:

1. ATV accidents were increasing dramatically:[121]
   Of all the fatalities over the five-year period, 165 involved children ages eleven and younger, while 47 percent of the total involved children ages sixteen and younger.[122]

	ATV-related emergency room admissions	Deaths from ATV accidents
1982	8,600	26
1983	26,900	85
1984	63,900	153
1985	85,900	246
1986	86,400	268

[120] Frederick M. Maynard, "Peril in the Path of All-Terrain Vehicles," Business and Society Review, Winter 1987, pp. 48–52.
[121] Daniel B. Moskowitz, "Why ATVs Could Land in a Heap of Trouble," Business Week, November 30, 1987, p. 38. The numbers do vary in press releases and according to various groups.
[122] James Bolger, "The High Gravity Risk of ATV's," Safety & Health, November 1987, pp. 48–49.

2. Of all ATV-related injuries, 90 percent involved people under the age of thirty and 70 percent involved those under the age of eighteen.
3. In some areas, ATV-related injuries accounted for 45 percent of all emergency care on weekends.
4. Ninety percent of all injuries happened to experienced ATV riders (those who had logged more than twenty-five hours of riding time).
5. Leg injuries were common, with spiral fractures being the most frequent form.
6. Many injuries requiring emergency care were leg burns caused by riders holding their legs too close to ATV engines.

Dr. Ralph R. Fine, codirector of the National Spinal Cord Injury Statistical Center, testified before a House committee about his concerns: "We were seeing a disproportionate number of spinal cord injuries resulting from three wheeler or ATV crashes. These are dangerously deceptive, deceptively dangerous vehicles."[123]

Honda was aware of the report and submitted a study to the Consumer Product Safety Commission that showed the accidents with injuries happened when ATVs were misused.[124] Referred to in the Honda report as "hotdogging," misuse included driving too fast, climbing hills at ninety-degree angles, going through rapidly moving water, and using ramps for jumping.[125]

Between 1982 and 1986, there were more than 50,000 ATV-related injuries. By 1986, 2.1 million ATVs at an average price of $2,000 each were in use. Between 1982 and 1988, 858 people were killed in ATV accidents, many of them young children. A Consumer Product Safety Commission report concluded, "Children under 12 years of age are unable to operate any size ATV safely."[126] State attorneys general began efforts to regulate ATV use in 1986. Texas Assistant Attorney General Stephen Gardner stated, "These are killer machines. They should not be allowed."[127] The CPSC tried to have the industry sales to sixteen-year-olds and younger banned, but was unsuccessful.[128]

After the report, Yamaha introduced a four-wheel ATV, including one model with two seats. Yamaha also undertook a dealer education program and issued an instruction manual with the vehicles to encourage responsible operation.[129]

Roy Janson of the American All-Terrain Vehicle Association, a subsidiary of the American Motorcyclist Association, stated at congressional hearings on ATVs:

Problems result primarily from how a vehicle is used rather than from its design. When ATVs are used as intended, they present no unreasonable risk to their operators. The major problems related to three-wheel ATV injuries are the failure of users to wear proper safety equipment while operating ATVs and using these vehicles in areas not recommended for

[123] "Public Safety: All-Terrain Vehicles," National Safety and Health News, August 1985, pp. 78–80.
[124] Jeff Riggenbach, "Regulation Not Needed; Danger Is Exaggerated," USA Today, November 6, 1986, p. 10A.
[125] "Safety Group Targets Use of ATVs by Young Riders," Mesa Tribune, November 20, 1986, p. A4.
[126] Randolph Schmid, "Safety Panel Tackles All-Terrain Cycle Issue," Phoenix Gazette, November 19, 1986, p. A14.
[127] Moskowitz, "Why ATVs Could Land in a Heap of Trouble," p. 38.
[128] "ATV Makers Warned to Halt Sales to Children or Face Ban," Mesa Tribune, October 2, 1986, p. A2.
[129] Alan R. Isley, "Industry Is Emphasizing Safety," USA Today, November 6, 1986, p. 1B.

ATV recreation. User education and information programs are clearly the most effective means for addressing the problems relating to misuse.[130]

In 1980, major nationally franchised rental centers ceased renting ATVs because of liability concerns.

In 1986, the Consumer Product Safety Commission published proposed ATV regulations that included these key provisions:

1. No ATVs below certain size limits would be manufactured. ATV riders would have to weigh at least 100 pounds and be at least sixteen years old.
2. All ATVs would have four wheels.
3. All manufacturers would undertake educational ad campaigns on the use and dangers of ATVs. No promotional advertising would be permitted in any media form.

While the proposed regulations were being debated, ATV accidents continued to climb steadily. Of particular concern was the marked increase in severe injuries, such as spinal cord and head injuries, to children six to ten years of age. At the same time, some manufacturers continued to provide studies to the Consumer Product Safety Commission indicating misuse, not design, was the primary cause of ATV accidents.

By 1987, the Association of Trial Lawyers of America had established a clearing-house for the exchange of information on ATV claims, and over 400 lawsuits had been filed. Three fourths of the suits were being settled for a typical payment of $1 million.

Because of increased, widely publicized objections from consumer groups, as well as a call for action from the American Academy of Pediatrics, the commission recalled three-wheel ATVs in May 1988 and halted their manufacture.[131] Meanwhile, manufacturers accelerated production of four-wheel vehicles. After judicial review of the commission's order and agreements were reached with the five manufacturers, the commission withdrew the recall but successfully implemented the ban on future sales.[132]

Some consumer groups, however, still felt a recall was necessary. James Florio, a Congressman from New Jersey, said, "How can anyone truly concerned with safety in effect say 'tough luck' to people who currently own these unsafe vehicles?"[133]

However, the manufacturers did agree to take the following steps:

• Offer cash incentives to encourage owners of ATVs purchased after December 30, 1987, to enroll in training programs.
• Revise warning labels and owner's manuals to outline the dangers of vehicle operation.
• Set up a consumer telephone hotline.
• Restrict sales of ATVs with engine displacements greater than ninety cubic centimeters displacement (CCD) to people sixteen years or older; children under twelve years would not be permitted to operate vehicles with engines greater than seventy CCD.

[130] "Public Safety," p. 79.
[131] "We Need Regulation of Dangerous ATVs," USA Today, November 14, 1986, p. 10A.
[132] "ATV Makers Agree to Warnings, Vehicle Ban," Arizona Business Gazette, May 9, 1988, Law 3.
[133] "Outlawing a Three-Wheeler," Time, January 11, 1988, p. 59.

- Scrap a provision in the preliminary agreement that would have required ATV purchasers to sign a form acknowledging the risks of operating the vehicle.[134]

Honda sent out the following "Safety Alert"[135] to owners of its ATVs in January 1988:

The Consumer Product Safety Commission has concluded that all-terrain vehicles (ATVs) may present a risk of death or severe injury in certain circumstances. While accidents may occur for many reasons:

- Over 900 people, including many children, have died in accidents associated with ATVs since 1982.
- Many people have become severely paralyzed or suffered severe internal injuries as a result of accidents associated with ATVs.
- Thousands of people have been treated in hospital emergency rooms every month for injuries received while riding an ATV.

Because of this, the United States government has filed a lawsuit against all manufacturers and distributors of ATVs asking the court to declare that ATVs are hazardous and to order the manufacturers and distributors to take actions to protect ATV riders. The distributors, while contesting the validity of the allegations made by the government, are presently engaged in discussions with the government to resolve these issues without litigation.

You should be aware that an ATV is not a toy and may be dangerous to operate. An ATV handles different [sic] from other vehicles, including motorcycles and cars. According to the Consumer Product Safety Commission, an ATV can roll over on the rider or violently throw the rider without warning, and even hitting a small rock, bump, or hole at low speed can upset the ATV.

To avoid death or severe personal injury:

Never drive an ATV without proper instruction. *Take a training course.* Beginning drivers should receive training from a certified instructor. . . .

- *Never* lend your ATV to anyone who has not taken a training course or has not been driving an ATV for at least a year.
- *Always* follow these age recommendations:
  - A child under 12 years old should never drive an ATV with engine size 70 CCD or greater.
  - A child under 16 years old should never drive an ATV with engine size greater than 90 CCD.
- *Never* allow a child under 16 years old to drive an ATV without adult supervision. Children need to be observed carefully because not all children have the strength, size, skills, or judgment needed to drive an ATV safely.
- *Never* drive an ATV after consuming alcohol or drugs.
- *Never* carry a passenger on an ATV; carrying a passenger may upset the balance of the ATV and may cause it to go out of control.
- *Never* drive an ATV on pavement. The vehicle is not designed to be used on paved surfaces and may be difficult to control.

---

[134] Matt DeLorenzo, *"ATV Companies Agree to Warn, Train Owners,"* Automotive News, *March 21, 1988, p. 58.*
[135] *Reprinted with permission of Honda Motor Company, Ltd.*

- *Never* drive an ATV on a public road, even a dirt or gravel one, because you may not be able to avoid colliding with other vehicles. Also, driving on a public road with an ATV may be against the law.
- *Never* attempt to do "wheelies," jumps, or other stunts.
- *Never* drive an ATV without a good helmet and goggles. You should also wear boots, gloves, heavy trousers, and a long-sleeve shirt.
- *Never* drive an ATV at excessive speeds.
- *Always* be extremely careful when driving an ATV, especially when approaching hills, turns, and obstacles and when driving on unfamiliar or rough terrain.
- *Always* read the owner's manual carefully and follow the operating procedures described.

Discussion Questions

1. Is the ATV too dangerous to be sold?

2. Are the warnings and the ban on future ATV sales sufficient?

3. If you were in marketing for one of the five firms, could you continue your sales efforts?

4. Should the three-wheel ATV have been recalled?

5. Is the cost of a recall just too high?

CASE 9.10

E. coli, Jack-in-the-Box, and Cooking Temperatures

On January 11, 1993, young Michael Nole and his family ate dinner at a Jack-in-the-Box restaurant in Tacoma, Washington, where Michael enjoyed his $2.69 "Kid's Meal." The next day, Michael was admitted to Children's Hospital and Medical Center in Seattle with severe stomach cramps and bloody diarrhea. Several days later, Michael died of kidney and heart failure.[136]

At the same time, 300 other people in Idaho, Nevada, and Washington who had eaten at Jack-in-the-Box restaurants were poisoned with *E. coli* bacteria, the cause of Michael's death. By the end of the outbreak, more than 600 people nationwide were affected.[137]

Jack-in-the-Box, based in San Diego, was not in the best financial health, having just restructured $501 million in debt. The outbreak of poisonings came at a difficult time for the company.

Federal guidelines require that meat be cooked to an internal temperature of 140 degrees Fahrenheit. Jack-in-the-Box followed those guidelines. In May 1992 and

---

[136] Catherine Yang and Amy Barrett, "In a Stew over Tainted Meat," Business Week, April 12, 1993, p. 36.

[137] Fred Bayles, "Meat Safety," USA Today, October 8, 1997, p. 1A.

September 1992, the state of Washington notified all restaurants, including Jack-in-the-Box, of new regulations requiring hamburgers to be cooked to 155 degrees Fahrenheit. The change would increase restaurants' costs because cooking to 155 degrees slows delivery of food to customers and increases energy costs.

At a news conference one week after the poisonings, Jack-in-the-Box president Robert J. Nugent criticized state authorities for not notifying the company of the 155-degree rule. A week later, the company found the notifications, which it had misplaced, and issued a statement.

After the Jack-in-the-Box poisonings, the federal government recommended that all states increase their cooking temperature requirements to 155 degrees. Burger King cooks to 160 degrees; Hardee's, Wendy's, and Taco Bell to 165 degrees. The U.S. Agriculture Department also changed its meat inspection standards.[138, 139]

The poisonings cut sales at Jack-in-the-Box by 20 percent.[140] Three store managers were laid off, and the company's plan to build five new restaurants was put on hold until sales picked up. Jack-in-the-Box scrapped 20,000 pounds of hamburger patties produced at meat plants where the bacteria was suspected to have originated. It also changed meat suppliers and added extra meat inspections of its own at an expected cost of $2 million a year.[141]

Consumer groups advocated a 160-degree internal temperature for cooking and a requirement that the meat no longer be pink or red inside.

A class action law suit brought by plaintiffs with minor *E. coli* effects was settled for $12 million. Two other suits, brought on behalf of children who went into comas, were settled for $3 million and $15.6 million, respectively.[142] All of the suits were settled by the end of 1997, most of the settlements coming from a pool of $100 million established by the company's ten insurers.[143]

Discussion Questions

1. In 1993, Jack-in-the-Box adopted tougher standards for its meat suppliers than those required by the federal government so that suppliers test more frequently for *E. coli*. Could Jack-in-the-Box have done more before the outbreak occurred?

2. The link between cooking to a 155-degree internal temperature and the destruction of *E. coli* bacteria had been publicly known for five years at the time of the outbreak. The federal Centers for Disease Control tests showed Jack-in-the-Box hamburgers were cooked to 120 degrees. Should Jack-in-the-Box have increased cooking temperatures voluntarily and sooner?

[138] Richard Gibson and Scott Kilman, "Tainted Hamburger Incident Heats Up Debate over U.S. Meat-Inspection System," The Wall Street Journal, February 12, 1993, pp. B1, B7.

[139] Martin Tolchin, "Clinton Orders Hiring of 160 Meat Inspectors," The New York Times, February 12, 1993, p. A11.

[140] Ronald Grover, Dori Jones Yang, and Laura Holson, "Boxed in at Jack-in-the-Box," Business Week, February 15, 1993, p. 40.

[141] Adam Bryant, "Foodmaker Cancels Expansion," The New York Times, February 15, 1993, p. C3.

[142] "Jack-in-the-Box Ends E-Coli Suits," National Law Journal, November 17, 1997, p. A8.

[143] Bob Van Voris, "Jack in the Box Ends E-Coli Suits," National Law Journal, November 17, 1997.

3. What does the misplacement of the state health department notices on cooking temperature say about the culture at Jack-in-the-Box?

4. Are there moral issues involved in deciding what temperature to cook meat to?

5. A plaintiff's lawyer praised Jack-in-the-Box saying, "They paid out in a way that made everybody walking away from the settlement table think they had been treated fairly." What do we learn about the company from this statement?

9c

Product Social Issues

Sometimes the product is legal, the quality is good, and yet the product does have its issues. In this section, the issues are ones of social responsibility.

CASE 9.11

The Mommy Doll

Villy Nielsen, APS, a Danish toy company, introduced the Mommy-To-Be doll in the United States. The doll, named Judith, looks like it is pregnant. When its belly is removed, a baby is revealed inside that can be popped out. Once the baby is removed, the doll's original stomach pops into place. The new stomach is flat and instantly restores Judith's youthful figure.

Teenage girls are intrigued by the doll, and call it "neat." However, Diane Welsh, the president of the New York chapter of the National Organization for Women, stated, "A doll that magically becomes pregnant and unpregnant is an irresponsible toy. We need to understand having a child is a very serious business. We have enough unwanted children in this world."[144]

Mommy-To-Be comes with Charles, her husband, and baby accessories. An eleven-year-old shopper said of the doll, "I don't think she looks like a mommy. . . . She looks like a teenager."[145]

Discussion Questions

1. Is the doll a socially responsible toy?

2. Would you carry the doll if you owned a toy store?

3. Would you want your children to have the doll?

[144] *"Mommy Doll Makes Birth a Snap," Mesa Tribune, May 9, 1992, p. A7.*
[145] Id.

Rock Music Warning Labels

In the summer of 1985, Tipper Gore, the wife of then-Senator Albert Gore of Tennessee, and Susan Baker, the wife of former U.S. Treasury Secretary James Baker, formed a citizens' group called the Parents Music Resource Center (PMRC). The group's concern was that rock music advocates "aggressive and hostile rebellion, the abuse of drugs and alcohol, irresponsible sexuality, sexual perversions, violence and involvement in the occult." Gore began the group after she listened to the song "Darling Nikki" from her eleven-year-old daughter's *Purple Rain* album by Prince. The song is about a girl masturbating as she looks at a magazine. Gore then discovered Sheena Easton singing about "genital arousal," Judas Priest singing about oral sex at gunpoint, and the lyrics in Motley Crue's top-selling *Shout at the Devil* album, describing killing a person and watching his face turn blue.

PMRC's strategy was to work with record companies to reach a mutually agreeable solution to the problem. PMRC met with the Recording Industry Association of America to request a ratings system for records, similar to that used for movies, and a requirement that printed lyrics be included with all records so that disc jockeys would know what they are sending out over the airwaves. In the first month after PMRC was organized, it received over 10,000 letters of support and inquiry. PMRC maintains a database with the following information:

- Teenagers listen to their music four to six hours per day for a total of 10,000 hours between grades seven and twelve.
- Of all violent crimes, 70 percent are committed by youths under the age of seventeen.
- Teenage suicide has increased by 300 percent since 1955.
- U.S. teenage pregnancy rates are the highest in the world.[146]

When PMRC failed to reach an agreement with the record industry, congressional hearings were held on a proposed bill to require labeling on records. Susan Baker and Tipper Gore testified, as did musicians Frank Zappa, former member of the Mothers of Invention, and Dee Snider of Twisted Sister. Zappa stated, "Putting labels on albums is the equivalent of treating dandruff by decapitation."[147]

Though nothing came of the hearings, by 1990 bills were pending in thirty-five state legislatures to require labeling of records. PMRC backed state groups lobbying for the legislation.[148] In Arizona, a reporter for *New Times* asked a sponsor of a labeling bill, Senator Jan Brewer, to read some of the objectionable lyrics. The reporter recorded the reading, set it to music, and played the tape over the speakers in the Capitol.[149]

In May 1990, with the state legislative debates on the label requirements still in progress, the Recording Industry Association of America introduced a uniform label

---

[146] William A. Henry, "Did the Music Say Do It?" Time, July 30, 1990, p. 65.
[147] "Musicians Mock Senators' Wives at Hearing," Mesa Tribune, September 20, 1995, p. A4.
[148] "Record Firm to Back Stores with Legal Aid," Mesa Tribune, June 5, 1990, p. A2.
[149] Ed Foster, "Music-Label Bill Shelved," Arizona Republic, March 24, 1990, p. A1.

for albums with explicit lyrics and expressed hope that its voluntary use by industry members would halt the passage of legislation.[150] The black-and-white label appears in the lower right-hand corner of the album and reads: "Parental Advisory—Explicit Lyrics."[151] The label is to be used on albums with lyrics relating to sex, violence, suicide, drug abuse, bigotry, or satanic worship. Use of the label is the decision of the record company and the artist.[152]

The PMRC and the National Parent and Teacher Association endorsed the warning system and asked state legislators to consider dropping proposed label legislation.[153]

Controversy continued to surround rock music lyrics. In the summer of 1990, parents of a teenager who committed suicide sued the rock group Judas Priest, alleging that its lyrics resulted in murderous mind control and the death of their son.[154] Their subliminal persuasion argument was unsuccessful.[155]

By 1995, the record industry's then ten-year-old warning label program was reviewed with the conclusion that parents don't know what the explicit-lyrics labels are.[156] A meeting between the Recording Industry Association of America and the National Association of Recording Merchandisers resulted in new plans to help the system work better.[157] The provisions included:

- Display signs in stores explaining the "Parental Advisory Explicit Lyrics" logo.[158]
- Ensure that record companies use the correct size (1-inch by ½-inch) and placement (lower right) on the record's permanent packaging.
- Alert reviewers of each record's sticker status.
- Encourage inclusion of a record's warning label in ads and promotional materials.

The attention to gangsta rap music also resulted in increased attention to lyrics. Recording company MCA was targeted in 1996 for marketing "death and degradation." MCA refused to make changes other than complying with warning labels and called Mr. William Bennett, a former secretary of education and author, a "warden of morality." Wal-Mart refused to stock explicit lyric music.

In late November 1997, the Senate began exploring the effects of music on children. One parent testified that his 15-year-old son committed suicide after listening to the Marilyn Manson album, *Antichrist Superstar*.

The issues of rock music, lyrics, and artists' rights had its usual cycle of relative quiet between 1997 and 2000. However, during the presidential election of 2000, the issues again surfaced because Mr. Gore was running for president and his wife Tipper again was in the news along with the issues that concerned her. In addition, George W. Bush chose Dick Cheney as his running mate. Mr. Cheney is married to Dr. Lynne

---

[150] "Warning: Rock Music Ahead," Time, May 21, 1990, p. 69.

[151] Robert M. Andrews, "Records Get Uniform Warning Tag," Arizona Republic, May 10, 1990, p. A1.

[152] Carrie White, "Rating Rock Music," Mesa Tribune, December 12, 1995, p. D1.

[153] "Record Firm to Back Stores with Legal Aid," p. A2.

[154] David Stout, "Senate Hearing Is Told Lyrics Led to Suicide," The New York Times, November 7, 1997, p. A1.

[155] Henry, "Did the Music Say Do It?" p. 65.

[156] Edna Gundersen, "Explicit Lyrics Warning Just Aren't Sticking," USA Today, October 25, 1995, p. 1D.

[157] Julia Malone, "Washington Wives Use Influence to Target Sex, Drugs in Rock Music," Christian Science Monitor, August 23, 1995, pp. 1, 36.

[158] "MCA 'Peddling Filth,' Critics Say," Arizona Republic, December 11, 1996, p. A7.

Cheney, who was the head of the Council on Humanities for Presidents Reagan and Bush, holds a PhD in literature, and is a resident scholar at the American Enterprise Institute.

During the presidential campaign of 2000, both Mrs. Cheney and Mrs. Gore became vocal about the lyrics of rock star Eminem. Eminem released his "The Marshall Mathers LP," which became the fastest-selling release ever, selling 5.2 million copies in two months. The album sold 8 million copies in nine months.[159] Mrs. Cheney stunned Congress when she read lyrics from Eminem's song, most too crude to reproduce here, but which included phrases such as:

Beat your bitches [sic] ass while your kids stare in silence

Went up inside the First National Bank broke, and left rich

Walking bio-hazard causing wreckage

His lyrics were described by various critics and commentators:

"Vile and full of frightening calls to violence." Jim Fouratt, *Billboard*

"In the hands of a more capable artist (say, Frank Zappa or Richard Pryor), this vitriol might be taken to such an extreme to make it a subversive farce; in Em's ego-fueled tirade, it's merely sickeningly offensive . . . about as funny as kiddie porn . . ." *Sonic Net.com*

"The first great pop record of the 21st Century . . . A-minus for artistry, D-plus for moral responsibility." *Entertainment Weekly*

"Crude, hostile, bigoted lyrics." Michael Medved, *USA Today*[160]

....

Discussion Questions

1. What are the ethical issues in the production of songs with explicit lyrics?

2. Will voluntary regulation work for the recording industry?

3. If you were a record producer, would your company sign artists who sing explicit lyrics?

4. If you were a record producer, would you feel an obligation to do more than put a warning label on albums with explicit lyrics?

5. You have just been informed that a teenager committed suicide while listening to the music of one of the artists your company produces. The music suggested suicide as an alternative to unhappiness. Would you feel morally responsible for the suicide? Should the artist feel morally responsible?

6. Does the reemergence of Eminem establish that rock music lyrics will always be an issue? Is there a danger that the bar is lowered with each discussion? For example, in this edition of the book, the Eminem lyrics are simply too crude to include whereas the lyrics from the last round could be included. Is this decline evidence of a decline in the social responsibility of record companies and artists?

[159] Edna Gundersen, "Eminem: What's With This Guy?" USA Today, July 27, 2000, p. 1D.
[160] Mim Udovitch, "Visible Man," New York Times Magazine, February 18, 2001, pp. 9–10.

CASE 9.13

Stem-Cell Research

During the summer of 2001, there was extensive debate over stem-cell research because President George W. Bush was faced with the decision of whether to allow federal funding for the extraction of stem cells from human embryos.

Stem-cell research has strong advocates in the medical and scientific community because of their belief that the research holds great potential for cures for Alzheimer's disease, cancer, spinal cord injuries, Parkinson's, diabetes, and a range of other related illnesses.[161] The advocates had strong support from Mrs. Nancy Reagan, wife of President Ronald Reagan, who had suffered from Alzheimer's for nearly a decade, and Christopher Reeve, a Hollywood actor with a spinal cord injury. Ron Reagan, Mr. Reagan's son, spoke at the Democrat National Convention in 2004 urging the delegates to support embryonic stem-cell research and to vote for John Kerry for president to ensure that the research developed with federal funding.

However, stem-cell research has its strong opponents among those who believe that life begins at conception and that the "harvesting" of stem cells from embryos is the taking of life, and that encouraging such research is likely to result in the creation of human embryos for purposes of harvesting the cells. These opponents tout adult stem-cell research as an alternative that has been pursued with some success and a solution that avoids what they see as a moral dilemma. They also fear the likelihood of the slippery slope to cloning.[162] Indeed, the House voted to ban human cloning during this time period because of concerns that any federal funding that would be approved might lead to further experimentation.[163] Richard M. Doerflinger, of the U.S. Conference of Catholic Bishops, has called the research "grotesque," and said, "Those who have become accustomed to destroying 'spare' embryos for research now think nothing of taking the next horrible step, creating human life for the purpose of destroying it."[164]

During the time of the debate, the media revealed that the Jones Institute, a private fertility clinic in Norfolk, Virginia, was mixing eggs and sperm to create human embryos.[165]

Mr. Bush, as a compromise position on a hotly debated issue, approved limited federal funding for lines of research on stem cells that were already "harvested." His reasoning was that the cells should not be thrown away.

While the public continued its debate, biotech businesses were gearing up for what they felt would be the new direction for medical research and treatment. For example, Advanced Cell Technology, Inc. began acquiring eggs from female donors for purposes

---

[161] Robert P. George, "Don't Destroy Human Life," The Wall Street Journal, July 30, 2001, p. A16.

[162] David Baltimore, "Don't Impede Medical Progress," The Wall Street Journal, July 30, 2001, p. A16.

[163] Sheryl Gay Stolberg, "House Backs Ban on Human Cloning for Any Objective," The New York Times, August 1, 2001, pp. A1, A11.

[164] Laurie McGinley, "Nancy Reagan Urges GOP to Back Stem-Cell Research," The Wall Street Journal, July 12, 2001, p. B2.

[165] Sheryl Gay Stolberg, "Bioethicists Find Themselves the Ones Being Scrutinized," The New York Times, August 2, 2001, pp. A1, A14.

of future research.[166] Later in 2001, Advanced Cell Technology announced that it has successfully cloned a human embryo.[167]

Universities such as Georgetown and Michigan, with extensive cancer research programs, stand to benefit substantially from federal research dollars. Upon President Bush's announcement of his partial approval, biotech stocks soared.

Discussion Questions

1. Is it ethical for the Jones Institute to create embryos? What of Advanced Cell Technology's cloning?

2. One bioethicist has questioned the role of bioethicists in the debate, raising the question, "Are we being ethical even as we say what is ethical?" What if they are funded by hospitals, biotech companies, and pharmaceutical firms in their research or at their colleges and universities?

3. Is stem-cell research a moral issue that breaks down along religious lines or are there implications for each side's position?

4. Pope John Paul II, believed to suffer from Parkinson's, has taken a strong position against stem-cell research and indicated, "The end never justifies the means."[168] What does he mean? Are businesses using this rationalization?

5. Would you work for a company that creates human embryos? That conducts stem-cell research? Why or why not? Be sure to refer to Unit 8 for a sample of a shareholder proposal on embryonic stem-cell research.

[166] "Cloning of Embryos for Research Raises Ethics Questions," The Wall Street Journal, July 12, 2001, p. B2.

[167] Sheryl Gay Stolberg, "Cloning Executive Presses Senate," The New York Times, December 5, 2001, p. A22.

[168] Robert A. Sirico, "No Compromise on Stem Cells," The Wall Street Journal, July 11, 2001, p. A16.

10

Business and Government

BUSINESSES ARE REGULATED BY GOVERNMENT AGENCIES, but they also provide goods and services to those same agencies. Unique ethical dilemmas arise on both sides when the private and public sectors cross.

> "I want a society that is based on truth. That means no longer hiding what we
> used to hide."
> —BORIS YELTSIN

> Dishonesty by government officials and employees not only costs us money, it
> undermines our faith in their integrity and that of our public institutions.
> Ethical breaches by government employees have far-reaching effects because
> they are so public.
> —MICHAEL JOSEPHSON

10^A

Government Employees

CASE 10.1

A Club in My Name

The Keds Corporation paid $7.2 million to the fifty state attorneys general to settle a complaint that the shoemaker had engaged in price fixing involving several lines of Keds' girls and womens shoes. The attorneys general each received a portion of the $7.2 million and had agreed to give the money to charities. Most donated the funds to Boys and Girls Clubs in their states.

Arizona's attorney general, Grant Woods, donated his state's share, $85,500, to the Mesa Boys and Girls Club, which used the money to help build a $3 million clubhouse that it then named after Woods.

A state representative noted:

It is a very good cause and I support the Boys and Girls Club, but that is not the point. The money is public money. It is not [Woods's] money.

My point is that no agency or director should be able to direct money to any specific personal cause or for personal use.[1]

Discussion Questions

1. What issues of propriety are raised?

2. Is it bad form to raise ethical issues when all the money went to charity?

3. How could the state representative's reaction have been anticipated?

[1] Kirk Mitchell, "Mesa Club Got Funds," Mesa Tribune, January 7, 1995, pp. A1, A6.

CASE 10.2

The Fireman and His Family

Robert "Hoot" Gibson served with the Phoenix Fire Department for nearly four decades. He was serving as deputy chief when he retired immediately after a four-month investigation revealed the following:

- Holiday pay of $5,000 to employees who had not actually worked those holidays;
- Three employees were permitted to store their pontoon boat at a city property;
- Design 10, a company owned by Gibson's wife and three children, had the contract for clothing sales to the fire department;
- Gibson's son was hired to open the department's print shop; and
- Relatives of Gibson and other employees were hired as temporary employees without going through standard hiring procedures.[2]

Discussion Questions

1. What ethical breaches could you see in this conduct?

2. What tests could have been applied to prevent these decisions from being made?

CASE 10.3

Commodities, Conflicts, and Clintons

In October 1978, Hillary Rodham Clinton, wife of then-attorney general of Arkansas and gubernatorial candidate William Jefferson Clinton, opened a margin account with a $1,000 investment at Refco, a commodities brokerage firm. Commodities market regulators had disciplined Robert L. "Red" Bone, Mrs. Clinton's chief broker at Refco, for his practice of allocating trades among his customers only after learning whether the actual trades made were positive or negative.[3]

Mrs. Clinton was given advice on her trades by James B. Blair, corporate counsel for Tyson Foods, Inc., which is the nation's largest producer of frozen chicken patties and pieces for grocery market sales and fast food franchises.[4] Like any poultry processor, Tyson is subject to strict federal and state regulation. Don Tyson, then-CEO of Tyson Foods, contributed to Mr. Clinton's campaigns for public office. Mr. Blair has stated that Mrs. Clinton alone decided the size of her commodities trades but that they discussed whether her trades should be short or long.

[2] Chris Fiscus, "Key Official Forced to Retire," Arizona Republic, October 18, 1996, pp. A1, A12.
[3] Michael K. Frisby and Bruce Ingersoll, "First Lady Turned $1,000 Investment Into a $98,000 Profit, Records Show," The Wall Street Journal, March 30, 1994, p. A1.
[4] "Hillary in the Pits," The Wall Street Journal, March 30, 1994, p. A18.

Between October 1978 and October 1979, Mrs. Clinton's $1,000 investment grew as follows:

Day 1—First Trade—profit of $5,300
October 1978—December 31, 1978—$49,069—profits
$22,548—losses
$26,541—net profit
January 1979—July 1979— $109,600—profits
$36,600—losses
$72,996—net profit[5]

After Mr. Clinton was elected governor of Arkansas in November 1978, he appointed several Tyson executives to state government positions, and Tyson received favorable regulatory decisions on several actions pending in state agencies. Tyson awarded its outside legal work to the Rose Law Firm in Little Rock, where Mrs. Clinton was a partner.[6] A Tyson spokesman has stated, "There is absolutely no evidence that Jim Blair's relationship with Bill or Hillary Clinton had any impact on our treatment."[7]

Commented a commodities trader: "The idea that Mrs. Clinton could turn $1,000 into $100,000 trading a cross-section of markets such as cattle, soybeans, sugar, hogs, copper and lumber just isn't believable. To make 100 times your money is possible, but it's difficult to understand how a newcomer could do it. I don't care who is advising her. It just isn't very likely."[8]

In 1992, Mr. Clinton was elected president of the United States. For more information on the role of Tyson at the federal government level following Mr. Clinton's election, see Case 10.4.

··

Discussion Questions

1. Did Mr. Blair have a conflict of interest in providing Mrs. Clinton with assistance on her trades?

2. Did Mrs. Clinton have a conflict of interest in accepting Mr. Blair's assistance on the trades?

3. Is there evidence of a quid pro quo?

4. Did Mr. Clinton have a conflict of interest?

5. Did Tyson's employment of the Rose Law Firm as outside counsel constitute a conflict of interest?

6. Evaluate all these decisions using the front-page-of-the-newspaper test.

7. What questions from Laura Nash's analysis provide insight into the ethical issues here?

8. Is the Tyson spokesperson's statement about there being no evidence of Mr. Blair's conduct having any influence relevant in determining whether a conflict of interest existed?

[5] Frisby and Ingersoll, "First Lady Turned $1,000 Investment Into a $98,000 Profit, Records Show," p. A1.
[6] "O Tempora! O Mores!" The Wall Street Journal, March 21, 1994, p. A18.
[7] Bruce Ingersoll, "Agriculture Chief's Handling of Chicken Industry Revives Questions About Clinton's Ties to Tyson," The Wall Street Journal, March 17, 1994, p. A16.
[8] Frisby and Ingersoll, "First Lady Turned $1,000 Investment Into a $98,000 Profit, Records Show," p. A1.

The Secretary of Agriculture, Chicken Processors, and Football Skybox Seats

Former President Bill Clinton appointed Mike Espy as Secretary of Agriculture in 1993. Mr. Espy accepted from Tyson Foods, Inc., the world's largest producer of fresh and processed poultry products, a ride on a Tyson corporate jet, free lodging at a lakeside cabin owned by Tyson, and seats in Tyson's skybox at a Dallas Cowboys/New York Giants playoff game. Later, a car paid for by the company took Mr. Espy and his friend, Pat Dempsey, shopping and then to the airport for the return trip to Washington.

Mr. Espy went to the 1994 Super Bowl at government expense, saying he made the trip because Smokey the Bear was being honored in public service announcements at the game. In addition, Mr. Espy's girlfriend, Pat Dempsey, received a $1,200 college scholarship from Tyson Foods.[9] At the time, Tyson and other regulators were fighting proposed Department of Agriculture guidelines (ultimately not implemented for poultry processors and withdrawn for other meat processors) that would have imposed a "zero tolerance" on the presence of fecal matter during processing. Tyson Foods also provided lodging at its management center in Russellville, Arkansas, to Mr. Espy and Pat Dempsey, while Mr. Espy was in the state to speak before the Arkansas Poultry Federation. A Tyson plane flew them back to Washington. Mr. Espy did reimburse Tyson for the cost of a first-class ticket from Washington, D.C., to Russellville and he also paid back the value of all the other flights and gifts he received from Tyson and others he regulated. These paybacks for flights and gifts such as luggage, limousine rides, and games brought the total of the benefits Mr. Espy received to $33,228.

As a former member of Congress, Mr. Espy felt the benefits he had accepted were so small in terms of monetary value that his accepting them was not an issue. However, public reaction to Mr. Espy's relationship with Tyson, despite the paybacks, was so intense that he was urged by the Clinton White House to resign. He did tender his resignation as Secretary of Agriculture as of December 31, 1994.[10–13] Donald Smaltz was appointed as a special prosecutor to investigate the legality of Mr. Espy's acceptance of the things Tyson had offered and whether he had granted any favors to Tyson in exchange.[14]

As Mr. Smaltz conducted his investigation there was an expanding web of issues involving others beyond Mr. Espy. Ronald Blackley, who became Mr. Espy's chief of staff at the Agriculture Department, has acknowledged that while a congressional aide

[9] Bruce Ingersoll, "Agriculture Chief's Handling of Chicken Industry Revives Questions About Clinton's Ties to Tyson," The Wall Street Journal, March 17, 1994, p. A16.

[10] Richard Benedetto, "Calls Ethics Accusations Distracting," USA Today, October 4, 1994, p. 1A.

[11] Richard Benedetto, "A Personnel Loss for Clinton," USA Today, October 4, 1994, p. 3A.

[12] David Johnston, "Agriculture Chief Quits as Scrutiny of Conduct Grows," The New York Times, October 4, 1994, pp. A1, A11.

[13] Bruce Ingersoll and Jeffrey H. Birnbaum, "Agriculture Secretary Espy Resigns under Pressure from the White House," The Wall Street Journal, October 4, 1994, p. A3.

[14] Bruce Ingersoll, "Espy Inquiry Focuses on Mystery Memo to Learn If Coverup Occurred over Industry Favoritism," The Wall Street Journal, January 16, 1995, p. A14.

to Mr. Espy, he was also on the payroll of farmers seeking support payments from the government. Mr. Blackley did close his consulting business before joining the Agriculture Department. While Mr. Espy was still secretary, Mr. Blackley ordered aides to stop work on proposals for tougher standards for poultry inspections.[15]

Mr. Smaltz also found benefits from other companies. For example, the chief executive of Quaker Oats, William D. Smithburg, gave Mr. Espy a ticket to a June 18, 1993, Chicago Bulls playoff game. The company indicated that it had received a request for the ticket from the Secretary of Agriculture's office.

Because Henry Espy, brother of Mike Espy, ran an unsuccessful campaign to take over his brother's Mississippi congressional seat, Mr. Smaltz examined campaign contributions in that run for office to determine the scope of contributions from agribusinesses to Mr. Espy's brother.[16]

All those who had given or offered Mr. Espy flights, tickets, and other benefits were also investigated. Richard Douglas, a longtime friend of Mr. Espy who was also the chief lobbyist for Sun-Diamond Growers of California, an almond and raisin cooperative based in California, and others were investigated largely because of a lavish birthday party Sun-Diamond paid for for Mr. Espy. The inspector general of the Department of Agriculture also investigated the party to determine whether any of the 150 Sun-Diamond employees in attendance were pressed for contributions to cover the party's cost.[17, 18]

As a result of the special prosecutor's investigation, the following charges, verdicts, and pleas occurred:

Party	Charge	Result
Arthur Schaffer III	Executive of Tyson charged with making illegal gifts	Convicted; judge granted judgment NOV; appellate court reinstated conviction
Sun-Diamond	Charged with making illegal gifts to Mr. Espy and illegal campaign contributions to Henry Espy ($4,000)	Convicted; fine of $1.5 million; conviction reversed; *U.S. v. Sun-Diamond Growers of California*, 526 U.S. 398 (1999), because the criminal statute required proof of some connection between the gifts and a specific pending matter, not a generic desire to seek goodwill

[15] Id.

[16] Jerry Seper, "Payments to Espy Brother Bring Big Fine," Washington Times, January 25, 1998, p. 10.

[17] Bruce Ingersoll, "Former Lobbyist for Sun-Diamond Gets Split Decision in Trial on Aiding Espys," The Wall Street Journal, November 26, 1997, p. B2.

[18] Bruce Ingersoll, "Lobbyist for Tyson Indicted in Espy Probe," The Wall Street Journal, September 18, 1996, p. B5.

Party	Charge	Result
Richard Douglas (lobbyist for Sun-Diamond Growers of California)	Charged with making illegal gifts (luggage plus a trip to the U.S. Open tennis tournament that cost $4,590)	Convicted[19, 20]
	Charged with furnishing Mr. Espy's girlfriend with a $3,100 plane ticket so that she could accompany him to Greece	Jury deadlocked[21]
James Lake (Washington lobbyist for Sun-Diamond)	Wire fraud, violations of Federal Election Campaign Act (a $4,000 gift to Henry Espy)	Convicted[22]
Crop Growers Corp.	Concealment of corporate campaign contributions to Henry Espy ($46,000)	Convicted[23]
American Family Life Assurance Co.	Illegal corporate conduit for campaign contributions to Henry Espy	Civil penalty of $80,000
John Hemmingson (Chairman of Crop Growers Corporation)	Fraud/money laundering; illegal campaign contributions to Henry Espy	Convicted
Tyson Foods, Inc.	Charged with making illegal gifts ($12,000 in tickets, travel, and lodging)	Guilty plea; $4 million in fines plus costs of the investigation ($2 million)[24, 25]
Jack Williams (lobbyist for Tyson Foods)	Four-count indictment for bribery and illegal gifts involving Mr. Espy; two counts for making false statements to regulators	Conviction; reversed on appeal; new trial ordered

[19] Jerry Seper, "Lobbyist for Tyson Indicted," Washington Times, October 12, 1997, p. 7.

[20] Bruce Ingersoll, "Sun-Diamond Gets Fine of $1.5 Million in Espy Affair," The Wall Street Journal, May 14, 1997, p. B7.

[21] Richard Douglas, a lobbyist for Sun Diamond, was found guilty of crimes related to his activities as a lobbyist and the resulting investigation, but the trial court did dismiss the gratuities charges against him. His appeal on these convictions was dismissed. U.S. v. Douglas, 161 F.3d 15 (9th Cir. 1999).

[22] Seper, "Lobbyist for Tyson Indicted," p. 7.

[23] Seper, "Payments to Espy Brother Bring Big Fine," p. 10.

[24] John Godrey, "Tyson Foods Is Fined $6 Million," Washington Times, January 11, 1998, pp. 1, 22.

[25] Jerry Seper, "Tyson Foods Is Named a Target in Espy Investigation," Washington Times, July 6, 1997, p. 8.

Party	Charge	Result
Don Tyson (CEO of Tyson Foods)		Granted immunity for everything except perjury in exchange for his testimony
Henry Espy (Mike Espy's brother)	Defrauding election authorities; false statements in loan applications	Charges dismissed for lack of evidence[26]
Ron Blackley (Mike Espy's chief of staff at Agriculture)	Lying to government authorities	Convicted/sentenced to 27 months in prison
Mike Espy	39-count indictment; accepting and soliciting gifts and favors (including Super Bowl tickets, a crystal bowl gift, and the $1,200 scholarship) from agribusinesses; witness tampering; procuring illegal campaign contributions	9 counts dismissed; pleaded innocent; acquitted on all 30 counts[27]

Mr. Smaltz obtained indictments against twenty individuals as part of his investigation and obtained more than fifteen convictions and $11 million in penalties.[28] However, many called for the elimination of the independent counsel statute that authorized these investigations of officials in the executive branch (the statute has since lapsed).

Mr. Espy now works for one of Mississippi's largest law firms as a trial attorney. He has been active in community service and has been mentioned as a possible candidate for the U.S. Senate as well as for lieutenant governor.

Discussion Questions

1. Is the value of these items an issue in determining whether Mr. Espy acted ethically? In a statement released by Tyson Foods on its indictment was the following sentence: "The company deplores the independent counsel's apparent view that acts of hospitality—consisting of a couple of meals and a football game—can rise to the level of criminal conduct." Is this a sound view for government relations?

2. Does Mr. Espy's reimbursement change the ethical issues?

3. What tests could Mr. Espy have used prior to accepting these items that would have required him to refuse them on ethical grounds?

4. Did Mr. Espy's conduct constitute a conflict of interest?

---

[26] Seper, "Payments to Espy Brother Bring Big Fine," p. 10.

[27] "Espy to Court," USA Today, September 11, 1997, p. 6A.

[28] Terry Eastland, "How Justice Tried to Stop Smaltz," The Wall Street Journal, December 22, 1997, p. A19.

5. Evaluate each of the matters the special prosecutor investigated. Are there ethical breaches regardless of any illegality?

6. Evaluate each of the following statements from an ethical perspective.

   a. "They used Mr. Espy's fondness for sports to get on his good side. He was easy pickings for companies that wanted to slip him something special," said Mr. Espy's attorney, Theodore Wells, in his opening statement in Mr. Espy's trial. Mr. Wells also noted, "He's completely innocent. He did not commit any criminal acts. He's not a crook."

   b. "I recall him saying something like in passing, in a very social setting . . . 'It's a bunch of junk. I'm going to do like I did in Congress.'" Former EPA Administrator, Carol Browner, during her testimony in Mr. Espy's trial when asked if he had ever discussed the Clinton Administration ethics rules with her. Ms. Browner said she could not remember the exact words but testified that Mr. Espy referred to the rules as "a bunch of junk."

   c. In sentencing Ronald Blackley for lying about his sources of income on a disclosure form and to investigators who asked him about the form, Judge Royce Lambreth said, "This court has a duty to send a message to other high government officials that there is a penalty to be paid for making false statements under oath." The judge ignored a sentencing recommendation of probation and sentenced Mr. Blackley to 27 months. An appellate court rejected Mr. Blackley's appeal.

7. Mr. Smaltz spent $11 million on his investigation. Is this amount justified for the size of the gifts? Mr. Smaltz stated when Tyson Foods entered its guilty plea, "Such conduct must continue to invite outrage, never passivity, from those who are regulated, the public, and our lawmakers." Is Mr. Smaltz correct?

Sources

"Asides," *The Wall Street Journal*, December 30, 1997, p. A10.

Behar, Richard, "On Fresh Ground," *Time*, December 26, 1994, p. 111.

Behar, Richard, and Michael Kramer, "Something Smells Fowl," *Time*, October 17, 1994, pp. 42–44.

Cauchon, Dennis, "Millionaire Tyson Stretches Political Limits," *USA Today*, October 5, 1994, p. 4A.

Clark, Kim, "Tough Times for the Chicken King," *Fortune*, October 28, 1996, pp. 88–97.

"Espy Quits with Push from Clinton," *Arizona Republic*, October 4, 1994, pp. A1, A9.

Fields, Gary, and Tom Squiteri, "Tough Term Is Warning in Intern Scandal," *USA Today*, March 19, 1998, p. 1A.

Ingersoll, Bruce, "Espy Case Figure, John Hemmingson, Is Indicted Again," *The Wall Street Journal*, August 7, 1996, p. B2.

Nichols, Bill, "Espy's Once-Promising Political Career Probably Over," *USA Today*, August 28, 1997, p. 4A.

Nichols, Bill, "Ex-Cabinet Member Indicted," *USA Today*, August 28, 1997, p. 1A.

Novak, Viveca, "The Peril of Prosecutorial Passion," *Time*, June 16, 1997, p. 42.

Seper, Jerry, "Illegal Gifts, Cover-Up Charged in Espy Indictment," *Washington Times*, September 7, 1997, p. 11.

Seper, Jerry, "Judge OK's Tyson Foods' Plea Deal," *Washington Times*, January 25, 1998, p. 10.

Stout, David, "Inquiry on Espy Leads to Indictment of Former Chief Aide," *The New York Times*, April 23, 1997, p. A12.

CASE 10.5

The City Council Member with Clout

The following chronology details the actions of Mr. Jim Stapley, a former member of the Mesa City Council.

March 1994

Stapley printed a photograph of him and former President Reagan in a campaign brochure for the City Council primary election. The photo was taken with a cardboard cutout of the former president, however.

April 1996

Councilwoman Joan Payne leaked word of a 15-month-old memo to the city manager in which she accused Stapley of putting his hand on her knee during a helicopter ride and of mailing her pornographic material. She asked the city manager to order Stapley to stay away from her.

In response, Stapley issued his own memo a few days later, saying that Payne touched his knee.

May 1997

Stapley called a Mesa justice of the peace about an eviction case proceeding against his son William. The case was later transferred to another Mesa Justice Court, but the judge said the two actions were not related.

June 1997

Stapley sought to have disorderly conduct charges dropped against Lee Watkins, a friend and political ally. In addition, Stapley sought to have the city prosecutor fired.[29] The council voted to censure Stapley after this incident, minutes after a measure to oust him failed by two votes.

July 1997

Stapley filed a lawsuit against Payne, saying she defamed him in two radio appearances by calling him a "pervert in polyester" and a "racist." The suit was settled in October 1997. Terms were not made public.

---

[29] Art Thomason, "Red Beets Less Luster in Scandal," *Arizona Republic*, June 19, 1997, p. EV1; see also Dan Nowicki, "Council Rebukes Stapley," *Mesa Tribune*, June 19, 1997, pp. A1, A4.

August 1997

Stapley possibly violated his censure by placing several calls to Mesa Firefighters Union President Chris Medrea about a $1,000 donation the union made to Payne's legal defense fund, established after Stapley sued her for defamation. Stapley said he feels he didn't violate the censure because he was contacting Medrea in his role with the union, not as a city firefighter.

October 1997

A memo surfaced in which Stapley was accused of impersonating a Pinal County sheriff's detective at a Florence courthouse in February 1995. Police records say Stapley flashed a police badge and said he was a detective when he visited the clerk's office at Pinal County Superior Court. He was looking for a search warrant affidavit on a narcotics case involving his son, Kenneth.

Stapley circulated petitions at a meeting attended by city employees. The action may have been illegal, since city policy forbids candidates to ask city employees to sign petitions in city buildings on city time.

Following the October 1997 impersonation, Mr. Stapley resigned.[30]

Discussion Questions

1. What ethical breaches do you feel occurred?

2. What impact would Mr. Stapley's conduct have on employees?

3. Would Mr. Stapley's involvement affect the wheels of justice?

4. Do you think employees would be comfortable complaining?

CASE 10.6

IRS Employees and Sensitive Data

In 1997, the IRS disciplined hundreds of employees for using agency computers and records to browse through the tax records of friends, relatives, and celebrities. The IRS fired 23 employees, disciplined 349, and provided counseling for 472.

During 1996 and 1997, the IRS investigated 1,515 cases of "snooping" among its 102,000 employees. Half of the employees have computer access to taxpayer returns.

Those employees who were counseled said they did not believe that what they did was wrong nor that there would be any sanctions for doing it. The law is not violated by "snooping;" it is violated only if the information is disclosed to others or used for personal purposes. However, in a case that reached the appellate level just as the IRS employees were disciplined, a court reached a different conclusion about their discipline.

---

[30] Chris Moeser, "Stapley Quits Mesa Council," Mesa Tribune, *November 1, 1997, p. A1.*

Richard Czubinski, an IRS employee in its Boston office, was a member of the IRS's Taxpayer Services Division and had full access to taxpayer files. He could retrieve taxpayer information on anyone in the United States who has filed a federal income tax return.

During lunch hours and breaks, Czubinski retrieved the tax returns of the following:

- An assistant district attorney in Boston who was prosecuting Czubinski's father
- A woman he was dating
- David Duke (at the time he was a presidential candidate)

Czubinski was charged with violations of the Computer Fraud and Abuse Act and convicted. The appellate court held that because he did not use the information to make up any dossiers, disclose the information to anyone, or even use the information beyond just looking at it, he had not violated the federal laws. The court added the following cautionary note at the end of its opinion:

> We add a cautionary note. The broad language of the mail and wire fraud statutes are [sic] both their blessing and their curse. They can address new forms of serious crime that fail to fall within more specific legislation. On the other hand, they might be used to prosecute kinds of behavior that, albeit offensive to the morals or aesthetics of federal prosecutors, cannot reasonably be expected by the instigators to form the basis of a federal felony. The case at bar falls within the latter category. Also discomforting is the prosecution's insistence, before trial, on the admission of inflammatory evidence regarding the defendant's membership in white supremacist groups purportedly as a means to prove a scheme to defraud, when, on appeal, it argues that unauthorized access in itself is a sufficient ground for conviction on all counts. Finally, we caution that the wire fraud statute must not serve as a vehicle for prosecuting only those citizens whose views run against the tide, no matter how incorrect or uncivilized such views are.[31]

Discussion Questions

1. What is so bad about snooping?

2. Should the law be the only standard?

3. What if the snooping was used only for clues to help in litigation?

4. What distinction does the most recent decision noted make between criminal violations, the law, and ethics?

CASE 10.7

The Generous and Profitable Foundation Board

Peggie Jean Gambarana was a real estate investor in the Las Vegas area whose substantial holdings enabled her to become one of the community's most generous philanthropists. In 1992, upon her death, her will provided that $1.5 million in cash

---

[31] U.S. v. Czubinski, *106 F.3d 1069 (1st Cir. 1997)*.

and property be given to the University of Nevada at Las Vegas Foundation to benefit the James R. Dickinson Library.

The $1.5 million testate donation, the largest ever for the library, included $350,000 in cash, three properties, and a leasehold interest in a souvenir shop located at Fourth and Fremont Streets in downtown Las Vegas. However, by the time the funds and properties were converted to permanent library endowments, their value had been reduced by one third. The reduction in value was the result of three real estate deals that involved members of the foundation.

The foundation sold all three donated properties below their appraised values. The Gambarana family home was sold to Arthur Nathan, who was moving from New Jersey to become the human resources director for the Mirage Hotel. The UNLV Foundation's chairwoman, Elaine Wynn, was an executive in Mirage Resorts, Inc., and her husband, Steve Wynn, was the corporation's chairman. Nathan purchased the home, which had an appraised value of $170,000, for $157,500. Golden Nugget, Inc., which later became Mirage Resorts, Inc., loaned Nathan the funds for the purchase. Wynn said she was not involved in the negotiations:

> It's possible for me to represent both interests without . . . creating a conflict of interest in this, especially since I didn't benefit personally nor did Mr. Nathan benefit personally.[32]

Ms. Wynn signed the sale documents for the property transaction.

The second property the foundation sold was appraised at $270,000 and sold for $206,628. The third property was appraised at $490,000 and sold for $320,000. After paying real estate commissions, the foundation received $296,200 from the sales. The commissions were paid to Madison Graves, a candidate for university regent in 1992 and a longtime friend of the foundation's director, Lyle Rivera. Rivera was also a broker for Graves' Flamingo Realty, the agency that handled the sales. Rivera saw no conflict of interest because Graves probably lost money on the sales, given the time it took to sell the property:

> We always ask them to do it at a lesser commission than standard so most of these guys don't relish doing business with the foundation.[33]

One of the purchasers of the third property was Shelli Lowe, who had also performed the appraisal on the property. Finally, with regard to the Las Vegas souvenir shop, the foundation lost $235,000 because it failed to exercise its option to renew the lease on the shop.

....

Discussion Questions

1. Was there a conflict of interest in the Nathan sale?

2. How would you have handled the Nathan sale differently?

3. Was there a conflict in having Madison Graves as the listing broker for the property appraised at $490,000?

---

[32] John Gallant, "UNLV's Gift Fails to Meet Projections," Las Vegas Review Journal, June 26, 1992, pp. 1A, 3A.
[33] Id.

4. Does a conflict exist when an appraiser purchases a property for which she has furnished the appraisal?

5. Did the foundation manage the funds as if they were its personal funds? Is this right or wrong?

6. What things would you have done differently if you had been a foundation member responsible for managing the gift?

7. Would disclosure forms and processes help the foundation's image?

CASE 10.8
....

One Foot in Government and the Other in the Private Sector

Richard N. Perle is a former chair of the Defense Policy Board, a position appointed by the Secretary of Defense. The Defense Policy Board consists of civilian experts from the private sector on military, security, and defense issues. At the time of Mr. Perle's appointment, the Secretary of Defense was Donald H. Rumsfeld. Following his appointment to the board, Mr. Perle was hired by Global Crossing, a telecommunications company in Chapter 11 bankruptcy, to work with the Defense Department because the Department opposes the sale of Global Crossing to Hutchison Whampoa and Singapore Technology, two foreign companies. Mr. Perle's agreement with Global Crossing provided that he was to be paid $725,000 for his work, plus an additional $600,000 if the Defense Department approved the sale. The Defense Department opposed the sale because it was using the Global Crossing fiberoptic network for its telecommunications needs, and the sale would put that network under Chinese control.

Mr. Perle filed an affidavit in the review process for the FBI and Defense Department (whose approvals are required) with the following language:

> As the chairman of the Defense Policy Board, I have a unique perspective on and intimate knowledge of the national defense and security issues that will be raised by the CFIUS review process that is not and could not be available to the other CFIUS professionals. [CFIUS is the Committee on Foreign Investment in the United States. It consists of representatives from the Defense Department and other agencies. CFIUS has the authority to block foreign acquisitions.][34]

When asked about his dual role, Mr. Perle said:

> I've abided by the rules. The question, I think, is have I recommended anything to the secretary or discussed this with the secretary, and I haven't. The alternative is if you are on the board, you can't have any action before the Defense Department. That isn't the rule. If that were the rule, I'd have to make a choice between being on an unpaid advisory board and my business.[35]

[34] Stephen Labaton, "Pentagon Adviser Is Also Advising Global Crossing," The New York Times, March 21, 2003, pp. C1, C2.
[35] Id., p. C2.

Objections to his service resulted in his resignation as chair of the Defense Policy Board in March 2003. In his letter of resignation, Mr. Perle indicated he would accept no compensation from Global Crossing for his work for them in order to avoid any questions about his role with the board. When questions from the press continued to hound him, Mr. Perle resigned from the board altogether in February 2004.

Discussion Questions

1. What ethical issue exists in Mr. Perle's conduct?

2. Mr. Perle is known as one of the country's foremost experts on war, weapons, and national security and defense. Does that change any of the issues?

3. What do we learn about dual relationships in government and business?

10B

Government Contracts

The existence of unlimited sources of funds often is used to justify behavior. In government contracts, the supply of funds seems endless, and the competition is stiff. These benefits and pressures often cause poor resolutions of ethical dilemmas. Pay particular attention to the impact of media coverage in the cases.

CASE 10.9

Stanford University and Government Overhead Payments

Included in government research grants to universities are indirect cost payments designed to compensate for the researchers' use of the schools' facilities.

Stanford University received approximately $240 million in federal research funds annually. About $75 million went to actual research, while Stanford billed the federal government $85 million, or 20 percent of its operating budget, for its overhead.[36] The rest of the research funds went toward employee benefits. An audit of Stanford's research program in 1990 by U.S. Navy accountant Paul Biddle revealed that the school billed the government $3,000 for a cedar-lined closet in president Donald Kennedy's home (Hoover House), $2,000 for flowers, $2,500 for refurbishing a grand piano, $7,000 for bedsheets and table linens, $4,000 for a reception for trustees following Kennedy's 1987 wedding, and $184,000 for depreciation for a seventy-two-foot yacht as part of the indirect costs for federally funded research.[37]

In response to the audit, Stanford withdrew requests for reimbursement totaling $1.35 million as unallowable and inappropriate costs. Stanford's federal funds were cut by $18 million per year.[38, 39]

[36] Colleen Cordes, "Universities Review Overhead Charges; Some Alter Policies on President's Home," Chronicle of Higher Education, April 3, 1991, p. A1.

[37] Maria Shao, "The Cracks in Stanford's Ivory Tower," Business Week, March 11, 1991, pp. 64–65.

[38] Gary McWilliams, "Less Gas for the Bunsen Burners," Business Week, May 20, 1991, pp. 124–126.

[39] Courtney Leatherman, "Stanford's Shift in Direction," Chronicle of Higher Education, September 7, 1994, p. A29.

Kennedy issued the following statements as the funding crisis evolved:

December 18, 1990: What was intended as government policy to build the capacity of universities through reimbursement of indirect costs leads to payments that are all too easily misunderstood.

Therefore, we will be reexamining our policies in an effort to avoid any confusion that might result.

At the same time, it is important to recognize that the items currently questioned, taken together, have an insignificant impact on Stanford's indirect-cost rate. . . .

Moreover, Stanford routinely charges the government less than our full indirect costs precisely to allow for errors and disallowances.

—From a university statement

January 14, 1991: We certainly ought to prune anything that isn't allowable—there isn't any question about that. But we're extending that examination to things that, although we believe are perfectly allowable, don't strike people as reasonable.

I don't care whether it's flowers, or dinners and receptions, or whether it's washing the table linen after it's been used, or buying an antique here or there, or refinishing a piano when its finish gets crappy, or repairing a closet and refinishing it—all those are investments in a university facility that serves a whole array of functions.

—From an interview with the Stanford Daily

January 23, 1991: Because acute public attention on these items threatens to overshadow the more important and fundamental issue of the support of federally sponsored research, Stanford is voluntarily withdrawing all general administration costs for operation of Hoover House claimed for the fiscal years since 1981. For those same years, we are also voluntarily withdrawing all such costs claimed for the operations of two other university-owned facilities.

—From a university statement

February 19, 1991: I am troubled by costs that are perfectly appropriate as university expenditures and lawful under the government rules but I believe ought not be charged to the taxpayer. I should have been more alert to this policy issue, and I should have insisted on more intensive review of these transactions.

—From remarks to alumni

March 23, 1991: Our obligation is not to do all the law permits, but to do what is right. Technical legality is not the guiding principle. Even in matters as arcane as government cost accounting, we must figure out what is appropriate and act accordingly. Over the years, we have not hesitated to reject numerous lawful and attractive business proposals, gifts, and even federal grants because they came with conditions we thought would be inappropriate for Stanford. Yet, with respect to indirect-cost recovery, we pursued what was permissible under the rules, without applying our customary standard of what is proper. . . .

The expenses for Hoover House—antique furniture, flowers, cedar closets—should have been excluded, and they weren't. That the amounts involved were relatively small is fortunate, but it doesn't excuse us. In our testimony before the subcommittee I did deal with this issue, but I obviously wasn't clear enough. I explained that we were removing Hoover House and some similar accounts from the cost pools that drew indirect-cost recovery because they plainly included inappropriate items. What came out in the papers was that Stanford removed the costs because it was forced to, not because it was wrong. . . . That is not so. To repeat, the allocation of these expenses to indirect-cost pools is inappropriate, regardless of its propriety under the law.

—*From remarks to alumni*[40]

By July 1991, Kennedy announced his resignation, effective August 1992, stating, "It is very difficult . . . for a person identified with a problem to be a spokesman for its solution."[41] Gerhard Casper, who was hired as Stanford's new president, said, "I just want this to remain one of the great universities in the world. I ask that we question what we are doing every day." Kennedy remains at Stanford, teaching biology.[42]

Stanford's donations declined that year; 1999 was the first time it saw an uptick in its donations since the time of this government overhead issue.[43]

Ultimately Stanford settled with the federal government for $1.3 million, a small percentage of the $185 million of alleged overcharges that appeared in Biddle's report. The federal government also concluded that there was no fraud by Stanford. Biddle filed suit, seeking recovery of the statutory whistleblower fee of 10 percent for finding the submitted costs that the government ultimately recovered from Stanford. His suit was dismissed.

Discussion Questions

1. Did Kennedy's ethics evolve during the crisis? Contrast his March 23, 1991, ethical posture with his December 18, 1990, assessment.

2. Is legal behavior always ethical behavior?

3. Do Casper's remarks reflect an ethical formula for Stanford's operations?

4. In a 2000 interview for an internal Stanford publication, Kennedy offered the following when asked about research and cost issues as he assumed the editorship of *Science*:

One of the factors in the explosive growth of Stanford during the '60s and continuing into the '70s and '80s was the availability of federal funding for research. The policy behind that support was always that the government benefited from basic research because it eventually produced findings that could be converted to human service in one way or another and so the government continually built that capacity and built that capacity in universities. Its policy was that it would pay the full cost of research, including not only the direct cost that could be associated with particular programs but the indirect costs that had to be made by the university in order to stay in the business of doing sponsored research.

[40] Karen Grassmuch, "What Happened at Stanford: Key Mistakes at Crucial Times in a Battle with the Government over Research Costs," Chronicle of Higher Education, May 15, 1991, p. A26.

[41] "Embattled Stanford President to Quit," Mesa Tribune, July 30, 1991, p. A6.

[42] Associated Press, "Stanford's Chief Resigns over Billing Controversy," Arizona Republic, July 30, 1991, p. A8.

[43] Leatherman, "Stanford's Shift in Direction," p. A29.

Over time, the percentage of all research funding that was allocated to indirect cost grew. And it grew to a point in the late '80s and early '90s when it seemed to many people, some in Congress and some on this faculty, that it was an unacceptably large percentage and we recognized that though, probably not soon enough, made some efforts to constrain it, but in fact it was high enough to trouble people and it was calculated, the indirect costs were calculated on the basis on a pool accounting mechanism no one in the public understood and indeed few people on the faculty understood. And when Congressman Dingell decided to make that the subject of a very high profile Congressional investigation and made Stanford the subject of it, we had a very, very bad time. And partly it was a bad time because we made some accounting mistakes, partly it was a bad time because it was not difficult at all for Chairman Dingell to make the pool accounting mechanism for indirect costs which were the subject of understandings, clear contractual understandings between the university and the government, sound like a scandal. We took a beating. It was sufficiently bad that after the hearings and during the summer of 1991, it became clear to me that there was so much faculty concern about the ruckus and whether Stanford would continue to be a target for this kind of thing that I decided that if you're part of a problem, you can't be part of a solution and so I resigned. I think that steadied things down considerably. It wasn't any fun to do that. It was not any fun to take a certain amount of newspaper abuse in connection with it. Stanford's recovered nicely. We're still not paid the indirect cost rate I think we are entitled to under articulated government policies, but the sequelae to the whole furor, I think, made it plain to everybody that Stanford hadn't engaged in any wrongdoing.

Flatté: Did you hear anything about the repercussions of cases like Stanford on other universities?

Kennedy: No, I think there were a few people in other institutions who got caught up in the problem later when it was revealed that they had engaged in exactly the same practices we had who did a little finger pointing and said "Well, Stanford was pushing the envelope." But in fact we weren't. Our indirect cost rate was high but it was in a cluster of other high rates, two or three or four other institutions which were comparable or within three or four percentage points. So you can't make the case that we were doing stuff that others weren't also doing.[44]

List the rationalizations you see in this statement. Does he think Stanford did anything unethical?

CASE 10.10

Casino Leases and the County Supervisor

Yvonne Atkinson Gates, the chairperson of the Clark County, Nevada, Commission, an elected office, also operated her own daiquiri business. Many of the new and expanding hotels in Clark County, where Las Vegas is located, have retail space available for shops and restaurants. Ms. Atkinson Gates, as a commissioner, makes decisions on whether proposed hotels and expansions will be approved.

---

[44] *http://becoming.stanford.edu/interview/donaldkennedy.html.*

Ms. Atkinson Gates was alleged to have approached executives from five casinos about leasing space for her daiquiri franchises. Ms. Atkinson Gates acknowledges the contacts but that they "were made in passing and cannot be considered solicitations."[45] She acknowledged actually seeking an arrangement with MGM Grand Resorts.

Sheldon Adelson, the chairperson of Las Vegas Sands, Inc. said, "I was shocked, absolutely shocked that Yvonne would come to me directly. I felt she was pressuring me to agree. And when I didn't, I think she went out of her way to vote against my project."[46] Adelson wanted to build a Sands Venetian Mall, but his proposal was not approved by the commission.

The state Ethics Commission is investigating Ms. Atkinson Gates' conduct with her daiquiri business.

Discussion Questions

1. Is there a conflict in Ms. Atkinson Gates' solicitations?

2. How should she handle the business solicitations?

3. What conclusions did Mr. Adelson draw? Is he justified?

4. Ms. Atkinson Gates says she is a silent partner. Does this status help?

CASE 10.11

Bids, Employees, and Conflicts

The state of Arizona awarded the contract for indemnity insurance for the state's 55,000 employees to Intergroup of Arizona. An investigation by the Attorney General's office found that the Department of Administration, the agency responsible for reviewing bids and awarding contracts, permitted a state employee who is the wife of an Intergroup executive to make key decisions about the insurance bids and the process.[47]

By the time the investigation was completed, the contract had been awarded.

Discussion Questions

1. What problems do you see with the process?

2. Why do you think no one said anything until the investigation was conducted?

3. How will Intergroup fare in the next round of contract bids?

[45] Susan Green, "Official Defines Role in Venture," Las Vegas Review Journal, October 4, 1997, pp. 1A, 2A.
[46] Susan Green, "Official Sought Casino Leases," Las Vegas Review Journal, October 3, 1997, pp. 1A, 2A.
[47] Jodie Snyder, "AG: Insurer Chosen Unfairly," Arizona Republic, August 2, 1991, pp. B1, B2.

CASE 10.12

Government Pricing and Finding a Way around It[48]

George Couto was a marketing manager with Bayer Corporation, the U.S. subsidiary of Bayer A.G., a German-based company. In 1995, Kaiser, the largest HMO in the United States, was demanding a discount for its bulk purchases of Cipro, an antibiotic manufactured by Bayer. Bayer could grant the discount to Kaiser; however, that discount meant that it had to sell at that price to the federal government (under Medicaid regulations).

To avoid having to give the federal government the discount, Couto oversaw the development and sale of a private label Cipro for Kaiser. The drug was manufactured in Connecticut and sold to Kaiser under a private label at a 40 percent discount. Kaiser had indicated it would turn to Johnson & Johnson if it were not given a deep enough discount by Bayer.

The plan was uncovered almost five years later and Bayer agreed to pay $257 million to the federal government, the largest Medicaid fraud settlement to date. Bayer also agreed to a $5.6 million criminal fine.

Couto was the person who led the federal government to Bayer and the plan, and such whistleblowers are entitled to as much as 30 percent of the amount of the penalty. According to his testimony, Couto wrote a letter outlining the private label plan that had been in effect for almost five years after attending an ethics class in which Bayer's CEO indicated that employees should follow not just the letter of the law but also the spirit of the law.

Couto was deposed in the case and admitted his role, but three months after his deposition and five months before Bayer settled the case, Couto (age 39) died of pancreatic cancer. However, despite his misgivings about the private label plan, he did seek to obtain a President's Achievement Award from the CEO of Bayer for his retention of the Kaiser account.

Couto, divorced, was awarded 24 percent of the federal government's share of the fine Bayer paid. His three children are the primary beneficiaries of the $34 million award. Mr. Couto's brother, Mark, has organized an annual golf tournament in Brewster, Massachusetts, in his brother's name with the proceeds going to fight pancreatic cancer.

Discussion Questions

1. Should a participant in the scam to defraud the government be permitted to collect the whistleblower fees?

2. Was what Bayer did a violation of the law or a creative interpretation of the statute?

3. How is this case similar to the Enron case (see Case 6.8)?

[48] Peter Aronson, "A Rogue to Catch a Rogue," National Law Journal, August 18–25, 2003, p. A1.

10^c

Government Responsibilities

How careful must government be with our money? The accountability of government employees for managing funds and resources is a critical area of focus in ethics.

CASE 10.13

Orange County: Derivative Capital of the United States

On December 6, 1994, Orange County, California, filed for bankruptcy protection.[49–51] The chairman of the Orange County Board of Supervisors said the step was necessary to prevent local agencies from withdrawing their funds from the county's investment fund of $7.5 billion, which might force a fire sale of the fund's assets.[52]

The investment pool had substantial holdings in risky financial instruments known as derivatives that would provide returns only if interest rates continued to fall. Interest rates rose, and Orange County had large debts from borrowing to invest in derivatives. As a result, the county could not pay its creditors and its investment pool lost $2.5 billion. The investments had been masterminded by County Treasurer Robert Citron.

Twelve different brokerage houses were left with loans to Orange County that might not be repaid.[53] The announcement of the county's bankruptcy caused the stock market to plunge fifty points. Litigation is pending by school districts and other government entities against the brokers who handled the derivatives sales. Hiring was frozen in the county, and many people with disabilities whose funds were in the Orange County investment pool could not withdraw their money because of the bankruptcy.[54] Mr. Citron and others entered pleas to various charges.

---

[49] "Orange County Seeks Protection under Bankruptcy Law," Mesa Tribune, December 7, 1994, p. A7.

[50] Karen Donovan, "Chapter 9: The Next Page," National Law Journal, December 26, 1994, p. A6.

[51] Sallie Hofmeister, "In Rare Move, California County Files for Bankruptcy Protection," The New York Times, December 7, 1994, pp. C1, C5.

[52] Del Jones, "County Seeks Bankruptcy Protection," USA Today, December 7, 1994, pp. 1C, 2C.

[53] "Orange County Fallout Hits Stocks," Arizona Republic, December 8, 1994, p. C3.

[54] "As Orange County Investments Flop, Kids' Money Is Frozen," Mesa Tribune, December 10, 1994, p. A9.

A report by the California state Bureau of Audits concludes as follows:

The Orange County (county) treasurer is responsible for receiving and keeping safe all funds belonging to the county and other monies deposited with the treasurer. However, we found that the former treasurer pursued an investment strategy that violated the basic principles of prudent investing, which are safety, liquidity, and yield, in that order. In fact, his investment strategies were diametrically opposed to these principles. The former treasurer's investments were unsafe, highly risky, and extremely volatile, and they lacked the liquidity needed to meet the portfolio's objectives. Further, he sacrificed safety and liquidity in a failed strategy to capture higher yields.[55] The former treasurer did this by leveraging the portfolio more than 2.7 times and purchasing highly volatile inverse floaters and other structured securities that comprised more than 40 percent of his investments.[56]

Discussion Questions

1. Should government investment decisions be based on factors different from those used in making private investment decisions?

2. List all the groups of people affected by the losses in Orange County.

3. What impact will Orange County's bankruptcy have on the ability of other government entities to sell their bonds?

4. Would you invest your own money in derivatives?

5. Should Orange County voters and investment pool participants have been given more information on the risk?

6. Should brokers who made the investments be held liable for advising Orange County to purchase unsuitable securities for its funds?

7. One of the recommendations of the Bureau of Audits report done by the state of California was as follows:

   In addition, we recommend that the board of supervisors establish strict rules regarding ethics, conflict of interest, and asset safekeeping for all the county's investment activities, and adopt and approve the treasurer's comprehensive investment policies.[57]

   Why are ethics and conflicts of interest important in preventing this from happening again?

Sources

Coffee, John C., "The Suitability Doctrine Revisited: Can Orange County Sue Its Broker for Recommending the Purchase of Unsuitable Securities for Its Funds?" *National Law Journal*, January 16, 1995, pp. B4, B6.

Craig, David, "Dow Plunges 50 as Investors Skitter," *USA Today*, December 9, 1994, p. 1B.

[55] *David J. Lynch, "How Golden Touch Turned into Crisis," USA Today, December 23, 1994, p. 1B.*
[56] *http://www.bsa.ca.gov/bsa/summaries/94026sum.html.*
[57] Id.

Craig, David, "Orange County Freezes Hiring as Markets Feel the Heat," *USA Today*, December 9, 1994, p. 1A.

Greenwald, John, "The California Wipeout," *Time*, December 19, 1994, p. 55.

Jereski, Laura, "How a Rescue Mission Failed, Just Barely, in Orange County," *The Wall Street Journal*, December 22, 1994, pp. A1, A14.

Jereski, Laura, "Orange County Fund Losses Put at $2.5 Billion," *The Wall Street Journal*, December 12, 1994, pp. A3, A5.

Jereski, Laura, "Who Bears Loss Becomes Critical Orange County Issue," *The Wall Street Journal*, January 10, 1995, p. C1.

Johnson, Kevin, and David J. Lynch, "California County Seeks Court Help on Debt," *USA Today*, December 7, 1994, p. 1A.

Memmott, Mark, "Orange County's Woes Won't Sway Fed's Course," *USA Today*, December 8, 1994, p. 1B.

Stevens, Amy, "Attorneys May Share Blame by Not Disclosing Risk in Orange County," *The Wall Street Journal*, December 16, 1994, p. B3.

Taylor, Jeffrey, "Hard-Charging Broker Draws the Spotlight in Orange County Miss," *The Wall Street Journal*, December 12, 1994, pp. A1, A7.

CASE 10.14

Cars and Conflicts

Maricopa County supervisors, Mary Rose Wilcox and Ed King (elected officials), turned in the county cars that they had been taking home with them. King's chief administrator also turned in his car. County policy is that employees may check out cars but should not drive them home without prior authorization, which is given only for night hearings or activities and next-day trips where distance to a car pick-up at the motor pool makes it time prohibitive.

Their use of vehicles was revealed in a public meeting by another supervisor who said it was "feeding off the taxpayers and sending the wrong message to county employees."[58]

Discussion Questions

1. Mrs. Wilcox apologized and said, "Sometimes, you get so immersed in things that you don't see what's right. I made a mistake, and for that, I'm sorry." What could have helped her see the issue?

2. What operational dangers for government agencies arise when elected officials don't follow the rules?

[58] David Schwartz, "2 Supervisors, Aide Turn in County Cars," *Arizona Republic*, May 4, 1994, pp. B1, B5.

Ethics and Nonprofits

GOOD INTENTIONS ARE NOT NECESSARILY THE SAME AS GOOD ETHICS. In this final segment of the book, we take a look at good intentions gone amuck. These organizations had the goodwill and donations of others but abused that trust, with resulting consequences that had far-reaching effects.

11A

Ethics and Nonprofits

Giving and Spending the United Way

The United Way, which evolved from the local community chests of the 1920s, is a national organization that funnels funding to charities through a payroll-deduction system.

Ninety percent of all charitable payroll deductions in 1991 were for the United Way. This system, however, has been criticized as coercive. Bonuses, for example, were offered for achieving 100 percent employee participation. Betty Beene, president of United Way of Tristate (New York, New Jersey, and Connecticut), commented, "If participation is 100 percent, it means someone has been coerced."[1] Tristate discontinued the bonuses and arm-twisting.

United Way's system of spending also came under fire through the actions of William Aramony, president of the United Way from 1970 to 1992. During his tenure, United Way receipts grew from $787 million in 1970 to $3 billion in 1990. But some of Aramony's effects on the organization were less positive.

In early 1992, the *Washington Post* reported that Aramony:

- Was paid $463,000 per year.
- Flew first class on commercial airlines.
- Spent $20,000 in one year for limousines.
- Used the Concorde for trans-Atlantic flights.[2]

The article also revealed that one of the taxable spin-off companies Aramony had created to provide travel and bulk purchasing for United Way chapters had bought a $430,000 condominium in Manhattan and a $125,000 apartment in Coral Gables, Florida, for his use. Another spin-off had hired Aramony's son, Robert Aramony, as its president.

[1] Susan Garland, "Keeping a Sharper Eye on Those Who Pass the Hat," Business Week, March 16, 1992, p. 39.
[2] As reported in "Ex-executives of United Way Indicted," Arizona Republic, September 14, 1994, p. A6.

When Aramony's expenses and salary became public, Stanley C. Gault, chairman of Goodyear Tire & Rubber Company, asked, "Where was the board? The outside auditors?"[3] Aramony resigned after fifteen chapters of the United Way threatened to withhold their annual dues to the national office.

Said Robert O. Bothwell, executive director of the National Committee for Responsive Philanthropy, "I think it is obscene that he is making that kind of salary and asking people who are making $10,000 a year to give 5 percent of their income."[4]

In August 1992, the United Way board of directors hired Elaine Chao, the Peace Corps director, to replace William Aramony at a salary of $195,000, with no perks.[5] She reduced staff from 275 to 185 and borrowed $1.5 million to compensate for a decline in donations. By 1995, United Way donations had still not returned to their 1991 $3.2 billion. Ms. Chao left the United Way and has served as secretary of labor for the Bush Administration since 2001. Ms. Chao is married to Republican Senator Mitch McConnell of Kentucky.

In September 1994, William Aramony and two other United Way officers, including the chief financial officer, were indicted by a federal grand jury for conspiracy, mail fraud, and tax fraud. The indictment alleged the three officers diverted more than $2.74 million of United Way funds to purchase an apartment in New York City for $383,000, interior decorating for $72,000, a condominium, vacations, and a lifetime pass on American Airlines. In addition, $80,000 of United Way funds were paid to Aramony's girlfriend, a 1986 high school graduate, for consulting, even though she did no work.

On April 3, 1995, Aramony was found guilty of twenty-five counts of fraud, conspiracy, and money laundering. Two other United Way executives were also convicted. Mr. Aramony was sentenced to 84 months in prison (and fined $300,000) and was released in 2004. He lives in Alexandria, Virginia, and United Way executives continue to refer to his tenure and all the problems as "the great unpleasantness."

By April 1998, donation levels were still not completely reinstated, but did increase (up 4.7 percent) for the first time since the 1992 Aramony crisis. Relationships between local chapters and the national organization were often strained and the recent Boy Scouts of America boycott has created additional tension. United Way's donations fell 11 percent since 1991 while overall charitable giving was up 9 percent.

In January 2000, a federal district court judge awarded Mr. Aramony the full value of his deferred compensation plan, or $4.2 million. Judge Shira Scheindlin ruled in favor of Mr. Aramony because she said there was no clause for forfeiting the money if Mr. Aramony committed a felony. Such a so-called "bad boy" clause had been discussed by the board when it was in the process of approving the deferred compensation plan for Mr. Aramony and other United Way executives. However, the "bad boy" clause never made it into the final agreement.[6]

---

[3] Garland, "Keeping a Sharper Eye on Those Who Pass the Hat," p. 39.

[4] Felicity Barringer, "United Way Head Is Forced Out in a Furor over His Lavish Style," The New York Times, February 28, 1992, p. A1.

[5] Desda Moss, "Peace Corps Director to Head United Way," USA Today, August 27, 1992, p. 6A; Sabra Chartrand, "Head of Peace Corps Named United Way President," The New York Times, August 27, 1992, p. A8.

[6] David Cay Johnston, "Ex-United Way Chief Owed $4.2 Million," The New York Times, January 5, 2000, p. C4.

However, Judge Scheindlin also ruled that United Way could withhold $2.02 million of the amount due to cover salary, investigation costs, and interest on those amounts. She did not award Mr. Aramony attorneys' fees for having to bring the suit against United Way to collect his deferred compensation.

Many in the nonprofit field say that the shadow of William Aramony looms over the nonprofit world.

Discussion Questions

1. Was there anything unethical about Aramony's expenditures?

2. Was the board responsible for the expenditures?

3. Is the perception as important as the acts themselves?

4. If Aramony were a CEO of a for-profit firm, would your answers change?

5. What obstacles did Chao face as she assumed the United Way helm?

6. Do you think Mr. Aramony should have asked for his deferred compensation funds?

Sources

Allen, Frank E., and Susan Pulliam, "United Way's Rivals Take Aim at Its Practices," *The Wall Street Journal*, March 6, 1992, pp. B1, B6.

Barringer, Felicity, "Ex-Chief of United Way Vows to Fight Accusations," *The New York Times*, April 10, 1992, p. A13.

Duffy, Michael, "Charity Begins at Home," *Time*, March 9, 1992, p. 48.

"Ex-executives of United Way Indicted," *Arizona Republic*, September 14, 1994, p. A6.

Kinsley, Michael, "Charity Begins with Government," *Time*, April 6, 1992, p. 74.

Moss, Desda, "Change Is Focus of United Way Meeting," *USA Today*, August 19, 1992, p. 7A.

Moss, Desda, "Former United Way Chief Charged with Looting Funds," *USA Today*, September 14, 1994, p. 1A.

Moss, Desda, "United Way's Ex-Chief Guilty of Using Funds," *USA Today*, April 14, 1995, p. 1A.

CASE 11.2

New Era—If It Sounds Too Good to Be True, It Is Too Good to Be True

The Foundation for New Era Philanthropy was founded in 1989 by Mr. John G. Bennett, Jr. New Era took in over $200 million between 1989 and May 1995, when the SEC brought suit against New Era and the foundation went into bankruptcy.

Mr. Bennett is a charismatic individual who was able to bring in many individual and institutional investors (most of them nonprofit organizations that included many colleges and universities) with the promise of a double-your-money return. Mr. Bennett often met personally with investors or their representatives and opened and closed his sessions with them with prayer.[7] Among the individual investors in New Era were Laurance Rockefeller, Pat Boone, then-president of Procter & Gamble John Pepper, and former Treasury Secretary William Simon. The institutional investors included the University of Pennsylvania, the Nature Conservancy, and the National Museum of American Jewish History.[8]

In 1991, Melenie and Albert Meyer moved from their native South Africa to Michigan, where Mr. Meyer took a tenure-track position as an accounting professor at Spring Arbor College. Because there were only three accounting majors at the time he was hired, Mr. Meyer was also required to work part-time in the business office.[9]

During his first month in the business office, Mr. Meyer found that the college had transferred $294,000 to Heritage of Values Foundation, Inc. He connected the term "Heritage" with Reverend Jim Bakker and went to the library to research Heritage of Values Foundation, Inc. While he found no connection to Jim Bakker, he could find no other information on the foundation. Mr. Meyer asked his supervisor, the vice president for business affairs, Ms. Janet M. Tjepkema, about Heritage of Values and the nature of the transfer. She explained that Heritage was the consultant that had found the New Era Foundation and had advised the college to invest in this "double your investment" fund.

Mr. Meyer attempted to research New Era but could find no registration for it in Pennsylvania, its headquarters location. He could not obtain information from New Era (there was no registration in Pennsylvania ever filed and no tax returns were filed until 1993). Mr. Meyer continued to approach administrators of the college, but they seemed annoyed. He continued to collect information about New Era for the next two years. He gathered income tax returns and even spoke directly with Mr. Bennett. Mr. Meyer remained silent during the time that he gathered information because he was untenured and on a temporary work visa.[10] He also had a family to support, with three children. He was convinced that his concerns were justified when he discovered that New Era had reported only $34,000 in interest income for one year. With the portfolio it purported to hold, the interest income should have been about $1 million.

After he had collected files of information on New Era, which he labeled "Ponzi File," Mr. Meyer wrote a letter to the president of Spring Arbor as well as the chairman of the board of trustees for the college warning them about his concerns regarding New Era. Mr. Meyer had also tried to talk with his colleagues about the information he had uncovered. He felt shunned by administrators and his colleagues and, by April 1994, he and his wife were no longer attending any social functions held by the college. He was told by administrators that raising funds was tough enough without

---

[7] Steve Wulf, "Too Good to Be True," Time, May 29, 1995, p. 34.

[8] Steve Secklow, "A New Era Consultant Lured Rich Donors Over Pancakes, Prayer," The Wall Street Journal, June 2, 1995, pp. A1, A4.

[9] Barbara Carton, "Unlikely Hero: A Persistent Accountant Brought New Era's Problems to Light," The Wall Street Journal, May 19, 1995, pp. B1, B10.

[10] Id.

his meddling. He repeatedly tried to convince administrators not to place any additional funds with New Era. His advice was ignored and Spring Arbor invested an additional $1.5 million in New Era in 1994. At that time, Spring Arbor College's total endowment was $6 million. The $1.5 million would later be lost as part of the New Era bankruptcy.

In March 1995, Mr. Meyer received tenure and began to try to help others by warning them about his concerns about New Era. He wrote to the SEC and detailed his information and concerns. The SEC then notified Prudential Securities, which was holding $73 million in New Era stock. Prudential began its own investigation and found resistance from New Era officers in releasing information. New Era began to unravel and by June 1995 it was in bankruptcy. There were 300 creditors named and net losses were $107 million. New Era was nothing but a Ponzi scheme. It was able to pay out double the investment, but only so long as it could recruit new participants. When it could no longer recruit participants, it was unable to pay on demands for withdrawal.

Mr. Bennett was indicted on 82 counts of fraud, money laundering, and tax code violations in March 1997.[11] He entered a no contest plea and was released after posting his daughter's $115,000 house to cover his bond.[12] Mr. Bennett entered a no-contest plea in 1997 and was sentenced to twelve years in prison following six days of testimony during his sentencing hearing, including emotional pleas from Mr. Bennett. In ordering a reduced sentence, the judge departed from the 24.5 years dictated by the federal sentencing guidelines because Mr. Bennett had been "extraordinarily cooperative" in the investigation and because he had voluntarily turned over $1.5 million in assets to the bankruptcy court to be distributed to New Era participants.[13] The judge also noted what he felt was Mr. Bennett's diminished capacity.[14] The judge, in particularly harsh language, lectured Mr. Bennett on the egregious nature of his conduct: "It is possible for an ostensibly good and reverent person who is a true believer to engage in egregiously reprehensible and societally disruptive behavior."[15]

The nonprofit organizations that had invested in New Era recovered two thirds of their investments and filed suit against Prudential Securities for recoupment of the remainder. That suit was settled without disclosure of its terms in 1996. The basis of the suit was that their funds were held in a single account at Prudential and that the funds were being used to repay New Era loans from Prudential instead of being invested as promised.

Mr. Meyer was still not embraced at his school for his efforts. Some still say that if Mr. Meyer had remained quiet Mr. Bennett could have worked out the problems of New Era. He was named a Michiganian of the Year for 1995.

[11] Steve Secklow, "Retired Judge Will Sort Out New Era Mess," The Wall Street Journal, June 29, 1995, pp. B1, B16.

[12] Steve Secklow, "How New Era's Boss Led Rich and Gullible Into a Web of Deceit," The Wall Street Journal, May 19, 1995, pp. A1, A5.

[13] Dinah Wisenberg Brin, "Philanthropy Scam Nets 12 Years," USA Today, September 23, 1997, p. 2A.

[14] Carton, "Unlikely Hero," pp. B1, B10.

[15] Joseph Slobodzian, "Bennett Gets 12 for New Era Scam," National Law Journal, October 6, 1997, p. A8.

Discussion Questions

1. Why did Mr. Meyer have so much difficulty convincing his college administrators that there was a problem with New Era?

2. Did Mr. Meyer follow the right steps in trying to bring New Era to the attention of the college officials?

3. What impact did Mr. Meyer's personal situation (visa and tenure issues) have on his desire to carry through with his concerns?

4. Why were administrators so reluctant to hear Mr. Meyer out? Mr. Bennett notified Spring Arbor College officials when Mr. Meyer called him and asked administrators to keep Mr. Meyer quiet. How would you read this kind of request? What would you do if you were an administrator?

5. About forty of the nonprofit organizations that had invested in New Era and withdrawn their funds and earnings prior to its collapse voluntarily agreed to return their money to the bankruptcy pool.[16] An administrator from Lancaster Bible College, in explaining the return of his college's funds to the trustee, quoted St. Paul's letter to the Philippians, "Let each of you look not only to his own interest, but also to the interests of others." Hans Finzel, head of CB International, a missionary fund, said his organization would not be returning the money: "It's true that it's tainted money, but it's also true that we received it in good faith."[17] Compare and contrast the positions of the parties. Would you return the money?

6. Bennett M. Weiner, head of the Philanthropic Advisory Service of the Council of Better Business Bureaus, says, "There's tremendous pressure on charities today to increase their revenues to meet expenses and growing public needs. Unfortunately, this can influence some organizations to take financial risks because of potential rewards."[18] Is this an indication that nonprofits operate as businesses and are susceptible to the same business ethics issues? Should nonprofits have ethics programs and training for their staff and volunteers?

Sources

Bloom, Michael A., "Key in New Era Settlement," *National Law Journal*, July 15, 1996, p. A4.

Davis, Ann, "Charity's Troubles Put Dechert in Bind," *National Law Journal*, May 29, 1995, p. A6.

Lambert, Wade, "Trustee in New Era Bankruptcy May Pursue 'Donations,'" *The Wall Street Journal*, May 22, 1995, p. B3.

Secklow, Steve, "A New Era Consultant Lured Rich Donors Over Pancakes, Prayers," *The Wall Street Journal*, June 2, 1995, pp. A1, A4.

Secklow, Steve, "New Era's Bennett Gets 12-Year Sentence," *The Wall Street Journal*, September 23, 1997, p. B13.

---

[16] *Andrea Gerlin, "Among the Few Given Money by New Era, Many See Blessings in Giving It Back," The Wall Street Journal, June 20, 1995, pp. B1, B10.*
[17] *Michael A. Bloom, "Key in New Era Settlement," National Law Journal, July 15, 1996, p. A4.*
[18] *William M. Bulkeley, "Charities Coffers Easily Become Crooks' Booty," The Wall Street Journal, June 5, 1995, pp. B1, B3.*

Secklow, Steve, "Prudential Securities Agrees to Settle New Era Suits by Paying $18 Million," *The Wall Street Journal*, November 18, 1996, p. A4.

Secklow, Steve, and Joseph Rebello, "IRS Is Studying Whether New Era's Donors Committed Fraud on Deductions," *The Wall Street Journal*, May 24, 1995, p. A3.

Slobodzian, Joseph, "New Era Founder Says: God Made Him Do It," *National Law Journal*, March 17, 1997, p. A9.

CASE 11.3

The Red Cross, New York, and Ground Zero

Following the September 11, 2001, attacks on the World Trade Center and Washington, there were many who had lost loved ones, their homes or businesses, or both.

The outpouring of support from the American public was overwhelming. The public donated $543 million for the September 11 disaster relief fund.[19] However, the Red Cross indicated it would use the funds for infrastructure support and not necessarily all of it would go to victims and their families.

When the decision to use the funds in this manner was made, Dr. Bernadine Healy resigned as president of the Red Cross, giving up her $450,010 annual salary and position.

The American public was outraged and demanded that the funds go to the victims and their families. The Red Cross eventually relented, admitted an error in judgment, and agreed to the limited and intended use of the funds.

Discussion Questions

1. Did the Red Cross commit an ethical violation in its initial decision?

2. What do you think of Dr. Healy's decision? Is she a whistleblower?

3. What policies should the Red Cross establish for the future in fund-raising and fund disbursement?

[19] *Marvin Olasky, "Charity Doesn't Have to Mean Bureaucracy," The Wall Street Journal, November 21, 2001, p. A15.*

Business Discipline Index

BUSINESS LAW

WHISTLE-BLOWING

Product/Company/Individuals/ Subject Index

Topic Index

HONESTY

INSIDE INFORMATION

INTERNAL AUDIT/CONTROLS

INTUITIONISM

WHISTLE-BLOWING

WORKPLACE SAFETY